'This book is a great combination of diverse scholars seeking to bridge the laboratory and the world of real social life. It tackles a wide range of personal and social problems, bringing psychology's methods and data to bear—sometimes with surprising results. If you care about the world today and what social psychology can do to help, this is the book for you.'

Roy F. Baumeister, Professor of Psychology, University of Queensland

'Social psychology's insights into major challenges confronting individuals and society are on impressive display in this volume. Whether it be children's aggression, tobacco addiction, eating disorders or depression, contributors to this valuable effort offer new and exciting understandings of problems that affect us all. This book is highly recommended for students, researchers, and professionals working in applied field, as well as everyone else who is interested in what social psychology can contribute to improving the human condition.'

Arie W. Kruglanski, Distinguished University Professor, University of Maryland

APPLICATIONS OF SOCIAL PSYCHOLOGY

This book explores what social psychology can contribute to our understanding of real-life problems and how it can inform rational interventions in any area of social life. By reviewing some of the most recent achievements in applying social psychology to pressing contemporary problems, Forgas, Crano, and Fiedler convey a fundamentally optimistic message about social psychology's achievements and prospects.

The book is organized into four sections. Part I focuses on the basic issues and methods of applying social psychology to real-life problems, discussing evolutionary influences on human sociability, the role of psychological 'mindsets' in interpreting reality, and the use of attitude change techniques to promote adaptive behaviors. Part II explores the applications of social psychology to improve individual health and well-being, including managing aggression, eating disorders, and improving therapeutic interactions. Part III turns to the application of social psychology to improve interpersonal relations and communication, including attachment processes in social relationships, the role of parent-child interaction in preventing adolescent suicide, and analyzing social relations in legal settings and online social networks. Finally, Part IV addresses the question of how social psychology may improve our understanding of public affairs and political behavior.

The book will be of interest to students and academics in social psychology, and professionals working in applied settings.

Joseph P. Forgas is Scientia Professor at the University of New South Wales. In recognition of his work, he received the Order of Australia, the Distinguished Scientific Contribution Award, and has been elected Fellow of the Australian and Hungarian Academies of Science.

William D. Crano is Oskamp Professor of Psychology at Claremont Graduate University. He was liaison scientist for the US Office of Naval Research, NATO Senior Scientist, and Fulbright Senior Scholar.

Klaus Fiedler is Professor of Psychology at the University of Heidelberg, Fellow of the German Academies of Science and the American Psychological Society and the Society for Personality and Social Psychology.

The Sydney Symposium of Social Psychology series

This book is Volume 21 in the *Sydney Symposium of Social Psychology* series. The aim of the Sydney Symposia of Social Psychology is to provide new, integrative insights into key areas of contemporary research. Held every year at the University of New South Wales, Sydney, each symposium deals with an important integrative theme in social psychology, and the invited participants are leading researchers in the field from around the world. Each contribution is extensively discussed during the symposium and is subsequently thoroughly revised into book chapters that are published in the volumes in this series. For further details see the website at www.sydneysymposium.unsw.edu.au

Previous Sydney Symposium of Social Psychology volumes:

SSSP 1. FEELING AND THINKING: THE ROLE OF AFFECT IN SOCIAL COGNITION★★ ISBN 0-521-64223-X (Edited by J.P. Forgas). *Contributors*: Robert Zajonc, Jim Blascovich, Wendy Berry Mendes, Craig Smith, Leslie Kirby, Eric Eich, Dawn Macauley, Len Berkowitz, Sara Jaffee, EunKyung Jo, Bartholomeu Troccoli, Leonard Martin, Daniel Gilbert, Timothy Wilson, Herbert Bless, Klaus Fiedler, Joseph Forgas, Carolin Showers, Anthony Greenwald, Mahzarin Banaji, Laurie Rudman, Shelly Farnham, Brian Nosek, Marshall Rosier, Mark Leary, Paula Niedenthal & Jamin Halberstadt.

SSSP 2. THE SOCIAL MIND: COGNITIVE AND MOTIVATIONAL ASPECTS OF INTERPERSONAL BEHAVIOR★★ ISBN 0-521-77092-0 (Edited by J.P. Forgas, K.D. Williams & L. Wheeler). *Contributors*: William & Claire McGuire, Susan Andersen, Roy Baumeister, Joel Cooper, Bill Crano, Garth Fletcher, Joseph Forgas, Pascal Huguet, Mike Hogg, Martin Kaplan, Norb Kerr, John Nezlek, Fred Rhodewalt, Astrid Schuetz, Constantine Sedikides, Jeffry Simpson, Richard Sorrentino, Dianne Tice, Kip Williams, and Ladd Wheeler.

SSSP 3. SOCIAL INFLUENCE: DIRECT AND INDIRECT PROCESSES★ ISBN 1-84169-038-4 (Edited by J.P. Forgas & K.D. Williams). *Contributors*: Robert Cialdini, Eric Knowles, Shannon Butler, Jay Linn, Bibb Latane, Martin Bourgeois, Mark Schaller, Ap Dijksterhuis, James Tedeschi, Richard Petty, Joseph Forgas, Herbert Bless, Fritz Strack, Eva Walther, Sik Hung Ng,

Thomas Mussweiler, Kipling Williams, Lara Dolnik, Charles Stangor, Gretchen Sechrist, John Jost, Deborah Terry, Michael Hogg, Stephen Harkins, Barbara David, John Turner, Robin Martin, Miles Hewstone, Russell Spears, Tom Postmes, Martin Lea, Susan Watt.

SSSP 4. THE SOCIAL SELF: COGNITIVE, INTERPERSONAL, AND INTERGROUP PERSPECTIVES** ISBN 978-1-84169-062-7 (Edited by J.P. Forgas & K.D. Williams). *Contributors*: Eliot R. Smith, Thomas Gilovich, Monica Biernat, Joseph P. Forgas, Stephanie J. Moylan, Edward R. Hirt, Sean M. McCrea, Frederick Rhodewalt, Michael Tragakis, Mark Leary, Roy F. Baumeister, Jean M. Twenge, Natalie Ciarocco, Dianne M. Tice, Jean M. Twenge, Brandon J. Schmeichel, Bertram F. Malle, William Ickes, Marianne LaFrance, Yoshihisa Kashima, Emiko Kashima, Anna Clark, Marilynn B. Brewer, Cynthia L. Pickett, Sabine Otten, Christian S. Crandall, Diane M. Mackie, Joel Cooper, Michael Hogg, Stephen C. Wright, Art Aron, Linda R. Tropp, and Constantine Sedikides.

SSSP 5. SOCIAL JUDGMENTS: IMPLICIT AND EXPLICIT PROCESSES** ISBN 978-0-521-82248-3. (Edited by J.P. Forgas, K.D. Williams & W. Von Hippel). *Contributors*: Herbert Bless, Marilynn Brewer, David Buss, Tanya Chartrand, Klaus Fiedler, Joseph Forgas, David Funder, Adam Galinsky, Martie Haselton, Denis Hilton, Lucy Johnston, Arie Kruglanski, Matthew Lieberman, John McClure, Mario Mikulincer, Norbert Schwarz, Philip Shaver, Diederik Stapel, Jerry Suls, William von Hippel, Michaela Waenke, Ladd Wheeler, Kipling Williams, Michael Zarate.

SSSP 6. SOCIAL MOTIVATION: CONSCIOUS AND UNCONSCIOUS PROCESSES** ISBN 0-521-83254-3 (Edited by J.P. Forgas, K.D. Williams & S.M. Laham). *Contributors*: Henk Aarts, Ran Hassin, Trish Devine, Joseph Forgas, Jens Forster, Nira Liberman, Judy Harackiewicz, Leanne Hing, Mark Zanna, Michael Kernis, Paul Lewicki, Steve Neuberg, Doug Kenrick, Mark Schaller, Tom Pyszczynski, Fred Rhodewalt, Jonathan Schooler, Steve Spencer, Fritz Strack, Roland Deutsch, Howard Weiss, Neal Ashkanasy, Kip Williams, Trevor Case, Wayne Warburton, Wendy Wood, Jeffrey Quinn, Rex Wright and Guido Gendolla.

SSSP 7. THE SOCIAL OUTCAST: OSTRACISM, SOCIAL EXCLUSION, REJECTION, AND BULLYING* ISBN 978-1-84169-424-5 (Edited by K.D. Williams, J.P Forgas & W. Von Hippel). *Contributors*: Kipling D. Williams, Joseph P. Forgas, William von Hippel, Lisa Zadro, Mark R. Leary, Roy F. Baumeister, and C. Nathan DeWall, Geoff MacDonald, Rachell Kingsbury, Stephanie Shaw, John T. Cacioppo, Louise C. Hawkley, Naomi I. Eisenberger Matthew D. Lieberman, Rainer Romero-Canyas, Geraldine

Downey, Jaana Juvonen, Elisheva F. Gross, Kristin L. Sommer, Yonata Rubin, Susan T. Fiske, Mariko Yamamoto, Jean M. Twenge, Cynthia L. Pickett, Wendi L. Gardner, Megan Knowles, Michael A. Hogg, Julie Fitness, Jessica L. Lakin, Tanya L. Chartrand, Kathleen R. Catanese and Dianne M. Tice, Lowell Gaertner, Jonathan Iuzzini, Jaap W. Ouwerkerk, Norbert L. Kerr, Marcello Gallucci, Paul A. M. Van Lange, and Marilynn B. Brewer.

SSSP 8. AFFECT IN SOCIAL THINKING AND BEHAVIOR★ ISBN 978-1-84169-454-2 (Edited by J.P. Forgas). *Contributors*: Joseph P. Forgas, Carrie Wyland, Simon M. Laham, Martie G. Haselton Timothy Ketelaar, Piotr Winkielman, John T. Cacioppo, Herbert Bless, Klaus Fiedler, Craig A. Smith, Bieke David, Leslie D. Kirby, Eric Eich, Dawn Macaulay, Gerald L. Clore, Justin Storbeck, Roy F. Baumeister, Kathleen D. Vohs, Dianne M. Tice, Dacher Keltner, E.J. Horberg, Christopher Oveis, Elizabeth W. Dunn, Simon M. Laham, Constantine Sedikides, Tim Wildschut, Jamie Arndt, Clay Routledge, Yaacov Trope, Eric R. Igou, Chris Burke, Felicia A. Huppert, Ralph Erber, Susan Markunas, Joseph P. Forgas, Joseph Ciarrochi, John T. Blackledge, Janice R. Kelly, Jennifer R. Spoor, John G. Holmes, Danu B. Anthony.

SSSP 9. EVOLUTION AND THE SOCIAL MIND★ ISBN 978-1-84169-458-0 (Edited by J.P. Forgas, M.G. Haselton & W. Von Hippel). *Contributors*: William von Hippel, Martie Haselton, Joseph P. Forgas, R.I.M. Dunbar, Steven W. Gangestad, Randy Thornhill, Douglas T. Kenrick, Andrew W. Delton, Theresa E. Robertson, D. Vaughn Becker, Steven L. Neuberg, Phoebe C. Ellsworth, Ross Buck, Joseph P. Forgas, Paul B.T. Badcock, Nicholas B. Allen, Peter M. Todd, Jeffry A. Simpson, Jonathon LaPaglia, Debra Lieberman, Garth J. O. Fletcher, Nickola C. Overall, Abraham P. Buunk, Karlijn Massar, Pieternel Dijkstra, Mark Van Vugt, Rob Kurzban, Jamin Halberstadt, Oscar Ybarra, Matthew C. Keller, Emily Chan, Andrew S. Baron, Jeffrey Hutsler, Stephen Garcia, Jeffrey Sanchez-Burks, Kimberly Rios Morrison, Jennifer R. Spoor, Kipling D. Williams, Mark Schaller, Lesley A. Duncan.

SSSP 10. SOCIAL RELATIONSHIPS: COGNITIVE, AFFECTIVE, AND MOTIVATIONAL PROCESSES★ ISBN 978-1-84169-715-4 (Edited by J.P. Forgas & J. Fitness). *Contributors*: Joseph P. Forgas, Julie Fitness, Elaine Hatfield, Richard L. Rapson, Gian C. Gonzaga, Martie G. Haselton, Phillip R. Shaver, Mario Mikulincer, David P. Schmitt, Garth J.O. Fletcher, Alice D. Boyes, Linda K. Acitelli, Margaret S. Clark, Steven M. Graham, Erin Williams, Edward P. Lemay, Christopher R. Agnew, Ximena B. Arriaga, Juan E. Wilson, Marilynn B. Brewer, Jeffry A. Simpson, W. Andrew Collins, SiSi Tran, Katherine C. Haydon, Shelly L. Gable, Patricia Noller, Susan Conway, Anita Blakeley-Smith, Julie Peterson, Eli J. Finkel, Sandra L. Murray, Lisa Zadro, Kipling D. Williams, Rowland S. Miller.

SSSP 11. PSYCHOLOGY OF SELF-REGULATION: COGNITIVE, AFFECTIVE, AND MOTIVATIONAL PROCESSES★ ISBN 978-1-84872-842-4 (Edited by J.P. Forgas, R. Baumeister & D.M. Tice). *Contributors*: Joseph P. Forgas, Roy F. Baumeister, Dianne M. Tice, Jessica L. Alquist, Carol Sansone, Malte Friese, Michaela Wänke, Wilhelm Hofmann, Constantine Sedikides, Christian Unkelbach, Henning Plessner, Daniel Memmert, Charles S. Carver, Michael F. Scheier, Gabriele Oettingen, Peter M. Gollwitzer, Jens Förster, Nira Liberman, Ayelet Fishbach, Gráinne M. Fitzsimons, Justin Friesen, Edward Orehek, Arie W. Kruglanski, Sander L. Koole, Thomas F. Denson, Klaus Fiedler, Matthias Bluemke, Christian Unkelbach, Hart Blanton, Deborah L. Hall, Kathleen D. Vohs, Jannine D. Lasaleta, Bob Fennis, William von Hippel, Richard Ronay, Eli J. Finkel, Daniel C. Molden, Sarah E. Johnson, Paul W. Eastwick.

SSSP 12. PSYCHOLOGY OF ATTITUDES AND ATTITUDE CHANGE★ ISBN 978-1-84872-908-7 (Edited by J.P. Forgas, J. Cooper & W.D. Crano). *Contributors*: William D. Crano, Joel Cooper, Joseph P. Forgas, Blair T. Johnson, Marcella H. Boynton, Alison Ledgerwood, Yaacov Trope, Eva Walther, Tina Langer, Klaus Fiedler, Steven J. Spencer, Jennifer Peach, Emiko Yoshida, Mark P. Zanna, Allyson L. Holbrook, Jon A. Krosnick, Eddie Harmon-Jones, David M. Amodio, Cindy Harmon-Jones, Michaela Wänke, Leonie Reutner, Kipling D. Williams, Zhansheng Chen, Duane Wegener, Radmila Prislin, Brenda Major, Sarah S. M. Townsend, Frederick Rhodewalt, Benjamin Peterson, Jim Blascovich, Cade McCall.

SSSP 13. PSYCHOLOGY OF SOCIAL CONFLICT AND AGGRESSION★ ISBN 978-1-84872-932-2 (Edited by J.P. Forgas, A.W. Kruglanski & K.D Williams). *Contributors*: Daniel Ames, Craig A. Anderson, Joanna E. Anderson, Paul Boxer, Tanya L. Chartrand, John Christner, Matt DeLisi, Thomas F. Denson, Ed Donnerstein, Eric F. Dubow, Chris Eckhardt, Emma C. Fabiansson, Eli J. Finkel, Gráinne M. Fitzsimons, Joseph P. Forgas, Adam D. Galinsky, Debra Gilin, Georgina S. Hammock, L. Rowell Huesmann, Arie W. Kruglanski, Robert Kurzban, N. Pontus Leander, Laura B. Luchies, William W. Maddux, Mario Mikulincer, Edward Orehek, Deborah South Richardson, Phillip R. Shaver, Hui Bing Tan, Mark Van Vugt, Eric D. Wesselmann, Kipling D. Williams, Lisa Zadro.

SSSP 14. SOCIAL THINKING AND INTERPERSONAL BEHAVIOR★ ISBN 978-1-84872-990-2 (Edited by J.P. Forgas, K. Fiedler & C. Sekidikes). *Contributors*: Andrea E. Abele, Eusebio M. Alvaro, Mauro Bertolotti, Camiel J. Beukeboom, Susanne Bruckmüller, Patrizia Catellani, Cindy K. Chung, Joel Cooper, William D. Crano, István Csertö, John F. Dovidio, Bea Ehmann, Klaus Fiedler, Joseph P. Forgas, Éva Fülöp, Jessica Gasiorek, Howard Giles, Liz

Goldenberg, Barbara Ilg, Yoshihisa Kashima, Mikhail Kissine, Olivier Klein, Alex Koch, János László, Anne Maass, Andre Mata, Elisa M. Merkel, Alessio Nencini, Andrew A. Pearson, James W. Pennebaker, Kim Peters, Tibor Pólya, Ben Slugoski, Caterina Suitner, Zsolt Szabó, Matthew D. Trujillo, Orsolya Vincze.

SSSP 15. SOCIAL COGNITION AND COMMUNICATION* ISBN 978-1-84872-663-5 (Edited by J.P. Forgas, O. Vincze & J. László). *Contributors*: Andrea E. Abele, Eusebio M. Alvaro, Maro Bertolotti, Camiel J. Beukeboom, Susanne Bruckmüller, Patrizia Catellani, István Cserto , Cindy K. Chung, Joel Coooper, William D. Crano, John F. Dovidio, Bea Ehmann, Klaus Fiedler, J. P. Forgas, Éva Fülöp, Jessica Gasiorek, Howard Giles, Liz Goldenberg, Barbara Ilg, Yoshihisa Kahima, Mikhail Kissine, Alex S. Koch, János László, Olivier Klein, Anne Maass, André Mata, Elisa M. Merkel, Alessio Nencini, Adam R. Pearson, James W. Pennebaker, Kim Peters, Tibor Pólya, Ben Slugoski, Caterina Suitner, Zsolt Szabó, Matthew D. Trujillo, Orsolya Vincze.

SSSP 16. MOTIVATION AND ITS REGULATION: THE CONTROL WITHIN* ISBN 978-1-84872-562-1 (Edited by J.P. Forgas & E. Harmon-Jones). *Contributors*: Emily Balcetis, John A. Bargh, Jarik Bouw, Charles S. Carver, Brittany M. Christian, Hannah Faye Chua, Shana Cole, Carsten K. W. De Dreu, Thomas F. Denson, Andrew J. Elliot, Joseph P. Forgas, Alexandra Godwin, Karen Gonsalkorale, Jamin Halberstadt, Cindy Harmon-Jones, Eddie Harmon-Jones, E. Tory Higgins, Julie Y. Huang, Michael Inzlicht, Sheri L. Johnson, Jonathan Jong, Jutta Joormann, Nils B. Jostmann, Shinobu Kitayama, Sander L. Koole, Lisa Legault, Jennifer Leo, C. Neil Macrae, Jon K. Maner, Lynden K. Mile, Steven B. Most, Jaime L. Napier, Tom F. Price, Marieke Roskes, Brandon J. Schmeichel, Iris K. Schneider, Abigail A. Scholer, Julia Schüler, Sarah Strübin, David Tang, Steve Tompson, Mattie Tops, Lisa Zadro

SSSP 17. SOCIAL PSYCHOLOGY AND POLITICS* ISBN 978-1-13882-968-8 (Edited by Joseph P. Forgas, Klaus Fiedler, William D. Crano). *Contributors*: Stephanie M. Anglin, Luisa Batalha, Mauro Bertolotti, Patrizia Catellani, William D. Crano, Jarret T. Crawford, John F. Dovidio, Klaus Fiedler, Joseph P. Forgas, Mark G. Frank, Samuel L. Gaertner, Jeremy Ginges, Joscha Hofferbert, Michael A. Hogg, Hyisung C. Hwang, Yoel Inbar, Lee Jussim, Lucas A. Keefer, Laszlo Kelemen, Alex Koch, Tobias Krüger, Mark J. Landau, Janos Laszlo, Elena Lyrintzis, David Matsumoto, G. Scott Morgan, David A. Pizarro, Felicia Pratto, Katherine J. Reynolds, Tamar Saguy, Daan Scheepers, David O. Sears, Linda J. Skitka, Sean T. Stevens, Emina Subasic, Elze G. Ufkes, Robin R. Vallacher, Paul A. M. Van Lange, Daniel C. Wisneski, Michaela Wänke, Franz Woellert, Fouad Bou Zeineddine

SSSP 18. The Social Psychology of Morality★ ISBN 978-1-138-92907-4 (Edited by Joseph P. Forgas, Lee Jussim, and Paul A. M. Van Lange). Contributors: Stephanie M. Anglin, Joel B. Armstrong, Mark J. Brandt, Brock Bastian, Paul Conway, Joel Cooper, Chelsea Corless, Jarret T. Crawford, Daniel Crimston, Molly J. Crockett, Jose L. Duarte, Allison K. Farrell, Klaus Fiedler, Rebecca Friesdorf, Jeremy A. Frimer, Adam D. Galinsky, Bertram Gawronski, William G. Graziano, Nick Haslam, Mandy Hütter, Lee Jussim, Alice Lee, William W. Maddux, Emma Marshall, Dale T. Miller, Benoît Monin, Tom Pyszczynski, Richard Ronay, David A. Schroeder, Simon M. Laham, Jeffry A. Simpson, Sean T. Stevens, William Von Hippel, Geoffrey Wetherell

SSP 19. The Social Psychology of Living Well★ ISBN 978-0-8153-6924-0 (Edited by Joseph P. Forgas and Roy F. Baumeister). Contributors: Yair Amichai-Hamburger, Peter Arslan, Roy F. Baumeister, William D. Crano, Candice D. Donaldson, Elizabeth W. Dunn, Ryan J. Dwyer, Shir Etgar, Allison K. Farrell, Klaus Fiedler, Joseph P. Forgas, Barbara L. Fredrickson, Megan M. Fritz, Shelly L. Gable, Karen Gonsalkorale, Alexa Hubbard, Chloe O. Huelsnitz, Felicia A. Huppert, David Kalkstein, Sonja Lyubomirsky, David G. Myers, Constantine Sedikides, James Shah, Kennon M. Sheldon, Jeffry A. Simpson, Elena Stephan, Yaacov Trope, William Von Hippel, Tom Wildschut

SSP 20. The Social Psychology of Gullibility★ ISBN 978-0-3671-8793-4 (Edited by Joseph P. Forgas and Roy F. Baumeister). Contributors: Stephanie M. Anglin, Joseph J. Avery, Roy F. Baumeister, Aleksandra Chicoka, Joel Cooper, Karen Douglas, David Dunning, Anthony M. Evans, Johanna K. Falbén, Klaus Fiedler, Joseph P. Forgas, Nicholas Fox, Marius Golubickis, Nathan Honeycutt, Lee Jussim, Alex Koch, Joachim I. Krueger, Spike W. S. Lee, C. Neil Macrae, Jessica A. Maxwell, Ruth Mayo, David Myers, Juliana L. Olivier, Daphna Oyserman, Jan-Willem van Prooijen, Norbert Schwarz, Sean T. Stevens, Fritz Strack, Robbie M. Sutton, Geoffrey P. Thomas, Christian Unkelbach, Kathleen D. Vohs, Claudia Vogrincic-Haselbacher

SSP 21. Applications of Social Psychology★ ISBN 978-0-367-41833-5 (Edited by Joseph P. Forgas, William Crano and Klaus Fidler). Contributors: Dana Atzil-Slomin, Hilary B. Bergsieker, Hart Blanton, Shannon T. Brady, Pablo Briñol, Christopher N. Burrows, Emily Butler, Akeela Careem, Susannah Chandhok, William D. Crano, Lianne P. de Vries, Suzanne Dikker, Klaus Fiedler, Joseph P. Forgas, William M. Hall, Nathan Honeycutt, Lee Jussim, Sander L. Koole, Margaret Bull Kovera, Barbara Krahé, Ethan Kross, Dorottya Lantos, Norman P. Li, Mario Mikulincer, Esther K. Papies, Richard E. Petty, Timothy Regan, Andrea L. Ruybal, Toni Schmader, Phillip R. Shaver, Anna Stefaniak, Sean T. Stevens, Wolfgang Tschacher, Mark van Vugt, Gregory M. Walton, Tom Wilderjans, Michael J. A. Wohl.

★ Published by Routledge
★★ Published by Cambridge University Press

APPLICATIONS OF SOCIAL PSYCHOLOGY

How Social Psychology Can Contribute to the Solution of Real-World Problems

Edited by Joseph P. Forgas, William D. Crano, and Klaus Fiedler

NEW YORK AND LONDON

First published 2020
by Routledge
52 Vanderbilt Avenue, New York, NY 10017

and by Routledge
2 Park Square, Milton Park, Abingdon, Oxon, OX14 4RN

Routledge is an imprint of the Taylor & Francis Group, an informa business

© 2020 selection and editorial matter, Joseph P. Forgas, William D. Crano and Klaus Fiedler; individual chapters, the contributors

The right of Joseph P. Forgas, William D. Crano and Klaus Fiedler to be identified as the authors of the editorial material, and of the authors for their individual chapters, has been asserted in accordance with sections 77 and 78 of the Copyright, Designs and Patents Act 1988.

All rights reserved. No part of this book may be reprinted or reproduced or utilized in any form or by any electronic, mechanical, or other means, now known or hereafter invented, including photocopying and recording, or in any information storage or retrieval system, without permission in writing from the publishers.

Trademark notice: Product or corporate names may be trademarks or registered trademarks, and are used only for identification and explanation without intent to infringe.

Library of Congress Cataloging-in-Publication Data
A catalog record for this title has been requested

ISBN: 978-0-367-41832-8 (hbk)
ISBN: 978-0-367-41833-5 (pbk)
ISBN: 978-0-367-81640-7 (ebk)

Typeset in Bembo
by Wearset Ltd, Boldon, Tyne and Wear

CONTENTS

Contributors   xvi
Preface   xviii

1 Applications of Social Psychology: History, Issues and Prospects   1
Joseph P. Forgas, Klaus Fiedler and William D. Crano

PART I
Basic Issues and Methods   **21**

2 Grounding Applied Social Psychology in Translational Research   23
Klaus Fiedler

3 The Evolutionary Mismatch Hypothesis: Implications for Applied Social Psychology   40
Mark van Vugt, Lianne P. de Vries and Norman P. Li

4 "Bad" Things Reconsidered   58
Gregory M. Walton and Shannon T. Brady

5 A Process Approach to Influencing Attitudes and Changing Behavior: Revisiting Classic Findings in Persuasion and Popular Interventions   82
Richard E. Petty and Pablo Briñol

PART II
Promoting Individual Health and Well-Being 105

6 Call of Duty – The Tobacco Wars: Opposing Effects of
  Tobacco Glorifying and Prevention Messages in
  Entertainment Video Games 107
  Hart Blanton, Christopher N. Burrows and Timothy Regan

7 The Development of Aggressive Behavior in Childhood
  and Adolescence: A Social Interactionist Perspective 124
  Barbara Krahé

8 Grounding Desire: The Role of Consumption and
  Reward Simulations in Eating and Drinking Behavior 142
  Esther K. Papies

9 In Sync with Your Shrink: Grounding Psychotherapy in
  Interpersonal Synchrony 161
  *Sander L. Koole, Dana Atzil-Slonim, Emily Butler, Suzanne
  Dikker, Wolfgang Tschacher and Tom Wilderjans*

PART III
Improving Interpersonal Relations and Communication 185

10 Applications of Attachment Theory and Research: The
   Blossoming of Relationship Science 187
   Mario Mikulincer and Phillip R. Shaver

11 Social Psychological Contributions to the Mitigation of
   Adolescent Depression 207
   William D. Crano and Andrea L. Ruybal

12 When Justice is Not Blind: The Effects of Expectancies
   on Social Interactions and Judgments in Legal Settings 231
   Margaret Bull Kovera

13 How Do Online Social Networks Influence People's
   Emotional Lives? 250
   Ethan Kross and Susannah Chandhok

PART IV
Public Affairs and Political Behavior 265

14 Understanding Populism: Collective Narcissism and the
    Collapse of Democracy in Hungary 267
    Joseph P. Forgas and Dorottya Lantos

15 Collective Nostalgia and the Desire to Make One's
    Group Great Again 292
    Michael J. A. Wohl and Anna Stefaniak

16 Do IAT Scores Explain Racial Inequality? 312
    *Lee Jussim, Akeela Careem, Nathan Honeycutt and
    Sean T. Stevens*

17 Cracking the Culture Code: A Tri-Level Model for
    Cultivating Inclusion in Organizations 334
    Toni Schmader, Hilary B. Bergsieker and William M. Hall

Index *356*

CONTRIBUTORS

Dana Atzil-Slonim, Bar-Ilan University

Hilary B. Bergsieker, University of Waterloo

Hart Blanton, Texas A&M University

Shannon T. Brady, Wake Forest University

Pablo Briñol, Universidad Autonoma de Madrid

Christopher N. Burrows, Texas A&M University

Emily Butler, University of Arizona

Akeela Careem, Rutgers University

Susannah Chandhok, University of Michigan

William D. Crano, Claremont Graduate University

Lianne P. de Vries, Vrije Universiteit Amsterdam

Suzanne Dikker, New York University

Klaus Fiedler, University of Heidelberg

Joseph P. Forgas, University of New South Wales

William M. Hall, Brock University

Nathan Honeycutt, Rutgers University

Lee Jussim, Rutgers University

Sander L. Koole, Vrije Universiteit Amsterdam

Margaret Bull Kovera, John Jay College of Criminal Justice, City University of New York

Barbara Krahé, University of Potsdam

Ethan Kross, University of Michigan

Dorottya Lantos, Goldsmiths, University of London

Norman P. Li, Singapore Management University

Mario Mikulincer, Interdisciplinary Center, Herzliya

Esther K. Papies, University of Glasgow

Richard E. Petty, Ohio State University

Timothy Regan, Texas A&M University

Andrea L. Ruybal, Claremont Graduate University

Toni Schmader, University of British Columbia

Phillip R. Shaver, University of California, Davis

Anna Stefaniak, Carleton University

Sean T. Stevens, New York University

Wolfgang Tschacher, University of Bern

Mark van Vugt, Vrije Universiteit Amsterdam

Gregory M. Walton, Stanford University

Tom Wilderjans, Leiden University

Michael J. A. Wohl, Carleton University

PREFACE

Although attempts to improve the quality of human life are as old as humanity itself, scientific methods have only been applied to this task in the last hundred years or so. Arguably, social psychology's proudest achievements have to do with its ability to generate theories and methods that can directly contribute to improving the human condition. The collection of chapters in this book review some of the most recent advances in applying social psychology to pressing contemporary problems. The chapters represent a variety of theoretical and methodological orientations, and deal with such applied issues as reducing teenage suicide, dealing with eating disorders, understanding political populism, exploring the social psychology of clinical encounters, reducing aggressive behavior, exploring the psychological consequences of online social network use, and the like.

The book aims to provide an up-to-date review of some of the most recent developments in applying social-psychological solutions to real-world problems, and offers an informative and scholarly yet readable overview of recent advances in this field. We argue that few topics are as important as the question of how human social life can be improved in the challenging environment of our complex post-industrial societies, using the most sophisticated empirical methods of our discipline.

The book is divided into four parts. Part I deals with general conceptual and methodological issues in applying social psychology to real-world problems. Part II features chapters that look at the contribution of applied social psychology to individual well-being and adjustment. Part III turns to applied contributions to promoting healthy interpersonal relationships and communication. Finally, Part IV looks at research focusing on public affairs and political behavior.

Of course, no single book could possibly include everything that is interesting and exciting in current research on the application of social psychology to real life. In selecting and inviting our contributors, we aimed to achieve a broad and varied coverage that is nevertheless representative of the major new developments in the applications of social-psychological research to everyday problems. The chapters included here represent some of the best recent examples of clear theorizing and careful research in this critically important area by leading international researchers.

The Origins of This Book: The Sydney Symposium of Social Psychology Series

This book is the twenty-first volume in the Sydney Symposium of Social Psychology series, supported over the years by the Australian Research Council, and the University of New South Wales, Sydney. Perhaps a few words are in order about the origins of this volume, and the Sydney Symposium of Social Psychology series in general. First, we should emphasize that this is not simply an edited book in the usual sense. The objective of the Sydney Symposia is to provide new, integrative understanding in important areas of social psychology by inviting leading researchers in a particular field to a three-day residential symposium. Most of our meetings have actually been held in Sydney, but in recent years the symposium has also moved to a number of new international locations. This symposium has received financial support from a variety of sources including the University of New South Wales and the Australian Research Council, allowing the careful selection and funding of a small group of leading researchers as contributors.

Draft papers by all contributors are prepared and circulated well in advance of the symposium and placed on a dedicated website. Thus, participants have an opportunity to review and revise their papers in the light of everybody else's draft contribution even before they arrive at the symposium. A vital part of the preparation of this book has been the intensive three-day face-to-face meeting between all invited contributors. Sydney Symposia are characterized by an open, free-ranging, critical, and often fun discussion between all participants, with the objective to explore points of integration and contrast between the papers. A further revision of each chapter is prepared soon after the symposium, incorporating many of the shared points that emerged in our discussions. Thanks to these intense collaborative procedures, the book does not simply consist of a set of chapters prepared by researchers in isolation. Rather, this Sydney Symposium volume represents a collaborative effort by a leading group of international researchers intent on producing an up-to-date review of research on the applications of social psychology to real-life issues.

We hope that the published papers will succeed in conveying some of the sense of fun and excitement we all shared during the symposium. For more information on the Sydney Symposium series and details of our past and future projects (as well as photos that show our contributors in more or less flattering situations, and other background information) please see our website at www.

sydneysymposium.unsw.edu.au. Books of the Sydney Symposium of Social Psychology series have in recent years been published by Psychology Press, New York, an imprint of Taylor & Francis Publishers. All previous volumes of the Sydney Symposium series can be inspected and ordered at their website, at www.crcpress.com/Sydney-Symposium-of-Social-Psychology/book-series/TFSE00262. Detailed information about our earlier volumes can also be found on the series page in this book, and also on our website.

Given its breadth of coverage, the present book should be useful both as a basic reference book, and as an informative textbook to be used in advanced courses dealing with applications of social psychology. The main target audience for this book comprises researchers, students, and professionals in all areas of the social and behavioral sciences, as well as applied professionals in areas such as counseling, clinical, organizational, communication, political psychology, and social work among others. The book is written in a readable yet scholarly style, and students at the undergraduate and graduate levels should find it an engaging overview of the field and thus useful as a textbook in courses dealing with applied social psychology. The book should also be of particular interest to people working in applied areas where dealing with and understanding the processes involved in understanding and managing individual well-being, relationships, interpersonal behavior and political behavior are important.

We want to express our thanks to the people and organizations who helped to make the Sydney Symposium of Social Psychology series, and this volume in particular, a reality. Producing a complex multi-authored book such as this is a lengthy and sometimes challenging task. We have been very fortunate to work with such an excellent and cooperative group of contributors. Our first thanks must go to them. Because of their help and professionalism, we were able to finish this project in record time and ahead of schedule. Past friendships have not been frayed, and we are all still on speaking terms; indeed, we hope that working together on this book has been a positive experience for all of us, that new friendships have been formed, and that all our contributors take happy memories with them about our time together.

We are especially grateful to Suellen Crano, who helped in more ways that we could list here. We also wish to acknowledge financial support from the Australian Research Council and the University of New South Wales, support that was of course essential to get this project off the ground. Most of all, we are grateful for the love and support of our families who have put up with us during the many months of work that went into producing this book.

Joseph Forgas, Klaus Fiedler and William Crano
Sydney, October 2019

1

APPLICATIONS OF SOCIAL PSYCHOLOGY

History, Issues and Prospects

Joseph P. Forgas, Klaus Fiedler and William D. Crano

Introduction

We may introduce this volume with a fundamental claim: at its heart, all social psychology is applied. From the earliest beginnings of our discipline, researchers have always been interested in exploring how their work might help to make the world a better place. And in turn, every theory-driven research program in social psychology has important applications in real life. This claim should not be surprising. Hardly any other discipline is as close to everyday life and experience as social psychology. The dramatic steps taken sometime at the end of the 19th century of finally applying scientific methods to study the most complex, most fascinating and least understood aspects of human life, sociability, heralded a new era in understanding ourselves and the world we live in. No matter where one sticks the pin on the dartboard of social psychology's inception, social psychology has been identified with, and most strongly celebrated, when it has turned to research on the practical implications of its evidence-based theories.

The ambition to be useful and applied can already be discerned in the classical experiments by Triplett (1898) to which experimental social psychology often traces its origins (Allport, 1924). Triplett discovered a spontaneous and difficult to explain improvement in motor performance when a task was performed in the company of others. This discovery held out the applied promise of an easily obtainable productivity benefit in simple motor tasks. We should not forget that this was the period of rapidly-improving industrial production, and the rational desire to increase performance was at the forefront of applied interest. Although Triplett's explanation for socially-induced improvements in motor performance was not much of a theory by today's standards, the explosive interest in his findings was no doubt fueled by an applied imperative.

The objective of this volume is to offer a review of the most recent achievements of applying social psychology to the real world. Our invited contributors are all internationally respected scholars who present cutting-edge work. Of course, no single volume can hope to address all of the many pressing concerns that currently occupy the world in which we find ourselves. However, we believe that the reader will find the issues addressed here of interest, spanning a range of concerns from teenage suicide, the effects of social media, clinical interactions, aggression, eating disorders, and the rise of political populism and illiberalism in the world today. We hope that the overall message of this volume is to offer hope that social psychologists can do a great deal to ameliorate some of the most vexing problems faced by contemporary society.

Theoretical vs Applied Research

One long-standing misunderstanding in social psychology is the often-voiced conflict between theoretical versus practical research. Kurt Lewin's (1943) dictum that "There is nothing as practical as good theory" (p. 118) has often been used to highlight the usefulness of applications outside the laboratory, a task many researchers still consider the ultimate aim of our discipline. Fiedler (this volume) has written eloquently on this issue in his discussion of translational science, and he clearly rejects claims about the priority of "basic science" over translational science.

We may consider a number of arguments in support of Lewin's statement. First of all, this claim is true historically. The most important practical contributions to psychological science were naturally embedded in strong theorizing. Alfred Binet's seminal work on intelligence testing – perhaps the most compelling practical contribution ever – was the result of deep theoretical thinking (Wolf, 1969), unfolding in relation to other intriguing topics such as the intelligence of the deaf (Binet & Simon, 1909). Hugo Münsterberg's (1915) foundation of modern legal psychology in his famous book *On the Witness Stand: Essays on Psychology and Crime*, was deeply rooted in theoretical reasoning about the pitfalls of witness reports under stress and under the influence of social taboos. This pioneering work continues to stimulate cutting-edge research today, as the chapter by Kovera (this volume) illustrates.

Another classic example of how theory-driven experimental research can tell us something profound about the human condition is Sherif's (1936) pioneering work on the spontaneous formation and maintenance of social norms. Notwithstanding the artificiality of the experiment itself, requiring participants to judge the illusory movement of stationary light sources, Sherif made a profound point about the fundamental evolutionary inclination of human beings to spontaneously establish and maintain consensual norms. More recently, the practical question of how to improve tolerance in a diverse society would not have been possible without a good theoretical understanding of human social cognition and social identity processes (Tajfel, 1969; see also Schmader, this volume).

Of course, the relationship between theory and practice cannot be a one-way street. Theorizing is not only antecedent to practical uses but is also improved by feedback from its practical applications. It is well to remember that many of our theories derive from practical problems which demanded solution and ultimately gave rise to research. Theoretical analysis is always essential to organize the mass of data collected in attempts to meet critical practical needs. Applied issues put selective evolutionary pressure on theorizing, calling for quantitative measurement, precise prediction, and maximization of cost-benefit ratios (see also Fiedler, this volume). This process was described by Campbell (1974) as "evolutionary epistemology." Based on Karl Popper's philosophy of science, Campbell suggested that science progresses by proposing new theoretical conjectures followed by a critical phase of selective elimination, a process that also occurs at the applied societal level in "experimenting societies" (Campbell, 1974).

Applications have been strong generators of new theories, whose derived insights are at least as valuable as those discovered within the more sterile and more confined walls of our laboratories. Indeed, application may be both the origin and the true end point in the evaluation process of scientific work (see also Koole et al.; Kross & Chandhok; Walton & Brady; and Jussim et al., this volume). Practical aims like better personality assessment, prevention of human suffering, conflict resolution, improving relationships or better learning outcomes in academic settings have given rise to ground-breaking theoretical work (see chapters by Crano & Ruybal; Krahé; Mikulincer & Shaver; and Papies, this volume).

Further, the ultimate progress in applied domains is often dependent on the methodological advances developed in basic science, often in distant domains. For example, the Purkinje effect (based on the differential sensitivity of rods and cones on the retina to light of different wave length) is crucial for the ergonomic optimization of work conditions for air traffic controllers (Mook, 1983). The Bayes theorem is essential for effective risk assessment and for diagnostic and prognostic problem-solving. Signal-detection analysis has been applied creatively in manifold applied areas. Swets, Dawes, and Monahan's (2000) synopsis of useful applications of signal-detection analysis in various domains is among the most fascinating pieces of applied work ever.

Finally, and perhaps most importantly, we must embrace Kurt Lewin's statement when we think about the likelihood, and the societal obligation, of applied (or translational) social research to contribute to the future. The challenges are obvious. As a result of unprecedented scientific progress, humanity now finds itself in a world to which it is not fully adapted – a situation we might label as "evolutionary mismatch" (van Vugt, this volume). There is hardly any other scientific discipline of similar relevance to present and future societal problems as social psychology. How can we deal with fake news, conspiracy theories, and uncontrolled influences in the social and electronic media (see for example Forgas & Baumeister, 2019)? How can democracy survive if individual thinking and opinions are no longer rational, but are confounded in an epidemic of emotionalism and conformity effects (see chapters by Forgas & Lantos; and Wohl & Stefaniak, this volume)? What will future workplaces look like given the fast development of machine learning and the growth of intrusive IT technologies? How can we manage racism, intolerance, and ethnocentrism in an increasingly diverse society (see chapters by Jussim et al.; Schmader, this volume)? What can psychology contribute to handling such existential problems as depression, addiction, obesity and aggression (see also chapters by Koole et al.; Kross and Chandhok; Krahé; Papies; Walton & Brady; and Crano & Ruybal, this volume)?

We cannot hope to cope with any of these challenges without good scientific theories that allow us to predict and evaluate the relative impact of different interventions. It is obvious that we cannot expect untested interventions to solve societal, economic, and ecological problems; only scientific theory-driven thinking can do so. This is indeed the ultimate purpose of a good theory – going beyond the present status quo, allowing us to simulate and reason about future outcomes, conditional on different causal conditions and enabling conditions.

With the growing importance of techniques of data collection in real life and powerful tools of data analysis, we can now precisely track and monitor consumer decisions, educational attainment, political and social preferences, physiological states, traffic movements, and much else besides. These techniques offer the promise of rapid feedback and evaluation of scientific theories in the real world. As an example, preconceived theoretical ideas about the role of implicit associations in real-life prejudice and discrimination should now be revised in the light of practical observations about the limited efficacy of such predictions (see Jussim et al., this volume). To maximize efficacy, basic science may model learning paradigms according to the architecture of real-world tasks, expand basic research on aggression to fit natural boundary conditions, and design experiments that take natural sampling processes and multi-causal structures of the real world into account (see also Fiedler; Krahé; Forgas & Lantos, this volume). Really good theories will almost certainly be applied practically, and practical observations – whether they are predicted or unexpected – constitute a crucial challenge for improving basic behavioral research.

History and Background

The origins of applied social psychology are often traced to Hugo Münsterberg, who came to Harvard at the invitation of William James from Berlin, Germany. In addition to his enduring interest in forensic psychology, he was also interested in motivation (purposive psychology) and the application of psychology to social problems. During his stay at Harvard, Münsterberg wrote several books applying psychology to work, education, and business. In no small measure due to Münsterberg's work, the establishment of the International Association of Applied Psychology (IAAP) in 1920 marked the creation of the first international scholarly society in psychology.

During the war years, applied social psychology came into its own and became a respected and sought-after profession. The services of applied social psychologists were recruited to assist the US war effort. The Office of Strategic Services employed numerous psychologists to work on tasks such as propaganda, leadership, improving troop morale, persuasion, and advertising. After the war, applied social psychologists became increasingly in demand outside the walls of academia in educational organizations, marketing, advertising, and a host of other fields. The growing success and attraction of social psychology as a university course owes much to the wide applicability of our discipline to numerous fields outside academia.

Yet, throughout the history of social psychology, relative interest in applied issues waxed and waned depending on the urgency of the demands of society and the historical circumstances. In a sense, our field is just now coming out of a neglect-of-application phase that favored more pure or basic research. A similar development also occurred after World War II, which had first forced a focus on applications at the expense of theory. Then, the necessity for psychology to serve national interests required researchers to adopt an often single-minded focus on using established knowledge to solve immediate and pressing problems, rather than on refreshing the knowledge base of human behavior. In reaction to this enforced applied focus, an 'applications exhaustion' ensued after the war, at least in academia, and the tide shifted to 'pure' science. For example, Carl Hovland's work after the war became heavily theory-oriented, specifically and by design, after Hovland had been devoted almost exclusively to the application of basic principles of memory and learning to foster persuasion goals during the war (Sears, 1961).

However, it would be a misreading of history to see these later efforts as eschewing applications. Hovland and others clearly recognized the need for a more theory-based social psychology, with his focus on communication and persuasion, but his research activities were anything but practically insignificant. Indeed, he laid the groundwork of much of what constitutes today's social psychology of attitudes, persuasion, and communication and much of that work was honed by the interplay of his own prior applied focus and its extension back to the laboratory (see also Blanton et al.; and Petty & Briñol, this volume).

Another illuminating historical example is Campbell's notion of the experimenting society (Campbell, 1969, 1974), a call to bring our theories *and* methodological tools to bear in the service of society. Campbell envisioned an enlightened and rational society in which competing social programs were put to the test and evaluated – did they succeed in their stated goals, did they produce better outcomes, did they avoid unexpected detrimental consequences?

His call for an experimenting society paved the way for the growing emphasis on *evaluation research*, an approach which has become a critical field of scientific endeavor in its own right, and which today is seen as a crucial factor in applied or translational research.

However, as a historical review of any scientific enterprise is bound to show, the application of social psychology to real-life problems has not been without its share of biases, false assumptions, and conceptual failures. We shall look at some of these issues in the following section in the hope that we can better learn to deal with the future by learning from the past.

Mistaken Assumptions

As in every field of human endeavor, applied social psychology also suffers from a number of false starts, mistaken assumptions, and ideological biases that have hindered its progress over the years. This section presents a brief discussion of some of these issues taken from the history of our field.

Ideological Assumptions

Researchers are not exempt from the usual ideological biases and assumptions of the normative society they live in. As Kuhn (1996) pointed out, scientific practice is always subject to normative distortions, and at any given time, practitioners of 'paradigmatic' science are usually not even aware of their ideological assumptions. This can be particularly noticeable when scientists deal with applied issues that touch directly on the dominant values and ideologies of the societies in which they live.

Perhaps the most interesting example of the emergence of such an ideological bias is the fluctuating fate of intelligence testing in Western societies we already alluded to above. The discovery of intelligence testing and the empirical construction of reliable and valid tests of intelligence is probably one of the greatest achievements of applied psychology. IQ scores indisputably remain by far the most reliable predictors of academic and career achievement, with conscientiousness (a personality trait) coming a distant second. The widespread adoption of intelligence testing in the educational institutions of many Western countries has been a major source of advancing social mobility, as talented individuals from disadvantaged socioeconomic groups were recognized and offered educational opportunities (Herrnstein & Murray, 1994).

Despite the unparalleled utility and highly socially desirable application of intelligence tests, the concept has come under ideological attack in recent decades. Any rational discussion of the construct of intelligence as a stable and inherited trait has now become controversial. How did this strange situation come about? Two ideological objections have driven the movement to discredit the concept of intelligence and intelligence testing.

First, the emergence of clear and consistent empirical evidence for racial differences in IQ in the US led to a powerful political backlash. Various mostly left-wing political groups sought to discredit the evidence, first unsuccessfully disputing its reliability and validity, and when this failed, labeling the very concept of intelligence and its testing as biased or racist. In the ensuing toxic climate, any objective discussion of the construct and its utility is becoming impossible. To the extent that intelligence testing is slowly abandoned, a very important tool for advancing meritocratic social mobility for members of disadvantaged groups is disappearing; surely a paradoxical outcome. The second ideological attack on the concept of intelligence and its testing came from the widespread anti-nativist beliefs among many social science practitioners, arguing that humans possess few if any biologically-determined characteristics worth worrying about. We shall have more to say about this assumption next.

Assumptions About Human Nature: The Situationist Bias

In addition to well-documented ideological bias, researchers practicing paradigmatic science are also influenced by their shared implicit assumptions about human nature. When those assumptions are inaccurate, as has often been the case in applied social psychology, the consequences can be serious. Applied social psychologists typically have an optimistic mindset; they believe in the almost limitless perfectibility of the human condition, and tend to assume that human beings are intrinsically flexible and thus improvable. These assumptions tend to minimize or even ignore the biological and evolutionary aspects of human nature and the intrinsic limits of human adaptability (Pinker, 1997; see also van Vugt, this volume).

Enthusiasm for applied social psychology is thus often based on the strong assumption that human social behavior is mostly situationally determined. The emphasis on situational causation is endemic in social-psychological textbooks, and is traceable to multiple conceptual sources. The first clear enunciation of this situationist assumption came from radical learning theorists, such as Watson (1929), who firmly believed that all human behavior is acquired and thus modifiable. This assumption continued to be popular among learning theorists. Skinner (1951) is also on record as claiming that manipulating the external rewards contingencies will provide an unlimited method for changing human behavior.

Situationism, and the neglect of internal factors in producing behaviors, gained further momentum in the 1960s, with the difficulty of establishing reliable links between individual personality traits and actual observable behaviors (Mischel, 1968). This research paradigm led to a renewed emphasis on the power of the situation in actually determining what people do (Forgas, 1979; Mischel, 1968). The situationist message was further reinforced by the emergence of attribution research in the 1970s, emphasizing as a major deficit the pervasive anti-situationist human tendency to incorrectly infer causation as residing inside the acting individual (the fundamental attribution error; Kelley, 1967), which gave further impetus to the study of external contingencies in the regulation of behavior.

We should note that such a situationist bias has characterized not only social psychology, but also most of the social sciences. Perhaps the most interesting example is the ferocious debate surrounding the anthropological work of Margaret Mead in Samoa. Mead was an adherent of absolute cultural determinism that entirely denies the role of biology and evolution in human behavior. She set out to show that even such deeply biologically anchored social behaviors as mate selection and sexuality are culturally variable, and therefore, manipulable. Her best-selling book, *Coming of Age in Samoa* (Mead, 1966) describes the easy, guilt-free, and unconstrained sexual mores and coming of age of Samoans, so different from the strait-laced and anxiety-ridden Western customs of the time. Her book became an all-time bestseller and a harbinger of the sexual revolution in the 1960s.

Unfortunately, Mead turned out to be mistaken in her assumptions and conclusions. An anthropologist at the Australian National University, Derek Freeman, initially a follower of Margaret Mead's work, returned to Samoa to continue her research, but to his surprise, found that almost nothing that Mead described about this idyllic South Pacific culture was actually true (Freeman, 1999). Samoans were violent and as hung up about issues of pre-marital sex, virginity and sexual mores as most other societies. Mead got her facts wrong by approaching her task with a powerful, preconceived situationist bias. She also spent too little time on field work, did not learn the language well, and relied almost exclusively on the second-hand verbal reports of two young girls (later located and identified by Freeman). Her informants were so embarrassed by Mead's intrusive questions about sexuality that they tricked her and gave her false, "joking" answers describing the opposite of their actual cultural customs.

An interesting feature of this ferocious controversy is just how deeply not only Mead, but the entire social science establishment was committed to the dominant ideology of situational explanations and cultural relativism. The entire social anthropology profession stood by her despite the evidence. When Derek Freeman's work questioning Mead's conclusions could no longer be ignored, professional associations felt compelled to take a stand – and they *voted to affirm that Mead was right, and Freeman wrong*. There are few more embarrassing chapters in the history of the social sciences. This episode shows just how deeply ingrained in our thinking is the belief that humans are somehow different from other species, have few if any important inherited traits, and so social behavior is relatively easily changeable by judicious social activism and social engineering.

The strong commitment to situationism also meant that social scientists have traditionally been deeply hostile to evolutionary explanations of social behavior (Forgas, Haselton, & von Hippel, 2007; von Hippel, 2018). The very idea that human beings were shaped by their evolutionary heritage, and carry certain wired-in and inflexible mind modules and ways of thinking and behaving has been anathema to most researchers. Yet precisely this conclusion is supported by numerous empirical research traditions in our field (Forgas et al., 2007; Pinker, 1997; von Hippel, 2018). Failure to recognize evolutionarily determined cognitive "mind modules" (van Vugt, this volume) is a particularly serious failure.

A bias toward cultural determinism is also noticeable in the voluminous research on stereotyping, where well-intentioned researchers regularly assume that categorizing people can be controlled or even eliminated with the right strategies (Judd & Park, 1993; Krueger, 1996). Work by Jussim (this volume) explains why this assumption can be seriously mistaken. Contrary to the evidence, most social psychologists have long assumed that stereotypes are false by definition, even though the originator of the term, Walter Lippmann (1922) argued that stereotypes, although simplifications, need not necessarily be false.

Contrary to received wisdom, stereotypes have considerable utility when it comes to describing the perceived characteristics of various groups, and as such, they have cognitive and social functions (Krueger, 1996). The tendency to categorize and simplify is one of the most fundamental cognitive habits of humankind (Kahneman, 2011; Tajfel, 1969). Suggesting that spontaneous categorization and stereotyping can be suspended or controlled in order to achieve socially desirable objectives appears misconceived when looked at from the perspective of evolutionary psychology (von Hippel, 2018). The ideological condemnation of stereotyping is unlikely to yield beneficial outcomes. Instead, in seeking to improve the human condition, applications of social psychology might be more effective if they recognized the fundamental evolutionary parameters of human cognition (Kahneman, 2011; Pinker, 1997), and adjust their recommendations to fit in with those constraints.

Focus on Individuals vs. Groups

As every social psychology textbook will confirm, social psychology is the science that studies the individual in social situations. Accordingly, the unit of analysis for our discipline is always the individual. However, this fundamental focus is often compromised in applied research as researchers are increasingly influenced by the growing contemporary ideological emphasis on the social group, and the identity individuals can derive from the groups to which they belong. Where does this preoccupation with group identity come from? Interest in the identity group as the basic unit of analysis overriding the individual owes much to Marxist collectivist social theorizing, where group membership in various social classes (defined by their relationship to the means of production) is assumed to be the key objective determinant defining the social nature of persons.

The bias toward focusing on group identity may also be traced to a questionable interpretation of Henri Tajfel's classical work on social identity and the minimal group paradigm (e.g., Tajfel, 1969; Tajfel & Forgas, 1981). Tajfel's classical work demonstrated one of the most important evolutionary universals characterizing human nature: our extreme propensity to prefer our in-group to any outgroup, a bias that had obvious survival advantages in our ancestral environment. Tajfel's experiments showed that even a simple and meaningless cognitive label is sufficient to produce powerful tendencies for intergroup discrimination. Numerous studies in this field lead to the conclusion: Homo Sapiens has a strong and universal inclination for in-group favouritism, even in otherwise empty and meaningless situations. The cumulative message of recent investigations about human information processing also confirms that in fundamental ways, human thinking was not shaped by evolution to maximize accuracy and objectivity, but rather, that we carry powerful mental habits designed to minimize errors that may be most costly (Kahneman, 2011; Pinker, 1997; von Hippel, 2018; see also van Vugt, this volume).

The real applied message of Tajfel's work may be understood as fundamentally cautionary: Beware of triggering group identifications. He showed that the tendency to classify and discriminate against outgroups is a dangerous human universal, yet his work has perversely been used to ever more strongly emphasize the importance of social identity group categories in modern life. The ideology of identity politics is the notion that humans can be reduced to exemplars of the categorical groups they belong to, and thus social progress and justice is best achieved by mobilizing "oppressed" groups to assert themselves against other groups. This group conflict ideology incorporates a fundamentally Marxist view of social progress, directly mirroring Marx's deeply mistaken idea of inevitable class conflict as the sole engine of historical progress. The disastrous consequences of this way of thinking – surprisingly embraced by many Western intellectuals who should have known better – are only now beginning to be recognized. The powerful backlash against identity-based politics and political correctness may have fostered the rise of populist right-wing politics all over the world (Albright, 2018; see also Forgas & Lantos; and Wohl & Stefaniak, this volume). Unfortunately, focus on identity groups as the basic unit of analysis has also been on the increase in the literature of both applied and laboratory social psychology. A more careful reading of the implications of Tajfel's work could have worked against our dangerous entanglement with identity politics (see also Jussim et al., this volume).

The Nominalist Fallacy

Another often discussed, but rarely addressed problem in studying social-psychological variables in real life is what epistemologists call the nominalist fallacy: the belief that just because we can name a construct and so give it symbolic reality, the construct actually exists in real life and can also be empirically studied, measured, and manipulated. Perhaps the most memorable example of the nominalist fallacy in psychology is associated with the thicket of various psychoanalytic theories and predictions. Creating a new vocabulary and a symbolic name for processes and structures such as id, ego, superego, or sublimation, or projection does not mean that these constructs can actually be established with a sufficient degree of reliability or validity in the real world. As Karl Popper convincingly showed, psychoanalysis and Marxism are not scientific theories, mainly because their concepts and predictions are not falsifiable as they are stated in an empirically inherently unfalsifiable manner, consistent with the nominalist fallacy.

Social psychology is subject to a number of similar problems. For example, early enthusiasm to study person perception accuracy as an important applied variable suffered a similar fate (Funder, 1995; Kenny, 1994). Understanding how human beings come to interpret and make sense of other people and the world around them remains a key concern for social psychologists to this day, even though the apparently simple objective of improving person perception "accuracy" remains elusive. Early experiments by Razran (1940) raised the troubling possibility that social perception is deeply flawed, and that people frequently misunderstand and misinterpret the communications by others. Razran (1940) found that the same message can be interpreted very differently, depending on whether the audience happens to be in a good mood (after a free lunch!), or in a bad mood (due to exposure to noxious smells). This line of research eventually inspired a rich and now thriving tradition of experimental work on the distorting effects of affective states on social judgments and behavior (see Forgas & Eich, 2012, for a review).

The accuracy of perceiving complex personal characteristics also turned out to be problematic. One major methodological issue in this field was the question of criterion measures. What is the proper yardstick to determine the accuracy of judgments of a person's friendliness, honesty, likeability, or warmth? As these characteristics are not directly observable, they must be inferred. The cognitive characteristics of such inferential processes were not properly explored until much later. Perhaps the final nail in the coffin of person perception accuracy research was the paper by Cronbach (1955) that demonstrated that person perception accuracy is actually *not* a single skill, or indeed a single measurable psychological process, but a complex constellation of multiple processes and abilities that often work against each other. Differential accuracy, the ability to perceive how a person differs from well-established types and categories, is a very different skill from stereotype accuracy, the ability to correctly classify a person as belonging to a particular type or category.

Cronbach's (1955) paper was a clear-cut demonstration of the nominalist fallacy in applied social psychology: the seductive belief that the ability to name a psychological phenomenon implies that such a phenomenon actually exists as a single and valid measurable construct. Just as Freud invented a rich new vocabulary for various psychoanalytic processes that could not be empirically demonstrated, the quest for person perception accuracy had a similar fate. It is telling that once the intuitively attractive concept of person perception accuracy has thus been deconstructed by Cronbach (1955), interest in studying it ceased almost immediately.

Of course, the nominalist fallacy still remains an issue for applied social psychology today. Potentially promising constructs such as stereotype threat, implicit prejudice, behavioral priming, or micro-aggression may well share a similar fate. The message is that words that offer an intuitively attractive symbolic, semantic function in describing high-level inferences and observations may not necessarily correspond to real psychological constructs with adequate reliability and validity.

Internal and External Validity and the Need for Representative Design

Another issue of applying social psychology to real-life problems has to do with the differential demands of maximizing internal and external validity. The demands to study a variable within the rarified atmosphere of the controlled laboratory are very different from the far more complex environment of the real world. As Fiedler (2011) and others noted, good experimental laboratory work in social psychology is predicated on creatively stage-managing a situation that is most conducive to producing the expected causal link between an independent and a dependent variable.

In seeking to test hypotheses in the laboratory, the skill of the experimenter is focused in controlling or eliminating any confounding variable that might influence the results. In the search for the best experimental design, the researcher seeks to maximize internal validity, with little regard to external validity. As a result, the carefully stage-managed laboratory situation will often bear little resemblance to the natural context in which the studied phenomena normally occur (in other words, it has low external validity).

The problem is more intractable if we consider that social psychologists still have not embraced the need for Brunswik's "representative design" – designs that are based on a valid taxonomy of the population of relevant social situations that we wish to explore. Even well-designed laboratory experiments often bear little resemblance to the natural ecology of the examined phenomenon. We also have little knowledge or understanding about exactly *how* the manipulated laboratory situation differs from, or deviates from, its natural equivalent. This issue has been repeatedly but unsuccessfully discussed within the social psychology literature (Brunswik, 1955). Arguments to develop "representative designs," that is, designs that represent real-life social situations in reliable ways, have rarely been followed, and we still do not pay much attention to the construction of reliable empirical taxonomies of various domains of social situations (Forgas, 1979).

One consequence is that the external validity and applicability of even our most striking and interesting discoveries remain under a cloud of uncertainty. A good example is the fate of Milgram's classic research on obedience (Milgram, 1963). Because the experiment was carried out in an artificial laboratory setting where the deceived participants were in some doubt about exactly what was happening, critics of the Milgram experiments claimed that the findings are inapplicable in real-life obedience settings. While this criticism is almost certainly overstated, it probably remains true that Milgram's studies mainly apply to one particular class of obedience situation (uninformed participants obeying an authority figure), but may not be generalized to all obedience phenomena.

Another similar example is the continuing debate around the interpretation of Zimbardo's famed Stanford prison study. Questions about the internal as well as the external validity and applicability of this study to real-life situations persist, again, because it remains unclear to what extent the situation as experienced by Zimbardo's participants is representative of the universe of similar situations in real life where such behavior actually occurs.

In summary, then, it seems that applications of social psychology are often subject to a trade-off between trying to maximize experimental control in laboratory settings, and the complexity of multiple uncontrolled influences that characterize the real-world environments where the studied phenomena actually occur. Yet in principle, internal and external validity could be simultaneously maximized with experimental designs that rely on the representative sampling of the situations (person, contexts, stimuli, etc.) to which the predictions are expected to generalize (Brewer & Crano, 2014; Brunswik, 1955). Thus, causal predictions could be developed and tested in environments that are representative and generalizable at the same time, instead of the present reliance on predominantly ad hoc experimental manipulations (Crano, in press).

In the next section we will offer a brief summary and overview of the contents of this book.

Overview of the Volume

Beyond this introductory chapter, our book is organized into four complementary sections, containing four chapters each. Part I deals with some of the *basic issues and methods of applying social psychology*. Part II explores the question of how applications of social psychology may *promote individual health and well-being*. Part III turns to the application of social psychology to *improve interpersonal relations and communication*. Finally, Part IV addresses the question of how social psychology may improve our *understanding of public affairs and political behavior*.

The next chapter, *Chapter 2* by *Fiedler*, suggests that translational research conducted in the lab under experimentally controlled conditions can often lead to more practically useful applications and more responsible interventions than less controlled research conducted under naturalistic conditions. The chapter describes several examples of this process, derived from sampling-theoretical approaches. The chapter concludes that, consistent with Kurt Lewin's (1943, p. 118) notion that "there is nothing as practical as a good theory," laboratory research often results in better understood interventions than applied research conducted in real life.

Van Vugt, de Vries and Li (Chapter 3) outline an evolutionary framework for applied social psychology looking at human social cognition, emotion, and behavior as products of psychological mechanisms that evolved to solve recurrent survival and reproduction challenges. The chapter introduces the concept of evolutionary mismatch, when previously adaptive psychological mechanisms may no longer produce the same beneficial outcomes in different environments and at different historical times. The chapter reviews evidence for mismatches affecting human well-being in applied domains, such as mating and parenting, physical and mental health, social decision-making, and work and organizations.

In *Chapter 4, Walton and Brady* analyze the nature of psychologically "wise" mindset interventions that address how specific events or experiences are represented can benefit human well-being. Drawing on examples from education, health, parenting, and intergroup relationships, the chapter argues that the key step is to identify and interpret pejorative events and experiences. The chapter describes a step-by-step methodology supported by laboratory and field experiments designed to explore how people commonly experience a negative event, and how its effects can be alleviated.

In *Chapter 5, Petty and Briñol* provide a brief review of the elaboration likelihood model (ELM) of persuasion as a basic conceptual framework for applying social-psychological interventions to influence beliefs and attitudes. The chapter describes five fundamental processes for influencing attitudes, and several areas of application of the model are discussed, including mental and physical health, consumer behavior, and political engagement. The reviewed research shows that judgments based on high thinking processes predict behavioral intentions and behavior better than judgments based on little thought.

Part II contains chapters dealing with questions of promoting individual well-being and adjustment.

Blanton, Burrows and Regan (Chapter 6) discuss health-related communication, and explore the ability of vivid imagery in video games to transport adolescent players into a compelling, fictional reality that exerts a beneficial influence on their health cognitions (a process they call "virtual transportation"). Their experiments show that by having a game avatar "vape" during play reduced the perceived riskiness of smoking e-cigarettes. Further, placing health messages into the background of first-person video games reduced players' willingness to engage in health risks. The chapter suggests that health communicators might use the same processes, including transporting and fantasy elements in video games to promote public health.

Krahé (Chapter 7) turns to the question of aggression and presents an extensive program of research looking at the development of the propensity to engage in aggressive behaviors, using longitudinal and multilevel designs. The review explores the role of interpersonal and environmental risk factors in middle childhood to early adulthood in producing aggression, and also discusses the way that individual dispositions and situational factors interact to predict the trajectories of aggressive behavior. The implications of the findings for effective interventions are also discussed.

Chapter 8 by *Papies* looks at the role of applied social psychology in understanding dysfunctional eating and drinking behaviors. She presents a grounded cognition theory of desire and motivated appetitive behaviors, suggesting that desire arises when internal or external cues trigger a simulation of an earlier appetitive experience. Empirical evidence supporting this account, using behavioral, physiological, and neuro-imaging methods is reviewed. The implications of this research for marketing and food labeling, and the design of effective interventions, are discussed.

Koole, Atzil-Slonim, Butler, Dikker, Tschacher and Wilderjans (Chapter 9) offer an applied social-psychological analysis of the therapeutic relationship, suggesting that interpersonal synchrony plays an important role in clinical settings. The chapter offers a model linking clinical research on psychotherapy and social-psychological research on interpersonal synchrony. The chapter reviews empirical research supporting the model and suggests that interpersonal synchrony has much promise as a basic social-psychology mechanism that contributes to clinical outcomes.

Part III turns to the contribution of applied social psychology to effective interpersonal relations and communication.

Mikulincer and Shaver (Chapter 10) review attachment theory, one of the most useful contemporary conceptual frameworks for understanding emotion regulation, interpersonal behavior, and social functioning. The availability of caring, supportive relationship beginning in infancy is crucial to developing a sense of safety and security. The chapter presents a theoretical model of the attachment behavioral system and describes the intrapsychic and interpersonal manifestations of attachment security. Empirical findings supporting the theory are reviewed, and the contributions of attachment theory to the fields of education, health, welfare, management, economics, and politics are considered.

In *Chapter 11, Crano and Ruybal* explore the role of parental monitoring in preventing adolescent suicide and depression, a leading cause of adolescent mortality. They review the epidemiological literature linking parental monitoring and warmth with adolescent drug use and depression and suggest that parental influence may sometimes play an unintended facilitative role in drug use among adolescents, and drug use, in turn, appears linked to exacerbated depressive symptoms among youth.

Kovera (Chapter 12) looks at the role that social interactions may play in biasing legal outcomes. The chapter documents how attorneys' expectations about potential jurors' attitudes influence the questions they ask, their assessments of their attitudes, and consequently the verdicts that jurors render. In another stream of research, the expectancies of lineup administrators produced suggestive behaviors that increased mistaken identifications. The chapter concludes that social interactions in legal settings can be a source of bias in legal decisions.

Kross and Chandhok (Chapter 13) discuss what we have learned about how online social networks such as Facebook influence people's emotional lives. The chapter offers a brief overview of research on the links between online social network use and emotional well-being, and describes a research program exploring how "active" and "passive" social network use influences how people feel in the lab and in daily life. The potential use of online social networks to promote well-being is considered.

Part IV of the book features chapters that discuss the beneficial role that applications of social psychology can play in public affairs and political behavior.

Forgas and Lantos (Chapter 14) explore the application of psychology to the political domain, and focus on the role of collective narcissism in explaining the recent rise of illiberal populist movements. The chapter adopts an integrative multi-method approach to document the emergence of collective narcissism as a key feature in the rise of anti-liberalism in a number of countries. These processes are illustrated through the recent history of Hungary, the prime exponent of illiberalism in Europe. The chapter reviews historical evidence, data from national surveys, and the analysis of linguistic narratives as well as empirical studies linking collective narcissism to populist politics.

In *Chapter 15, Wohl and Stefaniak* explore the role of another group emotion: collective nostalgia in political behavior. Collective nostalgia is often experienced when the in-group is perceived to be losing the connection to its cherished past, and leads to a desire to re-establish a sense of collective continuity. Inspired by literature on social representations of history, the chapter argues that the content of collective nostalgia holds predictive utility in understanding political reactions. Nostalgia for an open society yields constructive intergroup responses (e.g., support for immigration), and nostalgia for a homogenous society yields destructive intergroup responses (e.g., anti-immigration sentiments). The authors discuss how collective nostalgia may be used by populist leaders as a political tool.

In *Chapter 16, Jussim, Careem, Honeycutt, and Stevens* critically evaluate the capacity of IAT (Implicit Association Test) scores to explain real-world racial inequality. Their review indicates that the IAT is not a clean measure of either implicit biases or of associations. A series of heuristic models show that IAT scores can only explain a modest portion of racial inequality. Given its serious shortcomings, the chapter concludes that much more research is needed to fully understand what the IAT measures and explains before its widespread application is justified.

Schmader (Chapter 17) argues that social psychology is uniquely positioned to understand the key components of workplace culture and to design and test interventions that might foster a more inclusive culture in organisations. The chapter considers three interrelated levels of workplace culture: the institutional, individual, and interpersonal. Schmader reviews research that examines subtle cues to exclusion experienced by women at each of these levels. The chapter also explores evidence showing that interventions might successfully target one or more levels to cultivate a more inclusive culture for women and other devalued groups.

In summary, our aim with this book is to explore applications of social psychology can contribute to a better understanding of real-life problems at the individual, interpersonal, and social levels of analysis. In this introductory chapter in particular, we tried to survey some of the most important historical, cultural, evolutionary, and psychological issues that have a bearing on how social psychology is applied to real life. Contributions to this volume were selected to offer a broad and representative overview of recent research developments in this important area. As editors, we are deeply grateful to all our contributors for accepting our invitation to attend this, the 21st Sydney Symposium of Social Psychology, and sharing their valuable ideas with our readers. We sincerely hope that the insights contained in these chapters will contribute not only to the science of applied social psychology, but also to a better understanding of the manifold roles that we as psychologists can play in improving human affairs.

References

Albright, M. (2018). *Fascism: A warning*. New York, NY: Harper Collins Press.
Allport, F. H. (1924). *Social psychology*. Boston: Houghton Mifflin Company.
Binet, A., & Simon, T. (1909). An investigation concerning the value of the oral method. *American Annals of the Deaf, 142*(3), 35–45. doi:10.1353/aad.2012.0573, PMID 9222149
Brewer, M. B., & Crano, W. D. (2014). Research design and issues of validity. In H. T. Reis & C. M. Judd (Eds.), *Handbook of research methods in social and personality psychology* (2nd ed., pp. 11–26). New York, NY: Cambridge University Press.
Brunswik, E. (1955). Representative design and probabilistic theory in a functional psychology. *Psychological Review, 62*(3), 193–217.
Campbell, D. T. (1969). Reforms as experiments. *American Psychologist, 24*, 409–429.
Campbell, D. T. (1974). Evolutionary epistemology. In P. A. Schilpp (Ed.), *The philosophy of Karl R. Popper* (pp. 412–463). LaSalle, IL: Open Court.
Crano, W. D. (in press). Reflections on a proposal designed to enhance the internal and internal validity of research in psychology. *Psychological Inquiry*.
Cronbach, L. J. (1955). Processes affecting scores on "understanding of others" and "assumed similarity." *Psychological Bulletin*, 52, 177–193.
Fiedler, K. (2011). Voodoo correlations are everywhere—not only in neuroscience. *Perspectives on Psychological Science, 6*(2), 163–171.

Forgas, J. P. (1979). *Social episodes: The study of interaction routines*. London and New York: Academic Press.
Forgas, J. P. & Baumeister, R. F. (Eds.). (2019). *The social psychology of gullibility: Fake news, conspiracy theories and irrational beliefs*. New York: Psychology Press.
Forgas, J. P. & Eich, E. (2012). Affective influences on cognition. In A. F. Healy & R. W. Proctor (Vol. Eds.), *Experimental psychology* (2nd ed.). Vol. 4 in I. B. Weiner, *Handbook of psychology*, pp. 61–82.
Forgas, J. P., Haselton, M., & von Hippel, W. (Eds.). (2007). *Evolution and the social mind: Evolutionary psychology and social cognition*. New York: Psychology Press.
Freeman, D. (1999). *The fateful hoaxing of Margaret Mead*. New York: Basic Books.
Funder, D. C. (1995). On the accuracy of personality judgment: A realistic approach. *Psychological Review, 102*, 652–670.
Herrnstein, R., & Murray, C. (1994). *The Bell curve: Intelligence and class structure in American society*. New York: Free Press.
Judd, C. M., & Park, B. (1993). Definition and assessment of accuracy in social stereotypes. *Psychological Review, 100*, 109–128.
Kahneman, D. (2011). *Thinking, fast and slow*. New York: Macmillan.
Kelley, H. H. (1967). Attribution theory in social psychology. In D. Levine (Ed.), *Nebraska symposium on motivation* (pp. 192–238). Lincoln, Nebraska: University of Nebraska Press.
Kenny, D. A. (1994). *Interpersonal perception: A social relations analysis*. New York: Guilford.
Krueger, J. (1996). Probabilistic national stereotypes. *European Journal of Social Psychology, 26*, 961–980.
Kuhn, T. S. (1996). *The structure of scientific revolutions*. (3rd ed.). Chicago, IL: University of Chicago Press.
Lewin, K. (1943). Psychology and the process of group living. *Journal of Social Psychology, 17*, 113–131.
Lippmann, W. (1922). *Public opinion*. New York: Macmillan.
Mead, M. (1966). *Coming of age in Samoa*. London: Penguin.
Milgram, S. (1963). Behavioral study of obedience. *Journal of Abnormal and Social Psychology, 67*, 371–378.
Mischel, W. (1968). *Personality and assessment*. New York: Wiley.
Mook, D. G. (1983). In defense of external invalidity. *American Psychologist, 38*(4), 379–387.
Münsterberg, H. (1915). *On the witness stand: Essays in psychology and crime*. New York, NY: Doubleday, Page & Company. doi.org/10.1037/10854-000
Pinker, S. (1997). *How the mind works*. New York: Norton.
Razran, G. H. (1940). Conditioned response changes in rating and appraising sociopolitical slogans. *Psychological Bulletin, 37*, 481–493.
Sears, R. R. (1961). Carl Iver Hovland: 1912–1961. *The American Journal of Psychology, 74*(4), 637–639.
Sherif, M. (1936). *The psychology of social norms*. Oxford: Harper.
Skinner, B. F. (1951). *Science and human behavior*. New York: The Free Press.
Swets, J. A., Dawes, R. M., & Monahan, J. (2000). Psychological science can improve diagnostic decisions. *Psychological Science in the Public Interest, 1*(1), 1–26. doi.org/10.1111/1529-1006.001
Tajfel, H. (1969). Cognitive aspects of prejudice. *Journal of Social Issues, 25*, 79–97.

Tajfel, S. & Forgas, J. P. (1981). Social categorisation: Cognitions, values and groups. In J. P. Forgas (Ed.), *Social cognition* (pp. 113–140). London & New York: Academic Press.

Triplett, N. (1898). The dynamogenic factors in pacemaking and competition. *The American Journal of Psychology, 9*(4), 507–533.

Von Hippell, W. (2018). *The social leap*. New York, NY: Harper Collins.

Watson, J. B. (1929). *Behaviorism*. New York, NY: Norton.

Wolf, T. H. (1969). The emergence of Binet's conception and measurement of intelligence: A case history of the creative process. *Journal of the History of the Behavioral Sciences, 5*(2), 113–134.

PART I
Basic Issues and Methods

2
GROUNDING APPLIED SOCIAL PSYCHOLOGY IN TRANSLATIONAL RESEARCH

Klaus Fiedler

Introduction: From "Applied" to "Translational" Research

Kurt Lewin's wisdom that there is nothing as practical as a good theory is frequently cited and it seems to be endorsed and embraced by almost everybody who cites this statement. However, what does the statement mean? Did Lewin intend to say that when basic research is inspired by a good theory, it can be applied immediately to the real world, or that good theories allow us to equate theoretical and practical research? For instance, can the finding that distributed learning is superior to massed learning (Kornell & Bjork, 2008), which derives from an approved, incontestable theoretical principle, be equated with practical improvements in academic settings and everyday learning practices? Or, does the growing body of recent evidence on the "wisdom of crowds" (Surowiecki, 2004), which is logically rooted in Bernoulli's (1713) law of large numbers imply that, practically, all groups are more rational than all individuals, and that the accuracy of all group decisions increases with group size (Sorkin, Hays, & West, 2001), or that test validity always increases with the number of test items?

The answer to all these questions is clearly: No. A good theory cannot be equated simply with a successful practical intervention. There is still a long way from having a good theory to achieving practical success in applied settings. Lewin certainly did not want to downplay the amount of work and willpower required to translate a fully convincing idea into practical benefits. It might therefore be more adequate to refer to translational science rather than to applied science. To quote from Wikipedia (https://en.wikipedia.org/wiki/Translational_research): "translational research applies findings from basic science to enhance human health and well-being." Various impressive examples testify to the huge potential of translational science (Bjork, 1994; Swets, Dawes,

& Monahan, 2000; Wells et al., 2000). Excellent examples can also be found in Kovera (this volume) on eyewitness identification, Papies (this volume) on eating behavior, and Krahé (this volume) on social context of aggression.

It has to be admitted, though, that there are countless examples of good theories that were never translated into improved practices. The advantage of distributed learning was never implemented in university curricula. The wisdom of crowds does not prevent democratic group decisions from being often biased and irrational. Or, to provide another memory example, more than a hundred years after Galton's (1907) insightful work on regression effects, the "regression trap" continues to fool laypeople and experts in all areas of applied science (Campbell & Kenny, 1999; Fiedler & Krueger, 2012; Fiedler & Unkelbach, 2014). The failure to acknowledge that in a noisy world, plotting a second measure as a function of a primary measure must always produce a regression line with a slope less than one,[1] is at the heart of countless misunderstandings and irrational decisions and actions. As I will show below, the failure to pursue essential lines of translational research can have serious costs and result in irresponsible practical decisions.

Thus, a more moderate interpretation of Kurt Lewin may sound more realistic and encouraging: Successful practical interventions represent an ambitious and rarely accomplished goal, the attainment of which is, however, greatly facilitated when translational research is anchored in a clearly spelled-out theory. Let us illustrate this notion with a few prominent examples of successful translational science. Fundamental research on face recognition in multiple-choice settings have led to distinct procedural changes and improvements in eyewitness identification procedures (Wells et al., 2000; Wixted & Wells, 2017). For example, theory-driven experimentation has shown that sequential lineups are less likely than simultaneous lineups to produce false positives, that is, false identifications and convictions of innocent suspects. As a consequence, sequential procedures have been implemented in many places. More generally, translational research has produced profound knowledge of how to render lineups pristine diagnostic procedures (Wixted & Wells, 2017): only one suspect per lineup; suspect never more salient than fillers; caution that lineup might not include offender; double-blind testing; online confidence statement at the time of testing. Note that all these features of a pristine lineup are imported from basic-research methodology, following the ideal of "line-ups as experiments" (Kovera, this volume; Wells & Luus, 1990).

Other telling examples of uncontested practical success of theory-anchored psychological science include, for instance, Johnson and Goldstein's (2003) memorable demonstration that willingness to become an organ donor depends to an amazing degree on legal default setting. In countries like Austria and France, in which people are by default registered as organ donors, unless they actively decline, almost all citizens do not change their default status and are therefore willing to donate their organs after they die. In contrast, willingness to be registered as an organ donor is conspicuously low in countries like Germany or the Netherlands, where the default setting is not to donate (see Walton, this volume, on wise interventions).

Another nice example would be Ritov's (1996) translational work on anchoring effects in competitive markets (such as eBay). This research has shown that the best predictor of the final selling price in an auction is the initial offer, indicating that too much modesty at the beginning is hardly a prudent strategy. It is interesting to note that even exceptional evidence that exaggerating starting claims (Ku, Galinsky, & Murnighan, 2006) may sometimes discourage competitors and thereby reduce the final price can be well understood in a theory-driven translational research framework.

Note, however, that a good theory originating in fundamental science doesn't only improve the chances of strong practical interventions. One could even argue that controlled lab experiments and refined theories developed in basic research can be practically more useful than any attempt to conduct "practical research" in the real world. Legal, ethical, and pragmatic constraints do not allow us to induce real phobia and depression, to expose participants to dangerous risks, to let people gamble with non-trivial sums of money, to induce strong emotions with serious side effects, to assign different teaching methods to different school classes, or even to access confidential personal data from therapy, negotiation, or decision protocols. Moreover, because internal validity always sets an upper limit for external validity (Campbell, 1957), scientific hypothesis testing under controlled lab conditions must be logically and pragmatically antecedent to testing the generality and the limitations of hypotheses under natural conditions.[2] As shown by Bjork (1994) and discussed by Mook (1983), the results of research that attempts to mimic reality in the lab may lead to less transferable evidence than the deliberate manipulations of theoretically motivated interventions under controllable research conditions.

Using Sampling-Theory Approaches to Inform Translational Social Psychology

In the remainder of this chapter, I try to demonstrate and illustrate the emergence of translational research as a natural side effect of basic research in a theory domain that has been shown to produce "good theories" on the assembly line, namely sampling approach to judgment and decision-making. Rather than providing further post-hoc examples of influential applied work that can be traced back to basic research, the strategy here is the other way around, namely, to start from cogent theoretical ideas that promise to have strong practical implications. It goes without saying that such practical implications are still waiting to be translated, cross-validated, and exploited in applied domains. However, the potential for applied research of practical importance should be vividly apparent in any case.

Sampling approaches are well suited for at least two reasons. First, statistical sampling theory imposes a number of strong constraints on psychological predictions, such as Bernoulli's (1713) law of large numbers (i.e., the advantage of increasing sample size), which come with a guarantee of being valid on a priori grounds. So, in the realm of sampling theories (Fiedler & Juslin, 2006; Fiedler & Kutzner, 2015) there can be no doubt about what a theory actually implies. Second, the very samples of observations supposed to mediate rational or irrational judgments and decisions can be assessed in a typical sampling study, independently of the behavior to be explained. So, they provide excellent opportunities to validate the supposed causal mediation process.

Base-rate Neglect and the Asymmetry of Conditional Samples

Let us start with an illustration of this crucial point, using an example related to a basic finding known as base-rate neglect (Bar-Hillel, 1984; Tversky & Kahneman, 1974). An uncontestable property of the empirical world is that sample estimates of conditional probabilities can be highly asymmetric. The conditional probability $p(\text{blood alcohol} | \text{accident})$ – that if a car driver is involved in an accident, he or she has an elevated blood alcohol level – is presumably much higher than the reverse conditional probability $p(\text{accident} | \text{blood alcohol})$ of an accident, given elevated blood alcohol. Assuming that the base rate of car accidents is (fortunately) much lower than the base rate of elevated blood alcohol – that is, $p(\text{accident}) < p(\text{blood alcohol})$ – the former conditional must be much lower than the latter conditional: $p(\text{accident} | \text{blood alcohol}) < p(\text{blood alcohol} | \text{accident})$. The general mathematical (Bayesian) rule says that the ratio of conditionals is equal to the ratio of base rates, $p(Y|X)/p(X|Y) = p(X)/p(Y)$. Thus, the conditional probability of a less likely event given a more likely event must be lower than the reverse conditional probability of a more likely event, given a less likely event.

However, laypeople like experts often exhibit a base-rate neglect, that is, their judgments fail to take the asymmetry of base rates into account, especially when the conditional structure of the problem is less apparent or is not available at all (Gavanski & Hui, 1992). For instance, when estimating the danger of blood alcohol, which calls for an estimate of $p(\text{accident} | \text{blood alcohol})$, the relevant statistics are not available, because one cannot assess the level of blood alcohol in a representative sample huge enough to yield a reasonable number of such rare events as car accidents. In such a situation, people commonly rely on the reverse conditional, $p(\text{blood alcohol} | \text{accident})$, which is easily available because virtually all drivers involved in an accident undergo an alcohol test. It should be obvious, though, that $p(\text{blood alcohol} | \text{accident})$ must grossly overestimate the danger of blood alcohol. Assuming that elevated blood alcohol is, say, ten times more likely than accidents, the available sample statistic exaggerates the danger by the same factor 10!

Self-evident and banal as this example may appear, it is at the heart of some of the strongest biases in risk assessment. Because the base rate $p(HIV)$ of people who have contracted the HIV virus is much lower than the base rate $p(+tested)$ of people who are tested positively on an HIV test, the probability $p(HIV\,|\,+tested)$ that a positively-tested person has the virus is by magnitudes smaller than the reverse probability (hit rate) that a carrier of the HIV virus is tested positively. Whereas the latter conditional is virtually perfect, $p(+tested\,|\,HIV) \sim 1.00$, the former conditional is as low as $p(HIV\,|\,+tested) \sim 0.15$, as nicely explained by Swets et al., 2000.

Presumably, the diagnosticians' strong tendency to avoid false negatives (i.e., not to miss cases of real HIV), maybe for liability reasons, has led to the implementation of diagnostic tests that are overly sensitive, producing clearly more positive test results than there are HIV cases in the population. As a consequence of such base-rate neglect (Bar-Hillel, 1984), a huge number of false positives mislead practitioners and lay people to drastically overestimate the certainty with which a positive test indicates the HIV virus. To repeat, if someone is tested positively in an unselective screening test, the true probability that the person actually has the virus is as low as 15 percent![3] (A related point regarding implicit bias is made by Jussim, this volume.)

However, crucially, within a sampling-theoretical framework, it is possible to elucidate the process leading to such dangerous judgment biases. Thus, Fiedler, Brinkmann, Betsch, and Wild (2000) provided participants with an index-card file of patients, with the diagnosis (breast cancer or no breast cancer) on one side and a mammography test result (positive vs. negative) on the other side of each patient's index card. The distribution of all 2×2 combinations of diagnoses and test results corresponded roughly to the actual base rates and conditionals in the population. However, because the two base rates, p(breast cancer) $< p$(positive mammogram), are highly unequal (as in the HIV example above), the final judgments of p(breast cancer | positive mammogram) were radically different in two sampling conditions. When in one condition the index-card file was organized by test results, participants understood that they only had to draw a sample from the slot with positive test results, and the observed proportions of breast cancer cases indicated on the back of the sampled cards provided a rather precise estimate of the conditionals in question. In contrast, when in another condition the index-card file was organized by diagnosis, offering a very large number of no-breast cancer cases in one slot but only very few cases of breast cancer in the other slot (corresponding to the low base rate), participants would typically draw all breast cancer cases along with roughly the same number of no breast cancer cases. Thus, when the relevant conditional was not easily available, the reverse conditionals misled participants to provide drastic overestimates of p(breast cancer | +mammogram) based on samples that contained breast cancer at a rate as inflated as 50 percent (i.e., inflated by 5000 percent)!

Recall that this approach to translational research on risk assessment does not rely on weak speculations but on uncontestable Bayesian probability theorems. It does not run the danger of producing wrong predictions or non-replicable results. Not surprisingly, these results have been replicated again and again (Fiedler, 2008; Fiedler et al., 2000; Fiedler, Hütter, Schott, & Kutzner, 2019) under varying boundary conditions. And most importantly for Lewin's notion of a "good theory," it can be shown that the process underlying the sign and size of faulty risk assessments (Bodemer & Gaissmaier, 2012) can be convincingly explained by the objectively available sampling data. The strength of individual judges' biases is clearly predictable from the strength of the biases inherent in the individual judges' conditional samples drawn from the index-card file.

Output-Bound Sampling

The research documented in Fiedler (2008) highlights the malicious role of output-bound sampling. Participants were asked to take the role of a leading manager whose task was to purchase two kinds of equipment – computers and telecommunication devices – offered by three providers. To make optimal purchasing decisions, they could sample information from an available database about prior customers' positive (+) versus negative (–) experience with all three providers, with regard to both product types. On every trial, they could specify as many aspects as they wanted, that is, they could either ask for a new random draw from all database entries pertaining to computers from Provider 1, or simply computers from any provider, or negative experience with telecom devices, or any outcome and product from Provider 2, or they could leave all aspects open and simply ask for the next random draw from the entire database. In fact, in the entire database, the true success rates were exactly the same across all providers and product domains. Only the base rates varied; the frequency ratio of positive to negative experiences was constantly 2:1 for all three providers and for both product domains. However, computer entries were twice as frequent as telecom entries, and Provider 1 was twice as frequent as Provider 2, who was twice as frequent as Provider 3.

Only by never (not even on a subset of trials) specifying any provider, domain, or experience condition, but by confining oneself to an unconditional sample from the whole database, could participants obtain unbiased evidence (as in the upper chart of Figure 2.1). Unsurprisingly, though, such a strategy was virtually never chosen by the participants. They rather focused on those conditions that were relevant to testing specific hypotheses. For instance, when asked to focus on Provider 3 and find out whether Provider 3 was preferable to Providers 1 and 2, they gathered relatively more observations about the focal Provider 3, thus producing a sample, as in the middle chart of Figure 2.1. Or, when the task called for diagnostic inferences about the sources of deficits or negative

Grounding Applied Social Psychology   29

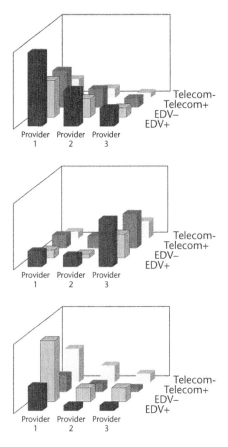

FIGURE 2.1 Frequency distribution of positive and negative experience with two product types (computers and telecom) from three different providers. The upper chart shows an unbiased (unconditional) sample; conditional samples from the same universe look quite different when comparing Provider 3 with Providers 1 and 2 (middle chart) or when trying to detect the origins of negative experiences, or deficits (lower chart).

experiences, they would conditionalize sampling on negative outcomes and leave providers and domains open. The resulting distribution in the bottom chart points to the high-base-rate Provider 1 as the major source of negative outcomes.

The final judgments and purchasing decisions were reflective of these distinct sampling biases. Samples of the first two types would reveal that most experiences were positive; such positive outcomes were more strongly associated with Provider 1 in the upper chart, but relatively more associated with Provider 3 in the middle chart. In contrast, when diagnosing deficits, sampling concentrated on negative outcomes, and the more frequently observed Provider 1 became the most frequent origin of the over-sampled negative outcomes. In any case, these distinct biases in the resulting preference judgments were predictable from the relative strength of the sampling biases experienced by participants who pursued different hypotheses.

Although judgments were highly sensitive to the sampled stimulus distributions in a three-dimensional space (providers × product domains × valence), they arrived at completely different evaluations, depending on the sampling perspective induced by the task instructions. An analysis of the underlying sampling processes revealed – thanks to the "good theory" that guided the entire investigation – one conspicuous source of irrational judgments biases: output-bound sampling. Output-bound sampling occurs when information search is selectively guided by the variable to be estimated from the sample. Thus, to diagnose the causes of product deficits, the sampling process focuses on mostly negative outcome, and based on the resulting (predominantly negative) sample, the most prevalent provider is found to be very negative.

But this negativity reflects the judge's own sampling bias. Although the most likely outcome in the database is clearly positive, the deliberate focus on the analysis of deficits produces highly biased samples that strongly over-represent negative outcomes, and this self-determined sampling bias misleads judges to provide mostly negative judgments of the provider with the highest base rate.

Practical importance of output-bound sampling biases in applied contexts. Output-bound sampling is at the heart of prominent translational research. An abstract concept from fundamental research turns out to be of enormous practical value in many applied domains. The likelihood p(HIV | positive HIV test) that a person who is tested positively actually has the HIV virus is strongly overestimated because the samples used for the estimate contain roughly the same 50 percent of HIV cases and non-HIV cases, even though the HIV base rate in the universe is much less than 1 percent (Fiedler et al., 2000; Fiedler et al., 2019). To be sure, the estimates accurately reflect the proportion of HIV cases in the sample, but the sample on which the estimate is based grossly over-represents the variable to be estimated.

Some manifestations of output-bound sampling appear blatant and almost unbelievable. For instance, the continued high reputation of polygraph lie detection is due to the systematic exclusion from study samples of those cases that could have invalidated the polygraph test. Only cases in which a positive polygraph test result is validated by a defendant's (genuine or strategic) confession are typically retained in the sample, because a confession is considered to be essential for a criterion of the "ground truth" (Fiedler, Schmid & Stahl, 2002). Innocent cases that do not confess are thus excluded by a sampling strategy that comes close to self-deception.

Another example from legal psychology concerns the composition of lineups for eyewitness identification. A severe case of output-bound sampling arises when the selection of a suspect for a lineup is based on a synthesized photo constructed from the witness's own report of the perpetrator's appearance. Given such output-bound sampling of the suspect's appearance, completely tuned to the witness's memory bias, it is no wonder that the same witness then often identifies the (innocent) suspect who resembles the witness's own memory biases (see Wixted & Wells, 2017, for a memorable review).

"MeToo" Movement. For a particularly prominent recent example of a media effect, consider the so-called MeToo movement, that is, the snowball effect of people revealing that they have also been the victim of rape or sexual assault or harassment. There can be no doubt that this public sensitization movement is meant to uncover intolerable and often criminal behavior and that we have to do all we can to tackle this problem. Nevertheless, the MeToo revelation process is seriously biased as an estimation procedure, because it is built on a severe form of output-bound sampling, mobilizing exactly the subset of sexual victims whose prevalence cannot be estimated from such a sample. Nevertheless, the absolute volume of the sample of women joining the MeToo movement is interpreted as an indicator of the prevalence of a serious social problem. This is irrational and strongly misleading, because the output-bound sampling design does not allow us to make any inferences about relative prevalence. One may also suspect that inflated estimates of sexual transgressions create a descriptive norm (Cialdini, 2012) that serves to downplay the severity of apparently "normal" habits.

Pitfalls of sampling truncation. An intriguing special case of output-bound sampling arises when sample size is not an independent variable, but when stopping depends on the information gathered so far. For example, an interview or interrogation is truncated as soon as sufficient information has been accrued; consumers cease sampling information and draw a purchasing decision when they know enough about different products; a democratic decision is made when a committee has formed its preferences; or an empirical study is closed at the moment the results look strong enough. Under such conditions of self-truncated information sampling, the law of the large number turns into the opposite: a small-sample advantage (Prager & Fiedler, in press; Prager, Krueger & Fiedler, 2018). A self-truncated small sample has remained so small exactly because it happened to provide such a clear-cut picture of the existing trend in the universe. In contrast, a larger sample had to grow to such a size because it did not reveal a clear-cut impression from the beginning. Thus, when sample size becomes a dependent variable that reflects the amount of information or diagnosticity of the initial evidence, a characteristic "less-is-more" effect can be exploited (Gigerenzer, Todd & the ABC group, 1999; Hogarth & Karelaia, 2005; Katsikopoulos, 2010). Quick actions and decisions can be made at high levels of confidence based on small samples causing little conflict and low information costs. In many situations, this may facilitate adaptive decisions at minimal levels of information cost. In other situations, for instance, in the public health domain, it is possible that strong initial test results motivate truncation of a test series, justifying the premature implementation of a medical treatment or a pharmacological agent that might not have approved in an extended test series.

Sampling at Different Aggregation Levels

Success and failure of evidence-based decision-making and political intervention depend on the analysis of the available data at an appropriate level of aggregation. Different aggregation levels can convey radically different pictures of the same reality. At the individual level, the rate of illiteracy is almost the same for Black and White people, but at the level of districts or social ecologies, the correlation between illiteracy and Black versus White race can be as high as $r = 0.92$ (Robinson, 1950). Economic wealth at the national level (in terms of the gross national product – GNP) can come along with a very high rate of poverty at the individual level. Or, the same consumer products may be sold at higher prices in cheaper than in more expensive supermarkets (Vogel, Kutzner, Fiedler, & Freytag, 2013).

As a consequence, many political debates and economic conflicts arise because different parties rely on different aggregation levels, often depending on which level provides a more favorable picture of one's own position. For instance, a rightist political party may praise the seemingly successful GNP in a country that minimizes taxes for industrial organizations, whereas a leftist party in the same country may complain about high individual-level rates of unemployment and poverty. Or, group-level preferences may diverge from the individual-level preferences in democratic decision-making (Fiedler, Hofferbert, Woellert, Krüger, & Koch, 2015), just as group-level research data may not tell us much about the behavior of individual participants in behavioral research.

The basic insight that different aggregation levels often reflect different causal mechanisms is of utmost importance for all applications of behavioral research. The danger of confusing highly divergent trends that may coexist at different aggregation levels is particularly striking in recent analyses of "big data," which come with the alleged guarantee of high reliability and robustness. It suffices to illustrate this point here with reference to a couple of recent studies of the relationship between air pollution and unethical behavior. One investigation by Lu, Lee, Gino, and Galinsky (2018), based on air pollution data and rates of six crime types in 9,360 American cities, found that all crime rates and all pollution indices jointly decreased regularly from 1999 to 2009. This led the authors to infer a systematic positive relationship between air pollution and ethical behavior. In contrast, in another recent big-data study using monthly data from British cities (Heck, Thielmann, Klein, & Hilbig, 2020), the authors found that air pollution is regularly higher in winter months, whereas the prevalence of different crime types increases strongly in summer time. This pattern is strongly suggestive of a marked negative relationship between pollution and immoral behavior. Not surprisingly, annual data reflect completely different causal influences (e.g., legal and political changes across an entire decade) than monthly data (e.g., seasonal temperature changes). At the same time, this example highlights the insight that the one and only true correlation between air pollution and immoral behavior does not exist. Completely different correlations seem to reflect different underlying processes at different levels of aggregation, calling for "good theories" that are sorely needed to understand the evidence gained from "big data."

Evading the Regression Trap in Translational Research

Let us finally consider the practical significance of the "regression trap" – another topic of basic and translational research that applied social psychology must keep in mind. Regressiveness is an essential property of the probabilistic world, which is however notoriously ignored or at least neglected. When predicting one variable Y from another variable X, an imperfect correlation $|r_{XY}| < 1$ means that predicted Y values must be less extreme than predictor values of X. That is, a regression slope of $|b| < 1$ implies that variance in the predicted values will be less than the variance in the predictor. To estimate the expected deviation $y = Y - M_Y$ of Y from the mean M_Y, the corresponding deviation score $x = X - M_X$ of the predictor has to be multiplied by the correlation r_{XY}. If $r_{XY} = 0.5$, the extremity or deviation scores of Y will shrink by one-half; if $r_{XY} = 0.67$, Y deviations shrink to two-thirds of the predictor values. Because the principle of regression is well understood, it makes for the kind of "good theory" that Lewin (1943) found to be so practical. Indeed, the failure to understand regressive shrinkage renders applied science worthless.

Overconfidence. Let us illustrate this point with respect to one of the most consequential topics in applied decision-making science, the so-called overconfidence bias. Let X be subjective confidence that a binary judgment or choice is correct and let Y be the objective accuracy rate. Granting that accuracy is not perfectly correlated with confidence, plotting accuracy as a function of confidence will be subject to regressive shrinkage. Assuming $r_{accuracy,confidence} = 0.50$, it can be expected that high confidence scores of, say, 0.40 or 0.30 above the midpoint will regress to accuracy scores of only 0.20 and 0.15 above the midpoint. Because the vast majority of all overconfidence studies plot accuracy as a function of confidence, overconfidence evidence reflects to a large extent a regression artifact. As Erev, Wallsten, and Budescu (1994) have shown, the same data set that seems to exhibit overconfidence can be shown to yield underconfidence, when in a reverse analysis, confidence is plotted as a function of accuracy. Then very high or high accuracy scores turn out to predict more moderate confidence scores. Ignoring this fundamental insight renders applied research faulty and incompetent. Genuine overconfidence must exceed the normal regression effect that can be expected from the less than perfect confidence-accuracy correlation.

Regression and unrealistic optimism. Because the degree of regression is an inverse function of reliability (r_{XY}), and because reliability increases with amount of information, many practical issues are subject to differential regression. For instance, self-judgments can be predicted to be less regressive than judgments of others, simply because a larger amount of information about the self raises the reliability to a higher level, compared to the lower amount of information about others. Pursuing this hardly contestable idea, Moore and Healy (2008) have greatly developed our understanding of unrealistic optimism, or the often-cited phenomenon that most people seem to be better than average. However, a more refined analysis informed by differential regression suggests how important it is to distinguish between three different variants of self-related overconfidence: (1) performance *overestimation* relative to objective performance; (2) *overplacement* of oneself relative to others, and (3) *overprecision* of subjective judgments relative to an actually much broader confidence interval.

In general, all judgments, whether they refer to the self or to others, overestimate the (actually low) true performance on difficult tasks and underestimate the (actually high) true performance on easy tasks, in line with the ubiquitous regression effect. However, this so-called hard-easy effect is less pronounced for self-referent than for other-referent judgments. Thus, the typical underestimation bias on easy tasks is stronger for others than for the self. Yet, on difficult tasks, overestimation is more pronounced in other-referent than in self-referent judgments. As a consequence, comparisons of self and others exhibit overplacement (i.e., relatively more positive self than other judgments) on easy tasks, but underplacement (i.e., relatively less positive self than other judgments) on actually difficult tasks. Finally, overprecision is more stable than the other two types of overconfidence. Regardless of whether hard or easy tasks produce (optimistic) overestimation versus (pessimistic) underestimation errors, or (self-devaluating) underplacement versus (self-serving) overplacement effects, subjective confidence intervals are generally too narrow. As reported by Moore and Healy (2008), 90 percent confidence intervals often contain the correct answer at a rate less than 50 percent (see also Juslin, Winman & Hansson, 2007). Apparently, then, subjective estimates of upper and lower boundaries of a confidence interval are also subject to "normal" regression. Subjective estimates are less extreme than the actual interval boundaries.

The ubiquitous regression trap. A plethora of evidence on biases in laypeople and experts falling into the regression trap highlight Campbell and Kenny's (1999, p. ix) conclusion that regression is "as inevitable as death and taxes." Its practical significance can hardly be overstated. For a very prominent example, the effectiveness of psychotherapy is often overestimated when interventions start in a crisis, which presumably exaggerates the patient's true pathological state (Campbell, 1996). Because the reliability with which a crisis can be measured is less than perfect, the apparent crisis may to some extent reflect an outlier, and the patient's true state can be expected to be less critical.

As a consequence, mere regression toward a less exaggerated measure of well-being can underlie an apparent therapy success.

For another example, the stock market is essentially regressive. Granting that stock prices are subject to stationary stochastic variation over time, a wise strategy is to invest anti-cyclically, that is, to buy stocks that are in a crisis and to sell stocks that are performing well. By analogy, empirical findings that yielded the strongest effect sizes in the original study produce relatively smaller effect sizes in a replication study, as demonstrated by Fiedler and Prager (2018) with respect to the 100 replications of the Open Science Collaboration (2015).

Stelzl (1982) discusses the question of why older teachers tend to give up the idealist educational theories of which they were fully convinced when they were young. As teachers get older, they replace their belief in the superiority of reward by the conviction that punishment is more effective than reward. This pessimistic shift may reflect a continuous influence of the regression trap: Assuming that student conduct underlies stochastic variation, positive conduct that is rewarded is typically followed by less positive conduct, whereas negative conduct that is punished is typically followed by more positive conduct. The resulting impression that punishment is more effective than reward may simply reflect the teacher's blindness for regression: Even in the absence of reward or punishment, positive states would have been followed by more negative conduct and vice versa.

Concluding Remarks

In a volume devoted to applied social psychology, the value of solid theorizing cannot be emphasized too much. While Kurt Lewin's (1943) famous parol concerning the practical value of a good theory is often cited and applauded, it is rarely explicitly explained why this is the case. Providing a twofold answer to this intriguing question was the purpose of the present chapter. On one hand, it was argued and illustrated that translational science – anchored in theory-driven fundamental research in the lab – often entails the potential to be translatable to diverse domains of real social life. Prominent examples include the enormous contributions made by memory researchers to improving eyewitness identification procedures (Wixted & Wells, 2017), the translation of basic insights on effective learning to academic learning contexts (Metcalfe & Kornell, 2007), the key role of base-rate neglect for risk assessment and risk communication (Fiedler, 2010), or the translation of anchoring effects to the applied domain of auctions and negotiations (Ritov, 1996). While the focus in this chapter was on the practical value of sampling theories in particular (Fiedler & Kutzner, 2015), a similar point could be made for practical implications and applications of several theoretical approaches, such as dissonance theory (Cooper, 2012), construal-level theory (Trope & Liberman, 2010), regulatory-focus theory (Higgins, 2012), or theories of affect regulation (Forgas & Ciarrochi, 2002).

On the other hand, however, Lewin's argument must not be reduced to generously granting theory a minor role in a field of applied psychology, which is otherwise dominated by "real" research conducted in the field, with reference to natural situations, political conflicts, social movements, migrants, patients, and victims of aggression and crime. Rather, a more offensive interpretation of Lewin is that such seemingly relevant work under naturalistic conditions can be error-prone, premature, and irresponsible if applied researchers fail to do their homework and take the warnings and insights from fundamental and translational research into account. An attempt was made to explain that the failure to beware of such theoretical and methodological issues as the output-bound sampling, the regression trap, and the pitfalls of different aggregation levels can undermine the value of even the most laborious and well-motivated applied work.

Finally, and reminiscent of the intriguing lesson conveyed by Bjork (1994), strictly controlled lab research under controlled conditions may be more transferrable to the real world than any attempt to mimic "real life" in a controlled study. Let us close this chapter with a quotation of a similar point made by Mook (1983, p. 379):

> ... psychological investigations are accused of "failure to generalize to the real world" because of sample bias or artificiality of setting ... such "generalizations" often are not intended. Rather than making predictions about the real world from the laboratory, we may test predictions that specify what ought to happen in the lab. We may regard even "artificial" findings as interesting because they show what can occur ...

even when the precise conditions in which they actually occur are not (yet) known.

Author Note

The work underlying the present article was supported by a grant provided by the Deutsche Forschungsgemeinschaft to the first author (FI 294/26–1). Email correspondence may be addressed to kf@psychologie.uni-heidelberg.de

Notes

1 For example, replication results must always be less pronounced than original results, for purely logical reasons (Fiedler & Prager, 2018).
2 Campbell also believed, to be sure, that empirical tests in natural environments can help refine basic theory.
3 When I included this evidence in a review article, which is based on authentic data analyzed by Swets et al. (2000), the editor wanted to intervene because a friend of his, an experienced radiologist, told him these statistics cannot be correct. However, the figures are valid. The problem is only that even experts like the editor's radiologist friend fall prey to base-rate fallacies.

References

Bar-Hillel, M. (1984). Representativeness and fallacies of probability judgment. *Acta Psychologica, 55*(2), 91–107. doi.org/10.1016/0001-6918(84)90062-3

Bernoulli, J. (1713). *Ars conjectandi, opus posthumum* [The art of conjecturing, posthumous work]. Basel, Switzerland: Thurneysen Brothers.

Bjork, R. A. (1994). Memory and metamemory considerations in the training of human beings. In J. Metcalfe, A. P. Shimamura, J. Metcalfe, A. P. Shimamura (Eds.), *Metacognition: Knowing about knowing* (pp. 185–205). Cambridge, MA: The MIT Press.

Bodemer, N., & Gaissmaier, W. (2012). Risk communication in health. In *Handbook of risk theory* (pp. 621–660). Dordrecht: Springer.

Campbell, D. T. (1957). Factors relevant to the validity of experiments in social settings. *Psychological Bulletin, 54*(4), 297–312.

Campbell, D. T. (1996). Regression artifacts in time-series and longitudinal data. *Evaluation and Program Planning, 19*, 377–389.

Campbell, D. T., & Kenny, D. A. (1999). *A primer on regression artifacts*. New York, NY: Guilford Press.

Cialdini, R. B. (2012). The focus theory of normative conduct. In P. A. M. Van Lange, A. W. Kruglanski, & E. T. Higgins (Eds.), *Handbook of theories of social psychology, Vol. 2*. (pp. 295–312). Thousand Oaks, CA: Sage Publications Ltd. doi.org/10.4135/9781446249222.n41

Cooper, J. (2012). Cognitive dissonance theory. In P. A. M. Van Lange, A. W. Kruglanski, & E. T. Higgins (Eds.), *Handbook of theories of social psychology, Vol. 1*. (pp. 377–397). Thousand Oaks, CA: Sage Publications Ltd. doi.org/10.4135/9781446249215.n19

Erev, I., Wallsten, T. S., & Budescu, D. V. (1994). Simultaneous over-and underconfidence: The role of error in judgment processes. *Psychological Review, 101*(3), 519–527. doi:10.1037/0033-295X.101.3.519

Fiedler, K. (2008). The ultimate sampling dilemma in experience-based decision making. *Journal of Experimental Psychology: Learning, Memory, and Cognition, 34*(1), 186–203. doi.org/10.1037/0278-7393.34.1.186

Fiedler, K. (2010). The asymmetry of causal and diagnostic inferences: A challenge for the study of implicit attitudes. In J. P. Forgas, J. Cooper, & W. D. Crano (Eds.), *The psychology of attitudes and attitude change* (pp. 75–92). New York, NY: Psychology Press.

Fiedler, K., Brinkmann, B., Betsch, T., & Wild, B. (2000). A sampling approach to biases in conditional probability judgments: Beyond base rate neglect and statistical format. *Journal of Experimental Psychology: General, 129*, 399–418.

Fiedler, K., Hofferbert, J., Woellert, F., Krüger, T., & Koch, A. (2015). The tragedy of democratic decision making. In J. P. Forgas, K. Fiedler, & W. D. Crano (Eds.), *Social psychology and politics*. (Vol. 17, pp. 193–208). New York, NY: Psychology Press.

Fiedler, K., Hütter, M., Schott, M., & Kutzner, F. (2019). Metacognitive myopia and the overutilization of misleading advice. *Journal of Behavioral Decision Making*. doi.org/10.1002/bdm.2109

Fiedler, K., & Juslin, P. (Eds.). (2006). *Information sampling and adaptive cognition*. Cambridge University Press.

Fiedler, K., & Krueger, J. I. (2012). More than an artifact: Regression as a theoretical construct. In J. I. Krueger (Ed.), *Social judgment and decision making* (pp. 171–189). New York, NY: Psychology Press.

Fiedler, K., & Kutzner, F. (2015). Information sampling and reasoning biases: Implications for research in judgment and decision making. In G. Keren & G. Wu (Eds.), *The Wiley Blackwell handbook of judgment and decision making* (pp. 380–403). New York: Wiley.

Fiedler, K., & Prager, J. (2018). The regression trap and other pitfalls of replication science—Illustrated by the report of the Open Science Collaboration. *Basic and Applied Social Psychology, 40*(3), 115–124. doi.org/10.1080/01973533.2017.1421953

Fiedler, K., Schmid, J., & Stahl, T. (2002). What is the current truth about polygraph lie detection? *Basic and Applied Social Psychology, 24*(4), 313–324. doi.org/10.1207/S15324834BASP2404_6

Fiedler, K., & Unkelbach, C. (2014). Regressive judgment: Implications of a universal property of the empirical world. *Current Directions in Psychological Science, 23*(5), 361–367.

Forgas, J. P., & Ciarrochi, J. V. (2002). On managing moods: Evidence for the role of homeostatic cognitive strategies in affect regulation. *Personality and Social Psychology Bulletin, 28*(3), 336–345. doi.org/10.1177/0146167202286005

Galton, F. (1907). Vox populi. *Nature, 75,* 450–451.

Gavanski, I., & Hui, C. (1992). Natural sample spaces and uncertain belief. *Journal of Personality and Social Psychology, 63*(5), 766–780. doi.org/10.1037/0022-3514.63.5.766

Gigerenzer, G., Todd, P. M., & the ABC Research Group (2000). *Simple heuristics that make us smart.* New York: Oxford University Press.

Heck, D. W., Thielmann, I., Klein, S. A., & Hilbig, B. E. (2020). On the limited generality of air pollution and anxiety as causal determinants of unethical behavior: Commentary on Lu, Lee, Gino, & Galinsky (2018). *Psychological Science.*

Higgins, E. T. (2012). Regulatory focus theory. In P. M. Van Lange, A. W. Kruglanski, E. T. Higgins, P. M. Van Lange, A. W. Kruglanski, & E. T. Higgins (Eds.), *Handbook of theories of social psychology (Vol 1)* (pp. 483–504). Thousand Oaks, CA: Sage Publications Ltd.

Hogarth, R. M., & Karelaia, N. (2005). Ignoring information in binary choice with continuous variables: When is less "more"? *Journal of Mathematical Psychology, 49*(2), 115–124.

Johnson, E. J., & Goldstein, D. G. (2003). Do defaults save lives? *Science, 302,* 1338–1339.

Juslin, P., Winman, A., & Hansson, P. (2007). The naïve intuitive statistician: A naïve sampling model of intuitive confidence intervals. *Psychological Review, 114*(3), 678–703.

Katsikopoulos, K. V. (2010). The less-is-more effect: Predictions and tests. *Judgment and Decision Making, 5*(4), 244–257.

Kornell, N., & Bjork, R. A. (2008). Learning concepts and categories: Is spacing the "enemy of induction?" *Psychological Science, 19*(6), 585–592. doi.org/10.1111/j.1467-9280.2008.02127.x

Ku, G., Galinsky, A. D., & Murnighan, J. K. (2006). Starting low but ending high: A reversal of the anchoring effect in auctions. *Journal of Personality and Social Psychology, 90*(6), 975–986.

Lewin, K. (1943). Psychology and the process of group living. *The Journal of Social Psychology, SPSSI Bulletin, 17,* 113–131.

Lu, J. G., Lee, J. J., Gino, F., & Galinsky, A. D. (2018). Polluted morality: Air pollution predicts criminal activity and unethical behavior. *Psychological Science, 29*(3), 340–355. doi.org/10.1177/0956797617735807

Metcalfe, J., & Kornell, N. (2007). Principles of cognitive science in education: The effects of generation, errors, and feedback. *Psychonomic Bulletin & Review, 14*(2), 225–229. doi.org/10.3758/BF03194056

Mook, D. G. (1983). In defense of external invalidity. *American Psychologist, 38*(4), 379–387.

Moore, D. A., & Healy, P. J. (2008). The trouble with overconfidence. *Psychological Review, 115*(2), 502–517. doi:10.1037/0033-295X.115.2.502

Open Science Collaboration. (2015). Estimating the reproducibility of psychological science. *Science, 349*, aac4716.

Prager, J., & Fiedler, K. (2019). *Forming impressions from self-truncated samples of traits: The interplay of Thurstonian and Brunswikian sampling effects*. Manuscript submitted for publication.

Prager, J., Krueger, J. I., & Fiedler, K. (2018). Towards a deeper understanding of impression formation—New insights gained from a cognitive-ecological perspective. *Journal of Personality and Social Psychology, 115*(3), 379–397. doi.org/10.1037/pspa0000123

Ritov, I. (1996). Anchoring in simulated competitive market negotiation. *Organizational Behavior and Human Decision Processes, 67*(1), 16–25. doi.org/10.1006/obhd.1996.0062

Robinson, W. S. (1950). Ecological correlations and the behavior of individuals. *American Sociological Review, 15*, 351–357. doi.org/10.2307/2087176

Sorkin, R. D., Hays, C. J., & West, R. (2001). Signal-detection analysis of group decision making. *Psychological Review, 108*(1), 183–203. doi.org/10.1037/0033-295X.108.1.183

Stelzl, I. (1982). *Fehler und fallen der statistik*. [*Errors and traps of statistics*]. Bern: Huber.

Surowiecki, J. (2004). *The wisdom of crowds: Why the many are smarter than the few and how collective wisdom shapes business, economies, societies, and nations*. New York, NY: Doubleday & Co.

Swets, J., Dawes, R. M., & Monahan, J. (2000). Psychological science can improve diagnostic decisions. *Psychological Science in the Public Interest, 1*, Whole No. 1.

Trope, Y., & Liberman, N. (2010). Construal-level theory of psychological distance. *Psychological Review, 117*(2), 440–463.

Tversky, A., & Kahneman, D. (1974). Judgment under uncertainty: Heuristics and biases. *Science, 185*(4157), 1124–1131. doi.org/10.1126/science.185.4157.1124

Vogel, T., Kutzner, F., Fiedler, K., & Freytag, P. (2013). How majority members become associated with rare attributes: Ecological correlations in stereotype formation. *Social Cognition, 31*(4), 427–442. doi.org/10.1521/soco_2012_1002

Wells, G. L., & Elizabeth Luus, C. A. (1990). Police lineups as experiments: Social methodology as a framework for properly conducted lineups. *Personality and Social Psychology Bulletin, 16*(1), 106–117.

Wells, G. L., Malpass, R. S., Lindsay, R. C., Fisher, R. P., Turtle, J. W., & Fulero, S. M. (2000). From the lab to the police station: A successful application of eyewitness research. *American Psychologist, 55*(6), 581–598.

Wixted, J. T., & Wells, G. L. (2017). The relationship between eyewitness confidence and identification accuracy: A new synthesis. *Psychological Science in the Public Interest, 18*(1), 10–65. doi.org/10.1177/1529100616686966

3

THE EVOLUTIONARY MISMATCH HYPOTHESIS

Implications for Applied Social Psychology

Mark van Vugt, Lianne P. de Vries and Norman P. Li

Introduction

Aliens visiting planet Earth would find Homo Sapiens a strange but remarkable species. They would discover astonishing examples of human intelligence and ingenuity such as airplanes, skyscrapers, electricity, and the internet. At the same time, they would also witness our miserable failure in preventing poverty, violence, disease, and ecological disasters. Humans are both highly intelligent and highly stupid, these alien anthropologists would probably conclude. It is true, we humans are very good at some things but very bad at others. People are able to recognize the faces of persons they met many years ago, but they easily misremember the telephone numbers of their best friends. People are very patient in accumulating knowledge and training skills through a long period of intense education, but they are not patient enough to save money for their pension or resist the temptation of a strawberry cheesecake. And, although most people would be reluctant to steal from shopkeepers, these same individuals have no moral reservations about illegally downloading music and movies from the internet.

Why are humans clever and moral in some situations, but stupid and amoral in others? Why do we exercise self-control in some contexts but not in others? Answers to these questions are highly relevant for both social psychologists and public policy-makers. If we can find out how the human mind has evolved, and how it operates in certain environments, then perhaps we can come up with policies and interventions that are effective in changing people's attitudes and decisions. So far, public policy programs have been built on the model of Homo Economicus, the idea that humans guide their actions on the basis of a rational calculation of costs and benefits (Fox & Sitkin, 2015; Loewenstein, Bryce,

Hagmann, & Rajpal, 2015). However, as we shall see, the behavior of Homo Sapiens is guided by a deeper evolutionary rationality that consists of a set of instincts, thought patterns (Kahneman, 2011), emotions (see also Wohl & Stefaniak; and Forgas & Lantos, this volume), and preferences (Kenrick, Griskevicius, Neuberg, & Schaller, 2010) that can depart dramatically from what appears to be rational (Johnson, Price, & van Vugt, 2013). Take an intervention program for increasing sign-up rates for post-mortem organ donations. Simply changing the default option from opt-in to opt-out doubles participation (from 42 percent to 82 percent) without any change in underlying beliefs or preferences (Johnson & Goldstein, 2003). Such "nudges" have been found to be fairly effective at changing people's behaviors, in part, because they pay attention to the constraints of human psychology (Baumard, 2015).

The core hypothesis put forward here is that the human mind evolved to solve particular challenges very efficiently. But these challenges were part of a relatively stable environment in which humans lived for many thousands of generations, the African savanna, out of which anatomically modern humans migrated some 60,000 years ago. Yet when environments change quickly – as they increasingly have been doing – new threats and opportunities emerge to which our minds may not be perfectly calibrated (see also Forgas et al., this volume). The result is evolutionary mismatch. In this contribution, we will first investigate the concept of mismatch as a core tenet of evolutionary theory and evolutionary psychology and how mismatch affects our preferences and decisions. We also discuss how to find evidence for mismatched behaviors. We will then discuss the implications of the mismatch hypothesis for some of the core domains of applied social psychology, from close relationships to work performance, politics, health, and sustainability. Finally, we note the implications of mismatch for public policy and how to design interventions, such as nudging strategies, that are better aligned with the core psychology of Homo Sapiens.

Evolutionary Challenges and Psychological Mechanisms

The mismatch hypothesis is one of the foundational principles of evolutionary psychology (Li, van Vugt, & Colarelli, 2018). Evolutionary psychology considers human cognition, emotion, and decision-making to be the products of psychological mechanisms that evolved to solve recurrent, adaptive challenges concerning survival and reproduction (Buss, 2015; Tooby & Cosmides, 1992). These psychological mechanisms are perfectly calibrated to the environment in which humans evolved, which is often referred to as the EEA, the environment of evolutionary adaptedness. The EEA for many of the more specialized human traits and their underlying mechanisms such as culture, cooperation, language, leadership, mate, and food preferences lies on the African savanna where the human lineage evolved over a period of several million years. Around 6 million years ago, the human lineage and that of our closest cousins – what are now bonobos and chimpanzees – split into separate branches. Over the course of hominid evolution, many key features of Homo evolved such as bipedal walking, retractable thumbs, and increased skull size. These physical changes can be easily determined from the fossil record (Kaplan, Hill, Lancaster, & Hurtado, 2000). The genus Homo that marks the beginning of our modern Homo Sapiens lineage evolved around 2 million years ago with the withdrawal of forests in East Africa and the emergence of the savannas, vast open grasslands. Paleo-archaeological and anthropological evidence supports the idea that our human ancestors lived in relatively small groups, essentially extended families, that were nomadic, and migrated with the seasons and available food resources (Foley, 1997).

Increased reliance on large game animals for nutrition increased cooperation and enhanced division of labor between hunters (usually men) and gatherers (usually women) (Tooby & DeVore, 1987). Food sharing emerged as a collective insurance system against hunger, and language emerged as a way to maintain social networks over increasingly large distances (Dunbar, 2003). Culture formed a buffer against perturbations in the environment which required novel social learning strategies based on imitation and teaching (Henrich, 2015). Prestigious individuals emerged as leaders to orchestrate coordinated group activities for group defense and collective movement (van Vugt & Ahuja, 2010). The uniquely human ability to accept abstract symbolic information from others as a substitute for reality was the foundation of all integrative belief systems, as well as gullibility and superstition throughout history (Harari, 2014; see also Kross; and Crano & Ruybal, this volume). The psychological mechanisms underlying these aspects of human behavior evolved over this long period, and were conserved when humans migrated out of Africa some 60,000 years ago. As a result of this transition, humans have begun living in ecologies and climatic conditions that are vastly different from the EEA. The reliance on intense agriculture that began after the agricultural revolution, which happened some 10,000 years ago in several places of the world (less than 1 percent of human evolutionary time), caused further dramatic shifts in the way we live and connect to each other, resulting in dietary and lifestyle changes to which our bodies and brains are not perfectly adapted (Lieberman, 2013). Similar seismic shifts in our physical and social organization have happened since the Industrial Revolution (some 250 years ago) when machines started to take over human physical work. Currently, more than half of the world's population lives in large, densely populated cities surrounded by millions of (genetic) strangers in tall buildings with little or no space to move, or access to nature. We are now in the middle of a digital revolution, blurring the distinction between the real world and the virtual world, with the potential to create increasingly more, novel mismatches (Giphart & van Vugt, 2018; Harari, 2014; see also contributions by Blanton; and Kross, this volume).

The evolutionary mismatch hypothesis asserts that in evolutionarily novel environments, the psychological mechanisms that evolved in a long and relatively stable period of human genetic evolution may not be appropriately functioning any more, producing behaviors that are suboptimal for the individual and for society as a whole (Li et al., 2018). If this is true, this has far-reaching consequences for human psychology and public policy. Mismatch ideas have been applied before in biology, economics, health, and medicine (Gluckman & Hanson, 2004; Lieberman, 2013; Lloyd, Wilson, & Sober, 2011; Nesse & Berridge, 1997). So far, however, there has been little interest in the implications for psychology and public policy, although some scholars in social psychology (Maner & Kenrick, 2010), organizational psychology (van Vugt & Ronay, 2014), and health psychology (Curtis & Aunger, 2011) have recently started taking an interest in this concept.

Mismatch is a by-product – and inevitable consequence – of the way evolution via natural selection works. Evolution produces psychological and behavioral mechanisms that have been retained via natural selection – and thus are species-typical, heritable, efficient, and developmentally stable – because they solved a particular adaptive challenge better than alternative solutions. These mechanisms operate as heuristics, or decision rules that are (a) activated by specific environmental cues acting as inputs and (b) produce adaptive outputs in terms of cognitions, emotions, and behaviors (Gigerenzer, 2007). However, biological evolution is a relatively slow process and therefore these mechanisms may not function properly when environments change. Evolutionary mismatch refers to the adaptive lag that occurs if the environment changes more rapidly than the time needed for the mechanism to adapt to the change, and this applies equally to humans and non-humans (Li et al., 2018). The human suite of psychological mechanisms, from culture to cooperation and language, evolved mainly during the period – 99 percent of human evolution – when people lived as hunter-gatherers on the African savanna. The subsequent agricultural, industrial, and digital revolutions have produced vast divergences from the past hunter-gatherer lifestyle (Giphart & van Vugt, 2018; Tooby & Cosmides, 1992; see also Forgas & Lantos, this volume).

Mismatch problems can arise through various causes. Some of these causes are natural, such as when a lack of sunlight exposure in Nordic climates results in vitamin D deficiency and a prevalence of people with seasonal affective disorders (Hidaka, 2012). Oftentimes, mismatches are human-induced, such as when industrial pollution affects the air quality such that it increases the number of people suffering from breathing problems. Mismatches can also be distinguished on the basis of whether living in a novel environment forces them upon us, such as our bodies having fewer opportunities to move in a sedentary environment. Alternatively, mismatches can occur when novel stimuli are favored by the mechanism over stimuli that these mechanisms evolved to process, such as when children prefer to eat candy, a sweet and sugary, human-made product, over fruit containing natural sugars (Krebs, 2009; see also Papies, this volume). Mismatches can also be distinguished in terms of their impact on our psychological mechanisms. Some mismatches occur when we try to apply evolved, intuitive psychological mechanisms to evolutionarily novel problems such as assessing the risks associated with airplane travel, or saving for a pension scheme. In fact, all kinds of cognitive biases, from the sunk cost fallacy to loss aversion, may be the result of this kind of mismatch. Alternatively, mismatch may occur by approaching evolutionarily old problems such as parenting, mating, or eating by utilizing more analytical, evolutionary novel psychological mechanisms, resulting in suboptimal decisions (see Crano & Ruybal, this volume). Thus, using the dichotomy popularized by Kahneman (2011), mismatch occurs when we apply System 1 thinking to evolutionary novel problems or, the reverse, when applying System 2 thinking to evolutionary ancient problems (for a similar distinction, see Petty & Briñol, this volume).

Mismatch can occur further because of significant changes in either the inputs or outputs of the evolved psychological mechanisms such that these mechanisms are not optimally calibrated. For instance, the lack of a supportive family network nearby may serve as an input into reproductive timing mechanisms causing married couples to delay the age at which they have their first child, resulting in suboptimal reproductive outcomes (Li et al., 2018). Or, the availability of internet porn may replace the search for romantic partners as inputs into mechanisms that trigger sexual excitement and induce reproductive activity. In terms of outputs, evolved mechanisms that capitalize status and wealth into reproductive success may not be functioning properly in a world with frequent and intense competition for jobs.

Although the focus here is on evolutionary mismatches, developmental and cultural mismatches are also possible. Developmental mismatches occur when the predicted state of the environment of a fetus or newborn turns out not to be the actual adult environment. For instance, one of the factors causing adult obesity is when a prenatally undernourished individual grows up in an environment with abundant food resources (Gluckman & Hanson, 2004). Cultural mismatches occur when individuals are spatially dispersed such that the psychological mechanisms that function well in one cultural environment, say a culture of honor, produces behaviors that are detrimental in a new environment, for instance, revenge killings in a culture of dignity. More generally, cultural and psychological mismatch occurs when a species naturally adapted for intense small group life where status and identity are a natural consequence of daily interactions, finds itself in a globalized, fragmented, and impersonal post-industrial society where status and identity needs can at best be expressed through spurious and meaningless consumer choices.

Finding Evidence for Evolutionary Mismatch

Finding evidence for evolutionary mismatches is not an easy feat and although it is possible that some of the social, psychological, and physical problems that humans experience in the modern post-agricultural, post-industrial world may be the result of mismatch, it is in many cases still a working hypothesis (Giphart & van Vugt, 2018). We should also note that not all negative behaviors or psychological states are the result of mismatch. Negative emotions like anxiety, fear, sadness, and anger may be adaptive in the sense that they are the result of properly functioning psychological mechanisms responding to real threats (e.g., the loss of a job or a loved one, fear of strangers, a threat or provocation; see also Koole, this volume).

To attribute a problem to mismatch we must first show (a) what an evolved mechanism is supposed to do: its function, (b) what the underlying decision-rules the mechanism uses are, and (c) what kinds of inputs (cues) and outputs the mechanisms evolved to process and produce. The mechanism itself must show evidence of adaptation, that is: Is it designed to solve a recurrent survival or reproductive challenge? Second, we should be able to describe how the mechanism operates in an ancestral environment and, third, how it is operating in the modern environment. We must then show evidence of a discrepancy between the ancestral environment and the modern environment in terms of a change in the inputs to which the mechanism responds (e.g., missing cues, a higher intensity of cues), or a change in the consequences of the outputs it produces (Li et al., 2018). Ultimately, we must show, or at least make a persuasive case, that the mechanism, as a result of mismatch, affects personal health and psychological well-being in a way that it is not designed to do.

Testing a mismatch hypothesis – like testing any evolutionary psychology hypothesis (Schmitt & Pilcher, 2004) – requires building up a nomological network of findings from different disciplines that have something to say about human-evolved psychology, from the knowledge gathered from experiments on psychological mechanisms (psychology and neuroscience) and insights into the small-scale societies in which humans evolved (anthropology), to genetics and measures of fertility, health, and well-being in modern populations (medicine, epidemiology). A well-documented mismatch is obesity, which occurs with food choices (Figure 3.1; inspired by Sbarra, Briskin, & Slatcher, 2019). Humans likely have evolved psychological mechanisms for preferring sweet, fatty, and salty foods, because these high-calorie foods were important for survival in ancestral environments (see Papies, this volume). In ancestral environments – as in current hunter-gatherer societies – these tastes are associated with natural foods like fruits, honey, and meat and these are scarce and highly prized, according to anthropologists. Today, however, the sweetest, fattiest foods are manufactured and processed with great amounts of sugar and salt (think of a bag of Lays crisps). Showing that adults and children prefer eating such processed foods

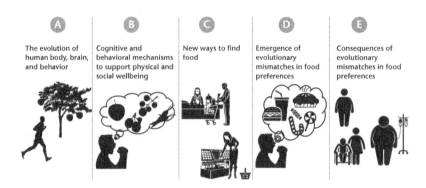

FIGURE 3.1 Obesity as a consequence of mismatch.

(inputs) over natural foods like fruits and honey is not enough. We also need to show that (a) these mismatched preferences produce health problems and (b) that these problems are considerably less prevalent in hunter-gatherer societies. In the case of food, there is clear evidence that our evolved preferences produce many maladies from obesity to type 2 diabetes and cardiovascular problems, because the physiological mechanisms involving insulin and glucagon did not evolve to repeatedly metabolize unnaturally large amounts of sugar (Gluckman & Hanson, 2006). Further, these diseases are virtually nonexistent in hunter-gatherer societies (Lieberman, 2013).

Studying Potential Mismatches in Social Psychology

What is the evidence for mismatch in applied social psychology? Are there mismatched conditions that result in a failure of our evolved psychological mechanisms to function properly in the modern human social context, such as in our relationships, work, economics, politics, and health and sustainability? Here, we review evidence from some of these domains that are aligned with, or at least can be interpreted in terms of mismatches operating in novel, modern environments.

Relationships

Some challenges associated with initiating and maintaining close relationships in the modern world may result from, or be aggravated by mismatch (Figure 3.2; see also Mikulincer & Shaver, this volume). Modern adolescents grow up living in areas with high population densities and the presence of a vast number of potential sexual partners and rivals – factors that increase both the intensity of intra- and intrasexual competition. What does this do to our mating psychology? We predict that this results in increased difficulty in initiating and maintaining long-term committed relationships, which were the norm for ancestral

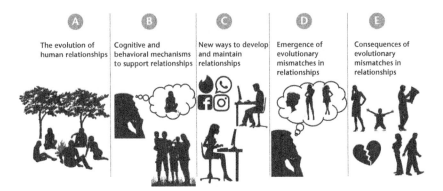

FIGURE 3.2 Relationship problems as a consequence of mismatch.

humans. Social psychologists showed men and women ten pictures of physically attractive female faces and found that this prime reduced men's commitment to their current long-term mate (Kenrick, Neuberg, Zierk, & Krones, 1994), as well as women's self-perceived desirability as a romantic partner (Gutierres, Kenrick, & Partch, 1999). This is consistent with various studies suggesting a link between frequent media consumption and social media use (e.g., Facebook) and particularly women's devaluation of their self-esteem and body image, resulting in problems associated with depression and eating disorders (like anorexia) (Li, Smith, Griskevicius, Cason, & Bryan, 2010; see also Kross, this volume). In addition, frequent use of internet porn has been linked to an inability in young men to seek and develop close intimate relationships with women (Short, Black, Smith, Wetterneck, & Wells, 2012). Divorce rates are much higher in modern, developed nations than in traditional, small-scale societies (Takyi, 2001).

A different consequence of high population density and intense sexual competition is the current fertility crisis in the modern world. Paradoxically, the wealthiest countries in the world – European and East-Asian countries – are now reproducing the least, with fertility rates well below population replacement levels. High population densities may lead to mismatched inputs into mating mechanisms because they point to an intense competition for resources. Both human and animal studies show that high population densities lead organisms to adopt a slower life-history strategy, an inclination to invest in building up physical (nutrition), mental (education), and social capital (friendship networks) at the expense of immediate reproductive success (Brumbach, Figueredo, & Ellis, 2009). Consistent with these ideas, a set of social-psychological experiments primed people with cues of high population density (e.g., images and noises of densely populated areas) and discovered that these cues increased the estimated age at which people want to get married and have kids (Sng, Neuberg, Varnum, & Kenrick, 2017).

Work

The modern workplace also offers various social and physical challenges that may be exacerbated by mismatch (Figure 3.3). Modern-day work organizations bear little resemblance to the organizational structures of hunter-gatherer societies that have no hierarchy, limited division of labor, high degrees of kinship, no real distinction between one's work life and private life, and a continuous physical engagement with the natural environment. Indeed, the design of many workplaces offers limited room for engaging actively with nature. Interventions that offer work spaces more green elements such as plants, natural sounds, and the presence of nearby parks for physical movement were found to increase job satisfaction, and reduce absenteeism and turnover intentions among employees (An, Colarelli, O'Brien, & Boyajian, 2016). Being exposed to natural rather than urban spaces enhances people's moods and increases their self-control, suggesting an attention-restoration function of nature (Van der Wal, Schade, Krabbendam, & van Vugt, 2013). Relatedly, an educational field experiment found that by inducing more play, interventions to green-up schoolyards have a positive impact on the attention and concentration levels of primary school children (van Dijk-Wesselius, Maas, Hovinga, van Vugt, & van den Berg, 2018).

Modern work contexts may also induce chronic work-related stress, enhancing the prevalence of modern diseases, such as burnout and depression, that are relatively rare in hunter-gatherer societies (Jacobsson, 1988). Our psychological mechanisms evolved in small-scale societies where humans lived and worked surrounded by family and friends on relatively simple production tasks. In contrast, modern work contexts present many novel inputs to evolved mechanisms, including intense social competition with genetic strangers that causes evolved status mechanisms to produce chronic feelings of insecurity, anxiety, and emotional exhaustion. Modern work also creates disconnects between inputs and outputs. Due to ambiguous and non-salient work outputs (e.g., electronic paychecks, extended deadlines, uncertain promotion criteria), the relation between

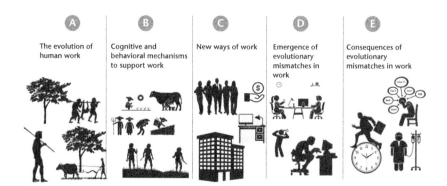

FIGURE 3.3 Work stress as a consequence of mismatch.

effort expended and rewards received is blurred. As such, our inbuilt information-gathering mechanisms are constantly on alert, perceiving uncertainty on what to work on, unfairness in the way we are treated, and frustration in choice of tasks. In addition, modern organizations contain steep hierarchies that are highly stratified, with individuals at the top earning thousands of times more than those at the bottom, leading our psychological mechanisms to perceive inequality and unfairness and reducing our sense of autonomy, competence, and relatedness. One of the consequences of these work-related mismatches is chronic work stress. Over 80 percent of Americans report being stressed by their work (Harris Interactive & Everest College, Work Stress Survey, 2013). Although some stress is beneficial to work performance, chronic stress can lead to various negative outcomes, including impairments to immune, cardiovascular, and metabolic functioning, as well as disease, psychological disorders, and mortality (Gluckman & Hanson, 2006). Chronic work stress also leads to job burnout – exhaustion, feelings of cynicism, and a sense of ineffectiveness (Maslach, Schaufeli, & Leiter, 2001).

Politics

Some challenges associated with modern-day politics may also be amplified by mismatch (see Figure 3.4). Humans evolved in small-scale societies with small-scale politics (Petersen, 2015). There was little or no hierarchy and conflicts were settled through informal leaders who had no authority beyond their domain of expertise. Excellent hunters, diplomats, warriors, and shamans offered valuable services and in return they received prestige, which culminated in some reproductive gains for these prestige leaders (Von Rueden & van Vugt, 2015; van Vugt & Smith, 2019). Ancestral humans knew their leaders intimately and so there was a tight relationship between someone's competence and their prestige as leader. This may not necessarily be the case in

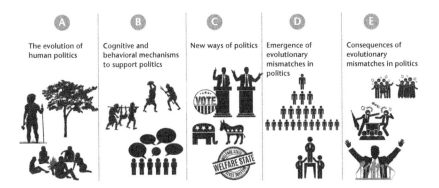

FIGURE 3.4 Emergence of mismatches in politics.

modern politics in which there is a vastly increased distance between leaders and followers (van Vugt & Ronay, 2014). As a consequence, political voting decisions are made with a great degree of uncertainty in an information-poor environment in which reliable competence cues are lacking. As a consequence, our psychological mechanisms are missing relevant inputs to make good judgments about which leaders to choose (see contributions by Fiedler & Forgas, this volume). Because much leadership in ancestral groups was based on physical properties, such as physical formidability, these cues are given increasing weight in our political decisions. Thus, voters have a preference for tall and dominant-looking leaders, especially in contexts that resemble ancestral threats such as intra- or intergroup conflicts (Laustsen & Petersen, 2015; van Vugt & Grabo, 2015). Further supporting this idea, voters who watch more television pay more attention to physical cues when choosing political candidates (Lawson, Lenz, Baker, & Myers, 2010).

Support for party policies is another domain that may suffer from mismatch. In small-scale systems, political decisions about the distribution of resources are often made on the basis of simple heuristics, such as deservingness: Who deserves to receive our help? (Petersen, 2015). Our psychological mechanisms have evolved to be constantly on the lookout for cheaters, individuals who free-ride on the efforts of others, or are otherwise unable or unwilling to contribute. This has implications for the way we view disadvantaged groups in society. We are more likely to support the temporarily ill than the chronically ill, we are more likely to help the ill rather than people who are unemployed, and we are more likely to support policies to give aid to members of ingroups rather than outgroups (McDonald, Navarrete, & van Vugt, 2012). Cues of physical formidability also matter in how people apply the deservingness heuristic. In ancestral groups, resource conflicts were often decided based on physical force. Surveys and experiments find that physically formidable men are (a) more prone to anger and (b) are less supportive of welfare policies unless they are a member of a disadvantaged group themselves, in which case, they are more supportive (Petersen, Sznycer, Sell, Cosmides, & Tooby, 2013). Thus, various cues, external and internal, activate our evolved political psychological mechanisms, resulting in preferences that may have detrimental consequences for our well-being, such as supporting dominant, aggressive leaders (see Forgas, this volume).

A final arena for political mismatch derives from our susceptibility to conspiracy theories which inform political preferences (Van Prooijen & van Vugt, 2018; see also Forgas & Baumeister, 2019). Humans are coalitional animals and possess various psychological mechanisms to detect coalitional threats. Being watchful for dangerous coalitions may have served us well in environments in which these threats were particularly lethal. This seems to be the case in ancestral environments in which killings were common. Through media exposure, we now receive constant information about potential conspiracies and we are highly susceptible. Almost half of Americans believe that the US government had advance knowledge of the 9/11 attacks, although there is no evidence for this. A significant portion of religious people believe that vaccinations are a conspiracy of Western governments liaising with the pharmaceutical industry to damage children's health. Our psychological mechanisms are biased to avoid dangers, and so they are calibrated to avoiding costly errors (error management). Because it is costlier to ignore a conspiracy when there is a genuine one, rather than recognize a conspiracy when there is nothing, our conspiracy detection mechanisms are very sensitive and on high alert. As a result, individuals make irrational decisions about their health and the well-being of close ones (Van Prooijen & van Vugt, 2018).

Sustainability and Health

The global environmental challenges that modern humans face may also be intensified by mismatch (van Vugt, Griskevicius, & Schultz, 2014). Climate change is something that humans have difficulty comprehending and responding to because the consequences are delayed in time and dispersed geographically. Ancestral humans may have struggled with local environmental problems, such as water or food shortages, but these problems were both immediate and visible. The problem is that our psychological mechanisms are not activated by inputs about global delayed environmental challenges. This is particularly true when information is presented in probabilistic terms (e.g., the chances of pollution in the 5-day weather forecast are 40 percent) rather than in frequentist numbers (e.g., in two out of five days there will be pollution). The latter is easier to comprehend. In order to tackle environmental mismatches, it is important that our psychological mechanisms receive the right input. For instance, associating meat consumption with immediate disease and disgust cues (Palomo-Vélez, Tybur, & van Vugt, 2018) is more effective than accentuating the long-term health (colon cancer) or environmental consequences of meat intake (deforestation). The idea is that humans respond more strongly to immediate sensory cues pointing out that something is wrong. In addition, humans have not evolved to be motivated by a concern for the planet. They are more likely to cooperate for a better environment if the consequences of their efforts benefit themselves and their children and grandchildren. Indeed, priming people with images of their own children helps increase their environmental intentions (Palomo-Vélez et al., 2018). Finally, our prosocial psychological mechanisms are triggered by social cues, that is, what we see others doing and by reciprocity cues – what they get in return. This can be used effectively in environmental campaigns. In one study, hotel guests were asked to reuse their towels either for the sake of the environment or to benefit themselves (a small discount on their hotel bill). The latter message was more effective than the first. The most effective message, however, when information was provided was that the majority of hotel guests were already reusing their towels (Goldstein, Cialdini, & Griskevicius, 2008).

Taken together, an understanding of the evolved social-psychological mechanisms that produce various human social behaviors, from close relationships to political preferences, along with insights into the relevant mismatched conditions – in terms of inputs and outputs – can lead to predictions about the consequences of mismatch for our behavior and contribute to an understanding of seemingly irrational, maladaptive human behaviors. We have reviewed evidence for mismatched behaviors in domains of relationships, work place behaviors, politics and health/sustainability challenges (Figures 3.2 and 3.3).

Implications for Public Policy

So how can the knowledge about human evolution and mismatch help to inform public policy? First, some cautionary comments are needed (see Walton, this volume). Although in the previous sections we provide considerable support for the idea that mismatch plays a role in various applied social psychology domains, further research is needed. For instance, is internet porn indeed causally related to relationship dissatisfaction and the ability to maintain a healthy partner relationship, or are there other confounding factors? Are preferences for physically formidable leaders in modern societies indeed mismatched such that having these leaders in charge is bad for these groups in the long run? Does frequent social media use lower people's self-esteem and makes them invest less in meaningful relationships (Sbarra et al., 2019; see also Kross, this volume)? The answer is that we need more research that explicitly starts from an evolutionary perspective, for instance, by examining factors that increase people's sensitivity to mismatch and treating this as an individual difference.

Additional evidence for mismatch should come from (a) comparing modern societies to the small-scale societies in which humans evolved and (b) showing that environmental factors, rather than genetics, are causing these behaviors. In the absence of a time machine, we have to rely on historical evidence (e.g., from ethnographies) and evidence from current small-scale societies such as the Hadza, Kung-San, or Tsimane. However, these societies are increasingly rare and many of them have interacted with modern societies for a while now (Von Rueden & van Vugt, 2015).

From an evolutionary perspective there are, in principle, three options available to deal with mismatches. The first option is to do nothing, and just wait and see. Biological evolution ultimately catches up with environmental changes and if there are profound negative selection consequences of certain traits or behaviors then they – and the individuals that carry these traits – will eventually disappear. Delaying the age of motherhood creates a selective disadvantage for women who are unable to remain fertile at a later age, and positive selection for women who do. Many mismatches are aggravated among people who are lacking in self-control, for instance, in what they eat or drink, how much physical risk they take, or how much they invest in education to achieve a high-status position (see Papies; and Krahé, this volume). By doing nothing, there will be positive selection for individuals who are able to control their impulses such that their genes can proliferate. Naturally, there will be selection consequences only when the mismatched behaviors affect someone's reproductive success; thus, lifestyle diseases that manifest themselves at an old age (e.g., certain forms of diabetes) are not likely to disappear rapidly via natural selection (Lieberman, 2013).

Doing nothing may be undesirable from a societal viewpoint, however, as there may be excessive costs placed upon individuals or societies if people do not change bad lifestyle choices. Therefore, society may decide to eliminate behavioral options that cause mismatch because they are too costly for society. Smoking addiction, a mismatched habit, is an example. Smoking clearly has a negative effect on one's health and costs society many billions of dollars in terms of disease treatment. The effects of passive smoking are also non-negligible. Accordingly, many modern societies have imposed fairly draconian measures to reduce people's freedom to smoke in public places. Constraining measures are also increasingly applied to limit unhealthy food options in sport canteens and schools, the use of smartphones in classrooms, and the access to day care centers of children who have not been vaccinated against infectious diseases. Yet, for many of the other mismatched problems we discussed here, from relationships to politics and the workplace, there is probably little public support for coercive measures.

Therefore, an alternative solution to reduce mismatch is to make alternative options more attractive, options that are ultimately better for individuals and for society. This can be done by applying nudging strategies to evolutionary mismatched behaviors (see Walton, this volume). Nudges are low-cost interventions that change people's behaviors through altering the choice architecture of the environment without removing their freedom to choose. For instance, climate change is an abstract problem for the human mind. Humans have evolved to pay attention to problems that are associated with direct sensory cues – what they can see, hear, or smell (see Papies, this volume). So, if we want people to behave in a more environmentally desirable manner, there is not much point in providing them with more education about the state of the environment ("The earth temperature will rise by two degrees"). Yet, by making some of these problems visual and directly noticeable, people may be persuaded to do something. So, providing households or offices with heat maps from their own buildings gives people a direct visible cue to what is needed to save more energy. Similarly, installing energy meters inside personal dwellings so that people can see their prepaid credits dwindling faster when air conditioners kick in, may be more effective than making general pleas to conserve energy.

As a different example, humans have evolved bodies which can engage in moderate physical exercise at late age (Lieberman, 2013). At the same time, humans have evolved not to waste calories by unnecessarily expending energy.

Hence, it can be difficult to get people to engage in regular physical exercise when there is no immediate need. Changing the choice environment through nudges can help. Elevators can be placed at the backside of buildings such that taking the stairs becomes more attractive. Closer to home, the staffrooms in our university building have been recently equipped with table tennis tables, pool tables, and high-quality coffee machines so that people are motivated to physically move during the working day. Finally, to solve the retirement savings issue identified at the beginning of this chapter, companies can enroll employees in default savings plans and place the burden on employees to opt out, rather than requiring them to opt in to such a program (Thaler & Sunstein, 2008).

In general, generating more effective solutions to important modern problems at both the individual and societal level will require knowledge of our evolved psychology and working with, rather than against or in ignorance of, the various mechanisms comprising that psychology. Well-meaning applied professionals sometimes fail to pay attention to this. There is a kind of arrogance in assuming that humans are so open, flexible, and intelligent that we can solve any problem with the right kind of social engineering. But an evolutionary perspective emphasizes the fact that we are far less flexible and adaptable than we would like to believe. We can try to reduce people's prejudices against immigrant groups, for instance, by educating them about the cultural and economic benefits these immigrants will bring to society. But an evolutionary perspective suggests a better strategy might be to make sure these immigrants elicit cues that they are healthy, harmless and accommodating – for instance, by smiling a lot, learning the language quickly, and wearing decent clothes (Ji, Tybur, & van Vugt, 2019).

Conclusion

In sum, evolutionary mismatch is an important concept in evolutionary psychology and it likely plays a substantial role in explaining various maladaptive behaviors and choice preferences of modern humans living in evolutionary novel environments. When we think of interventions to deal with various mismatched behaviors, such as restrictive or nudging strategies, it would be wise to consider the constraints and opportunities offered by the evolved psychological mechanisms that characterize this amazing species, Homo Sapiens.

Author Note

This work was supported by the Singapore Ministry of Education (MOE) Academic Research Fund (AcRF) Tier 1 grant.

References

An, M., Colarelli, S. M., O'Brien, K., & Boyajian, M. E. (2016). Why we need more nature at work: Effects of natural elements and sunlight on employee mental health and work attitudes. *PloS One*, *11*(5), e0155614.

Baumard, N. (2015). Evolutionary psychology and public policy. In D. Buss (Ed), *The handbook of evolutionary psychology* (pp. 1123–1142). New York: Wiley.

Brumbach, B. H., Figueredo, A. J., & Ellis, B. J. (2009). Effects of harsh and unpredictable environments in adolescence on development of life history strategies. *Human Nature*, *20*(1), 25–51.

Buss, D. (2015). *Evolutionary psychology: The new science of the mind*. London: Psychology Press.

Curtis, V., & Aunger, R. (2011). Motivational mismatch: Evolved motives as the source of – and solution to – global public health problems. *Applied Evolutionary Psychology*, 259–275.

Dunbar, R. I. (2003). The social brain: Mind, language, and society in evolutionary perspective. *Annual Review of Anthropology*, *32*(1), 163–181.

Foley, R. (1997). *Humans before humanity: An evolutionary perspective*. London: Blackwell.

Forgas, J. P., & Baumeister, R. F. (2019). Homo credulus: On the social psychology of gullibility. In *The social psychology of gullibility* (pp. 1–18). London: Routledge.

Fox, C. R., & Sitkin, S. B. (2015). Bridging the divide between behavioral science & policy. *Behavioral Science & Policy*, *1*(1), 1–12.

Gigerenzer, G. (2007). *Gut feelings: The intelligence of the unconscious*. London: Penguin.

Giphart, R., & van Vugt, M. (2018). *Mismatch: How our stone age brain deceives us every day (and what we can do about it)*. London: Hachette UK.

Gluckman, P. D., & Hanson, M. A. (2004). Living with the past: Evolution, development, and patterns of disease. *Science*, *305*(5691), 1733–1736.

Gluckman, P. D., & Hanson, M. A. (2006). The developmental origins of health and disease. In *Early life origins of health and disease* (pp. 1–7). Boston, MA: Springer.

Goldstein, N. J., Cialdini, R. B., & Griskevicius, V. (2008). A room with a viewpoint: Using social norms to motivate environmental conservation in hotels. *Journal of Consumer Research*, *35*(3), 472–482.

Gutierres, S. E., Kenrick, D. T., & Partch, J. J. (1999). Beauty, dominance, and the mating game: Contrast effects in self-assessment reflect gender differences in mate selection. *Personality and Social Psychology Bulletin*, *25*, 1126–1134.

Harari, Y. N. (2014). *Sapiens: A brief history of humankind*. London: Random House.

Harris Interactive & Everest College. (2013). *Work stress survey*. Los Angeles, CA: Everest College

Henrich, J. (2015). *The secret of our success: How culture is driving human evolution, domesticating our species, and making us smarter*. Los Angeles: Princeton University Press.

Hidaka, B. H. (2012). Depression as a disease of modernity: Explanations for increasing prevalence. *Journal of Affective Disorders*, *140*(3), 205–214.

Jacobsson, L. (1988). On the picture of depression and suicide in traditional societies. *Acta Psychiatrica Scandinavica*, *78*(S344), 55–63.

Ji, T., Tybur, J. M., & van Vugt, M. (2019). Generalized or origin-specific out-group prejudice? The role of temporary and chronic pathogen-avoidance motivation in intergroup relations. *Evolutionary Psychology*, *17*(1), doi:1474704919826851

Johnson, E. J., & Goldstein, D. (2003). Do defaults save lives? *Science*, *302*, 1338–1339.

Johnson, D. D., Price, M. E., & van Vugt, M. (2013). Darwin's invisible hand: Market competition, evolution and the firm. *Journal of Economic Behavior & Organization, 90*, S128–S140.

Kahneman, D. (2011). *Thinking, fast and slow*. New York, NY: Farrar, Straus and Giroux.

Kaplan, H., Hill, K., Lancaster, J., & Hurtado, A. M. (2000). A theory of human life history evolution: Diet, intelligence, and longevity. *Evolutionary Anthropology: Issues, News, and Reviews, 9*(4), 156–185.

Kenrick, D. T., Griskevicius, V., Neuberg, S. L., & Schaller, M. (2010). Renovating the pyramid of needs: Contemporary extensions built upon ancient foundations. *Perspectives on Psychological Science, 5*(3), 292–314.

Kenrick, D. T., Neuberg, S. L., Zierk, K. L., & Krones, J. M. (1994). Evolution and social cognition: Contrast effects as a function of sex, dominance, and physical attractiveness. *Personality and Social Psychology Bulletin, 20*(2), 210–217.

Krebs, J. R. (2009). The gourmet ape: Evolution and human food preferences. *The American Journal of Clinical Nutrition, 90*(3), 707S–711S.

Laustsen, L., & Petersen, M. B. (2015). Does a competent leader make a good friend? Conflict, ideology and the psychologies of friendship and followership. *Evolution and Human Behavior, 36*(4), 286–293.

Lawson, C., Lenz, G. S., Baker, A., & Myers, M. (2010). Looking like a winner: Candidate appearance and electoral success in new democracies. *World Politics, 62*(4), 561–593.

Li, N. P., Smith, A. R., Griskevicius, V., Cason, M. J., & Bryan, A. (2010). Intrasexual competition and eating restriction in heterosexual and homosexual individuals. *Evolution and Human Behavior, 31*, 365–372.

Li, N. P., van Vugt, M., & Colarelli, S. M. (2018). The evolutionary mismatch hypothesis: Implications for psychological science. *Current Directions in Psychological Science, 27*(1), 38–44.

Lieberman, D. E. (2013). *The story of the human body: Evolution, health, and disease*. New York, NY: Pantheon.

Lloyd, E., Wilson, D. S., & Sober, E. (2011). *Evolutionary mismatch and what to do about it: A basic tutorial*. Florida: The Evolution Institute, Wesley Chapel.

Loewenstein, G., Bryce, C., Hagmann, D., & Rajpal, S. (2015). Warning: You are about to be nudged. *Behavioral Science & Policy, 1*(1), 35–42.

Maner, J. K., & Kenrick, D. T. (2010). When adaptations go awry: Functional and dysfunctional aspects of social anxiety. *Social Issues and Policy Review, 4*(1), 111–142.

Maslach, C., Schaufeli, W. B., & Leiter, M. P. (2001). Job burnout. *Annual Review of Psychology, 52*(1), 397–422.

McDonald, M. M., Navarrete, C. D., & van Vugt, M. (2012). Evolution and the psychology of intergroup conflict: The male warrior hypothesis. *Philosophical Transactions of the Royal Society B: Biological Sciences, 367*(1589), 670–679.

Nesse, R. M., & Berridge, K. C. (1997). Psychoactive drug use in evolutionary perspective. *Science, 278*(5335), 63–66.

Palomo-Vélez, G., Tybur, J. M., & van Vugt, M. (2018). Unsustainable, unhealthy, or disgusting? Comparing different persuasive messages against meat consumption. *Journal of Environmental Psychology, 58*, 63–71.

Petersen, M. B. (2015). Evolutionary political psychology: On the origin and structure of heuristics and biases in politics. *Political Psychology, 36*, 45–78.

Petersen, M. B., Sznycer, D., Sell, A., Cosmides, L., & Tooby, J. (2013). The ancestral logic of politics: Upper-body strength regulates men's assertion of self-interest over economic redistribution. *Psychological Science*, *24*(7), 1098–1103.

Sbarra, D., Briskin, J., & Slatcher, R. B. (2019). Smartphones and close relationships: The case for an evolutionary mismatch. *Perspectives in Psychological Science*.

Schmitt, D. P., & Pilcher, J. J. (2004). Evaluating evidence of psychological adaptation: How do we know one when we see one? *Psychological Science*, *15*(10), 643–649.

Short, M. B., Black, L., Smith, A. H., Wetterneck, C. T., & Wells, D. E. (2012). A review of internet pornography use research: Methodology and content from the past 10 years. *Cyberpsychology, Behavior, and Social Networking*, *15*(1), 13–23.

Sng, O., Neuberg, S. L., Varnum, M. E., & Kenrick, D. T. (2017). The crowded life is a slow life: Population density and life history strategy. *Journal of Personality and Social Psychology*, *112*(5), 736.

Takyi, B. K. (2001). Marital instability in an African society: Exploring the factors that influence divorce processes in Ghana. *Sociological Focus*, *34*(1), 77–96.

Thaler, R. H., & Sunstein, C. R. (2008). *Nudge: Improving decisions about health, wealth, and happiness*. New Haven, CT: Yale University Press.

Tooby, J., & Cosmides, L. (1992). The psychological foundations of culture. In J. Barkow, L. Cosmides, L., & J. Tooby (Eds.), *The adapted mind: Evolutionary psychology and the generation of culture* (pp. 19–136). New York: Oxford University Press.

Tooby, J., & DeVore, I. (1987). The reconstruction of hominid behavioral evolution through strategic modeling. In W. G. Kinzey (Ed.), *The evolution of human behavior: Primate models* (pp. 183–273). New York, NY: State University of New York Press.

Van der Wal, A. J., Schade, H. M., Krabbendam, L., & van Vugt, M. (2013). Do natural landscapes reduce future discounting in humans? *Proceedings of the Royal Society B: Biological Sciences*, *280*(1773), 20132295.

van Dijk-Wesselius, J. E., Maas, J., Hovinga, D., van Vugt, M., & van den Berg, A. E. (2018). The impact of greening schoolyards on the appreciation, and physical, cognitive and social-emotional well-being of schoolchildren: A prospective intervention study. *Landscape and Urban Planning*, *180*, 15–26.

van Prooijen, J. W., & van Vugt, M. (2018). Conspiracy theories: Evolved functions and psychological mechanisms. *Perspectives on Psychological Science*, *13*(6), 770–788.

van Vugt, M., & Ahuja, A. (2010). *Selected: Why some people lead, why others follow and why it matters*. London: Profile Books.

van Vugt, M., & Grabo, A. E. (2015). The many faces of leadership: An evolutionary-psychology approach. *Current Directions in Psychological Science*, *24*(6), 484–489.

van Vugt, M., Griskevicius, V., & Schultz, P. W. (2014). Naturally green: Harnessing Stone-Age psychological biases to foster environmental behavior. *Social Issues and Policy Review*, *8*(1), 1–32.

van Vugt, M., & Ronay, R. (2014). The evolutionary psychology of leadership: Theory, review, and roadmap. *Organizational Psychology Review*, *4*(1), 74–95.

van Vugt, M., & Smith, J. E. (2019). A dual model of leadership and hierarchy: Evolutionary synthesis. *Trends in Cognitive Sciences*.

Von Rueden, C., & van Vugt, M. (2015). Leadership in small-scale societies: Some implications for theory, research, and practice. *The Leadership Quarterly*, *26*(6), 978–990.

4
"BAD" THINGS RECONSIDERED

Gregory M. Walton and Shannon T. Brady

"Bad" Things Reconsidered

Bad things happen. And when they do, it's good to know that they can happen to everyone; that they don't make you a bad person, and that they need not portend future problems.

In the title song in *Singin' In the Rain*, Gene Kelly (playing Don Lockwood) has just left Debbie Reynolds (playing Kathy Selden), with whom he has fallen in love, when he emerges into a rainstorm. He does not deny the rain, bemoan it, or shudder from it. Instead, he finds joy, swinging around light poles and stomping in puddles (see Figure 4.1). How can we help people see light where only darkness is commonly found?

Every day, people struggle or get criticized in school or at work, feel sick from medical treatments, or fight with their kids. And when bad things happen, people can react badly. They can draw negative conclusions about themselves, other people, or their future prospects. Those inferences often lead people to behave in ways that are maladaptive and self-reinforcing, and that have the effect of undermining their outcomes over time.

Yet if the struggles people experience arise, in part, from interpretations they draw, we have an opportunity. "Wise" psychological interventions can help reframe challenges (Figure 4.1; Walton & Wilson, 2018). As we will see, randomized controlled field trials in diverse contexts have found that messages and experiences that anticipate and forestall predictable pejorative interpretations can help people function better over time. For instance:

- Reframing placement on academic probation can reduce shame and stigma and help college students recover (Brady et al., 2019a).

"Bad" Things Reconsidered 59

FIGURE 4.1   Gene Kelly in "Singin' In The Rain" (1952).

- Reframing side symptoms of treatment for peanut allergies can improve patient outcomes (Howe et al., 2019).
- Reframing challenges with a new baby can prevent child abuse (Bugental et al., 2002).

In each case, people risk viewing an event in negative, even catastrophic ways—evidence that they can't succeed in college, that they will never overcome a serious allergy, or that they are a bad parent. Standard messages often permit, and sometimes reinforce, such toxic views. Yet more neutral, even positive ways of understanding the very same experience are possible. In each case, well-designed efforts to reframe the experience in authentic and non-pejorative ways improved outcomes for individuals, collectives (e.g., a parent and child), and/or institutions (e.g., a school or hospital).

Often, bad events arise in institutional contexts, in direct response to institutional messages. A student is told of her poor performance by a school official. She looks to the official to learn what that performance means to the institution and how the institution regards her now. A patient learns about possible side effects of a treatment from his doctor. He looks to the doctor to learn how to interpret these side effects. In these cases, institutions have a special role and obligation to help people make sense of challenges productively (cf. Murphy,

Kroeper, & Ozier, 2018; Schmader, Bergsieker, & Hall, this volume). Often, institutions overlook this responsibility. They act as though all they convey to people is an objective circumstance—such as placement on probation or the possibility of side effects. Yet, when institutions fail to help people make good sense of bad events, they hurt their own outcomes.

In this chapter, we review the science behind people's interpretations of bad events and the opportunities for improvement this work affords. We begin by comparing the kinds of interventions we focus on here—which address how people make sense of discrete experiences—with broader "mindset" interventions. Next, we review paradigmatic interventions that recast bad events. Finally, we close by discussing how institutions can anticipate when people risk drawing pejorative, self-undermining interpretations, and design steps that institutions can use to understand and change these interpretations productively.

What is "Bad"?

Before proceeding, let us define "bad." We put the word in quotes because these events may not be bad in an objective sense. Rather, we refer to events that readily or predictably lead people to draw global or fixed pejorative interpretations of themselves, other people, or a situation they are in. They are "bad" because of the interpretations commonly drawn from them. A Friday night to yourself is not so bad in itself. But if you are a first-year college student and you think this means that you are excluded from the social scene at your college, it may be deeply upsetting (Walton & Cohen, 2011). Even placement on academic probation may not be so bad unto itself. After all, a student placed on probation presumably already knows that she is struggling. Placement may come with access to resources to promote recovery. What may be shameful and stigma-inducing is the perception that probation reflects a negative judgment from the institution; that it is a marker of difference and deficiency. Similarly, an occasional feeling of nausea is part of being human. But if you think that nausea means your peanut allergy is resisting treatment, that may be threatening.

Mindset Interventions vs. Reframing "Bad" Events

We focus here on how people make sense of *specific* events and experiences, including seminal and repeated ones, and efforts to reframe their meaning. Such interventions represent one form of psychologically "wise" intervention, which address in general how people make sense of themselves, other people, or social situations to help them function more effectively (Walton & Wilson, 2018). Our focus on the representation of discrete events complements interventions that address broad beliefs or "mindsets" people have about qualities in people or experiences in general, such as whether a quality can change or is fixed, or whether something is positive or negative. Rather than reframing a specific experience, such interventions invite people to reflect on that quality or kind of experience *in general*.

The breadth of mindsets gives them a special power to shape how people interpret and thus respond to whole classes of experiences. For instance, one hour-long intervention represented challenges to belonging in general as normal in the transition to college and as improving with time. This exercise raised African-American students' achievement over the next three years, cutting the racial achievement gap in half (Walton & Cohen, 2011). It did so, in part, by changing how students interpreted their daily stream of social experience, preventing diverse challenges—from difficulty making friends, to receiving critical feedback, to feelings of homesickness—from seeming to mean that they did not belong in college in general (Walton & Cohen, 2007, 2011). Other mindsets include people's beliefs about the malleability of intelligence, which can enhance resilience and learning in the face of academic setbacks (Dweck & Yeager, 2019); beliefs about whether personality can change, which can help adolescents cope with bullying (Yeager, Johnson, et al., 2014); beliefs about whether stress is enhancing (vs. debilitating), which can improve performance and health (Crum, Salovey, & Achor, 2013); the belief that willpower can be self-enhancing (rather than reliant on an easily depleted resource), which predicts sustained self-regulatory efforts (Job, Dweck, & Walton, 2010; Job, Walton, Bernecker, & Dweck, 2015); and beliefs about the adequacy of the self, which can improve functioning in situations of psychological threat (Cohen & Sherman, 2014). There is even the idea that winter is "delightful," which predicts life satisfaction and mental health in Tromsø, Norway, 69 degrees north, a city of more than 75,000 that receives no direct sunlight in the middle of winter (Leibowitz & Vittersø, 2019).

Given the power of mindset interventions, why reframe specific events? One reason involves the role of institutions. Although mindset interventions can be embedded productively in institutional contexts (e.g., Yeager, Walton, et al., 2016), they can be an awkward fit. Institutions and institutional actors (people acting on behalf of institutions) are not social psychologists who begin each day thinking about the belief systems of those with whom they interact; typically, they are focused on day-to-day happenings. What *is* in their wheelhouse, however, is constructing daily experiences and communicating routine information to people. It is a school administrator's job to communicate a probation status to a struggling student. It is a doctor's job to communicate a diagnosis or course of treatment to a patient. Institutional actors would do well to consider how critical experiences and communications land with recipients and to work to communicate interpretations that will be adaptive for both individuals and the institutions they serve (Murphy et al., 2018). In focusing on the representation of bad events, we hope to help institutional actors do their existing work better. Moreover, institutional actors are well-placed to observe bad events. They know better than anyone else what moments can provoke negative reactions. By taking a formal approach to learning how people understand these experiences, they can develop systematic changes to common practices to improve outcomes.

Moreover, the interpretation of specific events can be life-altering. This is especially the case when the event is seminal (e.g., placement on academic probation; see Brady, Fotuhi et al., 2019), repeated (ongoing difficulties with a baby; see Bugental et al., 2002), or symbolic (whether critical academic feedback is seen as evidence a teacher can, or cannot, be trusted; see Yeager, Purdie-Vaughns, Hooper, & Cohen, 2017). In these circumstances, change in a interpretation can change ongoing cycles and thus improve people's outcomes long into the future, as several of our examples will illustrate.

Five Principles for Representing Bad Events Effectively

How can you productively reframe a "bad" event? Here we describe five principles, which can be used as tools to guide this reframing. Although it is useful to distinguish them, these principles are interrelated and typically work in concert to facilitate a more adaptive narrative. Further, different specific representations are available in different contexts, making certain principles more or less central.

1. **Prevent negative labels.** When people experience negative events, they risk labeling themselves in fixed, negative ways or perceiving that others could label them as such. Effective reframings forestall negative labels, and encourage a fundamentally positive view of the self, of factors that led to the bad news (e.g., normal, malleable), and of the person's future prospects.
2. **Communicate "You're not the only one."** People can think that they are the only one facing a particular challenge. Effective reframings recognize others who have faced the same challenge (and describe how they addressed that challenge productively).
3. **Recognize specific non-pejorative causes.** People can fear that bad things reflect, or could be seen as reflecting, their own deficiency (e.g., laziness, stupidity, immorality). Effective reframings acknowledge specific, non-pejorative causes of challenges or setbacks and legitimize these as normal obstacles that arise for many people.
4. **Forecast improvement.** People can fear that negative events forecast a fixed, negative future. Effective reframings emphasize the possibility of improvement, focus on process, and often represent this process collectively (we're on the same team/I'm not judging you).
5. **Recognize opportunities.** In some cases, it is possible to represent aspects of the "bad" event as positive, meaningful, or useful, and thus not just as something to be overcome, but as a harbinger of, or opportunity for, growth and improvement.

Even as these principles can be used to help people construct a coherent, adaptive narrative for making sense of challenges, an important function is also simply to displace the most negative and disempowering interpretations available. Knowing what meanings *not* to draw can forestall catastrophizing or globalizing responses.

As we will see, there is important variability in *how* these principles are implemented. In some cases, the role of the intervener is quite direct, as in how a university official represents academic probation to a student (Brady, Fotuhi et al., 2019; see also Howe et al., 2019; Yeager, Purdie-Vaughns, et al., 2014). In other cases, especially when people are making sense of very personal experiences, less direct approaches may be appropriate. They may involve asking people questions that suggest a new way of understanding a challenge, which people can then elaborate upon and internalize, as in work helping new parents make sense of difficulties with a baby (Bugental et al., 2002), or structuring a written reflection that helps people construct a more adaptive narrative about an experience on their own, such as a trauma (Pennebaker, 1997) or test anxiety (Ramirez & Beilock, 2011). At the end of the day, it is essential that people fully endorse the proffered interpretation; they must "own" it for themselves. In this sense, psychological interventions are always conducted *with* people not *on* people (Walton & Yeager, in press). Still, in each situation, the aforementioned principles can help describe what a more adaptive narrative for understanding a challenge might look like.

Reframing Bad News: Paradigmatic Examples

Here we illustrate the opportunity to reframe bad news with paradigmatic examples in four problem spaces (for a sample, see Table 4.1). We highlight examples tested with randomized controlled trials in field contexts and important real-life outcomes, though this field-experimental work is often supported by other methodologies (e.g., qualitative approaches, laboratory experiments). We also note cases ripe for reframing that have not yet been subject to direct research.

Education

Academic probation. Placement on academic probation is a seminal challenge for college students and it is common. Nearly one in ten students in the United States are placed on probation at least once during their college careers (National Center for Education Statistics, 2012), typically for poor grades or for failing to earn the requisite credits. Even by conservative estimates, more than half a million students are placed on probation every year (Brady, Fotuhi et al., 2019).

Evidence suggests that students readily experience probation as a mark of shame, a sign that they are, or are seen as, stupid, or lazy, or lesser than others.

TABLE 4.1 "Bad" news reconsidered: A sample.

Situation	Typical, Default, or Risked Meaning	Neutral or Positive Meaning Available	Primary Principles Used	Consequence of Reframing
Education: Academic probation (Brady, Fotuhi et al., 2019)	A college student is placed on academic probation.	I'm (seen as) stupid or lazy or deficient. I'm looked down on. I don't belong.	It's normal to face challenges in college, and it doesn't make you lesser or worse. Many students recover to succeed. The institution expects this and creates resources to support students facing such challenges. That's the purpose of the probation process.	1. Prevent negative labels 2. Communicate "you're not the only one" 3. Recognize specific, non-pejorative causes 4. Forecast improvement 5. Recognize opportunities	Reduced shame and stigma Reduced thoughts of dropping out Greater engagement with academic support resources Improved academic recovery (in some trials)
Health: Medical symptoms (Howe et al., 2019)	A child undergoing exposure therapy for a peanut allergy experiences minor symptoms (e.g., itchy mouth, nausea).	An unfortunate part of treatment. A sign my allergy is especially severe and resisting treatment.	My body is responding positively to treatment. My body is getting stronger.	5. Recognize opportunities	Report fewer symptoms at the end of treatment Less worry about symptoms Less likely to contact treatment staff about symptoms Greater biomarker of allergy tolerance at the end of treatment

Close relationships: Difficulties with an infant (Bugental et al., 2002)	A new mother, at risk of committing child abuse, struggles with a baby (e.g., to get the baby to nurse, to take a bottle, to sleep, etc.)	I'm a bad mom; my baby is a bad baby.	These are normal challenges to be solved in parenting	1. Prevent negative labels 2. Communicate "you're not the only one" 3. Recognize specific, non-pejorative causes 4. Forecast improvement	At age 1: Reduced rates of child abuse, especially for high-risk infants; improved child health; reduced mother depression At age 3: Increased maternal investment, for high-risk infants; reduced child aggression and stress; improved child cognitive functioning
Economic development: Receipt of cash aid (Thomas et al., 2019)	Low-income people receive cash aid	I am (seen as) poor, helpless, unable to meet my basic needs. I am lesser than others.	This is an opportunity to pursue my goals, to become financially independent, and to better support my family and community.	1. Prevent negative labels 5. Recognize opportunities	Chose to watch more videos teaching business skills Greater self-efficacy to accomplish important life goals Greater anticipated social mobility

Importantly, this interpretation may arise, not just from the challenges that led to the student's placement on probation, but from how institutions represent probation. In telling stories of their experience on probation, students often describe themes of shame and stigma and reference the official notification they received informing them of their placement on probation (Brady, Fotuhi et al., 2019). Could revising this notification using the principles described above improve students' experience? A series of studies tested this question, by comparing schools' existing probation letters to "psychologically attuned" letters, which incorporated the five principles (Brady, Fotuhi et al., 2019. See Table 4.2). The attuned letters also included stories of prior students' experience on probation, which illustrated how each key principle had played out in their lives, promoting relevance and authenticity. As compared to standard institutional letters, attuned letters reduced the shame and stigma and thoughts of dropping out that students anticipated if they were to be placed on probation. Moreover, in at least some field tests, they increased the use of academic support resources among students placed on probation and their likelihood of return to good standing a year later (Brady, Fotuhi et al., 2019; Waltenbury et al., 2018).[1]

TABLE 4.2 Reframing academic probation (Brady, Fotuhi et al., 2019).

	School's Standard Probation Notification Letter	Reframed "Psychologically Attuned" Notification Letter
Principle #1: Prevent negative labels	"Placement on academic Probation"	"The process for academic probation"
Principle #2: Communicate "You're not the only one"	[no related content]	"You should also know that you're not the only one experiencing these difficulties…"
Principle #3: Recognize specific non-pejorative causes	"Whatever difficulties [you] have experienced…"	"There are many reasons students enter the academic probation process. These reasons can include personal, financial, health, family, or other issues…"
Principle #4: Forecast improvement	[no related content]	"By working with their advisors, many [students on probation] leave the process and continue a successful career at [school]…"
Principle #5: Recognize opportunities	[no related content]	"I learned something important in the process, about how to face up to challenges, to reach out to others for help, and find a way forward."

Critical academic feedback. The receipt of critical academic feedback further illustrates how a "bad" event can be reframed as an opportunity (Principle #5: Recognize opportunities). Even as constructive critical feedback is among the most valuable resources for learning, why teachers give critical feedback can be ambiguous to students. They may wonder if it reflects a negative judgment or bias on the part of the feedback-giver. When teachers explicitly convey their growth-oriented reasons for providing critical feedback, however, students may trust and be motivated by that feedback more. In one study, 7th grade students wrote an essay about their hero, received critical feedback from their teacher, and had the opportunity to revise their work for a higher grade (Yeager, Purdie-Vaughns, et al., 2014). All that varied was a paper-clipped note appended from the teacher. When the note highlighted the growth-oriented reasons why the teacher provided feedback—"I'm giving you these comments because I have very high standards and I know that you can reach them"—more students took up the opportunity to turn in a revision. The increase was greatest for Black students, who can otherwise worry that teachers' critical feedback might reflect racial stereotypes. Just 27 percent of Black students revised their essay following a placebic control note ("I'm giving you these comments so that you'll have feedback on your paper"), but 64 percent did with the treatment note. Moreover, this single but clear experience disambiguating a teacher's motive for giving critical feedback bolstered Black students' trust in their teachers in general over the rest of the school year and caused lasting downstream benefits. Black students who had received the treatment note received fewer discipline citations the next year and were more likely to enroll in a four-year college immediately after high school (Yeager, Purdie-Vaughns, et al., 2017).

Arousal and anxiety in test-taking. A third challenge in school involves the arousal and anxiety many students experience before a test. Often this experience is seen as portending failure but it can also be represented as the body getting ready to take on a challenge (e.g., "[arousal] doesn't hurt … and can actually help performance"; Principle #5: Recognize opportunities). This representation can raise test scores (Brady, Hard, & Gross, 2018; Jamieson, Mendes, Blackstock, & Schmader, 2010; Rozek, Ramirez, Fine, & Beilock, 2019). Similarly, giving students structured ways to reframe test anxiety on their own, such as to write down their thoughts and feelings before an exam, can improve scores (Ramirez & Beilock, 2011; Rozek et al., 2019).

Reframing can also help students recover from a disappointing score. In other studies, representing a "2" on an Advanced Placement (AP) test—a score just below the mark that commonly earns college credit—as not a failure but a step of progress experienced by many students in their AP trajectories (Principle #4: Forecast improvement) improved test-takers' evaluation of their experience and motivation to take future AP courses (Brady, Kalkstein, Rozek, & Walton, 2019).

Health

Symptoms of treatment. As with challenges in school, health challenges can be readily understood in negative terms, yet authentically reframed. Consider the case of children with severe peanut allergies. These children and their families face the terrifying prospect of spending their entire lives trying to avoid a ubiquitous substance that could cause serious illness or death. In oral immunotherapy treatment (OIT), children consume small but increasing doses of peanuts to build desensitization (Sampath, Sindher, Zhang, & Nadeau, 2018). Often OIT comes with symptoms such as an itchy mouth, nausea, hives, or stomach pain. Though these symptoms are minor, they can provoke anxiety because of their association with serious allergic reactions (e.g., anaphylaxis). Practitioners typically express sympathy for patients' experience and try to minimize symptoms. While well-intended, this response permits negative representations to persist. At best, patients may infer only that symptoms are uncomfortable and to be minimized. But they could also see symptoms as evidence that their allergy is particularly severe and that the treatment is not working. Yet symptoms can be a sign that the body is healing (e.g., fever is a sign the body is fighting infection), including that the body is desensitizing to allergens (Sampath et al., 2018). Howe and colleagues (2019) tested the effect of informing children undergoing OIT for peanut allergies that non-life-threatening symptoms can indicate that the treatment is progressing (Principle #5: Recognize opportunities), using both written information and activities (e.g., writing a letter to remind themselves of this idea). As compared to a treatment-as-usual ("symptoms as side effects") control condition, those in the "symptoms as positive signals" condition reported less anxiety about non-life-threatening symptoms over the six-month treatment period; were less likely to contact treatment staff about such symptoms (9.4 percent vs. 17.5 percent); reported fewer symptoms at the end of treatment, when dosage increased; were marginally less likely to skip or reduce doses (4 percent vs. 21 percent); and showed greater biomarker of allergy tolerance at the end of treatment.

Painful medical procedures. Painful medical procedures may discourage people from undergoing future procedures, even if they could benefit their health. Yet it is possible to tweak a procedure to change how people represent it later, so they recall it as less painful, even if not positive (a variant of Principle #5: Recognize opportunities). Basic research shows that the level of pain felt at the end of an experience has a disproportionate effect on people's recall of the experience (the peak-end effect; Kahneman, Fredrickson, Schreiber, & Redelmeier, 1993). Building on this work, one study modified a standard colonoscopy to leave the colonoscope inside patients' rectums for up to three additional minutes before withdrawing it slowly (Redelmeier, Katz, & Kahneman, 2003). This lengthened the procedure, yet reduced the level of pain people experienced at the end. In turn, people recalled the experience as less painful and this difference in memory mattered. People who underwent the modified procedure were 41 percent more likely to agree to another colonoscopy several years later if needed.

Trauma. Traumatic experiences can trigger reverberating negative thoughts and feelings that undermine health and functioning. Yet similar to research on test-taking (Ramirez & Beilock, 2011), structured, open-ended writing activities can help people process their emotions more effectively. In this case, people are given the opportunity to write concretely about the most traumatic experiences in their lives for 20 minutes a day over several days. Across multiple trials, this experience has been shown to improve health and immune function and raise achievement among college students and other populations (Pennebaker, 1997). Given the open-ended nature of the task, it is likely that a variety of processes issue from writing to achieve these benefits. However, evidence suggests that among these are the construction of a coherent causal narrative (e.g., the use of causality and insight words) with which to understand the traumatic experience (Principle #3: Recognize specific non-pejorative causes) and the use of positive emotion words (Principles #4 and #5: Forecast improvement, Recognize opportunities), both of which can predict better health (Pennebaker & Francis, 1996). Similarly, the effectiveness of in-person therapy may depend on a relationship in which people are in tune with their therapist, rather than feel they are judged (Principle #1: Prevent negative labels; Koole, this volume).

Threatening diagnoses. The receipt of a negative medical diagnosis is an obvious instance of "bad" news. Yet despite recognition that how a doctor frames diagnoses and other health news is important (e.g., Paul, Clinton-McHarg, Sanson-Fisher, & Webb, 2009) and doctors' own interest in wanting to do this well (Monden, Gentry, & Cox, 2016), thus far, little field research has examined the consequences of different ways of presenting diagnoses for either patients' health or psychological outcomes (cf. Mast, Kindlimann, & Langewitz, 2005; van Osch, Sep, van Vliet, van Dulmen, & Bensing, 2014). More broadly, some evidence suggests that physicians' skills in working with emotionally distressed patients can be enhanced and that doing so can reduce patients' distress over time (Roter et al., 1995).

Close Relationships

Challenges with a new baby. Close relationships are among the most inherently rewarding aspects of people's lives, yet they pose significant challenges. Take new, sleep-deprived parents who struggle to get a baby to stop crying or to sleep. Consider, especially, a single mom, with a low income and little support, who herself was abused as a child. Struggling to meet these challenges day after day and night after night, she may begin to experience parenting as a power struggle with a tyrannical being. She may even begin to think, "I'm a bad mom" or "My baby is a bad baby."

In this case, it is important to help the mother see that the challenges she faces are part of the normal experience of parenting and that she can work to solve them. To help mothers get there, Bugental and colleagues (2002) partnered with a state program in which paraprofessionals visited at-risk new mothers an average of 17 times over the baby's first year. In the standard program, mothers learned about healthy development and relevant services. In an "enhanced" condition, the paraprofessionals also asked mothers to describe their greatest challenges (e.g., "I can't get the baby to take a bottle") and why they thought they were having those challenges. Although mothers often gave self- or child-blaming reasons, the visitors were trained to keep asking, "Could it be something else?" until the mother suggested a reason that was not pejorative (e.g., "Maybe the baby needs a new bottle") (cf. Petty & Briñol, this volume). The paraprofessionals then asked the mother how she could work on that and, on the next visit, asked how it went. This approach (1) discourages mothers from labeling themselves or their baby negatively (Principle #1: Prevent negative labels); (2) implies that other parents also experience such challenges (Principle #2: Communicate "You're not the only one"); (3) implies that normal factors cause challenges in parenting and, importantly, encourages mothers to identify these for themselves (Principle #3: Recognize specific non-pejorative causes); and (4) suggests the possibility of improvement and encourages mothers to problem-solve how to achieve this (Principle #4: Forecast improvement). As compared to both the standard visit condition and a condition with no visits, this experience reduced the rate of child abuse during the first year from 23 percent to 4 percent, with the greatest reduction for mothers with more difficult, higher-risk infants (58 percent vs. 10 percent). The intervention also improved children's health, increased mothers' sense of power relative to their baby, and reduced their depression at the child's first birthday. Subsequent studies have found reductions in corporal punishment (from 35 percent to 21 percent) and child injuries, and have documented improved health and cognitive functioning and reduced aggression and stress for the child through their third birthday (Bugental, Beaulieu, & Silbert-Geiger, 2010; Bugental, Corpuz, & Schwartz, 2012; Bugental, Schwartz, & Lynch, 2010).

Marital conflict. People also experience challenges in romantic relationships, even those that they have committed to through marriage. If conflict begins to reverberate between the couple, this can undermine marital quality over time. In one study, inviting married couples to consider how "a neutral third party who wants the best for all" would think about a conflict in their marriage, and how they could take this perspective in future conflict situations, halted a normative decline in marital satisfaction over a year (Finkel, Slotter, Luchies, Walton, & Gross, 2013). This targets Principle #4: Forecast improvement most directly, but in practice, likely involves other principles as well.

Economic Development

Even experiences that appear positive and, in some ways are, can be framed inadvertently in ways that incur a psychological toll. Anti-poverty cash aid, for instance, can be an essential resource for those living in poverty. Yet aid also risks conveying a representation of recipients as deficient or helpless (Edin, Shaefer, & Tach, 2017; Walker et al., 2013). One study tested the effects of representing aid, instead, as a means to empower people in their lives (Thomas, Otis, Abraham, Markus, & Walton, 2019). Low-income residents of informal settlements in Nairobi, Kenya received a small cash payment equivalent to two days' wages. For some residents, this payment was attributed to the "Poverty Alleviation Organization" whose goal involved "reducing poverty and helping the poor meet their basic needs," a common representation of aid. For others, the payment was attributed to the "Individual Empowerment Organization" or the "Community Empowerment Organization" whose goals, respectively, were to enable people "to pursue personal goals and become more financially independent" and "to support those they care about and help communities grow together." These representations avoided labeling recipients as poor (Principle #1: Prevent negative labels) and highlighted an opportunity for growth (Principle #5: Recognize opportunities). Both led residents to view more videos introducing business skills of relevance in the informal settlements in which they worked (e.g., how to calculate a profit), rather than leisure videos (e.g., soccer highlights), to feel greater self-efficacy to accomplish life goals, and to anticipate greater improvement in their social standing over the next two years.

Nuances of Effective Reframings

Not Generic "Think Positive!", Not Hiding the Facts

None of the examples given above urges people to just "look on the bright side." None obfuscates or hides "the facts." They do not pretend it's not raining. Simply suppressing a negative experience would not allow people to learn from it, even if they could do so; more likely, the act of suppression would rebound in thought and feeling to undermine people's outcomes and functioning (Gross, 2014; Logel, Iserman, Davies, Quinn, & Spencer, 2009). Instead, the interventions help people understand "the facts" in more appropriate and adaptive ways. Each helps people develop a specific, plausible, and authentic narrative about a challenge they face. They acknowledge the rain and see it as an opportunity to dance or, at least, not as a fixed and global barrier.

Consider sexual assault. It would be wrong and unhelpful to say to a survivor, "It was actually good for you" or "It didn't happen." But it could be essential to ensure that the survivor understands what the assault does *not* mean:

It doesn't mean that you're a bad, tainted, unlovable person; it doesn't mean you did something wrong. The challenge is how to convey this more positive narrative persuasively.

How You Say It Matters

Earlier we noted that interventions vary in how directive they are, from directly controlling a narrative (e.g., Brady, Fotuhi et al., 2019) to simply posing questions or creating an experience that helps people develop a more positive narrative on their own (e.g., Bugental et al., 2002; Pennebaker, 1997). Although the effectiveness of different methods requires more research, this is likely to matter (see Crano & Ruybal, this volume, on misdirection; Petty & Briñol, this volume). For instance, if people feel a message is inauthentic (Walton & Yeager, in press) or if they see it as overly controlling, a view they do not have choice over (Silverman, Logel, & Cohen, 2013), they may reject it even if it would benefit them.

It can also be helpful to convey a narrative not only in terms of a recipient's own experience but to show how that narrative has played out in other people's lives (e.g., Walton & Cohen, 2011). Such social models can increase authenticity and thus the power of a narrative. One study found considerably greater reductions in shame and stigma when psychologically attuned probation notification letters were paired with stories from prior students about their experience on probation that reflected the more adaptive narrative than when such stories were absent (Brady & Walton, 2019).

Practical Guidance for Institutions

Unfortunately, institutions often bear bad news. From schools (probation letters, rejections), to clinics (negative test results), to banks (overdraft notices, missed payment warnings), to social media companies (removing content labeled as inappropriate), institutions routinely communicate information that threatens people's well-being, health, sense of adequacy, or belonging in a valued context. Especially potent are experiences that reasonably appear to a person unique to them, or to a small number of people like them, and that may carry fixed, negative consequences. That perception gives negative experiences a destructive power. Why is the phrase "shit happens" reassuring? Perhaps because it punctures the perception that the shit that one is currently experiencing is unique to the self, rare, and damning. Shit happens to other people too, perhaps often, and need not have enduring consequences.

Relying on the five principles and the examples given here, institutions can intentionally develop messages that provide appropriate, coherent, authentic, and adaptive representations of the person and a challenge they face. But this is easier said than done. How can institutions learn how people experience common negative events in their context and whether efforts to reframe these events have succeeded? Table 4.3 outlines a series of design and developmental steps institutions can use to begin to answer these questions, each of which we have used in our own past work (see also Fiedler, this volume). Given the specialized knowledge this work may require, it may be helpful to do so in partnership with people with relevant psychological expertise (see Yeager & Walton, 2011).

Guiding these steps is a critical assumption: *We cannot guess how other people experience things, but we can begin to find out by asking them.* In a series of 25 studies, Eyal, Steffel, and Epley (2018) show that simply asking people to take the perspective of others does not improve the accuracy with which people understand other's thoughts, feelings, and attitudes; if anything, people become somewhat *less* accurate. Yet when people had a brief conversation about the subject at hand, they became considerably more accurate in understanding one another. To understand others' experiences, we need to perspective-*get*, not perspective-*take*. As Eyal and colleagues write, "Increasing interpersonal accuracy seems to require gaining new information rather than utilizing existing knowledge about another person" (p. 547). The steps outlined in Table 4.3 provide a way to begin this process.

Positive and Neutral Things Too

We have focused on the representation of bad things. Yet how people represent positive events and experiences can also be important for catalyzing benefits. Moreover, the five principles mentioned earlier have variants that apply to positive experiences.

This is clearly illustrated in studies of the placebo effect, where the beliefs and expectations surrounding a beneficial treatment can contribute to its effects. For instance, when people do not know they have been injected with well-established pharmacological drugs, such as those to reduce pain, anxiety, and arousal, these drugs are considerably less effective than when their injection is visible to the patient (Principle #4: Forecast improvement; Benedetti et al., 2003). People's productive expectations work in tandem with the active properties of the drug to cause improvement.

In relationships, people with low self-esteem can dismiss compliments from romantic partners, for instance as "something she *had* to say." But asking people to describe how a compliment has a broad and general meaning can catalyze benefits for the relationship, helping people feel more secure in their partner's regard and improving patterns of interaction between the couple over at least several weeks (Marigold, Holmes, & Ross, 2007, 2010). This intervention encourages a positive label, inverting Principle #1.

Relatively banal experiences can also be reframed to good effect. Healthy options at the cafeteria may not seem attractive. Then, representing vegetables in indulgent terms (e.g., "rich buttery roasted sweet corn" instead of "corn") can increase consumption (Principle #5; Recognize opportunities; Turnwald

TABLE 4.3 Design steps institutions can use to learn (a) how people in a context experience and make sense of a "bad" event (Column 1) and (b) how they might change existing or default representations to alter people's interpretations and improve outcomes (Columns 2–5). In general, efforts should start with steps on the left and move right as warranted. Notably, these steps can be useful both in understanding how people make sense of specific negative events and experiences (our focus here) (e.g., Brady, Fotuhi et al., 2019), and in broader mindsets, and how to change them productively (e.g., Yeager, Romero et al., 2016).

	Step 1: Open-Ended Qualitative Work (e.g., Brady, Fotuhi et al., 2019; Yeager, Romero et al., 2016)	Step 2: User-Centered Design (e.g., Yeager, Romero et al., 2016)	Step 3: A/B Tests (e.g., Brady, Fotuhi et al., 2019; Yeager, Romero et al., 2016)	Step 4: Randomized Field Experiments (e.g., Brady, Fotuhi et al., 2019; Yeager, Romero et al., 2016)	Step 5: Improvement Science (e.g., Bryk et al., 2015; see also Brady, Fotuhi et al., 2019)
What is it?	Ask people about their experience with the challenge. Get them to articulate their thoughts and feelings in and about it.	Create revised messages or representations. Give them to people and ask for their response.	A randomized scenario experiment with immediate proxy and/or psychological outcome measures.	A randomized field experiment with psychological or non-psychological outcomes of importance, often over time.	Delivery of the revised message to all relevant people along with other relevant improvement efforts.
Tools	Interviews Focus groups Surveys	Talk alouds Interviews Focus groups Surveys	"Lab studies" with randomized experimental materials and immediate self-report or other outcome measures.	Randomized controlled field experiments Collection of institutional records Follow-up surveys	Pre/post design Interrupted time series analyses

Example from probation	Open-ended survey prompts or interviews with students who have gone through probation about their experience: "Tell me your story of academic probation. How did it begin? What was it like?" "What felt good or positive/bad or negative? How so?"	Create a revised probation notification letter. Ask students to imagine being placed on probation and receiving the revised or existing probation notification letter. Ask them to describe their reactions: what they think and feel as they read each letter.	Ask students to imagine being placed on probation. Give them either the revised or the existing notification letter. Assess anticipated feelings of shame, stigma, and the likelihood students say they would consider dropping out.	Randomize students being placed on probation to receive either the revised or the existing notification letter. Assess students' feelings of shame or stigma, academic engagement (e.g., choice to meet promptly with an advisor), and/or subsequent recovery from probation.	Provide all students being placed on probation with the revised notification letter. Revise institutional policies and implement advisor training to reinforce more adaptive representations of probation. Compare outcomes (e.g., shame, stigma, academic recovery) from cohorts before to cohorts after implementation.
What can you learn from it?	How people experience an event or context; what they think and feel about it. What kinds and ranges of interpretations are possible. What triggering events led to positive or negative experiences and representations.	What makes people feel good or bad; what they like/do not like; differences in responses to the revised and existing messages. What is confusing; whether recipients understand the revised message as intended. Which examples are compelling or not. Appropriateness of language level and style.	Whether the revised message can improve immediate outcomes either of importance on their own or that may shape downstream consequences of importance.	Whether the revised message can cause improvement in important real-world outcomes.	Whether institutional outcomes shift with full-scale implementation.

continued

TABLE 4.3 Continued

	Step 1: Open-Ended Qualitative Work (e.g., Brady, Fotuhi et al., 2019; Yeager, Romero et al., 2016)	Step 2: User-Centered Design (e.g., Yeager, Romero et al., 2016)	Step 3: A/B Tests (e.g., Brady, Fotuhi et al., 2019; Yeager, Romero et al., 2016)	Step 4: Randomized Field Experiments (e.g., Brady, Fotuhi et al., 2019; Yeager, Romero et al., 2016)	Step 5: Improvement Science (e.g., Bryk et al., 2015; see also Brady, Fotuhi et al., 2019)
What can't you learn from it?	Whether a specific change will alter individuals' experience or improve real-world outcomes.	Whether a specific change will alter individuals' experience or improve real-world outcomes.	Whether the revised message will improve important real-world outcomes.	Whether institutional outcomes will improve with full-scale implementation.	What exactly caused any observed shifts in institutional outcomes.

et al., 2019). Getting to the polls may seem like a chore. But considering how this could make one "a voter" can increase turnout (Principle #1: Encourage positive labels; Bryan, Walton, Rogers, & Dweck, 2011). Calling alumni for money may seem boring. But having a five-minute conversation with a scholarship recipient can increase fundraising (Principle #5: Recognize opportunities; Grant et al., 2007; see also Grant, 2008). In each case, tasks relatively devoid of positive meaning can be enhanced to promote engagement and success (see also Hulleman & Harackiewicz, 2009; Yeager, Henderson et al., 2014).

Conclusion

In the classic children's book *Harold and the Purple Crayon* (Johnson, 1955), Harold has a magic crayon he uses to meet his every need. When he is hungry, he draws pies. When he is drowning, he draws a boat. Sometimes it can seem subjective meanings are like this—wholly under a person's control. "I only need wish to think it so!" From this perspective, it is frustrating when people become stuck in pejorative ways of thinking that undermine their outcomes. "Snap out of it," we want to say.

The truth is that meanings are not just up to us (Asch, 1952; Hardin & Higgins, 1996). As people navigate the world, they strive, in large part, to draw reasonable inferences about who they are, how they relate to others, and how they are regarded (Walton & Wilson, 2018). They look to others, in part, to construct these meanings. We need to help each other find ways to sing in the rain. Thus, it is essential that institutions and other gatekeepers of meaning attend to how people make sense of bad experiences and, where appropriate, create representations and experiences that reinforce positive, non-pejorative ways of making sense of the self and of one's circumstances.

Author Note

We thank Bill Crano, Beth Genné, Lauren Howe, Catherine Thomas, and Sean Zion for feedback on an earlier draft, and participants in the 2019 Sydney Symposium of Social Psychology for helpful discussion.

Note

1 The principles we articulate in this paper grew out of our work on academic probation. In papers on probation, we describe similar though more situationally-specific principles.

References

Asch, S. E. (1952). *Social psychology*. Englewood Cliffs, NJ: Prentice Hall.

Benedetti, F., Maggi, G., Lopiano, L., Lanotte, M., Rainero, I., Vighetti, S., & Pollo, A. (2003). Open versus hidden medical treatments: The patient's knowledge about a therapy affects the therapy outcome. *Prevention & Treatment, 6*, 1–19. doi.org/10.1037/1522-3736.6.0001a

Brady, S. T., Fotuhi, O., Gomez, E., Cohen, G. L., Urstein, R., & Walton, G. M. (2019). *A scarlet letter? Revising institutional messages about academic probation can mitigate students' feelings of shame and stigma*. Manuscript in preparation.

Brady, S. T., Hard, B. M., & Gross, J. J. (2018). Reappraising test anxiety increases academic performance of first-year college students. *Journal of Educational Psychology, 110*, 395–406. doi.org/10.1037/edu0000219

Brady, S. T., Kalkstein, D. A., Rozek, C. S., & Walton, G. M. (2019). *Reframing a "2" on an AP test to reduce negative emotions and enhance motivation*. Manuscript in preparation.

Brady, S. T., & Walton, G. M. (2019). *Testing the independent contribution of attuned letters and stories from other students*. Unpublished data.

Bryan, C. J., Walton, G. M., Rogers, T., & Dweck, C. S. (2011). Motivating voter turnout by invoking the self. In *Proceedings of the National Academy of Sciences of the United States of America, 108*, 12653–12656. doi.org/10.1073/pnas.1103343108

Bryk, A. S., Gomez, L. M., Grunow, A., & LeMahieu, P. G. (2015). *Learning to improve: How America's schools can get better at getting better*. Cambridge, MA: Harvard Education Publishing.

Bugental, D. B., Beaulieu, D. A., & Silbert-Geiger, A. (2010). Increases in parental investment and child health as a result of an early intervention. *Journal of Experimental Child Psychology, 106*, 30–40. doi.org/10.1016/j.jecp.2009.10.004

Bugental, D. B., Corpuz, R., & Schwartz, A. (2012). Preventing children's aggression: Outcomes of an early intervention. *Developmental Psychology, 48*, 1443–1449. doi.org/10.1037/a0027303

Bugental, D. B., Ellerson, P. C., Lin, E. K., Rainey, B., Kokotovic, A., & O'Hara, N. (2002). A cognitive approach to child abuse prevention. *Journal of Family Psychology, 16*, 243–258.

Bugental, D. B., & Schwartz, A. (2009). A cognitive approach to child mistreatment prevention among medically at-risk infants. *Developmental Psychology, 45*, 284–288. doi.org/10.1037/a0014031

Bugental, D. B., Schwartz, A., & Lynch, C. (2010). Effects of an early family intervention on children's memory: The mediating role effects of cortisol levels. *Mind, Brain and Education, 4*, 156–218. doi.org/10.1111/j.1751-228X.2010.01095.x

Cohen, G. L., & Sherman, D. K. (2014). The psychology of change: Self-affirmation and social psychological intervention. *Annual Review of Psychology, 65*, 333–371.

Crum, A., Salovey, P. & Achor, S. (2013). Rethinking stress: The role of mindsets in determining the stress response. *Journal of Personality and Social Psychology, 104*(4), 716–733.

Dweck, C. S. & Yeager, D. S. (2019). Mindsets: A view from two eras. *Perspectives on Psychological Science*.

Edin, K., Shaefer, H. L., & Tach, L. (2017). A new anti-poverty policy litmus test. *Pathways Spring 2017*, 9–13.

Eyal, T., Steffel, M., & Epley, N. (2018). Perspective mistaking: Accurately understanding the mind of another requires getting perspective, not taking perspective. *Journal of Personality and Social Psychology, 114*(4), 547–571.

Finkel, E. J., Slotter, E. B., Luchies, L. B., Walton, G. M., & Gross, J. J. (2013). A brief intervention to promote conflict reappraisal preserves marital quality over time. *Psychological Science, 24*, 1595–1601.

Grant, A. M. (2008). The significance of task significance: Job performance effects, relational mechanisms, and boundary conditions. *Journal of Applied Psychology, 93*, 108–124. doi.org/10.1037/0021-9010.93.1.108

Grant, A. M., Campbell, E. M., Chen, G., Cottone, K., Lapedis, D., & Lee, K. (2007). Impact and the art of motivation maintenance: The effects of contact with beneficiaries on persistence behavior. *Organizational Behavior and Human Decision Processes, 103*, 53–67. doi.org/10.1016/j.obhdp.2006.05.004

Gross, J. J. (Ed.). (2014). *Handbook of emotion regulation* (2nd ed.). New York, NY: Guilford Press.

Hardin, C. D., & Higgins, E. T. (1996). Shared reality: How social verification makes the subjective objective. In R. M. Sorrentino & E. T. Higgins (Eds.), *Handbook of motivation and cognition. The interpersonal context* (Vol. 3, pp. 28–84). New York, NY: The Guilford Press.

Howe, L. C., Leibowitz, K. A., Perry, M. A., Bitler, J. M., Block, W., Kaptchuk, T. J., Nadeau, K. C., & Crum, A. J. (2019). Changing patient mindsets about non-life-threatening symptoms during oral immunotherapy: A randomized clinical trial. *The Journal of Allergy and Clinical Immunology: In Practice*.

Hulleman, C. S., & Harackiewicz, J. M. (2009). Promoting interest and performance in high school science classes. *Science, 326*, 1410–1412. doi.org/10.1126/science.1177067

Jamieson, J. P., Mendes, W. B., Blackstock, E., & Schmader, T. (2010). Turning the knots in your stomach into bows: Reappraising arousal improves performance on the GRE. *Journal of Experimental Social Psychology, 46*, 208–212.

Job, V., Dweck, C. S., & Walton, G. M. (2010). Ego depletion – Is it all in your head? Implicit theories about willpower affect self-regulation. *Psychological Science, 21*, 1686–1693.

Job, V., Walton, G. M., Bernecker, K., & Dweck, C. S. (2015). Implicit theories about willpower predict self-regulation and grades in everyday life. *Journal of Personality and Social Psychology, 108*, 637–347.

Johnson, C. (1955). *Harold and the purple crayon*. New York, NY: Harper & Brothers.

Kahneman, D., Fredrickson, D. L., Schreiber, C. A., & Redelmeier, D. A. (1993). When more pain is preferred to less: Adding a better end. *Psychological Science, 4*, 401–405.

Leibowitz, K. & Vittersø, J. (2019). *Winter is coming: Wintertime mindset and wellbeing in Norway*. Manuscript under review.

Logel, C., Iserman, E. C., Davies, P. G., Quinn, D. M., & Spencer, S. J. (2009). The perils of double consciousness: The role of thought suppression in stereotype threat. *Journal of Experimental Social Psychology, 45*, 299–312.

Marigold, D. C., Holmes, J. G., & Ross, M. (2007). More than words: Reframing compliments from romantic partners fosters security in low self-esteem individuals. *Journal of Personality and Social Psychology, 92*, 232–248. doi.org/10.1037/0022-3514.92.2.232

Marigold, D. C., Holmes, J. G., & Ross, M. (2010). Fostering relationship resilience: An intervention for low self-esteem individuals. *Journal of Experimental Social Psychology, 46*, 624–630. doi.org/10.1016/j.jesp.2010.02.011

Mast, M. S., Kindlimann, A., & Langewitz, W. (2005). Recipients' perspective on breaking bad news: How you put it really makes a difference. *Patient Education and Counseling, 58*(3), 244–251.

Monden, K. R., Gentry, L., & Cox, T. R. (2016). Delivering bad news to patients. *Proceedings (Baylor University Medical Center), 29*(1), 101–102.

Murphy, M. C., Kroeper, K. M., & Ozier, E. M. (2018). Prejudiced places: How contexts shape inequality and how policy can change them. *Policy Insights from the Behavioral and Brain Sciences, 5,* 66–74.

National Center for Education Statistics. (2012). *Baccalaureate and beyond longitudinal study (B&B: 08/09)* [Data file]. Washington, DC: U.S. Department of Education, Institute for Education Sciences. Retrieved from http://nces.ed.gov/surveys/b&b

Paul, C. L., Clinton-McHarg, R. W., Sanson-Fisher, H., & Webb, D. G. (2009). Are we there yet? The state of the evidence base for guidelines on breaking bad news to cancer patients. *European Journal of Cancer, 45,* 2960–2966.

Pennebaker, J. W. (1997). Writing about emotional experiences as a therapeutic process. *Psychological Science, 8,* 162–166. doi.org/10.1111/j.1467-9280.1997.tb00403.x

Pennebaker, J. W., & Francis, M. E. (1996). Cognitive, emotional, and language processes in disclosure. *Cognition & Emotion, 10*(6), 601–626.

Ramirez, G., & Beilock, S. L. (2011). Writing about testing worries boosts exam performance in the classroom. *Science, 331,* 211–213. doi.org/10.1126/science.1199427

Redelmeier, D. A., Katz, J., & Kahneman, D. (2003). Memories of colonoscopy: A randomized trial. *Pain, 104,* 187–194. doi.org/10.1016/S0304-3959(03)00003-4

Roter, D. L., Hall, J. A., Kern, D. E., Barker, L. R., Cole, K. A., & Roca, R. P. (1995). Improving physicians' interviewing skills and reducing patients' emotional distress: A randomized clinical trial. *Archives of Internal Medicine, 155,* 1877–1884. doi:10.1001/archinte.1995.00430170071009

Rozek, C. S., Ramirez, G., Fine, R. D., & Beilock, S. L. (2019). Reducing socioeconomic disparities in the STEM pipeline through student emotion regulation. *Proceedings of the National Academy of Sciences, 116,* 1553–1558.

Sampath, V., Sindher, S. B., Zhang, W., & Nadeau, K. C. (2018). New treatment directions in food allergy. *Annals of Allergy, Asthma, and Immunology, 120*(3), 254–262.

Silverman, A. M., Logel, C., & Cohen, G. L. (2013). Self-affirmation as a deliberate coping strategy. *Journal of Experimental Social Psychology, 49,* 93–98. doi.org/10.1016/j.jesp.2012.08.005

Thomas, C. C., Otis, N. G., Abraham, J. R., Markus, H. R., & Walton, G. M. (2019). *How to deliver aid with narratives that empower: Experimental evidence and local forecasts from Kenya.* Manuscript under review.

Turnwald, B. P., Bertoldo, J. D., Perry, M. A., Policastro, P., Timmons, M., Bosso, C., Connors, P., Valgenti, R. T., Pine, L., Challamel, G., Gardner, C. G., & Crum, A. J. (2019). Increasing vegetable intake by emphasizing tasty and enjoyable attributes: A randomized controlled multisite intervention for taste-focused labeling. *Psychological Science, 30*(11), 1603–1615. doi.org/10.1177/0956797619872191

Van Osch, M., Sep, M., van Vliet, L. M., van Dulmen, S., & Bensing, J. M. (2014). Reducing patients' anxiety and uncertainty, and improving recall in bad news consultations. *Health Psychology, 33*(11), 1382–1390.

Walker, R., Kyomuhendo, G., Chase, E., Choudhry, S., Gubrium, E., Nicola, J., Lødemel, I., Mathew, L., Mwiine, A., Pellissery, S., & Ming, Y. (2013). Poverty in global perspective: Is shame a common denominator? *Journal of Social Policy, 42*(2), 215–233. doi:10.1017/S0047279412000979

Waltenbury, M., Brady, S. T., Gallo, M., Redmond, N., Draper, S., & Fricker, T. (2018). *Academic probation: Evaluating the impact of academic standing notification letters on students* (Interim Report). Toronto, ON: Higher Education Quality Council of

Ontario. Available from www.heqco.ca/SiteCollectionDocuments/Formatted_ARC_Mohawk.pdf.

Walton, G. M. & Cohen, G. L. (2007). A question of belonging: Race, social fit, and achievement. *Journal of Personality and Social Psychology, 92*, 82–96.

Walton, G. M. & Cohen, G. L. (2011). A brief social-belonging intervention improves academic and health outcomes of minority students. *Science, 331*, 1447–1451.

Walton, G. M & Wilson T. D. (2018). Wise interventions: Psychological remedies for social and personal problems. *Psychological Review, 125*, 617–655.

Walton, G. M. & Yeager, D. S. (in press). Seed and soil: Psychological affordances in contexts help to explain where wise interventions succeed or fail. *Current Directions in Psychological Science*.

Yeager, D. S., Henderson, M. D., Paunesku, D., Walton, G. M., D'Mello, S., Spitzer, B. J., & Duckworth, A. L. (2014). Boring but important: A self-transcendent purpose for learning fosters academic self-regulation. *Journal of Personality and Social Psychology, 107*, 559–580. doi.org/10.1037/a0037637

Yeager, D. S., Johnson, R., Spitzer, B., Trzesniewski, K., Powers, J., & Dweck, C. S. (2014). The far-reaching effects of believing people can change: Implicit theories of personality shape stress, health, and achievement during adolescence. *Journal of Personality and Social Psychology, 106*(6), 867–884.

Yeager, D. S., Purdie-Vaughns, V., Garcia, J., Apfel, N., Brzustoski, P., Master, A., … Cohen, G. L. (2014). Breaking the cycle of mistrust: Wise interventions to provide critical feedback across the racial divide. *Journal of Experimental Psychology: General, 143*, 804–824. doi.org/10.1037/a0033906

Yeager, D. S., Purdie-Vaughns, V., Hooper, S. Y., & Cohen, G. L. (2017). Loss of institutional trust among racial and ethnic minority adolescents: Consequence of procedural injustice and a cause of lifespan outcomes. *Child Development, 88*, 658–676. doi.org/10.1111/cdev.12697

Yeager, D., Romero, C., Hulleman, C., Schneider, B., Hinojosa, C., Lee, H. Y., O'Brien, J., Flint, K., Roberts, A., Trott, J., Greene, D., Walton, G. M., & Dweck, C. (2016). Using design thinking to make psychological interventions ready for scaling: The case of the growth mindset during the transition to high school. *Journal of Educational Psychology, 108*, 374–391.

Yeager, D. S. & Walton, G. M. (2011). Social-psychological interventions in education: They're not magic. *Review of Educational Research, 81*, 267–301.

Yeager, D. S., Walton, G. M., Brady, S. T., Akcinar, E. N., Paunesku, D., Keane, L., Kamentz, D., Ritter, G., Duckworth, A. L., Urstein, R., Gomez E., Markus, H. R., Cohen, G. L., & Dweck, C. S. (2016). Teaching a lay theory before college narrows achievement gaps at scale. *Proceedings of the National Academy of Sciences of the United States of America, 113*, E3341–3348.

5

A PROCESS APPROACH TO INFLUENCING ATTITUDES AND CHANGING BEHAVIOR

Revisiting Classic Findings in Persuasion and Popular Interventions

Richard E. Petty and Pablo Briñol

Introduction

Many psychological interventions designed to improve people's lives rely on attempts to form or change peoples' beliefs and attitudes in a desired direction (e.g., I am a good fit for this school, I like eating a healthy diet) so that these beliefs and attitudes will be capable of influencing relevant behaviors (e.g., staying in school, eating more vegetables). In this review, we rely on the *elaboration likelihood model of persuasion* (ELM) (Petty & Cacioppo, 1986; Petty & Briñol, 2012) as a conceptual framework for understanding how to produce beliefs and attitudes that will have important consequences. Although the ELM identifies five core psychological processes by which variables can influence judgments, in this review we focus on two of those processes that have proven particularly useful in producing judgments that are consequential.

One important insight from the ELM is that people's judgments can be changed by relatively low or high thought processes, and that high thought processes are more likely to produce impactful judgments. Thus, it is important to understand what variables are effective in producing high amounts of elaboration regarding an influence attempt. Second, when thinking is already high, research shows that it not only matters what people's thoughts are (i.e., whether they are favorable or unfavorable toward the advocacy), but what people think about their thoughts (Briñol & Petty, 2009). Thus, in addition to discussing elaboration processes, we focus on thought validation processes.

Throughout our review, we include suggestions useful for designing practical interventions that take into consideration these psychological processes. Although many studies are guided by the ELM, the ones we have chosen illustrate how to produce consequential judgments (i.e., persistent over time, resistant to change, and impactful on behavior; Krosnick & Petty, 1995). We do not focus on changes based on low thought processes, such as those that stem from reliance on simple heuristics. Such changes, though sometimes equal in magnitude to high thought changes in the short term, are not as consequential (see Petty, Haugtvedt, & Smith, 1995).

Elaboration

As noted, the ELM distinguishes relatively thoughtful from non-thoughtful processes of belief and attitude change and holds that variables (e.g., source credibility, a person's mood) can influence judgments by affecting one of five core processes. These core processes are (1) serving as a simple cue, (2) serving as a persuasive argument, (3) biasing thinking, (4) validating thinking, and (5) determining the extent of thinking.

A focus on thinking (elaboration) highlights the importance of considering the amount and direction of people's thoughts in response to persuasive attempts. One of the most studied variables affecting the degree of message elaboration is the personal relevance of the communication (Petty & Cacioppo, 1979). The importance of personal relevance has also been highlighted among researchers and practitioners who have recommended increasing personal involvement to make applied programs more successful (e.g., Bryan, Walton, Rogers, & Dweck, 2011; Cohen & Andrade, 2018; Walton & Wilson, 2018; Harackiewicz, Rozek, Hulleman, & Hyde, 2012). However, by focusing on the process by which involvement helps persuasion to succeed (i.e., elaboration) we demonstrate that involvement can either be good or bad for persuasion (i.e., produce change in the desired direction or not). According to the ELM, when the personal relevance of a message is high, people scrutinize the evidence more carefully than when it is low. This results in higher personal relevance being associated with more favorable thoughts and attitudes when the message arguments are strong and compelling, but with more unfavorable thoughts and attitudes when the arguments are weak and specious (Petty & Cacioppo, 1990).

In one prototypical early study illustrating this point, Petty, Cacioppo, and Schumann (1983) varied participants' interest in an advertisement for the "Edge razor" by informing them that they would receive a razor (high relevance) or a tube of toothpaste (low relevance) for participating in the experiment. Subsequently, participants were exposed to a razor advertisement containing either strong arguments (e.g., "In direct comparison tests, the Edge blade gave twice as many close shaves as its nearest competitor") or weak ones (e.g., "In direct comparison tests, the Edge blade gave no more nicks or cuts than its competition"). In addition to argument quality, this study varied whether the two endorsers featured in the ad were famous athletes or ordinary people. The results revealed a larger argument quality effect on attitudes (i.e., more persuasion for the strong than weak arguments) when the razor advertisement was high as opposed to low in personal relevance. However, the simple cue of endorser attractiveness had a larger impact on attitudes when the ad was of low rather than high personal relevance (see also Haugtvedt, Petty, & Cacioppo, 1992).

Processing arguments mattered more when relevance was high, but the simple source cue mattered more when relevance was low. Does it matter which kind of persuasion was produced? In addition to measuring attitudes toward the razor, participants were also asked about their likelihood of purchasing the razor the next time they needed one. Under high relevance conditions, not only did argument quality affect attitudes, but it also affected purchase intentions. In stark contrast, under low relevance, although positive endorsers produced more favorable product attitudes than neutral endorsers, these positive endorsers failed to produce more favorable purchase intentions. Positive attitudes failed to translate into behavior in the low relevance condition. This result is also demonstrated in the finding that people's product attitudes predicted their intentions less strongly in the low than in the high relevance conditions. In short, the greater thinking involved in changing attitudes under high than low relevance also led those attitudes to be more consequential.

Why were the attitudes formed under high thinking more consequential than those formed under low thinking? Subsequent research has pointed to at least two benefits of high thinking. First, when thinking is high, people tend to access their attitudes as they update them with each new argument processed. This updating leads high-thought attitudes to be more readily accessible when the attitude object is encountered (Tormala & Petty, 2001). The more likely attitudes are to come to mind quickly and spontaneously, the more people can use them to guide their behavior (Fazio, 1990). Second, attitudes based on high thought are held with more confidence than those based on little thought (Barden & Petty, 2008). When people are deciding what to do, they are more likely to act on an attitude if they are sure it is correct than if they are not (e.g., Rucker & Petty, 2004).

Elaboration and Intentions to Use Doping Substances

As explained, whether attitude change occurs as the result of relatively high or low amounts of thinking matters not only for determining what attitude is formed, but also how consequential or strong that attitude is over time (Petty & Krosnick, 1995). The more a judgment is based on thinking, the more it tends to persist over time, resist attempts at change, and have consequences for other judgments and behavior (Petty et al., 1995).

In a recent illustration of the elaboration-strength link in an applied context, Horcajo and Luttrell (2016) showed that influencing athletes' attitudes about doping through a high (vs. low) elaboration process made the newly-formed attitudes more predictive of behavioral intentions and more resistant to subsequent attacking messages. The participants in this study were all Spanish soccer players from registered teams. Elaboration was manipulated by varying personal involvement. In the high elaboration condition, the athletes were told that the legalization of doping proposal was being analyzed by the Fédération Internationale de Football Association (FIFA) and that legalization could be implemented in soccer rules the next season. Participants in the low elaboration condition were told that it was being analyzed by a relatively less powerful organization, the (fictional) World Anti-Doping Agency (WADA), and that legalization could be implemented only in other sports (cycling and athletics) in ten years.

Following this manipulation, participants received a persuasive message that presented strong arguments either against, or in favour of, the legalization of doping. These strong messages also included some peripheral cues (e.g., credible sources, a large number of arguments), which can lead to persuasion, even when people do not think carefully about the arguments. After participants read the first message, they reported their attitudes and behavioral intentions regarding the legalization proposal.

Next, all participants received a second message that argued for the opposite conclusion as the first message. Thus, someone who first received a strong message arguing in favor of legalization would receive a message arguing against that proposal, and vice versa. Attitudes toward the legalization proposal were then assessed again. In accord with the ELM predictions, participants showed greater attitude-consistent intentions when they formed their initial attitudes through thoughtful (vs. non-thoughtful) consideration of the first message (i.e., in the high vs. low relevance conditions). Moreover, there was also more resistance to the subsequent attacking message when participants formed their initial attitudes through a thoughtful vs. non-thoughtful process.

Elaboration and Prejudiced Attitudes

As another illustration of the elaboration–attitude strength link, consider the modification of prejudiced attitudes. In two studies, Cárdaba, Briñol, Horcajo, and Petty (2014) presented participants with a persuasive message composed of compelling arguments in favor of a minority group or a control message in favor of vegetables. In one study, the degree of elaboration was measured by asking people how much they had thought about the message and in a second study, motivation and ability to think about the message were manipulated by framing the message as personally relevant or not and by presenting a distraction task along with the message or not which would impair participants' ability to process the message. The relevance and distraction inductions were combined in a compatible way to create the high- and the low-thinking conditions.

Following the message, one study assessed the perceived strength of participants' attitudes (i.e., how much they believed their attitudes would change in the future) and the other study measured actual resistance to a subsequent attacking message. The results showed that even though the obtained attitude change to the first message (vs. control) was equivalent under low- and high-thinking conditions, the attitudes were stronger when thinking was high; participants not only rated their attitudes toward the minority group as less likely to change, but they were also more resistant to an actual attacking message. As this research demonstrates, understanding the nature of the processes by which attitudes change is essential because it is informative about the consequences of persuasion (see also Cárdaba, et al., 2014; Wegener, Clark, & Petty, 2006).

Elaboration and Personal Involvement Revisited

As described, prior research suggests that making a persuasive message more self-relevant by linking the advocacy to one's values, outcomes, or identity, can enhance information processing (Petty & Cacioppo, 1990; Fleming and Petty, 2000). When relevance is high versus low, people become more persuaded if the evidence is found to be strong, but if the evidence is found to be weak, less persuasion occurs with high relevance. It is important to highlight this fact because intervention programs typically recommend increasing personal relevance to enhance effectiveness (e.g., Bryan et al., 2011; Cohen & Andrade, 2018; Galton & Wilson, 2018; Harackiewicz, et al., 2012; Hulleman, Kosovich, Baron, & Daniel, 2017). However, as described, personal involvement increases elaboration leading to more persuasion for strong arguments, but to *reduced* persuasion if the arguments presented are specious.

Since these initial demonstrations of an interaction between personal involvement and argument quality on attitudes, this outcome has been replicated many times by independent labs using a variety of materials and inductions (see Carpenter, 2015). Notably, in all of this prior work, to form an accurate opinion, message recipients were plausibly motivated by their desire to learn about the issue advocated. Indeed, one of the major motivations that governs human thought and action is the *need to know*. Gaining accurate knowledge is the typical or default goal orientation assumed by contemporary persuasion theories such as the ELM (see also Chaiken, Liberman, & Eagly, 1989).

Importantly, in some recent research on personal involvement, researchers compared the motivation to gain knowledge to an alternative one in which people aim to process information to be entertained – a *hedonic* rather than an *epistemic* goal. The goal of seeking entertainment is an important motivation within communications (e.g., see Slater, 2002; Zillman & Bryant, 2002; Bridges & Florsheim, 2008). In fact, some authors have considered the hedonic mindset as one of the most predominant precursors of communication processing strategies (Bartsch & Schneider, 2014; Green, Brock, & Kaufman, 2004). When people have hedonic goals, they look to become transported into fictional characters, moving focus away from themselves (Green, 2006) and identifying with other people in a story, real or imagined (Cohen, 2001). Within social psychology, hedonic goals have also received recent attention (Wilson, Westgate, Buttrick, & Gilbert, in press). Thinking for pleasure with the deliberate intention of having fun has been found to be difficult, requiring more concentration than other kinds of thinking (e.g., for epistemic goals) and more concentration than engaging in certain external activities (e.g., playing a video game; Wilson, et al., 2014).

So, what would the impact of personal relevance be on information processing if people had a hedonic rather than an epistemic goal prior to receipt of a persuasive message? We hypothesized that people having an explicit knowledge goal would elaborate more under high vs. low involvement conditions; the typical effect observed in the prior literature. In contrast, people having a hedonic goal would elaborate less under high vs. low involvement conditions. Furthermore, consistent with the *elaboration-strength* notion of the ELM, conditions fostering greater elaboration were predicted to produce attitudes that were stronger and more predictive of behavioral intentions.

In a study examining this idea (Cancela, Briñol, & Petty, 2019), participants were informed that they would take part in a mass media study and were then given one of two goals. In the *epistemic goal* condition, participants read: "The goal of this editorial is for people to learn and have an informative and knowledgeable experience." This goal likely comports with the default goal in most persuasion studies. In the *hedonic goal* condition, participants read: "The goal of this editorial is for people to enjoy the experience and have a pleasurable and fun experience." This induction was pretested to produce the intended goal. Next, personal involvement was manipulated by framing the communication as high or low in personal relevance. In the high involvement condition, participants were told the message had to do with their self-concept. In the low involvement condition, they were simply told the topic of the message (Briñol, Petty, & Wheeler, 2006). Then, participants received a persuasive message composed of either strong or weak arguments about consuming more vegetables. Finally, participants completed the dependent measures – attitudes and behavioral intentions toward vegetables.

The study's results revealed that information processing goals and personal involvement interacted as predicted to affect elaboration and persuasion (see Figure 5.1). Increasing personal involvement increased information processing (and argument quality effects on attitudes) over low involvement when people had epistemic goals (see top panel, Figure 5.1). The reverse was true when people had hedonic goals (see bottom panel, Figure 5.1). Furthermore, conditions with greater elaboration produced attitudes that were more predictive of behavioral intentions than conditions with lower elaboration (see Figure 5.2).

This research has important implications for practical interventions. The research indicates that people can be motivated to think in different ways when they are in different contexts. For example, in educational contexts, teachers

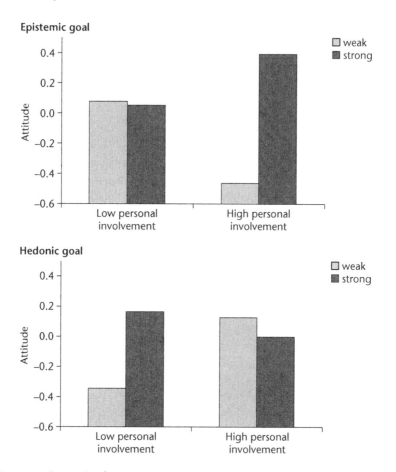

FIGURE 5.1 Interaction between personal involvement and argument quality as a function of epistemic goals (top panel) and hedonic goals (bottom panel) (adapted from Cancela, Briñol, & Petty, 2019).

could increase students' motivation by making the communication more personally relevant for them. Similarly, because patients usually come to a doctor's office in a high personal involvement circumstance, the doctor is better off using strong arguments in an epistemic rather than an entertainment appeal. Also, in these examples, making the communication more personally relevant would translate into stronger attitudes in guiding behavior as the arguments would receive greater elaboration and thus, would be translated into better adherence, healthier behaviors, better grades, and so forth (see also Higgins, Cesario, Hagiwara, Spiegel, & Pittman, 2010).

Although this advice fits with conventional wisdom, the research we reviewed also points to clear limits of invariably making communications more personally relevant. The research by Cancela and colleagues (2019) is noteworthy in its

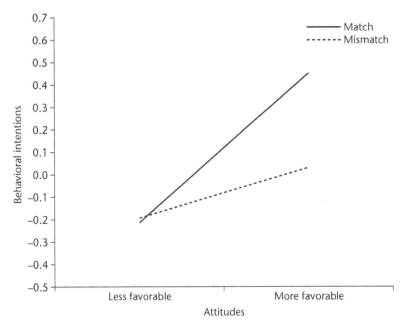

FIGURE 5.2 A match between goal orientation and involvement (i.e., epistemic orientation and high personal involvement and hedonic orientation and low personal involvement) led attitudes to be more predictive of behavioral intentions than a mismatch between goal orientation and involvement (i.e., epistemic orientation and low personal involvement and hedonic orientation and high personal involvement) (adapted from Cancela, Briñol, & Petty, 2019).

implications for people processing communications in the context of entertainment programs. Whereas past research might have led practitioners to think that communications always should be high in self-relevance to maximize thinking, the research we reviewed suggests that this is more likely to be an effective strategy for messages embedded in a news program than an entertainment program (see also Wilson et al., in press). Indeed, in the latter case, increasing personal involvement might even be counterproductive if people maintain their hedonic orientation during the message.

Summary

In sum, the core elaboration idea from the ELM appears applicable to topics as diverse as attitudes toward doping, prejudice toward minority groups, and views about healthy eating (e.g., vegetables, see also Papies, this volume). Across these and other domains, attitudes that came about through relatively thoughtful processes were more resistant to change, as well as particularly impactful on behavioral intentions. However, as demonstrated, simply having attitudes is not sufficient for behavioral influence. Those attitudes must come to mind and when they do, people must have confidence in them (Rucker, Tormala, Petty, & Briñol, 2014), two outcomes of high elaboration. The persuasion research we describe in the next section demonstrates that for thoughts to affect attitudes and behaviors, they should also be perceived as valid.

Validation

The process of validation highlights the distinction between primary and secondary cognition, and emphasizes the importance of considering what people think and feel about their thoughts. As in our discussion of elaboration, we explain that variables that are sometimes seen as invariably good for persuasion (e.g., making people feel confident via empowerment; see Burgmer & Englich, 2012; Hertwig & Grüne-Yanoff, 2017; Lammers, Dubois, Rucker, & Galinsky, 2013; Pratto, 2016), are not always good for producing change. Also, greater confidence in thoughts does not imply that thoughts are any more accurate or unbiased (see Fiedler, this volume; Kovera, this volume; Mikulincer & Shaver, this volume).

We have seen that one way in which interventions can change behavior is by creating strong attitudes through high elaboration. Another way is to produce confident thoughts via validation. The ELM holds that variables not only affect the extent of elaboration but can also influence what people think and feel about the thoughts they have generated. These meta-cognitions can then determine the extent to which people use their thoughts in forming judgments to ultimately guide their behavior. This general notion of people's reactions to their own thoughts determining their use is referred to as the *self-validation hypothesis* (Petty, Briñol, & Tormala, 2002), whose key tenet is that merely having favorable thoughts stemming from high elaboration is not sufficient to predict subsequent judgments and behavior. Rather, people must also perceive their thoughts as valid. Thus, any variables that increase perceptions of thought validity will increase use of thoughts in forming evaluations and guiding actions. In contrast, perceiving thoughts as invalid attenuates their use.

Unlike elaboration, which focuses on first-order cognition (e.g., vegetables are nutritious), validation emphasizes secondary or meta-cognition (e.g., I am sure that vegetables are nutritious). Given its meta-cognitive nature, validation requires relatively high thinking. Petty and colleagues (2002) demonstrated that self-validation is more likely to operate when people have the motivation and ability to think about their thoughts (e.g., if participants are high in need for cognition; Cacioppo & Petty, 1982; when there is high personal relevance of the persuasion topic; Petty & Cacioppo, 1979). Thus, for validation processes to matter, people need to have some thoughts to validate, and also to be motivated and able to consider thought validity. Another boundary condition on the operation of validation processes is that confidence from the validating variable should be salient during or following thought generation rather than prior to it.

In an early study examining self-validation, Briñol and Petty (2003) had participants nod or shake their heads while listening to a message containing strong or weak arguments advocating that students be required to carry personal identification cards on their campus. Head movements were varied because nodding one's head is associated with more confidence in what one is thinking than is shaking. Thus, when people listened through headphones to strong advocacy arguments, vertical head movements led to more favorable attitudes than horizontal movements. This is the effect expected if vertical movements increased confidence in and use of one's favorable thoughts. However, when people listened to weak arguments, vertical movements led to less favorable attitudes than horizontal movements – the result that would be expected if vertical movements increased confidence in and use of one's negative thoughts. These results were obtained in conditions that fostered high motivation and ability to think, and when head movements were performed during the generation of thoughts. Furthermore, the attitude changes resulting from head nodding were mediated by perceptions of thought confidence.

Although prior research had shown that head movements during a message could affect attitudes (Wells & Petty, 1980), the study just described was the first to show that the mechanism responsible for attitude change was self-validation. This is because unlike the prior research, which had used only strong arguments and showed a positive effect of head nodding versus shaking on attitudes, the more recent study showed that head nodding could also reduce persuasion if thoughts to the message were negative (see also Briñol, DeMarree, & Petty, 2015; Wichman et al., 2010).

Embodied Validation Influences Sport Performance

To illustrate the potential applications of self-validation processes, in a recent experiment on sport performance (Horcajo, Paredes, Higuero, Briñol, & Petty, 2019), cross fit athletes were recruited for an experiment while practicing at the gym. The athletes were randomly assigned to generate and then record on a smartphone either positive or negative statements about themselves. We relied on this thought-direction induction because extensive research has found that what athletes say to themselves through self-talk can influence their performance (e.g., Tod, Hardy, & Oliver, 2011; Van Raalte, Vincent, & Brewer, 2016). Meta-analyses of this literature have documented the robustness of this positive effect of self-talk (Hatzigeorgiadis, Zourbanos, Galanis, & Theodorakis, 2011; Tod, Edwards, McGuigan, & Lovell, 2015).

We predicted a self-validation framework could specify when and why self-statements can influence physical performance. Athletes were randomly assigned to a validating induction (nodding or shaking their heads) while listening over headphones to the self-statements they had recorded. Finally, after listening to the self-statements, physical performance was assessed in various tasks (e.g., vertical jump). Consistent with the self-validation hypothesis, athletes' self-statements were significantly more impactful on their physical performance in the head nodding than in the head shaking condition. As illustrated in Figure 5.3, listening to positive self-statements while nodding increased physical performance relative to shaking. However, listening to negative self-statements while nodding reduced performance relative to shaking. Thus, this study showed that bodily movements can either magnify or attenuate the impact of what people say to themselves. As noted, this self-validation effect is most likely when conditions foster thinking and the validation variable comes during or after thought generation. If the head movements had occurred prior to generating self-statements, other processes would be more likely to occur (e.g., head movements could have affected the amount and direction of the thoughts that came to mind; see Briñol, Petty, & Hinsenkamp, 2018).

Also relevant, given that the cover story used in this study (i.e., testing the use of headphones at the gym) aimed to hide the connection between head movements and subsequent physical performance, an important matter to consider for applied interventions in this and other domains is whether head movements could also be used to *intentionally* produce changes in performance. Indeed, people not only use their self-talk to intentionally improve their own performance, but they also use their non-verbal behavior to deliberately influence their own performance or the performance of others (e.g., when an audience smiles or cheers for their team). However, it remains to be seen if people

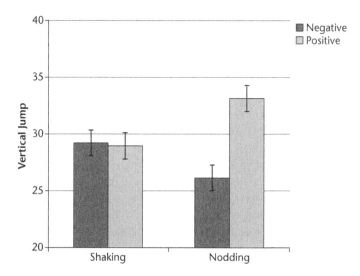

FIGURE 5.3 Vertical jump (in centimeters) as a function of self-talk and head movements (adapted from Horcajo et al., 2019).

can use their own nodding and shaking head movements to deliberately improve their performance by intentionally validating their thoughts. Thus, future research should examine to what extent the findings of Horcajo and colleagues (2019) can be generalized to interventions including intentional overt behaviors performed with the explicit goal of improving performance (see also Koole, this volume).

Validation Increases Goal-Behavior Correspondence

We have reviewed how variables associated with validity (head nodding) can validate mental constructs (thoughts from self-talk) affecting behavior (sport performance). We now focus on how other variables associated with validity (felt power, ease of recall) can influence behavior (e.g., academic performance, donations). Across three experiments, we manipulated participants' sense of power, the ease with which goal-relevant behavior was recalled, and an episodic recall of participants' own past experiences of confidence versus doubt to examine whether these variables affected subsequent behavior via thought validation.

In one study, DeMarree et al. (2012) examined whether felt power could validate people's goals of competition versus cooperation. Participants were first primed with words related to competition (e.g., compete, win) or cooperation (e.g., help, share), using a word completion task (i.e., filling in the missing letters of words). Following this, participants wrote about times when they had power over someone else or when someone else had power over them. Finally, they engaged in simulated economic games where they had an opportunity to share money with another participant. Consistent with the idea that power produces confidence (and powerlessness produces doubt; see Briñol, Petty, Valle et al., 2007), the primed goal affected participants' behavior in the economic games to a greater extent when they subsequently wrote about high power. Specifically, in the high versus low power conditions, cooperation-primed participants gave more money to their partner in the economic games than did competition-primed participants.

A second study by DeMarree et al. (2012) used a new prime to vary initial cognitions, a different variable to induce validity, and also a new behavioral-dependent measure. In this study, an achievement goal was first primed in all participants by having them recall past instances of achievement striving. The number of examples recalled served as a manipulation of participants' subjective ease of retrieval (Schwarz et al., 1991). Participants were randomly assigned to recall few (easy) or many (difficult) achievement memories. Research on self-validation had demonstrated that ease of thought retrieval affects confidence in the recalled content (Tormala, Petty, & Briñol, 2002; Tormala, Falces, Briñol, & Petty, 2007). Therefore, ease was the validating variable in this study. After completing the ease induction, all participants completed a series of difficult anagram items and were given a chance to raise their score on the task by completing additional, easy, items. The amount of time spent on the second anagram task served as the behavioral measure of achievement striving. In line with self-validation predictions, the achievement goal initially primed had a larger effect on task persistence when people associated the primes with the experience of ease (confidence) vs. difficulty (doubt).

In a third experiment, DeMarree et al. (2012) primed participants with a self-improvement or a money saving goal immediately prior to having them reflect on times when they experienced confidence or doubt. After the priming and confidence inductions, participants' intentions to donate to charity were recorded and served as the main dependent measure. Consistent with self-validation logic, participants who articulated past instances of confidence relied on the primed goal more than those who reflected upon instances of doubt. Specifically, confident participants in the self-improvement condition were willing to donate more than twice as much money ($13.00) as people in the confident saving money condition ($5.28). In the doubt conditions, no significant priming effects emerged. Taken together, this research on goal validation reveals that the extent to which prime-related mental contents are viewed as valid can determine whether a primed concept influences motivated behavior.

Power Validates Ambivalence Leading to Inaction

As described, power can influence behavior through validation processes. In a recent review, we have shown that a wide variety of power inductions can magnify the impact of any current thoughts via the self-validation process (Briñol, Petty, Durso, & Rucker, 2017). But, as noted, for power to influence judgment via a self-validation mechanism, elaboration must be sufficiently high for individuals to generate thoughts and to consider their validity. Second, power inductions are more likely to influence judgments by self-validation when the induction accompanies or follows the generation of thoughts rather than precedes it. According to the ELM, power serves in other roles when elaboration is not high or the feeling of power precedes the message (Briñol et al., 2017).

Given that the validation effect that emerges from power can be applied to any cognition, an interesting issue is whether power can also validate ambivalence. This is interesting because past research suggests that more power generally leads people to be more likely to take action (Galinsky, Gruenfeld, & Magee, 2003; Keltner, Gruenfeld, & Anderson, 2003), whereas ambivalence (the feeling of being mixed or conflicted; Priester & Petty, 1996), leads to *less* action than univalence (van Harreveld, van der Pligt, & de Liver, 2009). These observations allow for the simple conclusion that two main effects could emerge in a situation where people vary both in power and ambivalence: people might be most inclined to act when they are powerful and have consistent thoughts and be least inclined to act when they are powerless and have ambivalent thoughts. However, if power can validate any mental content including individuals' ambivalent thoughts, then power should magnify the extent to which this ambivalence was trusted and thus reduce participants' propensity to act, a novel hypothesis from the self-validation approach.

A recent experimental test of this unique prediction regarding power and ambivalence (Durso, Briñol, & Petty, 2016) had participants read information about an employee whose behavior was either consistent (entirely good or bad) or ambivalent (both good and bad). Subsequently, participants were induced to feel more or less powerful. Next, they indicated the extent to which they preferred action versus inaction in making a decision about an employee. Finally, participants were required to make a decision as to whether the employee should be promoted or fired. The time invested in making that decision was recorded.

Consistent with previous work demonstrating that power leads to action, among participants who received univalent information, those induced to feel powerful were more likely to express a preference for taking action and make quicker decisions than low power participants. In contrast, among participants who received ambivalent information, those who were made to feel powerful were more likely to prefer inaction and make their decisions more slowly than low-power participants (see Figure 5.4). These results are informative as to the conditions under which feeling powerful leads to more versus less action (see also, DeMarree, Briñol, & Petty, 2014; Hirsh, Galinsky, & Zhong, 2011). This is important because empowering people to take action has been shown to play a critical role in many interventions (Burgmer & Englich, 2012; Hertwig & Grüne-Yanoff, 2017; Lammers, et al., 2013; Pratto, 2016).

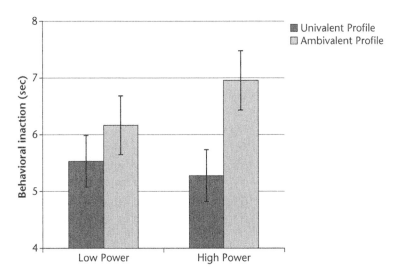

FIGURE 5.4 Behavioral inaction (decision time) as a function of ambivalence and power (adapted from Durso, Briñol, & Petty, 2016).

Elaboration and Validation: Practical Tips for Separating Processes

As noted throughout this review, maximizing the chances of designing effective interventions depends in part on understanding the psychological processes by which variables produce change. This review focused on two fundamental mechanisms of influence from the ELM – elaboration and validation – which are critical for predicting whether change occurs in the desired direction and are also relevant for specifying how consequential changed mental constructs (e.g., attitudes, goals) are in guiding behavior over time.

Given that many variables (power, ease, body movements) can affect judgments and behaviors through these two processes, a natural concern is how researchers and practitioners can explain and test the effects of interventions on influence in any given context of interest. Fortunately, systematic methods exist to help identify the fundamental process by which any given variable operates to produce influence. As noted, the effects of variables such as power can be predicted a priori based on contextual factors, such as the general background levels of elaboration as well as the order in which events occur. To examine the methods for systematically separating the processes by which variables can influence judgments and behaviors, researchers and practitioners can use moderation and mediation approaches. Indeed, a number of methods have been identified for both separating out and predicting when different processes occur.

One means to test for particular processes involves manipulating elaboration and the quality of the arguments contained in the critical intervention. Because different processes operate at distinct levels of elaboration, manipulating elaboration is an excellent tool to isolate and understand the nature of an underlying effect. Manipulating argument quality helps determine if a variable is affecting amount of thinking (elaboration) or reliance on the thoughts generated (validation). As alluded to earlier, the time at which variables are made salient can systematically alter the process by which argument quality affects persuasion. Variables are more likely to influence judgments by a process of thought validation when introduced after, rather than before individuals generate their thoughts, but are more likely to influence extent of thinking (elaboration) when induced before, rather than after. For instance, enhancing feelings of power after a message allows people to feel more confident in and use their generated thoughts about the message, whereas inducing power before a message decreases their likelihood of processing the message because people already feel confident in what they believe (Briñol, Petty, Valle, Rucker, & Becerra, 2007).

In addition to identifying moderators such as timing and elaboration, research has also developed mediators of attitude change that can be used to understand how variables affect influence. Measuring both the type (valence) of thoughts participants generate as well as their perceptions of thought validity can help determine the underlying processes involved in social influence. Affecting persuasion by increasing individuals' amount of thinking should result in a shift in the proportion of message-relevant thoughts that are consistent with the message (i.e., the valence of thoughts – favorable or unfavorable – becomes more congruent with the strong or weak quality of the message as thinking increases). Alternatively, if a variable affects persuasion by validating thoughts, then differences should be observed in participants' perceived thought validity, and this should mediate persuasion. In contrast, if a variable has no effect at all on message-relevant thoughts or thought validity, this can signal that the variable is serving as a peripheral cue, a process most likely to occur when thinking is low (see Petty, Schumann, Richman, & Strathman, 1993). In sum, thought favorability and validity can be measured to help examine the underlying process by which variables affect persuasion in a given context.

Revisiting Popular Interventions by Taking Process into Consideration

As should be clear so far, changing people is complex. However, taking a process-orientation to intervention can be helpful in understanding such complexity. The research we reviewed suggests some important caveats to popular interventions that propose relatively simple "tricks" for changing people's lives (Nair, Sagar, Sollers, Consedine, & Broadbent, 2014; Wiseman, 2012, 2013; see Walton & Wilson, 2018, for a review). For example, our work has qualified a recent trend of emphasizing feeling powerful as a means of becoming more successful across different domains of life (Lammers, Dubois, Rucker, & Galinsky 2013; Wiseman, 2013). Rather than being inherently beneficial, we explained how the confidence that comes from body postures or feelings of power can magnify whatever mental content is accessible, at least when power operates through a self-validation mechanism. Self-validation research has shown that feelings of power or confidence can increase self-esteem (Briñol, Petty, & Wagner, 2009) and physical performance (Horcajo et al., 2019) when people are thinking about their strengths, but decrease self-esteem and performance when they are thinking about their weaknesses.

Beyond power, other popular interventions often rely on additional positive inductions, such as getting people to express positive affect (smiling; Lyubomirsky, Dickerhoof, Boehm, & Sheldon, 2011; Lyubomirsky & Layous, 2013) and expressing one's values (self-affirmation; Cohen, Garcia, Purdie-Vaughns, Apfel, & Brzustoski, 2009). Our process-oriented approach suggests inductions of happiness and self-affirmation techniques would increase influence in some cases, but decrease it in others. For example, like the effects of feeling powerful, feeling happy or affirmed can influence attitudes by affecting one or more of the five ELM processes of attitude change. For example, if thinking is low, simple valenced cues such as feeling powerful, happy, or affirmed can serve as simple cues to evaluation in accord with their valence (e.g., if I am happy, I must like it). If thinking is high, however, these same variables work in other ways, such as biasing thinking (e.g., happiness can make positive thoughts more accessible), serving as arguments (e.g., happiness can be seen as evidence that a joke is good), or validating thoughts (e.g., happiness can make people view their thoughts as more valid). If thinking is not constrained to be high or low, these same inductions can affect how much thinking occurs (e.g., see Petty & Briñol, 2015, for an extensive review of multiple processes of emotion; Briñol, Petty, Gallardo, & DeMarree, 2007, for multiple roles of self-affirmation; and Briñol et al., 2017, for multiple roles for power).

Although in the examples just described, feelings of happiness (or affirmation or power) may often produce positive attitudes, the underlying process by which this occurs can vary, and therefore, we argue that the attitudinal consequences are also likely to differ (e.g., with high-thinking processes leading to more attitude-behavior-correspondence). Positive variables like happiness (or affirmation or power) can also lead to negative attitudes when these variables reduce elaboration of strong arguments or validate negative thoughts (e.g., Briñol, Petty, & Barden, 2007; Paredes, Stavraki, Briñol, & Petty, 2013).

Other popular interventions have succeeded in getting people to self-distance when feelings were analyzed. For example, cueing people to analyze past negative experiences from a self-distanced (vs. from a self-immersed) perspective makes a significant difference in health-related outcomes (Finkel, Slotter, Luchies, Walton, & Gross, 2013; Kross, Gard, Deldin, Clifton, & Ayduk, 2012; Kross et al., 2014). According to our self-validation analysis, however, creating distance from thoughts (either through perspective, mindfulness, or other means; Lee & Schwarz, 2011) will decrease the use, not only of negative thoughts (making people feel better), but also of positive thoughts (making people feel worse). In fact, recent research has demonstrated that physical distance from one's thoughts can either increase or decrease positive outcomes (Briñol, Gascó, Petty, & Horcajo, 2013). In short, our approach reinforces the notion that taking the psychological processes underlying change into account can provide a fruitful framework for understanding many different intervention paradigms in psychology.

Conclusion

In this review, we have argued that practical initiatives and applied interventions can be designed by considering elaboration and validation processes. Doing so can increase the likelihood that the induced mental contents (e.g., thoughts, attitudes, goals) will have an impact and also guide behavior. The research we reviewed indicates that judgments based on high-thinking processes predict behavioral intentions and behavior better than judgments based on little thought. As noted, elaboration processes are relevant for understanding short and long-term change, and illustrate how the same treatment can produce the same initial response (e.g., positive attitudes) but lead to very different behavioral outcomes depending on how much thought goes into the judgment. Validation processes are also important for understanding judgment and behavioral change and illustrate how the same treatment can produce the same initial response (e.g., positive thoughts), but lead to very different judgmental and behavioral outcomes depending on how people perceive the validity of those thoughts.

References

Barden, J., & Petty, R. E. (2008). The mere perception of elaboration creates attitude certainty: Exploring the thoughtfulness heuristic. *Journal of Personality and Social Psychology, 95,* 489–509.

Bartsch, A., & Schneider, F. M. (2014). Entertainment and politics revisited: How non-escapist forms of entertainment can stimulate political interest and information seeking. *Journal of Communication, 64,* 369–396.

Bridges, E., & Florsheim, R. (2008). Hedonic and utilitarian shopping goals: The online experience. *Journal of Business Research, 61*(4), 309–314.

Briñol, P., DeMarree, K. G., & Petty, R. E. (2015). Validating a primed identity leads to expectations of group-relevant outcomes. *International Journal of Social Psychology, 30,* 614–630.

Briñol, P., Gascó, M., Petty, R. E., & Horcajo, J. (2013). Treating thoughts as material objects can increase or decrease their impact on evaluation. *Psychological Science, 24,* 41–47.

Briñol, P., & Petty, R. E. (2003). Overt head movements and persuasion: A self-validation analysis. *Journal of Personality and Social Psychology, 84,* 1123–1139.

Briñol, P., & Petty, R. E. (2009). Persuasion: Insights from the self-validation hypothesis. In M. P. Zanna (Ed.), *Advances in Experimental Social Psychology, 41,* 69–118. New York: Elsevier.

Briñol, P., Petty, R. E., & Barden, J. (2007). Happiness versus sadness as determinants of thought confidence in persuasion: A self-validation analysis. *Journal of Personality and Social Psychology, 93,* 711–727.

Briñol, P., Petty, R. E., Durso, G. R. O., & Rucker, D. D. (2017). Power and persuasion: Processes by which perceived power can influence evaluative judgments. *Review of General Psychology, 21,* 223–241.

Briñol, P., Petty, R. E., Gallardo, I., & DeMarree, K. G. (2007). The effect of self-affirmation in non-threatening persuasion domains: Timing affects the process. *Personality and Social Psychology Bulletin, 33,* 1533–1546.

Briñol, P., Petty, R. E., & Hinsenkamp, L., (2018). Embodiment in sports: Strength, readiness, competitiveness, aggression, and beyond. In B. Jackson, J. A. Dimmock, & J. Compton (Eds.), *Persuasion and communication in sport, exercise, and physical activity* (pp. 201–216). Abingdon, UK: Routledge.

Briñol, P., Petty, R. E., Valle, C., Rucker, D. D., & Becerra, A. (2007). The effects of message recipients' power before and after persuasion: A self-validation analysis. *Journal of Personality and Social Psychology, 93,* 1040–1053.

Briñol, P., Petty, R. E., & Wagner, B. C. (2009). Body postures effects on self-evaluation: A self-validation approach. *European Journal of Social Psychology, 39,* 1053–1064.

Briñol, P., Petty, R. E., & Wheeler, S. C. (2006). Discrepancies between explicit and implicit self-concepts: Consequences for information processing. *Journal of Personality and Social Psychology, 91,* 154–170.

Bryan, C. J., Walton, G. M., Rogers, T., & Dweck, C. S. (2011). Motivating voter turnout by invoking the self. *Proceedings of the National Academy of Sciences, USA, 108,* 12653–12656.

Burgmer, P., & Englich, B. (2012). Bullseye! How power improves motor performance. *Social Psychological and Personality Science, 4*(2), 224–232.

Cacioppo, J. T., & Petty, R. E. (1982). The need for cognition. *Journal of Personality and Social Psychology, 42*(1), 116–131.

Cancela, A., Briñol, P., Petty, R. E., (2019). Hedonic vs. epistemic goals in processing persuasive communications: Revisiting the classic personal involvement by argument quality interaction. Manuscript under review.

Cárdaba, M. A. M., Briñol, P., Horcajo, J., & Petty, R. E. (2014). Changing prejudiced attitudes by thinking about persuasive messages: Implications for resistance. *Journal of Applied Social Psychology, 44,* 343–353.

Carpenter, C. J. (2015). A meta-analysis of the ELM's argument quality X processing type predictions. *Human Communication Research, 41,* 501–534.

Chaiken, S., Liberman, A., & Eagly, A. H. (1989). Heuristic and systematic information processing within and beyond the persuasion context. In J. S. Uleman & J. A. Bargh (Eds.), *Unintended thought* (pp. 212–252). New York, NY: Guilford.

Cohen, G. L., Garcia, J., Purdie-Vaughns, V., Apfel, N., & Brzustoski, P. (2009). Recursive processes in self-affirmation: Intervening to close the minority achievement gap. *Science, 324,* 400–403.

Cohen, J. (2001). Defining identification: A theoretical look at the identification of audiences with media characters. *Mass Communication and Society, 4,* 245–264.

Cohen, J. B., & Andrade, E. B. (2018). The ADF framework: A parsimonious model for developing successful behavioral change interventions. *Journal of Marketing Behavior, 3,* 81–119.

DeMarree, K. G., Briñol, P., & Petty, R. E. (2014). The effects of power on prosocial outcomes: A self-validation analysis. *Journal of Economic Psychology, 41,* 20–30.

DeMarree, K. G., Loersch, C., Briñol, P., Petty, R. E., Payne, B. K., & Rucker, D. D. (2012). From primed construct to motivated behavior: Validation processes in goal pursuit. *Personality and Social Psychology Bulletin, 38,* 1659–1670.

Durso, G. R. O., Briñol, P., & Petty, R. E. (2016). From power to inaction: Ambivalence gives pause to the powerful. *Psychological Science, 27,* 1660–1666.

Fazio, R. H. (1990). Multiple processes by which attitudes guide behavior – The mode model as an integrative framework. *Advances in Experimental Social Psychology, 23,* 74–109.

Finkel, E. J., Slotter, E. B., Luchies, L. B., Walton, G. M., & Gross, J. J. (2013). A brief intervention to promote conflict reappraisal preserves marital quality over time. *Psychological Science, 24,* 1595–1601.

Fleming, M. A., & Petty, R. E. (2000). Identity and persuasion: An elaboration likelihood approach. In M. A. Hogg & D. J. Terry (Eds.), *Attitudes, behavior, and social context: The role of norms and group membership* (pp. 171–199). Mahwah, NJ: Lawrence Erlbaum.

Galinsky, A. D., Gruenfeld, D. H., & Magee, J. C. (2003). From power to action. *Journal of Personality and Social Psychology, 85,* 453–466.

Green, M. C. (2006). Narratives and cancer communication. *Journal of Communication, 56,* 163–183.

Green, M. C., Brock, T. D., & Kaufman, G. F. (2004). Understanding media enjoyment: The role of transportation into narrative worlds. *Communication Theory, 14*, 311–327.

Harackiewicz, J. M., Rozek, C. S., Hulleman, C. S., & Hyde, J. S. (2012). Helping parents to motivate adolescents in mathematics and science: An experimental test of a utility-value intervention. *Psychological Science, 23*, 899–906.

Hatzigeorgiadis, A., Zourbanos, N., Galanis, E., & Theodorakis, Y. (2011). Self-talk and sport performance: A meta-analysis. *Perspectives on Psychological Science, 6*, 354–362.

Haugtvedt, C. P., Petty, R. E., & Cacioppo, J. T. (1992). Need for cognition and advertising: Understanding the role of personality variables in consumer behavior. *Journal of Consumer Psychology, 1*, 239–260.

Hertwig, R., & Grüne-Yanoff, T. (2017). Nudging and boosting: Steering or empowering good decisions. *Perspectives on Psychological Science, 12*, 973–986.

Higgins, E. T., Cesario, J., Hagiwara, N., Spiegel, S., & Pittman, T. (2010). Increasing or decreasing interest in activities: The role of regulatory fit. *Journal of Personality and Social Psychology, 98*, 559–572.

Hirsh, J. B., Galinsky, A. D., & Zhong, C. B. (2011). Drunk, powerful, and in the dark: How general processes of disinhibition produce both prosocial and antisocial behavior. *Perspectives on Psychological Science, 6*(5), 415–427.

Horcajo, J., & Luttrell, A. (2016). The effects of elaboration on the strength of doping-related attitudes: Resistance to change and behavioral intentions. *Journal of Sport and Exercise Psychology, 38*, 236–246.

Horcajo, J., Paredes, B., Higuero, G., Briñol, P., & Petty, R. E. (2019). The effects of overt head movements on physical performance after positive versus negative self-talk. *Journal of Sport and Exercise Psychology, 41*, 36–45.

Hulleman, C. S., Kosovich, J. J., Baron, K. E., & Daniel, D. B. (2017). Making connections: Replicating and extending the utility value intervention in the classroom. *Journal of Educational Psychology, 109*, 387–404.

Keltner, D., Gruenfeld, D. H., & Anderson, C. (2003). Power, approach, and inhibition. *Psychological Review, 110*, 265–284.

Krosnick, J. A., & Petty, R. E. (1995). Attitude strength: An overview. In R. E. Petty & J. A. Krosnick (Eds.), *Attitude strength: Antecedents and consequences* (pp. 1–24). Mahwah, NJ: Erlbaum.

Kross, E., Bruehlman-Senecal, E., Park, J., Burson, A., Dougherty, A., Shablack, H., … Ayduk, O. (2014). Self-talk as a regulatory mechanism: How you do it matters. *Journal of Personality and Social Psychology, 106*(2), 304–324.

Kross, E., Gard, D., Deldin, P., Clifton, J., & Ayduk, O. (2012). "Asking why" from a distance: Its cognitive and emotional consequences for people with major depressive disorder. *Journal of Abnormal Psychology, 121*(3), 559–569.

Lammers, J., Dubois, D., Rucker, D. D., & Galinsky, A. D. (2013). Power gets the job: Priming power improves interview outcomes. *Journal of Experimental Social Psychology, 49*, 776–779.

Lee, S. W. S., & Schwarz, N. (2011). Wiping the slate clean: Psychological consequences of physical cleansing. *Current Directions in Psychological Science, 20*(5), 307–311.

Lyubomirsky, S., Dickerhoof, R., Boehm, J. K., & Sheldon, K. M. (2011). Becoming happier takes both a will and a proper way: An experimental longitudinal intervention to boost well-being. *Emotion, 11*, 391–402.

Lyubomirsky, S., & Layous, K. (2013). How do simple positive activities increase well-being? *Current Directions in Psychological Science, 22*, 57–62.

Nair, S., Sagar, M., Sollers III, J., Consedine, N., & Broadbent, E. (2014). Do slumped and upright postures affect stress responses? A randomized trial. *Health Psychology*.

Paredes, B., Stavraki, M., Briñol, P., & Petty, R. E. (2013). Smiling after thinking increases reliance on thoughts. *Social Psychology, 44*, 349–353.

Petty, R. E. & Briñol, P. (2012). The Elaboration Likelihood Model. In P. A. M. Van Lange, A. Kruglanski, & E. T. Higgins (Eds.), *Handbook of theories of social psychology* (Vol. 1, pp. 224–245). London: Sage.

Petty, R. E., Briñol, P., & Tormala, Z. L. (2002). Thought confidence as a determinant of persuasion: The self-validation hypothesis. *Journal of Personality and Social Psychology, 82*, 722–741.

Petty, R. E., & Cacioppo, J. T. (1979). Issue involvement can increase or decrease persuasion by enhancing message-relevant cognitive responses. *Journal of Personality and Social Psychology, 37*, 1915–1926.

Petty, R. E., & Cacioppo, J. T. (1986). The Elaboration Likelihood Model of persuasion. In L. Berkowitz (Ed.), *Advances in experimental social psychology* (Vol. 19, pp. 123–205). New York: Academic Press.

Petty, R. E., & Cacioppo, J. T. (1990). Involvement and persuasion: Tradition versus integration. *Psychological Bulletin, 107*, 367–374.

Petty, R. E., Cacioppo, J. T., & Schumann, D. (1983). Central and peripheral routes to advertising effectiveness: The moderating role of involvement. *Journal of Consumer Research, 10*, 135–146.

Petty, R. E., Haugtvedt, C., & Smith, S. M. (1995). Elaboration as a determinant of attitude strength: Creating attitudes that are persistent, resistant, and predictive of behavior. In R. E. Petty & J. A. Krosnick (Eds.), *Attitude strength: Antecedents and consequences* (pp. 93–130). Mahwah, NJ: Erlbaum.

Petty, R. E., & Krosnick, J. A. (Eds.) (1995). *Attitude strength: Antecedents and consequences*. Hillsdale, NJ: Erlbaum.

Petty, R. E., Schumann, D. W., Richman, S. A., & Strathman, A. J. (1993). Positive mood and persuasion: Different roles for affect under high and low elaboration conditions. *Journal of Personality and Social Psychology, 64*, 5–20.

Pratto, F. (2016). On power and empowerment. *British Journal of Social Psychology, 55*, 1–20.

Priester, J. M. & Petty, R. E. (1996). The gradual threshold model of ambivalence: Relating the positive and negative bases of attitudes to subjective ambivalence. *Journal of Personality and Social Psychology, 71*, 431–449.

Rucker, D. D., & Petty, R. E. (2004). When resistance is futile: Consequences of failed counter-arguing for attitude certainty. *Journal of Personality and Social Psychology, 86*, 219–235.

Rucker, D. D., Tormala, Z. L., Petty, R. E., & Briñol, P. (2014). Consumer conviction and commitment: An appraisal-based framework for attitude certainty. *Journal of Consumer Psychology, 24*(1), 119–136.

Schwarz, N., Bless, H., Strack, F., Klumpp, G., Rittenauer-Schatka, H., & Simons, A. (1991). Ease of retrieval as information: Another look at the availability heuristic. *Journal of Personality and Social Psychology, 61*, 195–202.

Slater, M. D. (2002). Involvement as goal-directed strategic processing: Extending the Elaboration Likelihood Model. In J. Dillard & M. Pfau (Eds.), *The persuasion handbook: Theory and practice* (pp. 175–195). Thousand Oaks, CA: Sage.

Tod, D., Edwards, C., McGuigan, M., & Lovell, G. (2015). A systematic review of the effect of cognitive strategies on strength performance. *Sports Medicine, 45*, 1589–1602.

Tod, D., Hardy, J., & Oliver, E. J. (2011). Effects of self-talk: A systematic review. *Journal of Sport & Exercise Psychology, 33*, 666–687.

Tormala, Z. L., Falces, C., Briñol, P., & Petty, R. E. (2007). Ease of retrieval effects in social judgment: The role of unrequested cognitions. *Journal of Personality and Social Psychology, 93*, 143–157.

Tormala, Z. L., & Petty, R. E. (2001). On-line versus memory based processing: The role of "need to evaluate" in person perception. *Personality and Social Psychology Bulletin, 12*, 1599–1612.

Tormala, Z. L., Petty, R. E., & Briñol, P. (2002). Ease of retrieval effects in persuasion: A self-validation analysis. *Personality and Social Psychology Bulletin, 28*, 1700–1712.

van Harreveld, F., van der Pligt, J., & de Liver, Y. N. (2009). The agony of ambivalence and ways to resolve it: Introducing the MAID model. *Personality and Social Psychology Review, 13*, 45–61.

Van Raalte, J. L, Vincent, A., & Brewer, B. W. (2016). Self-talk: Review and sport-specific model. *Psychology of Sport and Exercise, 22*, 139–148.

Walton, G. M. (2014). The new science of wise psychological interventions. *Current Directions in Psychological Science, 23*, 73–82.

Walton, G. M., & Wilson, T. D. (2018). Wise interventions: Psychological remedies for social and personal problems. *Psychological Review, 125*, 617–655.

Wegener, D. T., Clark, J. K., & Petty, R. E. (2006). Not all stereotyping is created equal. Differential consequences of thoughtful versus non-thoughtful stereotyping. *Journal of Personality and Social Psychology, 90*, 42–59.

Wells, G. L., & Petty, R. E. (1980). The effects of overt head movements on persuasion: Compatibility and incompatibility of responses. *Basic and Applied Social Psychology, 1*, 219–230.

Wichman, A. L., Briñol, P., Petty, R. E., Rucker, D. D., Tormala, Z. L., & Weary, G. (2010). Doubting one's doubt: A formula for confidence. *Journal of Experimental Social Psychology, 46*, 350–355.

Wilson, T. D., Reinhard, D. A., Westgate, E. C., Gilbert, D. T., Ellerbeck, N., Hahn, C., Brown, C., & Shaked, A. (2014). Just think: The challenges of the disengaged mind. *Science, 345*(6192), 75–77.

Wilson, T. D., Westgate, E. C., Buttrick, N. R., & Gilbert, D. (in press). The mind is its own place: The difficulties and benefits of thinking for pleasure. *Advances in Experimental Social Psychology*.

Wiseman, R. (2012). *Rip it up: How small movements can change your live*. New York, NY: Free Press.

Wiseman, R. (2013). *The as if principle: The radically new approach to changing your life*. London: Pan Books.

Zillmann, D., & Bryant, J. (2002). Entertainment as media effect. In J. Bryant & D. Zillmann (Eds.), *Media effects: Advances in theory and research* (2nd ed., pp. 549–582). Mahwah, NJ: Lawrence Erlbaum Associates.

PART II
Promoting Individual Health and Well-Being

6

CALL OF DUTY – THE TOBACCO WARS

Opposing Effects of Tobacco Glorifying and Prevention Messages in Entertainment Video Games

Hart Blanton, Christopher N. Burrows and Timothy Regan

Call of Duty: The Tobacco Wars

The line between the real and the unreal is blurring. In work and play, people are spending an increasing amount of time in computer-mediated experiences – virtual realities, augmented realities, and the merging of the two in what is being called mixed reality. As successive generations continue this migration from the real to the unreal, psychological theories will need to shift with them. We attempt to do this by considering the way that influence processes change when individuals become fully immersed in virtual worlds, and how those processes can then impact real-world attitudes. Most of the research that has considered this question has applied social learning principles to posit a link between simulated in-game violence and real-world aggression in children (e.g., Anderson, Gentile, & Buckley, 2007). This work has come under attack recently, with some arguing that social psychologists working in this tradition have failed to give humans credit for their ability to distinguish reality from fiction (Ferguson & Dyck, 2012).

In the work that follows, we turn this argument on its head. We argue that it is precisely because humans can distinguish reality from fiction that video games can at times have consequential, real-world effects. We explore this possibility as it relates to gaming influence on health decisions, with particular attention to the ways video games might influence nicotine and tobacco use among adolescents who play them. As we demonstrate, many of the most popular commercial video games that adolescents play are rich in imagery and storylines that promote nicotine and tobacco use (NTU). We further argue that it is the obviously *fictional* quality of these presentations that might make them a threat to public health. We then present research suggesting that health communicators should fight fire with fire, by learning how to conduct informative (factual) health campaigns from within immersive (fictional) gaming worlds.

Virtual Transportation

We propose that by immersing players in compelling, life-like simulations, video games can exert powerful and consequential influence on the players' own attitudes and beliefs. We advance this hypothesis from two interrelated lines of research. First is research on persuasion through fiction. History points to many instances in which fictional texts have had consequential effects on public opinion. Historians might point to Harriet Beecher Stowe's *Uncle Tom's Cabin*, which furthered the Abolitionist cause in the run up to the US Civil War, or to Upton Sinclair's *The Jungle*, which led to changes in the meat-packing industry and promoted public support for food safety. Social psychology points to research on emulative suicide, which had as its early inspiration documented spikes in suicide that followed publication of Wolfgang von Goethe's novel, *The Sorrows of Young Werther* (Phillips, 1982).

Prentice, Gerrig and Bailis (1997), and Gerrig & Prentice (1991) argued that in instances such as these, it is possible that stories shaped public opinions and altered personal decisions, not *despite* their fictional nature, but in part *because* of this quality. To enjoy a piece of fiction or to be entertained by the twists and turns in the plot is in some way to accept the "reality" it presents. Stories become exciting to the extent that the characters and the characters' experiences feel and are experienced, as if they are real (resulting in what Coleridge 1817/1906 referred to as the "willing suspension of disbelief," p. 161). This shift in perception might leave individuals more open to and less critical of the information they encounter in fictional stories, perhaps even information with real-world relevance. In a series of studies, Prentice and Gerrig found support for this proposition. When untrue information was embedded in a story dialogue, it shaped later belief to the extent that it had been embedded in a written text thought to be fictitious (Gerrig & Prentice, 1991), especially if set in an unfamiliar location that would divorce the story from the reader's own reality (Prentice, Gerrig & Bailis, 1997).

Research on persuasion through fiction has inspired a second, broader line of research that explores the role that "narrative transportation" might play in enhancing persuasion and influence. Green and Brock (2000) proposed that as individuals become "transported" into the storyline of a text (such that they can visualize the story events as if from a lived experience, identify with the narrator or connect emotionally with other story characters), they might become less critical of and more open to the ideas they encounter. In a range of supporting studies, they have found that as transportation into a story narrative increases, the influence of the content of those stories increases in kind (and they have found this to be true whether a story is presented as fiction or nonfiction).

Follow-up studies suggested that this result occurs, in part, because people engage in less elaborate counter-arguing of the ideas when transported (Green, Garst, & Brock, 2004). This finding has clear implications for health communication, where resistance in its many forms can be an obstacle to persuasion and influence (Brehm, 1966; Knowles & Linn, 2004; Petty & Briñol, this volume; Witte, 1992). To the extent that health communicators can fold messages into a story with a compelling narrative, they may exert greater influence on real-world health decisions (see Green, 2006).

These two frameworks, persuasion through fiction and persuasion through narrative transportation, provide a basis for predicting that video games might have the potential to have consequential effects on a person's attitudes and beliefs. Not only do many modern games immerse players in rich narratives that can unfold over time, they have other elements that might heighten immersion into the game – what we term *virtual transportation*, as distinct from narrative transporation.[1] Among features of video games that likely promote this form of immersion are vivid and life-like graphics (Sollins, 2011), high levels of interactivity and opportunities for character identification (Carpentier, Rogers, & Barnard, 2015; Lin, 2013; Williams, 2011), and in-game consequences for a player's in-game choices and actions (Carnagey & Anderson, 2005; Sauer, Drummond, & Nova, 2015). By using such gaming features to help players leave their real worlds behind, video games might also help them leave behind some of their real-world resistance to influence, opening them up to ideas that they would otherwise reject (see Crano & Ruybal, this volume). Resistance might be further diminished by the cognitive states that games can promote. Video games, by their nature, generate cognitive load, and players often persist in playing commercial games long past the point of fatigue – factors that can further reduce resistance and increase influence (e.g., Burkley, 2008; Gilbert, 1991). All of this suggests that the compelling fiction of commercial video games might at times break through and become real by altering the attitudes and opinions of players in ways that can affect later decisions. Unfortunately, when we look at the influences commercial games are possibly having on public health in general, and on adolescent nicotine and tobacco use in particular, there is good reason to suspect that current influences are most typically for the worse.

Video Game Effects on Public Health

A large body of research suggests that movie and television storylines that promote or glorify risk can expand the range of risks that individuals themselves are willing to take – not just the rates of nicotine and tobacco use, but also of alcohol use and abuse, unprotected sex, reckless driving, and other risk behaviors which can be driven upward by risk glorification (Brown & Witherspoon, 2002; Escobar-Chaves & Anderson, 2008). As the term is commonly operationalized, media "glorifies" risk to the extent that it positively portrays the actions of individuals who knowingly endanger their health and well-being and/or put at risk other positive life outcomes. The most comprehensive support for the hypothesized influence of risk-glorifying media on actual risk-taking can be found in a meta-analysis by Fischer and colleagues (2011). They analyzed 105 independent effect sizes, taken from studies on over 80,000 individuals participating in a range of experimental, cross-sectional, and longitudinal studies. They found sizable Hedge's point estimates for the effects of risk-glorifying media exposure on risk-taking behaviors ($g=0.41$), including smoking ($g=0.44$). No studies in their meta-analytic review specifically linked video-game presentation of risk to nicotine or tobacco use, but a longitudinal study by Hull and colleagues is informative. They tracked the media habits and risky behaviors of a sample of adolescents over three waves and four years and found that self-reported exposure to mature-rated video games predicted cigarette smoking (as well as alcohol use, aggression, delinquency, and risky sex). This effect held, controlling for past behavior, as well as a range of demographic, household, and parenting variables. This one study provides a needed longitudinal link to many prior cross-sectional studies that suggested the possibility of a causal effect of video game use on smoking (e.g., Raiff, Jarvis, & Rapoza, 2012; Van Rooij et al., 2014).

A common interpretation of risk glorification effects on health risk behavior is that, by promoting counter-normative or socially "deviant" actions, risky media in general, and video games in particular, might promote norm-violating behaviors, including norm-violating health risks. This interpretation focuses attention on the mature-themed nature of many of today's games, which often involve violence, crime and other adult themes. There is reason to suspect, however, that modern games promote more than just general risk taking. They might also promote NTU, directly. Many of the most popular commercial video games played by adolescents and young adults also contain high levels of overt and covert promotion of nicotine and tobacco products; levels that we suspect are unknown to many parents and public health researchers (and see Papies, this volume).

We recently administered an elicitation survey to a large sample of adolescents, aged 18–24, drawn from college students (participant pool) and the community (Mechanical Turk). We had them complete an open-ended survey describing the types of tobacco imagery and promotion they have witnessed in commercial games, and they provided many dramatic examples. Consider the following: a version of *Guitar Hero* (a game that is rated appropriate for teens to play) at times places players in front of large audiences of bar patrons who are smoking. Players of popular games such as *Call of Duty*, *Mass Effect 3*, and *Medal of Honor* directly interact with and team up with heroic, glamorized characters who smoke cigars and cigarettes. Players in *Grand Theft Auto* and *Assassin's Creed* can purchase and sell cigarettes for profit (and must do so if they wish to advance in the game). Those in *Grand Theft Auto* are exposed to in-game tobacco marketing that glamorizes a fictitious brand of cigarettes (*Redwood Cigarettes*), and players in *Grand Theft Auto, Fallout, Guns of the Patriot, Bioshock,* and *Red Dead Redemption 2* can elect to have their characters smoke or "vape" and from these simulated acts, be rewarded in the game by having increased character energy, attention, perception, and/or agility.

The sheer volume of tobacco content in commercial games caused us to reconsider some of the findings in the study by Hull and colleagues (2014). Perhaps with regards to tobacco promotion specifically, the most consequential "risk" that is being glorified is nicotine and tobacco use. The US Surgeon General (2014) has already concluded that there is sufficient evidence to assume a causal and consequential effect of positive tobacco imagery from movies on adolescent smoking. In our view, movie promotion of tobacco imagery pales in comparison to what can be found in commercial video games that adolescents play, and when combined with the "transporting" qualities of video games, it seems quite plausible that this type of imagery will exert even stronger influence on adolescent decision-making than anything yet encountered. However, we know of only one study that has examined exposure to tobacco imagery in games as a risk factor. Cranwell and colleagues (2016) coded the content of video games played by a sample of 1,094 adolescents aged 11–17 and found that those who played games with tobacco and alcohol content were more likely to experiment with these substances. The cross-sectional nature of their study leaves their finding open to interpretation, however.

To get some clarity on this question, we decided to perform a laboratory test examining the influence of gaming content on health cognitions. At the start of the semester, we (Blanton, Burrows, & Regan, 2019) had participants in our university participant pool make baseline ratings of their attitudes toward "vaping" (e-cigarette smoking). Over the course of the semester, we then recruited students into a study that was presented to them as an investigation into factors shaping video game enjoyment. All played a skateboarding video game that we had designed from the ground up, using the Unity game engine. Players of our game navigated three-dimensional scenes on a skateboard – from a nightline cityscape to a colorful casino showroom. To maintain enjoyment, they could jump over ramps and off buildings while performing tricks and collecting objects to run up their point totals. What they were not told was that we included a single, subtle manipulation of their character. All participants played a character that matched their own gender but based on random assignment, this character either smoked an e-cigarette while skateboarding or it did not. If the character was smoking, players could hear the character at times inhaling smoke into the device, after which a smoke-puff "vape trail" would trail behind. After playing this game, we then had participants rate their level of transportation into the game and then through use of a bogus "two study" procedure, asked them to make a number of seemingly unrelated ratings, including one page of ratings that assessed the perceived risk of smoking e-cigarettes.

We found that the more positively participants felt toward e-cigarettes at the start of the semester, the more "transported" they reported feeling into the game as a function of "virtual vaping." This finding suggests that there may be some marketing synergy between the promotion of nicotine and tobacco products by the tobacco industry and the promotion of video games by the gaming industry. To the extent that tobacco marketing promotes youth interest in nicotine and tobacco products, it might also promote enjoyment of games that allow them to simulate nicotine and tobacco use. Gaming companies can thus benefit from including nicotine and tobacco imagery in their games, to the extent that nicotine and tobacco promotion is effective. More important for the influence of games on health decisions, we also found evidence that the gaming experience helped crystalize attitudes toward e-cigarettes. We found that the more transported participants were into the game, the lower the perceived risk of vaping among those who played the e-cigarette version of the game, and this was particularly true of those who had some initially positive attitudes toward e-cigarettes.

These findings come from a single study that requires replication and extension before any strong conclusion can be drawn, but these initial findings suggest troubling influence of common commercial gaming content on adolescent health cognitions. The majority of current adult smokers began experimenting during their adolescence (US Surgeon General, 2014) and gaming is at near-saturation levels in this same age group (Entertainment Software Association, 2014). These statistics suggest to us that attention should be turned to asking questions about how this new source of media influence might be shaping adolescent attitudes in ways that promote nicotine and tobacco use.

Tobacco (Gaming) Regulation?

If it appears that the Surgeon General's analysis of movie effects on adolescent smoking extends to video gaming effects, we can anticipate one class of countermeasures that will appeal to some. This is to adopt new tobacco-control regulations designed to protect youths from nicotine and tobacco glorifying imagery. One might, for instance, add warning labels to games that contain nicotine and/ or tobacco content. Alternatively, the presence of nicotine and tobacco use could be deemed sufficient to make a game lose its E (for "Everyone") or T (for "Teen") rating, moving such games up to M (for "Mature"), making it harder for adolescents to purchase the game.

However well intentioned, regulatory approaches are likely to have limited impact on adolescent gaming or health choices, as they are currently failing. It so happens that the Entertainment Software Rating Board (ESRB), the self-regulatory organization that assigns age and content ratings to games for American consumers, is meant to code games for the presence of "tobacco references" in the gaming content. However, we accessed their online database and looked up all of the aforementioned games that contained often vivid examples of tobacco and nicotine use. In no case could this content be discerned from the information provided to consumers.[2] To complicate matters, if warning labels were to more accurately convey the actual content of games, this change might increase the appeal of such games to players looking for risky/adult simulations (see Bushman, 2006). Also worth noting, most parents have limited understanding of the meaning of ESRB ratings and so have limited ability to use them to control access (Harris Interactive, 2013), and it is unclear how many would view nicotine and tobacco content as a concern. Although we think there can be a role for regulations to guide parents who wish to be involved in the gaming decisions of their children, we think health communicators should consider more creative approaches if they wish to play a part (and see Fiedler, this volume).

In fact, we suggest that health communicators continue to do what they have always done – fight fire with fire. The tobacco industry has long benefited from the presence of a media industry that often helps them promote their products, and health communicators have long responded to this threat by creating media campaigns that advance counter-messaging. Researchers concerned about the influence of media on adolescent smoking have waged war against the imagery found in movies and television. Now with the rise of video games that contain even stronger content, this fight must shift to a new (virtual) battlefield. By making this move, health communicators can also benefit from the transporting qualities of video games, using the immersive features of virtual gaming environments as a lever to reduce the forms of message resistance they often encounter when conducting campaigns in the real world.

A Virtual Transportation Model of Health Communication

In a series of studies (Burrows & Blanton, 2016, 2018), we tested whether 'Virtual Transportation' might be harnessed to increase the influence of prevention messages embedded in the background of video gaming scenes. As a first step in this work, we sought to design an immersive, first-person video game, in the hopes that we might engage and entertain players to such an extent that we generated levels of transportation sufficient to alter influence dynamics. We focused our initial energy on building a first-person shooter (FPS) game, where players had to navigate a three-dimensional world from the perspective of an armed individual tasked with shooting armed opponents. We chose to use an FPS for our initial work for three reasons. First, FPS games are the most popular format for commercial video games with adolescents (Entertainment Software Association, 2014). Second, games with a fast pace and first-person navigation of a three-dimensional world have key elements that have been shown to magnify the effects of violent games on aggression (e.g., Krahé, this volume; Slater, Lotto, Arnold, & Sanchez-Vives, 2009; Tamborini et al., 2004), and so we thought our game might be sufficiently transporting that it would magnify the effects of health messaging on health attitudes. Third, and perhaps most importantly, mature-themed games such as these are precisely the ones Hull and colleagues found might increase risk-taking tendencies in adolescents (Hull, Brunelle, Prescott, & Sargent, 2014; Hull, Draghici, & Sargent, 2012). We thus pursued a strong test of our hypothesis by trying to use such a game to *reduce* risk-taking attitudes.

As our first test of what we term the *Virtual Transportation Model of Health Communication*, we embedded messages designed to reduce participants' willingness to drive a car under the influence of alcohol (DUI). We focused on this behavior in our initial work because anti-DUI messages are easy to communicate graphically, even in a fast-paced game. Also, we knew that most college students in our research participant pool drove a car and also drank alcohol, making this topic relevant to a large percentage of those we could recruit. In the game we designed, players viewed an animation scene that placed them in a storyline that would explain their actions. They observed a helicopter landing on what was described as a "government office complex" that had been overtaken by space aliens. They were told that their task was to move floor-to-floor, shooting the armed aliens they encountered, to get to the basement. All participants then shot their way through the different levels of the building, with each floor presenting to them the offices of a particular government agency (e.g., a Department of Taxation, Army Recruitment, etc.). All eventually worked their way down to the lowest level, where we introduced our experimental manipulation. This final floor was presented as the former offices of the Division of Motor Vehicles, now overrun by alien humanoids. For half the players, this room had posters on the wall with graphic health warnings taken from real-world anti-DUI campaigns, developed by such groups as *Mothers Against Drunk Driving*. For the other half, these images were replaced with landscape paintings. After 30 minutes of play, the game came to an end, and players then completed a measure assessing their transportation into the game (with items asking the extent to which they felt physically present in the game while playing and the degree to which the game felt real to them during play). This was followed by a bogus two-study deception, where a research assistant entered and asked them if they would mind completing a second questionnaire, ostensibly as part of an unrelated study. On the 12th page of this inventory was a series of items asking their willingness to DUI in the future (e.g., how willing they would be to drive after feeling a "slight buzz" from drinking alcohol).

The results pointed to two opposing ways that transportation into the game might magnify influence. When willingness to DUI was regressed on to experimental condition, transportation, and the interaction term, a significant bilinear interaction was revealed. The nature of this interaction was that in the control condition that exposed participants to landscape art, higher transportation into the game was associated with an *increase* in willingness to DUI. This result offers further support of the findings in Hull's research (Hull et al., 2014; Hull, Draghici, & Sargent, 2012). It suggests that when players become transported into mature-themed games that glorify risk, the interest in general risk-taking increases. However, it was against the pull of this current that the positive effects of the anti-DUI messages were revealed. Among those who were exposed to anti-DUI messages, transportation resulted in a significant *decrease* in willingness to DUI.

It thus appeared that by transporting players into an immersive game – even though it had risk-promoting elements to it – openness to health-prevention messages increased. A set of replication studies extended these findings in a number of ways. First, we found that transportation effects were largest among those who reported relatively high baseline willingness to DUI (Burrows & Blanton, 2016, Studies 2 & 3). This pattern is consistent with effects of narrative transportation, documented by Green and Brock (2000; Green, Garst & Brock, 2004). It suggests that virtual transportation might increase influence from background health messages by short-circuiting message resistance. This interpretation follows because in the absence of transportation, those with the highest baseline risk would typically be the ones most likely to resist prevention messages (e.g., Gerrard, Gibbons, & Warner, 1991).

We have also replicated this effect with both high and low-fear messages, using both high and low-fear games. For instance, participants in Burrows and Blanton (2018) played a car-racing game that included background billboards with simple text reminders of the dangers of DUI (e.g., "Drive Sober or Get Pulled Over"). As with the FPS using high-fear messages, transportation into this game was associated with decreased willingness to DUI, controlling for baseline attitudes. And, most important to the current analysis, we have begun adapting these games to deliver anti-smoking messages. In a recent study, we embedded graphic anti-smoking messages (versus control and/or anti-DUI messages) in the background of a treasure-hunt game (where participants navigated a three-dimensional building in search of objects that increased point totals). We found that anti-smoking messages reduced willingness to smoke and anti-DUI messages decreased willingness to DUI, relative to the control condition and as a function of self-reported virtual transportation. Unexpectedly, we also found that the messages were more "leaky" than we would expect with real-world exposure: anti-DUI messages lowered willingness to smoke as a function of transportation, just as anti-smoking messages lowered willingness to DUI. This suggests that although message resistance is reduced, the level of message processing that occurs is not as deep as one would expect with greater elaboration of the message content (Petty & Briñol, this volume).

Importantly, we have also found that messages we embed in games can exert influence on willingness, whether we forewarn participants of the intent to include persuasive health messages or not. In one study, we explicitly informed participants that we were placing images in the games because we wished to study their impact. Inclusion of a warning like this could cause participants to feel targeted and produce some form of reactance, but we instead observed the same decrease in risk willingness, as a function of transportation. Much like consumer advertising – where it is readily apparent to anyone who cares to think about it that the intent is to exert influence – this finding suggests that health messages might continue to influence attitudes, even when their inclusion in a game is perceived to be intentional and strategic.[3] Here, again, however, the influence of messages on willingness was "leaky," in that prevention messages in one domain appeared to influence willingness in another (see Peña, Khan, Burrows, & Blanton, 2018).

Implications and Applications

This research is admittedly in its early stages. We have found encouraging results in the laboratory, suggesting that we can exert momentary, state changes on behavioral willingness by embedding health-promotion messages in immersive games. A next step will be to test real-world extensions, with the goal of exerting longer-term influence on attitudes and impacting real-world behaviors. We are currently pursuing research that will scale up our laboratory work in a number of ways. We are exposing participants to game-based anti-tobacco messaging for longer periods of time and we are measuring their influences immediately and at longer-term follow-up. We cannot yet report what level of influence we can exert with subtle in-game messaging, but we will be finding out.

Is Game-Based Messaging Feasible?

One concern about our work is that, perhaps, we are studying an intervention approach that can never be implemented on any meaningful scale. The commercial gaming industry is not going to stop designing and distributing mature-themed games (nor would we want them to). And, they will likely continue to market games to adolescents that contain a fair amount of imagery that in various ways glorifies nicotine and tobacco use (even though we do not want them to). In contrast, there is little reason to expect the industry to leap at the chance to redesign commercially successful games to deliver graphic health warnings. However, we do not count out some level of engagement from commercial gaming companies in the future. A defining feature of game developers is their creativity, and we should not underestimate their potential interest in meeting a challenge, nor their ability to embed messages into games in subtle ways that promote realism. Also, we note that it was through public pressure that studios began moving cigarettes out of scenes and seatbelts in to scenes. We may see some similar transformation among game producers, as this new industry considers ways of increasing public support for its products.

More importantly, health communicators need not always rely on the industry to create games for them. Some popular games are hosted online and allow interested users to create their own variants. For instance, in pilot studies, we have hosted gaming tournaments by having participants compete in teams against one another playing the popular first-person shooter game *Counter-Strike* (an objective-based version of an FPS). Health communicators who wish to deliver health messages through games can thus harness the popularity of such platforms by using them to deliver messages they design.

Of course, it may never be possible for health communicators to distribute their messages at a level that can rival the distribution of nicotine and tobacco imagery in commercial gaming, and many games simply do not allow modification. One possibility that might become of increasing interest is to buy the equivalent of "billboard space" in video games, in much the way that advertising space is purchased in the course of running real-world campaigns. Our work might help to implement effective campaigns from within virtual environments, focusing attention on the best ways to deliver messages in ways that might enhance the fiction created – by, for example, placing the anti-tobacco messages in the hospital scene, not the alien spaceship. Moreover, with the growth of "e-sports" – where it is estimated that by 2023, as many as 600 million people will use video game play as a form of entertainment (Tran, 2018) – it will also be relevant for communicators to consider how their virtual messages might impact third parties. Finally, we note that video games represent one of the many ways that people increasingly interact with information and others through computer-mediated realities. We see that the challenge ahead is for psychologists to develop a broader science of psychology and influence that can adapt to this new terrain; one that includes research within virtual gaming worlds, but that is not limited to it.

Expanding the Model

We have focused our attention on one quality of games, which we term virtual transportation. There are other ways that health communicators can seek to increase influence through immersive games. For one, we think attention should be turned back on *narrative transportation*. Most of the work on the concept has oriented around story narratives built into written texts. We think new attention should be focused on uses of narrative through gaming. Many of today's video games take players on journeys that can unfold over the span of days, weeks, months or considerably longer. For researchers who wish to use such devices to deliver impactful messages, there will be non-trivial challenges. It will be daunting for researchers to create video games or other virtual experiences that have the types of expansive stories found in modern commercial games, but current evidence suggests that this investment of time and resources could yield important information on how to impact health decisions from campaigns mounted in virtual environments.

A new science of "serious games" has begun laying this foundation. Education game designers have begun creating video games that educate players on everything from STEM (Science, Technology, Engineering, and Math) to world history, through game play. Much of this work focuses on the role of "gamification" (where the puzzle or challenge of the game introduces incentives that motivate learning) and simulation (where aspects of the game provide opportunities to acquire behavioral skills and build feelings of efficacy). We see signs that this work is moving to focus attention on the transporting features of serious games. Educators are considering the importance of adding narrative elements and surprise, as ways to more fully engage learning (Mustaro & Mendonça, 2012; De Troyer, van Broeckhoven, & Vlieghe, 2017; Wouters et al., 2017). We think, by extension, this work should consider ways that (for better or worse) compelling narratives can open players to subtle forms of influence. Our earlier examples of how tobacco imagery has been folded into the complex storylines of popular video games suggests to us that, if anything, this type of influence is currently for the worse, and so we think attention should be given to how to introduce counter-narratives.

Another defining feature of modern games is that players may identify with their own character or avatars to a far higher degree than they identify with characters in books or movies. In many ways, players of modern games seem to *become* the actor in the game. At the extremes, researchers have even proposed a virtual embodiment phenomenon that might result. Termed the *Proteus Effect* (in reference to the shape-changing Greek god Proteus; Yee, Bailenson & Ducheneaut, 2009), researchers propose that the physical features of a gaming avatar can alter players' own behaviors. This might cause them to do such things as slow down when playing an avatar that looks heavy (Peña, Khan, & Alexopoulos, 2016) or elderly (Yoo, Peña, & Drumwright, 2015), or they might otherwise act in ways that suggest they are navigating the "body" of the character they are playing. This research is suggestive of how reactions to in-game events might be altered by fusion of the self with the character being played. Going forward, we see a great deal of promise for health communicators to create new strategies of health education and influence by linking it to the concerns of the characters that adolescents play.

Rethinking Real and Unreal

We began this chapter by positing that technology has perhaps blurred the line between what is real and what is unreal. We moved from this argument to suggesting that it may be the unreal aspects of video games that in some cases promote influence on real-world attitudes and actions. We drew inspiration for this hypothesis from research on fiction and persuasion, and from research on narrative transportation. These lines of research suggest that by embracing a fiction or a storyline, individuals can become more open to new realities. There is an odd contradiction at the heart of our analysis, however. We have hypothesized that openness to influence increases as a linear function of what we term "virtual transportation." However, the way we measured virtual transportation was to ask our players how "realistic" they found our games, and how much they experienced our video games *as if they were real*. This would seem to suggest that if we continue to increase the realism of our game, we will continue to increase influence (see Blascovich et al., 2002 for a similar analysis). However, if realism were to increase until it was total or complete, then the games we design become indistinguishable from reality. It seems plausible that at this point, real-world resistance might return.

This analysis suggests to us that there must be some middle ground of realism and of virtual transportation, where influence from computer-simulated experiences are at their height and where further increases would only diminish influence. Influence would then be at its height when a virtual world is experienced as sufficiently "realistic" that it promotes transportation and immersion in all its different flavors, but also as sufficiently "unrealistic" that it continues to be perceived as a fiction; an alternative reality that must be sustained through openness to perception and experience. We are reminded in this analysis of the "uncanny valley" concept. This is a hypothesized curvilinear relationship between empathy for fictional or simulated "minds" or characters, and their level of realism. When applied to virtual reality, it suggests that the emotional connection players experience when interacting with a simulated being will increase the more realistic this character becomes – up until the point that it becomes so realistic that it elicits feelings of eeriness or other-worldliness (see Stein & Ohler, 2017). Health communicators can build off this idea when they design virtual campaigns. They wish to communicate real-world health information from within fictional worlds; worlds that are sufficiently immersive that players get lost in the experience, but not so realistic that everyday defenses come along for the ride.

Author Note

Hart Blanton, Department of Communication, Texas A&M University
Christopher N. Burrows, Department of Communication, Texas A&M University
Timothy Regan, Department of Psychology, Texas A&M University
This research was supported by funding from National Cancer Institute [1 R01 CA 214587–01]

Notes

1 We term the experience of immersion into a computer simulation as "virtual transportation," as this allows us to draw more clear parallels to past research linking narrative transportation to persuasion and influence. However, this concept is roughly equivalent or no different from earlier concepts of "telepresence" and/or "presence"

that are employed by researchers (largely from computer engineering) who study the immersion into computer-mediated realities (see Barfield, Zeltzer, Sheridan, & Slater, 1995). We do not wish to contribute to the proliferation of new or interchangeable terms, but in peer review, we found editors and reviewers sharply divided on which term we *had* to use, with the edge going to transportation.

2 The ESRB is a body formed by the trade association of the commercial video game industry (the Entertainment Software Association) and so arguably has a conflict of interest in assigning labels that will turn parents away.

3 This result suggests that strategic messaging might be fine but it should be so heavy-handed that it reduces transportation. An anti-drug poster in the background of a virtual guidance counselor's office might seem realistic to players, even if the scene is strategically introduced. An anti-drug poster in an alien spaceship might seem not only strategic but also so unrealistic that it could disrupt transportation.

References

Anderson, C. A, Gentile, D. A., & Buckley, K. E. (2007). *Violent video game effects on children and adolescents: Theory, research, and public policy*. New York: Oxford University Press.

Barfield, W., Zeltzer, D., Sheridan, T., & Slater, M. (1995). Presence and performance within virtual environments. In W. Barfield & T. A. Furness, III (Eds.), *Virtual environments and advanced interface design*. New York, NY: Oxford University Press.

Blanton, H., Burrows, C. N., & Regan, T. (2019). Unpublished manuscript.

Blascovich, J., Loomis, J., Beall, A., Swinth, K., Hoyt, C., & Bailenson, J. (2002). Immersive virtual environment technology as a methodological tool for social psychology. *Psychological Inquiry*, *13*(2), 103–124.

Brehm, J. W. (1966). *A theory of psychological reactance*. Oxford: Academic Press.

Brown, J. D., & Witherspoon, E. (2002). The mass media and American adolescents' health. *Journal of Adolescent Health*, *31*, 153–170.

Burkley, E. (2008). The role of self-control in resistance to persuasion. *Personality and Social Psychology Bulletin*, *34*(3), 419–431.

Burrows, C. N., & Blanton, H. (2016). Real-world persuasion from virtual-world campaigns: How transportation into virtual worlds moderates in-game influence. *Communication Research*, *43*(4), 542–570.

Burrows, C. N., & Blanton, H. (2018). In-game health communication: Delivering low-fear health messages in a low-fear videogame. *Games for Health Journal*, 7(3), 182–187.

Bushman, B. J. (2006). Effects of warning and information labels on attraction to television violence in viewers of different ages. *Journal of Applied Social Psychology*, *36*(9), 2073–2078.

Carnagey, N. L., & Anderson, C. A. (2005). The effects of reward and punishment in violent video games on aggressive affect, cognition, and behavior. *Psychological Science*, *16*(11), 882–889.

Carpentier, F. R. D., Rogers, R. P., & Barnard, L. (2015). Eliciting behavior from interactive narratives: Isolating the role of agency in connecting with and modeling characters. *Journal of Broadcasting & Electronic Media*, *59*(1), 76–93.

Coleridge, S. T. (1906). *Biographia literaria*. London: J. M. Dent & Sons (Original work published 1817).

Cranwell, J., Whittamore, K., Britton, J., & Leonardi-Bee, J. (2016). Alcohol and tobacco content in UK video games and their association with alcohol and tobacco use among young people. *Cyberpsychology, Behavior, and Social Networking, 19*(7), 426–434.

De Troyer, O., Van Broeckhoven, F., & Vlieghe, J. (2017). Linking serious game narratives with pedagogical theories and pedagogical design strategies. *Journal of Computing in Higher Education, 29*(3), 549–573.

Entertainment Software Association. (2014). Essential facts about the computer and video game industry: Sales, demographic, and usage data. *The Entertainment Software Association.* Retrieved from www.theesa.com/wp-content/uploads/2014/10/ESA_EF_2014.pdf

Escobar-Chaves, S. L., & Anderson, C. A. (2008). Media and risky behaviors. *The Future of Children, 18,* 147–180.

Ferguson, C. J., & Dyck, D. (2012). Paradigm change in aggression research: The time has come to retire the General Aggression Model. *Aggression and Violent Behavior, 17*(3), 220–228.

Fischer, P., Greitemeyer, T., Kastenmüller, A., Vogrincic, C., & Sauer, A. (2011). The effects of risk-glorifying media exposure on risk-positive cognitions, emotions, and behaviors: A meta-analytic review. *Psychological Bulletin, 137*(3), 367–390.

Gerrard, M., Gibbons, F. X., & Warner, T. D. (1991). Effects of reviewing risk-relevant behavior on perceived vulnerability among women marines. *Health Psychology, 10*(3), 173–179.

Gerrig, R. J., & Prentice, D. A. (1991). The representation of fictional information. *Psychological Science, 2*(5), 336–340.

Gilbert, D. T. (1991). How mental systems believe. *American Psychologist, 46*(2), 107–119.

Green, M. C. (2006). Narratives and cancer communication. *Journal of Communication, 56* (Suppl 1), S163–S183.

Green, M. C., & Brock, T. C. (2000). The role of transportation in the persuasiveness of public narratives. *Journal of Personality and Social Psychology, 79*(5), 701–721.

Green, M. C., Garst, J., & Brock, T. C. (2004). The power of fiction: Determinants and boundaries. In L. J. Shrum (Ed.), *The psychology of entertainment media: Blurring the lines between entertainment and persuasion* (pp. 161–176). Mahwah, NJ: Lawrence Erlbaum Associates Publishers.

Harris Interactive (2013, February 27). Harris Poll #10. Majority of Americans see connection between video games and violent behavior in teens. *Harris Interactive.* Online publication. Retrieved from https://bit.ly/2J1U4on.

Hull, J. G., Brunelle, T. J., Prescott, A. T., & Sargent, J. D. (2014). A longitudinal study of risk-glorifying video games and behavioral deviance. *Journal of Personality and Social Psychology, 107*(2), 300–325.

Hull, J. G., Draghici, A. M., & Sargent, J. D. (2012). A longitudinal study of risk-glorifying video games and reckless driving. *Psychology of Popular Media Culture, 1*(4), 244–253.

Knowles, E. S., & Linn, J. (Eds.). (2004). *Resistance and persuasion.* Mahwah, NJ: Lawrence Erlbaum Associates Publishers.

Lin, J. (2013). Identification matters: A moderated mediation model of media interactivity, character identification, and video game violence on aggression. *Journal of Communication, 63*(4), 682–702.

Mustaro, P. N., & Mendonça, R. L. (2012). Immersion, narrative, and replayability as the motivational and attractiveness factors in serious games. In M. M. Cruz-Cunha

(Ed.), *Handbook of research on serious games as educational, business and research tools* (Vols. I & II., pp. 991–1008). Hershey, PA: Information Science Reference/IGI Global.

Peña, J., Khan, S., & Alexopoulos, C. (2016). I am what I see: How avatar weight affects physical activity among male gamers. *Journal of Computer-Mediated Communication, 21*, 195–209.

Peña, J., Khan, S., Burrows, C., & Blanton, H. (2018). How persuasive are in-game health messages in first-person shooter games? Exploring knowledge-activation and thought-disruption mechanisms. *Communication Reports, 35*(4), 293–302.

Phillips, D. P. (1982). The impact of fictional television stories on U.S. adult fatalities: New evidence on the effect of the mass media on violence. *The American Journal of Sociology, 87*(6), 1340–1359.

Prentice, D. A., & Gerrig, R. J. (1999). Exploring the boundary between fiction and reality. In S. Chaiken & Y. Trope (Eds.), *Dual-process theories in social psychology* (pp. 529–546). New York, NY: Guilford Press.

Prentice, D. A., Gerrig, R. J., & Bailis, D. S. (1997). What readers bring to the processing of fictional texts. *Psychonomic Bulletin & Review, 4*(3), 416–420.

Raiff, B. R., Jarvis, B. P., & Rapoza, D. (2012). Prevalence of video game use, cigarette smoking, and acceptability of a video game-based smoking cessation intervention among online adults. *Nicotine & Tobacco Research, 14*(12), 1453–1457.

Sauer, J. D., Drummond, A., & Nova, N. (2015). Violent video games: The effects of narrative context and reward structure on in-game and postgame aggression. *Journal of Experimental Psychology: Applied, 21*(3), 205–214.

Slater, M., Lotto, B., Arnold, M., & Sanchez-Vives, M. V. (2009). How we experience immersive virtual environments: The concept of presence and its measurement. *Anuario De Psicología, 40*, 193–210.

Sollins, B. (2011). Predictors of presence in virtual reality. *HIM 1990-2015.* 1759. http://stars.library.ucf.edu/honorstheses1990-2015/1759

Stein, J.-P., & Ohler, P. (2017). Venturing into the uncanny valley of mind – The influence of mind attribution on the acceptance of human-like characters in a virtual reality setting. *Cognition, 160*, 43–50.

Tamborini, R., Eastin, M. S., Skalski, P., Lachlan, K., Fediuk, T. A., & Brady, R. (2004). Violent virtual video games and hostile thoughts. *Journal of Broadcasting & Electronic Media, 48*, 335–357.

Tran, K. (2018). Why the esports audience is set to surge — and how brands can take advantage of increased fans and viewership. *Business Insider*. Retrieved from www.businessinsider.com/the-esports-audience-report-2018-11.

US Surgeon General. (2014). *The health consequences of smoking—50 years of progress: A report of the Surgeon General*. Washington, DC: US Department of Health and Human Services.

Van Rooij, A. J., Kuss, D. J., Griffiths, M. D., Shorter, G. W., Schoenmakers, T. M., & Van De Mheen, D. (2014). The (co-)occurrence of problematic video gaming, substance use, and psychosocial problems in adolescents. *Journal of Behavioral Addictions, 3*(3), 157–165.

Williams, K. D. (2011). The effects of homophily, identification, and violent video games on players. *Mass Communication & Society, 14*(1), 3–24.

Witte, K. (1992). Putting the fear back into fear appeals: The extended parallel process model. *Communication Monographs, 59*(4), 329–349.

Wouters, P., van Oostendorp, H., ter Vrugte, J., vanderCruysse, S., de Jong, T., & Elen, J. (2017). The effect of surprising events in a serious game on learning mathematics. *British Journal of Educational Technology, 48*(3), 860–877.

Yee, N., Bailenson, J. N., & Ducheneaut, N. (2009). The Proteus effect: Implications of transformed digital self-representation on online and offline behavior. *Communication Research, 36*(2), 285–312.

Yoo, S.-C., Peña, J., & Drumwright, M. (2015). Virtual shopping and unconscious persuasion: The priming effects of avatar age and consumers' age discrimination on purchasing and prosocial behaviors. *Computers in Human Behavior, 48*, 62–71.

7
THE DEVELOPMENT OF AGGRESSIVE BEHAVIOR IN CHILDHOOD AND ADOLESCENCE

A Social Interactionist Perspective

Barbara Krahé

Introduction

The propensity to engage in aggressive behavior shows a high stability across the lifespan, comparable in magnitude to the stability of intelligence (Olweus, 1979). Defined as behavior intended to cause harm to others, aggression is a form of antisocial behavior that entails a host of negative consequences at the individual, interpersonal, intergroup, and society level (Krahé, 2013). Therefore, understanding how aggression develops from childhood to early adulthood is a task of paramount importance, not only from a scientific, but also from a societal point of view. This chapter presents findings from an extensive program of research with children, adolescents, and young adults in Germany that seeks to identify risk factors for the development and persistence of aggressive behavior.

The analysis presented in this chapter is grounded in a social interactionist perspective that goes back to Lewin's (1936) formula of social behavior as a function of both the person and the environment. He emphasized that individual differences interact with characteristics of the social environment in shaping behavior in a specific situation, requiring both theoretical perspectives and methodological approaches that jointly consider these two sources of influence (see Krahé, 1992, for a more detailed discussion). Accordingly, analyzing the dynamic interplay of individual differences and environmental influences is a task that brings together different sub-disciplines of psychology, most notably social psychology, personality psychology, and developmental psychology. The program of research presented in this chapter was designed to contribute to this task by examining the development of aggressive behavior in childhood and adolescence as a function of individuals, social environments, and their dynamic interactions over time.

Using longitudinal, multilevel and experimental designs and relying on multiple measures of aggressive behavior, the research presented in this chapter addresses three main questions: (1) What are *intrapersonal risk factors* for the development and persistence of aggressive behavior from middle childhood to adolescence? This part will discuss the role of deficits in anger regulation, theory of mind, and executive function for the development of aggressive behavior; (2) What factors in the *social environment* contribute to the development of aggressive behavior? Here, the focus will be on social rejection by nonaggressive peers and affiliation with aggressive peers, the impact of being surrounded by aggressive peers in the classroom, and exposure to violent role models in the media; and (3) How do individual *dispositions and environmental risk factors interact* to explain developmental trajectories of aggressive behavior? This part will show how exposure to risk factors of aggressive behavior in the social environment affects individuals differently, defining the boundary conditions within which individual differences in aggression may be magnified or reduced. The chapter concludes with discussing the implications of the findings for efforts to prevent and reduce aggressive behavior in the critical periods of childhood and adolescence.

Development of Aggression from an Interactionist Perspective

Like any social behavior, aggressive behavior is shaped by both individual dispositions and environmental influences. The interactive effects between those two sources of variability explain why not all individuals behave in the same fashion in a particular social context and why the same individual may be more likely to show aggressive behavior in certain contexts than in others. Current theories of aggression, such as the General Aggression Model (Anderson & Bushman, 2018), conceptualize the development of an aggressive personality as the result of the interplay of biological and environmental modifiers. A broad research literature has offered evidence on the critical variables on either side, for instance, genetic dispositions on the one hand and exposure to violence in the family on the other. As reflected in transactional models of development, individuals are not only shaped by their social environment but also impact that environment through their personal dispositions (Sameroff, 2009).

Socio-cognitive models of the development of aggression in childhood and adolescence reflect this mutual dependency of personality and environmental influences (Huesmann, 2018). For example, Huesmann's (1998) script theory proposes that individuals develop mental representations about when and how to act aggressively based on their social experiences on the one hand and their habitual modes of information processing and emotion regulation on the other. Similarly, Dodge's (2011) Social Information Processing (SIP) model conceptualizes aggressive behavior as the outcome of a sequence of perceiving and interpreting social stimuli on the basis of characteristic styles of information processing. According to both models, the resulting level of aggressive behavior elicits negative social reactions that may lead to further aggressive behavior, resulting in a downward spiral of the chronification of aggression.

In the following sections, we first present longitudinal evidence on the role of intrapersonal risk factors for the development of aggressive behavior, focusing on both cognitive and affective variables. This analysis is followed by a discussion of environmental risk factors, in particular peer rejection, the level of aggression in the peer environment, and exposure to violence in the media, again using longitudinal designs. After considering these "main effects," person-environment interactions are demonstrated by studies using multilevel analysis.

Intrapersonal Risk Factors for the Development and Persistence of Aggressive Behavior

Individual differences in aggressive behavior emerge in childhood as soon as children are able to form an intention to harm, which is the defining feature of aggression. An intention to harm presupposes a level of cognitive development at which children are able to anticipate that their actions will lead to harm to another person (Krahé, 2013). In the search for variables predicting a higher disposition to engage in aggressive behavior in childhood and adolescence, both cognitive and affective variables have been identified. In our longitudinal program of research, we examined deficits in executive function and theory of mind as cognitive risk factors for aggression and maladaptive anger regulation as a risk factor in the domain of affect regulation. These factors were studied in a large sample of children aged between six and eight years at the beginning of the study, who were followed over a period of three years.

Deficits in executive function and theory of mind

Executive function (EF) is a cognitive activity that governs goal-directed action and planning of behavior, and allows for adaptive responses to novel, complex, or ambiguous situations. It is important for self-regulation, including anger regulation, and comprises four main components: Inhibition, working memory updating, shifting, and planning (Karr et al., 2018). Previous studies have shown that lower executive function is related to antisocial behavior (Ogilvie, Stewart, Chan, & Shum, 2011). As a set of cognitive skills allowing people to exert self-control in challenging situations, it is unsurprising that good executive function may help to reduce aggression. However, few studies have examined the link between childhood executive function and aggression over time. Similarly, the relationships between executive function, specific types of aggression, and other contributing factors, such as how easily someone becomes angry, are not well understood.

In a three-wave longitudinal study, we investigated the relationship between childhood executive function and different types of aggression to test the prediction that deficits in executive function would predict aggressive behavior in later years (Rohlf, Holl, Kirsch, Krahé, & Elsner, 2018). Primary school children aged between 6 and 11 years old were assessed at the start of the study, and at two subsequent data waves approximately one and three years later. To assess differences in executive function, including memory, planning abilities, and self-restraint, the children completed written tests, and to measure aggression, their teachers recorded their aggressive behavior, distinguishing between different forms and functions. Forms included physical aggression, such as hitting or kicking, or relational aggression, such as damaging others' social relationships by excluding them or spreading false information about them. In addition, the study distinguished between two functions that may motivate aggressive behavior: reactive aggression, referring to the child's tendency to react aggressively to provocation, and proactive aggression, denoting the child's tendency to behave aggressively in "cold blood" without being angered or provoked. Finally, parents reported how often and how easily their child tended to get angry. Using structural-equation modeling, we investigated the reciprocal relations between EF and teacher-rated aggression over time. To be able to assess change at the individual level separately from stable between-person differences, we used a Random-Intercept Cross-Lagged Panel Model (RI-CLPM) as proposed by Hamaker, Kuiper, and Grasman (2015).

The findings supported the predicted path from deficits in EF to aggressive behavior over time: the lower children scored on the measure of EF at the start of the study, the higher their aggression was rated by their teachers one and three years later, controlling for initial levels of aggressive behavior. This was true for both physical and relational forms of aggression. We also found that an increased tendency to get angry in children with lower EF may partly explain their increased aggression over time. With regard to the different functions of aggressive behavior, deficits in EF were related to increased reactive aggression over time, but did not predict proactive aggression. This ties in with the idea of proactive aggression as "cold-blooded," planned aggression for which affect control is less critical than for reactive aggression, which is more strongly based on anger and therefore may be more strongly affected by deficits in EF (Rathert, Fite, Gaertner, & Vitulano, 2011).

A second basic ability relevant for understanding the development of aggressive behavior is Theory of Mind (ToM), which is a mental representation of the internal states of other people. It is conceptually related to EF and typically differentiated into two facets: Making inferences regarding others' beliefs, intentions, or desires, refers to *cognitive* ToM, and inferring others' emotions refers to *affective* ToM (Derksen, Hunsche, Giroux, Connolly, & Bernstein, 2018). Numerous studies have examined the relation between ToM and aggressive behavior in children (see Wellman, Cross, & Watson, 2001, for a meta-analysis and critique). However, the evidence is limited in several ways: Many studies have yielded mixed results, were limited to children of preschool age, used cross-sectional designs, or did not control for earlier levels of aggressive behavior.

To address some of these limitations, we used the same sample of elementary school children to conduct a three-wave analysis of the reciprocal relations of ToM with aggressive behavior (Holl, Kirsch, Rohlf, Krahé, & Elsner, 2018). Again, both forms (physical and relational) and functions (proactive and reactive) of aggression were included in the analysis. Using structural-equation modeling, we investigated the relations between a latent factor of ToM, composed of both cognitive and affective ToM, and aggressive behavior. To be able to separate change at the individual level from stable between-person differences, we again employed a Random-Intercept Cross-Lagged Panel Model to identify intraindividual trajectories of change in aggressive behavior in relation to deficits in ToM.

Consistent with our theoretical assumption, we found that lower ToM prospectively predicted higher physical and relational aggression as rated by the children's class teachers. This was true for the paths from T1 to T2 as well as from T2 to T3. Even though we did not examine mediating processes in our study, these results are in line with the predictions derived from the SIP model (Dodge, 2011) that deficits in ToM may lead to biased or deficient social information processing, which in turn may lead to more aggressive behavior.

Anger and maladaptive anger regulation

In the final set of analyses based on the sample of elementary school children, we examined the role of *maladaptive anger regulation* as a risk factor for the development of aggression. Children of that age are not yet able to provide valid self-reports of their anger regulation and anger expression strategies (Parker et al., 2001). Therefore, the study by Rohlf, Busching, and Krahé (2017) examined the prospective links between maladaptive anger regulation and aggressive behavior in middle childhood over a ten-month period using an observational measure to assess anger regulation *in situ*. The anger induction measure consisted of asking the children to build a tower of bricks that was manipulated so as to keep collapsing, and their reactions were coded. The same children were studied again another three years later using an age-adapted version of the tower-building task. Children's behavioral strategies for regulating their anger were observed, distinguishing between maladaptive (e.g., venting the anger, verbal and visual focus on the frustrating stimulus) and adaptive (solution orientation) behavioral strategies (Kirsch, Busching, Rohlf, & Krahé, 2019; Rohlf & Krahé, 2015). Maladaptive anger regulation was correlated with teacher ratings obtained ten months later of how frequently the child had shown physical and relational aggression in the past six months, and to what degree the aggressive behavior was reactive, that is, shown in response to a provocation (Rohlf et al., 2017). Extending the longitudinal analysis to a total of three years, the path from maladaptive anger regulation to teacher-rated aggressive behavior was still significant (Kirsch et al., 2019). By then, children were old enough to provide reliable and valid self-reports of aggressive behavior, and these reports also correlated significantly with maladaptive anger regulation observed three years earlier. Moreover, maladaptive anger regulation was a significant prospective predictor of problems with peers (assessed through self-, parent-, and teacher ratings).

In combination, the findings presented in this section show that individual differences in executive function, theory of mind, and anger regulation predict individual differences in aggressive behavior over time in the developmental period of middle childhood. The next section takes a closer look at the role of environmental risk factors in the development of aggression.

Risk Factors in the Social Environment

A host of environmental factors affect the extent to which children and adolescents acquire patterns of aggressive behavior and shape individual differences in the tendency to respond aggressively in specific situations. These include proximal factors, such as experiencing and witnessing aggression in their family, and more distal factors, such as high ambient temperatures (see Krahé, 2013, for an overview). In our program of research, we focused on two sources of environmental influences that are relevant for understanding the development and persistence of individual differences in aggression: exposure to violence in the media and peer relations.

Exposure to violence in the media

Content analyses have shown the strong presence of violence in movies, video games, books, and song lyrics (Dill, Gentile, Richter, & Dill, 2005; Herd, 2009; Potts & Belden, 2009; Shor, 2018). A large research literature has documented a link between exposure to violent media contents and aggressive behavior (see meta-analyses by Anderson et al., 2010; Greitemeyer & Mügge, 2014; Prescott, Sargent, & Hull, 2018). Findings from experimental studies demonstrating short-term effects of a single exposure to violent content, and longitudinal studies identifying habitual use of violent media as a predictor of aggressive behavior over time, support the conclusion that exposure to violence in the media has a causal impact on the development of aggressive behavior. Although the magnitude of the effects is on the small side, its size is comparable to other known risk factors for aggression.

In our program of research on violent media effects, we demonstrated the long-term effects of habitual use of violent media in adolescence (Krahé, 2014). Controlling for a number of other potential risk factors of aggression, we demonstrated a significant path from habitual use of media violence to aggressive behavior over a period of up to three years (Krahé & Busching, 2015; Krahé, Busching, & Möller, 2012; Möller & Krahé, 2009). Using latent-class analysis, we identified three trajectories of media violence over four data waves separated by one-year intervals: consistently low users, consistently high users, and "desisters," that is, adolescents starting off with a high level of media use that declines over time. Using membership in these groups to predict trajectories of aggressive behavior during the same period revealed a high similarity between both trajectories: low media violence users remained consistently low and high media users consistently high on aggressive behavior, whereas the decrease in media violence among the desisters was accompanied by a parallel decrease in aggression (Krahé et al., 2012).

Importantly, nonviolent media use was unrelated to aggressive behavior, which is consistent with an explanation based on observational learning, postulating that the effects are specific to the observation of violent behavioral models. In addition, we conducted a combined experimental-longitudinal study to show that when exposure to violence in the media was reduced through a systematic intervention, aggressive behavior also declined over time (Krahé & Busching, 2015; Möller, Krahé, Busching, & Krause, 2012). These findings are consistent with the hypothesis of a causal influence of media violence in the development of aggressive behavior.

In addition to the role of observational learning from media models that engage in violent behavior, we identified further mediating processes by which violent media contents may impact aggressive behavior. One such process is the acquisition of normative beliefs that justify aggressive behavior (Möller & Krahé, 2009). The more violent video game use adolescents reported at the first data wave, the more physical aggression they showed 30 months later, and the path was mediated by a higher acceptance of aggressive behavior as normative and appropriate. These findings show that being exposed to violence in the media or engaging in violent behavior in the virtual reality of a video game contributes to the development of aggressive scripts that are then used in guiding behavior in the real world.

A second mediating process is emotional desensitization, which works at the affective level and means that individuals who are used to media violence show less subjective and physiological arousal in response to graphic depictions of violence. In an experiment studying responses to violent film clips in young adults, we showed that greater habitual use of violent media predicted stronger positive and weaker negative affective responses to violent clips and also reduced physiological arousal as measured by skin conductance levels (Krahé et al., 2011). Furthermore, the use of violent media contributes to the development of aggression by increasing the accessibility of aggressive thoughts. The more time research participants spent on using violent media, the shorter their response latency in recognizing aggressive (but not nonaggressive) words (Busching & Krahé, 2013). In the same study, we showed that participants who had engaged in violent video game play in a ship context also showed shorter response latencies to ship-related words, whereas participants who had engaged in violent video game play in a city environment showed shorter response times in recognizing city-related words. The fact that city-related words facilitated a faster response to aggressive words in participants who had played the game in a city context, and ship-related words served as primes for aggression-related words among participants who had played the game in a ship context, indicates that initially neutral stimuli (the city- and ship-related terms) are imbued with aggressive meaning if they are presented in association with violent cues, consistent with a conceptualization of aggressive behavior as resulting from an associative network of aggressive affect and cognition (Berkowitz, 2008).

In summary, the research reviewed in this section has shown that exposure to violence in the virtual reality of the media is an environmental influence that contributes to the development of aggression. It has also identified several interlocking psychological mechanisms by which this process may be explained.

Peer relations and the development of aggression

Children and adolescents who are unable to regulate their anger in a socially accepted way and show aggressive behavior are likely to encounter problems with their peers and experience social rejection (Godleski, Kamper, Ostrov, Hart, & Blakely-McClure, 2015) or victimization (e.g., Rosen, Milich, & Harris, 2012)). Due to the marginalization by nonaggressive peers, aggressive children tend to affiliate with other aggressive peers, forming social groups in which aggressive behavior is normative (Patterson, DeBaryshe, & Ramsey, 1989).

In line with this reasoning, Rohlf et al., 2017 proposed that problems in relationships with peers would be both a consequence of deficits in anger regulation and a predictor of aggression. With regard to the frequency of aggression, they proposed that maladaptive anger regulation at T1 would predict higher levels of aggression at T2 via more peer problems at T1, which in turn would lead to a higher frequency of aggressive behavior at T2. They further predicted that maladaptive anger regulation would be indirectly linked to both proactive and reactive aggression through the influence of peer problems at T1. As expected, the frequency of aggression, as well as reactive and proactive aggression at T2, were indirectly predicted by T1 maladaptive anger regulation through T1 peer problems. Thus, the more maladaptive anger regulation children showed, the more peer problems they experienced, and the more socially rejected they were at T1, the higher their scores were on the measures of the frequency and functions of aggression at T2.

Jung, Krahé, Bondü, Esser, and Wyschkon (2018) studied the link between antisocial behavior, social rejection, academic failure, and affiliation with deviant peers in a sample of 6- to 15-year-old participants who took part in three measurement waves (T1 to T3) over a time period of about five years. Teacher ratings were used as indicators of participants' antisocial behavior, academic failure, social rejection, and affiliation with deviant peers. In addition, parents provided ratings of antisocial behavior and social rejection. Consistent with their predictions, and in line with previous research (Laird, Jordan, Dodge, Pettit, & Bates, 2001; Ostrov, Murray-Close, Godleski, & Hart, 2013), higher antisocial behavior at T1 predicted higher peer rejection at T2, controlling for the stability of social rejection between T1 and T2. T2 social rejection was a positive predictor of affiliation with deviant peers at T2, and T2 social rejection indirectly predicted T3 antisocial behavior through a stronger affiliation with deviant peers. The direct effect from T2 social rejection to T3 antisocial behavior was non-significant, indicating that affiliation with deviant peers is, indeed, a crucial process underlying the pathway from social rejection to antisocial behavior.

In addition to the responses peer groups show to the aggressive behavior of individuals, a social interactionist perspective on the development of aggression also needs to look at the responses of individuals to the aggressive peer group behavior to which they are exposed. A fruitful line of thinking to conceptualize the effect of aggressive peer groups on the individual is captured by the metaphor of aggression as a *"contagious disease"* (Dishion, 2015; Huesmann, 2018). Just as people's immune systems are affected by the germs they catch from others and that make them ill as a result, initially nonaggressive individuals may become infected with the aggressive behavior patterns of the peers around them.

Whereas past research on the peer contagion of aggression focused either on self-selected peer groups or on groups with a high level of aggression (see Jung, Busching, & Krahé, 2019 for a review), our research analyzed the contagious nature of aggression in groups where self-selection is minimized, namely classroom communities. Because students are assigned to their classes by the school administration, studying the contagion of aggression in classroom communities is particularly suitable for disentangling the socializing influence of peers from the selective affiliation with peers with similar levels of aggression. In a sample of approximately 1,300 male and female students in middle childhood, Rohlf, Krahé, and Busching (2016) investigated the effect of classroom aggression on both physical and relational aggression. They found that the higher the level of both physical and relational aggressive behavior in their class, the more aggressive individual class members were ten months later, even after controlling for the temporal stability of aggression as well as participants' gender and age.

Similar results were found in studies with adolescents that investigated the contagion of peer aggression in the broader context of antisocial behaviors, such as delinquency, vandalism, or substance abuse, which often co-occur with aggressive behavior. In a large multilevel study with almost 17,000 male and female adolescents distributed across approximately 1,300 classrooms, Busching and Krahé (2018) observed a significant main effect of class-level antisocial behavior on individual antisocial behavior across a one-year period. Again, the effect remained significant after controlling for the stability of individual antisocial behavior and relevant third variables, such as migration background, school track, academic performance, gender, and age. In another study, Busching and Krahé (2015) found that both physical and relational aggression at the class level significantly predicted future aggression at the class level across four measurement points, which indicates that peer contagion operates not only at the individual, but also at the group level. In the case of relational aggression, the autoregressive path coefficients were significantly higher at the class level than at the individual level, indicating that the level of relational aggression is more stable in the class communities as a whole than in the individuals of whom they are formed.

In summary, this body of evidence suggests that being surrounded by aggressive peers increases children and adolescents' risk of becoming more aggressive over time. Furthermore, recent findings support the idea that the contagious effect of aggression not only spreads within systems but also permeates other, interconnected ecosystems: Individuals who are surrounded by aggressive friends are at risk of introducing aggression into other spheres of their life and affecting individuals that had no direct contact with the original source of the aggressive behavior (Greitemeyer, 2018). The studies considering antisocial behavior suggest that the concept of peer contagion is not limited to aggression, but operates in a similar way across different kinds of problem behavior, including vandalism or substance abuse.

Interaction of Intrapersonal and Social Risk Factors

Personal characteristics and social environment shape the development of aggression not only as main effects, but also in interaction. In our program of research, we looked specifically at the interaction between individual-level and class-level variables in relation to peer norms and aggressive behavior. This enabled us to address the question whether the same classroom environment differentially affects the development of individual aggression depending on the individual's pre-existing level of aggressive behavior.

Multilevel modeling offers a statistical approach for addressing the question of whether exposure to an aggressive peer environment has the same effect on all individuals, or varies in relation to the level of aggression the individuals bring to the environment. In our program of research, we could take advantage of the fact that in the German school system, students remain in the same class community for several years, creating a stable class environment. This enabled us not only to quantify the main effects of classroom level of aggression on the developmental trajectories of aggressive behavior for the individual class members, but also to test possible cross-level interactions. These reflect the extent to which classrooms with a high overall level of aggression affect students differently depending on their individual level of aggression. In a series of analyses with elementary and secondary school students, we showed that aggressive classroom environments have a greater impact on initially nonaggressive children than on those with higher levels of aggression at the start of the analysis (Jung et al., 2019).

In their sample of children of elementary school age, Rohlf et al. (2016) found a significant cross-level interaction between individuals' relational aggression and the level of relational aggression among the remaining members of the class. Individuals who showed low initial levels of relational aggression scored significantly higher on measures of relational aggression ten months later if they were in classrooms with a high level of relational aggression. By contrast, individuals with initially high levels of relational aggression were unaffected by the level of relational aggression in their classroom, which means that they remained at a high level even in classes in which the overall level of aggression was low. Similarly, Busching and Krahé (2018) analyzed cross-level interactions between individual and classroom antisocial behavior in an adolescent sample. In line with their hypotheses, initially non-antisocial participants showed more antisocial behavior one year later the higher the level of classroom antisocial behavior had been in their class at the beginning of the study. By contrast, participants with initially high levels of antisocial behavior were largely unaffected by their peers' level of antisocial behavior. In a further study, we showed that not just the collective behavior in a class, but also the collective normative belief that aggression is acceptable, contributes to the development of aggressive behavior in individual class members by increasing the acceptance of aggression at the individual level (Busching & Krahé, 2015).

In all three studies, participants attended mainstream schools, and the overall level of aggression in the classrooms was in the lower half of the scale range. So the finding that children who were more aggressive initially were less affected by the level of aggression in their classroom cannot be attributed to a ceiling effect that would have reduced the potential for variability among the more aggressive individuals.

Consistent with the metaphor of aggression as a contagious disease, this finding indicates that being part of an aggressive environment "infects" initially "healthy" class members, whose aggression levels move toward the class level over the course of time, whereas it has little effect on those who have already "caught" the aggressive behavior. However, a similar cross-level interaction could not be observed for physical aggression in the Rohlf et al. (2016) study. For this form of aggression, only a classroom-level main effect was found, indicating that aggressive classrooms promoted aggressive behavior in class members regardless of their individual levels of aggression.

In addition to the contagious effect of peers' aggressive behavior, we also examined the impact of peers' normative beliefs about aggression, defined as subjective beliefs about the appropriateness and acceptance of aggressive behavior in different kinds of social situations, on individuals' aggressive behavior. For example, in the aforementioned study by Busching and Krahé (2015), a significant cross-level interaction between class-level normative beliefs and individual physical aggression was observed. Individuals with low levels of aggressive behavior at the start of the study showed more physical aggression 12 months later if they had been in a class with a high tolerance of aggression than if they had been surrounded by classmates with a low tolerance of aggression. By contrast, individuals with initially high levels of physical aggression were more aggressive 10 months later, regardless of their peers' tolerance of physical aggression.

It was noted earlier that aggressive children and children with maladaptive anger regulation are at risk of being socially rejected by their peers. By looking at cross-level interactions in the path from aggression to social rejection over time, we were able to show that aggressive students become less socially rejected over time if they are in a class with a high collective level of aggression (Rohlf et al., 2016). No effect of class level on social rejection of initially nonaggressive students was found. This finding suggests that aggressive behavior becomes normalized in aggressive classrooms, changing the normative and social context in the direction of making aggressive behavior more acceptable. As a result, aggressive children meet with less social rejection.

In addition to the proximal factor of exposure to aggressive peers, we found that the more distal factor of exposure to aggressive behavior in the media has a similar effect. Adolescents with an initially low level of aggressive behavior showed a stronger increase in the normative acceptance of aggression the more they used violent media, whereas little influence of media violence use was apparent for the initially more aggressive participants (Krahé & Busching, 2015).

In the reported studies, we also examined the role of gender differences as a possible moderator of class-level effects and cross-level interactions. Although significant moderator effects of gender were identified, the results did not yield a consistent pattern. In the younger sample studied by Rohlf et al. (2016), class members were more affected by the collective levels of relational aggression of their same-sex than their opposite-sex peers. In their adolescent sample, Busching and Krahé (2015) found that the aggression level of girls in a class had a greater impact on both male and female class members than the aggression levels of boys in predicting increases in aggressive behavior over a period of three years. This finding is compatible with an evolutionary perspective, proposing that females control mate selection. To the extent that boys become more interested in being accepted as dating partners by girls, moving in the direction of the girls' collective norms on aggressive behavior may be an adaptive strategy (see van Vugt, de Vries & Li, this volume, for an evolutionary perspective more generally). More research examining cross-level interactions broken down by gender are needed to explain these findings.

Implications for Prevention and Intervention

Gaining a better understanding of the risk factors for aggressive behavior in the individual and the social context is a precondition for developing promising intervention strategies (see Petty & Briñol, and Walton & Brady, this volume, for further discussions of interventions). The findings from our program of research have several implications for intervention efforts. For example, the results by Rohlf et al. (2018) suggest that training programs that help children to regulate their anger in a more socially acceptable way could reduce their aggression. A meta-analysis of anger management trainings directed at school-aged children showed that such programs can be successful in reducing anger and aggressive behavior, although the effect sizes across 60 studies were moderate in size (-0.33 for anger and -0.34 for aggressive behavior; Candelaria, Fedewa, & Ahn, 2012). In addition, a recent meta-analysis showed that interventions to foster executive function among both typically and nontypically developing children are effective in the region of moderate effect sizes (Takacs & Kassai, 2019).

Based on the Social Information Processing model, a program designed to reduce the normative acceptance of aggression also reported positive results (Dodge & Godwin, 2013). Reviewing a broader range of intervention approaches, Hendriks, Bartels, Colins, and Finkenauer (2018) concluded that intervention effects are larger among children with higher starting levels of aggressive behavior. However, our findings consistently showed that the initially less aggressive individuals are more negatively affected by a high level of aggression in their class, which speaks against focusing intervention efforts on the more aggressive individuals. Instead, the aim should be to prevent them from catching aggressive behavior from their peers, by focusing on changing classroom norms and behaviors and bolstering the "immune system" of non-aggressive peers so that they are better able to reject aggressive norms and behaviors in the class around them.

Based on our findings on the impact of violent media use on aggressive cognitions and behaviors, we specifically targeted adolescents' use of violent media in an effort to reduce aggressive behavior and the normative acceptance of aggression as a critical antecedent. We conducted a combined experimental-longitudinal study in which we randomly assigned adolescents to an intervention group designed to reduce media violence use, or to a non-treated control group, and followed the effects of the intervention on reducing media violence use, the normative acceptance of aggression, and aggressive behavior over a period of 30 months (Krahé & Busching, 2015). After the six-week intervention implemented in a school context, participants in the intervention group reported significantly less use of violent media than did participants in the control group, and the difference remained stable over the next 24 months. Reduced media violence use prospectively predicted lower normative acceptance of aggression and less self-reported physical aggression up to 18 months post-intervention. While it is not ethically feasible to increase the dosage of violent media contents in an experimental design, using an intervention to reduce the use of violent media is a viable approach (see Blanton, Burrows, & Regan, this volume, for a similar approach with regard to smoking). It may not only break the cycle from media violence to aggression but also provide a rigorous test of causal hypotheses about long-term effects of violent media use on aggressive behavior.

Summary and Conclusions

The program of research presented in this chapter was designed to identify risk factors for the development of aggressive behavior in childhood and adolescents based on a social-interactionist perspective on the mutual dependency of personal and environmental factors in shaping social behavior. Using a multimethod approach that comprised experimental, longitudinal, and multilevel studies, our research yielded the following conclusions.

First, looking at the main effects of intrapersonal risk factors for aggression, we showed that deficits in executive function (EF) and theory of mind (ToM) as well as maladaptive anger regulation, predicted increases in aggressive behavior over time. Mediational analyses suggest both intrapersonal and social pathways in this developmental process: Deficits in EF predicted aggression via maladaptive anger regulation, and maladaptive anger regulation predicted aggression via social rejection.

Second, we examined social environmental risk factors and showed that social rejection by nonaggressive peers and ensuing affiliation with deviant peers were linked to increases in aggressive behavior over time. Moreover, we found that deviant peer groups contribute to the development of aggression via the normative acceptance of aggression. Habitual exposure to violence in the media was another risk factor linked to the social context that led to increases in aggression over time.

Third, developmental trajectories of individual differences in aggression were shown to be moderated by social influences in the peer group: being surrounded by aggressive peers increases aggressive behavior over time. This is true especially for individuals with initially low levels of aggression, consistent with the metaphor of aggression as a contagious disease. By studying the impact of aggressive peer group behavior in classroom communities to which individuals are assigned by the school administration, this contagion effect could be identified largely uncontaminated by self-selection effects.

The findings provide a starting point for theory-based efforts to intervene in the transactional process of personal and environmental influences. For example, at the personal level, programs are needed to promote anger regulation with the aim to break the path from maladaptive anger regulation via social rejection to aggressive behavior. The existing literature shows that such approaches may yield at least moderate success. At the level of the social environment, interventions to reduce media violence use may have sustained effects on reducing the normative acceptance of aggression as well as aggressive behavior. Finally, identifying individual differences in the susceptibility to risk factors for aggression in the social environment alerts researchers and practitioners to the contagious effect of aggressive peer groups, especially among those individuals who enter such environments with a low level of aggressive behavior, and highlights the need to closely monitor class-level norms and behavior patterns. Given the negative effects of aggressive behavior on healthy development in childhood and adolescence in a broad range of domains, as well as the social costs involved for society, recognizing the interaction between individual and environmental risk factors for aggressive behavior and designing appropriate intervention tools remains a task of paramount importance for psychological research.

Author Note

The significant contributions of Robert Busching, Janis Jung, Fabian Kirsch, Ingrid Möller, and Helena Rohlf to the research presented in this chapter are gratefully acknowledged.

References

Anderson, C. A., & Bushman, B. J. (2018). Media violence and the General Aggression Model. *Journal of Social Issues, 74*, 386–413. doi:10.1111/josi.12275

Anderson, C. A., Shibuya, A., Ihori, N., Swing, E. L., Bushman, B. J., Sakamoto, A., ... Saleem, M. (2010). Violent video game effects on aggression, empathy, and prosocial behavior in Eastern and Western countries: A meta-analytic review. *Psychological Bulletin, 136*, 151–173. doi:10.1037/a0018251

Berkowitz, L. (2008). On the consideration of automatic as well as controlled psychological processes in aggression. *Aggressive Behavior, 34*, 117–129. doi:10.1002/ab.20244

Busching, R., & Krahé, B. (2013). Charging neutral cues with aggressive meaning through violent video game play. *Societies, 3*, 445–456. doi:10.3390/soc3040445

Busching, R., & Krahé, B. (2015). The girls set the tone: Gendered classroom norms and the development of aggression in adolescence. *Personality & Social Psychology Bulletin, 41*, 659–676. doi:10.1177/0146167215573212

Busching, R., & Krahé, B. (2018). The contagious effect of deviant behavior in adolescence. *Social Psychological and Personality Science, 9*, 815–824. doi:10.1177/1948550617725151

Candelaria, A. M., Fedewa, A. L., & Ahn, S. (2012). The effects of anger management on children's social and emotional outcomes: A meta-analysis. *School Psychology International, 33*, 596–614. doi:10.1177/0143034312454360

Derksen, D. G., Hunsche, M. C., Giroux, M. E., Connolly, D. A., & Bernstein, D. M. (2018). A systematic review of theory of mind's precursors and functions. *Zeitschrift für Psychologie, 226*, 87–97. doi:10.1027/2151-2604/a000325

Dill, K., Gentile, D. A., Richter, W. A., & Dill, J. (2005). Violence, sex, race, and age in popular video games: A content analysis. In E. Cole & J. H. Daniel (Eds.), *Featuring females: Feminist analyses of media* (pp. 115–130). Washington, D.C: American Psychological Association.

Dishion, T. J. (2015). A developmental model of aggression and violence: Microsocial and macrosocial dynamics within an ecological framework. In M. Lewis & K. D. Rudolph (Eds.), *Handbook of developmental psychopathology* (pp. 449–465). New York: Springer.

Dodge, K. A. (2011). Social information processing patterns as mediators of the interaction between genetic factors and life experiences in the development of aggressive behavior. In P. R. Shaver & M. Mikulincer (Eds.), *Human aggression and violence: Causes, manifestations, and consequences* (pp. 165–185). Washington, D.C: American Psychological Association.

Dodge, K. A., & Godwin, J. (2013). Social-information-processing patterns mediate the impact of preventive intervention on adolescent antisocial behavior. *Psychological Science, 24*, 456–465. doi:10.1177/0956797612457394

Godleski, S. A., Kamper, K. E., Ostrov, J. M., Hart, E. J., & Blakely-McClure, S. J. (2015). Peer victimization and peer rejection during early childhood. *Journal of Clinical Child and Adolescent Psychology, 44*, 380–392. doi:10.1080/15374416.2014.940622

Greitemeyer, T. (2018). The spreading impact of playing violent video games on aggression. *Computers in Human Behavior, 80*, 216–219. doi:10.1016/j.chb.2017.11.022

Greitemeyer, T., & Mügge, D. O. (2014). Video games do affect social outcomes: A meta-analytic review of the effects of violent and prosocial video game play. *Personality & Social Psychology Bulletin, 40*, 578–589. doi:10.1177/0146167213520459

Hamaker, E. L., Kuiper, R. M., & Grasman, R. P. P. P. (2015). A critique of the cross-lagged panel model. *Psychological Methods, 20*, 102–116. doi:10.1037/a0038889

Hendriks, A. M., Bartels, M., Colins, O. F., & Finkenauer, C. (2018). Childhood aggression: A synthesis of reviews and meta-analyses to reveal patterns and opportunities for prevention and intervention strategies. *Neuroscience and Biobehavioral Reviews, 91*, 278–291. doi:10.1016/j.neubiorev.2018.03.021

Herd, D. (2009). Changing images of violence in rap music lyrics: 1979–1997. *Journal of Public Health Policy, 30*, 395–406. doi:10.1057/jphp.2009.36

Holl, A. K., Kirsch, F., Rohlf, H., Krahé, B., & Elsner, B. (2018). Longitudinal reciprocity between theory of mind and aggression in middle childhood. *International Journal of Behavioral Development, 42*, 257–266. doi:10.1177/0165025417727875

Huesmann, L. R. (1998). The role of social information processing and cognitive schema in the acquisition and maintenance of habitual aggressive behavior. In R. G. Geen & E. Donnerstein (Eds.), *Human aggression: Theories, research, and implications for social policy* (pp. 73–109). San Diego, CA: Academic Press.

Huesmann, L. R. (2018). An integrative theoretical understanding of aggression. In B. J. Bushman (Ed.), *Aggression and violence: A social psychological perspective* (pp. 3–21). New York: Routledge.

Jung, J., Busching, R., & Krahé, B. (2019). Catching aggression from one's peers: A longitudinal and multilevel analysis. *Social and Personality Psychology Compass, 13*, e12433. doi:10.1111/spc3.12433

Jung, J., Krahé, B., Bondü, R., Esser, G., & Wyschkon, A. (2018). Dynamic progression of antisocial behavior in childhood and adolescence: A three-wave longitudinal study from Germany. *Applied Developmental Science, 22*, 74–88. doi:10.1080/10888691.2016.1219228

Karr, J. E., Areshenkoff, C. N., Rast, P., Hofer, S. M., Iverson, G. L., Garcia-Barrera, M. A. (2018). The unity and diversity of executive functions: A systematic review and re-analysis of latent variable studies. *Psychological Bulletin, 144*, 1147–1185. doi:10.1037/bul0000160

Kirsch, F., Busching, R., Rohlf, H., & Krahé, B. (2019). Using behavioral observation for the longitudinal study of anger regulation in middle childhood. *Applied Developmental Science, 25* (Advance online publication), 1–14. doi:10.1080/10888691.2017.13 25325

Krahé, B. (1992). *Personality and social psychology: Towards a synthesis.* London: Sage.

Krahé, B. (2013). *The social psychology of aggression* (2nd ed.). Hove: Psychology Press.

Krahé, B. (2014). Media violence use as a risk factor for aggressive behaviour in adolescence. *European Review of Social Psychology, 25*, 71–106. doi:10.1080/10463283.2014.9 23177

Krahé, B., & Busching, R. (2015). Breaking the vicious cycle of media violence use and aggression: A test of intervention effects over 30 months. *Psychology of Violence, 5*, 217–226. doi:10.1037/a0036627

Krahé, B., Busching, R., & Möller, I. (2012). Media violence use and aggression among German adolescents: Associations and trajectories of change in a three-wave longitudinal study. *Psychology of Popular Media Culture, 1*, 152–166. doi:10.1037/a0028663

Krahé, B., Möller, I., Huesmann, L. Rowell, Kirwil, L., Felber, J., & Berger, A. (2011). Desensitization to media violence: Links with habitual media violence exposure, aggressive cognitions, and aggressive behavior. *Journal of Personality and Social Psychology, 100*, 630–646. doi:10.1037/a0021711

Laird, R. D., Jordan, K. Y., Dodge, K. A., Pettit, G. S., & Bates, J. E. (2001). Peer rejection in childhood, involvement with antisocial peers in early adolescence, and the development of externalizing behavior problems. *Development and Psychopathology, 13*, 337–354. doi:10.1017/S0954579401002085

Lewin, K. (1936). *Principles of topological psychology.* New York: McGraw-Hill.

Möller, I., & Krahé, B. (2009). Exposure to violent video games and aggression in German adolescents: A longitudinal analysis. *Aggressive Behavior, 35*, 75–89. doi:10. 1002/ab.20290

Möller, I., Krahé, B., Busching, R., & Krause, C. (2012). Efficacy of an intervention to reduce the use of media violence and aggression: An experimental evaluation with adolescents in Germany. *Journal of Youth and Adolescence, 41*, 105–120. doi:10.1007/ s10964-011-9654-6

Ogilvie, J. M., Stewart, A. L., Chan, R. C. K., & Shum, D. H. K. (2011). Neuropsychological measures of executive function and antisocial behavior: A meta-analysis. *Criminology, 49*, 1063–1107. doi:10.1111/j.1745-9125.2011.00252.x

Olweus, D. (1979). Stability of aggressive reaction patterns in males: A review. *Psychological Bulletin, 86*, 852–875. doi:10.1037/0033-2909.86.4.852

Ostrov, J. M., Murray-Close, D., Godleski, S. A., & Hart, E. J. (2013). Prospective associations between forms and functions of aggression and social and affective processes during early childhood. *Journal of Experimental Child Psychology, 116*, 19–36. doi:10.1016/j.jecp.2012.12.009

Parker, E. H., Hubbard, J. A., Ramsden, S. R., Relyea, N., Dearing, K. F., Smithmyer, C. M., & Schimmel, K. D. (2001). Children's use and knowledge of display rules for anger following hypothetical vignettes versus following live peer interaction. *Social Development, 10*, 528–557. doi:10.1111/1467-9507.00179

Patterson, G. R., DeBaryshe, B. D., & Ramsey, E. (1989). A developmental perspective on antisocial behavior. *American Psychologist*, *44*, 329–335. doi:10.1037/0003-066X. 44.2.329

Potts, R., & Belden, A. (2009). Parental guidance: A content analysis of MPAA motion picture rating justifications 1993–2005. *Current Psychology*, *28*, 266–283. doi:10.1007/s12144-009-9065-y

Prescott, A. T., Sargent, J. D., & Hull, J. G. (2018). Metaanalysis of the relationship between violent video game play and physical aggression over time. *Proceedings of the National Academy of Sciences of the United States of America*, *115*, 9882–9888. doi:10.1073/pnas.1611617114

Rathert, J., Fite, P. J., Gaertner, A. E., & Vitulano, M. (2011). Associations between effortful control, psychological control and proactive and reactive aggression. *Child Psychiatry and Human Development*, *42*, 609–621. doi:10.1007/s10578-011-0236-3

Rohlf, H., Busching, R., & Krahé, B. (2017). Longitudinal links between maladaptive anger regulation, peer problems, and aggression in middle childhood. *Merrill-Palmer Quarterly*, *63*, 282. doi:10.13110/merrpalmquar1982.63.2.0282

Rohlf, H., Holl, A. K., Kirsch, F., Krahé, B., & Elsner, B. (2018). Longitudinal links between executive function, anger, and aggression in middle childhood. *Frontiers in Behavioral Neuroscience*, *12*, 27. doi:10.3389/fnbeh.2018.00027

Rohlf, H., & Krahé, B. (2015). Assessing anger regulation in middle childhood: Development and validation of a behavioral observation measure. *Frontiers in Psychology*, *6*, 453. doi:10.3389/fpsyg.2015.00453

Rohlf, H., Krahé, B., & Busching, R. (2016). The socializing effect of classroom aggression on the development of aggression and social rejection: A two-wave multilevel analysis. *Journal of School Psychology*, *58*, 57–72. doi:10.1016/j.jsp. -2016.05.002

Rosen, P. J., Milich, R., & Harris, M. J. (2012). Dysregulated negative emotional reactivity as a predictor of chronic peer victimization in childhood. *Aggressive Behavior*, *38*, 414–427. doi:10.1002/ab.21434

Sameroff, A. (2009). The transactional model. In A. Sameroff (Ed.), *The transactional model of development: How children and contexts shape each other* (pp. 3–21). Washington, D.C: American Psychological Association. doi:10.1037/11877-001

Shor, E. (2018). Age, aggression, and pleasure in popular online pornographic videos. *Violence Against Women*, 1077801218804101. doi:10.1177/1077801218804101

Takacs, Z. K., & Kassai, R. (2019). The efficacy of different interventions to foster children's executive function skills: A series of meta-analyses. *Psychological Bulletin*. Advance online publication. doi:10.1037/bul0000195

Wellman, H. M., Cross, D., & Watson, J. (2001). Meta-analysis of theory-of-mind development: The truth about false belief. *Child Development*, *72*, 655–684. doi:10.1111/1467-8624.00304

8
GROUNDING DESIRE
The Role of Consumption and Reward Simulations in Eating and Drinking Behavior

Esther K. Papies

How does desire arise in the human mind? Most people experience a variety of desires throughout the day, with desires for food, drink, and social interactions most prevalent (Hofmann, Baumeister, Förster, & Vohs, 2012). Often, these desires lead to self-control conflict, as acting on them would interfere with the pursuit of a long-term investment goal. Such conflicts take up cognitive resources, and they typically lead to self-control failures sooner or later (Hofmann, Vohs, & Baumeister, 2012). Thus, desire can have a variety of intrapersonal and interpersonal consequences, making it a topic of key significance in social-psychological research. In this chapter, I will present a grounded cognition approach to understanding the emergence of desire, which we have defined previously as the conscious or unconscious state of motivation for a specific stimulus or experience that is anticipated to be rewarding (Papies & Barsalou, 2015). The grounded cognition theory of desire attempts to explain how desire and motivated behavior arise in response to external cues, using basic cognitive and memory processes, which are often unconscious (Papies & Barsalou, 2015; Papies, Best, Gelibter, & Barsalou, 2017; Papies, Pronk, Keesman, & Barsalou, 2015). Thus, in contrast to work on, for example, the elaborated intrusion theory of desire (Kavanagh, Andrade, & May, 2005), which argues that conscious elaboration of sensory imagery related to consumption plays a key role in desire, the grounded cognition framework assumes that both the desire itself, as well as the processes that contribute to it, can be conscious or nonconscious.

After briefly describing the theory, I will review evidence supporting it in the domains of eating and drinking behavior. Then, I will discuss how interventions can regulate problematic desires by targeting consumption and reward simulations. Finally, I will briefly address the possible role of simulations in self-regulation and social psychology more generally, and discuss directions for future research.

A Grounded Cognition Theory of Desire

The grounded cognition theory of desire suggests that desire arises from consumption and reward simulations in response to appetitive cues, based on previous consumption experiences. Every time we consume a food or drink, we lay down a rich situated memory of this experience that integrates various streams of information, which is referred to as a situated conceptualization (Barsalou, 2003, 2009; Papies & Barsalou, 2015). Such situated conceptualizations can include, for example, sensory information on the taste and texture of the food or drink; visual information on the food or drink and one's surroundings; actions such as reaching out, using utensils, and chewing; information about one's physical state and the social, time, and physical context of eating or drinking; information about accompanying foods or drinks; immediate (bodily, cognitive, emotional, and hedonic) consequences of consumption; and short-term or long-term goals related to consumption. As Barsalou and colleagues describe (Barsalou, 2016; Wilson-Mendenhall, Barrett, Simmons, & Barsalou, 2011), these "local" streams of information get integrated into "global" representations that facilitate coherent conceptual interpretations of the events in a given situation (Papies et al., 2017).

When a relevant cue is encountered later, for example a visual food cue, this will reactivate the best matching situated conceptualization available from previous experiences. From a Bayesian perspective, the best matching situated conceptualization is one that has been used frequently in the past, and that seems to provide a good fit with current situational cues. Thus, the brain continually attempts to categorize the type of situation that is occurring, by mapping current information onto previously stored situated conceptualizations and activating the conceptualization that matches what is encountered in the moment (Barsalou, 2009; Papies et al., 2017). Non-present elements of the situated conceptualization can then be simulated via pattern completion inferences. As a result, an external cue, such as the mere picture of a food, can activate a vivid re-experience of eating the food, including a representation of its taste and texture, motor actions of picking it up to eat it, and other features of a consumption episode, despite no actual food being present. The theory further suggests that this matching process is sensitive to state and trait individual differences, such that, for example, an image of pizza encountered when hungry is likely to activate a situated conceptualization of previously eating pizza when hungry. This will make the pizza in the image appear more rewarding than when encountered in a satiated state, when eating pizza previously produced less reward.

Such situated conceptualizations are useful for understanding situations, anticipating likely events, and planning and executing goal-directed action

(Barsalou, 2009, 2016). Imagine, for example, passing a cafe in a new city where you have just arrived for a conference. Although you have never been to this cafe or even this city, you recognize this establishment as a place where you can drink coffee and eat snacks. You know how to line up at the counter when you enter, you know that a barista will prompt you for your order, and you know which coffee to choose based on your previous experiences with similar beverages. These predictions and preferences can be generated effortlessly through simulations within the situated conceptualizations of having coffee in a cafe.

Importantly, simulations within situated conceptualizations not only help to interpret situations as they occur and align our behavior, they can also lead to novel – and possibly problematic – desires (Papies & Barsalou, 2015; Papies et al., 2017). Imagine having entered the cafe in the example above to drink coffee before the start of the conference. As you stand at the counter waiting to order your drink, you see a variety of baked goods in front of you. You spontaneously simulate eating them, imagining their taste, texture, and the resulting hedonic experience. To the degree that any aspect of this simulated experience is rewarding, this will trigger the motivation to enact it. This may lead you to either impulsively purchase a piece of cake, or to experience a conscious craving, which may or may not lead you to order some cake. Critically, the consumption simulations triggered by the sight of the cake help you predict what eating the cake would be like, and the associated reward will determine whether this creates a desire. Thus, consumption simulations within previously stored situated conceptualizations can both help navigate known and less known environments, and also create novel desires and lead to unplanned motivated behavior, or impulses.

The research reviewed in the next sections supports the core tenets of this theory. It shows that food and drink stimuli trigger consumption and reward simulations, especially if they are attractive, as evidenced in both spontaneous language and in behavioral and neuro-imaging findings. Further evidence shows that consumption and reward simulations lead to desire for the simulated foods and drinks, as shown in behavioral and physiological data. Finally, self-regulation techniques that target consumption and reward simulations can reduce desire.

Appetitive Stimuli Trigger Consumption and Reward Simulations

A variety of research findings suggest that food and drink cues trigger consumption and reward simulations, especially if they are attractive. In initial studies on this topic, a feature listing task was used to assess participants' mental representations of food and drinks, and the possible role of simulations in these representations, or situated conceptualizations (Papies, 2013). Previous research using the feature listing paradigm has shown that participants describe objects by listing diverse features such as components of the object, visual properties, properties of background situations, and interoceptive states (Wu & Barsalou, 2009). In addition, when participants were asked to simply list typical properties, this led to similar types of properties being generated as asking participants to construct and describe a mental image of the object. This suggests that people spontaneously use conscious mental imagery, or nonconscious simulations, during feature listing (Wu & Barsalou, 2009).

Consumption and reward simulations of food. Applying this paradigm in the food domain (Papies, 2013) participants were asked to list typical features of four attractive foods and four neutral foods (e.g., chips, cookie; cucumber, rice), presented as food words, mixed with non-food filler items (e.g., mattress, sheep). All features were then coded in a hierarchical coding scheme, categorizing them as consumption and reward simulation features when they referred to the sensory properties of the food (e.g., taste, texture, temperature), eating context (e.g., time, social setting, physical setting) and immediate positive consequences (e.g., hedonic or bodily consequences). Non-eating simulation categories included visual features, purchase, preparation and storage features, features describing long-term consequences of eating a food, and category and linguistic features, and others. Again, participants were not instructed to simulate or imagine eating the food, or to describe an eating experience, but simply to describe the features that are typically true of the food. Therefore, if they list words that describe the mouthfeel of the food, or a specific eating situation, this may suggest that they simulate eating the food in a relevant context, and describe characteristics of that experience in the feature listing task.

The results of this study are in line with this account and suggest that participants spontaneously simulate eating the food they are asked to describe, especially if it is attractive. Specifically, the findings showed that participants listed large numbers of consumption and reward simulation features when describing the foods. This was especially the case for the attractive foods, where 53 percent of listed features were consumption and reward features, compared to 26 percent for the neutral foods. Neutral foods, on the other hand, were described more heavily in terms of visual features, and production and preparation features. As an example, for the food "chips," participants listed features such as *salty, crunchy, tasty, at night, with drinks*; whereas for the food "rice," participants listed features such as *white, small, long, from Asia, neutral taste, has to be cooked*. Additional analyses showed that for attractive foods, the proportion of consumption and reward simulation features correlated with their perceived attractiveness. These findings provide initial support for the hypothesis that attractive foods are represented through simulations of eating and enjoying them. From the perspective of the grounded cognition theory of desire, this may reflect people's own eating experiences, as well as vicarious learning through the eating experiences of others, and advertisements. Indeed, even menu descriptions of unhealthy foods have been shown to focus more on rewarding, sensory eating experiences than the descriptions for healthy food (Turnwald, Jurafsky, Conner,

& Crum, 2017), which may contribute to culturally shared representations of these foods.

Consumption and reward simulations of drinks. In a recent set of studies, we extended these findings to understanding the representations of non-alcoholic beverages (Rusz, Best, & Papies, 2019). Participants completed a feature listing task for two sugar-sweetened beverages, bottled water, tap water, and a number of control drinks. In one experiment, the feature listing was implemented with the standard instructions to "list features that are typically true of ...," and drinks were presented as words; in the other experiment, instructions were changed to ask participants "How would you describe this drink right now?," and images of drinks were presented. In both experiments, participants listed more consumption and reward features for the sugar-sweetened beverages than for water, with sensory features being particularly salient for the sugar-sweetened beverages. In addition, the proportion of consumption and reward features correlated with consumption frequency, especially for the sugary drinks. Thus, consuming a drink more often was associated with listing more consumption and reward simulation features, describing its taste, texture, mouthfeel, and hedonic and refreshing properties. In line with the findings for food, this again suggests that appetitive stimuli are represented in terms of consuming and enjoying them, and that these representations are learned from previous experiences.

Similar patterns have been observed for participants' representations of alcoholic drinks (Keesman et al., 2018). Here, we found that participants listed more consumption and reward features for alcoholic beverages that they frequently consume compared to alcohol they don't typically consume, and compared to water (but not compared to sugary drinks, which were again heavily represented in terms of sensory features). Critically, the alcoholic drinks were represented particularly in terms of sensory features and in terms of drinking context, more so than in terms of the immediate consequences of consumption, which include hedonic consequences. Within the category of context features, it was particularly the social context that dominated participants' descriptions, with example features being *friends* and *having a good time*. In other words, when asked to list features that are "typically true" of their typical alcoholic drink, participants were more likely to mention social drinking situations than the fact that it tastes good. These findings show that alcoholic drinks are strongly represented in terms of consuming them in social situations, or through situated consumption simulations.

Neural evidence for consumption and reward simulations. Neuroimaging research provides further evidence that food cues trigger consumption and reward simulations. Across a variety of studies, the processing of food images during fMRI activates the same brain areas that are implicated in actual eating (for reviews, see Chen, Papies, & Barsalou, 2016; van der Laan, de Ridder, Viergever, & Smeets, 2011). This "core eating network" involves, among others, the primary visual cortex and fusiform gyrus for viewing and recognizing the food in an image, the insula and frontal operculum as primary taste areas, the amygdale to attribute attentional salience, the orbitofrontal cortex and ventral striatum for reward prediction and experience, and the cerebellum for anticipated motor activity (Chen et al., 2016). From the grounded cognition perspective, and consistent with the feature listing findings reviewed above, this suggests that people simulate the taste and reward from a food when they process a food picture. Across studies, these brain activations in response to mere food pictures are especially pronounced for palatable foods, again suggesting that consumption and reward simulations are especially likely for attractive stimuli. Again, this may partially reflect direct eating experiences and culturally shared representations (see Turnwald, Jurafsky, et al., 2017), as well as an "evolutionary mismatch" such that our brains have evolved to respond strongly to high-calorie foods, while acting on these responses is not beneficial in today's food-rich environments (Stroebe, Papies, & Aarts, 2008; van Vugt, de Vries, & Li, 2020, this volume).

Consumption and Reward Simulations Contribute to Desire

The research discussed so far has demonstrated that attractive foods and drinks can elicit simulations of consuming and enjoying them. Next, I will review findings showing that these simulations in turn contribute to desire for these stimuli, and that this is again especially likely for attractive foods and drinks.

Correlational findings. In an initial test of the association between simulations and desire, we assessed the relation of consumption and reward simulation features produced for eight unhealthy food words with participants' self-reported desire for these foods. We found that, indeed, the proportion of consumption and reward simulation features predicted desire (Papies, Tatar, Best, Barsalou, & Tavoulari, 2018). Importantly, this relationship remained when controlling for participants' typical frequency of consuming each food, which itself was a strong predictor of desire to eat it. Thus, consumption and reward simulations explained unique variance in people's consumption motivation in addition to consumption habits.

In our recent experiments assessing representations of non-alcoholic beverages (Rusz et al., 2019), we also assessed desire by asking how much participants would currently like to drink each drink. We further assessed consumption habits by asking participants how often they typically consume each drink. As in the desire for food described above, we found that consumption habits were the strongest predictor of desire to consume a drink. In line with the grounded cognition theory of desire, however, when controlling for habits, consumption and reward simulations predicted desire for sugary drinks, but not for water. Together, these studies suggest that attractive foods and drinks are not only more likely to elicit consumption and reward simulations, but that these simulations are also more likely to predict the motivation to consume, compared to neutral foods and drinks.

We also assessed the relation between simulations and desire in the domain of alcohol. In the feature listing study described above (Keesman et al., 2018), we measured participants' desire to consume alcohol by assessing their current cravings, and by probing their preference for a voucher for an alcoholic drink or a non-alcoholic drink as an additional reward for participating in the study. In line with our findings that social context features were especially salient for frequently consumed alcoholic drinks, we found that these features were also correlated with alcohol cravings, and with participants' preference for an alcohol voucher, as a behavioral measure of alcohol desire. Social context features were also correlated with a higher frequency of intrusive alcohol-thoughts in participants' daily lives. Together, these findings suggest that thinking about alcohol in terms of the social situations one consumes it in makes it particularly attractive and hard to resist.

Experimental findings. While the work discussed so far has provided correlational evidence for the relation between consumption and reward simulations and desire, there is also some experimental evidence for this relationship, suggesting a causal effect. In one recent experiment, we used the amount of saliva in response to viewing foods as an implicit measure of desire (Keesman, Aarts, Vermeent, Häfner, & Papies, 2016). Salivary responses to food and food cues have been argued to reflect the body's preparation to eat (Nederkoorn, Smulders, & Jansen, 2000; Tepper, 1992), and can therefore be seen as a measure of desire. Critically, they occur without effort or intention on the part of the participant, and they are difficult or even impossible to control, thus showing key features of automatic measurement processes and implicit measures (De Houwer, Teige-Mocigemba, Spruyt, & Moors, 2009). Thus, simply measuring the amount of salivation produced in response to different foods may be particularly suited to studying the motivation to eat these foods, without effects of socially desirable responding. Participants in this experiment were exposed to three different food stimuli one at a time, namely a neutral food (bread with cheese), an attractive food (bowl of crisps), and a sour food (slice of lemon), in addition to a non-food stimulus for a baseline saliva measure (block of wood). Half of participants were instructed to merely look at the object for one minute, while the other half of participants were instructed to vividly imagine eating the object for one minute. During this time, participants let all saliva accumulate in the mouth, which was then spit into a cup and weighed by the experimenter. Afterwards, we assessed participants' eating simulations in response to each stimulus ("I imagined that I was eating the object"), as well as their desire ("I would have liked to eat the object").

In line with previous findings, we found that even without being instructed to imagine eating the food, participants reported stronger eating simulations for the attractive compared to the neutral and the sour food, and for neutral food compared to the non-food item. This again suggests that participants spontaneously simulate eating a food to which they are exposed, especially if this is attractive. The pattern for salivation was very similar, with higher salivation for the attractive than for the neutral food, and for the neutral food than for the non-food object. The level of salivation in response to the sour food was highest, probably reflecting the body's response to protect the teeth from the acidity of the lemon. Importantly, the instruction to imagine eating the object increased salivation for all stimuli, but most strongly for the attractive food. In other words, eating simulations increased the body's preparation to eat, especially when the presented food was attractive. Thus, both correlational and experimental evidence demonstrate that consumption simulations increase desire, especially for attractive food and drink.

We also tested whether eating and drinking simulations can be affected by cues signaling consumption situations. Appetitive stimuli are typically not encountered and enjoyed in isolation, but in rich situations that, according to the grounded cognition theory of desire, are stored as part of the situated conceptualizations of these stimuli. Thus, situational cues should be able to trigger consumption and reward simulations, or to increase the likelihood that an appetitive stimulus activates a situated conceptualization of consuming and enjoying a food or drink, and therefore increase consumption simulations and desire.

To test whether information about consumption situations can indeed affect desire, we conducted an experiment comparing situated and non-situated alcohol stimuli. We manipulated whether a variety of alcoholic drinks were presented in a congruent drinking context (e.g., an ale in a pub), an incongruent drinking context (e.g., a cocktail in a business meeting), or no context. Participants were assigned to one of these conditions and briefly immersed themselves in each image, before rating their consumption simulations ("I imagined that I was drinking the …," "It was as if I could taste the …") and desire. Results showed that desire was higher for drinks presented in a congruent compared to an incongruent context, with the no-context control condition in between. Importantly, the effect of congruence on desire was mediated by consumption simulations. In other words, an image of an appropriate drinking situation increased participants' spontaneous simulations of drinking the alcohol presented, which in turn increased desire to drink it. In a similar series of experiments in the domain of food, we found that presenting a food in a congruent eating context, compared to an incongruent or no context, increased eating simulations, expected liking, salivation, and desire (Papies, Stekelenburg, Smeets, Zandstra, & Dijksterhuis, 2019). Context had an indirect effect on expected liking, desire, and actual liking, through eating simulations. In other words, viewing a food in a matching eating context increased simulations of eating it, which increased desire to eat it and actual enjoyment. This is in line with the grounded cognition theory of desire, as it suggests that situational information is stored along with information of the sensory features of products, and can contribute to rewarding re-experiences and desire through pattern completion inferences. These experiments provide further evidence that consumption and reward simulations, which can be enhanced by context features, play a key role in the emergence of desire in response to appetitive cues.

Findings from food marketing. Evidence from the domain of marketing research shows that specific motor simulations, for example of picking up a food, may also play an important role in desire. These findings extend previous work showing that people spontaneously simulate interacting with objects they are presented with in their habitual way, for example picking up a teapot with one's dominant hand (Tucker & Ellis, 1998). Indeed, for images of both household products and food, people spontaneously simulate picking them up and engaging with or consuming them with their dominant hand, and being able to do this contributes to their preference for these products or their motivation to consume them (Eelen, Dewitte, & Warlop, 2013; Elder & Krishna, 2012). As an example, when the fork next to a piece of apple pie or the spoon in a bowl of yoghurt face the dominant hand of the perceiver, this increases spontaneous eating simulations and purchase intentions for desirable products. However, when the dominant hand is blocked, for example because participants press a clamp in their hand, this effect disappears (Elder & Krishna, 2012) – presumably because blocking the physical resource required for the action of picking up the spoon or fork interferes with mentally simulating this action, in turn reducing desire for the food. Other work, too, has shown that preventing the simulation of holding or interacting with a food or drink by occupying one's dominant hand can reduce the perceived attractiveness of the objects; conversely, engaging in relevant movements (e.g., approaching an image) or holding an object that facilitates interacting with the food can increase desire (Shen & Sengupta, 2012; Shen, Zhang, & Krishna, 2016). These findings suggest that motor simulations of picking up a food, as a specific aspect of consumption simulations, play an important role in the desire for food.

Finally, research on food labels and food descriptions provides further support for the role of simulations in desire, albeit indirectly. Field experiments by Turnwald, Boles, and Crum (2017) and Turnwald and Crum (2019), for example, have shown that labeling vegetable-based dishes with sensory-focused terms (e.g., "Sweet Sizzlin' Green Beans and Crispy Shallots"), compared to health-focused terms (e.g., "Light 'n Low Carb Green Beans and Shallots"), increased consumers' choices and taste ratings of these dishes. Research from our own lab further suggests that eating simulations may be underlying these effects, as self-reported eating simulations in response to such labels correlated strongly with desire (Papies et al., 2018). Conversely, foods that are labeled by emphasizing their healthy features, for example being low in salt or low in fat, are expected by consumers to taste less salty and fatty and to be liked less. Consequently, they are indeed liked less in taste tests, compared to the same products without such health-relevant labels (e.g., Kahkonen & Tuorila, 1998; Liem, Miremadi, Zandstra, & Keast, 2012). These findings make sense from a simulation perspective, as they suggest that the health labels induce a specific simulation of eating food low in salt or fat, based on previous experiences, which is likely associated with reduced reward. Even though these simulations may not reach conscious awareness, they nevertheless affect expectancies and actual experiences of a product.

Previous work indeed supports the account that eating simulations created by food descriptions and food labels may create expectancies around the sensory and hedonic properties of a food, which then affect motivation to consume, and also actual consumption experiences. The central role of expectancies was demonstrated in a seminal study by Yeomans and colleagues (2008), who offered their participants a novel food; smoked salmon ice-cream. When this was presented as "ice-cream," it was liked much less than when it was presented as "frozen savoury mousse" or with the uninformative label "Food 386," as the label "ice-cream" led to the expectation of a sweet and fruity flavor. Thus, it seems that the eating simulations that are triggered by food labels can be experienced as expectancies of what a food will taste like, which then affect actual experiences.

Consistent with this reasoning, neuro-imaging research (Grabenhorst, Rolls, & Bilderbeck, 2008) has shown that tasting a savoury solution that is labeled as having a "rich and delicious flavor" leads to higher pleasantness ratings and stronger associated reward activations in the brain, compared to tasting the same solution labeled as "boiled vegetable water." Similarly, tasting orange juice labeled as "extra sweet," compared with the same juice labeled as "less sweet," was associated with stronger activations in primary taste areas and higher sweetness ratings (Woods et al., 2011). Thus, food labels may trigger very specific sensory and reward simulations, which are then superimposed on the actual taste perception and affect consumer experience (for similar effects in the domain of color, see Hansen, Olkkonen, Walter, & Gegenfurtner, 2006). Such experiences, in turn, will update existing situated conceptualizations of the products involved, and affect future consumption decisions.

Targeting Consumption and Reward Simulations can Reduce Desire

The research discussed so far has described how simulations are triggered by external cues, how they are based on previous experiences, and how they contribute to desires for foods and drinks. What are the implications of these findings for self-regulation? Given that desires often lead to costly self-control conflicts, how can problematic desires be prevented, or how can they be reduced once they have arisen?

Cueing and training interventions. In previous work, I have introduced the distinction between cueing interventions and training interventions to target the nonconscious processes that often lead to self-control failure (Papies, 2016a, 2016b, 2017b), to facilitate the development of interventions that are grounded in strong theory and fundamental research (Fiedler, 2020, this volume). In brief, this approach assumes that the failure to enact conscious intentions in health behavior (i.e., the intention-behavior gap) often results from situational cues triggering nonconscious cognitive processes that affect behavior outside of conscious awareness. As an example, while a consumer may have the intention to purchase only healthy, unprocessed foods during grocery shopping, a highly salient promotion of savoury snacks in the store may lead to an impulsive purchase of unhealthy foods, thereby creating an intention-behavior gap. From this perspective, to prevent such effects and thus bridge the intention-behavior gap, interventions should either change the situational cues (e.g., remove salient promotions of unhealthy foods; see Best & Papies, 2017) or change the cognitive structures that lead to unhealthy behaviors when triggered by situational cues (e.g., reduce the positive affect or approach impulses associated with unhealthy foods). I will now discuss cueing and training interventions in more detail, and address how they relate to consumption and reward simulations.

Effective cueing interventions should be designed to ensure that external cues no longer trigger consumption and reward simulations that lead to problematic desires. As discussed in Best & Papies (2017), such "cueing interventions" have been implemented successfully, for example, in the domain of smoking, where the introduction of bland packaging for cigarettes, and the salience of other people smoking and of smoking paraphernalia through smoking bans in public spaces, has markedly reduced the prevalence of smoking and rates of uptake among adolescents. Such interventions targeting the micro-environment around where a consumer behavior takes place (Hollands et al., 2017) have the benefit that they can easily be scaled up to affect large groups of consumers at relatively low cost. Again, their effectiveness rests in ensuring that external cues don't trigger problematic consumption and reward simulations, either by removing "tempting" cues, or by introducing cues that will reduce the reward of appetitive cues (e.g., cues that activate health goals, or health implications of an appetitive stimulus; see Best & Papies, 2017; Stroebe, van Koningsbruggen, Papies, & Aarts, 2013). Cueing interventions can also be used to trigger consumption and reward simulations for desirable foods and drinks, as recent work has shown that, for example, food labels that trigger consumption and reward simulations can increase the attractiveness and choice of meat-free foods (Papies, Daneva, & Semyte, 2019; Turnwald & Crum, 2019; see Walton & Brady, this volume, for other "positive" interventions that may work through changing the situated conceptualizations that are activated to interpret a situation).

Alternatively, "training interventions" can be designed to change the situated conceptualizations that lead to problematic desires and behaviors once they are activated by situational cues (Papies, 2016b, 2017b). For example, a computerized training where one repeatedly processes negative affective stimuli along with specific foods or drinks (i.e., evaluative conditioning), or repeatedly withholds motor approach responses to tempting stimuli (i.e., inhibitory control training) could change the content of one's situated conceptualizations involving those food or drink items, such that they are less likely to later evoke problematic desires or approach impulses (e.g., Hollands & Marteau, 2015; Stice, Lawrence, Kemps, & Veling, 2016). Thus, the goal of these types of interventions is to reduce the likelihood that problematic desires or appetitive behaviors are enacted automatically in response to external cues.

Mindfulness-based training interventions. Recently, we have specifically investigated the potential of mindfulness-based training interventions to reduce impulses, cravings, and choices of attractive, unhealthy foods. In these brief interventions, participants are shown images of attractive foods, among other stimuli, and are instructed to observe all responses that they may have to these stimuli as "mere mental events." Specifically, without any mention of mindfulness or meditation, they are asked to simply notice all thoughts, emotions, and experiences in response to the pictures, and to consider them as mental states that arise and dissipate, without one having to act on them (Papies, 2017a; Papies, Barsalou, & Custers, 2012; Papies et al., 2015). In essence, then, participants are trained to observe their consumption and reward simulations, and to see them come and go (Keesman, Aarts, Häfner, & Papies, 2017; Papies et al., 2015; Tapper, 2017). Indeed, participants' responses to open-ended questions in various studies show that this is indeed what happens, as participants describe observing thoughts about eating the food, enjoying its taste and texture, and eating situations (e.g., Keesman, Aarts, Häfner, & Papies, 2019). Results from two sets of experiments show that applying this so-called "decentering" perspective to various food stimuli in a training phase can reduce impulsive approach responses, hypothetical and actual choices, and explicit cravings for unhealthy foods to the same and similar food stimuli in a subsequent test phase (Papies et al., 2012, 2015). Similar work has suggested that applying such a "decentering" or "cognitive defusion" approach to chocolate can reduce chocolate consumption over a five-day period (Jenkins & Tapper, 2014), and that it can also reduce cravings for addictive substances (e.g., cigarettes; Westbrook et al., 2013). Among experienced meditators, the degree to which they report spontaneously applying a "decentered" perspective to food thoughts throughout their daily lives is associated with reduced food cravings (Keesman, Papies, Aarts, & Häfner, 2019; Papies, Winckel, & Keesman, 2016).

Recent work provides more insight into the mechanisms underlying these effects. In a series of studies (Keesman, Aarts, et al., 2019), participants were instructed to first retrieve a memory of an attractive food, or in another study, they were exposed to a tasty snack on the table in front of them. Then, they were asked to apply the "decentering" perspective of viewing their thoughts as mere mental events, or a control perspective. We then measured the strength and vividness of participants' imagery of eating the food (i.e., their consumption simulations), as well as their cravings, by assessing self-reported food cravings and salivation in response to the food. Results showed that applying decentering did not reduce consumption and reward simulations compared to the control perspective, but it reduced cravings and salivation (Keesman, Aarts, et al., 2019). Indeed, our ongoing work suggests that applying decentering reduces the association between consumption and reward simulations and desire (Tatar, Barsalou, & Papies, 2019). In other words, applying decentering does not reduce the degree to which participants spontaneously think about eating and enjoying the food, but it reduces the degree to which these thoughts lead to desire to actually consume the food.

These findings suggest that the mechanisms underlying decentering effects may be slightly different than those of another prominent technique to address consumption simulations or imagery, namely loading working memory. Food cravings and the underlying conscious consumption imagery require working memory capacity, especially its visual subcomponent (Harvey, Kemps, & Tiggemann, 2005; Meule, Skirde, Freund, Vögele, & Kübler, 2012). This is consistent with predictions of the elaborated intrusion theory of desire (Kavanagh et al., 2005). Importantly, substantial research on interventions derived from this theory has shown that once food cravings have been induced, loading working memory, for example, by visual imagery instructions or visually demanding tasks, can effectively reduce cravings (e.g., Andrade, Pears, May, & Kavanagh, 2012; Hamilton, Fawson, May, Andrade, & Kavanagh, 2013; Kemps, Tiggemann, & Christianson, 2008). Presumably, working memory load reduces cravings because it interferes with the imagery that sustains them – in contrast to "decentering" interventions that, rather than reducing imagery itself, reduce its effect on desire.

Together, research so far on "decentering" and working memory load as intervention tools seems to suggest that targeting consumption and reward simulations early on can *prevent* their effect to produce cravings, and that targeting conscious consumption and reward imagery can *reduce* cravings, once they have fully developed. In any case, conscious and nonconscious simulations of eating and enjoying a food contribute to problematic desires, and tools that target these simulations are promising in the context of health interventions.

Summary and Future Research

This chapter has reviewed research on key predictions of the grounded cognition theory of desire, which proposes that consumption and reward simulations contribute to desire. The studies have shown that people spontaneously describe food and drink in terms of sensory, contextual, and hedonic features of consuming it, especially if they consume it often, and especially if it is attractive. Images of attractive food have been shown to activate the same brain areas for sensory and reward processing that are involved in actually eating attractive food, again suggesting that people simulate eating when they process food cues. These consumption and reward simulations, whether indexed by participants' spontaneous descriptions or self-reports, or experimentally induced, contribute to the motivation to consume the respective foods and drinks, again especially if they are attractive. Labeling products with words that reflect consumption and reward simulations, or showing products in background situations that facilitate such simulations, increases simulations and in turn, desire. Finally, interventions that target consumption and reward simulations, either by diffusing them as "mere mental events" or by reducing the working memory capacity needed to sustain them as conscious mental imagery, can prevent and reduce problematic cravings.

Key areas for future research include, for example, the degree of automaticity of these consumption and reward simulations. Previous research has suggested that simulations may require some cognitive resources, as research has shown that the hedonic value of attractive foods is not fully activated if a perceiver is under high cognitive load (Van Dillen, Papies, & Hofmann, 2013). However, no work so far has tested directly whether, for example, working memory capacity affects consumption and reward simulations in a similar way as it affects conscious mental imagery (Harvey et al., 2005). Future research should also examine in more detail how rewarding simulations of long-term goal pursuit can most effectively be stimulated (Andrade, Khalil, Dickson, May, & Kavanagh, 2016), and whether techniques that have been shown to validate or invalidate attitudes, for example nodding or shaking one's head while processing attitudinal messages, similarly affect how people relate to simulations (see Petty & Briñol, 2020, this volume). Related to this, little is known about how individual differences in health motivation affect consumption and reward simulations, and how external reminders of long-term goals (e.g., health goal primes) affect simulations that typically contribute to problematic desires.

Finally, future work could integrate this perspective with related research on simulations in social psychology more broadly. Simulations could play a role, for example in prejudice reduction, prosocial behavior, action control, episodic future thinking, the anticipation of reward from social media behavior or substance use, deciding whether one will fit into a prospective workplace, or preventing aggressive behavior if one anticipates that aggression is not accepted by one's peers (e.g., Atance & O'Neill, 2001; Blanton, Burrows, & Regan, 2020, this volume; Crisp & Turner, 2009; Gaesser, Shimura, & Cikara, 2019; Krahé, 2020, this volume; Kross & Chandhok, 2020, this volume; Martiny-Huenger, Martiny, Parks-Stamm, Pfeiffer, & Gollwitzer, 2017; Schmader, Bergsieker, & Hall, 2020, this volume). Establishing these mechanisms in more detail could help to generate a comprehensive account of the role of simulations in motivated behavior, and thus facilitate effective, empirically-grounded interventions.

References

Andrade, J., Khalil, M., Dickson, J., May, J., & Kavanagh, D. J. (2016). Functional Imagery Training to reduce snacking: Testing a novel motivational intervention based on Elaborated Intrusion theory. *Appetite*, *100*, 256–262. doi.org/10.1016/j.appet.2016.02.015

Andrade, J., Pears, S., May, J., & Kavanagh, D. J. (2012). Use of a clay modeling task to reduce chocolate craving. *Appetite*, *58*(3), 955–963. doi.org/10.1016/j.appet.2012.02.044

Atance, C. M., & O'Neill, D. K. (2001). Episodic future thinking. *Trends in Cognitive Sciences*, *5*(12), 533–539. doi.org/10.1016/S1364-6613(00)01804-0

Barsalou, L. W. (2003). Situated simulation in the human conceptual system. *Language and Cognitive Processes*, *18*, 513–562.

Barsalou, L. W. (2009). Simulation, situated conceptualization, and prediction. *Philosophical Transactions of the Royal Society B: Biological Sciences*, *364*(1521), 1281–1289. doi.org/10.1098/rstb.2008.0319

Barsalou, L. W. (2016). Situated conceptualization offers a theoretical account of social priming. *Current Opinion in Psychology*, *12*, 6–11.

Best, M., & Papies, E. K. (2017). Right here, right now: Situated interventions to change consumer habits. *Journal of the Association for Consumer Research*, *2*(3), 333–358.

Blanton, H., Burrows, C. N., & Regan, T. (2020). Call of duty – The tobacco wars. In J. Fargas, W. D. Kano, and K. Fiedler (Eds), *Applications of social psychology* (pp. 107–123). New York: Routledge.

Chen, J., Papies, E. K., & Barsalou, L. W. (2016). A core eating network and its modulations underlie diverse eating phenomena. *Brain and Cognition*, *110*, 20–42. doi.org/10.1016/j.bandc.2016.04.004

Crisp, R. J., & Turner, R. N. (2009). Can imagined interactions produce positive perceptions? Reducing prejudice through simulated social contact. *American Psychologist*, *64*(4), 231–240. doi.org/10.1037/a0014718

De Houwer, J., Teige-Mocigemba, S., Spruyt, A., & Moors, A. (2009). Implicit measures: A normative analysis and review. *Psychological Bulletin*, *135*(3), 347–368.

Eelen, J., Dewitte, S., & Warlop, L. (2013). Situated embodied cognition: Monitoring orientation cues affects product evaluation and choice. *Journal of Consumer Psychology*, *23*(4), 424–433. doi.org/10.1016/j.jcps.2013.04.004

Elder, R. S., & Krishna, A. (2012). The "visual depiction effect" in advertising: Facilitating embodied mental simulation through product orientation. *Journal of Consumer Research*, *38*(6), 988–1003. doi.org/10.1086/661531

Fiedler, K. (2020). Grounding applied social psychology in translational research. In J. Fargas, W. D. Kano, and K. Fiedler (Eds), *Applications of social psychology* (pp. 23–39). New York: Routledge.

Gaesser, B., Shimura, Y., & Cikara, M. (2019). Episodic simulation reduces intergroup bias in prosocial intention and behavior. *Journal of Personality and Social Psychology*.

Grabenhorst, F., Rolls, E. T., & Bilderbeck, A. (2008). How cognition modulates affective responses to taste and flavor: Top-down influences on the orbitofrontal and pregenual cingulate cortices. *Cerebral Cortex*, *18*(7), 1549–1559. doi.org/10.1093/cercor/bhm185

Hamilton, J., Fawson, S., May, J., Andrade, J., & Kavanagh, D. J. (2013). Brief guided imagery and body scanning interventions reduce food cravings. *Appetite*, *71*, 158–162. doi.org/10.1016/j.appet.2013.08.005

Hansen, T., Olkkonen, M., Walter, S., & Gegenfurtner, K. R. (2006). Memory modulates color appearance. *Nature Neuroscience*, *9*(11), 1367–1368. doi.org/10.1038/nn1794

Harvey, K., Kemps, E., & Tiggemann, M. (2005). The nature of imagery processes underlying food cravings. *British Journal of Health Psychology*, *10*(1), 49–56. doi.org/10.1348/135910704X14249

Hofmann, W., Baumeister, R. F., Förster, G., & Vohs, K. D. (2012). Everyday temptations: An experience sampling study of desire, conflict, and self-control. *Journal of Personality and Social Psychology*, *102*(6), 1318–1335. doi.org/10.1037/a0026545

Hofmann, W., Vohs, K. D., & Baumeister, R. F. (2012). What people desire, feel conflicted about, and try to resist in everyday life. *Psychological Science*, *23*(6), 582–588. doi.org/10.1177/0956797612437426

Hollands, G. J., Bignardi, G., Johnston, M., Kelly, M. P., Ogilvie, D., Petticrew, M., ... Marteau, T. M. (2017). The TIPPME intervention typology for changing environments to change behaviour. *Nature Human Behaviour*, *1*, 1–9. doi.org/10.1038/s41562-017-0140

Hollands, G. J., & Marteau, T. M. (2016). Pairing images of unhealthy and healthy foods with images of negative and positive health consequences: Impact on attitudes and food choice. *Health Psychology*, *35*(8), 847–851. doi.org/10.1037/hea0000293

Jenkins, K. T., & Tapper, K. (2014). Resisting chocolate temptation using a brief mindfulness strategy. *British Journal of Health Psychology*, *19*(3), 509–522. doi.org/10.1111/bjhp.12050

Kahkonen, P., & Tuorila, H. (1998). Effect of reduced-fat information on expected and actual hedonic and sensory ratings of sausage. *Appetite*, *30*(1), 13–23. doi.org/10.1006/appe.1997.0104

Kavanagh, D. J., Andrade, J., & May, J. (2005). Imaginary relish and exquisite torture: The elaborated intrusion theory of desire. *Psychological Review*, *112*(2), 446–467.

Keesman, M., Aarts, H., Häfner, M., & Papies, E. K. (2017). Mindfulness reduces reactivity to food cues: Underlying mechanisms and applications in daily life. *Current Addiction Reports*, *4*(2), 151–157. doi.org/10.1007/s40429-017-0134-2

Keesman, M., Aarts, H., Häfner, M., & Papies, E. K. (2019). Decentering reduces reactions to mental imagery. *Motivation Science*.

Keesman, M., Aarts, H., Ostafin, B. D., Verwei, S., Häfner, M., & Papies, E. K. (2018). Alcohol representations are socially situated: An investigation of beverage representations by using a property generation task. *Appetite*, *120*, 654–665. doi.org/10.1016/j.appet.2017.10.019

Keesman, M., Aarts, H., Vermeent, S., Häfner, M., & Papies, E. K. (2016). Consumption simulations induce salivation to food cues. *PLoS One*, *11*(11), e0165449. doi.org/10.1371/journal.pone.0165449

Keesman, M., Papies, E. K., Aarts, H., & Häfner, M. (2019). *Benefits of meditation experience on resilience and craving occur through decentering but not awareness*. Manuscript in preparation.

Kemps, E., Tiggemann, M., & Christianson, R. (2008). Concurrent visuo-spatial processing reduces food cravings in prescribed weight-loss dieters. *Journal of Behavior Therapy and Experimental Psychiatry*, *39*(2), 177–186. doi.org/10.1016/j.jbtep.2007.03.001

Krahé, B. (2020). The development of aggressive behavior in childhood and adolescence: A social interactionist perspective. In J. Fargas, W. D. Kano, and K. Fiedler (Eds), *Applications of social psychology* (pp. 124–141). New York: Routledge.

Kross, E., & Chandhok, S. (2020). How do online social networks influence people's emotional lives? In J. Fargas, W. D. Kano, and K. Fiedler (Eds), *Applications of social psychology* (pp. 250–263). New York: Routledge.

Liem, D. G., Miremadi, F., Zandstra, E. H., & Keast, R. S. (2012). Health labelling can influence taste perception and use of table salt for reduced-sodium products. *Public Health Nutrition*, *15*(12), 2340–2347. doi.org/10.1017/S136898001200064X

Martiny-Huenger, T., Martiny, S. E., Parks-Stamm, E. J., Pfeiffer, E., & Gollwitzer, P. M. (2017). From conscious thought to automatic action: A simulation account of action planning. *Journal of Experimental Psychology: General, 146*(10), 1513–1525. doi.org/10.1037/xge0000344

Meule, A., Skirde, A. K., Freund, R., Vögele, C., & Kübler, A. (2012). High-calorie food-cues impair working memory performance in high and low food cravers. *Appetite, 59*(2), 264–269. doi.org/10.1016/j.appet.2012.05.010

Nederkoorn, C., Smulders, F. T. Y., & Jansen, A. (2000). Cephalic phase responses, craving and food intake in normal subjects. *Appetite, 35*(1), 45–55. doi.org/10.1006/appe.2000.0328

Papies, E. K. (2013). Tempting food words activate eating simulations. *Frontiers in Psychology, 4*, 838. doi.org/10.3389/fpsyg.2013.00838

Papies, E. K. (2016a). Goal priming as a situated intervention tool. *Current Opinion in Psychology, 12*, 12–16. doi.org/10.1016/j.copsyc.2016.04.008

Papies, E. K. (2016b). Health goal priming as a situated intervention tool: How to benefit from nonconscious motivational routes to health behaviour. *Health Psychology Review, 10*(4), 408–424. doi.org/10.1080/17437199.2016.1183506

Papies, E. K. (2017a). Mindfulness and health behavior: Examining the roles of attention regulation and decentering. In *Current issues in social psychology. Mindfulness in social psychology* (pp. 94–108). London: Routledge.

Papies, E. K. (2017b). Situating interventions to bridge the intention-behaviour gap: A framework for recruiting nonconscious processes for behaviour change. *Social and Personality Psychology Compass, 11*(7), e12323. doi.org/10.1111/spc3.12323

Papies, E. K., & Barsalou, L. W. (2015). Grounding desire and motivated behavior: A theoretical framework and review of empirical evidence. In *The psychology of desire* (pp. 36–60). New York, NY: Guilford Press.

Papies, E. K., Barsalou, L. W., & Custers, R. (2012). Mindful attention prevents mindless impulses. *Social Psychological and Personality Science, 3*(3), 291–299. doi.org/10.1177/1948550611419031

Papies, E. K., Best, M., Gelibter, E., & Barsalou, L. W. (2017). The role of simulations in consumer experiences and behavior: Insights from the grounded cognition theory of desire. *Journal of the Association for Consumer Research, 2*(4), 402–418. doi.org/10.1086/693110

Papies, E. K., Daneva, T., & Semyte, G. (2019). *Using consumption and reward simulations to increase sustainable food choices*. Manuscript in preparation.

Papies, E. K., Pronk, T. M., Keesman, M., & Barsalou, L. W. (2015). The benefits of simply observing: Mindful attention modulates the link between motivation and behavior. *Journal of Personality and Social Psychology, 108*(1), 148–170. doi.org/10.1037/a0038032

Papies, E. K., Stekelenburg, A. van, Smeets, M. A. M., Zandstra, L., & Dijksterhuis, G. B. (2019). *Context cues increase desire for food through eating simulations*. Manuscript under review.

Papies, E. K., Tatar, B., Best, M., Barsalou, L. W., & Tavoulari, A. (2018). *Consumption and reward simulations lead to desire*. Manuscript in preparation.

Papies, E. K., Winckel, M. van, & Keesman, M. (2016). Food-specific decentering experiences are associated with reduced food cravings in meditators: A preliminary investigation. *Mindfulness, 7*(5), 1123–1131. doi.org/10.1007/s12671-016-0554-4

Petty, R. E., & Briñol, P. (2020). A process approach to influencing attitudes and changing behavior: Revisiting classic findings in persuasion and popular interventions. In J. Fargas, W. D. Kano, and K. Fiedler (Eds), *Applications of social psychology* (pp. 82-103). New York: Routledge.

Rusz, D., Best, M., & Papies, E. K. (2019). *The role of consumption and reward simulations in the motivation for sugar-sweetened beverages*. Manuscript in preparation.

Schmader, T., Bergsieker, H. B., & Hall, W. M. (2020). Cracking the culture code: A tri-level model for cultivating inclusion in organizations. In J. Fargas, W. D. Kano, and K. Fiedler (Eds), *Applications of social psychology* (pp. 334-355). New York: Routledge.

Shen, H., & Sengupta, J. (2012). If you can't grab it, it won't grab you: The effect of restricting the dominant hand on target evaluations. *Journal of Experimental Social Psychology, 48*(2), 525–529. doi.org/10.1016/j.jesp.2011.11.003

Shen, H., Zhang, M., & Krishna, A. (2016). Computer interfaces and the "direct-touch" effect: Can iPads increase the choice of hedonic food? *Journal of Marketing Research, 53*(5), 745–758. doi.org/10.1509/jmr.14.0563

Stice, E., Lawrence, N. S., Kemps, E., & Veling, H. (2016). Training motor responses to food: A novel treatment for obesity targeting implicit processes. *Clinical Psychology Review, 49*, 16–27. doi.org/10.1016/j.cpr.2016.06.005

Stroebe, W., Papies, E. K., & Aarts, H. (2008). From homeostatic to hedonic theories of eating: Self-regulatory failure in food-rich environments. *Applied Psychology: Health and Well-Being, 57*, 172–193.

Stroebe, W., van Koningsbruggen, G. M., Papies, E. K., & Aarts, H. (2013). Why most dieters fail but some succeed: A goal conflict model of eating behavior. *Psychological Review, 120*(1), 110–138. doi.org/10.1037/a0030849

Tapper, K. (2017). Can mindfulness influence weight management related eating behaviors? If so, how? *Clinical Psychology Review, 53*, 122–134. doi.org/10.1016/j.cpr.2017.03.003

Tatar, B., Barsalou, L. W., & Papies, E. K. (2019). *The effects of domain-specific and general decentering inductions on food cravings*. Manuscript in preparation.

Tepper, B. J. (1992). Dietary restraint and responsiveness to sensory-based food cues as measured by cephalic phase salivation and sensory specific satiety. *Physiology and Behavior, 52*(2), 305–311.

Tucker, M., & Ellis, R. (1998). On the relations between seen objects and components of potential actions. *Journal of Experimental Psychology: Human Perception and Performance, 24*(3), 830–846. doi.org/10.1037/0096-1523.24.3.830

Turnwald, B. P., Boles, D. Z., & Crum, A. J. (2017). Association between indulgent descriptions and vegetable consumption: Twisted carrots and dynamite beets. *JAMA Internal Medicine, 177*(8), 1216–1218. doi.org/10.1001/jamainternmed.2017.1637

Turnwald, B. P., & Crum, A. J. (2019). Smart food policy for healthy food labeling: Leading with taste, not healthiness, to shift consumption and enjoyment of healthy foods. *Preventive Medicine, 119*, 7–13. doi.org/10.1016/j.ypmed.2018.11.021

Turnwald, B. P., Jurafsky, D., Conner, A., & Crum, A. J. (2017). Reading between the menu lines: Are restaurants' descriptions of "healthy" foods unappealing? *Health Psychology, 36*(11), 1034–1037. doi.org/10.1037/hea0000501

van der Laan, L. N., de Ridder, D. T. D., Viergever, M. A., & Smeets, P. A. M. (2011). The first taste is always with the eyes: A meta-analysis on the neural correlates of processing visual food cues. *NeuroImage, 55*(1), 296–303. doi.org/10.1016/j.neuroimage.2010.11.055

Van Dillen, L. F., Papies, E. K., & Hofmann, W. (2013). Turning a blind eye to temptation: How task load can facilitate self-regulation. *Journal of Personality and Social Psychology, 104*(3), 427–443.

van Vugt, M., de Vries, L. P., & Li, N. P. (2020). The evolutionary mismatch hypothesis: Implications for applied social psychology. In J. Fargas, W. D. Kano, and K. Fiedler (Eds), *Applications of social psychology* (pp. 40–57). New York: Routledge.

Walton, G. M., & Brady, S. T. (2020). "Bad" things reconsidered. In J. Fargas, W. D. Kano, and K. Fiedler (Eds), *Applications of social psychology* (pp. 58-81). New York: Routledge.

Westbrook, C., Creswell, J. D., Tabibnia, G., Julson, E., Kober, H., & Tindle, H. A. (2013). Mindful attention reduces neural and self-reported cue-induced craving in smokers. *Social Cognitive and Affective Neuroscience, 8*(1), 73–84. doi.org/10.1093/scan/nsr076

Wilson-Mendenhall, C. D., Barrett, L. F., Simmons, W. K., & Barsalou, L. W. (2011). Grounding emotion in situated conceptualization. *Neuropsychologia, 49*(5), 1105–1127. doi.org/10.1016/j.neuropsychologia.2010.12.032

Woods, A. T., Lloyd, D. M., Kuenzel, J., Poliakoff, E., Dijksterhuis, G. B., & Thomas, A. (2011). Expected taste intensity affects response to sweet drinks in primary taste cortex: *NeuroReport, 22*(8), 365–369. doi.org/10.1097/WNR.0b013e3283469581

Wu, L., & Barsalou, L. W. (2009). Perceptual simulation in conceptual combination: Evidence from property generation. *Acta Psychologica, 132*(2), 173–189. doi.org/10.1016/j.actpsy.2009.02.002

Yeomans, M. R., Chambers, L., Blumenthal, H., & Blake, A. (2008). The role of expectancy in sensory and hedonic evaluation: The case of smoked salmon ice-cream. *Food Quality and Preference, 19*(6), 565–573. doi.org/10.1016/j.foodqual.2008.02.009

9
IN SYNC WITH YOUR SHRINK

Grounding Psychotherapy in Interpersonal Synchrony

Sander L. Koole, Dana Atzil-Slonim, Emily Butler, Suzanne Dikker, Wolfgang Tschacher and Tom Wilderjans

Every day, millions of people worldwide turn to psychotherapy to deal with a wide variety of mental health problems, including depression, anxiety disorders, psychotic disorders, eating disorders, personality disorders, and substance abuse (see also Crano & Ruybal; Walton; and Papies, this volume). Although there are over a thousand psychotherapies, virtually all of them involve structured interactions between a patient (or patients) and a therapist. The working relationship between patient and therapist is thus a central part of psychotherapy. Indeed, the quality of the therapeutic relationship ranks among the most robust predictors of better outcomes in psychotherapy (Horvath, Del Rey, Flückiger, & Symonds, 2011).

What determines whether patient and therapist in psychotherapy establish a good working relationship? In the present chapter, we suggest that the answer to this question may be found in basic processes of social psychology, the scientific discipline that studies how people relate with one another (see also Fiedler, this volume). In particular, we highlight the significance of *interpersonal synchrony* as a foundational principle to establish a beneficial working relationship between patient and therapist. Interpersonal synchrony is defined here as the temporal coordination of social agents' mutual behavioral, physiological, and neurological functions. By synchronizing their functioning, patient and therapist may find themselves "on the same wavelength" and literally "in sync" with another. This, in turn, may contribute to therapeutic goals and self-regulatory skills of the patient, especially when it comes to the patient's ability to self-regulate her or his emotional states.

The remainder of this chapter is organized into five parts. In Part 1, we begin by briefly reviewing clinical-psychological research on psychotherapy. In this review, we focus especially on research that pertains to the working relationship between patient and therapist, also known as the *therapeutic alliance*. In Part 2, we turn to social-psychological research on interpersonal synchrony, zooming in on the question of how this basic research can be used to understand the alliance between patient and therapist. In Part 3, we show how the clinical- and social-psychological literatures are integrated in the INterpersonal SYNChrony (IN-SYNC) model of psychotherapy (Koole & Tschacher, 2016). In Part 4, we review empirical research that bears on the IN-SYNC model. Finally, in Part 5, we summarize our main conclusions and consider the broader implications of this work for social psychology and its applications.

Part 1: The Alliance

The working relationship between patient and therapist has inspired an extensive literature in clinical psychology, where it is designated by various terms such as the alliance, the therapeutic bond, therapeutic relationship, treatment alliance, helping alliance, or working alliance. Research on the alliance has a long and rich history, a history that continues to color scientific debates in the present day and age. We therefore briefly consider the historical development of alliance research, after which we review the main findings of modern alliance research.

Historical Background

The importance of the patient-therapist relationship has been noted since the first psychotherapies were pioneered by psychoanalysts, around the start of the 20th century (Elvins & Green, 2008). The founder of the psychoanalytic movement, Sigmund Freud, discussed the importance of the analyst maintaining a supportive attitude toward the patient (Freud, 1912). Freud further observed that the patient may transfer experiences from earlier relationships into her or his dealings with the therapist. These early observations, particularly the notion of transference, were subsequently elaborated and translated into theoretical models of the patient-therapist relationship (Shedler, 2010). The psychoanalytic tradition has thus emphasized the patient's contributions to the alliance.

The rise of experimental psychology during the 20th century led to the development of new behavioral treatments in the 1950s, complemented by cognitive therapies in the 1960s and 1970s (Keegan & Holas, 2009). The resulting cognitive-behavioral tradition focused on problematic behaviors and maladaptive thinking styles of the individual patient, which were to be countered with an array of behavioral and cognitive interventions (see also Walton, this volume). Within the cognitive-behavioral tradition, at least initially, psychologists did not explicitly theorize about the possible therapeutic benefits of the patient-therapist relationship.

The patient-therapist relationship was given more attention from practitioners of humanistic or existential psychotherapies, a therapeutic tradition that emerged around the same time as cognitive-behavioral therapy. In contrast to the psychoanalysts, however, humanistic-existential psychologists emphasized the therapist's contributions to the alliance (Cain, 2002; Van Deurzen, 2012; Yalom, 1980). Particularly influential has been client-centered therapy (Rogers, 1951), which suggests that the therapist should relate authentically with the patient, while offering acceptance and empathy for the patient's perspective.

From the 1980s onward, the notion of the alliance increasingly found its way into mainstream psychology. Two developments are notable here. First, the psychoanalytic and humanistic notions of the alliance were merged into a transactional conception, in which the alliance is the product of the interactions between patient and therapist (Hougaard, 1994). Second, the notion of the alliance was increasingly extended across all psychotherapies (Bordin, 1979). Definitions of the alliance were stripped from elements belonging to a specific therapeutic tradition. In effect, the alliance became a "pantheoretical construct" that subsumed all collaborative elements within the therapeutic relationship (Horvath & Luborsky, 1993). For instance, one influential formulation defined the alliance as consisting of the patient and therapist (1) agreeing on the *goals* of the therapy; (2) dividing *tasks* among each other; and (3) developing *bonds* between them (Bordin, 1979). These conceptions were influential in guiding the development of empirical measures of the alliance.

The Great Psychotherapy Debate

As alliance research was broadened and popularized, it became caught up in what some have called "the great psychotherapy debate" (Wampold & Imel, 2015). This debate revolves around the question "what makes psychotherapy work?" Two sides of the debate have proposed different answers to this question. One side holds that psychotherapy is effective because of the effects of specific treatment methods. For instance, cognitive-behavioral therapy might cure depression because it replaces maladaptive thought patterns with adaptive ones. The other side of the debate believes that psychotherapy is effective because of processes that are common across different treatment factors, such as patients' hope that the treatment will be effective.

The great psychotherapy debate has pitted the effectiveness of specific treatments against the effects of the alliance, which operates across different treatments and can thus be seen as a common factor. However, this way of framing the debate is itself debatable (Norcross & Lambert, 2011). First, treatment methods and the alliance have a profound synergy. When the alliance functions well, patients are much more motivated to adhere with the treatment. Conversely, specific treatments will inevitably affect the alliance, and can thus be viewed as relational acts. Even when specific treatments and the alliance have distinct effects, there is no inherent reason why the effects of the one should come at the expense of the other. Pitting the alliance against specific treatments is thus artificial and misleading.

Second, the great psychotherapy debate has had a polarizing effect on the discipline, leading to something akin to culture wars (Norcross & Lambert, 2011). Rival camps have published endless critiques going back and forth, leading to entrenched positions on both sides. The problem has been exacerbated by the complexity of determining what makes psychotherapy work, which requires multiple, very large studies with complicated designs, along with experimental studies and theoretical work (Cuijpers, Reijnders, & Huibers, 2019; Kazdin, 2007). This means that it could take decades to determine the relative importance of the alliance and specific treatments (to the extent that this can be determined at all).

Despite these difficulties, the foregoing debates do not take away from the larger agreement that clinical psychologists have reached on the importance of the alliance. To be sure, some clinicians place more importance on the alliance than others. However, the authors of this chapter have never met a psychotherapist who deemed the alliance completely irrelevant to her or his clinical work, even though one of us has been in the field for decades. There thus exists a near-universal consensus among clinicians that a good working relationship between patient and therapist is desirable and conducive to good outcomes in psychotherapy. This consensus provides a firm foundation for modern alliance research.

Modern Alliance Research

It is not straightforward how patients can be experimentally assigned to different levels of the alliance. Consequently, alliance research has generally used correlational designs. Typically, the patient and the therapist (or sometimes an external observer) rate the alliance on a standard questionnaire. For instance, the widely used Working Alliance Scale has items such as "My therapist and I understand each other" and "We agree on what is important for me to work on" (Horvath & Greenberg, 1989). Factor-analytic research indicates that the core of patients' view of the alliance consists of being confident in and committed to a process that feels promising and helpful (Hatcher & Barends, 1996). Items relating to goals and tasks tend to be correlated (Elvins & Green, 2008), suggesting that the goal-task distinction may not matter so much on a psychological level.

In a meta-analysis of 190 independent studies, Horvath et al. (2011) found a positive correlation between the alliance and psychotherapy outcomes. Thus, stronger alliances are associated with better therapeutic outcomes. The alliance-outcome association is robust across different kinds of studies (randomized controlled trials or other), types of psychotherapy (cognitive-behavior therapies or other), different alliance measures, and types of outcomes (e.g., specific symptoms or general well-being). This makes the alliance-outcome association one of the most robust findings in modern clinical psychology. The strength of the alliance-outcome association is, statistically speaking, modest. It is estimated to be around 0.28 which means that alliance measures on average account for about 7.5 percent of psychotherapy outcomes. However, the statistical strength of an effect is difficult to interpret, and it is generally understood that statistically small effects can still be clinically relevant (Cuijpers, Turner, Koole, Van Dijke, & Smit, 2014).

Because the alliance-outcome association is correlational in nature, it is open to various explanations other than that a better alliance promotes good therapeutic outcomes. One obvious alternative explanation is that patients report a better alliance after they notice they benefited from the therapy. However, studies using autoregressive cross-lagged modeling and similar analyses have shown that the alliance usually precedes symptom reduction (Zilcha-Mano, 2017). Consequently, the alliance-outcome association seems to be more than a side effect of therapeutic success.

A second alternative explanation is that patients who are easier to treat may form a better alliance with the therapist. To address this idea, recent studies have begun to use advanced statistical techniques to separate the trait-like differences in forming the alliance from state-like, relationship-specific variations in the alliance (see Zilcha-Mano, 2017). The state-like component relates to the therapeutic nature of the alliance as an active ingredient sufficient in itself to bring about therapeutic change. The trait-like component relates to the patient's general trait-like ability to form strong and satisfying relationships. The trait-like component may enable the use of other aspects of treatment that may induce change, such as effective techniques. Importantly, research indicates that state-like changes in the alliance across treatment predict therapeutic outcomes, independently of the patient's general trait-like ability to form a strong and satisfying alliance. Thus, the alliance-outcome link does not arise simply because "easier" patients form a stronger alliance.

Summary and Outlook

Clinical psychologists have achieved important progress in studying the therapeutic alliance. First, researchers have converged on a transtheoretical definition of the alliance. Second, evidence supports a robust relation between the alliance and therapeutic outcomes, which cannot be attributed to reverse causality or trait variations in the ability to form beneficial relationships. At the same time, alliance research has limitations: First, it has largely relied on subjective ratings, ignoring objective aspects of the alliance. Second, alliance research has made little contact with disciplines outside clinical psychology. Third, alliance research so far lacks a theoretical framework for explaining why and how the alliance works. To address these limitations, we turn to social psychology.

Part 2: Interpersonal Synchrony

Social psychologists have long noted people's universal tendency to bond and form relationships with one another (Baumeister & Leary, 1995; Bowlby, 1969; Butler, 2011) (see also Mikulincer & Shaver, this volume). One foundational principle in regulating relationships is *interpersonal synchrony* (Feldman, 2007; Koole & Tschacher, 2016; Semin & Cacioppo, 2008). Interpersonal synchrony may be defined as the temporal coordination of people's mutual behavioral, physiological, and neurological functions. Everyday examples of interpersonal synchrony can be found when people spontaneously start walking at the same pace (van Ulzen, Lamoth, Daffertshofer, Semin, & Beek, 2008), when people are engaged in a naturally flowing conversation (Koudenburg, Postmes, & Gordijn, 2017), or when people are dancing together (Koch & Fischman, 2011).

The emergence of interpersonal synchrony is characteristic of positive, mutually beneficial social exchanges. In part, this is because people synchronize more readily with others with whom they seek to develop positive relationships (Miles, Lumsden, Richardson, & Macrae, 2011). However, interpersonal synchrony itself also contributes to the fluency of social interaction. Social-psychological experiments have shown that leading people to move in synchrony promotes cooperation and helping (Wiltermuth & Heath, 2009), while increasing liking, compassion, and rapport (Hove & Risen, 2009; Vacharkulksemsuk & Fredrickson, 2012; Valdesolo & DeSteno, 2011) and the sensitivity of responding to interaction partners (Valdesolo, Ouyang, & DeSteno, 2010). Interpersonal synchrony thus appears to be a fundamental mechanism for promoting social coordination.

As further testimony to its fundamental nature, interpersonal synchrony has been observed in multiple response modalities. The four most important response modalities of interpersonal synchrony are: (a) movement, (b) physiological responding, (c) language; and (d) brain-to-brain responding. These response modalities are meaningfully interrelated (Koole & Tschacher, 2016; Shamay-Tsoory, Saporta, Marton-Alper, & Gvirts, 2019). Nevertheless, they have mostly been studied separately in, respectively, movement science/social psychology, psychophysiology, cognitive linguistics, and social-cognitive neuroscience. We therefore discuss each response modality in turn.

Movement Synchrony

The first and most readily recognizable type of interpersonal synchrony emerges in people's bodily movements. It is well-established that people quickly and efficiently synchronize their movements in controlled laboratory environments, such as finger-tapping tasks (Repp & Su, 2013). In more recent years, new technologies have enabled non-invasive movement registration during naturalistic social interactions (Leclère et al., 2016). Using these technologies, and armed with increasingly sophisticated statistical techniques (Moulder, Boker, Ramseyer, & Tschacher, 2018; Ramseyer & Tschacher, 2010), researchers have been able to show that people spontaneously synchronize their movements in free and unstructured situations, both with strangers and familiar others (Feldman, 2007; Richardson, Marsh, Isenhower, Goodman, & Schmidt, 2007; van Ulzen et al., 2008). In addition, movement synchrony is associated with a sense of being mutually attuned in a shared present (Tschacher, Ramseyer, & Koole, 2018).

The latter findings have been complemented and extended by experimental studies, which have shown that moving in synchrony fosters social bonding and cooperation (Tarr, Launay, & Dunbar, 2016; Wiltermuth & Heath, 2009). Experimental studies have further been able to distinguish synchrony from mimicry (Chartrand & Lakin, 2013). Synchrony and mimicry both involve behavioral matching, but they differ in what is being matched. In mimicry, people match the identity of their actions. By contrast, in synchrony, people match the timing of their actions, regardless of which actions are involved. To see if synchrony has effects over and above mimicry, several experiments have manipulated whether participants display the same behavior in or out of synchrony (Hove & Risen, 2009; Valdesolo et al., 2010; Wiltermuth & Heath, 2009). The results have consistently shown that participants affiliate more with another when they move in (rather than out of) synchrony. These and related studies indicate that synchrony promotes affiliative responses, even when mimicry levels are held constant.

Physiological Synchrony

A second type of interpersonal synchrony emerges in physiological responding. In utero, human infants already adopt their mother's biological rhythms (Ivanov, Ma, & Bartsch, 2009; Van Leeuwen et al., 2009). After birth, physiological synchrony between caretaker and child sets the stage for autonomous emotion regulation (Feldman, 2007). Furthermore, adults physiologically synchronize in close relationships (Palumbo et al., 2017). Physiological synchronization may further occur among strangers, for instance, when they are observing or performing a collective ritual (Konvalinka et al., 2011). Research on physiological synchrony has so far concentrated on the autonomous nervous system, which is divided into the sympathetic system—which supports activation, or the "fight-flight" response—and the parasympathetic system (PNS), which supports restoration, or the "rest-and-digest" response.

Researchers have distinguished three major patterns of interpersonal physiological regulation (Butler & Randall, 2013). The first pattern is *emotional contagion*, and occurs when interaction partners directly adopt another's arousal levels. Emotional contagion can be regarded as a form of interpersonal synchrony. Nevertheless, emotional contagion can lead to excessive arousal when one interaction partner is highly distressed. It is likely for this reason that covariation of cortisol, an important stress hormone, among partners, has been found to be negatively associated with relationship satisfaction (Timmons, Margolin, & Saxbe, 2015). The second pattern is stress buffering, and occurs when one partner lowers the arousal level of the other partner. Although stress buffering is likely adaptive (Coan & Sbarra, 2015), it is not a reciprocal process and therefore it does not qualify as a form of synchrony. The third and last pattern is co-regulation, and occurs when interaction partners synchronize their emotional responses within a stable range. Co-regulation theoretically represents a beneficial form of interpersonal regulation that contributes to the person's physiological adaptability to changing circumstances. Consistent with this, statistical markers of the co-regulation are positively associated with relationship satisfaction (Helm, Sbarra, & Ferrer, 2014).

Linguistic Synchrony

A third type of interpersonal synchrony occurs in language. Part of the regulatory effects of language occur through the behavioral and physiological modalities of interpersonal synchrony: Conversation partners coordinate their postural sway and match another's eye gaze, even when they cannot see each other (Shockley, Richardson, & Dale, 2009). Moreover, conversation synchronizes breathing rates (McFarland, 2001), which in turn regulates cardiovascular responding (Lehrer & Gevirtz, 2014).

Cognitive linguists have further documented how the linguistic representations of conversation partners become aligned as a result of largely automatic processes (Pickering & Garrod, 2004). Such linguistic alignment involves a blend of mimicry (i.e., matching the identity of another's linguistic utterances) and synchrony (i.e., matching the timing of these utterances). It is often hard to tell linguistic mimicry and linguistic synchrony apart. Nevertheless, it seems fair to say that synchrony is a key aspect of linguistic alignment. Notably, linguistic alignment is complex, in that it occurs simultaneously at multiple levels, such that conversation partners become aligned in their intonation, speech sounds, pronunciation, word use, and grammar. These levels appear to be mutually reinforcing, such that linguistic alignment at one level promotes alignment at other levels (Pickering & Garrod, 2004). For instance, conversation partners who use the same grammatical structures are more likely to reach a common understanding of the situation. Conversely, conversation partners who have reached a mutual understanding are also more likely to use the same grammatical structures.

Brain-to-Brain Synchrony

Finally, a fourth type of interpersonal synchrony occurs between the brains of people who are interacting. The notion of brain-to-brain synchrony may initially seem esoteric, given that modern neuroscience has traditionally focused on individual brains. Nevertheless, brain-to-brain synchrony does not require extrasensory abilities, given that it builds on the brain's ability to be coupled to signals from the physical world (Hasson, Ghazanfar, Galantucci, Garrod, & Keysers, 2012; Konvalinka & Roepstorff, 2012; Nummenmaa, Lahnakoski, & Glerean, 2018). In brain-to-brain synchrony, the signal is generated by another person (or person's) living body and brain, rather than by inanimate objects.

More than research on other synchrony modalities, research on brain-to-brain synchrony has depended on recent technological innovations. In so-called hyperscanning studies, the conventional neuroimaging techniques of EEG and fMRI have been adapted to simultaneously record brain activity of interaction partners (Babiloni & Astolfi, 2014; Dikker et al., 2017; Mu, Cerritos, & Khan, 2018). Both techniques still have disadvantages. For instance, fMRI requires that people lie flat on their back with their head still inside a narrow, highly noisy magnet. EEG equipment can be made portable, but EEG signals suffer strongly from movement and speech interference. These problems may be resolved with new technological developments. For instance, functional near-infrared spectroscopy (fNIRS), which allows neuroimaging while people are sitting without head or body fixation, though fNIRS can currently only measure cortical activity up to 4 cm into the brain (Ferrari & Quaresima, 2012).

To date, hyperscanning studies have been able to demonstrate that joint action leads to brain-to-brain synchrony, for instance, among guitarists playing together (Müller, Sänger, & Lindenberger, 2018) and among students following the same lecture (Dikker et al., 2017). Brain-to-brain synchrony further emerges in emotionally charged relationships, such as parent-child dyads (Reindl, Gerloff, Scharke, & Konrad, 2018) and romantic partners (Kinreich, Djalovski, Kraus, Louzoun, & Feldman, 2017). One mechanism that promotes brain-to-brain synchrony appears to be the sharing of perspectives, particularly when it comes to emotional events. This was shown in a series of "pseudo-hyperscanning" studies in which the synchronization of participants' brains is recorded while they are watching or listening to a pre-recorded video or audio recording. In one of these studies, participants who were viewing similar emotional events in a movie showed synchronized brain activity in lower- and higher-order sensory areas and in corticolimbic emotion circuits (Nummenmaa et al., 2012). Analogous effects have been found for emotional speech (Nummenmaa et al., 2014). Such brain-to-brain synchrony is greatest when participants are led to adopt a similar psychological perspective on events (Lahnakoski et al., 2014). Brain-to-brain synchrony thus reflects shared emotions and a shared understanding of the situation.

Summary and Outlook

Growing research has documented interpersonal synchrony in movements, physiology, language, and neural activations. This work converges on the notion that synchrony is a fundamental mechanism of social coordination. At the same time, synchrony research has been somewhat scattered, given that it has been conducted in diverse disciplines, including movement science/social psychology, psychophysiology, cognitive linguistics, and social-cognitive neurosciences. Research in these disciplines has so far largely progressed in parallel, with little exchange taking place between traditional disciplinary boundaries. This is unfortunate, given that it is theoretically plausible that there is crosstalk between the different types of interpersonal synchrony. Moreover, in applied domains, the different types of interpersonal synchrony cannot be neatly separated, as they must always work together in real-life situations. In the next section, we therefore consider the integration of the different types of interpersonal synchrony in psychotherapy.

Part 3: The IN-SYNC Model

To integrate the different types of synchrony, we have proposed the Interpersonal Synchrony (IN-SYNC) model of psychotherapy (Koole & Tschacher, 2016). The IN-SYNC model is a theoretical framework that combines processes that have traditionally been studied in movement science, social psychology, psychophysiology, and social-cognitive neuroscience, and cognitive linguistics. In addition, the IN-SYNC model draws insights from developmental science, relationship science, and emotion science. The IN-SYNC model was developed to stimulate integration of the different literatures on interpersonal synchrony. Moreover, the IN-SYNC model seeks to promote clinical applications that harness the beneficial effects of the patient-therapist relationship.

A visual overview of the IN-SYNC model is provided in Figure 9.1. In brief, the model proposes that: (1) moment-to-moment synchronization of movement and physiological responses sets the stage for (2) a good working relationship between patient and therapist, which, across sessions, (3) strengthens patients' emotion-regulatory skills. The IN-SYNC model thus distinguishes between psychotherapy processes at three different timescales. For the sake of simplicity, our discussion here covers only the causal flow from faster (elementary) to slower (more complex) levels. In reality, however, higher levels may also regulate the lower levels. Such bidirectional loops are represented as double-sided arrows in Figure 9.1.

Level 1: Phasic Processes

At Level 1, synchrony processes operate at a phasic timescale, which runs from hundreds of milliseconds to about one minute. Automatic perceptual-motor

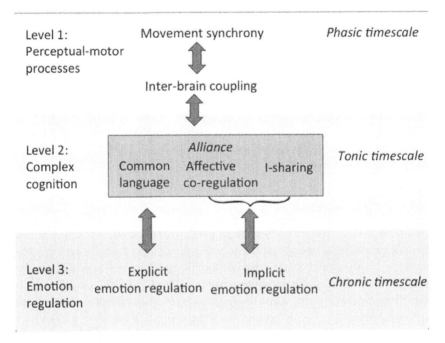

FIGURE 9.1 The IN-SYNC Model of Psychotherapy

processes at this level (Hommel, Müsseler, Aschersleben, & Prinz, 2001) give rise to movement synchrony. Most processes at this level are not consciously experienced. Nevertheless, movement synchrony is linked to a sub-linguistic form of brain-to-brain synchrony (Shamay-Tsoory et al., 2019). The latter may be partly subjectively experienced as sharing the present moment (Tschacher et al., 2018) or a state of mutual attunement (Geller & Porges, 2014). Although little is known about the physiological effects of movement synchrony, it is already established that movement synchrony can foster emotional security (Tschacher, Rees, & Ramseyer, 2014) and may even raise pain thresholds (Tarr et al., 2016). According to the IN-SYNC model, the latter effects indicate that movement synchrony may evoke mutual parasympathetic activation (the "rest-and-digest" system), which represents an important form of physiological synchrony at Level 1.

Level 2: Tonic Processes

Level 1 synchrony sets the stage for more complex interpersonal coordination at Level 2, which operate at a tonic timescale, from several minutes to one or more hours. Tonic processes are more accessible to conscious awareness, so they may be captured (at least, in part) by self-report scales that assess the quality of the patient-therapist relationship (Horvath et al., 2011). The IN-SYNC model distinguishes three processes that constitute the alliance. The first process is linguistic alignment (Pickering & Garrod, 2004), which gives rise to a common language that facilitates the task- and goal-related aspects of the alliance (Bordin, 1979). The second process consists of the sharing of subjective experiences by the patient and therapist, or 'I-sharing' (Pinel, Bernecker, & Rampy, 2015), which promotes social bonding and the personal aspects of the alliance (Bordin, 1979). The third and last process is co-regulation (Butler & Randall, 2013), or mutual regulation of emotional responses within a stable range. Effective therapists will make sure to keep mutual physiological arousal during the therapy within homeostatic boundaries.

Level 3: Chronic Processes

Finally, at Level 3, the effects of multiple psychotherapy sessions accumulate at a chronic timescale, over days, weeks, months, even years. To the extent that the working relationship between patient and therapist has been successful, the patient should display notable improvements. The IN-SYNC model assumes that these improvements particularly pertain to the patient's capacity for emotion regulation. This is because the interpersonal dynamics of psychotherapy closely parallel how people acquire emotion-regulatory skills in everyday life, through interactions with caregivers (Feldman, 2007) and loved ones (Butler & Randall, 2013). Emotion-regulatory improvements of the patient may pertain to conscious or explicit forms of emotion regulation, which have been traditionally the focus of psychotherapy research (Gratz, Weiss, & Tull, 2015). However, the patients' improvements may also extend to more implicit forms of emotion regulation (Koole, Webb, & Sheeran, 2015; Remmers et al., 2018).

Summary and Outlook

The IN-SYNC model addresses the role of interpersonal synchrony in psychotherapy. According to the model, interpersonal synchrony in movements, physiology, language, and neural activations (at the phasic timescale) sustain the working relationship of the patient and therapist in psychotherapy (at the tonic timescale). This, in turn, promotes therapeutic gains (at the chronic timescale), especially with regard to the patient's emotion-regulatory skills. The IN-SYNC model thus provides an integrative framework for understanding how moment-to-moment exchanges between patient and therapist may translate into more complex forms of social cognition and, eventually, improvements in emotion regulation and mental health.

Part 4: Empirical Research on Synchrony in Psychotherapy

A growing literature has examined interpersonal synchrony in psychotherapy. In this section, we review this emerging literature using the framework of the IN-SYNC model (Koole & Tschacher, 2016). Our review is selective in four ways. First, we focus only on the most studied relationships within the IN-SYNC model. Second, our discussion only covers the main studies that appeared in our earlier review of 2016. Third, we prioritize research that has been published since 2016, the year of our first publication on the IN-SYNC model. Fourth, for each point that we discuss, we highlight key questions that still need to be addressed in future research.

Level 1: Movement Synchrony

The first comprehensive study of movement synchrony in psychotherapy was conducted by Ramseyer and Tschacher (2011). These researchers selected 104 sessions from an archive of videotaped psychotherapies at an outpatient psychotherapy clinic in Switzerland. Patients suffered from a wide range of problems, including anxiety disorders and affective disorders. Automated video analyses showed that movement synchrony between patient and therapist was significantly higher than would be expected by chance. Moreover, movement synchrony, assessed at the start of the psychotherapy, was predictive of the quality of alliance, as rated by patients at the end of each session. Finally, movement synchrony between patient and therapist was a longitudinal predictor of symptom reduction at the end of psychotherapy. These findings provide some of the strongest evidence to date for the contribution of movement synchrony to the alliance and therapeutic outcomes.

In a conceptual replication of Ramseyer and Tschacher (2011), Paulick and associates conducted an automated video analysis of 136 videotaped sessions between 27 psychotherapists and 143 German patients who received integrative cognitive-behavioral therapy (Paulick, Deisenhofer, et al., 2018). As in Ramseyer and Tschacher (2011), movement synchrony occurred at above-chance levels between patients and therapists. However, there was no relation between movement synchrony and patient-rated alliance. Nonetheless, movement synchrony was predictive of therapeutic outcomes, when it was considered in combination with drop-out rates: The lowest amount of movement synchrony was found among non-improved patients who dropped out of therapy. A medium level of movement synchrony was found among improved patients. Finally, the most movement synchrony was found among non-improved patients who consensually terminated treatment. The latter could mean that patient and therapist can overdo it in synchronizing their movements, although more research is needed to confirm this finding.

More generally, the Paulick et al. study suggests that movement synchrony in early sessions can predict premature termination of psychotherapy. The latter effect was subsequently replicated in a study among 267 German patients who received cognitive-behavioral therapy or psychodynamic therapy for social anxiety disorder (Schoenherr et al., 2019). These findings suggest that movement synchrony may play an important role in motivating patients to continue treatment. According to the IN-SYNC model (Koole & Tschacher, 2016), the latter effect may be due to the improved alliance that is likely to be fostered by movement synchrony.

Another study (Paulick, Rubel, et al., 2018) examined movement synchrony in 173 cognitive-behavioral therapy sessions between 23 therapists-in-training and patients diagnosed with either depressive disorders ($N=68$) or anxiety disorders ($N=25$). Again, movement synchrony emerged within the psychotherapy sessions at levels that were significantly above chance. However, associations between movement synchrony and outcomes were not as expected. The association was statistically non-significant (though in the predicted direction) for patients with anxiety disorders, which could have been due to the small sample size of 25 patients. For patients with depressive disorders, the association was statistically significant, but in the opposite direction to what was expected: Less movement synchrony at the start of psychotherapy was associated with greater symptom reduction.

The findings of Paulick, Rubel, et al. (2018) remain somewhat puzzling. One possibility is that the findings resulted from a statistical confound. In the Paulick, Rubel et al. (2018) study, movement synchrony scores from when the patient began psychotherapy were used to assess its association with therapeutic outcomes. This analysis confounds between-patient differences, which are personality-based, and within-patient dynamics, which are a relationship-specific reflection of the alliance (Zilcha-Mano, 2017). It should be noted that this confound also applies to Ramseyer & Tschacher (2011). As far as we know, there has been only one study of within-patient variations in movement synchrony: A single-case study (Ramseyer & Tschacher, 2016) observed that patient-therapist synchrony of hand movements (assessed by an accelerometer) during 27 psychotherapy sessions was greater than chance, and positively associated with post-session therapeutic progress. This is a first indication that within-patient dynamics may drive the therapeutic benefits of movement synchrony. However, larger samples will be needed to statistically disentangle between- and within-patient components and their associations with the alliance and clinical outcomes.

Another possibility is that movement synchrony is not always beneficial to psychotherapy. When patients are in a negative emotional state (like the depressed patients in the Paulick, Rubel et al., 2018 study), it is conceivable that movement synchrony with the therapist serves to maintain this negative emotion. Studies showing beneficial effects of movement synchrony may have been limited to patients who were in a better emotional state. To test the viability of this second possibility, future work should jointly study patients' emotions and movement synchrony. If it turns out that patients' emotions determine the direction of the effects of movement synchrony, the IN-SYNC model (Koole & Tschacher, 2016) would have to be revised.

Level 2: Language, I-Sharing, and Co-Regulation

The IN-SYNC model (Koole & Tschacher, 2016) distinguishes three objective components of the patient-therapist alliance: Common language, I-sharing, and co-regulation. Because clinical psychologists usually assessed the alliance only with self-report scales, the objective components of the alliance have been understudied. Nevertheless, recent work has begun to make important headway here.

Linguistic Alignment. The first objective component of the alliance is linguistic alignment between patient and therapist. At a basic level (closely related to the perceptual-motor processes of Level 1), this linguistic alignment may become apparent in the synchronization of patient and therapist's rates of speaking. Relevant to this idea, one study examined speaking rates within 30 clinical sessions among five patients at a psychological facility in Italy (Rocco et al., 2018). As expected, speaking rates of patient and therapist speech became synchronized over the course of the sessions. At a more abstract level, patient and therapist may synchronize their word use. This notion was tested in a study of written transcripts of 122 sessions by 122 therapists in the US (Lord, Sheng, Imel, Baer, & Atkins, 2015). Patient and therapist were found to converge in their use of similar function words (e.g., personal pronouns, prepositions) at each conversational turn. Moreover, this form of linguistic style synchrony was positively correlated with observer-rated empathy of the therapist.

I-sharing. The second objective component of the alliance is I-sharing, that is, the sharing of deeply felt experiences (Pinel et al., 2015). The assessment of I-sharing in psychotherapy is still in its infancy. Nevertheless, a recent study on brain-to-brain synchrony (Zhang, Meng, Hou, Pan, & Hu, 2018) seems potentially relevant here. Using fNIRS (see Section 2), this study examined brain-to-brain synchrony among 34 participants who were randomly assigned to engage in either psychotherapy or casual chatting with one of three female professional counselors. The study showed that brain-to-brain synchrony was enhanced during psychotherapy (versus casual chatting) in the right temporo-parietal junction, a region associated with social connectedness and mentalizing (Cacioppo & Cacioppo, 2012). Notably, greater brain-to-brain synchrony was associated with a better quality of the alliance, as rated by the patients. Though preliminary, these results suggest that measures of brain-to-brain synchrony during psychotherapy may be useful in assessing the quality of I-sharing.

Co-Regulation. Finally, the third objective component of the alliance is co-regulation; mutual regulation of emotions within a stable range (Butler & Randall, 2013). A pioneering study observed that patient-therapist congruence in skin conductance of 20 patient-therapist dyads is associated with higher therapist empathy and more positive interactions between patients and therapists (Marci, Ham, Moran, & Orr, 2007). A more recent study found statistically significant physiological synchrony across various cardiovascular indexes recorded in 55 psychotherapy sessions with four clients and one female psychotherapist (Tschacher & Meier, 2019). Moreover, alliance rated by the client or therapist was positively associated with physiological synchrony.

Another recent study examined synchrony in skin conductance among 31 patients that were treated by ten therapists across five sessions (Bar-Kalifa et al., 2019). The latter study contrasted segments where the therapy used an emotion-focused technique (i.e.., imagery of emotionally charged situations) with segments that involved less emotion-focused techniques (e.g., psycho-education). The results showed that physiological synchrony was strong between patient and therapists during emotion-focused segments, but absent during more neutral segments. Moreover, physiological synchrony during emotion-focused segments was associated with the therapeutic bond aspects of the alliance, but not with the task/goal aspects of the alliance. These intriguing findings suggest that physiological synchrony is especially relevant to the emotionally-charged aspects of psychotherapy, as the IN-SYNC model (Koole & Tschacher, 2016) would predict.

An alternative way to operationalize co-regulation could be to assess the degree to which patients and therapists converge in their experienced emotions. A recent study examined such emotional convergence between 109 Israeli patients who were treated by 62 therapists (Atzil-Slonim et al., 2018). Ratings of patients' and therapists' emotions were obtained after each session. When patients and therapists displayed incongruent emotions, this predicted a worsening in the patients' symptoms during the next session. Other studies, however, have observed that congruency in patient-therapist emotional responding is negatively associated with therapist empathy and therapeutic outcomes (Reich, Berman, Dale, & Levitt, 2014).

The congruency pattern (see in Atzil-Slonim et al., 2018; Marci et al., 2007; Tschacher & Meier, 2019) and the incongruency patterns (as in Reich et al., 2014) superficially seem to be at odds. However, both patterns fit with a co-regulation account, which suggests that effective therapists are emotionally attuned to their patients, while sometimes dampening the patient's emotions to prevent emotional escalation (Butler & Randall, 2013). Future work in this area could benefit from the use of more sophisticated statistical models, which are capable of distinguishing co-regulation from alternative patterns like emotional contagion and stress buffering (e.g., coupled oscillator models; see Butler, 2017).

Level 3: Long-term Therapeutic Outcomes

Throughout our discussion of Levels 1 and 2 research, we observed that several studies of synchrony in psychotherapy have been related to therapeutic outcomes, in either cross-sectional or longitudinal studies. The results of these studies offer preliminary support for some of the core tenets of the IN-SYNC model (Koole & Tschacher, 2016). However, the available research on clinical outcomes has so far been limited in important respects. First, outcome studies so far have assessed only one type of synchrony at a time. On the basis of the IN-SYNC model, it is likely that different synchrony types (i.e., movement, physiology, language, emotion, brain-to-brain) make separate (though interrelated) contributions to psychotherapy. It is therefore important to assess multiple synchrony types in a single study. Second, outcome studies so far have been conducted over a limited time span, usually several weeks or months. It would be important to study the effects of synchrony in psychotherapy over longer timespans. Third, outcome studies so far have used relatively small samples, which limits their informational value (Lakens & Evers, 2014).

Future researchers should ideally address all three aforementioned limitations in a single study. An example of such a study can be found in developmental research that tracked the associations between various social-cognitive outcomes and multiple types of synchrony between children and their caregivers over a period of ten years (Feldman, 2015). It stands to reason that conducting analogous work among adult psychotherapy patients would afford profound new insights into the role of interpersonal synchrony in psychotherapy.

Summary and Outlook

Synchrony in psychotherapy has been the focus of a growing amount of research. There is now strong evidence that patients and therapists display significant amounts of synchrony in their movements, physiological responding, language, emotions, and brain activations. These different types of synchrony have been found to have meaningful (usually positive) relations with the patient-therapist alliance and therapeutic benefits. These findings provide preliminary evidence for the validity of the IN-SYNC model (Koole & Tschacher, 2016).

Part 5: Conclusions and Outlook

In the present chapter, we have highlighted the importance of interpersonal synchrony to psychotherapy. During psychotherapy, patient and therapist spontaneously synchronize their movements, language, physiological responses, and neural activations. The extent of this patient-therapist synchrony predicts the quality of the therapeutic relationship and therapeutic success. The patient-therapist relationship thus appears to rely on interpersonal synchrony as a fundamental mechanism of social coordination. In this way, psychotherapy can be said to be grounded in interpersonal synchrony.

Explicating the role of synchrony in psychotherapy is not only beneficial for scientific reasons, but it may also lead to new ways for improving psychotherapy. For instance, there are currently large differences between psychotherapists in how much success they achieve with their patients (Wampold & Imel, 2015). The reasons for these differences are poorly understood. From the present perspective, it seems likely that differences in therapists' effectiveness are at least partly due to differences in their ability to synchronize with patients. The IN-SYNC model (Koole & Tschacher, 2016) offers several inroads into identifying which specific social-cognitive skills may be involved, how to assess them, and how to improve them. Along similar lines, the IN-SYNC model may point to new ways of assessing and enhancing clinical-psychological expertise, a topic that has long eluded scientific analysis (Tracey, Wampold, Lichtenberg, & Goodyear, 2014).

In moving forward, one major challenge is formed by the rise of new modalities for social interaction. People increasingly interact with another online (see also Blanton, Burrows, & Regan, this volume), and there are considerable efforts in progress to develop online psychotherapy programs (Donker & Kleiboer, 2018). Online psychotherapy appears to be effective (Karyotaki et al., 2017). Nevertheless, online and face-to-face interaction differ in important respects, including in how they may impact emotion regulation (see Kross & Chandhok, this volume). The IN-SYNC model (Koole & Tschacher, 2016) may provide a framework for analyzing the similarities and differences between that online and face-to-face interaction. Such an analysis could prove useful in understanding how psychotherapy may be optimally administered.

Because interpersonal synchrony is a fundamental social-psychological principle, insights from research on synchrony in psychotherapy could also inform research on other kinds of interpersonal relationships (see also Mikulincer & Shaver, this volume). Here, we see an important potential integrative function for psychotherapy research. Synchrony in movement, physiology, emotion, language, and between brains have so far largely been studied separately. Nevertheless, these types of interpersonal synchrony all converge in psychotherapy. Psychotherapy may thus allow synchrony researchers from different disciplines to join forces, so that they can develop and test ideas about the interplay of various types of interpersonal synchrony. The resulting insights may be used to inform many other interpersonal domains, from close relationships to educational settings and business negotiations.

Coda

Throughout this chapter, we have seen that research on interpersonal synchrony is on its way to transforming clinical psychological science. If this trend continues, the day may come when interpersonal synchrony will be regarded as primarily a clinical-psychological phenomenon. When that point is reached, it will be important to remember that interpersonal synchrony was originally conceived as a basic social-psychological mechanism and rigorously investigated using controlled experiments (e.g., Repp & Su, 2013). Research on synchrony in psychotherapy thus testifies to the value of basic social-psychological experiments in generating insights that can inform practical interventions (see also Fiedler, this volume).

References

Atzil-Slonim, D., Bar-Kalifa, E., Fisher, H., Peri, T., Lutz, W., Rubel, J., & Rafaeli, E. (2018). Emotional congruence between clients and therapists and its effect on treatment outcome. *Journal of Counseling Psychology, 65*(1), 51.

Babiloni, F., & Astolfi, L. (2014). Social neuroscience and hyperscanning techniques: Past, present and future. *Neuroscience & Biobehavioral Reviews, 44*, 76–93.

Bar-Kalifa, E., Prinz, J. N., Atzil-Slonim, D., Rubel, J. A., Lutz, W., & Rafaeli, E. (2019). Physiological synchrony and therapeutic alliance in an imagery-based treatment. *Journal of Counseling Psychology, 66*(4), 508.

Baumeister, R. F., & Leary, M. R. (1995). The need to belong: Desire for interpersonal attachments as a fundamental human motivation. *Psychological Bulletin, 117*(3), 497–529.

Bordin, E. S. (1979). The generalizability of the psychoanalytic concept of the working alliance. *Psychotherapy: Theory, Research & Practice, 16*(3), 252–260.

Bowlby, J. (1969). *Attachment and loss v. 3* (Vol. 1). New York: Random House.

Butler, E. A. (2011). Temporal interpersonal emotion systems: The "TIES" that form relationships. *Personality and Social Psychology Review, 15*, 367–393.

Butler, E. A. (2017). Emotions are temporal interpersonal systems. *Current Opinion in Psychology, 17*, 129–134.

Butler, E. A., & Randall, A. K. (2013). Emotional coregulation in close relationships. *Emotion Review, 5*(2), 202–210.

Cacioppo, S., & Cacioppo, J. T. (2012). Decoding the invisible forces of social connections. *Frontiers in Integrative Neuroscience, 6*, 51.

Cain, D. J. (2002). *Humanistic psychotherapies: Handbook of research and practice*. Washington, D.C: American Psychological Association.

Chartrand, T. L., & Lakin, J. L. (2013). The antecedents and consequences of human behavioral mimicry. *Annual Review of Psychology, 64*, 285–308.

Coan, J. A., & Sbarra, D. A. (2015). Social baseline theory: The social regulation of risk and effort. *Current Opinion in Psychology, 1*, 87–91.

Cuijpers, P., Reijnders, M., & Huibers, M. J. H. (2019). The role of common factors in psychotherapy outcomes. *Annual Review of Clinical Psychology, 15*, 207–231.

Cuijpers, P., Turner, E. H., Koole, S. L., Van Dijke, A., & Smit, F. (2014). What is the threshold for a clinically relevant effect? The case of major depressive disorders. *Depression and Anxiety, 31*(5), 374–378.

Dikker, S., Wan, L., Davidesco, I., Kaggen, L., Oostrik, M., McClintock, J., ... Poeppel, D. (2017). Brain-to-brain synchrony tracks real-world dynamic group interactions in the classroom. *Current Biology, 27*(9), 1375–1380. doi.org/10.1016/J.CUB.2017.04.002

Donker, T., & Kleiboer, A. (2018). e-health innovations for global mental health. *Global Mental Health, 5.*

Elvins, R., & Green, J. (2008). The conceptualization and measurement of therapeutic alliance: An empirical review. *Clinical Psychology Review, 28*(7), 1167–1187.

Feldman, R. (2007). Parent–infant synchrony: Biological foundations and developmental outcomes. *Current Directions in Psychological Science, 16*, 340–345.

Feldman, R. (2015). Mutual influences between child emotion regulation and parent-child reciprocity support development across the first 10 years of life: Implications for developmental psychopathology. *Development and Psychopathology, 27*(4pt1), 1007–1023.

Ferrari, M., & Quaresima, V. (2012). A brief review on the history of human functional near-infrared spectroscopy (fNIRS) development and fields of application. *Neuroimage, 63*(2), 921–935.

Freud, S. (1912). The dynamics of transference. In *The standard edition of the complete psychological works of Sigmund Freud, Volume XII (1911–1913): The case of Schreber, papers on technique and other works* (pp. 97–108). London: Hogarth Press.

Geller, S. M., & Porges, S. W. (2014). Therapeutic presence: Neurophysiological mechanisms mediating feeling safe in therapeutic relationships. *Journal of Psychotherapy Integration, 24*(3), 178.

Hasson, U., Ghazanfar, A. A., Galantucci, B., Garrod, S., & Keysers, C. (2012). Brain-to-brain coupling: A mechanism for creating and sharing a social world. *Trends in Cognitive Sciences, 16*(2), 114–121.

Hatcher, R. L., & Barends, A. W. (1996). Patients' view of the alliance in psychotherapy: Exploratory factor analysis of three alliance measures. *Journal of Consulting and Clinical Psychology, 64*(6), 1326–1336.

Helm, J. L., Sbarra, D. A., & Ferrer, E. (2014). Coregulation of respiratory sinus arrhythmia in adult romantic partners. *Emotion, 14*(3), 522.

Hommel, B., Müsseler, J., Aschersleben, G., & Prinz, W. (2001). The theory of event coding (TEC): A framework for perception and action planning. *Behavioral and Brain Sciences, 24*(5), 849–878.

Horvath, A. O., Del Rey, A. C., Flückiger, C., & Symonds, D. (2011). Alliance in individual psychotherapy. *Psychotherapy, 48*(1), 9–16.

Horvath, A. O., & Greenberg, L. S. (1989). Development and validation of the Working Alliance Inventory. *Journal of Counseling Psychology, 36*(2), 223–233.

Horvath, A. O., & Luborsky, L. (1993). The role of the therapeutic alliance in psychotherapy. *Journal of Consulting and Clinical Psychology, 61*(4), 561–573.

Hougaard, E. (1994). The therapeutic alliance–A conceptual analysis. *Scandinavian Journal of Psychology, 35*(1), 67–85.

Hove, M. J., & Risen, J. L. (2009). It's all in the timing: Interpersonal synchrony increases affiliation. *Social Cognition, 27*(6), 949–960.

Ivanov, P. C., Ma, Q. D. Y., & Bartsch, R. P. (2009). Maternal–fetal heartbeat phase synchronization. *Proceedings of the National Academy of Sciences, 106*(33), 13641–13642.

Karyotaki, E., Riper, H., Twisk, J., Hoogendoorn, A., Kleiboer, A., Mira, A., ... Littlewood, E. (2017). Efficacy of self-guided internet-based cognitive behavioral therapy in the treatment of depressive symptoms: A meta-analysis of individual participant data. *JAMA Psychiatry, 74*(4), 351–359.

Kazdin, A. E. (2007). Mediators and mechanisms of change in psychotherapy research. *Annual Review of Clinical Psychology, 3,* 1–27.

Keegan, E., & Holas, P. (2009). Cognitive-behavior therapy. Theory and practice. In R. Carlstedt (Ed.), *Integrative clinical psychology, psychiatry and behavioral medicine* (pp. 605–643). New York: Springer.

Kinreich, S., Djalovski, A., Kraus, L., Louzoun, Y., & Feldman, R. (2017). Brain-to-brain synchrony during naturalistic social interactions. *Scientific Reports, 7*(1), 17060.

Koch, S. C., & Fischman, D. (2011). Embodied enactive dance/movement therapy. *American Journal of Dance Therapy, 33*(1), 57.

Konvalinka, I., & Roepstorff, A. (2012). The two-brain approach: How can mutually interacting brains teach us something about social interaction? *Frontiers in Human Neuroscience, 6,* 215.

Konvalinka, I., Xygalatas, D., Bulbulia, J., Schjødt, U., Jegindø, E.-M., Wallot, S., … Roepstorff, A. (2011). Synchronized arousal between performers and related spectators in a fire-walking ritual. *Proceedings of the National Academy of Sciences, 108*(20), 8514–8519.

Koole, S. L., & Tschacher, W. (2016). Synchrony in psychotherapy: A review and an integrative framework for the therapeutic alliance. *Frontiers in Psychology, 7*(862), 1–17.

Koole, S. L., Webb, T. L., & Sheeran, P. L. (2015). Implicit emotion regulation: Feeling better without knowing why. *Current Opinion in Psychology, 3,* 6–10.

Koudenburg, N., Postmes, T., & Gordijn, E. H. (2017). Beyond content of conversation: The role of conversational form in the emergence and regulation of social structure. *Personality and Social Psychology Review, 21*(1), 50–71.

Lahnakoski, J. M., Glerean, E., Jääskeläinen, I. P., Hyönä, J., Hari, R., Sams, M., & Nummenmaa, L. (2014). Synchronous brain activity across individuals underlies shared psychological perspectives. *NeuroImage, 100,* 316–324.

Lakens, D., & Evers, E. R. K. (2014). Sailing from the seas of chaos into the corridor of stability: Practical recommendations to increase the informational value of studies. *Perspectives on Psychological Science, 9*(3), 278–292.

Leclère, C., Avril, M., Viaux-Savelon, S., Bodeau, N., Achard, C., Missonnier, S., … Cohen, D. (2016). Interaction and behaviour imaging: A novel method to measure mother–infant interaction using video 3D reconstruction. *Translational Psychiatry, 6*(5), e816.

Lehrer, P. M., & Gevirtz, R. (2014). Heart rate variability biofeedback: How and why does it work? *Frontiers in Psychology, 5,* 756.

Lord, S. P., Sheng, E., Imel, Z. E., Baer, J., & Atkins, D. C. (2015). More than reflections: Empathy in motivational interviewing includes language style synchrony between therapist and client. *Behavior Therapy, 46*(3), 296–303.

Marci, C. D., Ham, J., Moran, E., & Orr, S. P. (2007). Physiologic correlates of perceived therapist empathy and social-emotional process during psychotherapy. *Journal of Nervous and Mental Disease, 195*(2), 103–111.

McFarland, D. H. (2001). Respiratory markers of conversational interaction. *Journal of Speech, Language, and Hearing Research, 44*(1), 128–143.

Miles, L. K., Lumsden, J., Richardson, M. J., & Macrae, C. N. (2011). Do birds of a feather move together? Group membership and behavioral synchrony. *Experimental Brain Research, 211*(3–4), 495–503.

Moulder, R. G., Boker, S. M., Ramseyer, F., & Tschacher, W. (2018). Determining synchrony between behavioral time series: An application of surrogate data generation for establishing falsifiable null-hypotheses. *Psychological Methods, 23*(4), 757.

Mu, Y., Cerritos, C., & Khan, F. (2018). Neural mechanisms underlying interpersonal coordination: A review of hyperscanning research. *Social and Personality Psychology Compass, 12*(11), e12421.

Müller, V., Sänger, J., & Lindenberger, U. (2018). Hyperbrain network properties of guitarists playing in quartet. *Annals of the New York Academy of Sciences, 1423*(1), 198–210.

Norcross, J. C., & Lambert, M. J. (2011). Psychotherapy relationships that work. *Psychotherapy, 48*, 4–8.

Nummenmaa, L., Glerean, E., Viinikainen, M., Jääskeläinen, I. P., Hari, R., & Sams, M. (2012). Emotions promote social interaction by synchronizing brain activity across individuals. *Proceedings of the National Academy of Sciences, 109*(24), 9599–9604.

Nummenmaa, L., Lahnakoski, J. M., & Glerean, E. (2018). Sharing the social world via intersubject neural synchronisation. *Current Opinion in Psychology, 24*, 7–14.

Nummenmaa, L., Saarimäki, H., Glerean, E., Gotsopoulos, A., Jääskeläinen, I. P., Hari, R., & Sams, M. (2014). Emotional speech synchronizes brains across listeners and engages large-scale dynamic brain networks. *NeuroImage, 102*, 498–509.

Palumbo, R. V, Marraccini, M. E., Weyandt, L. L., Wilder-Smith, O., McGee, H. A., Liu, S., & Goodwin, M. S. (2017). Interpersonal autonomic physiology: A systematic review of the literature. *Personality and Social Psychology Review, 21*(2), 99–141.

Paulick, J., Deisenhofer, A.-K., Ramseyer, F., Tschacher, W., Boyle, K., Rubel, J., & Lutz, W. (2018). Nonverbal synchrony: A new approach to better understand psychotherapeutic processes and drop-out. *Journal of Psychotherapy Integration, 28*(3), 367.

Paulick, J., Rubel, J. A., Deisenhofer, A.-K., Schwartz, B., Thielemann, D., Altmann, U., ... Lutz, W. (2018). Diagnostic features of nonverbal synchrony in psychotherapy: Comparing depression and anxiety. *Cognitive Therapy and Research, 42*, 539–551.

Pickering, M. J., & Garrod, S. (2004). Toward a mechanistic psychology of dialogue. *Behavioral and Brain Sciences, 27*(2), 169–190.

Pinel, E. C., Bernecker, S. L., & Rampy, N. M. (2015). I-sharing on the couch: On the clinical implications of shared subjective experience. *Journal of Psychotherapy Integration, 25*(2), 59.

Ramseyer, F., & Tschacher, W. (2010). Nonverbal synchrony or random coincidence? How to tell the difference. In *Development of multimodal interfaces: Active listening and synchrony* (pp. 182–196). New York: Springer.

Ramseyer, F., & Tschacher, W. (2011). Nonverbal synchrony in psychotherapy: Coordinated body movement reflects relationship quality and outcome. *Journal of Consulting and Clinical Psychology, 79*(3), 284–295.

Ramseyer, F., & Tschacher, W. (2016). Movement coordination in psychotherapy: Synchrony of hand movements is associated with session outcome. A single-case study. *Nonlinear Dynamics, Psychology, and Life Sciences, 20*, 145–166.

Reich, C. M., Berman, J. S., Dale, R., & Levitt, H. M. (2014). Vocal synchrony in psychotherapy. *Journal of Social and Clinical Psychology, 33*(5), 481–494.

Reindl, V., Gerloff, C., Scharke, W., & Konrad, K. (2018). Brain-to-brain synchrony in parent-child dyads and the relationship with emotion regulation revealed by fNIRS-based hyperscanning. *Neuroimage, 178*, 493–502.

Remmers, C., Zimmermann, J., Buxton, A., Unger, H. P., Koole, S. L., Knaevelsrud, C., & Michalak, J. (2018). Emotionally aligned: Preliminary results on the effects of a mindfulness-based intervention for depression on congruence between implicit and explicit mood. *Clinical Psychology & Psychotherapy, 25*(6), 818–826.

Repp, B. H., & Su, Y.-H. (2013). Sensorimotor synchronization: A review of recent research (2006–2012). *Psychonomic Bulletin & Review, 20*(3), 403–452.

Richardson, M. J., Marsh, K. L., Isenhower, R. W., Goodman, J. R. L., & Schmidt, R. C. (2007). Rocking together: Dynamics of intentional and unintentional interpersonal coordination. *Human Movement Science*, 26(6), 867–891.

Rocco, D., Pastore, M., Gennaro, A., Salvatore, S., Cozzolino, M., & Scorza, M. (2018). Beyond verbal behavior: An empirical analysis of speech rates in psychotherapy sessions. *Frontiers in Psychology*, 9, 978.

Rogers, C. (1951). *Client-centered therapy*. Boston: Houghton Mifflin.

Schoenherr, D., Paulick, J., Worrack, S., Strauss, B. M., Rubel, J. A., Schwartz, B., ... Altmann, U. (2019). Quantification of nonverbal synchrony using linear time series analysis methods: Lack of convergent validity and evidence for facets of synchrony. *Behavior Research Methods*, 1–23.

Semin, G. R., & Cacioppo, J. T. (2008). *Grounding social cognition: Synchronization, coordination, and co-regulation*. New York: Cambridge University Press.

Shamay-Tsoory, S. G., Saporta, N., Marton-Alper, I. Z., & Gvirts, H. Z. (2019). Herding brains: A core neural mechanism for social alignment. *Trends in Cognitive Sciences*, 23, 174–186.

Shedler, J. (2010). The efficacy of psychodynamic psychotherapy. *American Psychologist*, 65(2), 98–108.

Shockley, K., Richardson, D. C., & Dale, R. (2009). Conversation and coordinative structures. *Topics in Cognitive Science*, 1(2), 305–319.

Tarr, B., Launay, J., & Dunbar, R. I. M. (2016). Silent disco: Dancing in synchrony leads to elevated pain thresholds and social closeness. *Evolution and Human Behavior*, 37(5), 343–349.

Timmons, A. C., Margolin, G., & Saxbe, D. E. (2015). Physiological linkage in couples and its implications for individual and interpersonal functioning: A literature review. *Journal of Family Psychology*, 29(5), 720.

Tracey, T. J. G., Wampold, B. E., Lichtenberg, J. W., & Goodyear, R. K. (2014). Expertise in psychotherapy: An elusive goal? *American Psychologist*, 69(3), 218.

Tschacher, W., & Meier, D. (2019). Physiological synchrony in psychotherapy sessions. *Psychotherapy Research*, 1–16.

Tschacher, W., Ramseyer, F., & Koole, S. L. (2018). Sharing the now in the social present: Duration of nonverbal synchrony is linked with personality. *Journal of Personality*, 86(2), 129–138.

Tschacher, W., Rees, G. M., & Ramseyer, F. (2014). Nonverbal synchrony and affect in dyadic interactions. *Frontiers in Psychology*, 5, 1323.

Vacharkulksemsuk, T., & Fredrickson, B. L. (2012). Strangers in sync: Achieving embodied rapport through shared movements. *Journal of Experimental Social Psychology*, 48(1), 399–402.

Valdesolo, P., & DeSteno, D. (2011). Synchrony and the social tuning of compassion. *Emotion*, 11(2), 262–266.

Valdesolo, P., Ouyang, J., & DeSteno, D. (2010). The rhythm of joint action: Synchrony promotes cooperative ability. *Journal of Experimental Social Psychology*, 46(4), 693–695.

Van Deurzen, E. (2012). *Existential counselling & psychotherapy in practice*. London: Sage.

Van Leeuwen, P., Geue, D., Thiel, M., Cysarz, D., Lange, S., Romano, M. C., ... Grönemeyer, D. H. (2009). Influence of paced maternal breathing on fetal–maternal heart rate coordination. *Proceedings of the National Academy of Sciences*, 106(33), 13661–13666.

van Ulzen, N. R., Lamoth, C. J. C., Daffertshofer, A., Semin, G. R., & Beek, P. J. (2008). Characteristics of instructed and uninstructed interpersonal coordination while walking side-by-side. *Neuroscience Letters*, 432(2), 88–93.

Wampold, B. E., & Imel, Z. E. (2015). *The great psychotherapy debate: The evidence for what makes psychotherapy work*. New York: Routledge.

Wiltermuth, S. S., & Heath, C. (2009). Synchrony and cooperation. *Psychological Science, 20*(1), 1–5.

Yalom, I. D. (1980). *Existential psychotherapy*. New York: Basic Books.

Zhang, Y., Meng, T., Hou, Y., Pan, Y., & Hu, Y. (2018). Interpersonal brain synchronization associated with working alliance during psychological counseling. *Psychiatry Research: Neuroimaging, 282*, 103–109.

Zilcha-Mano, S. (2017). Is the alliance really therapeutic? Revisiting this question in light of recent methodological advances. *American Psychologist, 72*(4), 311–325.

PART III
Improving Interpersonal Relations and Communication

10
APPLICATIONS OF ATTACHMENT THEORY AND RESEARCH

The Blossoming of Relationship Science

Mario Mikulincer and Phillip R. Shaver

Attachment theory is one of the most influential contemporary conceptual frameworks for understanding mental health, psychological functioning, and social behavior. In his seminal exposition of the theory, Bowlby (1982) explained why the availability of caring, loving relationship partners, beginning in infancy, is so important to developing a sense of safety and security (see also Crano & Ruybal, this volume). This sense facilitates emotion regulation, promotes harmonious and satisfying interpersonal interactions, and sustains psychological well-being and mental health. In this chapter, we briefly review basic concepts of attachment theory, focusing on the "broaden and build" cycle of attachment security (Mikulincer & Shaver, 2003) and the growth-enhancing consequences of secure attachments. We then review and assess empirical findings concerning the ways in which attachment theory is being applied in the fields of psychotherapy, education, health and medicine, and leadership and management.

Attachment Theory: Basic Concepts

According to attachment theory (Bowlby, 1982), human beings are born with an innate and evolutionarily determined psychobiological system (the *attachment behavioral system*) that motivates them to seek proximity to protective others (*attachment figures*) in times of need (see also van Vugt et al., this volume). According to Bowlby (1988), attachment figures function as a "safe haven" in times of need – i.e., they provide protection, comfort, and relief – and a "secure base," encouraging autonomous pursuit of non-attachment goals while remaining available if needed. In this way, attachment figures provide a sense of attachment security (confidence that one is worthy and lovable and that others will be supportive when needed). Provision of this sense of security normally terminates proximity-seeking bids and allows a person to function better in a wide array of non-attachment activities, such as exploration, learning, interpersonal exchanges, and sexual mating.

Bowlby (1973) also described important individual differences in the extent to which a person holds a solid sense of security. In his view, these individual differences are rooted in reactions of one's attachment figures to bids for proximity and support in times of need, and the incorporation of these reactions into mental representations of self and others (*internal working models*). Interactions with attachment figures who are sensitive and responsive to one's proximity bids facilitate the smooth, normal functioning of the attachment system, promote a sense of connectedness and security, and contribute to positive working models of self and others. When a person's attachment figures are not reliably available and supportive, however, worries about one's social value and others' harmful intentions are strengthened, and the person becomes less secure in interpersonal relationships and less confident in dealing with threats and challenges (Bowlby, 1973).

Pursuing these theoretical ideas in adulthood, researchers have focused on a person's *attachment orientation*, a systematic pattern of relational expectations, emotions, and behaviors that results from a particular history of interactions with attachment figures (Fraley & Shaver, 2000). These orientations can be conceptualized as regions in a continuous two-dimensional space (e.g., Brennan, Clark, & Shaver, 1998). One dimension, attachment-related *avoidance*, reflects the extent to which a person distrusts others' intentions and defensively strives to maintain excessive behavioral and emotional independence. The other dimension, attachment-related anxiety, reflects the extent to which a person worries that others will not be available in times of need and anxiously seeks love and care. A person's general attachment orientation can be viewed as the top node in a complex network of attachment representations, some of which apply only to specific people and relationships and others which apply only in certain relational contexts (Collins & Read, 1994). These more specific mental representations can be activated by actual or imagined encounters with supportive or unsupportive others even if they are incongruent with the dominant attachment orientation (Mikulincer & Shaver, 2007).

We (Mikulincer & Shaver, 2003) have proposed that individuals' location in the two-dimensional anxiety-by-avoidance space reflects both their sense of attachment security and the ways in which they deal with threats and challenges. People who score low on both insecurity dimensions are generally secure, hold positive working models of self and others, and tend to employ constructive and effective affect-regulation strategies. Those who score high on either attachment anxiety or avoidance, or both, suffer from attachment insecurities and worries, and tend to use secondary attachment strategies that we, following Cassidy and Kobak (1988), characterize as attachment-system "hyperactivation" or "deactivation" when coping with threats, frustrations, rejections, and losses. People who score high on attachment anxiety rely on hyperactivating strategies – energetic attempts to achieve support and love combined with lack of confidence that these desired resources will be provided, and with feelings of anger and despair when they are not provided (Cassidy & Kobak, 1988). In contrast, people who score high on attachment-related avoidance tend to use deactivating strategies, attempting not to seek proximity to others when threatened, denying vulnerability and needs for other people, and avoiding closeness and interdependence in relationships. People who score high on both dimensions (labeled "fearfully avoidant" by Bartholomew, 1990) exhibit inconsistent, conflicted relational strategies based on desiring comfort and closeness while simultaneously fearing it.

The Broaden-and-Build Cycle of Attachment Security

According to our model of adult attachment-system functioning (Mikulincer & Shaver, 2003, 2016), appraisal of the availability and supportiveness of an attachment figure in times of need automatically activates mental representations of attachment security. These representations include both declarative and procedural knowledge organized around a relational prototype or "secure-base script" (Waters & Waters, 2006), which contains something like the following if-then propositions: "If I encounter an obstacle and/or become distressed, I can approach a significant other for help; he or she is likely to be available and supportive; I will experience relief and comfort as a result of proximity to this person; I can then return to other activities." Having many experiences that contribute to the construction of this script makes it easier for a person to confront stressful situations with optimistic expectations and to feel relative calm while coping with problems. Indeed, adolescents and adults who score lower on attachment anxiety or avoidance scales (more secure) are more likely to hold rich and fully developed secure-base scripts in mind when narrating threat-related stories or dreams (e.g., Mikulincer, Shaver, Sapir-Lavid, & Avihou-Kanza, 2009).

Attachment-figure availability also fosters what we, following Fredrickson (2001), call a broaden-and-build cycle of attachment security, which increases a person's resilience and expands his or her perspectives, coping flexibility, and skills and capabilities. By imparting a pervasive sense of safety, assuaging distress, and evoking positive emotions, interactions with responsive attachment figures allow secure people to remain relatively unperturbed in times of stress and to experience longer periods of positive affect, which in turn contributes to their sustained emotional well-being and mental health (see also Crano & Ruybal; Kross; and Walton & Brady, this volume). This heightened resilience is further sustained by a reservoir of core positive mental representations and memories derived from interactions with responsive attachment figures. During these interactions, people learn that distress is manageable and that others are benevolent, trustworthy, and kind. They also learn to view themselves as strong and competent, because they can effectively mobilize a partner's support when needed and can function autonomously when conditions warrant. Moreover, they perceive themselves as valuable, lovable, and special, thanks to being valued, loved, and regarded as special by caring attachment figures. Research has consistently shown that hope, optimism, and positive views of self and others are characteristic of secure persons (e.g., Baldwin, Fehr, Keedian, Seidel, & Thomson, 1993; Collins & Read, 1990; Mikulincer & Florian, 1998).

Besides building one's strength and resilience, experiences of attachment-figure availability have beneficial effects on pro-relational cognitions (beliefs that closeness is rewarding and that one can trust partners), thereby heightening secure people's chances of establishing and maintaining intimate and harmonious relationships. In addition, this heightened resilience allows secure people to feel safe and protected without having to deploy defensive strategies that can distort perception and generate tension and conflict (see also Krahé, this volume). Rather, they can devote mental resources that otherwise would be employed in preventive, defensive maneuvers to the pursuit of other non-attachment goals (e.g., exploration, affiliation). Moreover, being confident that support is available when needed, secure people can take calculated risks and accept important challenges that contribute to the broadening of their perspectives and facilitate the pursuit of self-actualization. Indeed, research has shown that adults scoring lower on attachment anxiety and/or avoidance scales form more stable and mutually satisfactory close relationships and tend to fully engage, enjoy, and thrive in non-attachment activities, such as learning, caregiving, and sex (see Feeney, 2016; Mikulincer & Shaver, 2016, for reviews).

Theoretically, the broaden-and-build cycle of security is renewed every time a person notices that an actual or imaginary caring attachment figure is available in times of stress. In examining this hypothesis, researchers have experimentally primed representations of a responsive attachment figure by exposing participants to the name or picture of this figure, or asking them to visualize this person's face or to imagine a security-enhancing interaction with him or her (see Mikulincer & Shaver, 2016, for a review of priming techniques, see also Papies, this volume, for the effects of priming food cues on eating). Findings have consistently shown that a contextual infusion of security (*security priming*) has positive effects on social cognitions, mood, and psychological functioning (e.g., Luke, Sedikides, & Carnelley, 2012; Mikulincer, Shaver, Gillath, & Nitzberg, 2005; Otway, Carnelley, & Rowe, 2014).

These laboratory findings have inspired attachment researchers to examine the renewal of the broad-and-build cycle of attachment security within real-life relational contexts (see Fiedler, this volume, for the need of well-controlled experiments in the laboratory before going to field studies). These field studies have consistently found that when a relationship partner's supportive behaviors are evident, personally significant, and repeated over time and situations, chronically insecure people tend to deal more effectively with life problems and adversities and to deploy mental resources in other non-attachment activities (see Mikulincer & Shaver, 2016, for a review). These theoretical ideas and research findings provide a foundation for applying attachment theory to a wide variety of life domains, such as marital relationships and educational and healthcare settings, with the goal of improving psychological functioning and quality of life in each such domain. In the next section, we briefly review some of these applications of attachment theory.

Applications of Attachment Theory

Originally, attachment theory (Bowlby, 1982) was formulated to explain infant-parent emotional bonding and its anxiety-buffering and growth-promoting functions in early childhood. However, based on Bowlby's (1979, p. 129) claim that attachment needs are active "from the cradle to the grave," attachment researchers have expanded the theory to examine the broaden-and-build cycle of attachment security and the psychological problems generated from attachment insecurities to other relational contexts and at other ages and developmental stages (see Mikulincer & Shaver, 2016, for a review). The expanded theory is being used to explain psychological functioning and thriving in a wide variety of life domains as well as to construct intervention programs that foster the broaden-and-build cycle of attachment security in those domains. Such applications are based on three principles:

(a) Threats and distress-eliciting events in a given life domain activate the attachment system and a person's dominant working models of self and others, which in turn shapes his or her motives, cognitions, and behaviors in that domain.
(b) A person's responses to stress and distress in a given life domain are also affected by the quality of interactions he or she has with others who fulfil the role of attachment figure in that context. That is, interactions with figures who are a target for proximity seeking in times of need and potential context-specific providers of a safe haven and/or a secure base.
(c) Interactions with a sensitive and responsive attachment figure in a given life domain set in motion a context-specific broaden-and-build cycle of security and the resulting cascade of positive outcomes derived from this cycle.

With those principles in mind, attachment theory can be applied to any life domain in which people feel threatened or distressed, and in which there is an actual person or symbolic figure who can provide a safe haven and secure base. This figure can have a close emotional relationship with the threatened person (e.g., parent, friend, spouse) or can occupy the formal role of a "stronger and wiser" caregiver in a specific context (e.g., teacher, therapist, manager, priest). In such cases, a person's dominant attachment orientation can be projected onto the potential security provider, thereby biasing the person's pattern of relating and responses to this figure. However, this figure's responsiveness to bids for proximity and support can counteract this projection and cause meaningful changes in a care recipient's psychological functioning. Hence, attachment-based interventions aimed at bringing positive psychological change to a given life domain (a) target the security provider as the agent of change and (b) attempt to heighten his or her responsiveness and capacity to provide empathic and effective care and support the distressed person's autonomous growth and thriving.

The original application of attachment theory occurred in the domain of parent-child relations. Numerous cross-sectional and prospective longitudinal studies consistently found that parents' responsiveness to their infants' signals and needs contributed to children's security in relation to parent (in Ainsworth's *Strange Situation*; Ainsworth, Blehar, Waters, & Wall, 1978) and more favorable developmental outcomes (see Thompson, 2015, for a review, see also Crano & Ruybal, this volume). There is also extensive evidence that parents' attachment orientations contribute to their child's attachment security and favorable psychological development (see Verhage et al., 2016, for a review and meta-analysis). Longitudinal studies have revealed that these effects tend to persist over time and contribute to adolescent and adult well-being and functioning (e.g., Haydon, Collins, Salvatore, Simpson, & Roisman, 2012).

Based on these findings, child psychologists have created attachment-based intervention programs aimed at heightening parents' responsiveness as a means of fostering children's positive development. Some of these programs include short-term interventions (5–16 weeks), mostly relying on parents' psycho-education and video feedback of their behavior during interactions with their infants. Research findings clearly indicate that infants' attachment security is enhanced when parents participate in these short-term programs, especially when parents themselves show improved post-intervention responsiveness (see Mountain, Cahill, & Thorpe, 2017, for review and meta-analysis). Similar positive effects have been obtained in studies of more intensive and longer (20 weeks to one year) intervention programs (e.g., Hoffman, Marvin, Cooper, & Powell, 2006; Lieberman, Ippen, & Van Horn, 2006; Slade, Sadler, & Mayes, 2005). Most of these interventions include not only psycho-education and video feedback, but also psychotherapeutic techniques aimed at correcting parents' attachment-related fears and defenses that interfere with the provision of empathic care.

In adulthood, a romantic or marital partner is often a person's primary attachment figure (e.g., Zeifman & Hazan, 2016). Therefore, attachment theory is being applied to the field of couple and marital counseling. During the past 40 years, hundreds of studies have documented the crucial contribution of a person's dominant attachment orientation to motives, cognitions, feelings, and behavior in the context of couple and marital relationships (see Feeney, 2016, and Mikulincer & Shaver, 2016, for reviews). At the same time, there is growing evidence that a sensitive and responsive romantic partner can counteract the destructive intrusion of the other partner's attachment insecurities into a couple relationship, buffering the detrimental effects of attachment anxiety and avoidance (see Arriaga, Kumashiro, Simpson, & Overall, 2018, for a review). Moreover, supportive and loving couple interactions have been found to attenuate partners' distress and contribute to psychological well-being, physical health, and longevity (see Holt-Lunstad & Smith, 2012, & Taylor & Broffman, 2011, for reviews). Correlational and experimental studies have also indicated that actual or imagined interactions with a responsive dating partner or spouse promote a wide variety of pro-relational cognitions and behaviors that heighten relationship stability and satisfaction (see Reis, 2014, for a review).

The increasing body of evidence highlighting the growth-promoting role of a partner's responsiveness within couple relationships led Sue Johnson (2003) to apply attachment theory to the field of couple therapy and to develop an attachment-based intervention – Emotion-Focused Therapy (EFT). Johnson (2003) conceptualizes relationship distress as resulting from one partner's lack of responsiveness to the other partner's support-seeking bids and from their own unacknowledged and unmet attachment needs (*attachment injuries*). EFT helps partners acknowledge basic attachment needs, insecurities, and injuries and improve their ability to respond to each other with sensitive and responsive care, resulting in more positive and pro-relational interactions (see also Walton & Brady on positive interventions, this volume). There is growing evidence that heightening partners' functioning as a secure base to one another within the context of EFT dramatically reduces relationship distress and improves the quality of the relationship (see Greenman, Johnson, & Wiebe, 2019, for a review).

Besides these two relational contexts – parent-child and couple relationships – attachment theory has been applied to other life domains in which a person formally occupies or is expected to occupy the role of security provider (e.g., teacher, therapist, supervisor). In the following sections, we review some of these applications to counseling and psychotherapy, education, health and medicine, and leadership and management.

Counseling and Psychotherapy

In applying attachment theory to counseling and psychotherapy, Bowlby (1988) emphasized that clients typically enter therapy in a state of frustration, distress, and psychological pain, which automatically activates their attachment system and causes them to yearn for support and relief. Attachment needs are easy to direct toward therapists, because therapists, at least when a client believes in their healing powers, are perceived as "stronger and wiser" caregivers. Therapists are expected to know better than their clients how to deal with the clients' problems, and they occupy the dominant and caregiving role in the relationship. As a result, the therapist can easily become a potential provider of security and a target of the client's projection of attachment-related worries and defenses. Moreover, the therapist's responsiveness to clients' support-seeking bids becomes crucial in facilitating clients' broaden-and-build cycle of attachment security and fostering positive therapy outcomes (see also Koole et al., this volume). With this in mind, Bowlby (1988) developed a model of therapeutic change focused on the ability of a responsive therapist to provide a secure base from which clients can explore and understand their painful attachment experiences, identify and revise insecure working models of self and others, and acquire more adaptive patterns of relating.

Bowlby (1988) discussed five therapeutic tasks that contribute to the revision of insecure mental representations and to the achievement of positive therapeutic outcomes. The first is to provide clients with a safe haven and secure base from which they can begin to explore painful memories and emotions and maladaptive beliefs and behaviors. This is a precondition for all of the other aspects of the therapeutic process. The second and third tasks are to encourage clients to consider how beliefs and expectations about themselves and others influence how they think, feel, and act in relationships, including in the therapeutic relationship itself. The fourth task is to help clients assess how current thoughts, feelings, and behaviors may have originated in childhood relationships with parents or other caregivers. The fifth task is to help clients understand that previous ways of thinking and behaving may not be well-adapted to their current lives and to imagine and practice alternative, healthier ways of coping and relating. In this way, therapists' encouragement of inner exploration in a secure environment can promote clients' broaden-and-build cycle of security and facilitate therapeutic change and personal growth (see also Walton & Brady, this volume).

Research has provided support for this attachment-focused conceptualization of psychotherapy. Numerous studies have shown that clients' pre-therapy attachment orientations bias their attitudes toward therapists and therapy, shape the establishment of a good working alliance, and affect therapeutic outcomes (see Bernecker, Levy, & Ellison, 2014; Levy, Kivity, Johnson, & Gooch, 2018; and Mikulincer & Shaver, 2016, for reviews and meta-analyses). In addition, there is evidence that clients tend to perceive therapists as security providers (Parish & Eagle, 2003) and that therapists' responsiveness has beneficial effects on therapy outcomes (e.g., Håvås, Svartberg, & Ulvenes, 2015). Studies have also found that the formation of clients' secure attachment to a therapist has beneficial effects on therapeutic change (see Mallinckrodt & Jeong, 2015, for a meta-analysis; see also Koole et al., this volume, for the important role played by therapist-client relational synchrony in fostering therapeutic change). There is also growing evidence that therapy can move clients away from insecure and toward secure attachment orientations, and that this movement is a good indication of effective treatment. For example, Travis, Bliwise, Binder, and Horne-Moyer (2001) found an increase in clients' reports of secure attachment across the course of time-limited dynamic psychotherapy, and this increase was associated with decreases in the severity of psychiatric symptoms. Similarly, Maxwell, Tasca, Ritchie, Balfour, and Bissada (2014) found that attachment insecurities decreased during group psychotherapy, and that this decrease predicted improvement in clients' well-being and functioning up to 12 months after therapy.

Several evidence-based therapies have incorporated Bowlby's (1988) principles of therapeutic change in both individual and group psychotherapy. Among these therapies are the following: *Mentalization-Based Therapy* (MBT, Bateman & Fonagy, 2004), *Accelerated Experiential-Dynamic Psychotherapy* (AEDP, Fosha, 2000), *Attachment-Based Group Psychotherapy* (ABGP, Marmarosh, Markin, & Spiegel, 2013) and *Group Psychodynamic Interpersonal Psychotherapy* (GPIP, Tasca, Mikail, & Hewitt, 2005). These attachment-based interventions explicitly recognize the trauma induced by rejection, separation, and loss, and the impact of these experiences on mental health, the self-fulfilling nature of attachment working models, and the positive therapeutic effects of interventions that focus on developing secure emotional connections with a therapist and other relationship partners. Moreover, they underscore the importance of the therapist providing a safe haven and secure base for the exploration and revision of maladaptive working models. There is growing evidence that these attachment-based approaches are more effective than other cognitive-behavioral or psychodynamic approaches in improving mental health and psychosocial functioning (e.g., Bateman & Fonagy, 2008; Marmarosh et al., 2013; Maxwell et al., 2014).

Education

Attachment theory has been applied to the field of education, where it provides a conceptual framework for understanding the relational basis of academic performance and socio-emotional adjustment to school (e.g., Ladd, Kochenderfer-Ladd, & Rydell, 2014; Pianta, 2016). Several studies have shown that a child who has a more secure attachment to parents tends to appraise teachers as more responsive and to elicit more caregiving behavior from them (see Ahnert, Pinquart, & Lamb, 2006, and Williford, Carter, & Pianta, 2016, for reviews and meta-analyses). Moreover, children's attachment security to parents has been reliably associated with more school readiness and better socio-emotional adjustment to school during the early school years (see Williford et al., 2016, for a review).

There is also a large theoretical and empirical literature concerning the effects of teachers' responsiveness on children's adjustment to school (see Ladd et al., 2014; Pianta, 2016, for reviews). Theoretically, teachers, mainly at the kindergarten and elementary school levels, function as context-specific attachment figures who can provide comfort and support within the school setting. Moreover, they can function as a secure base from which children can explore and learn, take risks, and even make mistakes, with the confidence that their teacher's support will be available when needed (Wentzel, 2016). As a result, children whose teacher functions as a security provider can maintain an open and confident attitude toward learning and remain calm while coping with school-related threats and challenges. In support of this view, many studies have shown that children whose teacher is warmer and more emotionally responsive tend to exhibit better socio-emotional and academic adjustment to school (see Roorda, Jak, Zee, Oort, & Koomen, 2017, for review and meta-analysis). Moreover, field experiments have found that improving teachers' responsiveness to students' needs improves the children's academic functioning and adjustment to school (e.g., Murray & Malmgren, 2005; Webster-Stratton, Reid, & Hammond, 2004).

Based on such research findings, Pianta, La Paro, and Hamre (2008) developed a systematic classroom observation system that captures the extent to which a teacher is responsive to children's support-seeking bids and provides a secure climate to explore and learn: The Classroom Assessment Scoring System (CLASS). The primary domains assessed in the CLASS are emotional support (teacher's ability to manage students' emotional needs), classroom organization (teacher's ability to manage students' behaviors), and instructional support (teacher's ability to provide constructive and supportive feedback on students' academic efforts and performance). The CLASS has been found to have good psychometric qualities and to predict students' academic functioning and adjustment to school (e.g., Hamre, Hatfield, Pianta, & Jamil, 2014; Mashburn et al., 2008).

The CLASS has also been used to evaluate a teacher's functioning as a secure base and improve student-teacher interactions. For example, Head Start uses CLASS scores to help determine the accreditation of new pre-kindergarten teachers (Hamre et al., 2014). In addition, evidence-based professional development programs, such as My Teaching Partner (MTP, Pianta, Mashburn, Downer, Hamre, & Justice, 2008), use the CLASS framework to analyze videotaped teacher-student interactions and provide feedback to teachers on their functioning as a secure base. In the MTP program, for example, teachers work with a personal coach throughout the program and are given the opportunity to watch videotaped teacher-student interactions of highly responsive teachers, identify security-enhancing responses to students' needs, and receive ongoing constructive feedback from the coach on their own interactions with students. The coach, working with the teacher, then creates an action plan for the teacher to change his or her interactions with students and improve his or her functioning as a secure base. Studies have found the MTP effective in improving teachers' responsiveness and heightening children's academic functioning and adjustment to school (see Williford et al., 2016, for a review).

Health and Medicine

From an attachment perspective, physical pain, injuries, and illnesses can provoke fear and distress, which automatically activates the attachment system. As a result, needs for protection and support and characteristic attachment orientations, including working models of self and others, are activated and directed toward people who can reduce illness-related worries and distress. According to Maunder and Hunter (2015), this kind of attachment-system activation is likely to be directed toward physicians and other healthcare providers in medical settings, because they are perceived as a source of knowledge, healing, and physical safety. That is, they generally occupy the role of "stronger and wiser" caregivers in the physician-client relationship. Thus, we can expect clients to appraise physicians as fulfilling, or not fulfilling, the attachment functions of a safe haven and secure base. Moreover, we can hypothesize that clients will project their attachment concerns and orientations onto their relationships with physicians, which may be relevant to explaining individual differences in the healing process. In addition, physicians' responsiveness to clients' support-seeking bids can be expected to contribute to patients' distress management, compliance with treatment, and the entire healing process.

Based on this reasoning, Maunder and Hunter (2016) constructed a self-report scale tapping whether a healthcare provider functions as a safe haven (e.g., "In some circumstances, I might count on this person to help me feel better") and a secure base (e.g., "This person makes me feel more confident about my health"). Patients were asked to nominate healthcare providers "who matter to you more than others" and to complete the scale for each of the identified providers. Ninety-one percent of the participants were able to identify at least one healthcare provider who mattered most, and the majority of them appraised these healthcare providers as fulfilling safe haven and secure-base functions.

Research also provides evidence that attachment orientations are relevant for explaining individual variations in health-related behaviors. For example, attachment anxiety and avoidance have been associated with less engagement in health-promoting behaviors, such as maintaining a healthy diet or engaging in physical activity, and more engagement in health-related risks, such as smoking, drinking, drug abuse, and eating disorders (e.g., Ahrens, Ciechanowski, & Katon, 2012; Davis et al., 2014, see also Papies, this volume). For example, Ciechanowski, Walker, Katon, and Russo (2002) assessed attachment orientations in a large sample of primary care patients and found that women scoring higher on attachment insecurities were less likely to make healthcare visits over a six-month period, despite reporting higher symptom levels.

There is also consistent evidence that attachment insecurities can intrude and interfere with medical treatment, the physician-client relationship, and the healing process. First, attachment insecurities have been found to interfere with adherence to medical regimens among people diagnosed with a wide variety of physical problems (e.g., Tuck & Consedine, 2015). Second, attachment insecurities have been found to foster catastrophic perceptions of physical illness, which in turn interfere with the healing process (e.g., Vilchinsky, Dekel, Asher, Leibowitz, & Mosseri, 2013). Third, attachment insecurities have been found to interfere with restorative biological processes (e.g., Robles, Brooks, Kane, & Schetter, 2013) and to heighten inflammatory stress-related responses that counteract the healing process (e.g., Kidd, Hamer, & Steptoe, 2013).

Research also indicates that patients' attachment insecurities are associated with more negative attitudes toward physicians and poorer trust in them (e.g., Calvo, Palmieri, Marinelli, Bianco, & Kleinbub, 2014). Maunder et al. (2006) asked physicians (who were blind to clients' attachment scores) to rate the difficulty of their relationships with particular patients. Physicians reported having more troubled relationships with insecure than secure patients. That is, insecure patients' relational problems were evident in physician-patient relationships.

Despite the cumulative evidence highlighting the relevance of attachment theory for health and medicine, there is no systematic research program on the contribution of physicians' responsiveness and ability to effectively manage client's emotional needs to the client's health and physical recovery. In our review of the literature, we found only one study reporting that physicians' attachment insecurities, which probably make them less responsive to clients, were associated with clients' lower satisfaction with treatment (Kafetsios, Hantzara, Anagnostopoulos, & Niakas, 2016). Moreover, there is no evidence-based medical training program aimed at cultivating physicians' responsiveness and functioning as a secure base (see Blanton, Burrows, & Regan, this volume, for video simulations in the field of health and medicine). However, in their pioneering book, *Love, Fear, and Health*, Maunder and Hunter (2015) provided practical recommendations to healthcare providers about how to manage clients' attachment-related worries and defenses and how to make clients feel more secure. We hope that these efforts will ultimately result in important changes in medical education and in the development of attachment-based training programs, which would aid healing and reduce expenses for both clients and the medical system.

Leadership and Management

From an attachment perspective, there is a close correspondence between leaders (e.g., managers, political and religious authorities, supervisors, and military officers) and attachment figures. "Leaders, like parents, are figures whose role includes guiding, directing, taking charge, and taking care of others less powerful than they and whose fate is highly dependent on them" (Popper & Mayseless, 2003, p. 42). That is, leaders often occupy the role of "stronger and wiser" caregivers and can provide a secure base for their subordinates (Mayseless & Popper, 2007). Like other security-enhancing attachment figures, effective leaders are likely to be responsive to their subordinates' needs; to provide advice, guidance, and emotional and instrumental resources to group members, affirm subordinates' ability to deal with challenges, and encourage learning and personal growth (Haslam, Reicher, & Platow, 2015).

Following this attachment-based conceptualization of leadership, a responsive leader can support the broaden-and-build cycle of attachment security in subordinates, increasing their self-esteem, competence, autonomy, and well-being. By the same token, as in other cases of unresponsive attachment figures, a leader's inability or unwillingness to respond sensitively and supportively to subordinates' needs can magnify their anxieties and lead to feelings of demoralization and an inclination to disengage. In these cases, a non-responsive leader can radically alter the leader-subordinate relationship and transform what began with the promise of a secure base into a destructive, conflicted, hostile relationship that is damaging to the leader, his or her subordinates, and the organization to which they belong.

In two studies conducted with Israeli combat soldiers and their direct officers, Davidovitz, Mikulincer, Shaver, Ijzak, and Popper (2007) provided empirical support for this attachment-focused conceptualization of leadership. In one study, an officer's ability to provide effective emotional and instrumental support to his soldiers in times of need (as rated by himself and his soldiers) contributed positively to his soldiers' instrumental and socio-emotional functioning. In a second study, Davidovitz et al. (2007) found that soldiers' appraisal of their officer as a secure base during combat training (i.e., the officer's ability and willingness to accept and care for his or her soldiers rather than rejecting and criticizing them) produced positive changes in soldiers' mental health two and four months later. These findings highlight the importance of a leader's responsiveness in sustaining subordinates' mental health.

Subsequent studies have built upon and extended Davidovitz et al.'s (2007) findings to business organizations, showing that managers' responsiveness contributes positively to workers' job satisfaction, organizational commitment, and psychological well-being (e.g., Lavy, 2014; Ronen & Mikulincer, 2012; Wu & Parker, 2017). Conceptually similar findings have been reported in studies of relationships between school directors and teachers (e.g., Kafetsios, Athanasiadou, & Dimou, 2014), and between coaches and athletes (e.g., Davis, Jowett, & Lafrenière, 2013). Using an experimental manipulation of supervisor behavior, Game (2008) found that less secure workers reacted to a manager's cold and rejecting behavior with greater distress.

Although these findings support the conceptualization of supervisors and managers as security providers, this role is still undervalued in some contemporary management literature, which advocates the creation of cool, and exciting organizational cultures to increase workers' engagement and satisfaction (Rheem, 2017). We know of no evidence-based leadership development program based on attachment-theory principles for enhancing leaders' ability to consider and react effectively to subordinates' emotional needs. These programs might be crucial in organizational contexts where a socially-oriented leader might be more effective than a task-oriented leader. However, some attachment-theory principles can be found in positive leadership programs that train leaders to be emotionally available, mentor their subordinates, attend to and validate their subordinates' needs, recognize their accomplishments, and encourage their autonomous growth (e.g., Cameron, 2012, see also Schmader, Bergsieker, & Hall, this volume, for positive interventions aimed at increasing inclusion in organizations). In fact, organizational scientists and professionals are becoming more aware of attachment theory and the benefits of cultivating emotionally safe organizations and transforming managers into security-enhancing attachment figures.

Conclusions

In this chapter, we have briefly reviewed theory and research findings concerning the application of attachment theory to the domains of parenting, of counseling and psychotherapy, education, health and medicine, and leadership and management. This is only a partial list of applications of attachment theory and research. Due to space limitations, we have not included findings showing the relevance of attachment theory for understanding individual differences in career development, work engagement, financial decisions, consumer behavior, moral judgments, group-related attitudes and behavior, religious orientations and spiritual development, and political attitudes and behavior (Mikulincer & Shaver, 2016). Moreover, we have not addressed how attachment theory and research inform social policy related to domestic violence, divorce, child custody, child maltreatment, foster care, adoption, and incarceration and rehabilitation of delinquent adolescents and adult criminals (Shaver, Mikulincer, & Feeney, 2009). We also did not have space to consider implications of attachment theory and research for political systems (e.g., the welfare state as a security provider; Gruneau Brulin, Hill, Laurin, Mikulincer, & Granqvist, 2018), terrorism, intergroup violence and war, and intergroup reconciliation and peace education (Mikulincer & Shaver, 2016).

Nevertheless, we hope we have demonstrated the broad relevance of attachment theory and research to many domains of life in which temporary or continuing close relationships matter greatly to the well-being of individuals, families, groups, and organizations. Human beings are, first and foremost, social beings; the human mind is a complex, highly-evolved device for dealing with social relationships; and the attachment processes evident from birth through the first years of life continue to show themselves, as Bowlby (1979) said, "from the cradle to the grave." Noticing and nurturing the attachment aspects of all relationships could make an enormous contribution to individuals' mental and physical health and the quality and benefits of their diverse relationships. There is now adequate basic and applied research to inspire future applications and interventions.

References

Ahnert, L., Pinquart, M., & Lamb, M. E. (2006). Security of children's relationships with non-parental care providers: A meta-analysis. *Child Development, 77*, 664-679.

Ahrens, K. R., Ciechanowski, P., & Katon, W. (2012). Associations between adult attachment style and health risk behaviors in an adult female primary care population. *Journal of Psychosomatic Research, 72*, 364–370.

Ainsworth, M. D. S., Blehar, M. C., Waters, E., & Wall, S. (1978). *Patterns of attachment: Assessed in the strange situation and at home.* Hillsdale, NJ: Erlbaum.

Arriaga, X. B., Kumashiro, M., Simpson, J. A., & Overall, N. C. (2018). Revising working models across time: Relationship situations that enhance attachment security. *Personality and Social Psychology Review, 22*, 71–96.

Baldwin, M. W., Fehr, B., Keedian, E., Seidel, M., & Thomson, D. W. (1993). An exploration of the relational schemata underlying attachment styles: Self-report and lexical decision approaches. *Personality and Social Psychology Bulletin, 19*, 746–754.

Bartholomew, K. (1990). Avoidance of intimacy: An attachment perspective. *Journal of Social and Personal Relationships, 7*, 147–178.

Bateman, A., & Fonagy, P. (2004). *Psychotherapy for borderline personality disorder: Mentalization-based treatment.* Oxford, UK: Oxford University Press.

Bateman A., & Fonagy, P. (2008). 8-year follow-up of patients treated for borderline personality disorder: Mentalization-based treatment versus treatment as usual. *American Journal of Psychiatry, 165*, 631–638.

Bernecker, S. L., Levy, K. N., & Ellison, W. D. (2014). A meta-analysis of the relation between patient adult attachment style and the working alliance. *Psychotherapy Research, 24*, 12–24.

Bowlby, J. (1973). *Attachment and loss: Vol. 2. Separation: Anxiety and anger.* New York: Basic Books.

Bowlby, J. (1979). *The making and breaking of affectional bonds.* London: Tavistock.

Bowlby, J. (1982). *Attachment and loss: Vol. 1. Attachment* (2nd ed.). New York: Basic Books. (Original ed. 1969)

Bowlby, J. (1988). *A secure base: Clinical applications of attachment theory.* London: Routledge.

Brennan, K. A., Clark, C. L., & Shaver, P. R. (1998). Self-report measurement of adult romantic attachment: An integrative overview. In J. A. Simpson & W. S. Rholes (Eds.), *Attachment theory and close relationships* (pp. 46–76). New York: Guilford Press.

Calvo, V., Palmieri, A., Marinelli, S., Bianco, F., & Kleinbub, J. R. (2014). Reciprocal empathy and working alliance in terminal oncological illness: The crucial role of patients' attachment style. *Journal of Psychosocial Oncology, 32*, 517–534.

Cameron, K. (2012). *Positive leadership: Strategies for extraordinary performance*. San Francisco, CA: Berrett-Koehler.

Cassidy, J., & Kobak, R. R. (1988). Avoidance and its relationship with other defensive processes. In J. Belsky & T. Nezworski (Eds.), *Clinical implications of attachment* (pp. 300–323). Hillsdale, NJ: Erlbaum.

Ciechanowski, P. S., Walker, E. A., Katon, W. J., & Russo, J. E. (2002). Attachment theory: A model for health care utilization and somatization. *Psychosomatic Medicine, 64*, 660–667.

Collins, N. L., & Read, S. J. (1990). Adult attachment, working models, and relationship quality in dating couples. *Journal of Personality and Social Psychology, 58*, 644–663.

Collins, N. L., & Read, S. J. (1994). Cognitive representations of attachment: The structure and function of working models. In K. Bartholomew & D. Perlman (Eds.), *Advances in personal relationships: Attachment processes in adulthood* (Vol. 5, pp. 53–92). London: Jessica Kingsley.

Davidovitz, R., Mikulincer, M., Shaver, P. R., Ijzak, R., & Popper, M. (2007). Leaders as attachment figures: Their attachment orientations predict leadership-related mental representations and followers' performance and mental health. *Journal of Personality and Social Psychology, 93*, 632–650.

Davis, C. R., Usher, N., Dearing, E., Barkai, A. R., Crowell-Doom, C., Neupert, S. D., Mantzoros, C. S., & Crowell, J. A. (2014). Attachment and the metabolic syndrome in midlife: The role of interview-based discourse patterns. *Psychosomatic Medicine, 76*, 611–621.

Davis, L., Jowett, S., & Lafrenière, M. K. (2013). An attachment theory perspective in the examination of relational processes associated with coach-athlete dyads. *Journal of Sport & Exercise Psychology, 35*, 155–167.

Feeney, J. A. (2016). Adult romantic attachment: Developments in the study of couple relationships. In J. Cassidy & P. R. Shaver (Eds.), *Handbook of attachment: Theory, research, and clinical applications* (3rd ed., pp. 435–463). New York: Guilford Press.

Fosha, D. (2000). *The transforming power of affect: A model for accelerated change*. New York: Basic Books.

Fraley, R. C., & Shaver, P. R. (2000). Adult romantic attachment: Theoretical developments, emerging controversies, and unanswered questions. *Review of General Psychology, 4*, 132–154.

Fredrickson, B. L. (2001). The role of positive emotions in positive psychology: The broaden-and-build theory of positive emotions. *American Psychologist, 56*, 218–226.

Game, A. (2008). Negative emotions in supervisory relationships: The role of relational models. *Human Relations, 61*, 355–393.

Greenman, P. S., Johnson, S. M., & Wiebe, S. (2019). Emotionally focused therapy for couples: At the heart of science and practice. In B. H. Fiese, M. Celano, K. Deater-Deckard, E. N. Jouriles, & M. A. Whisman (Eds.), *APA handbook of contemporary family psychology* (pp. 291–305). Washington, D.C: American Psychological Association.

Gruneau Brulin, J., Hill, P. C., Laurin, K., Mikulincer, M., & Granqvist, P. (2018). Religion vs. the welfare state—The importance of cultural context for religious schematicity and priming. *Psychology of Religion and Spirituality, 10*, 276–287.

Hamre, B., Hatfield, B., Pianta, R., & Jamil, F. (2014). Evidence for general and domain-specific elements of teacher-child interactions: Associations with preschool children's development. *Child Development, 85*, 1257–1274.

Haslam, S. A., Reicher, S. D., & Platow, M. J. (2015). Leadership: Theory and practice. In M. Mikulincer, P. R. Shaver, J. F. Dovidio, & J. A. Simpson (Eds.), *APA handbook of personality and social psychology: Group processes* (pp. 67–94). Washington, D.C: American Psychological Association.

Håvås, E., Svartberg, M., & Ulvenes, P. (2015). Attuning to the unspoken: The relationship between therapist nonverbal attunement and attachment security in adult psychotherapy. *Psychoanalytic Psychology, 32,* 235–254.

Haydon, K. C., Collins, W. A., Salvatore, J. E., Simpson, J. A., & Roisman, G. I. (2012). Shared and distinctive origins and correlates of adult attachment representations: The developmental organization of romantic functioning. *Child Development, 83,* 1689–1702.

Hoffman, K. T., Marvin, R. S., Cooper, G., & Powell, B. (2006). Changing toddlers' and preschoolers' attachment classifications: The Circle of Security intervention. *Journal of Consulting and Clinical Psychology, 74,* 1017–1026.

Holt-Lunstad, J., & Smith, T. B. (2012). Social relationships and mortality. *Social and Personality Psychology Compass, 6,* 41–53.

Johnson, S. M. (2003). Attachment theory: A guide for couple therapy. In S. M. Johnson & V. E. Whiffen (Eds.), *Attachment processes in couple and family therapy* (pp. 103–123). New York: Guilford Press.

Kafetsios, K., Athanasiadou, M., & Dimou, N. (2014). Leaders' and subordinates' attachment orientations, emotion regulation capabilities and affect at work: A multilevel analysis. *The Leadership Quarterly, 25,* 512–527.

Kafetsios, K., Hantzara, K., Anagnostopoulos, F., & Niakas, D. (2016). Doctors' attachment orientations, emotion regulation strategies, and patient satisfaction: A multilevel analysis. *Health Communication, 31,* 772–777.

Kidd, T., Hamer, M., & Steptoe, A. (2013). Adult attachment style and cortisol responses across the day in older adults. *Psychophysiology, 50,* 841–847.

Ladd, G. W., Kochenderfer-Ladd, B., & Rydell, A. (2014). Children's interpersonal skills and school-based relationships. In P. K. Smith & C. H. Hart (Eds.), *The Wiley Blackwell handbook of childhood social development* (pp. 181–206). New York: Wiley-Blackwell.

Lavy, S. (2014). Supervisor security provision: Correlates and related mechanisms. *Psychological Reports, 114,* 758–783.

Levy, K. N., Kivity, Y., Johnson, B. N., & Gooch, C. V. (2018). Adult attachment as a predictor and moderator of psychotherapy outcome: A meta-analysis. *Journal of Clinical Psychology, 74,* 1996–2013.

Lieberman, A. F., Ippen, C. G., & Van Horn, P. J. (2006). Child-parent psychotherapy: Six-month follow-up of a randomized control trial. *Journal of the American Academy of Child and Adolescent Psychiatry, 45,* 913–918.

Luke, M. A., Sedikides, C., & Carnelley, K. (2012). Your love lifts me higher! The energizing quality of secure relationships. *Personality and Social Psychology Bulletin, 38,* 721–733.

Mallinckrodt, B., & Jeong, J. (2015). Meta-analysis of client attachment to therapist: Associations with working alliance and client pretherapy attachment. *Psychotherapy, 52,* 134–139.

Marmarosh, C., Markin, R., & Spiegel, E. (2013). *Attachment in group psychotherapy.* Washington, D.C: American Psychological Association.

Mashburn, A. J., Pianta, R. C., Hamre, B. K., Downer, J. T., Barbarin, O. A., Bryant, D., ... Howes, C. (2008). Measures of classroom quality in prekindergarten and children's development of academic, language, and social skills. *Child Development, 79,* 732–749.

Maunder, R. G., & Hunter, J. J. (2015). *Love, fear, and health*. Toronto, Canada: Toronto University Press.

Maunder, R. G., & Hunter, J. J. (2016). Can patients be "attached" to healthcare providers? An observational study to measure attachment phenomena in patient-provider relationships. *BMJ Open, 6*, e011068.

Maunder, R. G., Panzer, A., Viljoen, M., Owen, J., Human, S., & Hunter, J. J. (2006). Physicians' difficulty with emergency department patients is related to patients' attachment style. *Social Science and Medicine, 63*, 552-562.

Maxwell, H., Tasca, G. A., Ritchie, K., Balfour, L., & Bissada, H. (2014). Change in attachment insecurity is related to improved outcomes 1-year post group therapy in women with binge eating disorder. *Psychotherapy, 51*, 57–65.

Mayseless, O., & Popper, M. (2007). Reliance on leaders and social institutions: An attachment perspective. *Attachment & Human Development, 9*, 73–93.

Mikulincer, M., & Florian, V. (1998). The relationship between adult attachment styles and emotional and cognitive reactions to stressful events. In J. A. Simpson & W. S. Rholes (Eds.,) *Attachment theory and close relationships* (pp. 143–165). New York: Guilford Press.

Mikulincer, M., & Shaver, P. R. (2003). The attachment behavioral system in adulthood: Activation, psychodynamics, and interpersonal processes. In M. P. Zanna (Ed.), *Advances in experimental social psychology* (Vol. 35, pp. 53–152). New York: Academic Press.

Mikulincer, M., & Shaver, P. R. (2007). Boosting attachment security to promote mental health, prosocial values, and inter-group tolerance. *Psychological Inquiry, 18*, 139–156.

Mikulincer, M., & Shaver, P. R. (2016). *Attachment in adulthood: Structure, dynamics, and change* (2nd ed.). New York: Guilford Press.

Mikulincer, M., Shaver, P. R., Gillath, O., & Nitzberg, R. A. (2005). Attachment, caregiving, and altruism: Boosting attachment security increases compassion and helping. *Journal of Personality and Social Psychology, 89*, 817–839.

Mikulincer, M., Shaver, P. R., Sapir-Lavid, Y., & Avihou-Kanza, N. (2009). What's inside the minds of securely and insecurely attached people? The secure-base script and its associations with attachment-style dimensions. *Journal of Personality and Social Psychology, 97*, 615–633.

Mountain, G., Cahill, J., & Thorpe, H. (2017). Sensitivity and attachment interventions in early childhood: A systematic review and meta-analysis. *Infant Behavior & Development, 46*, 14–32.

Murray, C., & Malmgren, K. (2005). Implementing a teacher-student relationship program in a high-poverty urban school: Effects on social, emotional, and academic adjustment and lessons learned. *Journal of School Psychology, 43*, 137–152.

Otway, L. J., Carnelley, K. B., & Rowe, A. C. (2014). Texting "boosts" felt security. *Attachment & Human Development, 16*, 93–101.

Parish, M., & Eagle, M. N. (2003). Attachment to the therapist. *Psychoanalytic Psychology, 20*, 271–286.

Pianta, R. C. (2016). Classroom processes and teacher-student interaction: Integrations with a developmental psychopathology perspective. In D. Cicchetti (Ed.), *Developmental psychopathology: Risk, resilience, and intervention* (pp. 770–814). Hoboken, NJ: Wiley.

Pianta, R. C., La Paro, K. M., & Hamre, B. K. (2008). *Classroom Assessment Scoring System Manual K-3*. Baltimore, MD: Brookes Publishing.

Pianta, R. C., Mashburn, A. J., Downer, J. T., Hamre, B. K., & Justice, L. (2008). Effects of web-mediated professional development resources on teacher-child interactions in pre-kindergarten classrooms. *Early Childhood Research Quarterly, 23*, 431–451.

Popper, M., & Mayseless, O. (2003). Back to basics: Applying a parenting perspective to transformational leadership. *Leadership Quarterly, 14*, 41–65.

Reis, H. T. (2014). Responsiveness: Affective interdependence in close relationships. In M. Mikulincer & P. R. Shaver (Eds.), *Mechanisms of social connection: From brain to group* (pp. 255–271). Washington, D.C: American Psychological Association.

Rheem, D. (2017). *Thrive by design*. Charleston, SC: Forbes Books.

Robles, T. F., Brooks, K. P., Kane, H. S., & Schetter, C. D. (2013). Attachment, skin deep? Relationships between adult attachment and skin barrier recovery. *International Journal of Psychophysiology, 88*, 241–252.

Ronen, S. & Mikulincer, M. (2012). Predicting employees' satisfaction and burnout from managers' attachment and caregiving orientations. *European Journal of Work and Organizational Psychology, 21*, 828–849.

Roorda, D. L., Jak, S., Zee, M., Oort, F. J., & Koomen, H. M. (2017). Affective teacher-student relationships and students' engagement and achievement: A meta-analytic update and test of the mediating role of engagement. *School Psychology Review, 46*, 239–261.

Shaver, P. R., Mikulincer, M., & Feeney, B. C. (2009). What's love got to do with it? Insecurity and anger in attachment relationships. *Virginia Journal of Social Policy & the Law, 16*, 491–513.

Slade, A., Sadler, L. S., & Mayes, L. C. (2005). Minding the baby: Enhancing parental reflective functioning in a nursing/mental health home visiting program. In L. J. Berlin, Y. Ziv, L. Amaya-Jackson, & M. T. Greenberg (Eds.), *Enhancing early attachments: Theory, research, intervention, and policy* (pp. 152–177). New York: Guilford Press.

Tasca, G. A., Mikail, S., & Hewitt, P. (2005). Group psychodynamic interpersonal psychotherapy: Summary of a treatment model and outcomes for depressive symptoms. In M. E. Abehan (Ed.), *Focus on psychotherapy research* (pp. 159–188). New York: Nova Science.

Taylor, S. E., & Broffman, J. I. (2011). Psychosocial resources: Functions, origins, and links to mental and physical health. In J. M. Olson & M. P. Zanna (Eds.), *Advances in experimental social psychology* (pp. 1–57). New York: Academic Press.

Thompson, R. A. (2015). Relationships, regulation, and early development. In M. E. Lamb & R. M. Lerner (Eds.), *Handbook of child psychology and developmental science: Socioemotional processes* (pp. 201–246). Hoboken, NJ: Wiley.

Travis, L. A., Bliwise, N. G., Binder, J. L., & Horne-Moyer, H. (2001). Changes in clients' attachment styles over the course of time-limited dynamic psychotherapy. *Psychotherapy, 38*, 149–159.

Tuck, N. L., & Consedine, N. S. (2015). Breast cancer screening: The role of attachment. *Psychology, Health & Medicine, 20*, 400–409.

Verhage, M. L., Schuengel, C., Madigan, S., Fearon, R. M. P., Oosterman, M., Cassibba, R., ... van Ijzendoorn, M. H. (2016). Narrowing the transmission gap: A synthesis of three decades of research on intergenerational transmission of attachment. *Psychological Bulletin, 142*, 337–366.

Vilchinsky, N., Dekel, R., Asher, Z., Leibowitz, M., & Mosseri, M. (2013). The role of illness perceptions in the attachment-related process of affect regulation. *Anxiety, Stress & Coping, 26*, 314–329.

Waters, H. S., & Waters, E. (2006). The attachment working models concept: Among other things, we build script-like representations of secure base experiences. *Attachment & Human Development, 8,* 185–198.

Webster-Stratton, C., Reid, M. J., & Hammond, M. (2004). Treating children with early-onset conduct problems: Intervention outcomes for parent, child, and teacher training. *Journal of Clinical Child and Adolescent Psychology, 33,* 105–124.

Wentzel, K. R. (2016). Teacher-student relationships. In K. R. Wentzel & D. B Miele (Eds.), *Handbook of motivation at school* (2nd ed., pp. 211–230). New York: Routledge.

Williford, A. P., Carter, L. M. & Pianta, R. C. (2016). Attachment and school readiness. In J. Cassidy & P. R. Shaver (Eds.), *Handbook of attachment: Theory, research, and clinical applications* (3rd ed., pp. 966–982). New York: Guilford.

Wu, C. H., & Parker, S. K. (2017). The role of leader support in facilitating proactive work behavior: A perspective from attachment theory. *Journal of Management, 43,* 1025–1049.

Zeifman, D., & Hazan, C. (2016). Pair bonds as attachments: Mounting evidence in support of Bowlby's hypothesis. In J. Cassidy & P. R. Shaver (Eds.), *Handbook of attachment: Theory, research, and clinical applications* (3rd ed., pp. 416–434). New York: Guilford Press.

11
SOCIAL PSYCHOLOGICAL CONTRIBUTIONS TO THE MITIGATION OF ADOLESCENT DEPRESSION

William D. Crano and Andrea L. Ruybal

Social psychological research has contributed to the betterment of society in many ways, but its present contributions to the prevention of adolescent depression, a leading cause of adolescent and young adult suicide, have not yet made the desired impact. Clinical scientists and practitioners have been most involved in research and treatment of depression in adolescents and young adults, but this observation does not negate the possible contributions of social psychology in preventing the harm involved with this crucial issue, which falls, at least to some degree, in the realm of social psychology. In this chapter, we will review the ways social psychologists have contributed to the amelioration of depression and subsequent suicide of youth. In addition, we will consider research on the role psychoactive substances play in the deadly dance and attempt to integrate findings on the evidence arising from the application of well-established theories of persuasion to drug prevention, which might moderate the terrible losses incurred when individuals take their own lives.

Significance

There is little need to establish the significance of adolescent depression-related suicide in contemporary society. Even trivial suicide rates are unacceptable, and today's research indicates that the frequency of adolescent self-destruction is far from trivial. In establishing significance in this instance, and the potential role of social psychology, more focus should be on the costs and benefits of social psychological interventions than in establishing the profundity of the problem. For social psychology, the issue becomes whether or not the field's potential contribution to moderating the solution of teen suicide justifies the direct or indirect (i.e., opportunity) costs involved in the attempt. Is not clinical psychology and psychiatry better equipped to deal with extraordinary interventions that treat acute manifestations of extreme depression? Would not resources be applied more wisely to treating teens with depression, rather than social-psychological attempts at prevention? In our view, the answer to the first of these questions must be stated in the affirmative. When the house is burning, the need for a good dousing is clearly preferable to recondite speculation on the concept of fire. However, the answer to the second question is moot. Social-psychological contributions to the solution of severe teen depression, apart from clinical interventions, may prove a wise line of attack on this perplexing and complex problem. We discuss some possible social-psychological contributions to understanding adolescent depression and invite the open-minded reader to consider them carefully when assessing their viability or suggesting alternatives that might add to their potential utility. However, before we begin, it is reasonable to gauge the severity of the problem. Afterwards, we will consider social psychology's role in its solution, with special emphasis on the application of persuasive prevention, and that of parents and drug use by both children and their parents, which have been shown to have a powerful bearing on the likelihood of adolescent drug initiation and its attendant outcomes, which may include teen suicide. Effects of both parents and drugs have been implicated in research on adolescent suicide, and in this context, social psychology may play its strongest hand.

Adolescent Depression and Suicide

Depression is a mental health condition resulting in persistent sadness and loss of usual interests. It can influence how a person thinks, feels, and behaves, resulting in serious emotional, physical, and functional problems. Depression is widespread in the United States and beyond. Worldwide, depression is the second most common illness following anxiety disorders. Among adolescents, depression is increasingly widespread. The National Institute of Mental Health (NIMH, 2011) found that teens with depression are at a substantially greater risk than those without this condition of experiencing serious episodes of depression in adulthood, and are more likely to become involved in the criminal justice system as adults.

Mental Health America (2010) estimated that 12.5 percent of teenagers experienced clinical depression, and 67 percent reported major depressive episodes that had caused issues with school, work, friends, or family. Changes in attitudes or behaviors about school and social activities, as well as problems at home, may be indicators of depression in youth. Compared to adults, adolescent depression may manifest in remarkably different ways. Youths in this age group tend to have issues not faced by adults, such as powerful and highly relevant peer pressures, academic expectations, and concurrent hormonal and bodily changes. Although depressive symptoms may vary widely among individuals, common emotional and behavioral changes in teenagers can be warning signs of depression or impending depression. According to findings reported by the Mayo Clinic (Hall-Flavin & McKean, 2018), some emotional changes include, among others, feelings of sadness, hopelessness, worthlessness, guilt, and pessimism. Teenagers experiencing depression also may experience crying spells, frustration or anger disproportionate to the situation, irritability, loss of interest or pleasure in usual activities, conflict with friends or family, low self-esteem, may ruminate or fixate on failures and self-blame, have trouble concentrating, poor decision-making or have trouble making decisions, and frequent thoughts of death or dying. Behavioral changes may include tiredness, changes in sleep patterns, changes in appetite with accompanying weight change, restlessness, choosing social isolation, poor school performance or truancy, less attention to self-appearance, disruptive behavior, use of alcohol or drugs, self-harm, and suicidal behaviors (Hall-Flavin & McKean, 2018).

Suicide rates are increasing. It is important to treat depression at any age to ameliorate and prevent progressive worsening of ongoing problems. Fortunately, most teenagers who receive treatment overcome depression. However, left untreated, adolescents are at substantially greater risk for suicide than older adults. In the United States, suicide is the second leading cause of death among persons aged 10 to 34 (NIMH, 2018). In adolescents and young adults, suicide is more common than cancer, heart disease, birth defects, pneumonia, and influenza combined (Kann et al., 2018).

Suicide obviously is not confined to adolescents; it occurs across the lifespan. Globally, suicide is the second leading cause of death among those aged 15 to 29. In this age group, it is the second leading cause of death for males, lagging behind only road accidents. For females, suicide is second only to childbirth related deaths (WHO, 2016). Across all age groups in the United States, the total suicide rate increased 31 percent from 2001 to 2017, with males experiencing a suicide rate four times that of females (NIMH, 2018). Suicide increased in almost every state during this time period. Worldwide, an estimated 793,000 known suicides occur annually in people of all ages. By this measure, a suicide occurs across the globe every 40 seconds (WHO, 2018).

Cross-sectional data from one of the longest ongoing investigations on suicide rates of US adolescents are available in the archives of the national Youth Risk Behavior Survey (YRBS: Kann et al., 2018), which since 1991 has monitored health behaviors of American youth using nationally representative samples of adolescents in grades 9–12 in public and private schools (Kann et al., 2018). Data have been available from this source every other year since its inception. Let us consider data from the 2017 survey, which found that in the previous year, roughly one-third of all high school students in this nationally representative sample felt sad or helpless almost every day for at least one two-week period, so much so that they stopped their usual activities. This figure accounts for just over 20 percent of the sampled males and 40 percent of the females. This result also is reflected in variations in self-reported depression severity. Among these same students, 17.2 percent of the sample had seriously considered attempting suicide. Divided by sex, this number included 11.9 percent of all male respondents and 22.1 percent of all female respondents. Considerable research indicates that making a suicide plan is highly predictive of impending suicide or attempted suicide. It was found that 13.6 percent of all students in the US made a suicide plan. Across the total sample, 9.7 percent of all males and 17.1 percent of all females sampled made suicide plans, and suicide attempts were made by 7.4 percent of students. Across the sample, 5.1 percent of all males and 9.3 percent of all females made an attempt at ending their lives. In the US, 2.4 percent of teens were injured, poisoned, or overdosed, requiring medical attention due to a suicide attempt. It is noteworthy that among these students, males accounted for 1.5 percent and females for 3.1 percent of serious injuries. Although females are more likely to consider suicide, make suicide plans, attempt suicide, and be injured from an attempt, males have higher rates of suicide completion (NIMH, 2018).

Rates of sadness and helplessness increased significantly in the adolescent population from 2009 to the present (Kann et al., 2018). Over a ten-year period from 2007 to 2017, the YRBS indicated an increase of about 3 percent in adolescents seriously considering suicide. Data suggest that rates of attempted suicide and attempts that resulted in serious injury have remained relatively stable since 1991, with minor variations across the years. Remarkably, *on an average day in the United States*, 3,041 students in grades 9 through 12 attempt suicide.

Eighty percent of adolescents who attempt suicide give clear warnings before they commit to this action (Kann et al., 2018). Many of these warning signs have been mentioned, including symptoms of severe depression; other signs include talking, writing, or drawing about death, distributing belongings, displaying aggressive behavior, running away from home, risky behaviors, or drastic changes in personality (HealthLinkBC, 2018).

Drug Involvement in Depression and Suicide

Several factors can contribute to the decision to take one's life, including severe mental health problems and high levels of psychotropic substance use. It has been estimated that nearly 30 percent of individuals who die by suicide have problems involving substance use (CDC, 2018). According to the Substance Abuse and Mental Health Services Administration (SAMHSA, 2013), suicide is the most common cause of death for individuals with substance use disorders. Furthermore, mental illness coupled with substance use disorders materially increases the risk of suicide. In 2011 alone, more than 200,000 emergency room visits were attributed to drug-related suicide attempts, and between 2004 and 2011, such attempts rose 41 percent (SAMHSA, 2013). Depression was found to be a precursor to both substance misuse and suicide, and continued substance misuse exacerbates depression.

The connection of depression and substance use problems practically compels the attention of social psychological research to contribute to understanding and perhaps help ameliorate depression leading to suicide. The field has proved highly relevant in research designed to help combat the use of dangerous psychotropic substances (e.g., Crano, Alvaro, Tan, & Siegel, 2017; Lac, Crano, Berger, & Alvaro, 2013; Griffin & Botvin, 2000; Hawkins, Catalano, & Miller, 1992; Lochman & van den Steenhoven, 2002; Newcomb & Locke, 2005; Siegel et al., 2014; Sloboda, Petras, Hingson, & Robertson, 2019; Sussman & Ames, 2008). Social psychological theory and research designed to provide greater understanding of the dangers of such use are commonplace and informative, and the field's contribution to understanding is impressive. This research has been used extensively to develop applications that moderate or eliminate the potential dangers involved in misuse of dangerous psychotropic substances. The transfer of social psychological principles and research into important areas involving the public good is not new (e.g., see Lewin, 1943, 1946, 1947), and over the years the application of social psychological principles to important issues has become ever more intense, after a brief hiatus following the Second World War (Crano & Lac, 2012; McGuire, 1973; Prislin & Crano, 2012).

Depression and self-medication. When dealing with the problem of depression-linked suicide, contemporary applied research on the relevance of social psychological theory makes clear the field's potential to contribute to the well-being of youth. Research has found that teenagers under stress often seek ways to self-medicate with marijuana; in the case of depression, however, marijuana uptake appears to intensify, rather than mollify the underlying problems of depression (Shrier, Ross, & Blood, 2014; Wilkinson et al., 2016). Research in a young adult population supports this finding. It indicates that marijuana use to self-medicate reduced negative anxiety symptoms, but in turn resulted in more marijuana use problems (Buckner, Bonn-Miller, Zvolensky, & Schmidt, 2007).

Marijuana has been proven a risky and ineffective solution to teen depression. Although research is limited in populations of participants under 18 years of age, considerable research on adults consistently reports linkages between depression, suicide, and substance use disorders. These results suggest strong, if not necessarily causal associations among these factors. Understanding the relation between drug use and suicide is important, insofar as more than 90 percent of people who die by suicide are found to have been dealing with either depression, psychotropic substance use issues, or both (Juergens & Hampton, 2018). Self-medication with psychoactive substances often appears to be used as a means to deal with depression, to numb pain, or to reduce negative emotions. Suicide is rarely caused by a specific ailment or circumstance. However, a number of co-occurring variables have been identified as commonly found in suicide, including such factors as depression, suicidal thoughts, past suicidal attempts, drug abuse, alcohol abuse, poor familial connections, or a troubled familial past (Juergens & Hampton, 2018). The relations among these co-occurring features deserve close scrutiny, although experimental designs that would allow a clearer understanding of the causal relations of the substance use-depression-suicide cycle remain elusive, owing to the very nature of the variables involved.

Adolescent Depression, Marijuana Use, and Legalization

The association of marijuana with adolescent depression is of particular interest, both because of the drug's popularity with youth and the fact that many US states have recently medicalized, legalized, or decriminalized (in practice or by law) the use of the substance. These recent changes render marijuana more accessible than ever before to adults, and indirectly, youth, who are the recipients of diverted legal marijuana. Coincident with these changes are the past decade's moderation in adolescents' perceptions of the risk posed by marijuana usage, and the disapproval rates of associating with consistent users of the drug (Johnston, O'Malley, Miech, Bachman, & Schulenberg, 2016; Siegel, Alvaro, Patel, & Crano, 2009).

Researchers and policy makers have become increasingly concerned with the ways increased accessibility of marijuana might affect adolescents (e.g., Hayatbakhsh, Williams, Bor, & Najman, 2013). It is our position that legalization has raised the risk of marijuana-involved depression in youth substantially, and as such, deserves close attention. For example, Johnston and colleagues (2016) identified marijuana as the illicit substance most commonly used by US adolescents in the eighth, tenth, and twelfth grades. Roughly 14 percent of adolescents report using marijuana between the ages of 14 and 16 (Wilkinson et al., 2016), and the average age of marijuana initiation is 15 years (Hayatbakhsh et al., 2013). Heavy and consistent marijuana usage can affect cognitive development, hindering associative learning processes and short-term memory (National Academies of Sciences, Engineering, and Medicine, 2017; WHO, 2014). Furthermore, marijuana use in teenagers has been associated with significantly higher odds of non-medical use of stimulants and opioids, if marijuana is adopted early and is used consistently (Nakawaki & Crano, 2012, 2015). Like adolescents with depression, those who initiate marijuana early are also likely to underperform educationally and are more susceptible to delinquency and other behavioral and mental health conditions (Copeland, Rooke, & Swift, 2013; Siegel et al., 2014). Because adolescents experiencing depression are twice as likely to use marijuana as those without depression (Office of National Drug Control Policy [ONDCP], 2008), it would seem almost obligatory that social psychologists explore this relation more fully. In a major review of the literature on the relation of marijuana use and psychosis, Radhakrishnan, Wilkinson, and D'Souza (2014, p. 5) found:

> Acute exposure to both cannabis and synthetic cannabinoids (Spice/K2) can produce a full range of transient psychotomimetic symptoms, cognitive

deficits, and psychophysiological abnormalities that bear a striking resemblance to symptoms of schizophrenia ... Exposure to cannabinoids in adolescence confers a higher risk for psychosis outcomes in later life and the risk is dose-related.

Radhakrishnan and colleagues' research indicating a strong and consistent linkage between depression and marijuana use has been bolstered by later studies (e.g., Gobbi et al., 2019; Hser et al., 2017; Ketcherside & Filbey, 2015; Wilkinson et al., 2016). Although these studies cannot be interpreted causally with high certainty, nor do they necessarily implicate or identify a path between marijuana-to-depression-to-suicide in adolescents, there can be little doubt of the association between high levels of marijuana use and depression. Whether marijuana antedates or follows depression remains an open question, but the importance of the question requires an attempt at an informed evidence-based answer, and we will present one such attempt in the pages that follow.

Depression and Self-medication

Once thought to be used socially, to fit in with friends or as a form of rebellion, current research indicates that marijuana and alcohol often are used by adolescents to self-medicate in an attempt to reduce symptoms of depression (Grunberg, Cordova, Bidwell, & Ito, 2015; Wilkinson et al., 2016). These findings and observations render the marijuana-depression linkage all the more interesting and ominous. Research in this area has been confined largely to adults, rather than adolescents (Buu et al., 2009; Consoli et al., 2013; Pacek, Martins, & Crum, 2013), but the extension of research into adolescent use seems pertinent and justified. Its goal is to uncover the psychological processes involved in the self-medicating process, and the temporal relation linking marijuana use and depression. Do teens use marijuana in response to a depressive episode, or are users more prone to progress from quotidian sadness that seems to be a part of normal adolescent life to more serious depression? Both sequences are plausible, but the *self-medicating hypothesis* suggests that symptoms of mental illness occur first, and substance use is adopted to alleviate its symptoms (Khantzian, 1985; Womack, Shaw, Weaver, & Forbes, 2016). Some evidence supports this hypothesized sequence. Individuals who become regular users of marijuana have reported that a major motive for consuming the substance is to relieve affective symptoms such as depression and anxiety (Bottorff, Johnson, Moffat, & Mulvogue, 2009). Repetto and colleagues' (2008) longitudinal study found depressive symptoms predicted later marijuana use in a sample of ninth-grade African-American students, even after controlling for several earlier-implicated factors including prior use, other substance use, grade point average, and socioeconomic status.

Although this evidence lends some credence to the self-medicating hypothesis, other studies have found no relation when examining the association of depression and marijuana use over the long term. As a result, some psychologists examining the interrelatedness of depression and marijuana use developed the concept of the *cannabis effect* (Womack et al., 2016), which holds that persistent and heavy use of marijuana may lead to the development of depression, not just to its exacerbation. Considerable research supports this possibility too (e.g., Radhakrishnan et al., 2014). Many disparate factors have been implicated in the development of adolescent depression. Evidence from a neurological perspective indicates that frontal lobe white matter abnormalities in adolescents with regular marijuana use can predict depressive symptoms (Medina, Nagel, Park, McQueeny, & Tapert, 2007). Shonesy and colleagues (2014) suggest that depressive symptomology may be caused by an "endocannabinoid deficiency," which may drive individuals to use marijuana to satiate symptoms. The neurological evidence is intriguing, but it is clear that much remains to be done on this front before effective solutions are reached. However, given the pace of research in this area, these solutions may arrive more quickly than anticipated.

An alternative to the self-medication hypothesis suggests that marijuana usage leads to social problems (e.g., isolation, poor peer and parental relations, low school achievement) that can result in subsequent depression in adolescents. However, much of this research has been considerably less directional, suggesting a correlational rather than causal relation between heavy marijuana use and depression. Perhaps the most scientifically acceptable interpretation of the available data is that these factors may act as mediators that link heavy marijuana usage and depression in early adulthood. Data are consistent with this possibility. For example, a comprehensive meta-analysis on the issue found that marijuana consumption in adolescence was related to the development of depression as well as suicidal ideation in young adulthood (Gobbi et al., 2019). The researchers suggested that more than 400,000 cases of adolescent depression could be a result of marijuana use. Fairman and Anthony (2012) found that early marijuana use in adolescence and early adulthood led to a 10 percent increase in depression during adulthood, even after controlling for several other plausible risk factors, and the ONDCP (2008) reported that adolescents with depression who were regular users of marijuana were at higher risk for other mental illnesses. Marmorstein and Iacono (2011) reported complementary results. They identified significant correlates of lower educational attainment, employment, and legal issues with cannabis use disorders in adolescence with subsequent adult depression. This view suggests a sequential ordering in which marijuana use affects later mental states. Consistent with this possibility, Hser and colleagues (2017) found in research with an adult sample that reducing marijuana intake was associated with improvements in anxiety, depression, and sleep quality in individuals with these ailments. These results lend support to the idea that marijuana may exacerbate later tendencies toward depression.

As there is evidence for both a *self-medicating hypothesis* and a *cannabis effect*, Womack and associates (2016) suggested the relation between depression and marijuana use may be bidirectional, fueling a vicious cycle of marijuana use to cope with depression, and depression becoming more severe as a result of marijuana use (see Pacek et al., 2013 for evidence of a bidirectional relationship in adults). Taylor (2011) found that marijuana use was a result of attempts to cope with feelings of sadness, and Moreira's (2007) research showed amounts of marijuana consumed was monotonically associated with severity of depression.

It seems reasonable to conclude that attempts to self-medicate with marijuana are likely to result in a worsening of depression as well as an increase in marijuana usage in an attempt to cope with resultant increases in depressive symptoms. The cyclical nature of this process would confound many of our standard non-experimental methods designed to identify causal priority (e.g., structural-equation models, path analysis, etc.), as outcomes of the analyses would be largely a function of an arbitrary identification of the starting point of the process. Practical and ethical restraints on assigning adolescent subjects with and without depression randomly to heavy marijuana use or a control (no use) condition has retarded our capacity to pinpoint the preponderant cause via experimentation (i.e., does heavy marijuana use induce depression in adolescents, or does adolescent depression lead to heavy use in the attempt to self-medicate?).

Our relative inability to crack the causal priority puzzle in the marijuana-depression association may not be as encumbering as might appear at first glance. We believe a definitive identification of the causal sequence may not be needed if we focus instead on approaches that might attenuate marijuana use. If marijuana use is prevented or curtailed, then an important link in the causal marijuana-depression or depression-marijuana chain may be broken, and for practical purposes, this may be sufficient to interrupt its ultimate and tragic outcome. Social psychological research is ideally suited to this task. It is in this way that social psychology can make perhaps its strongest contribution to a major and heretofore intractable and mounting social issue. On the pages that follow, we consider some social psychological approaches designed to understand the relation between marijuana use and depression in adolescents.

Parental Influences on Marijuana Use and Depression

Parental influences are crucial factors in adolescent development (Castro-Schilo et al., 2013; Crano & Donaldson, 2018; Donaldson, Handren, & Crano, 2016). Two key parental influences that have been studied at length are parental warmth and parental monitoring. Parental monitoring involves surveillance. It refers to parents knowing where their children are, what they are doing, and whom they are with (Dishion & McMahon, 1998; Donaldson, Nakawaki, & Crano, 2015). Lac and Crano's (2009) meta-analysis examining marijuana use prevention revealed that parental monitoring was predictive of lower marijuana use. The research also identified larger effect sizes for females than males, suggesting that parents monitored their girls more closely than boys. This result supports speculation regarding males' greater likelihood of engaging in delinquent behaviors because they are not as heavily monitored (Pedersen, Mastekaasa, & Wichstrøm, 2001; Peters, 1994). In Lac and Crano's (2009) research, more intense monitoring was related to less marijuana use across 23 different samples, involving more than 35,000 independent observations – regardless of the age of adolescents. Thus, parental monitoring is viewed as a protective factor for marijuana usage in adolescent samples. Research on adolescent marijuana use found that high parental knowledge was associated with less positive attitudes toward marijuana in teens. As well, the belief that they had behavioral control over using marijuana, and subjective norms that proscribed marijuana use, also supported lower pro-marijuana use (Lac, Alvaro, Crano, & Siegel, 2009).

A second factor that determines parental influence is warmth, which describes how adolescents interpret their parents' feelings toward them. Warmth includes perceived love and care, as well as responsiveness to their needs (Lowe & Dotterer, 2013). Parental warmth also can be categorized as perceived acceptance, support, positive reinforcement, affection, and involvement from parents, as well as setting reasonable limits for behavior (Donaldson et al., 2016; Morrill, Hawrilenko, & Córdova, 2016). Adolescents' perceptions of parental warmth foster higher levels of life satisfaction and well-being (Schwarz et al., 2011) and may work as a buffer against delinquency (Menting, Van Lier, Koot, Pardini, & Loeber, 2016), factors associated with adolescent depression. Parental warmth also has been associated inversely with pro-marijuana attitudes and subjective norms. Youths who perceived their parents as cold were more likely to favor marijuana consumption and felt other important people in their life also were pro-marijuana (Lac, Alvaro, Crano, & Siegel, 2009). In our research on adolescent substance use prevention, participants usually are divided into users, vulnerable nonusers, and resolute nonusers. We have found this categorization useful in developing research to prevent initiation or continuance of substance use (typically, marijuana). Operationally, our categorization system distinguished *resolute nonusers*, who have never used an indicated substance (e.g., marijuana, inhalants, etc.) and who state that they would *definitely not* initiate usage, from *vulnerable nonusers*, who have also have never used an indicated substance, but who do not respond "definitely not" when asked if they might initiate use someday. This classification has proved useful in identifying adolescents who are likely to begin substance use from those who are likely to maintain abstinence. Research on marijuana use has indicated that resolute nonusers reported significantly higher levels of parental warmth than vulnerable nonusers and users (Crano, Siegel, Alvaro, Lac, & Hemovich, 2008; see Figure 11.1).

Although research on adolescent risk behaviors has long indicated the importance of parents' influence on their children's outcomes, more recent studies

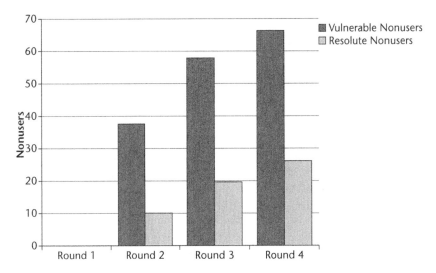

FIGURE 11.1 Percentage of initially marijuana abstinent youth who initiate use over a three-year period (adapted from Crano et al., 2008).

have focused on the growing influence of peers, certainly a proper focus of attention. However, the emphasis on peers often comes at the expense of underrating parental influences. Considerable research indicates that for good or ill, parental influences throughout the lifespan are considerably more powerful than might be inferred from an over-focus on peer influence, and this has prompted attempts at developing more refined understanding of parental effects.

The work of Kerr, Stattin, and their associates remains a beacon of excellent research in this field (Kerr & Stattin, 2000; Kerr, Stattin, & Burk, 2010; Kerr, Stattin, & Engels, 2008; Stattin & Kerr, 2000). This research stream suggests that it is not monitoring, per se, that affects adolescent behavior, but rather the quality of monitoring. Knowing how children behave can be observed by simple surveillance. However, whether knowledge born of surveillance is of much value was called into serious question by Kerr and associates (2010), who found in a two-year longitudinal investigation of more than 900 parent-child dyads that simple control (surveillance) or solicitation did not predict accurate parental knowledge of their children's behavior. However, youths' disclosures of their activities when out of earshot (or sight) of their parents was significantly linked to accuracy of parental knowledge.

What would motivate a child's disclosure of *private* actions when *unobserved by parents*? The answer arising from considerable research is simple – parental warmth, combined with reasonable and reasonably enforced guidelines for proper behavior (Donaldson, Handren, & Crano, 2016). In a number of recent studies, the importance of children's perceptions of parental warmth, or the strength of the parent-child bond, has been identified as a powerful predictor of their behavior, at least as it reflects the use of dangerous substances (alcohol, inhalants, marijuana, etc.). For example, Donaldson and associates (2016) identified crucial and continuing effects of early parental warmth in controlling adolescents' use of alcohol (see also Crano & Donaldson, 2018; Handren, Donaldson, & Crano, 2016; Lac et al., 2009). A series of longitudinal path analyses by Hemovich and colleagues also showed the crucial effects of parental warmth, along with simple surveillance, as indirect influences on children's use of a variety of proscribed substances (Hemovich & Crano, 2009; Hemovich, Lac, & Crano, 2011). These path analytic studies showed the indirect influence of parental monitoring and warmth on children's attitudes toward various substances and their friendship choices, which were directly implicated in substance use.

This research was reinforced by findings showing the importance of child-parent relations and their children's initiation of marijuana use. Considerable research indicates that the initial use of proscribed substances is in reaction to an offer of the substance by a friend or acquaintance. This *exposure opportunity* has been implicated as a strong precursor of substance use initiation (Frost, 1927; Wagner & Anthony, 2002). Beyond opportunity, those predisposed to initiate usage also are more likely to accept an offer of a drug (Voelkl & Frone, 2000). Siegel, Tan, Navarro, Alvaro, and Crano (2015) found adolescents engaged in close positive relations with their parents were significantly less likely to initiate substance use as a result of opportunity exposure. The reason for the strong parental influence effects found throughout the literature is quite plausible in retrospect, but not one that comes immediately to mind. Positive parental monitoring mitigated the opportunity effect in adolescents' marijuana initiation by attenuating the number of offers the adolescent received. The friendship choices of well-monitored adolescents mediated the likelihood of being offered a proscribed substance, because their friendship groups were less likely to include users. This finding is compatible with those of Hemovich and colleagues (2011), who found that the effects of parental monitoring and warmth indirectly affected adolescent substance use through adolescents' attitudes toward the substance *and their choice of friends*. Children with friends who got into trouble were more likely to get into trouble themselves. Your mother was right when she warned you about the dangers of associating with delinquent friends.

Parents' own substance use also has proven a strong predictor of their children's usage (Miller, Siegel, Hohman, & Crano, 2013). Past parental marijuana use, and their recency of use, significantly predicted their children's marijuana use. This effect was mediated by three critical factors implicated in prior research on adolescent marijuana use – expectation of punishment for use, expectations of the positivity of the experience of marijuana, and attitudes toward marijuana.

A telling example of parents' behavior on their children's substance use, which clearly is associated with, if not causative of depression and its sequelae, was provided in research by Lamb and Crano (2014) in their secondary analytic research on a nationally representative sample of US adolescents. The study was designed to test effects of parental self-fulfilling prophecies on their children's substance use. The researchers asked children if they had ever used marijuana. Separately, they also asked the children's parents to report their speculations on the child's use of the substance. One year later, the children were asked if they had used marijuana in the previous 12 months. The results were striking. The odds of a self-described abstinent child initiating marijuana use in the second year were 4.4 times greater if the parent voiced the impression that the child had used drugs in a data collection session one year earlier. The ascription of this result to social desirability response effects (i.e., the parents in year one were correct; the children merely gave a socially desirable answer to the interviewer) begs the question why the child became honest in year two. Another way of considering the question of a potential self-presentation bias in the children's year one self-report is to consider the year two responses of those adolescents who in year one admitted to having used drugs in the past. These respondents apparently were not particularly concerned with presenting a positive (i.e., socially desirable) image in the initial interview. In this analysis, results showed that children whose parents ventured the guess one year earlier that their child had never used drugs were 2.7 times less likely to continue marijuana use as their peers whose parents at year one believed their child had already initiated drug use (which their child had admitted in a separate interview one year earlier).

This research, and the others reviewed to this point, are examples of the futility of the "don't do as I do, do as I say" approach to parenting, as if another example is needed, in addition to showing how subtle cues emitted by parents can have important implications for children's behavior. In this case, the implications of parental actions over parental advice carry a heavy weight. If children's usage is affected by parents' behaviors, even very subtle behaviors, and if usage has an effect on their offspring's mental health, then the conclusion is inescapable that parental drug-related actions are implicated in children's likelihood of experiencing depression and its attendant dangers. We do not dismiss the possibility that there are many factors that may incline an adolescent toward use of dangerous substances, nor do we dismiss the possibility that genetic predispositions may affect the likelihood that an individual will initiate dangerous drug use, and that this use may well prove exceptionally disruptive psychologically. But we strongly suggest that the research on parental behavior and its impact on children's mental health be viewed with serious consideration.

Positive relations between parents and adolescents reduce risky behaviors, promote well-being (e.g., Hemovich et al., 2011; Lac et al., 2009), and lower levels of stress in children (Lippold, Davis, McHale, Buxton, & Almeida, 2016). With respect to depression, parental indifference toward adolescents has been associated with more severe depression (Long et al., 2014), whereas greater parental warmth has been associated with lower depression levels in adolescents (Ozer, Flores, Tschann, & Pasch, 2013). Poor parental-child relationships also have been associated with more suicidal ideation in teens with clinical depression (Field, Diego, & Sanders, 2001). Parent-child discussions about substance use have been linked to reduced use in teens (Huansuriya, Siegel, & Crano, 2014; ONDCP, 2008). Stattin and Kerr (2000) have argued that knowledge-based monitoring, based on a child's self-disclosure, one outcome of warm parent-child relations, is a critical factor for positive child behaviors as well. Individuals with depression who had poor parental relationships also consumed more marijuana than their counterparts without depression (Field et al., 2001). The increase in research on parental influences is likely to improve our understanding of the depression-marijuana link and how parents can serve as buffers against negative outcomes (Consoli et al., 2013; Lac et al., 2009; Ozer et al., 2013). The upshot of all of this is that parental behaviors play a major role in their children's mental health. Even subtle interactions powerfully influence their children's behaviors, for good or ill. Prevention of adolescent substance use may depend heavily on proper parental responses to their children. This means not only providing proper models of behavior, but actively creating and maintaining a clear set of reasonable requirements for proper behavior and providing an environment that is both warm and attentive to the child's needs and behaviors. Parental substance use has been shown in the studies reviewed here to have a deleterious effect on children's own actions. Lack of proper monitoring, which involves not only attention to the child's actions, but also a warm environment in which children feel free to disclose issues of importance to them, put the child at risk for substance use and the attendant psychological effects of usage on mental health. Social psychology can provide the kinds of persuasive information useful in facilitating parents' proper behavior vis-à-vis their children.

Although causal priority is difficult to establish in this area of research, Ruybal and Crano (2020) made an attempt to identify the structural relationships linking parental monitoring, warmth, and depression. This path analytic study made use of data from the National Survey on Drug Use and Health (NSDUH). Youths from 12–17 years of age were included in the analysis ($N=12,115$). These respondents, who were operationally identified as having had a major depressive episode in the past year, had experienced lower levels of parental warmth and monitoring, and an increased use of marijuana (see Figure 11.2). All of the paths in the model were statistically significant, which exhibited good fit with the obtained data. The results indicated that parental warmth and monitoring were related significantly. Parental warmth was not associated directly with marijuana use, but parental monitoring was; low monitoring was linked to greater marijuana use. The predicted indirect effect of depression on parental warmth and parental monitoring on marijuana use was statistically significant. As shown in Figure 11.2, low levels of parental warmth and

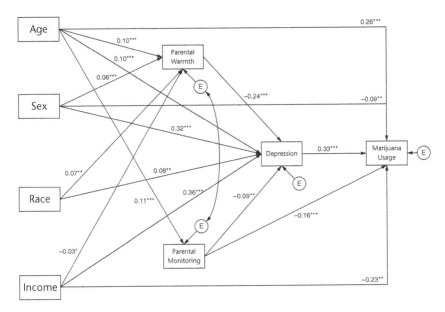

FIGURE 11.2 Path analytic model of relations involving parental warmth, parental monitoring, depression, and marijuana use with covariates age, sex, race, and income ($N = 12,115$). Non-significant paths were removed for clarity; $p = 0.07†$, $p < 0.05*$, $p < 0.01**$, $p < 0.001***$.

monitoring have a significant influence on depression, which in turn is associated with marijuana use. These results must be interpreted with caution, insofar as the NSDUH provides only cross-sectional data. If longitudinal data were available, causal inference could be made with greater confidence (Crano, Brewer, & Lac, 2015).

Media Research

In research framed with Fishbein and Ajzen's theory of planned behavior (TPB), Huansuriya and colleagues (2014) investigated parents' exposure to substance prevention messages presented in a major mass media drug prevention campaign of four years' duration. The research disclosed that parents who were more highly exposed to the campaign's anti-drug communications in the first year of the campaign had more favorable attitudes than less media-exposed parents toward talking to their children about marijuana, felt significant others would value this behavior more positively, and hence, intended to have the "drug talk" with their offspring. When the parents' children were interviewed one year later, those whose parents were more heavily exposed to the campaign reported a higher frequency of drug discussions with parents, less positive attitudes toward drugs, and lower intentions to use marijuana.[1] When this analysis was conducted on data from the final two years of the campaign, the results were identical to the first analysis. If drugs are implicated in adolescent depression and suicide, then these results indicate a clear path for parents to help break the marijuana-depression cycle.

Attempts to directly persuade individuals experiencing depression to seek help have been unsuccessful on numerous occasions (Costin et al., 2009; Gulliver et al., 2012; Klimes-Dougan & Lee, 2010; Lienemann & Siegel, 2016; Lienemann, Siegel, & Crano, 2013). Research devoted to processes of persuasion for individuals with depressive symptomatology is difficult due to the very nature of depression. Many individuals suffering from depression appear to have a negative bias toward attempts designed to convince them to seek help (Siegel, Lienemann, & Rosenberg, 2017). It appears that the more severe their depressive symptoms become, the less likely people are to seek help (Keeler, Siegel, & Alvaro, 2013). Research has hypothesized that a negative bias characterizes individuals' information processing when helpful information was offered if they have depression. It was as if they concluded, "Yes, this treatment option may help most other people, but it will not help me" (Beck, 2008; Bradley & Mathews, 1983; Watters & Williams, 2011).

A way to overcome this bias was inspired by Walster and Festinger's (1962) overheard communication technique. Crano, Siegel, Alvaro, and Patel (2007) assumed that directly targeted persuasive prevention communications would be met with some degree of resistance, especially by vulnerable nonusers or users. To overcome counter-argumentation, they hypothesized that a communication apparently directed to another would elicit less resistance, more openness to persuasion, and thus, would have a positive preventive effect. In a sample of nearly 900 middle school students, the researchers found that mass media messages dealing with inhalant prevention that were apparently meant for the children's parents were significantly more effective than directly targeted communications for vulnerable nonusers and users. These subjects evaluated the indirectly targeted messages more favorably, and message evaluation was significantly associated with inhalant usage intentions.

Siegel and colleagues applied this approach in research to individuals with depression. Their research showed that people with depression were resistant to offers of help, and the more severe the depression, the more resistant they were. They reasoned that to persuade people with elevated depressive symptomatology, public service announcements that appeared to be targeting a friend of someone with depression (e.g., "Do you have a friend who is depressed?") might have a better chance of success if the misdirection effect held, as it might circumvent counter-argumentation, or negative self-biases (Siegel, Lienemann, & Tan, 2015). As such, people with depression, the true target of the message, would be more likely to process the help-seeking information and to resist it less forcefully (why counter-argue a message meant for one's mother, or a friend?) than they would if they were the direct target of the communication.

Misdirection operated as hoped. In a media-based investigation, misdirection resulted in more positive attitudes about seeking help and intentions to seek help than a direct public service announcement (Siegel et al., 2015). This approach has considerable appeal in persuasive prevention models. Its use will be seen with increasing frequency across a number of approaches designed to prevent the initiation or continuance of self-destructive behaviors.

Where We Go from Here: Reading the Tea Leaves

Although confident causal interpretation of the interaction of parental monitoring, warmth, and psychotropic substance use on depression cannot be made with great confidence at this time, there can be no doubt that these factors are intimately interrelated in a cycle that may bode ill for many adolescents. We will unravel this riddle eventually, but while we are attempting to do so, we face the undeniable possibility that a demonstrably dangerous and destructive substance has become the darling of a number of state legislatures in the United States, based on no good scientific evidence, and plenty of evidence by our best and brightest arguing the contrary position. Whether or not this finance-driven judgment will prove worth the risk remains unknowable, but it is certain that the children of this generation will pay the price if this social experiment fails.

Legalization, which renders the substance considerably more available to youths, could not help but play into the sad outcomes that await many of them. Arguments regarding the direction of causation are beside the point. If marijuana causes adolescent depression, or whether marijuana use is caused by depression is immaterial. The substance is part of the marijuana-depression-suicide cycle. Where one cuts into the cycle may not be as important as the fact that the cycle may be broken or moderated if one of its central components, marijuana, is made unavailable or its availability is strongly circumscribed. Legalization does anything but this. Legislators who have not succumbed to the siren of legalization need to come to grips with this issue and decide if they are willing to gamble a number of their constituents' futures, perhaps lives, for the additional promised revenues that may or may not materialize.

Notes

1 In this sentence, "drugs" refer to marijuana, as this was the substance measured in the end of each year of the panel survey.

References

Beck, A. T. (2008). The evolution of the cognitive model of depression and its neurobiological correlates. *American Journal of Psychiatry, 165*, 969–977. doi.org.ccl.idm.oclc.org/10.1176/appi.ajp.2008.08050721

Bottorff, J. L., Johnson, J. L., Moffat, B. M., & Mulvogue, T. (2009). Relief-oriented use of marijuana by teens. *Substance Abuse Treatment, Prevention & Policy, 4*, 1–10. doi-org.ccl.idm.oclc.org/10.1186/1747-597X-4-7

Bradley, B., & Mathews, A. (1983). Negative self-schema in clinical depression. *British Journal of Clinical Psychology, 22*, 173–181. doi.org.ccl.idm.oclc.org/10.1111/j.2044-8260.1983.tb00598.x

Buckner, J. D., Bonn-Miller, M. O., Zvolensky, M. J., & Schmidt, N. B. (2007). Marijuana use motives and social anxiety among marijuana using young adults. *Addictive Behaviors, 32*, 2238-2252. doi.org.ccl.idm.oclc.org/10.1016/j.addbeh.2007.04.004

Buu, A., DiPiazza, C., Wang, J., Puttler, L. I., Fitzgerald, H. E., & Zucker, R. A. (2009). Parent, family, and neighborhood effects on the development of child substance use and other psychopathology from preschool to the start of adulthood. *Journal of Studies on Alcohol and Drugs, 70*, 489–498. doi.org.ccl.idm.oclc.org/10.15288/jsad.2009.70.489

Castro-Schilo, L., Taylor, Z. E., Ferrer, E., Robins, R. W., Conger, R. D., & Widaman, K. F. (2013). Parents' optimism, positive parenting, and child peer competence in Mexican-origin families. *Parenting: Science and Practice, 13*, 95–112. doi:10.1080/15295192.2012.709151

Center for Disease and Control. (2018). CDC's national violent death reporting system, data from 27 states participating in 2015. Retrieved from: www.cdc.gov/vitalsigns/suicide/infographic.html#graphic3

Consoli, A., Peyre, H., Speranza, M., Hassler, C., Falissard, B., Touchette, E., Cohen, D., Moro, M. R., & Révah-Lévy, A. (2013). Suicidal behaviors in depressed adolescents: Role of perceived relationships in the family. *Child and Adolescent Psychiatry and Mental Health, 7*. doi:10.1186/1753-2000-7-8

Copeland, J., Rooke, S., & Swift, W. (2013). Changes in cannabis use among young people: Impact on mental health. *Current Opinions in Psychiatry, 26*, 325–329. doi.org.ccl.idm.oclc.org/10.1097/YCO.0b013e328361eae5

Costin, D. L., Mackinnon, A. J., Griffiths, K. M., Batterham, P. J., Bennett, A. J., Bennett, K., & Christensen, H. (2009). Health e-cards as a means of encouraging help seeking for depression among young adults: Randomized controlled trial. *Journal of Medical Internet Research, 11*, 1–14. doi-org.ccl.idm.oclc.org/10.2196/jmir.1294

Crano, W. D., Alvaro, E. M., Tan, C. N., & Siegel, J. T. (2017). Social mediation of persuasive media in adolescent substance prevention. *Psychology of Addictive Behaviors, 31*, 479–487. doi.org.ccl.idm.oclc.org/10.1037/adb0000265

Crano, W. D., Brewer, M. B., & Lac, A. (2015). *Principles and methods of social research.* New York, NY: Routledge.

Crano, W. D., & Donaldson, C. D. (2018). Positive parenting, adolescent substance use prevention, and the good life. In J. P. Forgas & R. Baumeister (Eds.), *Social psychology of living well* (pp. 277–297). New York, NY: Routledge.

Crano, W. D., & Lac, A. (2012). The evolution of research methodologies in social psychology: A historical analysis. In A. W. Kruglanski & W. Stroebe (Eds.). *Handbook of the history of social psychology* (pp. 159–174). New York, NY: Taylor & Francis.

Crano, W. D., Siegel, J. T., Alvaro, E. M., Lac, A., & Hemovich, V. (2008). The at-risk adolescent marijuana nonuser: Expanding the standard distinction. *Prevention Science, 9*, 129–137. doi-org.ccl.idm.oclc.org/10.1007/s11121-008-0090-0

Crano, W. D., Siegel, J., Alvaro, E. M., & Patel, N. M. (2007). Overcoming adolescents' resistance to anti-inhalant messages. *Psychology of Addictive Behaviors, 21*, 516–524. doi.org.ccl.idm.oclc.org/10.1037/0893-164X.21.4.516

Dishion, T. J., & McMahon, R. J. (1998). Parental monitoring and the prevention of child and adolescent problem behavior: A conceptual and empirical formulation. *Clinical Child and Family Psychology Review, 1*, 61–75. doi:10.1023/A:1021800432380

Donaldson, C. D., Handren, L. M., & Crano, W. D. (2016). The enduring impact of parents' monitoring, warmth, expectancies, and alcohol use on their children's future binge drinking and arrests: A longitudinal analysis. *Prevention Science, 17*, 606–614. doi:10.1007/s11121-016-0656-1

Donaldson, C. D., Nakawaki, B., & Crano, W. D. (2015). Variations in parental monitoring and predictions of adolescent prescription opioid and stimulant misuse. *Addictive Behaviors, 45*, 14–21. doi:10.1016/j.addbeh.2015.01.022

Fairman, B. J., & Anthony, J. C. (2012). Are early-onset cannabis smokers at an increased risk of depression spells? *Journal of Affective Disorders, 138*, 54–62. doi-org.ccl.idm.oclc.org/10.1016/j.jad.2011.12.031

Field, T., Diego, M., & Sanders, C. (2001). *Adolescent depression and risk factors*. US: Libra Publishers.

Frost, W. H. (1927). *Public health and preventive medicine* (Vol. 2). London: Nelson.

Gobbi, G., Atkin, T., Zytynski, T., Wang, S., Askari, S., Boruff, J., ... Mayo, N. (2019). Association of cannabis use in adolescence and risk of depression, anxiety, and suicidality in young adulthood: A systematic review and meta-analysis. *JAMA Psychiatry, 76*, 426–434. doi:10.1001/jamapsychiatry.2018.4500

Griffin, K. W., & Botvin, G. (2000). Evidence-based interventions for preventing substance use disorders in adolescents. *Child and Adolescent Psychiatric Clinics, 19*, 505–526.

Grunberg, V. A., Cordova, K. A., Bidwell, L. C., & Ito, T. A. (2015). Can marijuana make it better? Prospective effects of marijuana and temperament on risk for anxiety and depression. *Psychology of Addictive Behaviors, 29*, 590–602. doi:10.1037/adb00001 0910.1037/adb0000109.supp (Supplemental).

Gulliver, A., Griffiths, K. M., Christensen, H., Mackinnon, A., Calear, A. L., Parsons, A., ... Stanimirovic, R. (2012). Internet-based interventions to promote mental health help-seeking in elite athletes: An exploratory randomized controlled trial. *Journal of Medical Internet Research, 14*, 120–137. doi-org.ccl.idm.oclc.org/10.2196/jmir.1864

Hall-Flavin, D. K., & McKean, A. J. (2018). Teen depression. *The Mayo Clinic*. Retrieved from www.mayoclinic.org/diseases-conditions/teen-depression/symptoms-causes/syc-20350985

Handren, L., Donaldson, C. D., & Crano, W. D. (2016). Adolescent alcohol use: Protective and predictive parent, peer, and self-related factors. *Prevention Science, 17*, 862–871. doi:10.1007/s11121-016-0695-7

Hawkins, J. D., Catalano, R. F., & Miller, J. Y. (1992). Risk and protective factors for alcohol and other drug problems in adolescence and early adulthood: Implications for substance abuse prevention. *Psychological Bulletin, 112*, 64–105. doi.org.ccl.idm.oclc.org/10.1037/0033-2909.112.1.64

Hayatbakhsh, R., Williams, G. M., Bor, W., & Najman, J. M. (2013). Early childhood predictors of age of initiation to use of cannabis: A birth prospective study. *Drug and Alcohol Review, 32*, 232–240. doi.org.ccl.idm.oclc.org/10.1111/j.1465-3362.2012.00520.x

HealthLinkBC. (2018). Warning signs of suicide in children and teens. Retrieved from www.healthlinkbc.ca/health-topics/ty6090

Hemovich, V., & Crano, W. D. (2009). Family structure and adolescent drug use: Findings from a national study. *Substance Use and Misuse, 44*, 1099–2013. doi.org.ccl.idm.oclc.org/10.3109/10826080902858375

Hemovich, V., Lac, A., & Crano, W. D. (2011). Understanding early-onset drug and alcohol outcomes among youth: The role of family structure, social factors, and interpersonal perceptions of use. *Psychology, Health & Medicine, 16*, 249–267. doi.org.ccl.idm.oclc.org/10.1080/13548506.2010.532560

Hser, Y.-I., Mooney, L. J., Huang, D., Zhu, Y., Tomko, R. L., McClure, E., ... Gray, K. M. (2017). Reductions in cannabis use are associated with improvements in anxiety, depression, and sleep quality, but not quality of life. *Journal of Substance Abuse Treatment, 81*, 53–58. doi-org.ccl.idm.oclc.org/10.1016/j.jsat.2017.07.012

Huansuriya, T., Siegel, J. T., & Crano, W. D. (2014). Parent-child drug communication: Pathway from parents' ad exposure to youth's marijuana use intention. *Journal of Health Communication, 19*, 244–259. doi-org.ccl.idm.oclc.org/10.1080/10810730.2013.811326

Johnston, L. D., O'Malley, P. M., Miech, R. A., Bachman, J. G., & Schulenberg, J. E. (2016). *Monitoring the Future national survey results on drug use, 1975–2015: Overview, key findings on adolescent drug use.* Ann Arbor, MI: Institute for Social Research, The University of Michigan.

Juergens, J., & Hampton, D. (2018). Suicide and substance abuse and addiction. *Addiction Center.* Retrieved from: www.addictioncenter.com/addiction/addiction-and-suicide/

Kann, L., McManus, T., Harris, W. A., Shanklin, S. L., Flint, K. H., Queen, B., ... Ethier, K. A. (2018). Youth risk behavior surveillance — United States, 2017. *Surveillance Summaries, 8*, 1–114.

Keeler, A. R., Siegel, J. T., & Alvaro, E. M. (2013). Depression and help seeking among Mexican–Americans: The mediating role of familism. *Journal of Immigrant and Minority Health, 16*, 1225–1231. doi:10.1007/s10903-013-9824-6

Kerr, M., & Stattin, H. (2000). What parents know, how they know it, and several forms of adolescent adjustment: Further support for a reinterpretation of monitoring. *Developmental Psychology, 36*, 366–380. doi-org.ccl.idm.oclc.org/10.1037/0012-1649.36.3.366

Kerr, M., Stattin, H., & Burk, W. J. (2010). A reinterpretation of parental monitoring in longitudinal perspective. *Journal of Research on Adolescence, 20*, 39–64.

Kerr, M., Stattin, H., & Engels, R. C. (2008). Introduction: What's changed in research on parenting and adolescent problem behavior and what needs to change? In M. Kerr, H. Stattin, & R. C. Engels (Eds.), *What can parents do?* doi:10.1002/9780470774113.ch

Ketcherside, A., & Filbey, F. M. (2015). Mediating processes between stress and problematic marijuana use. *Addictive Behaviors, 45*, 113–118. doi-org.ccl.idm.oclc.org/10.1016/j.addbeh.2015.01.015

Khantzian, E. J. (1985). The self-medication hypothesis of addictive disorders: Focus on heroin and cocaine dependence. *The American Journal of Psychiatry, 142*, 1259–1264. doi-org.ccl.idm.oclc.org/10.1176/ajp.142.11.1259

Klimes-Dougan, B., & Lee, C. S. (2010). Suicide prevention public service announcements. Perceptions of young adults. *Crisis, 31*, 247–254. doi.org.ccl.idm.oclc.org/10.1027/0227-5910/a000032

Lac, A., Alvaro, E. M., Crano, W. D., & Siegel, J. T. (2009). Pathways from parental knowledge and warmth to adolescent marijuana use: An extension to the theory of planned behavior. *Prevention Science, 10*, 22–32. doi.org.ccl.idm.oclc.org/10.1007/s11121-008-0111-z

Lac, A., & Crano, W. D. (2009). Monitoring matters: Meta-analytic review reveals the reliable linkage of parental monitoring with adolescent marijuana use. *Perspectives on Psychological Science, 4*, 578–586. doi.org.ccl.idm.oclc.org/10.1111/j.1745-6924.2009.01166.x

Lac, A., Crano, W. D., Berger, D. E., & Alvaro, E. M. (2013). Attachment theory and theory of planned behavior: An integrative model predicting underage drinking. *Developmental Psychology, 49,* 1579–1590. doi.org.ccl.idm.oclc.org/10.1037/a0030728

Lamb, C. S., & Crano, W. D. (2014). Parents' beliefs and children's marijuana use: Evidence for a self-fulfilling prophecy effect. *Addictive Behaviors, 39,* 127–132. doi:10.1016/j.addbeh.2013.09.009

Lewin, K. (1943). *The relative effectiveness of a lecture method and a method of group decision for changing food habits.* Washington, D.C: National Research Council, Committee on Food Habits.

Lewin, K. (1946). Action research and minority problems. *Journal of Social Issues,* 34–46. doi.org.ccl.idm.oclc.org/10.1111/j.1540-4560.1946.tb02295.x

Lewin, K. (1947). Frontiers in group dynamics II. Channels of group life; social planning and action research. *Human Relations, 1,* 143–153. doi.org.ccl.idm.oclc.org/10.1177/001872674700100201

Lienemann, B. A., & Siegel, J. T. (2016). State psychological reactance to depression public service announcements among people with varying levels of depressive symptomatology. *Health Communication, 31,* 102–116. doi-org.ccl.idm.oclc.org/10.1080/10410236.2014.940668

Lienemann, B. A., Siegel, J. T., & Crano, W. D. (2013). Persuading people with depression to seek help: Respect the boomerang. *Health Communication, 28,* 718–728. doi.org.ccl.idm.oclc.org/10.1080/10410236.2012.712091

Lippold, M. A., Davis, K. D., McHale, S. M., Buxton, O. M., & Almeida, D. M. (2016). Daily stressor reactivity during adolescence: The buffering role of parental warmth. *Health Psychology, 9,* 1027–1035. doi:10.1037/hea0000352

Lochman, J. E., & van den Steenhoven, A. (2002). Family-based approaches to substance abuse prevention. *Journal of Primary Prevention, 23,* 49-114. doi.org/10.1023/A:1016591216363

Long, K., Fan, F., Chen, S., Tang, K., Wang, H., Zhang, Y., & Wang, Z. (2014). Parenting styles and depressive symptoms in senior high school students: The mediating effect of gratitude. *Chinese Journal of Clinical Psychology, 22,* 864–867.

Lowe, K., & Dotterer, A. M. (2013). Parental monitoring, parental warmth, and minority youths' academic outcomes: Exploring the integrative model of parenting. *Journal of Youth and Adolescence, 42,* 1413–1425. doi:10.1007/s10964-013-9934-4

Marmorstein, N. R., & Iacono, W. G. (2011). Explaining associations between cannabis use disorders in adolescence and later major depression: A test of the psychosocial failure model. *Addictive Behaviors, 36,* 773–776. doi-org.ccl.idm.oclc.org/10.1016/j.addbeh.2011.02.006

McGuire, W. J. (1973). The yin and yang of progress in social psychology: Seven koan. *Journal of Personality and Social Psychology, 26,* 446–456. doi.org/10.1037/h0034345

Medina, K. L., Nagel, B. J., Park, A., McQueeny, T., & Tapert, S. F. (2007). Depressive symptoms in adolescents: Associations with white matter volume and marijuana use. *Journal of Child Psychology and Psychiatry, and Allied Disciplines, 48,* 592–600. doi:10.1111/j.1469-7610.2007.01728.x.

Mental Health America. (2010) Factsheet: Depression in children. Retrieved from www.mentalhealthamerica.net.

Menting, B., Van Lier, P. A. C., Koot, H. M., Pardini, D., & Loeber, R. (2016). Cognitive impulsivity and the development of delinquency from late childhood to early adulthood: Moderating effects of parenting behavior and peer relationships. *Development and Psychopathology, 28,* 167–183. doi:10.1017/S095457941500036X

Miller, S. M., Siegel, J. T., Hohman, Z., & Crano, W. D. (2013). Factors mediating the association of the recency of parent's marijuana use and their adolescent children's subsequent initiation. *Psychology of Addictive Behaviors, 27,* 848–853. doi:10.1037/a0032201

Moreira, F. A. (2007). Serotonin, the prefrontal cortex, and the antidepressant-like effect of cannabinoids. *Journal of Neuroscience, 27,* 13369–13370. doi.org.ccl.idm.oclc.org/10.1523/JNEUROSCI.4867-07.2007

Morrill, M. I., Hawrilenko, M., & Córdova, J. V. (2016). A longitudinal examination of positive parenting following an acceptance-based couple intervention. *Journal of Family Psychology, 30,* 104–113. doi.org.ccl.idm.oclc.org/10.1037/fam0000162

Nakawaki, B., & Crano, W. D. (2012). Predicting adolescents' persistence, nonpersistence, and recent onset of nonmedical use of opioids and stimulants. *Addictive Behaviors, 37,* 716–721. doi.org.ccl.idm.oclc.org/10.1016/j.addbeh.2012.02.011

Nakawaki, B., & Crano, W. D. (2015). Patterns of substance use, delinquency, and risk factors among adolescent inhalant users. *Substance Use & Misuse, 50,* 114–122. doi.org.ccl.idm.oclc.org/10.3109/10826084.2014.961611

National Academies of Sciences, Engineering, and Medicine. (2017). *The health effects of cannabis and cannabinoids: The current state of evidence and recommendations for research.* Washington, D.C: The National Academies Press. doi:10.17226/24635.

National Institute of Mental Health. (2011). Depression. *U.S. Department of Health & Human Services,* 3511–3561.

National Institute of Mental Health. (2018). Suicide. *U.S. Department of Health & Human Services.* Retrieved from: www.nimh.nih.gov/health/statistics/suicide.shtml

Newcomb, M. D. & Locke, T. (2005). Health, social, and psychological consequences of drug use and abuse. In Z. Sloboda (Ed.), *Epidemiology of drug abuse* (pp. 45–59). New York, NY: Springer.

National Institute of Mental Health. (2018). Suicide: Leading cause of death in the United States (2017). Retrieved from: www.nimh.nih.gov/health/statistics/suicide.shtml

Office of National Drug Control Policy. (2008). *National drug control strategy: 2008 annual report.* The White House.

Ozer, E. J., Flores, E., Tschann, J. M., & Pasch, L. A. (2013). Parenting style, depressive symptoms, and substance use in Mexican American adolescents. *Youth and Society, 45,* 365–388. doi:10.1177/0044118X11418539

Pacek, L. R., Martins, S. S., & Crum, R. M. (2013). The bidirectional relationship between alcohol, cannabis, co-occurring alcohol and cannabis use disorders with major depressive disorder: Results from a national sample. *Journal of Affective Disorders, 148,* 188–195. doi.org.ccl.idm.oclc.org/10.1016/j.jad.2012.11.059

Pedersen, W., Mastekaasa, A., & Wichstrøm, L. (2001). Conduct problems and early cannabis initiation: A longitudinal study of gender differences. *Addiction, 96,* 415–431. doi-org.ccl.idm.oclc.org/10.1046/j.1360-0443.2001.9634156.x

Peters, J. F. (1994). Gender socialization of adolescents in the home: Research and discussion. *Adolescence, 29,* 913–934. Retrieved from http://search.ebscohost.com.ccl.idm.oclc.org/login.aspx?direct=true&db=psyh&AN=1995-17060-001&site=ehost-live&scope=site

Prislin, R., & Crano, W. D. (2012). A history of social influence research. In A. Kruglanski & W. Stroebe (Eds.), *Handbook of the history of social psychology* (pp. 321–339). New York, NY: Psychology Press.

Radhakrishnan, R., Wilkinson, S. T., & D'Souza, D. C. (2014). Gone to pot – A review of the association between cannabis and psychosis. *Frontiers in Psychiatry*, 5–54. doi.org/10.3389/fpsyt.2014.00054

Repetto, P. B., Zimmerman, M. A., & Caldwell, C. H. (2008). A longitudinal study of depressive symptoms and marijuana use in a sample of inner-city African Americans. *Journal of Research on Adolescence*, 18, 421–447. doi:10.1111/j.1532-7795.2008.00566.x.

Ruybal, A. L. & Crano, W. D. (2020). *Parental influences on adolescent major depressive symptoms and marijuana usage*. Manuscript under review.

Schwarz, B., Mayer, B., Trommsdorff, G., Ben-Arieh, A., Friedlmeier, M., Lubiewska, K. ... Peltzer, K. (2011). Does the importance of parent and peer relationships for adolescents' life satisfaction vary across cultures? *The Journal of Early Adolescence*, 32, 55–80. doi.org.ccl.idm.oclc.org/10.1177/0272431611419508

Shonesy, B. C., Bluett, R. J., Ramikie, T. S., Baldi, R., Hermanson, D. J., Kingsley, P. J., ... Patel, S. (2014). Genetic disruption of 2-arachidonoylglycerol synthesis reveals a key role for endocannabinoid signaling in anxiety modulation. *Cell Reports*, 9, 1644–1653. doi.org/10.1016/j.celrep.2014.11.001

Shrier, L. A., Ross, C. S., & Blood, E. A. (2014). Momentary positive and negative affect preceding marijuana use events in youth. *Journal of Studies on Alcohol and Drugs*, 75, 781–789. doi.org.ccl.idm.oclc.org/10.15288/jsad.2014.75.781

Siegel, J. T., Alvaro, E. A., Patel, N., & Crano, W. D. (2009). "... you would probably want to do it. Cause that's what made them popular": Exploring perceptions of inhalant utility among young adolescent non-users and occasional users. *Substance Use and Misuse*, 44, 597–615. doi.org.ccl.idm.oclc.org/10.1080/10826080902809543

Siegel, J. T., Crano, W. D., Alvaro, E. M., Lac, A., Hackett, J. D., & Hohman, Z. P. (2014). Differentiating common predictors and outcomes of marijuana initiation: A retrospective longitudinal analysis. *Substance Use & Misuse*, 49, 30–40. doi.org.ccl.idm.oclc.org/10.3109/10826084.2013.817427

Siegel, J. T., Lienemann, B. A., & Rosenberg, B. D. (2017). Resistance, reactance, and misinterpretation: Highlighting the challenge of persuading people with depression to seek help. *Social and Personality Psychology Compass*, 11. doi-org.ccl.idm.oclc.org/10.1111/spc3.12322

Siegel, J. T., Lienemann, B. A., & Tan, C. N. (2015). Influencing help-seeking among people with elevated depressive symptomatology: Mistargeting as a persuasive technique. *Clinical Psychological Science*, 3, 242–255. doi-org.ccl.idm.oclc.org/10.1177/2167702614542846

Siegel, J. T., Tan, C. A., Navarro, M. N., Alvaro E. A., Crano, W. D. (2015). The power of the proposition: Frequency of marijuana offers, parental monitoring, and adolescent marijuana use. *Drug Use and Dependence*, 148, 34–39. doi.org/10.1016/j.drugalcdep.2014.11.035

Sloboda, Z., Petras, H., Hingson, R. W., & Robertson, E. B. (Eds.). (2019). *Prevention of substance use*. New York: Springer.

Stattin, H., & Kerr, M. (2000). Parental monitoring: A reinterpretation. *Child Development*, 71, 1072–1085. doi-org.ccl.idm.oclc.org/10.1111/1467-8624.00210

Substance Abuse and Mental Health Services Administration. (2013). *Drug Abuse Warning Network, 2011: National estimates of drug-related emergency department visits*. HHS Publication No. (SMA) 13-4760, DAWN Series D-39. Rockville, MD: Substance Abuse and Mental Health Services Administration.

Substance Abuse and Mental Health Services Administration. (2019). *Behavioral health barometer: United States, Volume 5: Indicators as measured through the 2017 National Survey* on *Drug Use and Health and the National Survey of Substance Abuse Treatment Services.* HHS Publication No. SMA-19-Baro-17-US. Rockville, MD: Substance Abuse and Mental Health Services Administration, 2019.

Sussman, S., & Ames, S. L. (2008). *Drug abuse: Concepts, prevention, and cessation.* New York, NY: Cambridge University Press.

Taylor, O. D. (2011). Adolescent depression as a contributing factor to the development of substance use disorders. *Journal of Human Behavior in the Social Environment, 21,* 696–710. doi:10.1080/10911359.2011.583519

Voelkl, K. E., & Frone, M. R. (2000). Predictors of substance use at school among high school students. *Journal of Educational Psychology, 92,* 583–592. doi:10.1037/0022-0663.92.3.583

Wagner, A., & Anthony, J. C. (2002). Into the world of illegal drug use: Exposure opportunity and other mechanisms linking the use of alcohol, tobacco, marijuana, and cocaine. *American Journal of Epidemiology, 155,* 918–925. doi.org/10.1093/aje/155.10.918

Walster, E., & Festinger, L. (1962). The effectiveness of "overheard" persuasive communications. *The Journal of Abnormal and Social Psychology, 65,* 395–402. doi:10.1037/h0041172

Watters, A. J., & Williams, L. M. (2011). Negative biases and risk for depression; integrating self-report and emotion task markers. *Depression and Anxiety, 28,* 703–718. doi:10.1002/da.20854

Wilkinson, A. L., Halpern, C. T., Herring, A. H., Shanahan, M., Ennett, S. T., Hussey, J. M., & Harris, K. M. (2016). Testing longitudinal relationships between binge drinking, marijuana use, and depressive symptoms and moderation by sex. *Journal of Adolescent Health.* doi:10.1016/j.jadohealth.2016.07.010

Womack, S. R., Shaw, D. S., Weaver, C. M., & Forbes, E. E. (2016). Bidirectional associations between cannabis use and depressive symptoms from adolescence through early adulthood among at-risk young men. *Journal of Studies on Alcohol and Drugs, 77,* 287–297. doi-org.ccl.idm.oclc.org/10.15288/jsad.2016.77.287

World Health Organization. (2014). Cannabis. Retrieved from www.who.int/substance_abuse/facts/cannabis/en/

World Health Organization. (2016). Suicide data. Retrieved from www.who.int/mental_health/prevention/suicide/suicideprevent/en/

World Health Organization. (2018). Mental Health: Suicide. Data Retrieved from www.who.int/mental_health/prevention/suicide/suicideprevent/en/

12

WHEN JUSTICE IS NOT BLIND

The Effects of Expectancies on Social Interactions and Judgments in Legal Settings

Margaret Bull Kovera

Actors within the criminal justice system are expected to be objective and decide issues without bias. Indeed, legal actors do, at least in part, rely on legally-relevant information when making decisions. For example, the single best predictor of juror decisions are variations in the strength of the evidence against the defendant (Visher, 1987). Attorneys use their discretion to prevent potential jurors with the most extreme bias from serving on juries (Johnson & Haney, 1994). Eyewitnesses are more likely to make a positive identification of a culprit than of an innocent suspect (Wells, Yang, & Smalarz, 2015).

Despite evidence that legal actors often make choices that should bolster our faith in their competence to carry out their duties objectively, biases have been documented in all sorts of legal decisions. Pretrial publicity influences jurors' verdicts (Steblay, Besirevic, Fulero, & Jimenez-Lorente, 1999), even when they receive instructions to disregard it (Fein, McCloskey, & Tomlinson, 1997). Prosecutors are more likely to dismiss Black than White jurors from jury service (Sommers & Norton, 2007). Eyewitnesses are more likely to misidentify someone of their own race than someone of another race (Meissner & Brigham, 2001; Platz & Hosch, 1988). In each of these cases, the decision-makers (jurors, attorneys, or witnesses) passively received information (pretrial publicity and evidence, a juror profile, a crime) and then made decisions (rendered a verdict, challenged the suitability of a juror, identified someone from a lineup).

Perhaps because of a preference for the ease of low-impact paradigms in which participants are passive recipients of information on which they base their decisions, scholars at the intersection of social psychology and law have relatively neglected the possibility that social interactions may bias legal outcomes. In particular, studies of jury decision-making infrequently include deliberations (Bornstein, 2017), the social setting in which jurors interactively discuss the trial evidence and the law. Similarly, studies of jury selection have only rarely examined the interaction between attorneys and potential jurors (also known as venirepersons) during voir dire (the procedure during which jury selection occurs; Kovera & Austin, 2016). Only recently have researchers explored the ways in which the interaction between a lineup administrator and a witness might influence witnesses' decisions (Kovera & Evelo, 2017). In contrast, newer paradigms, which provide opportunities for participants to interact with each other, allow for an examination of how the expectancies of legal actors influence their interactions in criminal justice settings, consequently influencing legal decisions. The reinsertion of the social context into the psychological examination of these legal situations has generated new insights into how expectancies bias consequential decisions in legal domains.

In the remainder of this chapter, I will review research on interpersonal expectancy effects, highlighting ways in which interpersonal expectancies likely play a role in legal decisions. I will then describe two programs of research in which I have examined how situating research paradigms within social interactions allows for a demonstration that interpersonal expectancies bias legal decision-making. The first program of research examines how attorneys' expectations about potential jurors' attitudes influence the jury selection process. The second research program demonstrates how lineup administrators' expectancies influence eyewitness identification decisions. Finally, I will argue that to gain a more complete understanding of legal decision-making, researchers must identify the social situations in which these decisions are often made and consider the extent to which social interactions influence the decision-making process.

Interpersonal Expectancy Effects

The study of interpersonal expectancy effects is rooted in Orne's (1962) early recognition that people are not passive subjects in experiments, but active participants. Active participants assume that all research has a purpose and attempt to discern the hypothesis. Orne coined the term *demand characteristic* to refer to any cue that communicates the hidden purpose of an experiment to participants. When participants believe that they have discerned the research hypothesis, they conform their behavior to that hypothesis in an effort to appear competent (Weber & Cook, 1972).

When experimenters have expectations for how research participants will behave, they can emit subtle cues that communicate their hypotheses to participants, even though they are unaware of doing so (for a research summary, see Rosenthal, 2002). When teachers were told that certain students would soon blossom, those students performed better over the course of the year, even though the students had been chosen at random (Rosenthal & Jacobson, 1968). When graduate students were given the expectation that some of their rats were bright and others were dull, the bright rats made fewer errors learning a T-maze than did dull rats, even though the two sets of rats were genetically identical (Rosenthal & Fode, 1963b). When experimenters were led to believe that facial stimuli expressed either success or failure (when the stimuli were, in fact, neutral), participants judged the emotion of the faces to be consistent with the experimenters' expectations (Rosenthal & Fode, 1963a). In essence, interpersonal expectancy effects occur when one person's expectations affect another person's (or rat's) behavior (Trusz & Bąbel, 2016).

Interpersonal expectancies influence a target's behavior by first influencing the behavior of the person holding the expectation (Rosenthal, 2002; Trusz & Bąbel, 2016). Holding an expectation of another changes the behavior of the expectation holder toward the target of the expectation. The changes in expectation holders' behavior cause targets to confirm the expectations through their behavior, a process known as behavioral confirmation. Mediating behaviors can take many forms (Harris & Rosenthal, 1985) and likely depend upon the context in which the behavioral confirmation occurs. In behavioral and medical studies, researchers routinely use double-blind procedures to control for expectancy effects. With double-blind methods, neither the researchers who interact with participants nor the participants themselves know to which condition of the experiment the participant has been assigned (Rosenthal & Rosnow, 1984; Shadish, Cook, & Campbell, 2002; Weber & Cook, 1972), removing the possibility that interpersonal expectancies can initiate the behavioral confirmation process.

The typical research designs used to study jury decision-making, jury selection, and eyewitness identifications preclude the investigation of interpersonal expectancy effects in legal decision-making. Yet the effects of interpersonal expectancies occur in many different contexts, and legal contexts should be no different. Indeed, there have been sporadic attempts to explore behavioral confirmation processes in legal settings. For example, judges' beliefs about a defendant's guilt influence the way they read pattern jury instructions, resulting in jurors rendering verdicts that confirm judges' beliefs (Halverson, Hallahan, Hart, & Rosenthal, 1997; Hart, 1995). Despite demonstrating the effects of interpersonal expectancies in a jury decision-making context, these investigations did not fundamentally change our understanding of legal decision-making or the operation of legal procedures.

In contrast, two programs of research examining the role of interpersonal expectancies in legal contexts necessitate a re-evaluation of whether two legal procedures operate as intended. The first program of research examined the extent to which attorneys' interpersonal expectancies about venirepersons' attitudes and beliefs interfere with voir dire's goal of uncovering bias and instead bias jurors' verdicts. The second research program investigated whether lineup administrators' expectations about which lineup member witnesses will identify influence witnesses' identification decisions. In the sections that follow, I will describe the typical paradigms used to study jury decision-making, jury selection, and eyewitness identification and how novel paradigms that allowed for social interaction among research participants were needed to demonstrate the role of interpersonal expectancies in legal decision-making.

The Role of Interpersonal Expectancies in Jury Selection and Decision-Making

Most scholars studying jury selection have focused their attention on identifying venireperson characteristics (e.g., demographics, traits, and attitudes) that predict verdict preferences (Kovera & Cutler, 2013). In the typical study, participants report on a characteristic of interest, read a written summary of trial evidence or watch a video-recorded trial simulation, and render a verdict. Researchers then examine correlations between jurors' characteristics and their verdicts. Similarly, studies of jury decision-making typically involve exposing participants to a trial simulation that manipulates some aspect of the evidence or trial procedure and measuring their verdicts (Kovera & Levett, 2015). There are some exceptions to this characterization of the literature, with a few studies examining the effects of different types of voir dire questioning (Crocker & Kovera, 2010; Dexter, Cutler, & Moran, 1992; Jones, 1987; Middendorf & Luginbuhl, 1995) and some studies allowing jurors to deliberate before rendering final verdicts (for an analysis of the prevalence of deliberations in jury simulation studies, see Bornstein, 2017). Other than a few outliers, most studies of jury selection and its relationship to jury decision-making have tackled a relatively simple question: Do juror characteristics predict verdicts?

In the past decade, perhaps because of an overreliance on a single paradigm—a paradigm that neglects the social interaction between attorney and venireperson that lies at the heart of voir dire—there have been few significant advances in our understanding of the interrelationship of voir dire, jury selection, and jury decision-making. Although psychology and law pioneer Larry Wrightsman (1987) noted years ago that the voir dire process may serve as a source of juror bias, this notion has received little empirical attention. It is true that a few studies have addressed the issue of whether exposure to the voir dire process influences the expression of juror bias in verdicts (Greathouse, Sothmann, Levett, & Kovera, 2011; Haney, 1984; Vitriol & Kovera, 2018). However, these studies treated participants as passive recipients of the voir dire process, manipulating the content of a video-recorded voir dire simulation that participants watched, rather than active participants in the trial process.

In our laboratory, we have turned our attention to investigating how interpersonal expectancies influence the interaction between attorneys and venirepersons during voir dire, subsequently influencing jurors' verdicts. Specifically, we have studied whether attorneys' expectations for venirepersons' attitudes influence the questions that they ask venirepersons during voir dire, the responses that they receive from venirepersons, their evaluations of what those responses mean, and the verdicts rendered by jurors. In essence, in a series of five studies we investigated whether attorneys' expectations cause them to engage in biased hypothesis testing, which results in jurors behaviorally confirming their expectations. Three of these studies employed high-impact methods designed to simulate the social interactions that occur in voir dire between attorneys and venirepersons.

Biased Hypothesis Testing in Voir Dire

During voir dire, attorneys generate hypotheses about which prospective jurors may be more favorable to their side, ask questions designed to elicit indications of bias from those venirepersons they deem unfavorable, and then attempt to remove those who appear least favorable to their case. They can remove venirepersons in one of two ways. Attorneys may challenge venirepersons for cause, arguing that they have demonstrated bias that makes them unfit to serve as a juror. Theoretically, the number of challenges for cause is limited only by the ability of an attorney to convince a judge that a venireperson is irremediably biased. The second method for removing a venireperson is a peremptory challenge. Peremptory challenges are limited in number, the exact number varying by jurisdiction, trial type (criminal vs. civil), and other trial factors like charge severity. In most cases, attorneys need not specify why they are removing a particular juror using a peremptory challenge, unless there are charges that the basis is race or gender, which are legally prohibited bases for challenging a venireperson (*Batson v. Kentucky*, 1986; *J.E.B. v. Alabama*, 1994).

Attorneys are tasked with exercising their challenges in a way that maximizes the likelihood that the venirepersons who are eventually seated on the jury will be favorably disposed to the arguments that they present. To successfully complete this task, attorneys generate hypotheses about the relationship between jurors' characteristics and their verdict preferences. Once they have generated their hypotheses, they formulate questions that will allow them to gather information from the venirepersons that tests these hypotheses. Once venirepersons have responded to the questions, attorneys infer whether the responses support their hypotheses and decide whether to challenge particular jurors. These stages of the information-gathering process in voir dire correspond well with social psychologists' proposed stages in testing hypotheses: hypothesis generation, information gathering, and inference (Trope & Liberman, 1996).

Attorneys' interpersonal expectancies about venirepersons may influence their jury selection decisions. If these expectancies are inaccurate, it could lead to an ineffective use of peremptory challenges. Indeed, only a small number of demographic and personality characteristics influence attorneys' evaluations of which venirepersons would be favorable to their side, and their beliefs about which characteristics predict venireperson favorability are often in error (Olczak, Kaplan, & Penrod, 1991). Presumably attorneys can gather information during voir dire that will help them recognize whether their initial hypotheses about venirepersons are supported. For example, attorneys could gather information that enables them to fairly test their expectancies are valid if they posed diagnostic questions to venirepersons designed to provide differential support for their hypotheses and alternative hypotheses (Skov & Sherman, 1986). However, people tend to ask questions at the information-gathering stage that are biased toward confirming their hypothesis, rather than questions that are designed to test the accuracy of their hypothesis (Snyder & Swann, 1978).

During the inference stage, attorneys evaluate whether the information they have received from venirepersons supports their hypotheses. Three different types of bias—based on the questions that they have asked and the answers that they received—may affect attorneys' inferences (Hodgins & Zuckerman, 1993). Hypothesis bias occurs when attorneys infer that their hypothesis is more likely to be true because the hypothesis (as opposed to its alternative) is more readily available in memory. Question bias occurs when attorneys infer that venirepersons hold attitudes that are consistent with the question asked. For example, attorneys may be more likely to infer that venirepersons endorse a presumption of innocence if they ask venirepersons "Do you believe that a defendant is innocent until proven guilty?" Finally, answer bias occurs when attorneys' inferences are overly influenced by the responses they receive to their questions, overconfirming their hypotheses when they receive confirmatory responses and overdisconfirming when they receive disconfirmatory responses. Thus, whether attorneys are successful at detecting bias during voir dire is likely restricted by the hypotheses that the attorneys wish to test, the questions that they ask to test these hypotheses, the responses that venirepersons provide, and by the inferences made by attorneys from the information they obtain.

In my laboratory, we have conducted two studies that test the effects that attorneys' expectations have on the questions that they propose to ask venirepersons, to discern whether they hold attitudes that are favorable to their side. In one study (Experiment 1; Otis, Greathouse, Kennard, & Kovera, 2014), prosecutors and defense attorneys read the profile of a hypothetical venireperson in a capital case. The description of the venireperson varied to manipulate participants' expectations about the extent to which the venireperson supported the death penalty. The attorneys then wrote two questions that they would ask the venireperson during voir dire to test one of two hypotheses: the venireperson supports the death penalty or the venireperson opposes the death penalty. For each question, they provided estimates of the percentage of people who supported and who opposed the death penalty if they answered yes to the voir dire question, opined whether venirepersons supported or opposed the death penalty given a yes or a no response to the question, and estimated the likelihood that the venirepersons supported the death penalty if they answered yes or if they answered no the question. These responses were subjected to a Bayesian analysis, in which attorneys' answers were compared with the responses they should have given if they were making normatively correct inferences.

Although attorneys in this study did not ask hypothesis-confirming questions, they did pose more diagnostic questions when the venireperson's death penalty attitudes were inconsistent with the hypothesis they had been instructed to test. Attorneys also made inferences that were biased by the questions that they asked and by the responses they expected to receive to those questions. For example, if attorneys asked a question that tested whether the venireperson opposed the death penalty, they would overestimate the probability that the venireperson opposed the death penalty. Attorneys would also be more likely to overestimate that a venireperson opposed the death penalty if the venireperson responded yes to a question that tested whether the person opposed the death penalty and no to a question testing the alternative hypothesis that the venireperson supported the death penalty.

Because attorneys are likely aware of the low base rate of death penalty opposition among the general public, it is possible that this knowledge could have affected attorneys' inferences about venirepersons' attitudes. This possibility seems likely as, when attorneys read the profile of a venireperson who was likely a death penalty opponent, they tended to overestimate the chances that the venireperson was in favor of the death penalty. Thus, we sought to test our hypotheses using a different set of venireperson profiles and a different target attitude. Specifically, we conducted a second study in which we asked attorneys and law students to test the hypothesis that a venireperson was a legal authoritarian, a civil libertarian, or either a legal authoritarian or a civil libertarian (the double hypothesis; Experiment 2; Otis et al., 2014). In addition to manipulating the hypothesis that the attorneys tested, we manipulated the base rate of legal authoritarianism among potential jurors (80 percent, 50 percent, or 20 percent likelihood). The remaining procedure was consistent with the earlier study.

In this second study, attorneys responded in a manner consistent with previous research on biased hypothesis testing (Hodgins & Zuckerman, 1993) by asking hypothesis-confirming questions. Moreover, the inferences that attorneys drew about the venireperson's attitudes were biased in predictable ways. Once again, attorneys' inferences were biased by the hypothesis they were instructed to test, with attorneys who tested the legal authoritarian hypothesis overestimating that the venireperson was a legal authoritarian. The actual question that attorneys asked also biased their inferences, with attorneys overestimating that the venireperson held attitudes consistent with the hypothesis they tested with their question. Consistent with the previous study, attorneys overestimated the value of a yes response that tested the hypothesis and undervalued no responses that tested the opposing hypothesis. These studies, taken together, suggest that attorneys engage in biased hypothesis-testing during voir dire. These biased strategies for testing their hypotheses bias the conclusions they reach about whether the retention of a particular venireperson during jury selection will benefit their side.

Behavioral Confirmation During Voir Dire

Many studies on dyadic interactions demonstrate that when one participant (the perceiver) is given an expectation about another participant (the target), the target of the expectation tends to behave in a manner consistent with the perceiver's expectation – a process called behavioral confirmation (e.g., Snyder, Tanke, & Berscheid, 1977; Stukas & Snyder, 2002). Similarly, attorneys' expectations about venirepersons may alter attorneys' behavior toward venirepersons during voir dire, consequently affecting venirepersons' responses to attorneys' questions and ultimately influencing the verdicts that they would render if they are seated on a jury. But the motivational goals of attorneys and venirepersons may influence whether behavioral confirmation occurs. Behavioral confirmation was more common when perceivers were tasked with gathering information about the target that would help them form a stable, reliable impression of that person than when they were tasked with having a smooth social interaction with the target (Snyder & Haugen, 1994). Thus in voir dire, behavioral confirmation may be more prevalent when attorneys use voir dire as an information-gathering process in which the attorneys' goal is to form a reliable evaluation of the jurors' attitudes and verdict leanings. Alternatively, if attorneys' goals during voir dire are to ingratiate themselves with jurors, behavioral confirmation may be less likely to occur. Similarly, venirepersons' motivations to achieve certain outcomes should affect whether behavioral confirmation occurs. For example, venirepeople who are motivated to get out of jury duty may be less likely to behaviorally confirm an attorney's expectation than would those jurors who are motivated to please the court.

To examine whether behavioral confirmation processes operate during voir dire, advanced law students prepared questions to ask a community member during a simulation of a voir dire in a death penalty case (Kovera, Greathouse, Otis, Kennard, & Chorn, 2019). We provided the attorney with information about the venirepersons' criminal justice attitudes to manipulate the mock attorneys' expectations about the mock venirepersons' favorability toward the prosecution or the defense. Rather than providing attorneys with attitudinal information that we obtained from the community members, we randomly assigned attorneys to receive information that the venireperson with whom they would be interacting held either pro-prosecution or pro-defense attitudes. In addition, we manipulated the motivation of the attorneys (i.e., either to ingratiate or gather accurate information) and the motivations of the venireperson (i.e., get on or off the jury). After interacting with the community member, attorneys rated the venireperson's desirability for their capital case and community members completed a measure of death penalty attitudes. Coders who were blind to condition watched the videos of the venirepersons' answers to the attorneys' questions and rated the extent to which they exhibited pro-prosecution behavior.

Interestingly, attorneys tended to ask general questions about the venireperson's background rather than questions that directly assessed the venireperson's attitudes about the death penalty. When attorneys did ask questions designed to test hypotheses about death penalty support/opposition, they tended to ask hypothesis-confirming questions. Specifically, attorneys who were given pro-prosecution expectations about the venireperson they were to question asked more questions testing a pro-prosecution hypothesis, and those given pro-defense expectations asked more questions testing a pro-defense hypothesis. Not only did attorneys ask hypothesis-confirming questions, venirepersons confirmed attorneys' expectations with their behavior during the simulated voir dire, as evidenced by naïve observers' ratings of the venirepersons' behavior. In addition, voir dire questioning influenced the post-voir dire attitudes that jurors held; attorney's expectations about the venireperson's attitudes caused venirepersons' self-reported attitudes toward the death penalty to shift in the direction of the attorneys' expectations. Finally, attorneys' pre-voir dire expectations explained significant variance in attorneys' ratings of the venireperson's attitudes post-voir dire, even after controlling for post-voir dire death penalty attitudes and independent coders' (blind to condition) ratings of jurors' pro-prosecution behavior. Note that this effect of pre-voir dire expectations survived the opportunity for attorneys to gather information during a one-on-one social interaction.

In another study, we examined whether behavioral confirmation processes negatively affected attorneys' abilities to make jury selection decisions that benefited their side (Kovera, Kennard, Otis, Chorn, & Zimmerman, 2019). Using snowball sampling, we recruited 40 practicing criminal attorneys from the New York City area (20 Assistant District Attorneys, 20 public defenders) to conduct voir dires of 12 jury-eligible community members. As in the previous study, we manipulated the attorneys' expectation of the attitudes (pro-prosecution or pro-defense) held by each of the community members; the expectation associated with each community member was randomly assigned. Based on this manipulated expectation and general demographic information that was collected from the community member, attorneys generated hypotheses about individual venirepersons, formulated questions to test their hypotheses, and then conducted a mock voir dire with the 12 community members. Attorneys conducted the voir dire with the goal of excusing six venirepersons, leaving them with a jury of six. Following the voir dire, community members reviewed evidence in a death penalty case and rendered a verdict.

As in the previous study, the randomly-assigned expectation about juror attitudes influenced attorneys' decisions. Prosecuting attorneys struck more venirepersons whom they expected to be pro-defense and defense attorneys struck more venirepersons whom they expected to be pro-prosecution. Again, the effect of attitudinal expectation on strike decisions survived attorneys' questioning of venirepersons. The effect of attitudinal expectation was not moderated by venirepersons' pre-voir dire attitude. Thus, voir dire may not be an effective method of identifying juror biases. Finally, we again found evidence of behavioral confirmation in voir dire. Venirepersons rendered more guilty verdicts when the attorney's expectation of the juror was pro-prosecution than when the attorney expected the venireperson to be pro-defense.

Behavioral confirmation and cognitive dissonance. When attorneys engaged in biased hypothesis testing, they elicited responses from jurors that were consistent with their expectations about the venireperson (i.e., behavioral confirmation). For some proportion of these venirepersons, the attitudes they express that behaviorally confirm the attorneys' expectations are at odds with the attitudes they held when they started the voir dire process. This attitude-behavior inconsistency may cause venirepersons to experience cognitive dissonance (Festinger, 1957). Because people desire consistency between attitudes and behavior, they may experience an uncomfortable psychological state (i.e., dissonance) when they are in conflict. Once people engage in a counterattitudinal behavior, they tend to endorse attitudes that are consistent with that behavior to reduce the unpleasant feeling associated with the inconsistency. In the case of voir dire, imagine that an attorney is trying to test the hypothesis that a venireperson is pro-prosecution and asks the hypothesis-confirming question: "If someone commits premeditated murder, do you think that person should be prosecuted to the full extent of the law?" Many people would likely respond affirmatively to this question. Not only is this question not particularly diagnostic of whether a venireperson tends to be pro-prosecution or pro-defense, pro-defense jurors might experience some discomfort with their response. Venirepersons who are uncomfortable for responding in a counterattitudinal manner may later attempt to relieve their discomfort by rendering a verdict that is consistent with the attitude they expressed during voir dire.

To test whether experienced dissonance mediated the effects of hypothesis-confirming questions during voir dire on jurors' verdicts that we saw in earlier studies, we conducted a final study that manipulated whether venirepersons responded to open-ended versus close-ended pro-prosecution voir dire questions in a simulated voir dire (Experiment 2; Zimmerman, Otis, Kennard, Chorn, & Kovera, 2019). People must feel personal responsibility for their counterattitudinal behavior to feel cognitive dissonance (Cooper & Fazio, 1984). Thus, we expected that venirepersons who provided a more detailed counterattitudinal expression would be more likely to experience cognitive dissonance and to shift their verdicts in the counterattitudinal direction than would venirepersons who provided a simple "yes" or "no" response to a counterattitudinal voir dire question.

In a voir dire simulation, confederates posed as attorneys and asked jury-eligible community members who were generally opposed to the death penalty either closed-ended or open-ended voir dire questions testing a pro-prosecution hypothesis. The mock venirepersons then completed a measure of experienced dissonance (Elliott & Devine, 1994) and watched a trial that varied in evidence strength (strong, ambiguous, or weak). After watching the trial, participants rendered a verdict and again completed the cognitive dissonance scale. We predicted that venirepersons who answered open-ended questions would experience cognitive dissonance as a result of their freely chosen counterattitudinal expression but those who answered closed-ended questions would not. As a result, we predicted that venirepersons who answered open-ended pro-prosecution questions would render a verdict consistent with the hypothesis tested by the confederate attorney, but only when the evidence strength was ambiguous. That is, if the evidence clearly supported a not guilty or guilty verdict, participants should not feel dissonance as a result of their counterattitudinal expression and should return a verdict consistent with the evidence. However, when the evidence is ambiguous, participants should experience dissonance as a result of their voir dire behavior and would render a verdict consistent with the hypothesis tested by the attorney.

Whether mock jurors behaviorally confirmed the hypothesis tested in the voir dire questioning depended on whether the mock attorney asked open-ended or closed-ended questions and the strength of the evidence. When the trial evidence was ambiguous and the confederate attorneys asked open-ended voir dire questions testing a pro-prosecution hypothesis, jurors rendered more guilty verdicts than when attorneys asked them closed-ended questions and the evidence was ambiguous. Consistent with our predictions, there were no effects of pro-prosecution hypothesis testing when the trial had strong or weak evidence against the defendant. In terms of dissonance reduction, jurors reported higher levels of cognitive dissonance after voir dire than after rendering a verdict, but the attorneys' questioning method or evidence strength did not influence participants' experienced dissonance. Post-trial, jurors expressed more support for the death penalty and more pro-prosecution attitudes post-trial than they did pretrial, consistent with our earlier findings that verdicts shift toward the hypothesis tested by voir dire questioning.

The Role of Interpersonal Expectancies in Eyewitness Identification

For decades, researchers studying eyewitness identification accuracy have relied on a paradigm in which participants watch a re-enactment of a crime and then attempt to identify the perpetrator of that crime (Cutler & Kovera, 2010). The crime re-enactment may be a live event or recorded on video. The identification procedure might vary in terms of the instructions given to the witness, whether the witness views only the suspect or the suspect plus a set number of known innocent people, whether the lineup members are shown simultaneously or sequentially, and whether the suspect is the culprit or innocent. Until recently, the presentation of the identification procedure to witnesses has been highly controlled, sometimes presented in mass testing sessions by projecting a photo array on a screen or to individuals by experimenters following rigid protocols, drastically minimizing any interaction of the lineup administrator with witnesses. Increasingly, studies have been conducted online with a computer presenting a photoarray to participants, completely eliminating any chance that a lineup administrator interacts with, let alone influences, a witness.

These conditions do not mimic the conditions of identification procedures conducted in the field. In real cases, identification procedures are rarely conducted using computer administration, with the exception of some field studies conducted by psychologists who intended to minimize administrator/witness contact (for example, Wells, Steblay, & Dysart, 2015). Instead, most lineups and photo arrays are administered by police officers who have the opportunity to interact with witnesses during the administration. How does this knowledge influence the expectations that the police officer holds about the witness? If the police officer is confident that the suspect is the culprit, it is likely that the officer expects that (a) the witness will make a positive identification (i.e., identify one of the lineup members as the culprit) and (b) that the lineup member identified will be the suspect.

Might these expectations change how the administrator behaves while administering the identification procedure? Given past research on interpersonal expectancies and behavioral confirmation, it is likely that administrators who know which lineup member is the suspect (non-blind administrators) could behave differently than administrators who do not know which lineup member is the suspect (blind administrators), potentially steering the witness toward picking the suspect. For example, a non-blind administrator might tell witnesses to look more closely or to take their time when they appear to be looking at the suspect, but tell them to make sure to look at all the photos if they appear to be considering a filler. If a witness is wavering between choosing a filler or the suspect, a non-blind administrator might ask what looks familiar about the photo of the suspect, but not ask a similar question about the filler. Might the witness be more likely to identify the suspect if an administrator, even unwittingly, engages in those behaviors?

Thus, in the context of lineups, administrators' expectations (i.e., that the witness will select the suspect) may cause witnesses to choose the suspect from the lineup. Before guidelines were issued recommending blind administration of lineups (Wells, Kovera, Douglass, Meissner, Brewer, & Wixted, 2020; Wells et al., 1998), almost all administrators of identification procedures knew which lineup member (or photo in a photo array) was suspected of committing the crime viewed by the eyewitness. Even today, only half of US states require—when feasible—that identification procedures be double-blind, that is, conducted by administrators and administered to witnesses who are blind to which lineup member is the suspect (Kovera & Evelo, 2017). Single-blind lineup administration is concerning because it is possible that the witness will not base their identification decision on their memory alone—as legally intended—but on behavioral cues from the administrator. In other words, administrators with knowledge of the suspect's identity may unconsciously and unintentionally contaminate the identification procedure (see Fiedler, this volume, for a discussion of other recommended lineup procedures).

Although several paradigms have been developed to test the extent to which the administrator's knowledge of the suspect's identity influences eyewitnesses' identification decisions, the paradigm that most faithfully models the full cycle of interpersonal expectancy effects and behavioral confirmation is the *double-blind paradigm* (Kovera & Evelo, 2017). In this paradigm, half of the participants are trained to serve as administrators; half of these administrators are told who the suspect is (single-blind administration) and half are not (double-blind administration). These participant administrators then conduct a photo array with participants who witnessed a crime (Evelo, Zimmerman, Rhead, Chorn, & Kovera, 2019; Greathouse & Kovera, 2009; Zimmerman, Chorn, Rhead, Evelo, & Kovera, 2017). These photo array administrations are video recorded surreptitiously, allowing for observers who are blind to condition to code the administrators' behaviors for cues that suggest which lineup member is the suspect. Thus, the paradigm allows for a test of whether knowing the suspect's identity changes administrators' behavior during the identification procedure and whether those behavioral changes subsequently influence the likelihood that witnesses will identify the suspect as opposed to a filler (i.e., a photo of a known innocent person).

In one of the first investigations using this paradigm (Greathouse & Kovera, 2009), we examined whether the effect of single-blind administration of photo arrays was greater when other conditions were present that promote witness guessing (i.e., witnesses are likely to make a choice from an identification procedure despite having a relatively weak memory trace for the perpetrator of the crime): simultaneous (as opposed to sequential) presentation of the photos and biased lineup instructions that imply that the culprit is present among the photos in the array. Indeed, non-blind administrators were more likely to obtain a positive identification of the suspect from witnesses, irrespective of whether the suspect was the culprit or was innocent, than were blind administrators, especially under conditions that promoted choosing.

Consistent with theory on interpersonal expectancy effects, changes in the administrators' behaviors during the photo array administration were instrumental in producing these increases in identifications of the suspect. Non-blind administrators were more likely than blind administrators to behave in potentially biasing ways (e.g., tell the witness to take another look if they did not make an identification; Greathouse & Kovera, 2009). Given the camera angle in this study, we were unable to determine whether these behaviors were directed toward suspects or fillers. However, observers who were unaware of whether the administrator knew which lineup member was the suspect reported that non-blind administrators put more pressure on the witness to choose someone than did blind administrators (Greathouse & Kovera, 2009).

We have also studied whether witnesses with weaker memory traces are more likely to be susceptible to administrator influence than are witnesses with stronger memories (Zimmerman et al., 2017). Within the double-blind paradigm, we manipulated memory strength by varying the retention interval between witnessing the crime and making an identification attempt (Deffenbacher, Bornstein, McGorty, & Penrod, 2008): 30 minutes vs. one week. We also manipulated simultaneous versus sequential presentation of the photos. Non-blind administrators did not influence the rate at which witnesses chose the suspect from sequential lineups for either retention interval. Nor did it influence the rate at which witnesses chose the suspect from a simultaneous photo array with only a 30-minute delay. In contrast, when a simultaneous photo array was administered after a one-week delay, witnesses were more likely to pick the suspect when the administrator knew which photo depicted the suspect than when the administrator did not. Once again, we observed evidence of suggestiveness in the behavior of non-blind administrators. When administrators asked witnesses about a particular photo in the array, non-blind administrators were more likely to ask about or point at the suspect's photo than were blind administrators, demonstrating the attempts of non-blind administrators to focus witness attention on the suspect rather than fillers.

An analysis of the pattern of identification decisions in these studies reveals that administrator influence is not operating by changing the rates at which witnesses make a positive identification from a photo. Witnesses report that the culprit is not present in the photo array at equal rates, irrespective of whether the administrator is blind to which lineup member is the suspect. The increase in identifications of suspects from single-blind administrations is accompanied by a decrease in filler identifications (Kovera & Evelo, 2017). Essentially, witnesses who would have chosen a filler without influence from the administrator shift their picks to the suspect when the administrator knows who the suspect is.

Conclusion

In sum, studies of social interactions in two simulated legal settings, voir dire and the administration of eyewitness identification procedures, introduced bias into legal decision-making through the expectancies of others. In voir dire, attorneys' expectations about the attitudes held by potential jurors changed jurors' self-reported attitudes toward the death penalty. These randomly-assigned expectations also influenced attorneys' perceptions of venirepersons' biases despite attorneys being allowed to gather information that could have disconfirmed their expectations. Indeed, the attorneys' expectancies influenced their perceptions of venirepersons' attitudes even after controlling for the change in venirepersons' attitudes that was a byproduct of the voir dire questioning and observers' ratings of the adversarial slant of the venirepersons' behavior (pro-prosecution versus pro-defense). In identification procedures, lineup administrators' expectations increased rates of the misidentification of innocent suspects. These findings suggest that reforms—like double-blind lineup administration—are needed to reduce the influence of interpersonal expectancies on legal decisions.

In addition, these two programs of research serve as a reminder of the importance of studying the role of social interaction on decision-making in the legal context. Other than the small fraction of jury simulation studies that include deliberations, very few studies at the intersection of social psychology and the law allow for social interaction among participants. It is difficult to find studies that include behavior either as a manipulation of an independent variable or as a dependent variable. This neglect of behavior in the design of experimental studies is not unique to the social-psychological study of the law. A similar neglect is manifest in the larger discipline as well (Baumeister, Vohs, & Funder, 2007). With an increasing reliance on brief online investigations conducted with samples from Amazon's Mechanical Turk as the empirical evidence gathered to test social-psychological hypotheses (Anderson, Allen, Plante, Quigley-McBride, Lovett, & Rokkum, 2019), we are in danger of missing the influence of important variables that influence the phenomena we hope to understand. It is encouraging that several chapters in this volume describe programs of research that either recognized the importance of social interaction for understanding particular phenomena (e.g., social interactions with attachment figures establish patterns of expectations, emotions, and behaviors related to relationships; Mikulincer & Shaver, this volume; the role of interpersonal interaction in communicating a workplace's culture regarding inclusion; Schmader, Bergsieker, & Hall, this volume) or measured qualities of social interaction to predict behavior (e.g., interpersonal synchrony between therapist and client; Koole, this volume; social rejection by nonaggressive peers is related to aggressive behavior; Krahé, Tschacher, Butler, Dikker, & Wilderjans, this volume). Our focus has been to infuse experimental designs with manipulations of behavior that are hypothesized to influence behaviors and legal decisions. Intentional decisions to infuse behavior into our experiments and situate our investigations within social interactions broaden our research questions beyond those that can be studied with convenient paradigms consisting of reading research stimuli and circling numbers on a questionnaire, and lead to new insights about decision-making in a legal context.

Author Note

This material is based upon work supported by the National Science Foundation under Grant Numbers SBE# 0520617, 0921408, 0922314, and 1728938.

Any opinions, findings, and conclusions or recommendations expressed in this material are those of the author and do not necessarily reflect the views of the National Science Foundation.

References

Anderson, C. A., Allen, J. J., Plante, C., Quigley-McBride, A., Lovett, A., & Rokkum, J. N. (2019). The MTurkification of social and personality psychology. *Personality and Social Psychology Bulletin, 45*, 842–850.

Batson v. Kentucky, 476 U.S. 79 (1986).

Baumeister, R. F., Vohs, K. D., & Funder, D. C. (2007). Psychology as the science of self-reports and finger movements: Whatever happened to actual behavior? *Perspectives on Psychological Science, 2*, 396–403.

Bornstein, B. H. (2017). Jury simulation research: Pros, cons, trends, and alternatives. In M. B. Kovera (Ed.), *The psychology of juries* (pp. 207–226). Washington, D.C: American Psychological Association.

Cooper, J., & Fazio, R. H. (1984). A new look at dissonance theory. *Advances in Experimental Social Psychology, 17*, 229–266. doi:10.1016/S0065-2601(08)60121-5

Crocker, C. B., & Kovera, M. B. (2010). The effects of rehabilitative voir dire on juror bias and decision making. *Law and Human Behavior, 34*, 212–226. doi:10.1007/s10979-009-9193-9

Cutler, B. L., & Kovera, M. B. (2010). *Evaluating eyewitness identification*. New York: Oxford University Press.

Deffenbacher, K. A., Bornstein, B. H., McGorty, E. K., & Penrod, S. D. (2008). Forgetting the once-seen face: Estimating the strength of an eyewitness's memory representation. *Journal of Experimental Psychology: Applied, 14*, 139–150. doi:10.1037/1076-898X.14.2.139.

Dexter, H. R., Cutler, B. L., & Moran, G. (1992). A test of voir dire as a remedy for the prejudicial effects of pretrial publicity. *Journal of Applied Social Psychology, 22*, 819–832. doi:10.1111/j.1559-1816.1992.tb00926.x

Elliot, A. J., & Devine, P. G. (1994). On the motivational nature of cognitive dissonance: Dissonance as psychological discomfort. *Journal of Personality and Social Psychology, 67*, 382–394. doi:10.1037/0022-3514.67.3.382

Evelo, A. J., Zimmerman, D. A., Rhead, L. M., Chorn, J. A., & Kovera, M. B. (2019). *Administrators in single-blind lineups bias results toward the suspect despite cognitive constraints* (Unpublished manuscript). City University of New York.

Fein, S., McCloskey, A. L., & Tomlinson, T. M. (1997). Can the jury disregard that information? The use of suspicion to reduce the prejudicial effects of pretrial publicity and inadmissible testimony. *Personality and Social Psychology Bulletin, 11*, 1215–1226.

Festinger, L. (1957). *A theory of cognitive dissonance*. Stanford University Press.

Greathouse, S. M., & Kovera, M. B. (2009). Instruction bias and lineup presentation moderate the effects of administrator knowledge on eyewitness identification. *Law and Human Behavior, 33*, 70–82. doi:10.1007/s10979-008-9136-x

Greathouse, S. M., Sothmann, F. C., Levett, L. M., & Kovera, M. B. (2011). The potentially biasing effects of voir dire in juvenile waiver cases. *Law and Human Behavior, 35*, 427–439. doi:10.1007/s10979-010-9247-z

Halverson, A. M., Hallahan, M., Hart, A. J., & Rosenthal, R. (1997). Reducing the biasing effects of judges' nonverbal behavior with simplified jury instruction. *Journal of Applied Psychology, 82*, 590–598. doi:10.1037/0021-9010.82.4.590

Haney, C. (1984). On the selection of capital juries: The biasing effects of the death-qualification process. *Law and Human Behavior, 8*, 121–132. doi:10.1007/BF01044355

Harris, M. J. & Rosenthal, R. (1985). Mediation of interpersonal expectancy effects: 31 meta-analyses. *Psychological Bulletin, 97*, 363–386. doi:10.1037/0033-2909.97.3.363

Hart, A. J. (1995). Naturally occurring expectancy effects. *Journal of Personality and Social Psychology, 68*, 109–115. doi:0.1037/0022-3514.68.1.109

Hodgins, H., & Zuckerman., M. (1993). Beyond selecting information: Biases in spontaneous questions and resultant conclusions. *Journal of Experimental Social Psychology, 5*, 387–407. doi:10.1006/jesp.1993.1018

J. E. B. v. Alabama ex rel. T. B., 511 U.S. 127 (1994).

Johnson, C., & Haney, C. (1994). Felony voir dire: An exploratory study of its content and effect. *Law and Human Behavior, 18*, 487–506.

Jones, S. E. (1987). Judge- versus attorney-conducted voir dire: An empirical investigation of juror candor. *Law and Human Behavior, 11*, 131–146. doi:10.1007/BF01040446

Kovera, M. B., & Austin, J. L. (2016). Juror bias: Moving from assessment and prediction to a new generation of jury selection research. In C. Willis-Esqueda & B. H. Bornstein (Eds.), *The witness stand and Lawrence S. Wrightsman, Jr.* (pp. 75–94). New York: Springer.

Kovera, M. B. & Cutler, B. L. (2013). *Jury selection*. New York: Oxford University Press.

Kovera, M. B., & Evelo, A. J. (2017). The case for double-blind lineup administration. *Psychology, Public Policy and Law, 23*, 421–437. doi:10.1037/law0000139

Kovera, M. B., Greathouse, S. M., Otis, C. C., Kennard, J. B., Chorn, J. L., & Kovera, M. B. (2014). *Attorney expectations influence the voir dire process* (Unpublished manuscript). City University of New York.

Kovera, M. B., Kennard, J. B., Otis, C. C., Chorn, J. L., & Zimmerman, D. M. (2019). *Behavioral confirmation in voir dire: Effects on jury selection and verdict choices* (Unpublished manuscript). City University of New York.

Kovera, M. B., & Levett, L. M. (2015). Jury decision making. In B. L. Cutler & P. A. Zapf (Eds.), *APA handbook of forensic psychology, Vol. 2: Criminal investigation, adjudication, and sentencing outcomes* (pp. 271–311). Washington, D.C: American Psychological Association.

Meissner, C. A., & Brigham, J. C. (2001). Thirty years of investigating the own-race bias in memory for faces: A meta-analytic review. *Psychology, Public Policy, and Law, 7*, 972–984.

Middendorf, K., & Luginbuhl, J. (1995). The value of a nondirective voir dire style in jury selection. *Criminal Justice and Behavior, 22*, 129–151. doi:10.1177/0093854895022002003

Olczak, P. V., Kaplan, M. F., & Penrod, S. (1991). Attorneys' lay psychology and its effectiveness in selecting jurors: Three empirical studies. *Journal of Social Behavior & Personality, 6*, 431–452.

Orne, M. T. (1962). On the social psychology of the psychological experiment: With particular reference to demand characteristics and their implications. *American Psychologist, 17*, 776–783. doi:10.1037/h0043424

Otis, C. C., Greathouse, S. M., Kennard, J. B., & Kovera, M. B. (2014). Hypothesis-testing in attorney-conducted voir dire. *Law and Human Behavior, 38*, 392–404. doi:10.1037/lhb0000092

Platz, S. J., & Hosch, H. M. (1988). Cross-racial/ethnic eyewitness identification: A field study. *Journal of Applied Social Psychology, 18*, 972–984.
Rosenthal, R. (2002). Covert communication in classrooms, clinics, courtrooms, and cubicles. *American Psychologist, 57*, 839–849. doi:10.1037/0003-066X.57.11.839
Rosenthal, R. & Fode, K. L. (1963a). Psychology of the scientist: V. Three experiments in experimenter bias. *Psychological Reports, 12*, 491–511. doi:10.2466/pr0.1963.12.2.491
Rosenthal, R., & Fode, K. L. (1963b). The effect of experimenter bias on the performance of the albino rat. *Behavioral Science, 8*, 183–189. doi:10.1002/bs.3830080302
Rosenthal, R., & Jacobson, L. (1968). Pygmalion in the classroom. *The Urban Review, 3*, 16–20. doi:10.1007/BF02322211
Rosenthal, R., & Rosnow, R. L. (1984). *Essentials of behavioral research: Methods and data analysis.* New York, NY: McGraw-Hill.
Shadish, W. R., Cook, T. D., & Campbell, D. T. (2002). *Experimental and quasi-experimental designs for generalized causal inference.* Boston, MA: Wadsworth Publishing.
Skov, R. B., & Sherman, S. J. (1986). Information-gathering processes: Diagnosticity, hypothesis-confirmatory strategies, and perceived hypothesis confirmation. *Journal of Experimental Social Psychology, 22*, 93–121. doi:10.1016/0022-1031(86)90031-4
Snyder, M., & Haugen, J. A. (1994). Why does behavioral confirmation occur? A functional perspective on the role of the perceiver. *Journal of Experimental Social Psychology, 30*, 218–246. doi:10.1006/jesp.1994.1011
Snyder, M., & Swann, W. B. (1978). Hypothesis-testing processes in social interaction. *Journal of Personality and Social Psychology, 36*, 1202–1212. doi:10.1037/0022-3514.36.11.1202
Snyder, M., Tanke, E. D., & Berscheid, E. (1977). Social perception and interpersonal behavior: On the self-fulfilling nature of social stereotypes. *Journal of Personality and Social Psychology, 35*, 656–666. doi:10.1037/0022-3514.35.9.656
Sommers, S. R., & Norton, M. I. (2007). Race-based judgments, race-neutral justifications: Experimental examination of peremptory use and the Batson Challenge procedure. *Law and Human Behavior, 31*, 261–273.
Steblay, N. M., Besirevic, J., Fulero, S. M., & Jimenez-Lorente, B. (1999). The effects of pretrial publicity on juror verdicts: A meta-analytic review. *Law and Human Behavior, 23*, 219–235.
Stukas, A., & Snyder, M. (2002). Targets' awareness of expectations and behavioral confirmation in ongoing interactions. *Journal of Experimental Social Psychology, 38*, 31–40. doi:10.1006/jesp.2001.1487
Trope, Y., & Liberman, A. (1996). Social hypothesis-testing: Cognitive and motivational mechanisms. In E. T. Higgins & A. W. Kruglanski (Eds.), *Social psychology: Handbook of basic principles* (pp. 239–270). New York: Guilford Press.
Trusz, S., & Bąbel, P. (2016). Two perspectives on expectancies. In S. Trusz & P. Bąbel (Eds.), *Interpersonal and intrapersonal expectancies* (pp. 1–19). New York, NY: Routledge.
Visher, C. A. (1987). Juror decision making: The importance of evidence. *Law and Human Behavior, 11*, 1–17.
Vitriol, J. A., & Kovera, M. B. (2018). Exposure to capital voir dire may not increase convictions despite increasing pretrial presumption of guilt. *Law and Human Behavior, 42*, 472–483. doi:10.1037/lhb0000304
Weber, S. J., & Cook, T. D. (1972). Subject effect in laboratory research: An examination of subject roles, demand characteristics, and valid inference. *Psychological Bulletin, 4*, 273–295. doi:10.1037/h0032351

Wells, G. L., Kovera, M. B., Douglass, A. B., Brewer, N., Meissner, C. A., & Wixted, J. (2020). Policy and procedure recommendations for the collection and preservation of eyewitness identification evidence. *Law and Human Behavior*.

Wells, G. L., Small, M., Penrod, S., Malpass, R. S., Fulero, S. M., & Brimacombe, C. A. E. (1998). Eyewitness identification procedures: Recommendations for lineups and photospreads. *Law and Human Behavior, 22*, 603–647.

Wells, G. L., Steblay, N. K., & Dysart, J. E. (2015). Double-blind photo lineups using actual eyewitnesses: An experimental test of a sequential versus simultaneous lineup procedure. *Law and Human Behavior, 39*, 1–14.

Wells, G. L., Yang, Y., & Smalarz, L. (2015). Eyewitness identification: Bayesian information gain, base-rate effect equivalency curves, and reasonable suspicion. *Law and Human Behavior, 39*, 99–122. doi:10.1037/lhb0000125

Wrightsman, L. S. (1987). The jury on trial: Comparing legal assumptions with psychological evidence. In N. E. Grunberg, R. E. Nisbett, J. Rodin, & J. E. Singer (Eds.), *A distinctive approach to psychological research: The influence of Stanley Schachter* (pp. 27–45). Hillsdale, NJ: Lawrence Erlbaum Associates, Inc.

Zimmerman, D. M., Chorn, J. A., Rhead, L. M., Evelo, A. J., & Kovera, M. B. (2017). Memory strength and lineup presentation moderate effects of administrator influence on mistaken identifications. *Journal of Experimental Psychology: Applied, 23*, 460–473. doi:10.1037/xap0000147

Zimmerman, D. M., Otis, C. C., Kennard, J. B., Chorn, J. A., & Kovera, M. B. (2019). *Behavioral confirmation during voir dire: The effects of biased voir dire questions on juror decision-making* (Unpublished manuscript). City University of New York.

13

HOW DO ONLINE SOCIAL NETWORKS INFLUENCE PEOPLE'S EMOTIONAL LIVES?

Ethan Kross and Susannah Chandhok

The advent of online social networking sites like Facebook have rapidly altered the way human beings interact. With a gentle tap of one's finger, people can share their inner thoughts and feelings with untold numbers of people. A gentle swipe down on one's smartphone reveals a compilation of updates on other people's lives from an endlessly populated newsfeed.

These features of social media aren't restricted to an exclusive set of technophiles; they have been widely embraced by humanity. Indeed, at the time of our writing this chapter, close to 2.8 billion people use social media, a number that is predicted to keep rising (Statista, 2019). Moreover, the average user spends approximately 50 minutes per day on Facebook, Instagram, and Facebook Messenger (Stewart, 2016).

But what consequence—if any—does engaging with these online social networks have on how people feel? When we and our colleagues became curious about this issue in the late 2000s, we did what most researchers do when we become interested in a new topic: we performed a literature review. That's when we came across what we now call *The Puzzle*.

On the one hand, several studies revealed negative cross-sectional associations between self-reported Facebook usage and emotional well-being (Farahani, Kazemi, Aghamohamadi, Bakhtiarvand, & Ansari, 2011; Labrague, 2014; Pantic et al., 2012). But other studies revealed the opposite (Datu, Valdez, & Datu, 2012; Ellison, Steinfield, & Lampe, 2007; Nabi, Prestin, & So, 2013; Valenzuela, Park, & Kee, 2009). Still other work suggested that the relationships between Facebook usage and well-being was more nuanced; it depended on additional factors like individual differences in loneliness (Kim, LaRose, & Peng, 2009) or the number of Facebook friends people had (Manago, Taylor, & Greenfield, 2012). At the end of the literature review, we were left with more questions than answers.

In this chapter, we will review the work that we and others have performed to systematically address this puzzle over the past decade. We begin by providing a brief overview of research on online social network usage and well-being, highlighting the conceptual and methodological challenges that prevented early work from drawing strong inferences about the links between these variables. We will then describe a program of research designed to address these concerns by focusing on the mechanisms underlying how two different types of online social network usage—active versus passive usage—shape the emotional outcomes people experience inside and outside of the laboratory. In addressing these issues, we will focus our discussion predominantly on Facebook, the world's largest online social network, because it has been the focus of the majority of empirical attention. We conclude by discussing (a) how researchers can draw inferences about emotion from "big data" and (b) whether online social networks can be strategically harnessed to promote well-being.

Facebook Use & Well-being: Early Research

Does using Facebook influence people's well-being? Our review of early research that focused on this question revealed two issues that made it difficult to answer. First, nearly all of the studies that had been performed on this issue involved asking participants to self-report how much they used Facebook and how they felt in general. While there is clear value to using trait self-report measures to address certain kinds of questions, concerns about using them to measure people's moment-to-moment behaviors and emotions are well-established (for discussion see Kahneman & Deaton, 2010; Kahneman, Krueger, Schkade, Schwarz, & Stone, 2004). Second, the majority of the studies on this topic had utilized cross-sectional, correlational designs that made it impossible to draw inferences about the causal or likely causal relationship between Facebook use and well-being.

As a first step toward overcoming these limitations, we used experience sampling, a methodology that is widely considered the "gold standard" for assessing in vivo behavior and psychological experiences over time and drawing inferences about the *likely* causal sequence of events between variables (Bolger, Davis, & Rafaeli, 2003; Larson & Csikszentmihalyi, 2014). Specifically, over the course of several months, we text messaged 82 participants five times per day between 10 a.m. and midnight for 14 consecutive days, resulting in a data set consisting of 4,589 observations. Each time we texted participants, we asked them to rate how positive and negative they felt. We also asked them to rate how much they had used Facebook since the last time we texted them. We then examined whether the amount of time participants spent using Facebook systematically predicted changes in how they felt from the start of that period to its end.

Our results indicated that the more participants reported using Facebook during one chunk of time, for example, between 9 a.m. and 11 a.m., the more their positive mood declined over the course of that time period. We also found that the reverse pattern of results was not true—i.e., feeling bad at one moment in time did not predict increases in subsequent usage. It was likewise not moderated by any of the individual differences we assessed—e.g., number of Facebook friends, motivation for using Facebook, perceptions of their Facebook network, gender, self-esteem, loneliness, or depressive symptoms.

Importantly, each time we text messaged participants, we also asked them to rate how much they had interacted with other people directly—i.e., face-to-face or via phone—since the last time we text messaged them, to rule out the possibility that any results we observed might be attributed to general social interaction. In fact, our analyses indicated that interacting with other people directly predicted the exact opposite set of results—the more people reported interacting with other people directly during one time period, the more their positive mood rose from the beginning of that time period to its end (Kross et al., 2013).

The paper reporting these results triggered a number of commentaries (e.g., Bohannon, 2013; Konnikova, 2013). In the exchanges that followed, a key question arose: How does Facebook use undermine subjective well-being? To address this question, we turned our attention to the different ways that people interact with Facebook and how it might differentially influence the way they feel.

Prior research had distinguished between two broad categories of Facebook usage: passive and active usage (Burke, Marlow, & Lento, 2010; Deters & Mehl, 2013; Krasnova, Wenninger, Widjaja, & Buxmann, 2013). Passive usage refers to voyeuristically consuming information on a social media site—e.g., scrolling through one's news feed to peer in on the lives of others without generating information. Active usage, on the other hand, involves producing information on the site and engaging in direct exchanges with others—e.g., chatting, uploading posts and pictures. Going into the next phase of the work, we predicted that passively using Facebook in particular might account for its harmful emotional outcomes.

We based this prediction on the idea that social media allows people to curate the way they present themselves to others to a degree that is not possible in daily life. We human beings, of course, always curate how we present ourselves to others to varying degrees (Goffman, 1956, 1963, 1967. Indeed, across multiple seminal works in sociology, Goffman (1956, 1963, 1967) argued that human beings are driven to present themselves in flattering terms. For example, most people think strategically about what clothing they should wear based on who they are going to interact with later on that day. An important meeting may warrant dress attire, whereas a casual get-together with one's friends calls for more relaxed garb. But on social media, the ability to manage the way we present ourselves to others takes on a new form. It allows us to curate the way we appear to others to a degree that is not possible in daily life. We can add filters to our photos, carefully edit our posts, or even send them to friends for review before sharing. Indeed, one study found that a key reason people use Facebook is to serve self-presentational needs (Nadkarni & Hofmann, 2012).

But what might the emotional consequences of scrolling through a world populated by the most glamorized portraits of other people's lives be? Classic research on social comparisons (Festinger, 1954; Goethals, 1986; Wood, 1996) provides a clear answer to this question: When we are exposed to the unobtainable glorified lives of other people, we engage in upward social comparisons that promote envy and lead us to feel worse (Salovey & Rodin, 1984). As argued by Blanton, Burrows and Regan (this volume) in their chapter on health messages in video games, even exaggerated or "unreal" experience with technology can influence real-world behavior. Thus, even if people are aware that a social media profile is augmented beyond something obtainable in reality, such experiences can still have significant consequences on well-being.

We tested these assumptions over the course of two studies (Verduyn et al., 2015). In the first study, we brought participants into the laboratory and randomly assigned them to use Facebook actively or passively for ten minutes. We then assessed how people felt both immediately after the manipulation and at the end of the day (via an email survey).

Immediately after the active versus passive Facebook use manipulations, participants in the two groups did not differ on how they felt. But by the end of the day, participants in the passive Facebook usage group displayed a significant positive emotion decline compared to both their baseline levels of emotion and the levels of end of the day affect that characterized the active Facebook users. The active Facebook usage condition, in contrast, did not display any changes in how they felt over the course of the three assessments.

But were the emotional well-being declines experienced by the passive Facebook users driven by envy? And would these findings be replicated in a more ecologically valid context? We shifted back to experience sampling to address these questions. Specifically, we repeated the experience sampling protocol that we had used in our initial study (Kross et al., 2013), but this time asked people to rate how much they had used Facebook actively and passively since the last time we text messaged them. We also asked them to rate how envious they felt of others each time we texted them.

Our findings indicated that most of the time that people were using Facebook, they were using it passively. In fact, participants used Facebook passively 50 percent more than they did actively. In retrospect, this finding explained why we observed emotional well-being declines linked with overall Facebook usage in our first study (Kross et al. 2013)—i.e., most of the time people were on Facebook, they were likely using it the harmful way. Critically, longitudinal mediation analyses indicated that passive Facebook usage predicted emotional well-being declines, and it did so by promoting feelings of envy. Conceptually replicating the laboratory results, active Facebook usage once again had no impact on people's emotions.

Together, the results from these initial studies began to paint a portrait that described how using Facebook influenced people's emotional lives; an image suggesting that the majority of the times people use Facebook, they do so passively, which in turn leads people to feel envious and predicts declines in their positive mood over time.

Does Counting Emotion Words Provide a Window into Emotion?

An early challenge to these findings came in 2014 when a group of researchers published a controversial experiment in which they manipulated the percentage of positive and negative emotional words contained in 689,003 Facebook users' news feeds for one week (Kramer, Guillory, & Hancock, 2014).[1] The researchers leading the study were interested in examining emotional contagion on social media—i.e., the idea that emotions could spread across social networks just like diseases are transmitted between people who come into physical contact with each other. They predicted that consuming different amounts of positive (or negative) information on social media should lead people to experience more positive or negative emotions in their own lives. They furthermore suggested that they could index people's emotional states by counting the number of emotion words contained in their Facebook posts.

Kramer and colleagues (2014) tested their prediction by manipulating the amount of positive and negative words contained in participants' Facebook news feeds for one week. As predicted, they observed a statistically significant effect of their manipulation. Participants who were exposed to news feeds that contained more (or less) positive (or negative) words ended up using more (or less) positive (or negative) words in their own news feed. They interpreted these findings in support of their predictions noting, "these results indicate that emotions expressed by others on Facebook influence our own emotions, constituting experimental evidence for massive-scale contagion via social networks" (Kramer et al., 2014).

At first blush, these findings directly contradicted the findings that had accumulated up to that point (Kross et al., 2013; Turkle, 2011; Verduyn et al., 2015; Vogel, Rose, Okdie, Eckles, & Franz, 2015). The results of our studies suggested that consuming positive information in other people's news feeds instigates a social comparison process that leaves people feeling worse, not an emotional contagion process that enhances how good people feel.

However, there was an important difference when characterizing these two lines of work. In prior studies on Facebook and well-being, emotional well-being was indexed by asking participants directly how they felt. Concerns about self-report measures notwithstanding, asking people how they feel remains the standard tool for indexing subjective experiences (Kahneman et al., 2004;

Kahneman & Riis, 2005). In the aforementioned study, however, the authors assumed that counting the number of emotion words contained in participants' online social network posts would provide an equally valid tool for drawing inferences about people's emotional experience. But was this a reasonable assumption? Shortly following the publication of the Kramer study, we noted that there were three reasons to question it.

First, word counting methods fail to take context into account. Consider, for example, the following two statements: "I am feeling so great" and "I am not feeling great." A word-counting algorithm that counts the percentage of positive words contained in each of these statements would produce the same result—20 percent (one out of five words in each statement contains a positive emotion word)—even though the two statements convey opposite meaning.

Second, it is well documented that people tend to self-present on social media in ways that may not be accurate or authentic (Nadkarni & Hofmann, 2012; Walther, Van Der Heide, Ramirez, Burgoon, & Peña, 2015). For example, in response to learning that a colleague received a job promotion, a person might write, "That's great news," but not really feel happy for their colleague. They might also simply try to mimic the person they are interacting with to enhance rapport, a common technique in face-to-face interactions (Chartrand & Bargh, 1999; Chartrand & Jefferis, 2003). Thus, we suggested that it was also possible that a person might say something online that on the surface conveyed positive (or negative) emotion, but didn't correlate with how they actually felt.

Finally, compounding these conceptual concerns was the fact that no validation evidence existed to support the idea that counting emotion words on online social networks does in fact track how people feel. Some studies had looked at the correlation between online social network emotional word usage and judges' ratings of the emotionality of participants' posts. But if participants' posts don't honestly convey how they feel, then there's no reason to expect judges to be able to accurately categorize participants' posts (for additional validation concerns see Kross et al., 2018).

So, do people's usage of emotion words in their posts actually reflect how they feel? To address this question, we collapsed four experience sampling data sets that contained two types of information: (a) participants' self-reports of how they felt throughout the day and (b) their Facebook wall posts corresponding to the same time period that they rated their emotions (Kross et al., 2018). For each participant, we computed the percentage of positive and negative words contained in their posts and then examined whether they correlated with how participants reported feeling around the same time that they made each post. Regardless of how we analyzed the data, our results did not reveal any significant associations between participants' usage of emotion words in their Facebook posts and their self-reports of how they felt—a set of findings that cast doubt on researchers' ability to draw inferences about people's emotional states by counting the number of emotion words contained in their online social network posts (for conceptual replication, see Sun, Schwartz, Son, Kern, & Vazire, in press).

The Broader Landscape

Between 2004 and 2012, 412 studies on Facebook were published. Yet, not a single one of those papers examined the relationship between Facebook usage and changes in people's well-being over time. Since that time, the literature on this topic has grown substantially. In 2017, we reviewed this literature, focusing specifically on longitudinal and experimental studies that had examined the relationship between Facebook usage and well-being up to that point (Verduyn, Ybarra, Résibois, Jonides, & Kross, 2017). We concluded that passive Facebook usage robustly predicts emotional well-being declines whereas the relationship between active Facebook usage and well-being was more tenuous. While some relationships revealed positive links between active Facebook usage and well-being improvements, many studies did not.

Since our 2017 review, several additional large-scale studies have been performed which broadly align with these conclusions. For example, Tromholt (2016) randomly assigned over a thousand Danish participants to either use Facebook as usual, or stop using it altogether. Results indicated that Facebook abstention led to an increase in both cognitive and affective well-being (also see Mosquera, Odunowo, McNamara, Guo, & Petrie, 2018; and Allcott, Braghieri, Eichmeyer, & Gentzkow, 2019).

In 2018, researchers at the University of Pennsylvania adopted a slightly different approach to experimentally examine the effects of online social network usage on emotionality (Hunt, Marx, Lipson, & Young, 2018). Rather than use a deprivation paradigm that cut off participants' Facebook usage entirely, they randomly assigned 143 participants to either keep using social media as usual or to limit social media use to ten minutes per day for three weeks. Their results indicated that the limited social media use group showed significant reductions in loneliness and depression over the course of the study period. However, there were no significant effects on social support, self-esteem, or psychological well-being—a pattern of differential results that points to the need for future research to examine how the nature and length of Facebook interventions may systematically impact different variables (Hunt et al., 2018).

Finally, in one particularly persuasive study, Shakya and Christakis (2017) used Facebook log data in conjunction with three waves of nationally representative data to examine the longitudinal relationship between Facebook usage and changes in well-being over time in a sample of 5,208 participants. Their prospective findings indicated that Facebook use predicted decreases in well-being over time (Shakya & Christakis, 2017). Interestingly, the authors found that the more often participants engaged in active usage behaviors like updating one's status or liking another post, the more likely they were to have lower self-reported well-being—a finding that further speaks to the potentially nuanced nature of the relationship between active social media usage and well-being.

Frequently Asked Questions

Given the prevalence of social media, and the somewhat counterintuitive nature of the findings suggesting that a technology built to connect people frequently ends up undermining rather than elevating their positive mood, it is perhaps not surprising that people often have several questions about the aforementioned findings. Here we address two common questions that often arise.

FAQ #1: Why do people continue to use social media if doing so consistently leads them to feel worse? It is well established that people are motivated to approach pleasure and avoid pain (e.g., Freud, 1920; Higgins, 1997). Given this feature of the human condition, why do people continue to engage in a behavior that undermines their positive mood? Although a definitive answer to this question has yet to emerge, here we suggest three possibilities.

First, human behavior is multiply determined; there are several goals activated at any moment. In the context of social media, for example, we may be motivated to engage in a behavior that improves the way we feel. But we may also be motivated by social goals that motivate us to stay abreast of how our social networks are functioning. In this vein, one study found that 88 percent of people report using social media to maintain social relationships (Whiting & Williams, 2013). Thus, it is possible that people use social media despite its negative emotional effects because doing so allows people to stay informed of what is happening in their social networks.

Second, it is well established that people engage in behaviors that they are addicted to even when they reap negative consequences—a phenomenon that neuroscience research has illuminated by highlighting the fact that different brain systems are involved in *wanting* and *liking* (Robinson & Berridge, 2001). These findings are noteworthy in the current context because a growing amount of evidence suggests that social media has addictive properties (Alter, 2017; Andreassen, 2015; Ryan, Chester, Reece, & Xenos, 2014). Further research could examine the role of desire and motivated behavior in social media use (for more details about real-world applications of this cognitive theory, see Papies, this volume).

Finally, some research suggests that people mispredict how using Facebook will make them feel. For example, one study found that participants predicted they would feel better after using Facebook for 20 minutes. In fact, they felt worse after doing so (Sagioglou & Greitemeyer, 2014). This misprediction might be captured by an evolutionary mismatch between how our brains evolved to seek social connections, and the negative consequences they yield on social media (see van Vugt et al., this volume, for a discussion about the concept of evolutionary mismatches).

Taken together, these different findings begin to explain why people may continue to engage in a behavior that leads to emotional well-being declines. However, future research is needed to examine the role that each of these and other factors play in isolation and interactively in predicting types of social media usage.

FAQ #2: Are there ways of harnessing social media to improve well-being? There are many attempts underway to address this important question. One route that we have pursued to examine this issue involves focusing on people suffering from depression. A large literature stretching back to the 1980s indicates that people with depression are characterized by impoverished social support networks (Fiore, Becker, & Coppel, 1983; Rook, 1984). One of the explanations that research has provided for why individuals with depression are characterized by low social support is because they talk frequently about their negative feelings (Blumberg & Hokanson, 1983; Kuiper & McCabe, 1985) in ways that end up pushing away those that care about them (Teichman & Teichman, 1990). In other words, there may be poor interpersonal synchrony between individuals with depression and others (for more details about interpersonal synchrony, please see Koole et al., this volume).

Park and colleagues (2016) were interested in whether these findings would generalize to social media. Given the psychological distance that social media provides people with, they wondered whether the social networks of depressed individuals might be more responsive in the online versus offline world. They addressed this question across two studies (Park et al., 2016).

In Study 1, they focused on an unselected sample of participants with varying levels of depressive symptoms; in Study 2 they recruited psychiatrically diagnosed individuals with Major Depressive Disorder and their age-matched control participants. Across both studies, the experimenters had judges code how supportive the posts of participants' Facebook friends were in response to any negative experiences described by participants on their Facebook accounts over the course of a month. They then compared the amount of support that depressed versus non-depressed participants received, controlling for the number of negative expressions that participants made during the month-long period. As expected, participants with depression self-disclosed negative information more and positive information less to their Facebook networks. However, in direct contrast to prior research examining the links between offline social support and depression, participants with depression received *more* social support from their Facebook friends.

These findings illustrate how social media may provide a platform for providing social support to individuals that may otherwise have difficulty acquiring it, highlighting the need for future research to extend these findings to other vulnerable populations. In particular, one application of social psychology to this line of research would be in testing which aspects of a social media platform could be manipulated to provide better social support for its members.

Concluding Comment

> The Internet does not, contrary to current popular opinion, have by itself the power or ability to control people, to turn them into addicted zombies, or make them dispositionally sad or lonely ... the Internet is one of several social domains in which an individual can live his or her life, and attempt to fulfill his or her needs and goals, whatever they happen to be.
>
> *McKenna & Bargh, 2000*

At the turn of the millennium, McKenna and Bargh concluded that the overall sentiment toward the internet was negative, if not "apocalyptic" (McKenna & Bargh, 2000). Over the course of the next few years, they documented the beneficial aspects of internet use, highlighting how it can foster social relationships and provide people with meaningful routes to express themselves authentically (Bargh, McKenna, & Fitzsimons, 2002; Bargh & McKenna, 2004).

Their work was notably published before the birth of Facebook in 2004. Since that time, the tide of research has drawn away from focusing on internet use to examining the links between social media and well-being instead. Yet, we see a similar pattern emerging. Some have voiced a concern that digital technology is destroying society (Twenge, 2017). Other have suggested that social networking addiction should be a clinically diagnosable disorder and have developed a Facebook Addiction Scale (Andreassen et al., 2012; Karaiskos et al., 2010; Ryan et al., 2014; also see Alter, 2017).

The goal of this chapter is not to paint a picture one way or the other about social media being good or bad. The social media world is multifaceted. Much like the offline terrestrial world, social media allows people to experience an infinite number of healthy and harmful emotional experiences. A critical challenge for future research is to illuminate the mechanisms that systematically predict these different kinds of emotional experiences. Doing so has the potential to enrich our understanding of how a ubiquitous technology can be harnessed to promote rather than undermine well-being.

Note

1 The controversy was a function of the fact that Facebook users were unaware that they were participating in this experiment (Kosinski, Matz, Gosling, Popov, & Stillwell, 2015; Puschmann & Bozdag, 2014; Shaw, 2016).

References

Allcott, H., Braghieri, L., Eichmeyer, S., & Gentzkow, M. (2019). *The welfare effects of social media*. 116.

Alter, A. (2017). *Irresistible: The rise of addictive technology and the business of keeping us hooked*. New York, NY: Penguin Press.

Andreassen, C. S. (2015). Online social network site addiction: A comprehensive review. *Current Addiction Reports, 2*(2), 175–184. doi.org/10.1007/s40429-015-0056-9

Andreassen, C. S., Torsheim, T., Brunborg, G. S., & Pallesen, S. (2012). Development of a Facebook addiction scale. *Psychological Reports, 110*(2), 501–517.

Bargh, J. A., & McKenna, K. Y. (2004). The Internet and social life. *Annual Review of Psychology, 55*, 573–590.

Bargh, J. A., McKenna, K. Y., & Fitzsimons, G. M. (2002). Can you see the real me? Activation and expression of the "true self" on the Internet. *Journal of Social Issues, 58*(1), 33–48.

Blumberg, S. R., & Hokanson, J. E. (1983). The effects of another person's response style on interpersonal behavior in depression. *Journal of Abnormal Psychology, 92*(2), 196–209. doi.org/10.1037/0021-843X.92.2.196

Bohannon, J. (2013, August 14). ScienceShot: Facebook is making you sad. *Science Magazine*. Retrieved from www.sciencemag.org/news/2013/08/scienceshot-facebook-making-you-sad.

Bolger, N., Davis, A., & Rafaeli, E. (2003). Diary methods: Capturing life as it is lived. *Annual Review of Psychology, 54*(1), 579–616. doi.org/10.1146/annurev.psych.54.101601.145030

Burke, M., Marlow, C., & Lento, T. (2010, April). Social network activity and social well-being. In *Proceedings of the SIGCHI conference on human factors in computing systems* (pp. 1909–1912). ACM.

Chartrand, T. L., & Bargh, J. A. (1999). The chameleon effect: The perception-behavior link and social interaction. *Journal of Personality & Social Psychology, 76*(6), 893–9101.

Chartrand, T. L., & Jefferis, V. E. (2003). Consequences of automatic goal pursuit and the case of nonconscious mimicry. In J. P. Forgas & K. D. Williams (Eds.), *Social judgments: Implicit and explicit processes* (pp. 290–305). New York: Cambridge University Press.

Datu, J. A. D., Valdez, J. P., & Datu, N. (2012). Does Facebooking make us sad? Hunting relationship between Facebook use and depression among Filipino adolescents. *International Journal of Research Studies in Educational Technology, 1*(2). doi.org/10.5861/ijrset.2012.202

Deters, F. große, & Mehl, M. R. (2013). Does posting Facebook status updates increase or decrease loneliness? An online social networking experiment. *Social Psychological and Personality Science, 4*(5), 579–586. doi.org/10.1177/1948550612469233

Ellison, N. B., Steinfield, C., & Lampe, C. (2007). The benefits of Facebook "friends:" Social capital and college students' use of online social network sites. *Journal of Computer-Mediated Communication, 12*(4), 1143–1168. doi.org/10.1111/j.1083-6101.2007.00367.x

Farahani, H. A., Kazemi, Z., Aghamohamadi, S., Bakhtiarvand, F., & Ansari, M. (2011). Examining mental health indices in students using Facebook in Iran. *Procedia – Social and Behavioral Sciences, 28*, 811–814. doi.org/10.1016/j.sbspro.2011.11.148

Festinger, L. (1954). A theory of social comparison processes. *Human Relations, 7*(2), 117–140. doi.org/10.1177/001872675400700202

Fiore, J., Becker, J., & Coppel, D. B. (1983). Social network interactions: A buffer or a stress. *American Journal of Community Psychology; New York, 11*(4), 423–439.

Freud, S. (1920). Beyond the pleasure principle. In J. Strachey, A. Freud, A. Strachey, & A. Tyson (Trans.), *Beyond the pleasure principle, group psychology and other works (1925-1926)* (pp. 1–64).

Goethals, G. R. (1986). Social comparison theory: Psychology from the lost and found. *Personality and Social Psychology Bulletin, 12*, 261–278. doi.org/10.1177/0146167286123001

Goffman, E. (1956). *The presentation of self in everyday life*. New York, NY: Anchor Books.

Goffman, E. (1963). *Behavior in public places*. New York: Free Press.

Goffman, E. (1967). *Interaction ritual*. New York: Pantheon.

Higgins, E. T. (1997). Beyond pleasure and pain. *American Psychologist, 52*(12), 1280–1300. doi.org/10.1037/0003-066X.52.12.1280

Hunt, M. G., Marx, R., Lipson, C., & Young, J. (2018). No more FOMO: Limiting social media decreases loneliness and depression. *Journal of Social and Clinical Psychology, 37*(10), 751–768. doi.org/10.1521/jscp.2018.37.10.751

Karaiskos, D., Tzavellas, E., Balta, G., & Paparrigopoulos, T. (2010). Social network addiction: A new clinical disorder? *European Psychiatry, 25*, 855.

Kahneman, D., & Deaton, A. (2010). High income improves evaluation of life but not emotional well-being. *Proceedings of the National Academy of Sciences, 107*(38), 16489–16493. doi.org/10.1073/pnas.1011492107

Kahneman, D., & Krueger, A. B., Schkade, D. A., Schwarz, N., & Stone, A. A. (2004). A survey method for characterizing daily life experience: The day reconstruction method. *Science, 306*(5702), 1776–1780. doi.org/10.1126/science.1103572

Kahneman, D., & Riis, J. (2005). Living, and thinking about it: Two perspectives on life. In F. A. Huppert, N. Baylis, & B. Keverne (Eds.), *The science of well-being* (pp. 284–305). doi.org/10.1093/acprof:oso/9780198567523.003.0011

Kim J., LaRose R., Peng, W. (2009). Loneliness as the cause and the effect of problematic Internet use: The relationship between Internet use and psychological well-being. *Cyberpsychology & Behavior: The Impact of the Internet, Multimedia and Virtual Reality on Behavior and Society, 12*, 451–455.

Konnikova, M. (2013, September 10). How Facebook makes us unhappy. *The New Yorker*. Retrieved from www.newyorker.com/tech/annals-of-technology/how-facebook-makes-us-unhappy

Kosinski, M., Matz, S. C., Gosling, S. D., Popov, V., & Stillwell, D. (2015). Facebook as a research tool for the social sciences: Opportunities, challenges, ethical considerations, and practical guidelines. *American Psychologist, 70*(6), 543–556. doi.org/10.1037/a0039210

Kramer, A. D. I., Guillory, J. E., & Hancock, J. T. (2014). Experimental evidence of massive-scale emotional contagion through social networks. *Proceedings of the National Academy of Sciences, 111*(24), 8788–8790. doi.org/10.1073/pnas.1320040111

Krasnova, H., Wenninger, H., Widjaja, T., & Buxmann, P. (2013). *Envy on Facebook: A hidden threat to users' life satisfaction?* 11th International Conference on Wirtschaftsinformatik (WI).

Kross, E., Verduyn, P., Boyer, M., Drake, B., Gainsburg, I., Vickers, B., … Jonides, J. (2018). Does counting emotion words on online social networks provide a window into people's subjective experience of emotion? A case study on Facebook. *Emotion, 19*, 97–107. doi.org/10.1037/emo0000416

Kross, E., Verduyn, P., Demiralp, E., Park, J., Lee, D. S., Lin, N., ... Ybarra, O. (2013). Facebook use predicts declines in subjective well-being in young adults. *PLoS One*, *8*(8), e69841. doi.org/10.1371/journal.pone.0069841

Kuiper, N. A., & McCabe, S. B. (1985). The appropriateness of social topics: Effects of depression and cognitive vulnerability on self and other judgments. *Cognitive Therapy and Research*, *9*(4), 371–379. doi.org/10.1007/BF01173087

Labrague, L. J. (2014). Facebook use and adolescents' emotional states of depression, anxiety, and stress. *Health Science Journal*, *8*(1), 80–89.

Larson, R., & Csikszentmihalyi, M. (2014). The experience sampling method. In M. Csikszentmihalyi, *Flow and the foundations of positive psychology* (pp. 21–34). doi.org/10.1007/978-94-017-9088-8_2

Manago, A. M., Taylor, T., & Greenfield, P. M. (2012). Me and my 400 friends: The anatomy of college students' Facebook networks, their communication patterns, and well-being. *Developmental Psychology*, *48*(2), 369–380.

McKenna, K. Y., & Bargh, J. A. (2000). Plan 9 from cyberspace: The implications of the Internet for personality and social psychology. *Personality and Social Psychology Review*, *4*(1), 57–75.

Mosquera, R., Odunowo, M., McNamara, T., Guo, X., & Petrie, R. (2018). The economic effects of Facebook. *SSRN Electronic Journal*. doi.org/10.2139/ssrn.3312462

Nabi, R. L., Prestin, A., & So, J. (2013). Facebook friends with (health) benefits? Exploring social network site use and perceptions of social support, stress, and well-being. *Cyberpsychology, Behavior, and Social Networking*, *16*(10), 721–727. doi.org/10.1089/cyber.2012.0521

Nadkarni, A., & Hofmann, S. G. (2012). Why do people use Facebook? *Personality and Individual Differences*, *52*(3), 243–249. doi.org/10.1016/j.paid.2011.11.007

Pantic, I., Damjanovic, A., Todorovic, J., Topalovic, D., Bojovic-Jovic, D., Ristic, S., & Pantic, S. (2012). Association between online social networking and depression in high school students: Behavioral physiology viewpoint. *Psychiatria Danubina*, *24*(1), 90–93.

Park, J., Lee, D. S., Shablack, H., Verduyn, P., Deldin, P., Ybarra, O., ... Kross, E. (2016). When perceptions defy reality: The relationships between depression and actual and perceived Facebook social support. *Journal of Affective Disorders*, *200*, 37–44. doi.org/10.1016/j.jad.2016.01.048

Puschmann, C., & Bozdag, E. (2014). Staking out the unclear ethical terrain of online social experiments. *Internet Policy Review*. Retrieved from https://policyreview.info/articles/analysis/staking-out-unclear-ethical-terrain-online-social-experiments

Robinson, T. E., & Berridge, K. C. (2001). Incentive-sensitization and addiction. *Addiction*, *96*(1), 103–114. doi.org/10.1046/j.1360-0443.2001.9611038.x

Rook, K. S. (1984). The negative side of social interaction: Impact on psychological well-being. *Journal of Personality and Social Psychology*, *46*(5), 1097–1108. doi.org/10.1037/0022-3514.46.5.1097

Ryan, T., Chester, A., Reece, J., & Xenos, S. (2014). The uses and abuses of Facebook: A review of Facebook addiction. *Journal of Behavioral Addictions*, *3*(3), 133–148. doi.org/10.1556/JBA.3.2014.016

Sagioglou, C., & Greitemeyer, T. (2014). Facebook's emotional consequences: Why Facebook causes a decrease in mood and why people still use it. *Computers in Human Behavior*, *35*, 359–363. doi.org/10.1016/j.chb.2014.03.003

Salovey, P., & Rodin, J. (1984). Some antecedents and consequences of social-comparison jealousy. *Journal of Personality and Social Psychology*, *47*(4), 780–792. doi.org/10.1037/0022-3514.47.4.780

Shakya, H. B., & Christakis, N. A. (2017). Association of Facebook use with compromised well-being: A longitudinal study. *American Journal of Epidemiology.* doi.org/10.1093/aje/kww189

Shaw, D. (2016). Facebook's flawed emotion experiment: Antisocial research on social network users. *Research Ethics, 12*(1), 29–34. doi.org/10.1177/1747016115579535

Statista. (2019). Number of social media users worldwide from 2010 to 2021 (in billions). Retrieved May 6, 2019 from www.statista.com/statistics/278414/number-of-worldwide-social-network-users/

Stewart, J. B. (2016). Facebook has 50 minutes of your time each day. It wants more. *The New York Times.* Retrieved from http://www.nytimes.com/2016/05/06/business/facebook-bends-the-rules-ofaudience-engagement-to-its-advantage.html. Retrieved October 12, 2016.

Sun, J., Schwartz, H. A., Son, Y., Kern, M. L., & Vazire, S. (in press). The language of well-being: Tracking fluctuations in emotion experience through everyday speech. *Journal of Personality and Social Psychology.*

Teichman, Y., & Teichman, M. (1990). Interpersonal view of depression: Review and integration. *Journal of Family Psychology, 3*(4), 349–367. doi.org/10.1037/h0080549

Tromholt, M. (2016). The Facebook experiment: Quitting Facebook leads to higher levels of well-being. *Cyberpsychology, Behavior, and Social Networking, 19*(11), 661-666.

Turkle, S. (2011). *Alone together: Why we expect more from technology and less from each other.* New York, NY: Basic Books.

Twenge, J. M. (2017, September). Have smartphones destroyed a generation? *The Atlantic.* Retrieved from www.theatlantic.com/magazine/archive/2017/09/ has-the-smartphone-destroyed-a-generation/534198/

Valenzuela, S., Park, N., & Kee, K. F. (2009). Is there social capital in a social network site? Facebook use and college students' life satisfaction, trust, and participation. *Journal of Computer-Mediated Communication, 14*(4), 875–901. doi.org/10.1111/j.1083-6101.2009.01474.x

Verduyn, P., Lee, D. S., Park, J., Shablack, H., Orvell, A., Bayer, J., ... Kross, E. (2015). Passive Facebook usage undermines affective well-being: Experimental and longitudinal evidence. *Journal of Experimental Psychology: General, 144*(2), 480–488. doi.org/10.1037/xge0000057

Verduyn, P., Ybarra, O., Résibois, M., Jonides, J., & Kross, E. (2017). Do social network sites enhance or undermine subjective well-being? A critical review. *Social Issues and Policy Review, 11*(1), 274–302. doi.org/10.1111/sipr.12033

Vogel, E. A., Rose, J. P., Okdie, B. M., Eckles, K., & Franz, B. (2015). Who compares and despairs? The effect of social comparison orientation on social media use and its outcomes. *Personality and Individual Differences, 86,* 249–256. doi.org/10.1016/j.paid.2015.06.026

Walther, J. B., Van Der Heide, B., Ramirez, A., Burgoon, J. K., & Peña, J. (2015). Interpersonal and hyperpersonal dimensions of computer-mediated communication. In S. S. Sundar (Ed.), *The handbook of the psychology of communication technology* (pp. 1–22). doi.org/10.1002/9781118426456.ch1

Whiting, A., & Williams, D. (2013). Why people use social media: A uses and gratifications approach. *Qualitative Market Research: An International Journal, 16*(4), 362–369. doi.org/10.1108/QMR-06-2013-0041

Wood, J. V. (1996). What is social comparison and how should we study it? *Personality and Social Psychology Bulletin, 22,* 520–537. doi.org/10.1177/0146167296225009

PART IV
Public Affairs and Political Behavior

14

UNDERSTANDING POPULISM

Collective Narcissism and the Collapse of Democracy in Hungary

Joseph P. Forgas and Dorottya Lantos

Introduction

In May 2019, Mr. Viktor Orbán, Prime Minister of Hungary, declared to the Austrian *Kleine Zeitung* that "If you are a Hungarian, your basic state of mind is the feeling of betrayal." (*Kleine Zeitung*, 2019). His regime and the country he rules has in turn been characterized as displaying "the same authoritarian nationalism practiced by thugs and charlatans throughout the 20th century – including Hungary's pro-Nazi World War II regime. Mr. Orbán has excluded himself from the democratic West; he and his government should be treated accordingly" (*Washington Post*, 2014). Is there a link between these two claims? Can a damaged sense of national identity facilitate the establishment of authoritarian anti-democratic political systems? Exploring this question is one of the main objectives of this chapter.

The last few decades saw the emergence of populist, illiberal political movements in a number of countries that have taken political scientists and psychologists by surprise (Gusterson, 2017; Inglehart & Norris, 2016; Zakaria, 2016). The rejection of the liberal democratic model is puzzling, considering that Western liberal democracies have produced previously unimaginable levels of freedom, justice, fairness, equality, prosperity, tolerance, and decency (Acemoglu & Robinson, 2013; Pinker, 2018; Rosling, 2019).

Given the indisputable superiority of the Western liberal model to illiberal systems, why do massive numbers of voters turn their backs on such a successful and well-tried formula? This turn to illiberal populism is occurring at the same time when millions of would-be migrants are voting with their feet, desperately seeking to *leave* authoritarian, illiberal regimes and move to the successful nations of Western *liberalism*. The rise of populism and illiberalism occurred in both highly developed Western countries (USA, Britain, France, Austria) and less developed nations (Hungary, Poland, Turkey, Russia). Applied social psychology may offer some explanations, and this is the objective of this chapter. Specifically, we will be concerned with exploring the psychological links that lead from feelings of betrayal and inferiority indicated by the first quotation above by Mr. Orbán, to the development of the kind of authoritarian nationalism described in the second quotation.

Applied Social Psychology and Political Behavior

Understanding the psychological reasons for the rise of illiberalism is a major challenge for applied social scientists, who are uniquely placed to offer a responsible empirical analysis of this phenomenon. This important task calls for a new type of scientific approach and methodology. Laboratory research and theoretical analysis alone are unlikely to offer a persuasive explanation of complex macro-social phenomena such as the rise of political populism. An alternative approach, advocated here, is to combine historical analysis and the conceptual armory of empirical social psychology to understand and interpret the psychological meaning of recent changes in voter behavior. Such a task necessarily calls for a theory-driven multi-method approach (see also Fiedler, this volume), relying on a combination of survey data, the analysis of linguistic narratives and the study of the themes employed by government propaganda to explain changes in voter behavior.

We know at least since Plato's seminal treatise on the "Republic" that all political systems rise or fall depending on their goodness of fit to the mental requirements of their citizens. Could there be some underlying, common psychological mechanism that can help to explain the rise of a narcissistic and often dishonest candidate like Trump to the presidency of the United States, the surprising decision by British voters to leave the EU against their own manifest interests, or the dramatic turning away from the liberal democratic model in such historically challenged countries like Russia, Poland, Turkey and Hungary?

This chapter will argue that there are some common psychological features to these events. In particular, the need for positive group identity − collective narcissism − may contribute to the growing receptivity of voters to misleading but highly effective populist propaganda not otherwise seen since the days of Mussolini, Hitler, and Stalin (Albright, 2018). Research suggests that collective narcissism − a belief that one's own group is exceptional and entitled to privileged treatment, but that it is not sufficiently recognized by others − lies at the core of many populist beliefs (for a review, see Golec de Zavala, Dyduch-Hazar, & Lantos, 2019). We will review evidence showing that collective narcissism is related to the endorsement of populist beliefs cross-culturally, in the US (Federico & Golec de Zavala, 2018), Britain (Golec de Zavala, Guerra, & Simão, 2017), Poland (Marchlewska, Cichocka, Panayiotou, Castellanos, & Batayneh,

2017), and Hungary (Lantos & Forgas, 2019). We will focus on the case of Hungary, as this country has undergone perhaps the most dramatic collapse of democracy in the last ten years. The role of government propaganda in exploiting collective narcissism and feelings of national inferiority will receive special attention.

The Link Between Mental Representations and Political Behavior

There is a veritable tradition in social psychology on translational research linking theoretical and practical concerns (see also Fiedler, this volume), and focusing especially on the mental representations of nations or cultures, reaching back to Wundt's classic work on "Voelkerpsychologie" (Borgida, Federico, & Sullivan, 2009; Forgas, 1980; Wundt, 1911). Humans have a strong tendency to believe in various shared fictions (Harari, 2014), and almost any symbolic narrative can influence political behavior (László, 2014; see also Wohl & Stefaniak, this volume). In the course of their history, nations form narratives that serve various integrative, psychological and identity functions (Harari, 2014; Hobsbawm, 1992; Koestler, 1959).

There is an abundance of evidence for what might be called such *consensual delusions*. For centuries, many Meso-American cultures believed that ripping out the beating hearts of thousands of captives in a single day was necessary to ensure a good harvest, and keep the sun-god happy. In the West, belief in witchcraft and the ritual burning of humans for the sake of their eternal souls was long considered essential to protect the community from evil influences. Barely distinguishable branches of Christianity fought a life-or-death struggle over hundreds of years, just as Sunni and Shiite Muslims continue to do today. Many of the fundamental beliefs of our Christian civilisation are also entirely fictional and indeed, absurd (virgin birth, resurrection, biblical miracles, transubstantiation, etc).

We should see collective narcissism in this light: as yet another fictional narrative extolling the virtues of the in-group (Rosling, 2019). Such narratives, once aroused, may be capable of undermining even well-designed democratic systems (Myers, 2019). Our objective of analysing collective narcissism as a feature of populism falls within this research tradition.

Collective Narcissism

Collective narcissism can be defined as an enduring belief and a feeling of emotional resentment that our own group (the in-group) is unfairly treated and insufficiently recognized, despite having exceptional qualities that should entitle it to privileged treatment (Golec de Zavala, 2018; Golec de Zavala, Cichocka, Eidelson, & Jayawickreme, 2009). Historically, the concept of narcissism has psychoanalytic origins. The possibility that entire groups, collectives, and even nations can become narcissistic, was first articulated by social scientists inspired by psychoanalytic ideas, and associated with the Frankfurt School (Adorno, 1997). For example, Fromm (1964/2010) understood narcissism as self-admiration and over-evaluation of one's own subjective perspective also marked by a "blindness" to objective reality.

Taking a somewhat different perspective, Adorno (1997) thought that collective narcissism involves attributing to the in-group the characteristics its members most admire but lack in themselves. Both authors suggested that collective narcissism arises especially in challenging situations that undermine self-worth and life satisfaction and often results in intergroup hostility. However, the contemporary understanding of collective narcissism differs from the psychoanalytic approach and makes no assumptions about pathological intrapsychic conflicts (Cichocka, 2016). Rather, we may view collective narcissism as the empirical manifestation of an interrelated set of social-psychological beliefs and ideas about the in-group that mirrors the way individual narcissists think about themselves vis-à-vis others.

We shall use a number of high-level nominal terms in this paper such as collective narcissism, populism, illiberalism, system derogation, collective victimhood, collective nostalgia, political hysteria, etc. Not all of these terms have a universally accepted and empirically validated definition, and the possibility of confound cannot be excluded. We shall consider collective narcissism as the key integrative concept here, as it does have a clear definition and an empirical operationalization.

We should also note that terms such as collective narcissism are not purely descriptive, but also have unfortunate pejorative connotations (Koole, personal communication). This is of course undesirable, but all too common in current political discourse where numerous terms have been created, not to illuminate genuine processes, but primarily to condemn those whose views are considered unacceptable in terms of political correctness (e.g., homophobe, islamophobe, climate change denier, patriarchal, etc.). For want of a better alternative, we shall use the well-established terminology of collective narcissism here (Golec de Zavala et al., 2009).

Collective Narcissism and Political Beliefs

Political propaganda can often exploit collective narcissism (Albright, 2018; see also Jussim; and Petty & Briñol, this volume). Dictators often rely on distorted interpretation of national history to generate collective narcissism and legitimacy (Skarżyńska, Przybyła, & Wójcik, 2012). For example, recent Hungarian state propaganda claims that Hungary (actually a secular country with low levels of church attendance) is a bastion defending Christian values against the twin onslaughts of Muslim migration, and godless Western liberalism as exemplified by the EU (see also Figure 14.3). Martyrdom, suffering and lost battles

(Hungary, Poland, Serbia) offer as fertile a ground for feelings of collective narcissism as do past victories and military might (Russia). Religious "sacred beliefs" can be especially powerful (Ginges, 2014). Both Poles and Hungarians (and some others as well) believe that the Holy Virgin has a special love for *their* nation. Claims about exceptional moral virtues such as honesty, decency, fairness, kindness, or hospitality are often employed to bolster collective narcissism (Żemojtel-Piotrowska et al., 2019).

Collective Narcissism and In-group Favoritism

Collective narcissism is closely related to Tajfel's original explanation for in-group favoritism in the minimal group experiments (Tajfel & Forgas, 1981). According to this view, intergroup discrimination is driven by the universal need for positive self-worth, achieved through maximizing positive in-group distinctiveness. This argument is supported by findings that allocations that maximize in-group/out-group *differences* are often preferred to allocations that simply maximize in-group *rewards* (Crocker & Park, 2004; Emmons, 1987; Tajfel & Forgas, 1981).

Collective narcissism is also closely related to well-known (and in our evolutionary past, highly adaptive) motivational tendencies for self-inflation, self-justification, and self-serving distortions, which can be generalized to how one feels about one's in-group (Putnam, Ross, Soter, & Roediger, 2018; Zaromb et al., 2018; von Hippel, 2018). As Golec de Zavala, Dyduch-Hazar, et al. (2019) conclude, just

> as people can demand special recognition and privilege for themselves (as individual narcissists do), they can claim the same for the groups they belong to (as collective narcissists do). ... the intergroup consequences of collective narcissism often parallel the interpersonal consequences of individual narcissism: hostility, exaggerated reactions to negative feedback and criticism, or lack of empathy.
>
> *p. 38*

Collective narcissism has been a common feature of fascist ideologies: in the 1930s, the Germans, Italians, and Japanese all believed in their innate racial and cultural superiority and deservingness (Albright, 2018). Collective narcissism is also characteristic of various Jihadist movements, who see their sacred religion and culture as inherently superior to others (Ginges, 2014; Kruglanski & Fishman, 2009).

The Measurement of Collective Narcissism

Collective narcissism can be empirically measured using tests such as the Collective Narcissism Scale, adapting psychological measures of individual narcissism to a group level. For example, items in the Narcissistic Personality Inventory (NPI; Emmons, 1987; Raskin & Terry, 1988) and narcissism-related items in the Millon Clinical Multiaxial Inventory-III (Millon, 2006) were re-written to refer to group-related beliefs rather than the individual (e.g., "I insist upon getting the respect that is due to me" was transformed to "I insist upon my group getting the respect that is due to it"; Golec de Zavala et al., 2009). People who score high on the Collective Narcissism Scale believe that their in-group's importance is not sufficiently recognized by others and that their in-group deserves special treatment.

Collective Narcissism and Populism in the USA and Britain

Both the Trump campaign, and the 2016 Brexit referendum used slogans designed to mobilize those with collective narcissistic beliefs, emphasizing that the intrinsic value of the national in-group has been undermined, and that it is time to restore the in-group's greatness (Golec de Zavala, Federico, et al., 2019; Golec de Zavala, Cichocka, & Iskra-Golec, 2013; Golec de Zavala, Peker, Guerra, & Baran, 2016).

American citizens who felt that the social status of their reference group (white males especially), and the international standing of their nation was challenged were especially responsive to slogans promising to prioritize "America First" and "Make America Great Again." A national representative survey of Americans before and after the elections showed that those who scored high on collective narcissism had more favorable views of Donald Trump, and were more likely to vote for him (Federico & Golec de Zavala, 2018). The study controlled for a number of demographic and psychological variables, and found that apart from partisanship, collective narcissism proved to be the strongest predictor of political preferences.

Another representative study in the US looked at belief in conspiracy theories (e.g., van Prooijen, 2019) and found that collective narcissism was significantly related to belief in conspiracy theories both before, and after the 2016 election (Golec de Zavala & Federico, 2018). Conspiracy theories may be especially attractive to collective narcissists as an explanation for the inadequate recognition of their in-group, and the 2016 US elections were marked by an uncommon level of conspiracy beliefs (Cichocka, Marchlewska, & Golec de Zavala, 2016; Golec de Zavala & Cichocka, 2012; Samuelsohn, 2016; van Prooijen, 2019).

The outcome of the 2016 Brexit referendum can also be interpreted through the mobilization of collective narcissists, who felt that the EU was undermining the political status and autonomy of their country. The emphasis on the threat from out-groups and "migrants" was a common feature of both the Trump and the Brexit campaigns (e.g., Clarke, Goodwin, & Whiteley, 2016). A recent study found that collective narcissism, social dominance orientation, and right-wing authoritarianism all predicted xenophobia and the Brexit vote (Golec de Zavala et al., 2017), even when demographic factors are controlled. Collective narcissism most directly relates to concerns over the image of the national group, its purity, grandiosity, and uniqueness.

Another experimental study found (Marchlewska et al., 2017) that reading about the long-term economic disadvantages that the EU caused for the UK led to an increase in endorsing collective narcissistic beliefs, compared to a control condition. These findings suggest that populist messages emphasizing long-term threat and decline may find particularly enthusiastic reception among voters holding collective narcissistic beliefs (Figure 14.1). A very similar pattern has also been observed in Poland, where collective narcissism was a significant predictor of the support for the right-wing populist party of Jaroslaw Kaczynski in the presidential elections (Marchlewska et al., 2017).

The Collapse of Democracy in Hungary: Social and Historical Context

Hungary presents a particularly interesting case for analyzing the role of collective narcissism in political behavior. Hungary today is no longer a democratic country, and is the only EU member country classified as having an only partially free press by Freedom House (2018). Since their election in 2010, the prime minister, Viktor Orbán, and his Fidesz party established a de-facto one-party state they call the "System of National Cooperation," who have

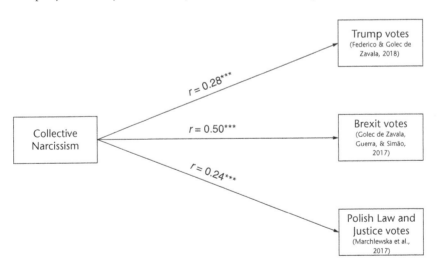

FIGURE 14.1   The link between collective narcissism and the tendency to support populist causes internationally.

Note
*** $p < 0.001$.

systematically dismantled democratic institutions and eliminated the usual checks and balances that limit executive power. They passed a new constitution entrenching the power of the ruling party, changed the electoral law that perpetuates their power, made the prosecutorial system subject to direct party control, and brought most of the media under single party rule. In the last eight years, Hungary has fallen from the 23rd to the 87th place on the international list of press freedom – below Sierra Leone (Majtényi & Miklosi, 2013; Scheppele, 2013; Tóth, 2013).

In an extraordinary speech on July 26th, 2014, Mr. Orbán openly declared that Hungary is turning its back on liberal democracy. Praising autocratic states such as Singapore, China, Turkey, and Russia, he stated that "we have to abandon liberal methods and principles of organizing society, as well as the liberal way of looking at the world … because liberal values today incorporate corruption, sex, and violence" (Orbán, 2014). Orbán often contrasts the "vitality of the work based economy of the healthy, Eastern peoples as against the tired, immoral, Western citizens subjugated by finance capitalism" (Tölgyessy, 2013, p. 2).

As Timothy Garton Ash concluded in the *Guardian*, Mr. Orbán has demolished liberal democracy in his country. He has misappropriated EU funds to consolidate his illiberal regime. Orbán's cronies and family members receive government contracts, while NGOs and opposition supporters are harassed with arbitrary tax investigations. State resources are routinely used for Fidesz party propaganda. Orbán has effectively demolished the independence of the judiciary, as also documented in an extensive report by Judith Sargentini for the European Parliament. Reports by Transparency International and the European Commission have found that in about 50 percent of public procurement procedures, there was only one tender, and the procedures are thoroughly corrupt (Garton Ash, 2019). In a similar vein, the *Washington Post* concluded in its editorial on August 16, 2014, that what Mr. Orbán offers

> is little more than the same authoritarian nationalism practiced by thugs and charlatans throughout the 20th century – including Hungary's pro-Nazi world War II regime. … Mr. Orbán has excluded himself from the democratic West; he and his government should be treated accordingly.

Mafia-like corruption is a central feature of the system, fueled by EU funds that are routinely misappropriated by Orbán's cronies. His childhood friend, until 2010 a humble gas fitter, has become one of the richest men in Hungary in just a few years. Orbán's son-in-law has been identified by OLAF, the European Union's anti-corruption agency, as being engaged in organized crime in stealing EU funds, but the Hungarian prosecutors have done nothing. While the facade of democracy is maintained, in reality institutions are now run by loyal party appointees. Criticism from the European Parliament, the Venice Commission, the European Commission and more recently, following the

Sargentini report, the commencement of EU sanctions against Hungary under Section 7 of the EU constitution had no discernible effect.

The unrelenting government propaganda appealing to narcissistic beliefs played a crucial role in legitimizing this process (Albright, 2018; see also Figure 14.3). The carefully fueled sense of nationalism, grievance and collective narcissism provide a crucial component, capitalizing on Hungary's traumatic history, as we will argue below.

The Role of Historical Traumas

Recurring historical traumas provide fertile ground for collective narcissism, and Hungarian history is replete with such events. Hungarian tribes settled in the Carpathian basin in 898, adopted Christianity and formed a unified state by AD 1000. In the middle ages, Hungary was an important country, possessing some of the richest gold and silver mines of the continent (Lendvai, 2004). However, in 1526, the expanding Ottoman Turkish empire defeated Hungary, resulting in 150 years of Turkish occupation, followed by centuries of Habsburg dominance and several failed revolutions, giving rise to endemic feelings of victimhood, betrayal, and injustice (Bibó, 1991; László & Fülöp 2010).

Whereas in Western Europe, the nation and the state evolved together, in countries like Hungary (as in Poland) the symbolic "nation" was traditionally mobilized *against* states of oppressive external occupation (Bibó, 1986). Thus, a romantic notion of sacred and inviolable nationalism has assumed an emotional significance unparalleled elsewhere (Lendvai, 2012). The dominant ideological values of the Enlightenment, such as individualism, liberalism, and the emergence of an autonomous and independent bourgeoisie, were late to reach Hungary, and whatever bourgeoisie emerged was repeatedly decimated by wars and the holocaust (Bibó, 1986; Lendvai, 2004; 2012).

Hungarian language was a powerful cause of cultural isolation, but paradoxically, also a salient source of distinct cultural identity. After the defeated 1848 revolution, in 1876, a historic treaty with the Habsburgs created the Austro-Hungarian Monarchy, producing 50 years of unprecedented economic, political, and cultural progress until the First World War. After the lost war, Hungary suffered probably its greatest national trauma, the loss of two-thirds of its historical territory in the Trianon peace treaty (Mihályi, 2010). The interwar years saw a bloody but short-lived communist dictatorship, followed by an autocratic, nationalistic, right-wing regime in the 1920s and 1930s. Having also lost the Second World War on Hitler's side, Hungary then became a communist dictatorship for 45 years under Soviet military occupation.

After the collapse of communism in 1989, more traumas followed the transition to a free-market democracy (Andorka, Kolosi, Rose, & Vukovich, 1999; Kolosi & Tóth, 2008; Lendvai, 2012; Mihályi, 2010). Many firms collapsed and unemployment skyrocketed, while large sections of the population experienced absolute, or relative impoverishment. Parties often pursued short-term, opportunistic agendas; crucial economic, education, health service, and administrative reforms have been neglected, and the national debt reached unmanageable levels (Andorka et al., 1999; Inotai, 2007; Tölgyessy, 2013). Since 2008, Hungary has made little progress to catch up with the more developed Western European nations (Inotai, 2007; Lendvai, 2012; Mihályi, 2010). Strikingly, many voters report nostalgia for the former dictatorial, but certainly more egalitarian, communist regime (see Question 2 in Table 14.2).

This traumatic history over the last 500 years produced a deep sense of grievance and a narcissistic sense of national identity. Surveys show that many Hungarian voters can still be characterized as living in a pre-modern age, comfortable with authoritarianism and strong leaders, and holding on to an archaic romantic, nationalistic, and ethnocentric sense of identity (Kelemen et al., 2014; Lendvai, 2004). In a recent survey, 67 percent of upper-middle class Hungarians were satisfied with the autocratic regime, and the majority also evaluated positively the earlier dictatorial communist regime (Table 14.2).

In summary then, Hungary had an uncommonly traumatic, and to this day, poorly comprehended history. Recurring traumatic experiences call for a narrative explanation, and frequently narcissistic narratives were constructed around themes of injustice, betrayal, powerlessness, and victimhood (Bibó, 1986; László & Ehmann, 2013; László & Fülöp, 2010).

Hungarian National Identity: Attitudes, Values, and Romantic Nationalism

In contrast with most Western democracies, Hungarians live in a mental world that is characterized by pessimism, grievance, and a closed-minded cognitive style (Keller, 2010), supported by a poorly elaborated understanding of the causal forces that shaped their nation's history (László, 2014). For example, Csepeli (2018) recently compared the text of the national anthem of Hungary with that of neighboring countries (see Table 14.1). While the anthems of neighboring countries focus on positive, optimistic, and dynamic characteristics, the phrases in the

TABLE 14.1 Comparison of imagery in national anthems (After Csepeli, 2018, TedX talk www.youtube.com/watch?v=Up9ry4AHbdY).

Neighbor Countries	*Hungary*
Pleasure, Joy, Health, Glory, Life, Lightning, Dawn, Freedom, Love, Luck, Pleasure, Faith, Trust, Wealth, Pride, Solidarity, Victory, Competition, Happiness, Ability, Strength, Heart, Faith.	Sin, Atonement, Defeat, Yoke, Slavery, Strife, Ill fate, Suffering, Grave, Anger, Thundering clouds, Corpses, Funeral urn, Freedom, Fugitive, Sword, Sadness, Despair, Blood, Ocean of flames, Heap of stones, Groans of death.

Hungarian national anthem are mostly about suffering, victimhood, despair, and injustice. Many Hungarian national holidays also celebrate traumatic rather than glorious and successful historical events (cf. Csepeli, 2018).

Data from the World Value Survey also confirms that Hungarians are more closed-minded, insecure, and less trusting than Western nations (Keller, 2010). While most Western countries tend to over-justify their political systems (Jost & Banaji, 1994), in a national survey (N = 1,000) Hungarians show the opposite trend; system derogation (Kelemen, 2010; Table 14.2). Paradoxically, despite this all-encompassing pessimism, almost 80 percent assert that Hungary is still the nicest place in the world, indicating a kind of romantic, narcissistic, fictional nationalism also identified by Bibó (1991), László (2014), and Lendvai (2004) (see Question 8 in Table 14.2).

TABLE 14.2 Hungarian attitudes: Disenchantment and pessimism in a national representative sample, and among a smaller sample of lawyers (after Kelemen, 2010).

	Representative National Sample N = 1000	
	(N=1000)	Lawyers (N = 100)
1. Democracy will not work as it should in Hungary for several decades.		
Disagree	21%	29%
Agree	79%	71%
2. People lived better before the change in the political system.		
Disagree	24%	40%
Agree	76%	60%
3. I think Hungarian society is honest.		
Disagree	70%	49%
Agree	30%	51%
4. Political parties do not have the interests of the country in mind.		
Disagree	18%	29%
Agree	82%	71%
5. A strong political leader should be in control to solve the problems of the country.		
Disagree	16%	19%
Agree	84%	81%
6. In Hungary, everybody has an equal chance to be wealthy and happy.		
Disagree	76%	69%
Agree	24%	31%
7. Social conditions get worse year by year.		
Disagree	14%	22%
Agree	86%	78%
8. For me, Hungary is the nicest place in the world.		
Disagree	22%	18%
Agree	78%	82%

Hungarians (and also Poles) score lower on just world beliefs than do citizens of Western nations (Sallay & Krotos, 2004; Dolinski, 1996), and report lower perceived justice and trust in the establishment (Kelemen, 2010). A "system derogation" bias indicating a stable psychological tendency to perceive socio-political systems as inherently bad, unfair, unjust, and illegitimate may also serve important defensive psychological objectives. If the system is fundamentally unfair, then individual failures can be safely attributed to a bad system (Dolinski, 1996).

In a national representative survey, we found that those with a right-wing party preference ($b = -0.101$, $SE = 0.024$, $\beta = -0.200$, $p < 0.001$), lower income ($b = 0.057$, $SE = 0.014$, $\beta = 0.186$, $p < 0.001$), and who were in a worse economic situation ($b = -0.097$, $SE = 0.030$, $\beta = -0.140$, $p = 0.001$), showed the strongest system derogation compared to voters of left-wing parties and those with higher income ($R2 = 0.105$, $F(8, 579) = 8.53$, $p < 0.001$) (Forgas, Kelemen, & László, 2014). System derogation can have corrosive political consequences, undermining trust and increasing the predisposition to abandon democracy in favor of autocratic alternatives. The ready acceptance of endemic corruption may be another symptom of system scepticism.

These results indicate that Hungarians have low expectations and take a highly sceptical view of their socio-political system and see the world as a fundamentally unjust and unfair place. Paradoxically, these attitudes coexist with an exaggerated sense of their nation's value, a pattern consistent with a narcissistic view of the in-group (Bibó, 1986; Tölgyessy, 2013). Analyzing the narrative language used when describing national events offers an additional important empirical method for analyzing such narcissistic beliefs in "folk psychology," as the next sections will show (Allport, 1924; Wundt, 1911).

The Language of Narcissism

Recent textual analyses of historical narratives in Hungarian school books, literary works, and everyday conversations by László (2014) and his colleagues offer illuminating empirical insights into how Hungarians think of themselves, showing a pattern of victimhood, distrust of foreigners, and romanticised ideas of an exaggerated sense of national identity and destiny (László, 2005; 2014; László & Ehmann, 2013). Using a quantitative computerized content analytic method (László & Ehmann, 2013), these studies analyzed descriptions of history in history textbooks, historical novels, newspaper texts, and everyday spoken narratives by respondents from a stratified sample of 500 participants.

For example, the words used to describe historical events in school books and in folk narratives can be revealing about perceptions of *agency*, or the opposite of it, *victimhood* (László, 2013; László, Szalai, & Ferenczhalmy, 2010). The authors found an overwhelming tendency for Hungarians to describe themselves as passive and out-groups as agentic and dominant in producing historical events

(Figure 14.2), suggesting a victim mentality and the inadequate cognitive elaboration of historical traumas.

The *emotional reactions* expressed in verbal narratives are also a critical aspect of "folk psychology" (Allport, 1924; László & Fülöp, 2010). Analyses of the descriptions of historical events used in textbooks, literary works, and personal narratives by László (2014) identified 57 emotion types with 918 occurrences. *Sadness* and *hope* were the two emotions that most distinguished Hungarians from other

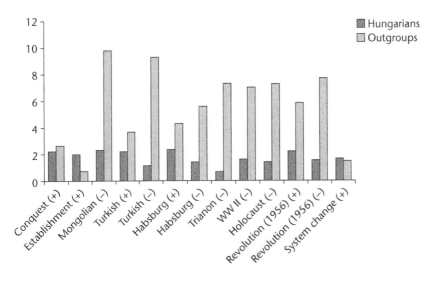

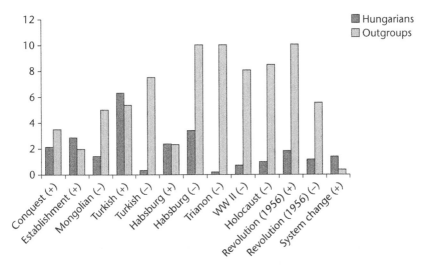

FIGURE 14.2 The use of narrative words indicating agency for 13 key historical events in (1) schoolbooks (top) and (2) in folk narratives.

nations, as also demonstrated by Csepeli (2018) analyzing the national anthem (Table 14.1). László and Ehmann (2013, pp. 216–217) concluded that

> the results portray a vulnerable Hungarian national identity and a long-term adoption of the collective victim role … The emotional and cognitive organization of the Hungarian national identity as it is expressed in historical narratives shows a deep attachment to the glorious past and a relatively low level of cognitive and emotional elaboration of the twentieth century and earlier traumas … suggesting that this historical trajectory is not the most favorable ground to build an emotionally stable identity.

This kind of collective affective predisposition marked by collective nostalgia and narcissism has also been identified by others (Bibó, 1986, 1991; Lendvai, 2004, 2012; see also Wohl & Stefaniak, this volume).

Despite the perceived lack of agency and negative emotionality, *self-evaluations* of Hungarians were paradoxically and consistently more positive for themselves than the out-groups, again consistent with a narcissistic mindset. Hungarians evaluated themselves positively for desirable events, but accepted no responsibility for negative events in folk stories and textbooks. Such inflated self-evaluations absolved Hungarians of blame, even for events where they were clearly the aggressors and perpetrators (such as the holocaust, lost wars, etc.). The propaganda of the current autocratic regime consistently promotes misleading historical narratives exploiting this tendency (e.g., the Germans as solely responsible for the holocaust), absolving Hungarians of all responsibility. Bar-Tal (2000) described this identity state as collective victimhood. Experiences of historical traumas make it difficult to maintain positive group beliefs, and ideas of collective victimhood, nostalgia, and narcissism may function as protective psychological devices, maintaining positive group identity by emphasizing moral superiority, refusing responsibility, avoiding criticism, and evoking sympathy from other groups (László, 2014; see also Wohl & Stefaniak, this volume).

Based on his extensive research, László (2014, p. 95) concludes that

> The emotional and cognitive organisation of Hungarian national identity is profoundly tied to … a distant glorious past and a subsequent series of defeats and losses … the characteristic emotions of the Hungarian national identity are fear, sadness, disappointment, enthusiasm and hope … Hungarian's sense of agency is very low.

Further, Hungarians' emotional landscape also "includes inflated self-evaluations accompanied by the degradation of outgroups" (p. 96), a pattern indicating collective narcissism and collective victimhood (Bar-Tal, 2000). This narcissistic narrative "provides moral justification … and ensures a sense of moral superiority, legitimizing aggression" (p. 96; see also Krahé, this volume). Such an emotional disposition, as a direct result of historical traumas, also produces an incapacity to empathize with the suffering of another group. It is analogous to narcissism and self-centeredness (László, 2014). These psychological processes were earlier also recognized by Bibó (1991), who suggested that recurring historical traumas distort the perception of reality, producing political illusions and generating a pathological state that he identified as an inclination to "political hysteria."

Collective Narcissism Predicts Political Preferences in Hungary

Autocratic regimes regularly use propaganda to appeal to a sense of grievance and collective narcissism, and this is also the case in Hungary (Albright, 2018). Regular propaganda campaigns included billboards plastered across the country advertising the need to "send messages to Brussels," including requesting more respect for Hungarians (see Figure 14.3). The objective of Hungarian state propaganda was to exploit the sense of victimhood and narcissism and turn it into political capital to support the legitimacy for the ruling party. In particular, the unrelenting promotion of absurd and misleading conspiracy theories (e.g., depicting George Soros, a philanthropist, as the manipulator of anti-Hungarian EU policies, and Juncker as his puppet) is unprecedented in an EU country (Figure 14.3d).

Rewriting history is also a hallmark of Hungary's autocratic regime. Numerous new "historical institutes" were financed by taxpayer funds, spreading propaganda absolving Hungarians of all responsibility for lost wars and the holocaust. Another propaganda strategy is the creation of absurd stories about the ancient virtues and glories of Hungarians. For example, *Magyar Hírlap*, the Fidesz daily, often publishes articles by self-styled "historians" suggesting that Hungarian civilisation preceded the Egyptians, that Hungarians invented writing and much else besides, and that these "achievements" are not sufficiently recognized because of a conspiracy by enemies and detractors. Rather than inviting well-deserved ridicule, such theories find fertile ground. For example, many Hungarian localities now proudly display locality names in runic writing that nobody can read (claimed to be an ancient Hungarian invention), as a visible affirmation of national superiority (Figure 14.3e).

By all accounts, this systematic exploitation of a wounded sense of national identity and collective narcissism has been highly effective. Two recent studies investigating two samples of Hungarian adults ($N1=284$; $N2=265$) recruited through social media confirmed that collective narcissism was significantly related to support for the populist Fidesz party and for Viktor Orbán (Lantos & Forgas, 2019). Participants scoring higher on collective narcissism were more likely to vote for Fidesz and Orbán in the 2014 and 2018 national elections. Higher narcissists also held more conservative views, had more favorable views about Hungary, and more negative views about the EU (Figure 14.4).

Further data, collected just before the 2018 Hungarian elections, replicated these results (Lantos & Forgas, 2019, Study 2, see Figure 14.5). Collective

FIGURE 14.3 Examples of Hungarian government propaganda: Top left: "Our message to Brussels: We demand respect for Hungarians!" Top right: "Let's not allow Soros to have the last laugh!" Middle left: "Let's not give in to blackmail: Defend Hungary." Middle right: "You have a right to know what Brussels is planning for you." Bottom left: Runic writing of locality names. Bottom right: "Hungary will not give in!"

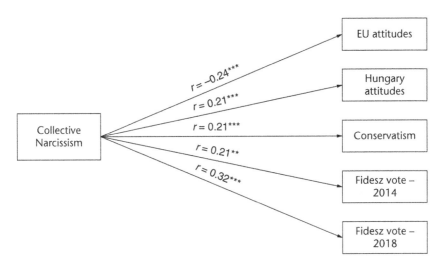

FIGURE 14.4 The relationship between collective narcissism and populist beliefs in Hungary in 2016.

Note
** $p<0.01$. *** $p<0.001$.

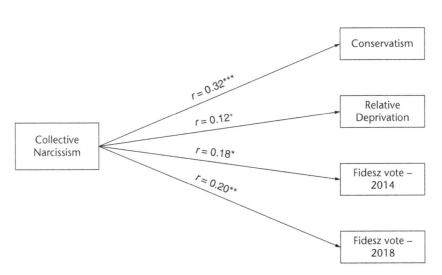

FIGURE 14.5 The relationship between collective narcissism and predictors of populism in Hungary in 2018.

Note
+ $p=0.06$. * $p<0.05$. ** $p<0.01$. *** $p<0.001$.

narcissism was again significantly associated with conservatism, greater support for Orbán and Fidesz, and higher levels of relative deprivation (poverty; see Figure 14.5).

As was the case in the Brexit and Trump campaigns, the Hungarian government also emphasizes the threat of immigrants to generate negative attitudes to the EU. The failure of the EU to deal with the problem of uncontrolled migration has clearly played into Orbán's hands. The threat of migrants has remained the centerpiece of xenophobic government propaganda for the last few years, creating an atmosphere of fear and hate, and turning Hungary into one of the most xenophobic countries in Europe. Research has confirmed an increase in hate speech and hate crime following the 2016 campaigns of Trump in the US (Levin, Nolan, & Reitzel, 2018), Brexit in the UK (Agerholm, 2016), the Fidesz party in Hungary (Wallen, 2018), and also following the election of the ultra-conservative Law and Justice party in Poland (Flückiger, 2017).

There is thus a clear pattern indicating a strong relationship between collective narcissism and support for populism across several nations, as summarized in Table 14.3. We also conducted a meta-analysis to summarize these results using Meta-Essentials (see Table 14.4; Suurmond, van Rhee, & Hak, 2017), confirming a clear and significant relationship between collective narcissism and populism across all studies reported, with a moderate positive overall correlation of 0.30.

Conclusions

In this chapter we explored the links between psychological representations and political behavior, and more specifically, the role of collective narcissism as a factor in the rise of populism across a number of nations. We focused especially on the case of Hungary, a country that has progressed perhaps furthest in actively embracing a populist, nationalist, and illiberal political agenda. In order to gain a deeper understanding of these developments, we considered some of the historical, psychological, and cognitive factors that may explain why democracy seems such a fragile institution in some newly democratic countries, such as Hungary.

The cultivation of a collective sense of national grievance and victimhood paired with a narcissistic over-evaluation of the in-group has been a recurring propaganda strategy used by populist leaders such as Mussolini, Hitler, Putyin, Erdogan, and Orbán to generate political legitimacy (Albright, 2018; Golec de Zavala et al., 2013; 2016). It seems that a vulnerable group identity can increase the effectiveness of populist and nationalist propaganda in Hungary and elsewhere. Claiming that Hungary is fighting a life-and-death struggle for recognition, defending Christianity, and resisting colonization by the EU and international Jewish conspirators may seem absurd, but such claims do resonate with significant portions of the Hungarian electorate (Kelemen, 2010; László, 2014). This is only possible because their understanding of history has been

TABLE 14.3 Summary of findings regarding the relationship between collective narcissism measured on the Collective Narcissism Scale (CNS) and support for populist political causes in the USA, Britain, Poland and Hungary.

Source	Study	N	Country	CN measure	α	Populism measure	r
1. Federico & Golec de Zavala, 2018	–	1730	USA	5-item CNS	0.83	Trump vote	0.28***
2. Golec de Zavala, Guerra, & Simão, 2017	1	280	UK	5-item CNS	0.87	Brexit vote	0.50***
3. Golec de Zavala, Guerra, & Simão, 2017	2	226	UK	5-item CNS	0.88	Brexit vote	0.37***
4. Lantos & Forgas, 2019	1	194	Hungary	5-item CNS	0.82	Orbán vote in 2014	0.21**
5. Lantos & Forgas, 2019	1	240	Hungary	5-item CNS	0.82	Orbán vote in 2018	0.32***
6. Lantos & Forgas, 2019	2	155	Hungary	5-item CNS	0.73	Fidesz vote in 2014	0.18*
7. Lantos & Forgas, 2019	2	207	Hungary	5-item CNS	0.73	Fidesz vote in 2018	0.20**
8. Marchlewska et al., 2017	1	1007	Poland	5-item CNS	0.87	Law and Justice vote	0.24***
9. Marchlewska et al., 2017	1	1007	Poland	5-item CNS	0.87	Jaroslaw Kaczynski vote	0.18***
10. Marchlewska et al., 2017	2	497	UK	9-item CNS	0.91	Brexit support	0.47***
11. Marchlewska et al., 2017	3	403	USA	5-item CNS	0.88	Trump support	0.29***

Note. * $p < 0.05$. ** $p < 0.01$. *** $p < 0.001$.

TABLE 14.4 Meta-analytical summary of the relationship between collective narcissism and support for populist movements across the ten studies summarized in Table 14.3.

N	k	r	T	Q	I^2
5,946	11	0.30	0.10	63.37***	84%

Notes

N = average sample size per study x k. k = number of studies. r = summary correlation coefficients. T = an estimate of the standard deviation of the distribution of true effect sizes, under the assumption that these true effect sizes are normally distributed. Q = heterogeneity. I^2 = proportion of unexplained variance. *** $p < 0.001$.

colored by historical narratives and metaphors that emphasize victimhood, exploitation, and conspiracy against a small but valiant people (see also Landau & Keefer, 2014; van Prooijen, 2019).

For democracy to flourish, it is important that individual citizens have trust in the "system," and think and act in an independent, autonomous, confident, individualistic, and assertive manner as citizens. Countries such as Hungary suffered from a traumatic past that provides few reasons for citizens to derive genuine positive identity and distinctiveness from their flawed history. Centuries of oppression produced a pessimistic victim mentality, and the ideology and mental habits of robust individualism have not had a chance to establish themselves. Representative national samples showed that Hungarians are characterized by a high degree of system scepticism and system derogation, and general beliefs in an unjust world (Kelemen, 2010; Kelemen, Szabó, Mészáros, László, & Forgas, 2014). Linguistic analyses of historical narratives confirmed that these attitudes are rooted in historical experiences, demonstrating a lack of agency and victimhood, and a lack of ability to take responsibility for historical traumas, paired with a defensive, unrealistically positive and poorly elaborated evaluation of the in-group and nation (Keller, 2010; Kelemen, 2010; László, 2014).

These data are consistent with what we may call a "narcissistic mindset." We also presented direct empirical evidence showing that higher scores on the Collective Narcissism Scale significantly correlate with right-wing ideology and a preference for the ruling authoritarian party. Government propaganda that now dominates both the public broadcaster as well as most of the printed and electronic media consistently emphasizes narcissistic themes, such as the demand for recognition, heroic virtues, and historical greatness. It seems then, that it is the combination of unresolved historical traumas, a vulnerable sense of national identity, and an absence of autonomous individualism that is most likely to make a society vulnerable to simplistic government messages exploiting collective narcissism, and emphasizing external enemies and victimhood.

Applied social psychologists need to adopt new methods to come to terms with such complex historical and psychological processes. In this paper we demonstrated how a multi-method approach, using historical analysis, empirical data from representative surveys, narrative linguistic analyses, and questionnaire studies can be used to produce convergent data documenting how social thinking and political behavior are intricately linked.

As Plato noted more than 2000 years ago, one of the greatest dangers for democracy is that ordinary people are all too easily swayed by the emotional and deceptive rhetoric of ambitious politicians. Evolutionary psychological research on the fundamental characteristics of human cognition now confirms that humans are indeed highly predisposed to embrace fictitious symbolic belief systems as a means of enhancing group cohesion and coordination (Harari, 2014; von Hippel, 2018; see also van Vugt et al., this volume). Populism is designed to exploit these tendencies. If democracy is to work and collective narcissism is to be controlled, it is essential for nations to face their historical traumas, develop a realistic sense of national identity, and reaffirm the Enlightenment values of autonomous individualism. Unfortunately, this difficult process now appears to have been set back, possibly by decades, in countries like Hungary.

References

Acemoglu, D., & Robinson, J. A. (2013). *Why nations fail: The origins of power, prosperity, and poverty*. New York, NY: Crown Books.

Adorno, T. (1997). *Gesammelte schriften in zwanzig bänden [Collected writings in 20 volumes]* (Vols. 8–9). Berlin, Germany: Suhrkamp/Insel.

Agerholm, H. (2016, June 26). Brexit: Wave of hate crime and racial abuse reported following EU referendum. *The Independent*. Retrieved from www.independent.co.uk/news/uk/home-news/brexit-eu-referendum-racial-racism-abuse-hate-crime-reported-latest-leave-immigration-a7104191.html

Albright, M. (2018). *Fascism: A warning*. New York, NY: Harper Collins Press.

Allport, F. H. (1924). *Social psychology*. Boston: Houghton Mifflin.

Andorka, R., Kolosi, T., Rose, R., & Vukovich, G. (1999). *A society transformed: Hungary in time-space perspective*. Budapest: CEU Press.

Bar-Tal, D. (2000). *Shared beliefs in a society: Social psychological analysis*. London: Sage.

Bibó I. (1986). A Kelet-európai kisállamok nyomorúsága. *Válogatott tanulmányok, 185–266*.

Bibó, I. (1991). *Democracy, revolution, self determination*. Budapest: Eastern European Monographs.

Borgida, E., Federico, C. M., & Sullivan, J. L. (Eds.). (2009). *The political psychology of democratic citizenship*. New York: Oxford University Press.

Cichocka, A. (2016). Understanding defensive and secure in-group positivity: The role of collective narcissism. *European Review of Social Psychology, 27*, 283–317.

Cichocka, A., Marchlewska, M., & Golec de Zavala, A. (2016). Does self-love or self-hate predict conspiracy beliefs? Narcissism, self-esteem, and the endorsement of conspiracy theories. *Social Psychological and Personality Science, 7*(2), 157–166.

Clarke, H. D., Goodwin, M., & Whiteley, P. (2016). *Why Britain voted for Brexit: An individual-level analysis of the 2016 referendum vote*. Paper Presented at EPOP Conference, Sept. 10. Kent.

Crocker, J., & Park, L. E. (2004). The costly pursuit of self-esteem. *Psychological Bulletin, 130*(3), 392–414.

Csepeli, G. (2018). *National character and a culture of complaint*. TedX Danubia, 18th November. www.ted.com/tedx/events/30245

Dolinski, D. (1996) Belief in an unjust world: An egotistic delusion. *Social Justice Research, 9*, 213–221.

Emmons, R. A. (1987). Narcissism: Theory and measurement. *Journal of Personality and Social Psychology, 52*, 11–17.

Federico, C. M., & Golec de Zavala, A. (2018). Collective narcissism and the 2016 United States presidential vote. *Public Opinion Quarterly, 82*(1), 110–121.

Flückiger, P. (2017, August 2). Poland's government stays silent as xenophobia worsens. *DW*. Retrieved from www.dw.com/en/polands-government-stays-silent-as-xenophobia-worsens/a-39941042

Forgas, J. P. (1980). Implicit representations of political leaders: A multidimensional analysis. *Journal of Applied Social Psychology, 10*, 95–310.

Forgas, J. P., Kelemen, L, & László, J. (2014). Social cognition and democracy: An eastern European case study. In J. P. Forgas, B. Crano, & K. Fiedler (Eds.) *Social psychology and politics* (pp. 263–285). New York: Psychology Press.

Freedom House. (2018). *Freedom in the world report, 2018*. Hungary. https://freedomhouse.org/report/freedom-world/2018/hungary

Fromm, E. (1964/2010). *The heart of man: Its genius for good and evil*. New York, NY: AMHF.

Garton Ash, T. (2019, June 20). Europe must stop this disgrace: Viktor Orban is dismantling democracy. *The Guardian*. Retrieved from www.theguardian.com/commentisfree/2019/jun/20/viktor-orban-democracy-hungary-eu-funding

Ginges, J. (2014). Sacred values and political life. In J. P. Forgas, B. Crano, & K. Fiedler (Eds.), *The social psychology of politics* (pp. 41–57). New York: Psychology Press.

Golec de Zavala, A. (2018). Collective narcissism: Antecedents and consequences of exaggeration of the in-group image. In A. Hermann, A. Brunell, & J. Foster (Eds.), *The handbook of trait narcissism: Key advances, research methods, and controversies* (pp. 79–89). New York, NY: Springer.

Golec de Zavala, A., & Cichocka, A. (2012). Collective narcissism and anti-Semitism in Poland. *Group Processes & Intergroup Relations, 15*(2), 213–229.

Golec de Zavala, A., Cichocka, A., Eidelson, R., & Jayawickreme, N. (2009). Collective narcissism and its social consequences. *Journal of Personality and Social Psychology, 97*(6), 1074–1096.

Golec de Zavala, A., Cichocka, A., & Iskra-Golec, I. (2013). Collective narcissism moderates the effect of in-group image threat on intergroup hostility. *Journal of Personality and Social Psychology, 104*(6), 1019.

Golec de Zavala, A., Dyduch-Hazar, K., & Lantos, D. (2019). Collective narcissism: Political consequences of investing self-worth in the ingroup's image. *Political Psychology, 40*, 37–74.

Golec de Zavala, A., & Federico, C. M. (2018). Collective narcissism and the growth of conspiracy thinking over the course of the 2016 United States presidential election: A longitudinal analysis. *European Journal of Social Psychology, 48*(7), 1011–1018.

Golec de Zavala, A., Federico, C. M., Sedikides, C., Guerra, R., Lantos, D., Cypryanska, C., & Baran, T. (2019). *Low self-esteem predicts outgroup derogation via collec-*

tive narcissism, but this relationship is obscured by in-group satisfaction. Manuscript under review.
Golec de Zavala, A., Guerra, R., & Simão, C. (2017). The relationship between the Brexit vote and individual predictors of prejudice: Collective narcissism, right wing authoritarianism, social dominance orientation. *Frontiers in Psychology, 8*, 2023.
Golec de Zavala, A., Peker, M., Guerra, R., & Baran, T. (2016). Collective narcissism predicts hypersensitivity to in-group insult and direct and indirect retaliatory intergroup hostility. *European Journal of Personality, 30*, 532–551.
Gusterson, H. (2017). From Brexit to Trump: Anthropology and the rise of nationalist populism. *American Ethnologist, 44*(2), 209–214.
Harari, Y. N. (2014). *Sapiens: A brief history of humankind.* London, UK: Random House.
Hobsbawm, E. J. (1992). *Nations and nationalism since 1780: Programme, myth, reality.* Cambridge: Cambridge University Press.
Inglehart, R., & Norris, P. (2016). *Trump, Brexit, and the rise of populism: Economic have-nots and cultural backlash.* Paper for the roundtable on "Rage against the machine: Populist politics in the U.S., Europe and Latin America," on 2 September 2016. Annual Meeting of the American Political Science Association, Philadelphia.
Inotai, A. (2007). *The European Union and Southeastern Europe. Troubled waters ahead?* College of Europe Studies No. 7. Peter Lang Editors, Brussels.
Jost, J. T., & Banaji, M. R. (1994). The role of stereotyping in system-justification and the production of false consciousness. *British Journal of Social Psychology, 33* (1), 1–27.
Keller, T. (2010). Hungary on the world values map. *Review of Sociology, 20*, 27–51.
Kelemen, L. (2010). *Mikent velekedjunk a jogrol?* Budapest: Line Design.
Kelemen, L., Szabó, Zs. P., Mészáros, N. Zs., László, J., & Forgas, J. P. (2014). Social cognition and democracy: The relationship between system justification, just world beliefs, authoritarianism, need for closure, and need for cognition in Hungary. *Journal of Social and Political Psychology, 2*, 197–219.
Kleine Zeitung. (2019, May 7). Interview with Viktor Orbán. Vienna, Austria. Retrieved from www.kleinezeitung.at/politik/aussenpolitik/5623229/Orban-im-ExklusivInterview_Budapest-ist-pulsierender-und-kreativer
Koestler, A. (1959). *Sleepwalkers: A history of man's changing vision of the universe.* Hutchinson: London.
Kolosi T., & Tóth I. Gy. (2008). A rendszerváltás nyertesei és vesztesei – generációs oldalnézetből. Tíz állítás a gazdasági átalakulás társadalmi hatásairól. *Társadalmi Riport*, 15–45.
Kruglanski, A. W., & Fishman, S. (2009). The psychology of terrorism: Syndrome versus tool perspectives. *Journal of Terrorism and Political Violence, 18*, 193–215.
Landau, M. J., & Keefer, L. A. (2014). The persuasive power of political metaphors. In J. P. Forgas, W. Crano, & K. Fiedler (Eds.), *Social psychology and politics.* New York: Psychology Press.
Lantos, D., & Forgas, J. P. (2019). *The role of collective narcissism in populist attitudes and the collapse of democracy in Hungary.* Manuscript under review.
László, J. (2005). A történetek tudománya: Bevezetés a narratív pszichológiába. *Pszichológiai Horizont, 3*, 209–223.
László, J. (2014). *Historical tales and national identity. An introduction to narrative social psychology.* London: Routledge.
László, J., & Ehmann, B. (2013). Narrative social psychology. In J. P. Forgas, O. Vincze, & J. László (Eds.), *Social cognition and communication.* New York: Psychology Press.

László, J., & Fülöp, É. (2010). A történelem érzelmi reprezentációja a történelemkönyvekben és naiv elbeszélésekben. *Történelemtanítás*, XLV/3, 1–13.

László J., Szalai K., Ferenczhalmy R. (2010). Role of agency in social representations of history. *Societal and Political Psychology International Review, 1*, 31–43.

Lendvai, P. (2004). *The Hungarians: A thousand years of victory in defeat*. Princeton: University Press.

Lendvai, P. (2012). *Hungary: Between democracy and authoritarianism*. Columbia University Press.

Levin, B., Nolan, J. J., & Reitzel, J. D. (2018, June 26). New data shows US hate crimes continued to rise in 2017. *The Conversation*. Retrieved from http://theconversation.com/new-data-shows-us-hate-crimes-continued-to-rise-in-2017-97989

Majtényi, L., & Miklosi, Z. (Eds.). (2013). *Es mi lesz az alkotmannyal?* Budapest: Eotvos Karoly Intezet.

Marchlewska, M., Cichocka, A., Panayiotou, O., Castellanos, K., & Batayneh, J. (2017). Populism as identity politics: Perceived in-group disadvantage, collective narcissism, and support for populism. *Social Psychological and Personality Science, 9*(2), 151–162. doi:10.1177/1948550617732393

Mihályi, P. (2010). *A magyar privatizacio enciklopediaja. [The encyclopaedia of Hungarian privatization]*. Budapest: Pannon Kiado.

Millon, T. (2006). *Millon Clinical Multiaxial Inventory-III manual*. (3rd ed.). Minneapolis, MN: NCS Pearson.

Myers, D. G. (2019). Psychological science meets a post-truth world. In J. P. Forgas & R. Baumeister (Eds.). *Gullibility: Fake news, conspiracy theories and irrational beliefs* (pp. 77–101). New York: Psychology Press.

Orbán, V. (2014, July 26). *Tusnadfurdoi beszed*. Re-published in https://mandiner.hu/cikk/20180728_orban_viktor_tusnadfurdoi_beszed.

Pinker, S. (2018). *Enlightenment now: The case for reason, science, humanism, and progress*. USA: Penguin Books.

Putnam, A. L., Ross, M. Q., Soter, L. K., & Roediger III, H. L. (2018). Collective narcissism: Americans exaggerate the role of their home state in appraising US history. *Psychological Science, 29*(9), 1414–1422.

Raskin, R., & Terry, H. (1988). A principal-components analysis of the narcissistic personality inventory and further evidence of its construct validity. *Journal of Personality and Social Psychology, 54*(5), 890–902.

Rosling, H. (2019). *Factfulness: Ten reasons we're wrong about the world – and why things are better than you think*. Flatiron Books: New York.

Sallay, H., & Krotos, H. (2004). The development of just world beliefs: A cross-cultural comparison between Japan and Hungary. *Pszichológia, 24*, 233–252.

Samuelsohn, D. (2016). A guide to Donald Trump's "rigged" election. Retrieved May 25, 2019 from www.politico.com/story/2016/10/donald-trump-rigged-election-guide-230302

Scheppele, K. L. (2013, July 3). In praise of the Tavares report. *Hungarian Spectrum*. Retrieved from http://hungarianspectrum.wordpress.com/2013/07/03/kim-lane-scheppele-in-praise-of-the-tavares-report/

Skarżyńska, K., Przybyła, K., & Wójcik, A. (2012). Grupowa martyrologia: Psychologicznefunkcje przekonańo narodowej krzywdzie [Group martyrdom: Psychological functions of beliefs about national victimhood]. *Psychologia Społeczna, 4*, 335–352.

Suurmond, R., van Rhee, H., & Hak, T. (2017). Introduction, comparison and validation of Meta-Essentials: A free and simple tool for meta-analysis. *Research Synthesis Methods, 8*(4), 537–553.

Tajfel, H., & Forgas, J. P. (1981). Social categorization: Cognitions, values and groups. In J. P. Forgas (Ed.), *Social cognition: Perspectives on everyday understanding*. New York: Academic Press.

The Washington Post (2014, August 16). Hungary's illiberalism should not go unchallenged. Retrieved from www.washingtonpost.com/opinions/hungarys-illiberalism-should-not-go-unchallenged/2014/08/16/b2dc72d4-1e5c-11e4-82f9-2cd6fa8da5c4_story.html

Tölgyessy, P. (2013). *Az Orbán rendszer természzete [The nature of the Orban system]*. Komment. Retrieved from www.komment.hu/szerzok/tolgyessy_peter/index.html

Toth, A. (2013). The collapse of the post-communist industrial system in Hungary. *Journal for Labour and Social Affairs in Eastern Europe, 1*, 5–19. www.seer.nomos.de/fileadmin/seer/doc/Aufsatz_SEER_13_01.pdf

van Prooijen, J-W. (2019). Belief in conspiracy theories: Gullibility or rational scepticism? In J. P. Forgas & R. Baumeister (Eds.), *Gullibility: Fake news, conspiracy theories and irrational beliefs* (pp. 319–333). New York: Psychology Press.

von Hippel, W. (2018). *The social leap*. New York: Harper Collins.

Wallen, J. (2018, July 13). "Hungary is the worst": Refugees become punch bag under PM Viktor Orbán. *The Independent*. Retrieved from www.independent.co.uk/news/world/europe/hungary-refugees-immigration-viktor-orban-rac-ism-border-fence-a8446046.html

Wundt, W. (1911). *Probleme der völkerpsychologie* [Problems of social psychology], Leipzig: Wiegandt.

Zakaria, F. (2016). Populism on the march: Why the West is in trouble. *Foreign Affairs, 95*, 9.

Zaromb, F. M., Liu, J. H., Páez, D., Hanke, K., Putnam, A. L., & Roediger III, H. L. (2018). We made history: Citizens of 35 countries overestimate their nation's role in world history. *Journal of Applied Research in Memory and Cognition, 7*(4), 521–528.

Żemojtel-Piotrowska, M., Piotrowski, J., Fatfouta, R., Gebauer, J., Rogoza, J., Czarna, A. … Sedikides, C. (2019). *Towards an agency-communion model of collective narcissism: Communal collective narcissism and its nomological network*. Manuscript under preparation.

15
COLLECTIVE NOSTALGIA AND THE DESIRE TO MAKE ONE'S GROUP GREAT AGAIN

Michael J. A. Wohl and Anna Stefaniak

The human mind is a master time traveler, with the past often being a place of refuge for people who perceive that a cherished group to which they belong (e.g., national, religious, ethnic) is under threat (Smeekes, Verkuyten, & Martinovic, 2015; Wohl, Tabri, & Halperin, in press). The human symbolic ability to project into the future and retrieve the past is also one of the greatest evolutionary accomplishments of our species (see also van Vugt et al., this volume). In terms of projection into the past, this can be accomplished psychologically via collective nostalgic reverie (i.e., sentimental longing or wistful reflection) for the way the group used to be—a time when the ingroup was perceived to be better off than current socioeconomic, cultural, and/or political realities suggest. Collective nostalgia, like other collective emotions such as collective narcissism (see also Forgas & Lantos, this volume), soothes because it strengthens a sense of connection to one's group and its longed-for past (Wildschut, Bruder, Robertson, van Tilburg, & Sedikides, 2014). In other words, it helps members to psychologically reclaim times gone by (i.e., re-establish collective continuity). Moreover, it motivates ingroup members to support ingroup-favoring collective action in the name of recreating the past in the present (e.g., Cheung, Sedikides, Wildschut, Tausch, & Ayanian, 2017; Wohl et al., in press). As such, collective nostalgia is functional group-based emotion.

The applied social-psychological significance of collective nostalgia lies in the perceived loss and change endemic in modernity (Boym, 2001; Davis, 1979), which has given rise to populism in Europe as well as North and South America (Mols & Jetten, 2018; Mudde & Kaltwasser, 2012; see also Forgas, this volume). Populist political entrepreneurs on the left and right have demonstrated a propensity to use collective nostalgic rhetoric (e.g., "Make America Great Again") as a political tool to galvanize the electorate in their favor (Gaston & Hilhorst,

2018). They do so by painting a picture of the in-group's past as having been identity consistent, prosperous, and certain in order to cement (and augment) discontent with the present and anxiety about the future. Critically, however, the picture painted of the ingroup's past may exist only in the minds of those who desire a particular present (i.e., the longed-for past may have never been; Cheung et al., 2017; Liu & Khan, 2014). Indeed, collective nostalgic rhetoric is often used to craft a version of the in-group's (glorious) past as a means to direct support for particular (anti-establishment) socioeconomic, cultural, and/or political agenda.

Although collective nostalgia is not an unfamiliar topic in both social and political psychology, both fields have been remarkably silent about the malleability of collective nostalgia for political ends. In contrast to this prevailing approach, we contend that collective nostalgia is more nuanced and complex than the nascent literature would suggest, and as such, worthy of further reflection and scholarly discourse (and research). In the current chapter, we provide support for this contention within the context of the pervasive extent to which contemporary politics uses collective nostalgia rhetoric to influence the electorate's attitudes about, among other things, the ingroup's security and status. Specifically, we put forth the supposition that the scant empirical work on collective nostalgia has unduly treated the content of the nostalgic reverie (i.e., what kind of past group members are longing for) as noise. The outcome is a dampening of collective nostalgia's predictive utility, which would be heightened by paying closer attention to the signal provided by the content of both political discourse that uses collective nostalgia rhetoric, as well as the collective nostalgia reported by group members. We argue that the content of collective nostalgia is highly informative, because it will determine the paths that group members and group leaders are likely to take to re-establish group continuity and secure a better future for the in-group.

Days of Future Past: Social (Mis)representations of Collective Continuity

Group history is the bedrock of social identity. The stories a group tells about its past provide members with a common understanding of current lived experiences (Bar-Tal, 2007). They do so by informing members who they are (i.e., they define the central values, beliefs, and norms of the group), where they came from (i.e., a shared history), and where they are going (i.e., a common fate; Liu & Hilton, 2005; Moscovici, 1988; Páez & Liu, 2011; Wohl, Squires, & Caouette, 2012). They also draw implicit as well as explicit connections between contemporary and future group members with those of the past (Hilton, Erb, McDermott, & Molian, 1996; Liu, Wilson, McClure, & Higgins, 1999). For example, during the Amidah—the central prayer of the Jewish liturgy—Jews read silently as well as sing the phrase "l'dor va'dor," which translates to "from generation to generation." The practice of "l'dor va'dor" is also a central tenet of Jewish education. Jews are instructed to make connections between generations via the adherence to, as well as the passing along of, Jewish traditions. The outcome is a sense that the group is collectively continuous and enduring through the vicissitudes of time (Reicher & Hopkins, 2001; Sani et al., 2007)—that core cultural traits (values, beliefs, and norms) are transmitted over time in a coherent manner with high fidelity.

The narratives that undergird stories about the group's past also tend to be communicated in such a way that members are instilled with a belief in the positive uniqueness of the ingroup relative to "others" (Reicher & Hopkins, 2001; Sani et al., 2007; Sani, Herrera, & Bowe, 2009; see also Forgas, this volume), and the conviction that the in-group holds a special (and exalted) place in the unfolding narrative of humanity (see Bar-Tal, 2007). Importantly, these narratives are weaved together into a representation or specific manifestation that positions the group as a temporally constituted and enduring community that stretches back into the past and forward into the future (Kahn, Klar, & Roccas, 2017; Sani et al., 2007, 2009). Such a sense of collective continuity affords group members existential security (i.e., "we were, we are, and we always will be"; Jetten & Wohl, 2012; Solomon, Greenberg, & Pyszczynski, 1991), and in so doing casts the group as a vehicle for symbolic immortality (see Smeekes & Verkuyten, 2013). Although one's corporeal form is finite, that part of the self that is derived by one's group membership is (perceived to be) eternal.

Despite the intent of groups' social representation of their past as collectively continuous, the central values, beliefs, and norms of the group are not static. Change can and does occur. For example, the current manifestation of "American values" would behest action to stop and bring to justice those who engage in human trafficking, despite the fact that it was once a normative and legal activity in America. Whether by way of economic recession or boom, intergroup cooperation or competition, or cultural shifts, all social groups undergo change. To co-opt an observation Woody Allen made about relationships, a social group is like a shark. It has to continually move forward, or it dies. In other words, groups need to adapt to their current environ, or they run the risk of going the way of the Assyrians, the Vikings, the Whigs, and the Know-Nothings, as well as the Shakers—groups that now lack a single member.

Despite the ubiquity (and arguably necessity) of change experienced by the ingroup over the course of its existence, its occurrence is frequently appraised to be a threat to collective continuity (Jetten & Hutchison, 2011; Jetten & Wohl, 2012). This is because the group provides the existential ground on which the social self stands, and thus perceived threat to the collective continuity of the in-group is unsettling to members (Lewin, 1948). Perceived threat also heightens the belief in the need of, and right to redress (Smeekes & Verkuyten, 2013; Wohl et al., 2012). For example, Jetten and Wohl (2012) presented English participants with narratives about their nation's history as being either connected to the present (collective continuity) or disconnected (collective discontinuity). Those who read that England is losing connection to its illustrious heritage (i.e., the English of today and the English of yesteryear are becoming two very different peoples) expressed greater opposition to immigration than those who read that the ingroup's past has strong connections with the present (i.e., the English of today have remained true to the English of yesteryear). Importantly, they also found that collective angst mediated the relation between perceived collective discontinuity and anti-immigration sentiments. That is, perceiving the group to be losing ties to its past increased concern for the group's future vitality and action perceived to protect the ingroup's future. These results provide evidence that change is perceived to endanger collective continuity, which is often met with resistance.

When change is detected, the result can lead to group schisms—as was the case with the American Baptist Church, which splintered over its decision to relax its policies on homosexuality in the denomination (Tomlin, 2006). More prevalent, however, is that the occurrence of change is underplayed or resisted to preserve a sense of collective continuity (Boym, 2007; Hamilton, Levine, & Thurston, 2008). One way that groups resist change is via narratives that elicit collective nostalgic reverie (i.e., sentimental longing) for the group's (real or imagined) *past* (Boym, 2001; Davis, 1979; Smeekes & Verkuyten, 2015; Wildschut et al., 2014). Specifically, in times of change, group members begin to feel that the past and present are becoming untethered. Collective nostalgia functions to motivate collective action to fortify those tethers and achieve and maintain collective continuity (Cheung et al., 2017).

The Applied Social Psychology of Collective Nostalgia

Nostalgia, a compound of the Greek *nostos* (return) and *algos* (pain), was coined by Swiss physician Johannes Hofer to describe the homesickness (i.e., longing for home) Swiss mercenaries expressed while fighting in foreign countries. Although originally positioned as indicative of the presence of an underlying psychiatric disorder (as is the case with collective narcissism; see also Forgas & Lantos, this volume), it is now understood to be a coping mechanism used in times of change or crisis (see Sedikides, Wildschut, Arndt, & Routledge, 2008; Sedikides, Wildschut, Routledge, & Arndt, 2015; Sedikides, Wildschut, Routledge, Arndt, Hepper, & Zhou, 2015). For example, Kim and Wohl (2015) found that people who are experiencing negative life events that are associated with problem drinking or disordered gambling report a greater willingness to engage in behavior change when they experience nostalgic (measured or manipulated) reverie for the life they lived before drinking or gambling entered their behavioral repertoire. More recently, in two longitudinal studies, Wohl et al., (2018) showed that nostalgic reverie for the pre-addicted self improved the odds of a self-reported quit attempt among those living with addiction. One reason for nostalgia's behavior change utility is that addiction is often accompanied by a feeling of "identity loss" or "identity spoilage" as a result of the addictive behavior (Best et al., 2016; Dingle, Cruwys, & Frings, 2015; Frings & Albery, 2015; McIntosh & McKeganey, 2000; Waldorf & Biernacki, 1981). Nostalgia helps people re-establish connection to the person they used to be, which heightens a sense of identity continuity (Iyer & Jetten, 2011).

The power of nostalgia also resides in its ability to fortify meaning in life (Routledge, Arndt, Sedikides, & Wildschut, 2008; Routledge et al., 2011), which is often at a deficit among those who experience significant life distress (Coleman, Kaplan, & Downing, 1986; Nicholson et al., 1994), including existential anxiety (i.e., concern about one's own mortality; Juhl, Routledge, Arndt, Sedikides, & Wildschut, 2010; Routledge, et al., 2008). Indeed, Routledge and colleagues (2011) showed that nostalgia is a psychological resource that can be harnessed to derive and sustain a sense of meaning in life. There is good reason why nostalgia provides people with meaning. Nostalgic episodes typically reference significant life events, which involve social connectedness and highlight one's values and traditions (see Wildschut, Sedikides, Arndt, & Routledge, 2006). In fact, although nostalgia is a self-relevant emotion, most significant events about which people were nostalgic are social in nature (e.g., a birthday party, trips with friends or family members, rites of passage; Sedikides & Wildschut, 2018).

Given the social aspect of nostalgia, it is only logical that nostalgia can also be experienced for a bygone time that is group-relevant. According to intergroup emotions theory (Mackie & Smith, 1998; Smith & Mackie, 2008, 2015), people experience emotions not only as a result of their personal experiences and thoughts, but also as a consequence of their membership in social groups. Such group-based emotions are experienced as a result of the process of social identification (Tajfel & Turner, 1986) and self-categorization as a group member (Turner & Oaks, 1986). Specifically, events that are appraised as being relevant to the ingroup elicit group-based emotions. The type of group-based emotion experiences is dependent on the appraisal process. For example, when people appraise the actions of their ingroup to be discordant with the ingroup's or their personal values, they are apt to feel collective guilt (Doosje, Branscombe, Spears, & Manstead, 1998). Crucially, people can feel this group-based emotion even for the misdeeds that were committed long before contemporary members were born (for a review see Wohl, Branscombe, & Klar, 2006). Via the same social identification process, people who appraise the ingroup's past in a more positive light than the ingroup's present may feel collective nostalgia (i.e., sentimental longing) for a bygone time in their ingroup's past (e.g., their nation), even if the past that they long for was not a part of their lived experience (Cheung et al., 2017; Smeekes & Verkuyten, 2015; Smeekes et al., 2015; Smeekes et al., 2018; Wildschut et al., 2014).

Importantly, the temporal comparison at the heart of collective nostalgia is often elicited by social change and transition (Boym, 2001; Davis, 1979).

Indeed, rapidly occurring social change, such as an influx of refugees in the European Union since 2015, or increased immigration and demographic racial shift in the United States, is often construed as a threat to collective continuity (Sedikides, Wildschut, & Baden, 2004), which elicits concern for the future vitality of one's (national) group (see Wohl et al., 2012). As a consequence, group members tend to turn to the past as a way to cope with a potentially unwanted future and, in the process, retain or regain collective continuity (Jetten & Wohl, 2012; Smeekes et al., 2018; see also Forgas, this volume). For example, a cross-cultural study involving 27 countries found that perceived threats to the group's future vitality elicited collective nostalgia, which was associated with an increased sense of group belonging and collective continuity (Smeekes et al., 2018). To the point, disruptions (real or perceived) to perceived collective continuity (i.e., collective discontinuity) elicit collective nostalgia, which helps re-establish collective continuity. In this way, collective nostalgia constitutes a coping strategy (see Milligan, 2003; Sedikides, Wildschut, Gaertner, Routledge, & Arndt, 2008).

Collective nostalgia also focuses people's attention on the perceived cause of the collective discontinuity, which can have ramifications for intergroup relations. For example, when young people in the Netherlands were manipulated to feel collective discontinuity, the result was increased willingness to restrict religious expression rights of Muslims (Smeekes & Verkuyten, 2013). Thus, besides the positive, continuity-restoring properties, research on collective nostalgia has also established its negative consequences for intergroup relations. Nostalgia refocuses people's attention on their group's past and through this, it also highlights that those who do not share this past (e.g., immigrants), are not a part of the ingroup. It therefore accentuates the "us" versus "them" distinction which, in line with the self-categorization theory, contributes to more negative attitudes toward outgroups (Mols & Jetten, 2014; Smeekes, 2015; Turner, Hogg, Oakes, Reicher, & Wetherell, 1987). In line with this argument, collective nostalgia has been shown to be associated with negative attitudes toward national minorities in the Netherlands (Smeekes, 2015; Smeekes et al., 2015), anger toward mainland China, and greater support for ingroup benefitting collective action among Hong Kongese (Cheung et al., 2017), negative views of new employees by old-timers following an organizational transition (Milligan, 2003), and hostile attitudes toward newcomers to an urban neighborhood in New York by more established inhabitants (Kasinitz & Hillyard, 1995).

Not all Sentimental Longings are Created Equal

Unfortunately, existing applied research on the consequences of collective nostalgia may be biased because it has treated the content of collective nostalgic reflection as noise, a common problem when theoretical concepts are translated into real-life applied settings (see also Fiedler, this volume). Doing so hinders the utility of collective nostalgia as a predictor of the ways in which members try to reclaim the ingroup's treasured past. This is because, undeniably, different group members may long for different aspects of the group's past. Although collective memory underscores the group's unique identity that endures through the vicissitudes of time, there is variance in the particular stories that members tell of their group's past (Liu & Hilton, 2005). In some instances, there is high consensus about what constitutes a group's *charter*—the representation of the most important events and figures, critical to the group's identity and its perceived mission (Hilton & Liu, 2008). However, even though members may agree on the significance of a given event in their group's past (e.g., World War II; Liu et al., 2005), social representations of the ingroup may also be polemic (Moscovici, 1984, 1988) and differ from one group member to the next.

The selection of what is remembered about that past may be shaped by the contemporary political agenda of group members (or a subset of group members) as well as group leaders. According to Hilton and Liu (2008):

> Changes in group agendas may render certain aspects of their history more relevant than others for political purposes. The existence of historical records (books, recordings, memorials) and professional groups dedicated to the preservation and interpretation of historical knowledge (archaeologists, archivists, historians etc.) means that events that have effectively disappeared from public consciousness can be resurrected as part of a historical charter when the need arises.
>
> *p. 348*

In line with this supposition, highly identified group members have been shown to recall fewer instances of historical wrongdoings of their groups (Sahdra & Ross, 2007). They also employ a host of strategies (e.g., selective "forgetting" of certain facts, reinterpretation, or blaming others for the ingroup's wrongdoings) to arrive at an acceptable version of group history (Baumeister & Hastings, 1997), thus maintaining a positive perception of the ingroup. To the point, social representation of the ingroup's past can be highly biased by the group-based goals (Baumeister & Hastings, 1997; Lewicka, 2008; 2011; Sahdra & Ross, 2007).

Representations of the ingroup's past can also be influenced by events that affect an individual group member. Bilewicz, Stefaniak, Barth, Witkowska, and Fritsche (2019), for example, found that people induced to feel they do not have control over their life compensated for this lack of (personal) general agency by expressing interest in aspects of their national history that evidenced moral agency. In a like manner, people may compensate for perceived personal-level threat by focusing on and longing for a (perceived) period in their group's past when such threats did not exist. For instance, if someone feels their personal safety or economic security is threatened by an immigrant group, they may compensate by focusing on a time when their society was more homogeneous. The net effect should be a desire to reclaim a time when the ingroup was more homogeneous. However, if the content of the collective nostalgia was different (e.g., a time when different groups lived together in a more harmonious manner), the outcome of the collective nostalgic reverie would likely be more prosocial.

To the point, the content of nostalgia matters for intergroup relations. In line with this supposition, Wohl and Smeekes (2019) found that while some group members long for a past in which the ingroup was more homogeneous (*homogeneity-focused collective nostalgia*) other group members long for a past in which the ingroup was more open and tolerant (*openness-focused collective nostalgia*). Specifically, they argued that homogeneity-focused collective nostalgia is triggered among group members who feel (or are manipulated to feel) that they live in a time of rapid social or cultural change. When threats of this ilk are experienced, group members should become motivated to strengthen adherence to ingroup's norms and values (see Riek, Mania, & Gaertner, 2006; Stephan & Stephan, 2000). Indeed, Wohl and Smeekes (2019) found that people who feel homogeneity-focused nostalgia (measured or manipulated) are apt to reject outgroups, particularly those seen as different from the ingroup in terms of culture and values (e.g., Muslim immigrants in the Western world; see also Smeekes & Verkuyten, 2013). They also found that some group members experience openness-focused nostalgia. This kind of collective nostalgia is experienced by group members who feel that their contemporaries are losing sympathy or indulgence for beliefs or practice that differ from or conflict with the ingroup. Put another way, group members who experience openness-focused nostalgia believe that the ingroup is becoming untethered from its moral core. In response, they are apt to support policies that demonstrate sympathy for outgroup's as well as their beliefs and practices.

To put a dark line under the issue, the content of the collective nostalgia group members report provides a signal for what is ailing a group and its members. That signal can then be used to predict as well as manipulate group members' attitudes and behavior. Group leaders have demonstrated an intuitive understanding of this process by attempting to amplify the experience of a particular collective nostalgia via their rhetoric—rhetoric they think will resonate with ordinary people to serve their political agenda. Indeed, political leaders are well aware of the mobilizing effect of referring to the ingroup's glorious past to gain political support (Hilton & Liu, 2008). For example, former US President Barack Obama used nostalgia to advance the rights of immigrants in the name of "allegiance to our founding principles" (see Obama, 2013). However, collective nostalgia has also been used to galvanize an electorate that has social, cultural, and economic grievances. Indeed, collective nostalgia and the associated promise to make the group great *again* has been argued to be central to the rise of populism in Europe and North America (see Betz & Johnson, 2004; Mudde

& Kaltwasser, 2012). Mobilizing collective nostalgia can also be method for identifying "enemies" and preparing aggression against deviants (see Krahé, this volume).

While the studies of collective nostalgia content conducted to date addressed its openness-focused and homogeneity-focused aspects, the content of collective nostalgia is likely more expansive. This is because collective nostalgia is shaped by the current (perceived) socio-political and cultural needs of the ingroup, and is therefore context-specific. At the personal level, the frustration of a basic human need (e.g., autonomy) motivates the desire to fulfill that basic need (Maslow, 1943; Kenrick, Griskevicius, Neuberg, & Schaller, 2010; Ryan & Deci, 2017). Likewise, at the group level we expect that frustration of specific group-based needs will motivate group members to seek consolation in their group's past as a mechanism to fulfil those needs. Nostalgia for communism in Poland, Hungary, and Russia, for instance, has been shown to be more common among people who did not fare well during political transformation (operationalized by lower income or living standards; Prusik & Lewicka, 2016; White, 2010; see also data in Forgas & Lantos, this volume). Similarly, it can be expected that groups that find themselves facing a financial crisis may nostalgize about former economic stability, those who live in a time of social unrest will likely look back fondly on times of relative tranquility, and inhabitants of former empires that are losing their dominant position may experience nostalgic reverie for the days of greater power.

Collective Nostalgia and Populism

Various theorists have argued that collective nostalgia is a core feature of populist ideology (e.g., Betz & Johnson, 2004; Taggart, 2004)—an ideology in which the past is portrayed as a closed and conflict-free whole, carried by ordinary people who shared similar beliefs, norms, and traditions (see Duyvendak, 2011). Populists seek to create a deep sense of longing among "ordinary people" for the good ol' days. More specifically, populists strategically appeal to people who believe they are losing out socially, culturally, and/or economically and try to instill such beliefs in others (Gaston & Hilhorst, 2018; Inglehart & Norris, 2016). The populist rhetoric focuses on a need to return to how things used to be, which can only be accomplished with the populist leader at the helm (Forgas & Lantos, this volume). Indeed, elicitation of collective nostalgia has been a critical tool in the arsenal of populist politicians who employ it to harness support and remove the establishment elites (who have allowed discontinuity to come about; Mols & Jetten, 2014).

Unfortunately, loss and change are endemic in modernity (Boym, 2001; Davis, 1979). According to Boym (2007), collective nostalgia-based rhetoric emerged as a reaction to and a defense against the rapidly-changing world and groups' inability to stop or slow down these changes. Similar cultural processes also occurred earlier in the 19th century when the romantic movement articulated a powerful sense of collective nostalgia about the pre-modern world. Populist politicians exploit people's need for collective continuity by creating versions of the ingroup's past that upregulate collective nostalgia. Importantly, these visions of the past need not have much in common with historical reality. They merely need to create a sense of connection to populist leaders' version of what the group used to be and promise to bring that version back to the present. In this way, populists tempt their followers to "relinquish critical thinking for emotional bonding" to the glories of what the group used to be and what it could once again become (Boym, 2007, p. 9). Donald Trump's electoral success constitutes a striking example of the efficacy of using collective nostalgia (i.e., "Make American Great Again") as a populist tool.

Providing empirical support for the connection between collective nostalgia and populism, Smeekes (in press) found that Dutch people who report feeling collective nostalgia are more apt to support Partij voor de Vrijheid (in translation: Party for Freedom), which is a right-wing populist party. Moreover, this link was mediated by the perception that "real" Dutch people must have Dutch roots (*nativist ideology*). Although collective nostalgia was assessed using general items (e.g., "I long for the Netherlands of the past"), and in light of the fact that nostalgia was associated with nativist ideology, it is very likely that participants were experiencing homogeneity-focused nostalgia. If so, this would suggest that homogeneity-focused nostalgia is a predictor of support for right-wing populism. This supposition is based on an understanding of conservatism and right-wing populism as being anchored in the rejection of social change coupled with a focus on established institutions and traditions framed as emanating from generational wisdom (see Eccleshall, 2003). Importantly, those who support traditional values of conformity and heightened attention to group-based security issues display a general opposition to change (Jost, Glaser, Kruglanski, & Sulloway, 2003).

Unfortunately, the existing nostalgia literature has treated nostalgia as being synonymous with homogeneity-focused nostalgia. For example, Lammers and Baldwin (2018) argued that not only are conservatives (i.e., people on the political right) more prone to experience nostalgia compared to liberals, but also that collective nostalgia can be used as a tool to harness support from conservatives. In support of this supposition, they demonstrated that conservatives can be manipulated to support traditionally liberal positions (e.g., restricting gun rights, greater leniency with regard to immigration or increasing social diversity) by framing these positions as a means to return the country to its roots. Conservatives' affinity for the past is perhaps why conservative (compared to liberal) news outlets and State of the Union addresses made by conservative (compared to liberal) US Presidents are more apt to use past-tense verbs than future-tense verbs (see Robinson, Cassidy, Boyd, & Fetterman, 2015). Being so anchored in the past plays well with a populist narrative that highlights the presence of unwanted change and the threat of additional unwanted change.

However, it is not only right-wing politicians who employ nostalgic rhetoric to achieve political goals. A broad analysis of collective nostalgia in Great Britain, Germany, and France (Gaston & Hilhorst, 2018) revealed that left-wing politicians also use collective nostalgia as a rhetorical tool to appeal to the general societal sense of decline and crisis in social, cultural, and economic domains. For instance, supporters of the "Remain" campaign in the Brexit referendum evoked images of British soldiers fighting for the unity of Europe in World War II (Johnston, 2016). Moreover, in the United States, Bernie Sanders, the left-wing political candidate for democratic presidential nomination in 2016, frequently appealed to the well-paying working-class jobs of the past in his campaign (Mudde, 2016).

In light of Wohl and Smeekes' (2019) distinction between homogeneity-focused and openness-focused collective nostalgia, we argue that conservatives may not be simply more prone to experiencing this collective emotion, but that investigations conducted to date simply focused on the former type and largely neglected the existence of the latter, which will likely be more prevalent among people on the left of the political spectrum. For example, whereas Donald Trump clearly used collective nostalgia in an attempt to cement anti-immigration sentiments, Barack Obama used collective nostalgia to advance the rights of immigrants in the name of "upholding the traditions of this country." In short, how ingroup history is represented conditions how group members relate to members of their own group and other groups (i.e., outgroups), as well as their position on current political issues.

On the Importance of Studying the Contents of Social-Psychological Processes

Investigating specific contents of collective nostalgic reverie, as well as their unique antecedents and consequences, fits into a broader trend to contextualize social-psychological processes. Indeed, John Turner (1999, p. 34) argued that "process theories such as social identity and self-categorization require the incorporation of specific content into their analyses before they can make predictions either in the laboratory or the field and are designed to require such an incorporation" (on a related point, see also Crano & Ruybal, this volume; Fiedler, this volume; Petty & Briñol, this volume). Although social psychology as a discipline recognizes the validity of paying closer attention to the contents of identity and group representations and the role that specific content plays in shaping people's thoughts and behavior, it rarely does so in practice (Reicher & Hopkins, 2001).

A notable exemption is provided by research on modes of ingroup identification, which shows that social identification is a complex and multifaceted phenomenon (e.g., Cameron, 2004; Jackson & Smith, 1999; Leach et al., 2008; Luhtanen & Crocker, 1992; Roccas, Klar, & Liviatan, 2006). One crucial distinction differentiates identification that is associated with pro-group adaptive behavior from identification that is primarily related to derogation and rejection of outgroups in aim to assert ingroup's dominance. These two types have been referred to as pseudo-patriotism and patriotism (Adorno, Frenkel-Brunswik, Levinson, & Sanford, 1950); insecure and secure social identity (Jackson & Smith, 1999); blind and constructive patriotism (Schatz, Staub, & Lavine, 1999); nationalism and patriotism (Kosterman & Feshbach, 1989; Mummendey, Klink, & Brown, 2001); or glorification and attachment (Roccas et al., 2006).

Recently, Cichocka (2016) proposed to systematize the understanding of these different types of identification under the umbrella terms of *secure* and an *insecure* (narcissistic) *in-group positivity*. The former is an emanation of a stable individual self while the latter stems from unfulfilled individual-level needs that people attempt to satisfy by belonging to a strong group. Recognizing the complexity of identity allowed researchers to better understand its origins and consequences and to explain research results previously regarded as contradictory (Forgas, this volume). For instance, social identity theory posits that outgroup derogation may be one way to achieve a positive social identity; however, strong social identification does not always correlate with outgroup-directed prejudice (e.g., Amiot & Aubin, 2013; Hopkins & Reicher, 2011; Jackson & Smith, 1999). Although strong insecure ingroup identification is related to greater prejudice (e.g., Cai & Gries, 2013; Golec de Zavala & Cichocka, 2012), secure ingroup positivity, without the narcissistic component, shows a *negative* relation with prejudice—that is, people who strongly identify with their groups in a secure manner are *less* prejudiced toward outgroups (Golec de Zavala, Cichocka, & Bilewicz, 2013).

Contents and meanings that people associate with membership in different social categories depend not only on their individual needs but are also powerfully shaped by social and historical context. Reicher and Hopkins (2001) point out that the meaning of the ingroup and outgroup categories should not be thought of as stable, but instead as a product of the current comparative context (see also Turner, Oakes, Haslam, & McGarty, 1994). Indeed, ingroup and outgroup stereotypes change as a function of the context (Haslam, Turner, Oakes, McGarty, & Hayes, 1992; Hopkins, Regan, & Abell, 1997; Rabinovich, Morton, Postmes, & Verplanken, 2012). For instance, Scots rated their own group as more aloof and hardworking when compared to Greeks, and as warmer and less aloof when the ratings were made in the context of the English (Hopkins et al., 1997).

Current interest in collective memory and social representations of history (see Assmann, 1995; Forgas & Lantos, this volume; Hilton & Liu, 2017; Liu & Hilton, 2005; Liu & László, 2007; Olick, 1999; Wertsch, 2002) demonstrates that scholars increasingly engage with the particulars of historical and cultural contexts (see also Blanton, Burrows, & Regan, this volume; Jussim et al., this volume; Kross & Chandhok, this volume; van Vugt et al., this volume). This allows them to better understand intergroup relations and explain situations in which groups react differently to ostensibly similar events because of their divergent representations of the past (Hilton & Liu, 2008). For instance, Hanke and colleagues (2013) investigated the role of interpretations of a violent intergroup conflict in shaping group members' willingness to forgive a historical perpetrator (see also Krahé, this volume). In a study carried out in Taiwan, the Philippines, China, France, Poland, and Russia the level of forgiveness for Japanese and German war atrocities was determined by different interpretations of World War II. Even such well-established processes as intergroup contact (Allport, 1954; Pettigrew & Tropp, 2011) have been shown to depend on the social context. Specifically, intergroup contact that occurs during intense conflict (Pettigrew & Tropp, 2011; Paolini, Harwood, & Rubin, 2010) or focuses on troubled intergroup history (Bilewicz, 2007), may lead to reinforcement of intergroup prejudice rather than to its reduction. Focusing on a difficult intergroup history seems to nullify the positive effects of intergroup contacts, even among people who were not involved in the traumatic historical events themselves (Bilewicz, 2007).

In a similar vein, we argue that collective nostalgia should not be treated as a unidimensional phenomenon. Unfortunately, the prevailing approach positions nostalgia as a characteristic of conservatives (Lammers & Baldwin, 2018) and right-wing populists, and threats the content of collective nostalgia as noise. One outcome is the overemphasis of the negative impacts of collective nostalgia (e.g., the absolution of guilt and shame of group members who do wrong in the name of bringing back the ingroup's glory days; see Boym, 2007; Kammen, 1991). Likewise, social scientists have almost exclusively focused on the adverse effects of collective nostalgia for intergroup relations (e.g., Smeekes & Verkuyten, 2013). Applying a more fine-grained approach to studying collective nostalgia allows us, in a way similar to the processes described above, to investigate different forms of nostalgic content and the circumstances under which people are more attracted to one or the other.

Conclusion

Experiencing a sense of discontinuity between a cherished ingroup's past and an unfavorably evaluated present elicits collective nostalgia. Recent electoral victories of populist right-wing politicians in many countries around the world underscore the relevance of collective nostalgia, which is eagerly utilized by populists to garner political support. So much so that arguments were put forward that nostalgia is a predominantly conservative/right-wing emotion (Lammers & Baldwin, 2018). In this chapter we demonstrated that investigating the contents of collective nostalgia (i.e., what exactly group members feel nostalgic about) provides a crucial piece of the puzzle, largely neglected in the extant literature. A greater focus on the content of the collective nostalgia that group members are experiencing will only serve to increase the predictive utility of this group-based emotion.

Author Note

The authors declare that there are no potential conflicts of interest with respect to authorship, and/or publication of this article. Preparation of this article was supported by a research grant from the Social Sciences and Humanities Research Council of Canada Insight Grant as well as the Ontario Ministry of Health and Long-Term Care to Wohl. Correspondence concerning this article should be addressed to Michael J. A. Wohl, Department of Psychology, Carleton University, 1125 Colonel By Drive, Ottawa, Ontario, Canada, K1S 5B6. Tel: (902) 520–2600 x 2908, Email: michael.wohl@carleton.ca

References

Adorno, T. W., Frenkel-Brunswik, E., Levinson, D. J., & Sanford, R. N. (1950). *The authoritarian personality*. New York, NY: Harper.

Allport, G. (1954). *The nature of prejudice*. Cambridge, MA: Perseus Books.

Amiot, C. E., & Aubin, R. M. (2013). Why and how are you attached to your social group? Investigating different forms of social identification. *British Journal of Social Psychology, 52*, 563–586.

Assmann, J. (1995). Collective memory and cultural identity. *New German Critique, 65*, 125–133.

Bar-Tal, D. (2007). Sociopsychological foundations of intractable conflicts. *American Behavioral Scientist, 50*, 1430–1453.

Baumeister, R. F., & Hastings, S. (1997). Distortions of collective memory: How groups flatter themselves. In J. W. Pennebaker, D. Páez & B. Rimé (Eds.), *Collective memory of political events. Social psychological perspective* (pp. 277–293). Mahwah, NJ: Lawrence Erlbaum Associates.

Best, D., Beckwith, M., Haslam, C. A., Jetten, J., Mawson, E., & Lubman, D. I. (2016). Overcoming alcohol and other drug addiction as a process of social identity transition: The social identity model of recovery (SIMOR). *Addiction Research & Theory, 24*, 111–123.

Betz, H-G., & Johnson, C. (2004). Against the current – Stemming the tide: The nostalgic ideology of the contemporary radical populist right. *Journal of Political Ideologies, 9*, 311–327.

Bilewicz, M. (2007). History as an obstacle: Impact of temporal-based social categorizations on Polish-Jewish intergroup contact. *Group Processes & Intergroup Relations, 10*, 551–563.

Bilewicz, M., Stefaniak, A., Barth, M., Witkowska, M., & Fritsche, I. (2019). The role of control motivation in Germans' and Poles' interest in history. *Social Psychological Bulletin, 14*(2).

Boym, S. (2001). *The future of nostalgia*. New York, NY: Basic Books.

Boym, S. (2007). Nostalgia and its discontents. *The Hedgehog Review, 9*, 7–19.

Cai, H., & Gries, P. (2013). National narcissism: Internal dimensions and international correlates. *PsyCh Journal, 2*, 122–132.

Cameron, J. E. (2004). A three-factor model of social identity. *Self and Identity, 3*, 239–262.

Cheung, W. Y., Sedikides, C., Wildschut, T., Tausch, N., & Ayanian, A. H. (2017). Collective nostalgia is associated with stronger outgroup-directed anger and participation in ingroup-favoring collective action. *Journal of Social and Political Psychology, 5*, 301–319.

Cichocka, A. (2016). Understanding defensive and secure in-group positivity: The role of collective narcissism. *European Review of Social Psychology, 27*, 283–317.

Coleman, S. B., Kaplan, J. D., & Downing, R. W. (1986). Life cycle and loss—The spiritual vacuum of heroin addiction. *Family Process, 25*, 5–23.

Davis, F. (1979). *Yearning for yesterday: A sociology of nostalgia*. New York, NY: Free Press.

Dingle, G. A., Cruwys, T., & Frings, D. (2015). Social identities as pathways into and out of addiction. *Frontiers in Psychology, 6*.

Doosje, B., Branscombe, N. R., Spears, R., & Manstead, A. S. (1998). Guilty by association: When one's group has a negative history. *Journal of Personality and Social Psychology, 75*, 872–886.

Duyvendak, J. W. (2011). *The politics of home: Belonging and nostalgia in Western Europe and the United States*. Basingstoke, UK: Palgrave Macmillan.

Eccleshall, R. (2003). Conservatism. In V. Geoghegan, R. Eccleshall, M. Lloyd, I. MacKenzie, R. Wilford, M. Kenny, & A. Findlayson (Eds.), *Political ideologies: An introduction* (3rd ed., pp. 47–72). Taylor & Francis: e-library.

Frings, D., & Albery, I. P. (2015). The social identity model of cessation maintenance: Formulation and initial evidence. *Addictive Behaviors, 44*, 35–42.

Gaston, S., & Hilhorst, S. (2018). *At home in one's past: Nostalgia as a cultural and political force in Britain, France and Germany*. Demos. Retrieved from: https://demos.co.uk/project/nostalgia/

Golec de Zavala, A., & Cichocka, A. (2012). Collective narcissism and anti-Semitism in Poland. *Group Processes & Intergroup Relations, 15*, 213–229.

Golec de Zavala, A., Cichocka, A., & Bilewicz, M. (2013). The paradox of in-group love: Differentiating collective narcissism advances understanding of the relationship between in-group and out-group attitudes. *Journal of Personality, 81*, 16–28.

Hamilton, D. L., Levine, J. M., & Thurston, J. A. (2008). Perceiving continuity and change in groups. In F. Sani (Ed.), *Self continuity: Individual and collective perspectives* (pp. 117–130). New York, NY: Psychology Press.

Hanke, K., Liu, J. H., Hilton, D. J., Bilewicz, M., Garber, I., Huang, L. L., ... & Wang, F. (2013). When the past haunts the present: Intergroup forgiveness and historical closure in post World War II societies in Asia and in Europe. *International Journal of Intercultural Relations, 37*, 287–301.

Haslam, S. A., Turner, J. C., Oakes, P. J., McGarty, C., & Hayes, B. K. (1992). Context-dependent variation in social stereotyping: The effects of intergroup relations as mediated by social change and frame of reference. *European Journal of Social Psychology, 22*, 3–20.

Hilton, D. J., Erb, H.-P., McDermott, M., & Molian, D. J. (1996). Social representations of history and attitudes to European unification in Britain, France, and Germany. In G. Breakwell & E. Lyons (Eds), *Changing European identities: Social psychological analyses of social change* (pp. 275–295). Oxford, UK: Butterworth-Heinemann.

Hilton, D. J., & Liu, J. H. (2008). Culture and inter-group relations. The role of social representations of history. In R. Sorrentino & S. Yamaguchi (Eds.), *The handbook of motivation and cognition: The cultural context* (pp. 343–368). New York, NY: Guilford Press.

Hilton, D., & Liu, J. (2017). History as a narrative of the people: From function to structure and content. *Memory Studies, 10*, 297–309.

Hopkins, N., Regan, M., & Abell, J. (1997). On the context dependence of national stereotypes: Some Scottish data. *British Journal of Social Psychology, 36*, 553–563.

Hopkins, N., & Reicher, S. (2011). Identity, culture and contestation: Social identity as cross-cultural theory. *Psychological Studies, 56*, 36–43.

Inglehart, R. F., & Norris, P. (2016). Trump, Brexit, and the rise of populism: Economic have-nots and cultural backlash. *HKS Working Paper No. RWP16-026*. Retrieved from: https://papers.ssrn.com/sol3/papers.cfm?abstract_id=2818659

Iyer, A., & Jetten, J. (2011). What's left behind: Identity continuity moderates the effect of nostalgia on well-being and life choices. *Journal of Personality and Social Psychology, 101*, 94–108.

Jackson, J. W., & Smith, E. R. (1999). Conceptualizing social identity: A new framework and evidence for the impact of different dimensions. *Personality and Social Psychology Bulletin, 25*, 120–135.

Jetten, J., & Hutchison, P. (2011). When groups have a lot to lose: Historical continuity enhances resistance to a merger. *European Journal of Social Psychology, 41*, 335–343.

Jetten, J., & Wohl, M. J. A. (2012). The past as a determinant of the present: Historical continuity, collective angst, and opposition to immigration. *European Journal of Social Psychology, 42*, 442–450.

Johnston, C. (2016, May 9). Second World War veterans say Brexit risks stability they fought for. *The Guardian*. Retrieved from www.theguardian.com/politics/2016/may/09/war-veterans-brexit-risk-stability

Jost, J. T., Glaser, J., Kruglanski, A. W., & Sulloway, F. (2003). Political conservatism as motivated social cognition. *Psychological Bulletin, 129*, 339–375.

Juhl, J., Routledge, C., Arndt, J., Sedikides, C., & Wildschut, T. (2010). Fighting the future with the past: Nostalgia buffers existential threat. *Journal of Research in Personality, 44*, 309–314.

Kahn, D. T., Klar, Y., & Roccas, S. (2017). For the sake of the eternal group: Perceiving the group as trans-generational and endurance of ingroup suffering. *Personality and Social Psychology Bulletin, 43*, 272–283.

Kammen, M. (1991). *Mystic chords of memory: The transformation of tradition in American culture*. New York, NY: Knopf.

Kasinitz, P., & Hillyard, D. (1995). The old-timers' tale: The politics of nostalgia on the waterfront. *Journal of Contemporary Ethnography, 24*, 139–164.

Kenrick, D. T., Griskevicius, V., Neuberg, S. L., & Schaller, M. (2010). Renovating the pyramid of needs: Contemporary extensions built upon ancient foundations. *Perspectives on Psychological Science, 5*, 292–314.

Kim, H. S. A., & Wohl, M. J. A. (2015). The bright side of self-discontinuity: Feeling disconnected with the past self increases readiness to change addictive behaviors (via nostalgia). *Social Psychological and Personality Science, 6*, 229–237.

Kosterman, R., & Feshbach, S. (1989). Toward a measure of patriotic and nationalistic attitudes. *Political Psychology, 10*, 257–274.

Lammers, J., & Baldwin, M. (2018). Past-focused temporal communication overcomes conservatives' resistance to liberal political ideas. *Journal of Personality and Social Psychology, 114*, 599–619.

Leach, C. W., Van Zomeren, M., Zebel, S., Vliek, M. L., Pennekamp, S. F., Doosje, B., ... & Spears, R. (2008). Group-level self-definition and self-investment: A hierarchical (multicomponent) model of in-group identification. *Journal of Personality and Social Psychology, 95*, 144–165.

Lewicka, M. (2008). Historical ethnic bias in urban memory: The case of central European cities. *Magazine for Urban Documentation: Opinion + Theory.* 50–57.

Lewicka, M. (2011). Historical ethnic bias in collective memory of places: Cognitive or motivational? In W. Brun, G. Keren, G. Kirkebøen, & H. Montgomery (Eds.), *Perspectives on thinking, judging, and decision making* (pp. 262–273). Oslo, Norway: Universitetsforlaget.

Lewin, K. (1948). *Resolving social conflicts: Selected papers on group dynamics.* New York, NY: Harper.

Liu, J. H., Goldstein-Hawes, R., Hilton, D. J., Huang, L. L., Gastardo-Conaco, C., Dresler-Hawke, E., ... & Hiddka, Y. (2005). Social representations of events and people in world history across twelve cultures. *Journal of Cross-Cultural Psychology, 36,* 171–191.

Liu, J. H., & Hilton, D. J. (2005). How the past weighs on the present: Social representations of history and their role in identity politics. *British Journal of Social Psychology, 44,* 537–556.

Liu, J. H., & Khan, S. S. (2014). Nation building through historical narratives in pre-independence India: Gandhi, Nehru, Sarvarkar, and Golwalkar as entrepreneurs of identity. In M. Hanne (Ed.), *Warring with words: Narrative and metaphor in domestic and international politics* (pp. 211–237). New York, NY: Psychology Press.

Liu, J. H., & László, J. (2007). A narrative theory of history and identity: Social identity, social representations, society and the individual. In G. Moloney & I. Walker (Eds.), *Social representations and identity: Content processes and power* (pp. 85–107). London, UK: Palgrave-Macmillan.

Liu, J. H., Wilson, M. S., McClure, J., & Higgins, T. R. (1999). Social identity and the perception of history: Cultural representations of Aotearoa/New Zealand. *European Journal of Social Psychology, 29,* 1021–1047.

Luhtanen, R., & Crocker, J. (1992). A collective self-esteem scale: Self-evaluation of one's social identity. *Personality and Social Psychology Bulletin, 18,* 302–318.

Mackie, D. M., & Smith, E. R. (1998). Intergroup relations: Insights from a theoretically integrative approach. *Psychological Review, 105,* 499–529.

Maslow, A. H. (1943). A theory of human motivation. *Psychological Review, 50,* 370–396.

McIntosh, J., & McKeganey, N. (2000). Addicts' narratives of recovery from drug use: Constructing a non-addict identity. *Social Science & Medicine, 50,* 1501–1510.

Milligan, M. J. (2003). Displacement and identity discontinuity: The role of nostalgia in establishing new identity categories. *Symbolic Interaction, 26,* 381–403.

Mols, F., & Jetten, J. (2014). No guts, no glory: How framing the collective past paves the way for anti-immigrant sentiments. *International Journal of Intercultural Relations, 43,* 74–86.

Mols, F., & Jetten, J. (2018). Beyond the "crisis and losers of globalization" thesis: Explaining the appeal of One Nation. *Queensland Review, 25,* 27–38.

Moscovici, S. (1984). The phenomenon of social representations. In M. Farr & S. Moscovici (Eds.), *Social representations* (pp. 3–69). New York, NY: Cambridge University Press.

Moscovici, S. (1988). Notes towards a description of social representations. *European Journal of Social Psychology, 18,* 211–250.

Mudde, C. (2016). Europe's populist surge: A long time in the making. *Foreign Affairs*, *95*, 25–30.

Mudde, C., & Kaltwasser, C. R. (Eds.). (2012). *Populism in Europe and the Americas: Threat or corrective for democracy?* Cambridge, UK: Cambridge University Press.

Mummendey, A., Klink, A., & Brown, R. (2001). Nationalism and patriotism: National identification and out-group rejection. *British Journal of Social Psychology*, *40*, 159–172.

Nicholson, T., Higgins, W., Turner, P., James, S., Stickle, F., & Pruitt, T. (1994). The relation between meaning in life and the occurrence of drug abuse: A retrospective study. *Psychology of Addictive Behaviors*, *8*, 24–28.

Obama, B. (2013). *Remarks by the President on comprehensive immigration reform* [Transcript]. Retrieved from https://obamawhitehouse.archives.gov/the-press-office/2013/01/29/remarks-president-comprehensive-immigration-reform.

Olick, J. K. (1999). Collective memory: The two cultures. *Sociological Theory*, *17*, 333–348.

Páez, D., & Liu, J. H. (2011). Collective memory of conflicts. In D. Bar-Tal (Ed.), *Intergroup conflicts and their resolution: A social psychological perspective* (pp. 105–124). New York, NY: Psychology Press.

Paolini, S., Harwood, J., & Rubin, M. (2010). Negative intergroup contact makes group memberships salient: Explaining why intergroup conflict endures. *Personality and Social Psychology Bulletin*, *36*, 1723–1738.

Pettigrew, T. F., & Tropp, L. R. (2011). *When groups meet: The dynamics of intergroup contact*. New York, NY: Psychology Press.

Prusik, M., & Lewicka, M. (2016). Nostalgia for communist times and autobiographical memory: Negative present or positive past? *Political Psychology*, *37*, 677–693.

Rabinovich, A., Morton, T. A., Postmes, T., & Verplanken, B. (2012). Collective self and individual choice: The effects of inter-group comparative context on environmental values and behaviour. *British Journal of Social Psychology*, *51*, 551–569.

Reicher, S., & Hopkins, N. (2001). *Self and nation*. London, UK: Sage.

Riek, B. M., Mania, E. W., & Gaertner, S. L. (2006). Intergroup threat and outgroup attitudes: A meta-analytic review. *Personality and Social Psychology Review*, *10*, 336–353.

Robinson, M. D., Cassidy, D. M., Boyd, R. L., & Fetterman, A. K. (2015). The politics of time: Conservatives differentially reference the past and liberals differentially reference the future. *Journal of Applied Social Psychology*, *45*, 391–399.

Roccas, S., Klar, Y., & Liviatan, I. (2006). The paradox of group-based guilt: Modes of national identification, conflict vehemence, and reactions to the in-group's moral violations. *Journal of Personality and Social Psychology*, *91*, 698–711.

Routledge, C., Arndt, J., Sedikides, C., & Wildschut, T. (2008). A blast from the past: The terror management function of nostalgia. *Journal of Experimental Social Psychology*, *44*, 132–140.

Routledge, C., Arndt, J., Wildschut, T., Sedikides, C., Hart, C., Juhl, J., Vingerhoets, A. J., & Scholtz, W. (2011). The past makes the present meaningful: Nostalgia as an existential resource. *Journal of Personality and Social Psychology*, *101*, 638–652.

Ryan, R. M., & Deci, E. L. (2017). *Self-determination theory: Basic psychological needs in motivation, development, and wellness*. New York, NY: Guilford Press.

Sahdra, B., & Ross, M. (2007). Group identification and historical memory. *Personality and Social Psychology Bulletin*, *33*, 384–395.

Sani, F., Bowe, M., Herrera, M., Manna, C., Cossa, T., Miao, X., & Zhou, Y. (2007). Perceived collective continuity: Seeing groups as entities that move through time. *European Journal of Social Psychology*, *37*, 1118–1134.

Sani, F., Herrera, M., & Bowe, M. (2009). Perceived collective continuity and ingroup identification as defense against death awareness. *Journal of Experimental Social Psychology, 45*, 242–245.

Schatz, R. T., Staub, E., & Lavine, H. (1999). On the varieties of national attachment: Blind versus constructive patriotism. *Political Psychology, 20*, 151–174.

Sedikides, C., & Wildschut, T. (2018). Finding meaning in nostalgia. *Review of General Psychology, 22*, 48–61.

Sedikides, C., Wildschut, T., Arndt, J., & Routledge, C. (2008). Nostalgia: Past, present, and future. *Current Directions in Psychological Science, 17*, 304–307.

Sedikides, C., Wildschut, T., & Baden, D. (2004). Nostalgia: Conceptual issues and existential functions. In J. Greenberg, S. Koole, & T. Pyszczynski (Eds.), *Handbook of experimental existential psychology* (pp. 200–214). New York, NY: Guilford Press.

Sedikides, C., Wildschut, T., Gaertner, L., Routledge, C., & Arndt, J. (2008). Nostalgia as enabler of self-continuity. Self-continuity: *Individual and Collective Perspectives*, 227–239.

Sedikides, C., Wildschut, T., Routledge, C., & Arndt, J. (2015). Nostalgia counteracts self-discontinuity and restores self-continuity. *European Journal of Social Psychology, 45*, 52–61.

Sedikides, C., Wildschut, T., Routledge, C., Arndt, J., Hepper, E. G., & Zhou, X. (2015). To nostalgize: Mixing memory with affect and desire. *Advances in Experimental Social Psychology, 51*, 189–273.

Smeekes, A. (2015). National nostalgia: A group-based emotion that benefits the ingroup but hampers intergroup relations. *International Journal of Intercultural Relations, 49*, 54–67.

Smeekes, A. (in press). Longing for the good old days of "our country": Understanding the triggers, functions and consequences of national nostalgia. In P. S. Salter & S. Mukherjee (Eds.), *History and collective memory: Its role in shaping national identities*. New York: Nova Science Publishers.

Smeekes, A., Jetten, J., Verkuyten, M., Wohl, M. J. A., Jasinskaja-Lahti, I., Ariyanto, A., ... & Butera, F. (2018). Regaining in-group continuity in times of anxiety about the group's future. *Social Psychology, 49*, 311–329.

Smeekes, A., & Verkuyten, M. (2013). Collective self-continuity, group identification and in group defense. *Journal of Experimental Social Psychology, 49*, 984–994.

Smeekes, A., & Verkuyten, M. (2015). The presence of the past: Identity continuity and group dynamics. *European Review of Social Psychology, 26*, 162–202.

Smeekes, A., Verkuyten, M., & Martinovic, B. (2015). Longing for the country's good old days: National nostalgia, autochthony beliefs, and opposition to Muslim expressive rights. *British Journal of Social Psychology, 54*, 561–580.

Smith, E. R., & Mackie, D. M. (2008). Intergroup emotions. In M. Lewis, J. M. Haviland-Jones, & L. F. Barrett (Eds.), *Handbook of emotions* (pp. 428–439). New York, NY: Guilford Press.

Smith, E. R., & Mackie, D. M. (2015). Dynamics of group-based emotions: Insights from intergroup emotion theory. *Emotion Review, 7*, 349–354.

Solomon, S., Greenberg, J., & Pyszczynski, T. (1991). A terror management theory of social behavior: The psychological functions of self-esteem and cultural worldviews. *Advances in Experimental Social Psychology, 24*, 93–159.

Stephan, W. G., & Stephan, C. W. (2000). An integrated threat theory of prejudice. In S. Oskamp (Ed.), *Reducing prejudice and discrimination* (pp. 23–45). Mahwah, NJ: Lawrence Erlbaum Associates.

Taggart, P. (2004). Populism and representative politics in contemporary Europe. *Journal of Political Ideologies, 9*, 269–288.

Tajfel, H., & Turner, J. C. (1986). An integrative theory of group conflict. In W. G. Austin & S. Worchel (Eds.), *The social psychology of intergroup relations* (pp. 7–24). Chicago, IL: Nelson-Hall.

Tomlin, G. (2006, May 18). Split among American Baptists over homosexuality is final. *Baptist Press*. Retrieved from: www.bpnews.net/23275/split-among-american-baptists-over-homosexuality-is-final

Turner, J. C. (1999). Some current issues in research on social identity and self-categorization theories. In N. Ellemers, R. Spears, & B. Doojse (Eds.), *Social identity* (pp. 6–34). Oxford, UK: Blackwell.

Turner, J. C., Hogg, M. A., Oakes, P. J., Reicher, S. D., & Wetherell, M. S. (1987). *Rediscovering the social group: A self-categorization theory*. Oxford, UK: Blackwell.

Turner, J. C., & Oakes, P. J. (1986). The significance of the social identity concept for social psychology with reference to individualism, interactionism and social influence. *British Journal of Social Psychology, 25*, 237–252.

Turner, J. C., Oakes, P. J., Haslam, S. A., & McGarty, C. (1994). Self and collective: Cognition and social context. *Personality and Social Psychology Bulletin, 20*, 454–463.

Waldorf, D., & Biernacki, P. (1981). The natural recovery from opiate addiction: Some preliminary findings. *Journal of Drug Issues, 11*, 61–74.

Wertsch, J. V. (2002). *Voices of collective remembering*. Cambridge, UK: Cambridge University Press.

Wildschut, T., Bruder, M., Robertson, S., van Tilburg, W. A., & Sedikides, C. (2014). Collective nostalgia: A group-level emotion that confers unique benefits on the group. *Journal of Personality and Social Psychology, 107*, 844–863.

Wildschut, T., Sedikides, C., Arndt, J., & Routledge, C.D. (2006). Nostalgia: Content, triggers, functions. *Journal of Personality and Social Psychology, 91*, 975–993.

White, S. (2010). Soviet nostalgia and Russian politics. *Journal of Eurasian Studies, 1*, 1–9.

Wohl, M. J. A., Branscombe, N. R., & Klar, Y. (2006). Collective guilt: Emotional reactions when one's group has done wrong or been wronged. *European Review of Social Psychology, 17*, 1–37.

Wohl, M. J. A., Kim, H. S., Salmon, M., Santesso, D., Wildschut, T., & Sedikides, C. (2018). Discontinuity-induced nostalgia improves the odds of a self-reported quit attempt among people living with addiction. *Journal of Experimental Social Psychology, 75*, 83–94.

Wohl, M. J. A., & Smeekes, A. (2019). *Longing is in the memory of the beholder: Collective nostalgia content determines the method members will support to make their group great again*. Manuscript in preparation.

Wohl, M. J. A., Squires, E. C., & Caouette, J. (2012). We were, we are, will we be? The social psychology of collective angst. *Social Psychology and Personality Compass, 6*, 379–391.

Wohl, M. J. A, Tabri, N., & Halperin, E. (in press). Emotional sources of intergroup atrocities. In L. S. Newman (Ed.), *Confronting humanity at its worst: The social psychology of genocide and extreme intergroup violence*. Oxford, UK: Oxford University Press.

16

DO IAT SCORES EXPLAIN RACIAL INEQUALITY?

Lee Jussim, Akeela Careem, Nathan Honeycutt and Sean T. Stevens

How much does whatever is measured by implicit association test (IAT) scores explain racial inequality? Our answer is, "probably not much." How is this even possible, given how much applied attention implicit bias (the pre-eminent measure of which is the IAT) has received in scientific journals (e.g., Bertrand & Mullainathan, 2004; Sabin & Greenwald, 2012), law journals (e.g., Jolls & Sunstein, 2006), the popular press (e.g., Baker, 2018), organizational anti-bias interventions (e.g., Department of Justice, Office of Public Affairs, 2016), and even US presidential elections (Hensch, 2016)?

In this chapter, we argue that, even after 20 years of research, the IAT remains poorly understood. We first review definitional, psychometric, interpretive, construct validity, and predictive validity issues regarding the IAT. We then present a series of heuristic models that may be useful for attempting to understand the likely role of IAT scores in accounting for important inequalities.

Definitional Issues

There is no widely-agreed upon consensus as to what "implicit bias" means. Numerous articles use the term without defining it at all (e.g., see Jussim, Careem, Goldberg, Honeycutt, & Stevens, 2019, for a review). Because those articles use the IAT to measure implicit bias (or refer to studies using it as having measured implicit bias), they appear to presume that it means "whatever is measured by the IAT."

Considering only cases where a definition is actually provided, the specific content varies so widely as to render it impossible for readers to be sure authors are discussing the same construct:

> Cultural stereotypes may not be consciously endorsed, but their mere existence influences how information about an individual is processed and leads to unintended biases in decision-making, so called "implicit bias."
>
> *Chapman, Kaatz, & Carnes, 2013, p. 1504*

> Here, we focus on implicit social bias, a measure of how strongly one associates a concept (e.g., pleasant/unpleasant) with one or another social group.
>
> *Stanley, Sokol-Hessner, Banaji, & Phelps, 2011, p. 7710*

> Whereas explicit bias is overt and freely expressed, implicit bias may not be consciously acknowledged and operates in more subtle ways. For example, a clinician with implicit bias may unconsciously exhibit negative behavior or poor communication with a black patient, as has been shown in laboratory research.
>
> *Blair et al., 2013, p. 44*

Greenwald (2017), at a special National Science Foundation (NSF) conference on controversies surrounding the IAT, provided this as the working definition of implicit bias provided for academics for most of the prior 20 years:

> Introspectively unidentified (or inaccurately identified) effects of past experience that mediate discriminatory behavior.

Inasmuch as this definition was offered by the developer of the IAT (Greenwald, McGhee, & Schwartz, 1998), this definition warrants close scrutiny. If this is the definition, it is not clear that the IAT measures implicit bias, because:

1. It is a reaction time measure that assesses the difference in time it takes to do two different yet related categorization tasks. Difference in reaction times is not discrimination.
2. It is a single variable. Although any single variable *might* be a mediator of the effect of one variable on some other variable, that is a separate empirical question that cannot be addressed simply by assessing a single variable. We can conduct research providing evidence that "B mediates the effect of A on C," but we cannot declare "merely by measuring B we have established that it mediates the effect of A on C." Defining the measure as "mediation" biases the communication of what the IAT captures by subterranean importation of the unverified assumption that it is involved in discrimination without having to provide any evidence that it actually is.
3. Nor are IAT scores "introspectively unidentified." People can quite accurately predict their IAT scores, r's ranged from about 0.60 to 0.70 (Hahn, Judd, Hirsh, & Blair, 2014). Inasmuch as well-elaborated attitudes more

strongly predict behavioral intentions (Petty & Briñol, this volume), questions can (and have – e.g., Schimmack, 2019) been raised about whether IAT scores predict behavior much beyond explicit attitudes.

Here is what is left of Greenwald's (2017) definition of implicit bias after we remove statements that do not apply to the IAT:

> ~~Introspectively unidentified (or inaccurately identified)~~ effects of past experience ~~that mediate discriminatory behavior~~.

What is left is "effects of past experience." This may not be pure coincidence as we discuss in the next section on construct validity.

Construct Validity

Exactly what the IAT measures remains muddled. Yet, there are large bodies of scholarship that presume that it is a clean measure of unconscious or automatic prejudice. For example, in 1998, Greenwald and Banaji held a press conference unveiling a "… new tool that measures the unconscious roots of prejudice" (Schwarz, 1998). In 2013, Banaji & Greenwald declared in their book *Blindspot* (Chapter 3, at 23 percent of the epub version) "… the automatic White preference expressed on the Race IAT is now established as signaling discriminatory behavior." Many, perhaps most, scholars who have published research using the IAT to assess implicit associations regarding demographic groups once interpreted it similarly (e.g., Jolls & Sunstein, 2006; Jost et al., 2009; McConnell & Leibold, 2001). However, two decades of research regarding exactly what the IAT measures have not converged on a consensus. Instead, the level of disagreement and controversy has escalated.

First, consider what the IAT is supposed to measure: *implicit associations* between concepts in memory. Let's temporarily put aside measurement, psychometric, or predictive validity issues, and stipulate that it succeeds at doing so. How do two concepts in memory become associated? One likely route is that they co-occur in the world in some way. Ham and eggs, for example, go together in the environment far more than do ham and quantum mechanics. Similarly, at least for North Americans, New York is probably more strongly associated with Yankees than with malaria. This analysis has a kinship to that of one of the earliest critiques of the IAT (Arkes & Tetlock, 2004). They argued that, rather than reflecting prejudice, the race IAT might reflect knowledge of cultural stereotypes.

Our argument, however, goes further. The associations tapped by the IAT may reflect implicit cognitive registration of regularities and realities of the social environment. Consistent with this analysis, IAT response times were faster when stimuli corresponded to ecologically valid base rates (Bluemke & Fiedler,

2009). What about evaluations of whether group membership is good or bad, pleasant or unpleasant (as used in so many IATs)? That depends on where evaluations come from. One possibility is that evaluations of groups come from knowledge of those groups' social conditions. Groups disproportionately living in unpleasant conditions (such as poverty, crime, rundown housing) may be associated with "unpleasant" more than other groups simply as the result of laypeople accurately associating them with unpleasant realities.

Research on stereotype accuracy has repeatedly demonstrated that the racial, gender, and age stereotypes of those who have been studied are often quite accurate in that people's beliefs about groups often correlate moderately to highly with credible measures of real group differences, such as census data and meta-analysis (Jussim, Crawford & Rubinstein, 2015). People who are better at detecting patterns regarding social groups also more efficiently learn, apply, and update their stereotypes (Lick, Alter, & Freeman, 2018).

Although both work on stereotype accuracy and pattern detection focused on explicit stereotypes, there are reasons to suspect similar processes underlie implicit associations. The earliest work on implicit cognition long predated social-psychological approaches. Reviewing two decades of that research, Reber (1989, p. 219, emphasis added) concluded:

> (a) Implicit learning produces a tacit knowledge base that is ***abstract and representative of the structure of the environment***; (b) such knowledge is optimally acquired independently of conscious efforts to learn; and (c) it can be used implicitly to solve problems and ***make accurate decisions about novel stimulus circumstances.***

A new theoretical perspective on implicit bias reached conclusions largely compatible with this view (Payne, Vuletich & Lundberg, 2017, p. 242): "... the reason that implicit bias is widespread in general is that the environment has a relatively constant level of disparities and systemic inequalities that repeatedly raise the accessibility of stereotypic concepts." Although Payne et al. (2017) emphasize bias and racism throughout their paper, in fact, the core claim above is plausibly interpretable as consistent with implicit accuracy. That is, systemic inequalities may not merely "raise the accessibility of stereotype concepts," they may *create* those stereotypic associations. This is exactly what would be expected to happen if, as Lick et al. (2018) and Reber (1989) indicate, people who are good at detecting patterns in the environment associate groups with their different and unequal social conditions.

Empirical research has begun to confirm the prediction that implicit associations are responsive to regularities in the social environment. In one series of studies, either African-American or White individuals were paired with images reflecting either intelligence (e.g., a brain) or stupidity (e.g., a paper with an "F" on it; Rubinstein & Jussim, 2019). When the African-American target was paired with smart images and the White target with stupid images, conventionally biased IAT scores (in a control condition without such associations) were not merely eliminated, they reversed (people completed Jamal/Smart and Luke/Stupid more quickly than Jamal/Stupid and Luke/Smart). Also consistent with this perspective, one recent study found that, in addition to results interpretable as racial bias, implicit stereotypes as assessed by the IAT correlated with geographic crime rates among blacks (Johnson & Chopik, 2019).

The weight of the evidence from multiple sources – explicit stereotypes, the earliest work on implicit cognition, and the recent theoretical and empirical work on sources of IAT scores – all converges on the conclusion that what was left in Greenwald's definition above is no coincidence. Whether or not IAT scores reflect prejudice or knowledge of cultural stereotypes, they likely capture the individual's past experiences with groups. After reviewing many other theoretically plausible or empirically demonstrated potential influences on IAT scores, Bluemke & Fiedler (2009, p. 1036) put it this way: "Whether an implicit attitude really underlies a latency difference is a question that cannot be answered from the magnitude of the association index alone."

Thus, one important area for future research is to more thoroughly test the role of experience and social realities in producing IAT scores. How well do census data on achievement gaps, wealth and income gaps, and health gaps correlate with IAT scores? Addressing such questions may shed light on the role of social realities in producing the implicit associations captured by the IAT.

But even that analysis presumes that the IAT is a clean measure of implicit associations, an assumption unlikely to be generally true (Fiedler, Messner, & Bluemke, 2006). The quad model (Conrey, Sherman, Gawronski, Hugenberg, & Groom, 2005) provided five experiments indicating that the IAT simultaneously reflected: implicit associations, discriminability (ability to identify a correct response), ability to overcome the bias produced by having such associations, and guessing biases (other systematic influences on responses). Because their model yields parameters for each of the four sources of IAT scores, it provides one way to make use of the IAT to assess implicit associations. However, it also showed that a presumption that IAT scores are a clean measure of "implicit associations" (let alone "implicit biases") was not justified. Additional research assessing and removing artifacts and measurement biases (see Fiedler et al., 2006) could also advance the understanding of what the IAT assesses.

Psychometric Issues

The internal consistency of IAT scores meets conventional standards of acceptability, and ranges from 0.60–.090 (LeBel & Paunonen, 2011). Test-retest reliabilities fare worse. Even when tested over only a few weeks, test-retest correlations average about $r=0.4$ (Payne et al., 2017).

For most of its existence, IAT effects have been assessed with D scores (Greenwald, Nosek, & Banaji, 2003). D scores are computed separately for each participant as:

$D = IATRAW/SDWI$. Raw scores are the mean difference in response times in milliseconds to two IATs (such as African-American/pleasant or white/unpleasant versus African-American/unpleasant or white/pleasant). $SDWI$ is the within individual standard deviation. Blanton, Jaccard, and Burrows (2015) were the first to point out a computational weakness of this method:

This change [to D scores] unwittingly produced a situation in which a reduction in trial error (typically something a researcher or practitioner would view as desirable) now results in more extreme bias scores, everything else being equal.

p. 431

Consider two people with identical raw reaction time differences (let's say, 100 ms). The first has an SD of 100; the second an SD of 25. The first will have $D = 1$, the second, $D = 4$, even though their levels of bias as indicated by the raw difference in response times are identical (in this example, both raw differences equal 100 ms).

Furthermore, IAT scores are difference scores, and difficulties with interpreting difference scores have been recognized for decades (e.g., Cronbach & Furby, 1970). Although a thorough review of such difficulties is beyond the scope of this chapter, fortunately, one applied specifically to IAT scores already exists (see Fiedler et al., 2006). For example, correlations of IAT scores with outcomes are difficult to interpret because they may reflect a correlation with the compatible trials (e.g., black/unpleasant v. white/pleasant), a correlation with the incompatible trials (e.g., black/pleasant v. white/unpleasant), or a correlation with the difference. The criterion may also correlate more strongly with the compatible vs. incompatible trials, further muddying the interpretation of the correlation with the difference. Fiedler et al. (2006) also explained why standardized IAT scores via the D statistic (Greenwald et al., 2003) do not solve these problems, and identify a slew of other issues with the IAT that derive from using difference scores.

The Curious Case of The Doubly-Computed Effect Size

D scores are computationally similar, but not quite identical to the common effect size, Cohen's d. This is explicitly acknowledged in the paper recommending D (Greenwald et al., 2003). This raises the question: Why, if D is a close relative of d, do many papers reporting IAT effects further transform the (already transformed from raw scores) effect size D into yet another effect size, d (e.g., Cao & Banaji, 2016; Lane, Banaji, Nosek, & Greenwald, 2007)? D is already a standardized effect size. Although we have never seen a rationale for recomputing a d from the D's in print, the consequence of doing so will be clear: If the standard deviation of the IAT D scores is less than 1, d will be larger than D; if the SD of each participant is larger than 1, d will be smaller than D. Although doing a comprehensive analysis of this issue is beyond the scope of this chapter, every paper of which we are aware that reported both D's and Cohen's d's reported d's that were larger than the mean D (e.g., Cao & Banaji, 2016; Lane et al., 2007; Charlesworth & Banaji, 2019). If this is not justified, the literature may be filled with exaggerated estimates of implicit bias effects. In the absence of a compelling and fully articulated reason to do otherwise, we recommend simply reporting the average D as *the IAT effect size*, rather than further computing Cohen's ds.

Interpretations of "Bias"

Let's temporarily put aside all the other problems involved in interpreting IAT scores and consider them to reflect "bias" as have others for over two decades. IAT scores that differ from 0 have routinely been interpreted as "implicit bias" (Greenwald et al., 1998; Greenwald et al., 2003; Lane et al., 2007). There are two separate problems with this. When researchers use conventional null hypothesis significance tests (as nearly all have when conducting research with the IAT), two factors contribute to concluding whether an IAT score is "different than 0." The first is that the score cannot equal 0. The second is statistical power. With sufficiently high power, almost any non-zero value will differ "significantly" from 0; the same IAT effect may significantly differ from 0 in a large sample, but not in a small sample. Presumably, however, "bias" (if any) or even implicit association, is a function of strength of association, not statistical power. Is a D score of 0.04 really "bias" if obtained in a sufficiently large sample? And if so, is it a bias of sufficient magnitude that it warrants being taken seriously, for either theoretical or applied reasons? If so, we have never seen such arguments articulated. Perhaps for these reasons, Nosek et al. (2007) recommended use of an absolute (if arbitrary) standard of $D \geq 0.15$ for "implicit biases" (or associations) to be considered sufficiently substantial to warrant being taken seriously.

Although Nosek et al.'s (2007) recommendations were definitely an improvement (and, in deference to this tradition, we have used it ourselves, e.g., in Rubinstein, Jussim, & Stevens, 2018 and Rubinstein & Jussim, 2019), it is not obvious that it is well-justified. This issue was first raised as a theoretical possibility on the grounds that the preponderance of positive race IAT scores (80 percent or more) could indicate that the base rate of positive IAT scores in the populations taking the test was simply much higher than the base rate of racist implicit attitudes (Fiedler et al., 2006).

Subsequent research supported this prediction. Research re-analyzing a slew of studies correlating IAT scores with other measures of bias (behavior, attitudes, evaluations, etc.) found that the IAT is consistently *right-biased* (Blanton, Jaccard, Strauts, Mitchell, & Tetlock, 2015). That is, rather than $D=0$ corresponding to unbiased responding on other measures, D's corresponding to unbiased responding ranged widely, but consistently fell well above 0 (most D's corresponding to egalitarian responding were between 0.3 and 0.6). Although the generality of this pattern is unclear, so is the interpretation of IAT scores as reflecting prejudice or bias. If the right bias pattern found by Blanton et al. (2015) is more general, it means not only is the Nosek et al. (2007) recommendation of $D \geq 0.15$ too conservative, but that it might actually reflect *reverse bias*. For example, if a $D=0.5$ corresponds to racial egalitarianism, $D=0.15$ might correspond to *anti-white bias!* This interpretation is given further credence by the facts that at least one study reporting supposedly anti-African-American IAT scores also found far more anti-white than anti-African-American behavioral discrimination (McConnell & Leibold, 2001; although it took a reanalysis by Blanton et al., 2009, to reveal this inconvenient finding). Many others reporting positive IAT scores also reported average patterns of unbiased behavior (e.g., Green et al., 2007; Rachlinski, Johnson, Wistrich, & Guthrie, 2009; Stanley, Sokol-Hessner, Banaji, & Phelps, 2011). Because the average of the predictor corresponds to the average of the outcome in bivariate regression, positive IAT scores corresponded to egalitarian behavior in all of these studies. In order to better understand what IAT scores mean, and especially what scores correspond to egalitarian versus biased beliefs and attitudes, whenever possible, research should report the D scores that correspond to egalitarian responding on criteria or outcome measures.

Predictive Validity Controversies

One might argue that the above issues are minor nit-picks if stereotype and prejudice-related IAT's predict discrimination well. Unfortunately, this issue is unclear. Dueling meta-analyses have appeared since 2009 (Greenwald, Poehlman, Uhlmann, & Banaji, 2009; Forscher et al., in press; Greenwald, Banaji, & Nosek, 2015; Oswald, Mitchell, Blanton, Jaccard, & Tetlock, 2013), yielding predictive validities in the 0.1 to 0.3 range. The upper range of 0.3 constitutes predictive validity comparable to many attitude measures (e.g., Fazio, 1990), but the extent to which such findings suffer from "allegiance bias," i.e., a pattern in which devotees to a method or phenomenon produce studies yielding higher effects than do other researchers (Dragioti, Dimoliatis, Fountoulakis, & Evangelou, 2015) is unclear. Even the lower predictive validities have been described as "socially important," in part, because small effects obtained in short-term studies may accumulate over time and across perceivers (Greenwald, Banaji, & Nosek, 2015). On the other hand, small effects do not necessarily actually accumulate, and any conclusion that they do requires empirical evidence; absent such evidence, the "socially important" argument has been criticized as a vague reference to what is, in essence, a compound interest formula, in the sense that any effect, if it compounds over multiple events, will increase (Oswald et al., 2013). Of course, *whether* it actually compounds over multiple events is itself an empirical question and one to which the best evidence strongly suggests "probably not" (see Jussim et al., 2019 for a review of theory and evidence regarding the accumulation of bias hypothesis).

We can imagine two areas of productive future research on predictive validity issues. First, can conditions be identified a priori under which IAT scores more strongly predict discrimination? Given the history of IAT conclusions being overstated, the registered replication format will probably be necessary to convince sceptics that conditions under which strong effects are systematically claimed to occur were actually predicted a priori rather than HARKed (Kerr, 1998). Second, do the discriminatory effects predicted by IAT scores actually accumulate over time, as predicted by Greenwald et al. (2015)? Or, like most self-fulfilling prophecies, are they more likely to dissipate than to accumulate (Jussim, 2017)? Addressing this question may not only help design interventions to ameliorate some sources of inequality by studying their role in naturally-occurring applied settings, it may theoretically advance our understanding of the nature and social effects of implicit beliefs and attitudes.

IAT, Implicit Bias, and Racial Inequality

Given the swirl of uncertainties about what the IAT measures, and its seeming modest ability to predict discrimination, it is probably scientifically premature to even speculate on the role of whatever it measures in producing large-scale social inequalities. Nonetheless, some clearly have.

> These studies testify to the enduring historical (and psychological) legacies of racism, sexism, and other forms of group-based inequality and they suggest, not so surprisingly after all, that these legacies have left behind at least some residue in our hearts and minds.
>
> *Jost et al., 2009, p. 64*

> *Conclusion 7: Implicit race attitudes (automatic race preferences) contribute to discrimination against African-American Americans.* ... a sizable collection of studies summarized in a 2009 journal publication made it clear that there now exists a substantial body of evidence that automatic White preference—as measured by the Race IAT—predicts discriminatory behavior even among people who fervently espouse egalitarian views. This evidence is far too substantial to ignore....
>
> *Banaji & Greenwald, 2013, at position 88 percent of epub*

Neither quote addresses *how much* implicit biases contribute to inequalities. The tone of both strongly suggests quite a lot, but both stop short of stating so explicitly. Thus, in the remainder of this chapter, we review theory and evidence to consider the likely extent of such contributions.

Before continuing, a note on nomenclature. In the remainder of this paper, we use the term "IAT scores" to refer to "whatever is measured by the IAT." It would be awkward to keep repeating "whatever is measured by the IAT." If there was a simple interpretation of IAT scores, say, as "unconscious prejudice" or "implicit bias," we would just use the term for the underlying construct. However, because what is captured by IAT scores is unclear, using a simple term such as "implicit bias" is not justified. The term "IAT scores" suffers no such uncertainties.

What, then, is scientifically known about the role of IAT scores in explaining large-scale social inequities? To attempt to understand this, we start from the phenomena that IAT scores might ultimately explain. A wide range of measures consistently show that, in the US, White people are advantaged over African-American people in income, wealth, higher levels of education, and longevity (e.g., Arias & Xu, 2018; Fontenot, Semega, & Kollar, 2018; Ryan & Bauman, 2016). In order to try to get some clarity on plausible contributions of IAT scores to differences such as these, we consider their possible effects in the context of other possible causes of inequality.

To this end, Figure 16.1 presents a heuristic pie chart of potential contributors to racial inequalities. The pie represents the total gap. Figure 16.1 identifies three broad sources: Past discrimination, group differences, and discrimination in the present. Although it depicts the contribution of each type of discrimination as equal to the others, this is just for heuristic purposes. The actual contribution of each may never be knowable, which is why we default to the simple heuristic of treating them as equal. Unless one wishes to argue that one of the

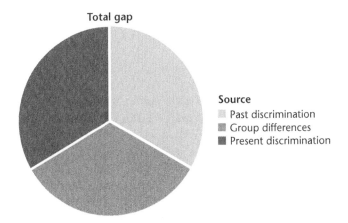

FIGURE 16.1 Pie represents total amount of some gap.

three sources of gaps identified here is trivial (which seems highly implausible), whether it contributes 20 percent or 33 percent or 50 percent to current gaps is not important with respect to our analysis. In other contexts when one is uncertain, identifying relevant predictors, weighting them all equally, and adding them, has proven to be an effective and robust heuristic approach to making decisions (Dawes, 1979).

Past Discrimination

In Figure 16.1, the right third represents the portion of a gap due to past racial discrimination. There is ample evidence for the long reach of past discrimination. For example, after analyzing the relationship of proportion of slaves in 1860 to income inequality within counties of 42 US states in 2000, Bertocchi & Dimico (2014) concluded (p. 208) that: "… the legacy of slavery still plays a major role in the US economy and society, since the past use of slave labor persistently affects current inequality …" Similarly, regarding the long reach of slavery and Jim Crow, Loury (1998) concludes: "… for some three centuries now, the communal experience of the slaves and their descendants has been shaped by political, social, and economic institutions that, by any measure must be seen as oppressive" (p. 41).

Modern IAT scores cannot possibly explain slavery, Jim Crow, or the long legacy of their ugly aftermaths. Furthermore, there was nothing "implicit" about such blatant laws and norms. Even if whatever is measured by IAT scores did cause discrimination in the past, such effects would *still* be considered past discrimination with respect to 2019. IAT scores in the present cannot possibly explain effects of past discrimination, because causality cannot run backwards in time. Thus, to whatever extent past discrimination has produced effects that manifest as modern gaps, modern IAT scores cannot possibly account for such effects.

Group Differences in the Present

In Figure 16.1, the bottom third represents reasons groups can differ unrelated to discrimination in the past or present; and, as such, cannot be explained by IAT scores. For example, higher sickle cell anemia rates among American African-Americans than Whites (Centers for Disease Control and Prevention, 2019) may contribute to mortality differences. A culture of honor may be more likely to explain violence among African-Americans than among Whites (Felson & Pare, 2010). There are also a wide range of other differences in beliefs, attitudes, values, habits, and other characteristics that could, at least possibly, contribute to racial gaps in wealth and income (Hughes, 2018). Those that result from discrimination do not belong in this section; those that do not result from discrimination do belong in this section.

Discrimination in the Present

Institutional Discrimination. IAT scores have the potential to explain individual discrimination in the present. However, not all discrimination in the present is individual. Institutional discrimination refers to laws, rules, norms, and policies of governments and other organizations that might have intentional or unintentional effects of discriminating. Any policy or practice that disproportionately disadvantages people of low socioeconomic status (SES) constitutes institutional racism in the US because African-Americans tend to be disproportionately poor. States that fund schools through property taxes advantage wealthier communities. Congressional districts that are gerrymandered to reduce African-American political influence constitute institutional racism. Even requiring lawyers in court cases can be viewed as a form of institutional racism, if it is harder for people from low SES backgrounds (disproportionately African-American) to hire good lawyers.

This situation is reflected in Figure 16.2, which is identical to Figure 16.1, with one exception. "Discrimination in the present" has been divided into two components: 1. Institutional discrimination (on the left); and 2. Individual discrimination (top left section).

IAT scores can only cause the portion of gaps represented by individual acts of discrimination. Gerrymandering to reduce African-American influence is clearly an explicit, not implicit process. Requiring lawyers in court reflects legal practices developed over centuries in European countries with little or no African presence, so the idea that they might reflect implicit racial biases is highly implausible. Nearly all forms of institutional discrimination reflect either intentional biases (e.g., Jim Crow, redlining) or practices that developed for reasons other than race (lawyers, paying for public schools via property taxes).

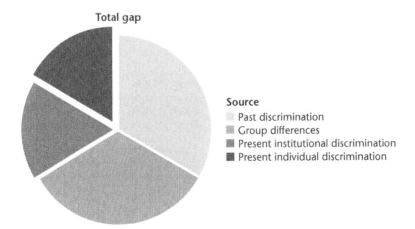

FIGURE 16.2 Pie represents total amount of some gap.

We know of no evidence linking IAT scores to institutional discrimination. Nonetheless, it is possible to hypothesize some role of individual IAT scores in creation of some degree of institutional discrimination. Perhaps, for example, IAT scores reflecting strong associations of African-Americans with unpleasantness, crime, or violence cause individuals to favor politicians claiming to be tough on crime, who then pass laws leading to disproportionate incarceration of African-Americans. Such effects would not be included in the left section because they start with the IAT scores of individuals (and, as such, would be represented by the top left section for individual discrimination shown in Figure 16.2).

Individual discrimination caused by explicit prejudice versus IAT scores. Of course, not all individual discrimination is necessarily caused by IAT scores. At most, IAT scores reflect implicit associations and perhaps implicit prejudice. Although a review of the literature on links between explicit prejudice and discrimination is beyond the scope of this chapter, much evidence exists demonstrating that explicit racial prejudice predicts discrimination (see e.g., the meta-analysis of 57 studies by Talaska, Fiske, & Chaiken, 2008). Inasmuch as well-elaborated attitudes (see also Petty & Briñol, this volume) and collective narcissism and collective nostalgia (see also Forgas & Lantos; and Wohl & Stefaniak, this volume) are plausibly viewed as influencing conscious attitudes, the evidence that they substantially predict behavior converges on the conclusion that the most powerful sources of prejudice may be explicit rather than implicit. Similarly, explicit expectations about workplace interactions, or forensic encounters can influence behaviors (see also Kovera; Schmader, this volume).

To the extent that explicit prejudice causes discrimination, it is contributing to racial inequality. However, explicit prejudice is not what is measured by IAT scores. Therefore, the "Present Individual Discrimination" pie slice in Figure 16.2 needs to be divided further, as shown in Figure 16.3, in which the portion of a gap explained by IAT scores is pulled out of the pie.

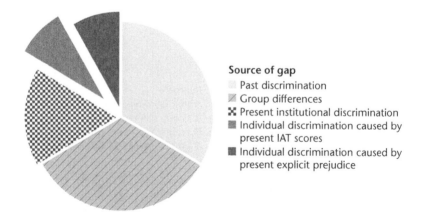

FIGURE 16.3 Pie represents total amount of some gap.

How much individual-level discrimination is there in the present? Whereas there is clear evidence that discrimination at the individual level occurs, exactly how much occurs or how much it explains racial disparities remains unclear (see Pager & Shepherd, 2008, for a review).

Research on discrimination at the individual level is characterized by conflicting results. Field and audit studies often find evidence of individual-level racial discrimination. For example, Quillian, Pager, Hexel, & Midtbøen's (2017) meta-analysis revealed that, during the hiring process, White applicants consistently received more interview call-backs than African-Americans and Latinos over a 25-year period. Further, hiring discrimination had not declined for African-Americans over time. Likewise, Pager, Western, & Bonikowski (2009) investigated the low-wage labor market in New York City and found that Black applicants were half as likely as equally qualified Whites to receive a call-back for an interview or a job offer. Furthermore, Black applicants with no criminal record fared no better than White applicants with a criminal record.

On the other hand, Heckman (1998) argued that audit and field studies on individual discrimination may be less informative than they seem. When the implications of discrimination audit studies were critically evaluated, Heckman concluded that such studies may overestimate the actual level of discrimination on several grounds:

1. "Discrimination at the individual level is different from discrimination at the group level" (p. 102).
2. "The impact of market discrimination is not determined by the ... average level of discrimination among firms" (p. 102).
3. The real-world level of actual discrimination is determined by "... where ethnic minorities or women actually end up buying, working, or borrowing" (p. 102).
4. "Purposive sorting within markets eliminates the worst forms of discrimination" (p. 103).

"Purposive sorting" refers to the idea that people can shift their efforts to contexts (jobs, banks) where they are not likely to be victimized by discrimination. This can limit the effects of discrimination. If, for example, half of all firms discriminate, but those targeted mostly avoid those firms by frequenting the other half, the effects of discrimination are mostly mitigated. As a result, after reviewing the evidence from discrimination audit studies up to that time, Heckman (1998, p. 105) concluded, "Only a zealot can see evidence in these data of pervasive discrimination in the U.S. labor market."

Heckman's (1998) arguments, however, are largely theoretical. More recent empirical data suggest that Blacks and African-Americans do not target or avoid particular job types. Instead, they tend to cast a wider net in their job search than similarly situated Whites (Pager & Pedulla, 2015). Thus, having to exert this extra effort is itself an effect of discrimination, and is unlikely to be detected in audit studies. Thus, Heckman's analysis (1998) may have underestimated the extent to which audit studies capture discrimination (for a more extensive review, see Pager, 2007).

Nonetheless, some empirical studies find little or no discrimination. One audit study sent out 9,000 resumes and did not find evidence of racial discrimination in seven major US cities, across six occupational categories (Darolia, Koedel, Martorell, Wilson, & Perez-Arce, 2016). In a similar vein, 17 unpublished studies finding no net bias against African-Americans were recently uncovered (Zigerell, 2018). These samples were nationally representative and included a total of over 13,000 respondents, 2,781 of whom were African-American. There was no evidence of bias on a variety of outcomes, including willingness to provide resources, evaluations of competence, and criminal culpability.

Some of the clearest evidence of non-discrimination comes from, surprisingly, work assessing the extent to which the IAT predicts discrimination. First, however, it is important to recognize that the IAT might correlate with some measure of discrimination, even in the absence of net anti-black bias. For example, let's say there is no anti-black bias in some study; bias outcomes range from anti-white to egalitarian. IAT scores could still positively correlate with this outcome if low IAT scores corresponded to anti-white bias, and high scores to egalitarianism. This is not hypothetical; it is exactly what McConnell & Leibold (2001) found, although this pattern was not reported in their paper. Instead, the pattern was reported in a reanalysis of their data by Blanton et al. (2009).

Another study found no overall racial discrimination among doctors (Green et al., 2007). The study has been cited almost 1,000 times according to Google Scholar, and is widely considered a classic in the "implicit bias" literature. For example, it is one of the ten studies "no manager should ignore" according to Jost et al. (2009). Thus, it may be best for us to quote the paper directly to report the largely ignored fact that, overall, they found no bias: "However, participants were *equally* **likely** to recommend thrombolysis [treatment for blood clots] for black (52%) and white (48%) patients [who complained of chest pain] …" (pp. 1234–1235).

Other research assessing the extent to which IAT scores predict discrimination have found similar results indicating egalitarian behavior. For example, a study of trial judges found that: "The judges' determinations [sentencing] were not influenced by race" (Rachlinski et al., 2009, p. 1214). Yet another study, an experimental laboratory investigation into economic decisions found that "There was no significant difference between the mean [monetary] offers to black (μ=$3.74, SD=$1.99) and white (μ=$3.75, SD=$1.72) partners …" (Stanley et al., 2011, p. 7713).

To be clear, we have not performed a comprehensive meta-analysis of IAT predictive validity studies assessing net levels of racial discrimination. Our prediction is that, overall, such research would probably find non-zero net racial discrimination, despite the presence of studies finding no net discrimination and at least one finding net anti-white discrimination (McConnell & Leibold, 2001; Blanton et al., 2009). Regardless, such a meta-analysis (of level of overall racial bias, not predictive validity of the IAT) would be valuable on its merits as yet another way to gain insights into the extent of discrimination.

It is possible that empirical studies may underestimate the amount of discrimination occurring. However, it is a fact that some research finding no discrimination has been published, but that the narratives around that research have focused on the predictive validity of the IAT rather than the evidence of net nonbias. It is also a fact that forensic work uncovered 17 previously unpublished studies finding no bias; this raises questions about how many other studies finding null bias results remain unpublished.

Thus, it is distinctly possible that there is less individual-level discrimination in the present than indicated by our Figure 16.3. If so, that would warrant the revised heuristic estimate shown in Figure 16.4.

Figure 16.4 is the same as Figure 16.3, except that the total proportion of the gap due to individual discrimination has been reduced. It is possible that both Figures 16.3 and 16.4 overestimate the contribution of IAT scores to individual discrimination, because they are insufficiently subdivided. Individual discrimination in Figures 16.3 and 16.4 is only accounted for by prejudice (either implicit or explicit). Other factors, such as conformity to social norms, can also explain individual acts of discrimination (e.g., Duckitt, 1992). If Figures 16.3 and 16.4 fail to capture all sources of individual-level discrimination, the proportion capable of being attributed to IAT scores would shrink further, if those other sources were adequately represented. Thus, Figures 16.3 and 16.4 probably have

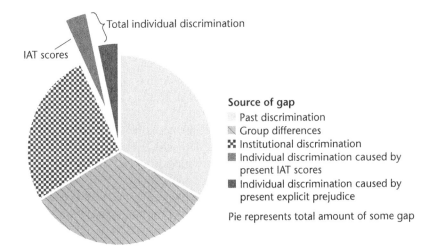

FIGURE 16.4 Pie represents total amount of some gap.

a greater risk of overestimating than of underestimating the role of IAT scores in producing individual-level discrimination.

Of course, our analysis here was heuristic, not empirical. No one knows how much IAT scores contribute to gaps between African-Americans and Whites in the US. Discrimination surely plays some role in those gaps; indeed, if one includes the effects of past discrimination and current discrimination, all of our models, despite their heuristic nature, are consistent with that total contribution being quite substantial. Consequently, interventions designed to reduce such gaps by focusing on individual, situational, and structural factors (see also Schmader, Bergsieker, & Hall, & Walton & Brady, this volume) are more likely to be effective than those focusing primarily on reducing "implicit biases." If Fiedler (this volume) is right in arguing that the most successful applications of social psychology need to be grounded in strong theories, so far, theories of implicit bias fall short, which may explain why changing implicit biases has little effect on discrimination (Forscher et al., 2019).

Regardless, our approach may provide some insight into the *potential for IAT scores* to contribute to those gaps, even if that potential cannot be precisely quantified. Unless one assumes that all or most other potential contributors to inequality – the legacy of slavery and Jim Crow, institutional discrimination, explicit prejudice – are trivial, we do not see how the conclusion can be avoided that the role of IAT scores in producing gaps is likely to be highly limited.

Conclusions

Should the IAT be scrapped? No, we are not suggesting that. Like most useful tools, from knives to planes, and computers to pesticides, it can be misused. The IAT has many imperfections: dubious construct validity, low test-retest reliability, various other psychometric oddities, its effect size has often been computed in a way that appears to exaggerate its size, it has been almost universally misinterpreted and misrepresented as measuring "implicit bias" when, by Greenwald's (2017) own definition, it does not do so, its predictive validity has been found to be modest at best, and even if we ignore all that, its ability to account for inequality in the present is likely to be limited.

This does not mean the IAT is useless. We could generate an equally long list for how cars have been misused. The IAT can be constructively used for both self-insight and research mainly by treating it for what it is – at best, a useful but imperfect measure of implicit *associations*. Each of those imperfections, however, can be a starting point for the next phase of research on and with the IAT. Whether and when such associations reflect norms, cultural stereotypes, social realities, or prejudice remains unclear after over 20 years of research on the IAT. Because so much emphasis was placed on the IAT as a measure of "implicit bias" or "unconscious prejudice," many alternative explanations for its effects received only modest attention. Intensified empirical attention to those alternatives is sorely needed.

Similarly, the IAT is not necessarily even a pure measure of implicit associations, and may reflect response biases, skill sets, and more. It is also possible that they may reflect different sources in different contexts, and some admixture in yet others. These possibilities, too, can serve as inspirations for future research. It is of course possible that in some contexts and under some circumstances, implicit associations *do* mostly reflect bias and such biases contribute to real-world inequalities. That, however, requires more evidence than a mere reaction time difference between two IATs.

References

Arias, E., & Xu, J. Q. (2018). United States life tables, 2015. *National Vital Statistics Reports, 67*(7).

Arkes, H. R., & Tetlock, P. E. (2004). Attributions of implicit prejudice, or "Would Jesse Jackson 'fail' the Implicit Association Test?" *Psychological Inquiry, 15*(4), 257–278. doi.org/10.1207/s15327965pli1504_01

Baker, A. (2018, July 18). Confronting implicit bias in the New York Police Department. *The New York Times*. Retrieved from www.nytimes.com/2018/07/15/nyregion/bias-training-police.html

Banaji, M. R., & Greenwald, A. G. (2013). *Blindspot: Hidden biases of good people* [epub]. New York, NY: Delacorte Press.

Bertocchi, G., & Dimico, A. (2014). Slavery, education, and inequality. *European Economic Review, 70*, 197–209.

Bertrand, M., & Mullainathan, S. (2004). Are Emily and Greg more employable than Lakisha and Jamal? A field experiment on labor market discrimination. *The American Economic Review, 94*(4), 991–1013.

Blair, I. V., Steiner, J. F., Fairclough, D. L., Hanratty, R., Price, D. W., Hirsh, H. K., Wright, L. A., Bronsert, M., Karimkhani, E., Magid, D. J., & Havranek, E. P. (2013). Clinicians' implicit ethnic/racial bias and perceptions of care among Black and Latino patients. *Annals of Family Medicine, 11*(1), 43–52. doi:10.1370/afm.1442

Blanton, H., Jaccard, J., & Burrows, C. N. (2015). Implications of the Implicit Association Test D-transformation for psychological assessment. *Assessment, 22*(4), 429–440. doi.org/10.1177/1073191114551382

Blanton, H., Jaccard, J., Klick, J., Mellers, B., Mitchell, G., & Tetlock, P. E. (2009). Strong claims and weak evidence: Reassessing the predictive validity of the IAT. *Journal of Applied Psychology, 94*(3), 567–582. doi.org/10.1037/a0014665

Blanton, H., Jaccard, J., Strauts, E., Mitchell, G., & Tetlock, P. E. (2015). Toward a meaningful metric of implicit prejudice. *Journal of Applied Psychology, 100*(5), 1468–1481. doi.org/10.1037/a0038379

Bluemke, M., & Fiedler, K. (2009). Base rate effects on the IAT. *Consciousness and Cognition, 18*(4), 1029–1038. doi.org/10.1016/j.concog.2009.07.010

Cao, J. & Banaji, M. R. (2016). Base rate principle and fairness principle. *Proceedings of the National Academy of Sciences, 113*(27), 7475–7480. doi.org/10.1073/pnas.1524268113

Centers for Disease Control and Prevention. (2019). Data and statistics on sickle cell disease. Retrieved from www.cdc.gov/ncbddd/sicklecell/data.html.

Chapman, E. N., Kaatz, A., & Carnes, M. (2013). Physicians and implicit bias: How doctors may unwittingly perpetuate health care disparities. *Journal of General Internal Medicine, 28*(11), 1504–1510. doi.org/10.1007/s11606-013-2441-1

Charlesworth, T. E. S., & Banaji, M. R. (2019). Patterns of implicit and explicit attitudes: I. Long-term change and stability from 2007 to 2016. *Psychological Science, 30*(2), 174–192. doi.org/10.1177/0956797618813087

Conrey, F. R., Sherman, J. W., Gawronski, B., Hugenberg, K., & Groom, C. J. (2005). Separating multiple processes in implicit social cognition: The quad model of implicit task performance. *Journal of Personality and Social Psychology, 89*(4), 469–487. doi.org/10.1037/0022-3514.89.4.469

Cronbach, L. J., & Furby, L. (1970). How we should measure "change": Or should we? *Psychological Bulletin, 74*(1), 68–80. doi.org/10.1037/h0029382

Darolia, R., Koedel, C., Martorell, P., Wilson, K., & Perez-Arce, F. (2016). Race and gender effects on employer interest in job applicants: New evidence from a resume field experiment. *Applied Economics Letters, 23*(12), 853–856.

Dawes, R. M. (1979). The robust beauty of improper linear models in decision making. *American Psychologist, 34*(7), 571–582.

Department of Justice, Office of Public Affairs. (2016, June 27). Department of Justice announces new department-wide implicit bias training for personnel [Press release]. Retrieved from www.justice.gov/opa/pr/department-justice-announces-new-department-wide-implicit-bias-training-personnel

Dragioti, E., Dimoliatis, I., Fountoulakis, K. N., & Evangelou, E. (2015). A systematic appraisal of allegiance effect in randomized controlled trials of psychotherapy. *Annals of General Psychiatry, 14*(25).

Duckitt, J. H. (1992). Psychology and prejudice: A historical analysis and integrative framework. *American Psychologist, 47*(10), 1182–1193.

Fazio, R. H. (1990). Multiple processes by which attitudes guide behavior: The mode model as an integrative framework. *Advances in Experimental Social Psychology, 23*, 75–109.

Felson, R. B., & Pare, P. (2010). Gun cultures or honor cultures? Explaining regional and race differences in weapon carrying. *Social Forces, 88*(3), 1357–1378.

Fiedler, K. (2020). Grounding applied social psychology in translational research. In J. Forgas, W. D. Crano, & K. Fiedler (Eds), *Applications of social psychology* (pp. 23–49). New York: Routledge.

Fiedler, K., Messner, C., & Bluemke, M. (2006). Unresolved problems with the "I", the "A", and the "T": A logical and psychometric critique of the Implicit Association Test (IAT). *European Review of Social Psychology, 17*(1), 74–147. doi.org/10.1080/10463280600681248

Fontenot, K., Semega, J., & Kollar, M. (2018). *Income and poverty in the United States: 2017*. U.S. Census Bureau, Current Population Reports, P60–263.

Forgas, J. P., & Lantos, D. (2020). Understanding populism: Collective narcissism and the collapse of democracy in Hungary. In J. Forgas, W. D. Crano, & K. Fiedler (Eds), *Applications of social psychology* (pp. 267–293). New York: Routledge.

Forscher, P. S., Lai, C. K., Axt, J. R., Ebersole, C. R., Herman, M., Devine, P. G., & Nosek, B. A. 2019. A meta-analysis of procedures to change implicit measures. *Journal of Personality & Social Psychology, 117(3)*, 522–559. https://doi.org/10.1037/pspa0000160

Green, A. R., Carney, D. R., Pallin, D. J., Ngo, L. H., Raymond, K. L., Iezzoni, L. I., & Banaji, M. R. (2007). Implicit bias among physicians and its prediction of thrombolysis decisions for black and white patients. *Journal of General Internal Medicine, 22*(9), 1231–1238. doi.org/10.1007/s11606-007-0258-5

Greenwald, A. G. (2017). *Twenty years of research on implicit social cognition.* Presented at the September 2017 National Science Foundation Conference on Implicit Bias.

Greenwald, A. G., Banaji, M. R., & Nosek, B. A. (2015). Statistically small effects of the Implicit Association Test can have societally large effects. *Journal of Personality and Social Psychology, 108*(4), 553–561. doi.org/10.1037/pspa0000016

Greenwald, A. G., McGhee, D. E., & Schwartz, J. L. (1998). Measuring individual differences in implicit cognition: The implicit association test. *Journal of Personality and Social Psychology, 74*(6), 1464–1480.

Greenwald, A. G., Nosek, B. A., & Banaji, M. R. (2003). Understanding and using the Implicit Association Test: I. An improved scoring algorithm. *Journal of Personality and Social Psychology, 85*(2), 197–216. doi.org/10.1037/0022-3514.85.2.197

Greenwald, A. G., Poehlman, T. A., Uhlmann, E. L., & Banaji, M. R. (2009). Understanding and using the Implicit Association Test: III. Meta-analysis of predictive validity. *Journal of Personality and Social Psychology, 97*(1), 17–41. doi.org/10.1037/a0015575

Hahn, A., Judd, C. M., Hirsh, H. K., & Blair, I. V. (2014). Awareness of implicit attitudes. *Journal of Experimental Psychology: General, 143*(3), 1369–1392. http://dx.doi.org/10.1037/a0035028

Heckman, J. J. (1998). Detecting discrimination. *Journal of Economic Perspectives, 12,* 101–116.

Hensch, M. (2016, September 26). Clinton: We must fight "implicit bias." *The Hill.* Retrieved from https://thehill.com/blogs/ballot-box/presidential-races/297939-clinton-i-think-implicit-bias-is-a-problem-for-everyone

Hughes, C. (2018, July 19). Black American culture and the racial wealth gap. *Quillette.* Retrieved from https://quillette.com/2018/07/19/black-american-culture-and-the-racial-wealth-gap/

Johnson, D. J., & Chopik, W. J. (2019). Geographic variation in the black-violence stereotype. *Social Psychological and Personality Science, 10*(3), 287–294. doi.org/10.1177/1948550617753522

Jolls, C., & Sunstein, C. R. (2006). The law of implicit bias. *California Law Review, 94,* 969.

Jost, J. T., Rudman, L. A., Blair, I. V., Carney, D. R., Dasgupta, N., Glaser, J., & Hardin, C. D. (2009). The existence of implicit bias is beyond reasonable doubt: A refutation of ideological and methodological objections and executive summary of ten studies that no manager should ignore. *Research in Organizational Behavior, 29,* 39–69. doi.org/10.1016/j.riob.2009.10.001

Jussim, L. (2017). Accuracy, bias, self-fulfilling prophecies, and scientific self-correction. *Behavioral and Brain Sciences, 40.* doi.org/10.1017/S0140525X16000339

Jussim, L., Careem, A., Goldberg, Z., Honeycutt, N., & Stevens, S. T. (2019). IAT scores, racial gaps, and scientific gaps. Chapter prepared for J. A. Krosnick, T. H. Stark, & A. L. Scott (Eds., under review), *The future of research on implicit bias.*

Jussim, L., Crawford, J. T., & Rubinstein, R. S. (2015). Stereotype (in)accuracy in perceptions of groups and individuals. *Current Directions in Psychological Science, 24*(6), 490–497. doi.org/10.1177/0963721415605257

Kerr, N. L. (1998). HARKing: Hypothesizing after the results are known. *Personality and Social Psychology Review, 2*(3), 196–217.

Kovera, M. B. (2020). When justice is not blind: The effects of expectancies on social interactions and judgments in legal settings. In J. Forgas, W. D. Crano, & K. Fiedler (Eds), *Applications of social psychology* (pp. 231–249). New York: Routledge.

Lane, K. A., Banaji, M. R., Nosek, B. A., & Greenwald, A. G. (2007). Understanding and using the Implicit Association Test: IV: What we know (so far) about the method. In B. Wittenbrink & N. Schwarz (Eds.), *Implicit measures of attitudes* (pp. 59–102). New York: Guilford Press.

LeBel, E. P., & Paunonen, S. P. (2011). Sexy but often unreliable: The impact of unreliability on the replicability of experimental findings with implicit measures. *Personality and Social Psychology Bulletin, 37*(4), 570–583. doi.org/10.1177/0146167211400619

Lick, D. J., Alter, A. L., & Freeman, J. B. (2018). Superior pattern detectors efficiently learn, activate, apply, and update social stereotypes. *Journal of Experimental Psychology: General, 147*(2), 209–227. doi.org/10.1037/xge0000349

Loury, G. C. (1998). An American tragedy: The legacy of slavery lingers in our cities' ghettos. *The Brookings Review, 16*(2), 38–42. doi.org/10.2307/20080781

McConnell, A. R., & Leibold, J. M. (2001). Relations among the Implicit Association Test, discriminatory behavior, and explicit measures of racial attitudes. *Journal of Experimental Social Psychology, 37*(5), 435–442. doi.org/10.1006/jesp.2000.1470

Nosek, B. A., Smyth, F. L., Hansen, J. J., Devos, T., Lindner, N. M., Ranganath, K. A., … Banaji, M. R. (2007). Pervasiveness and correlates of implicit attitudes and stereotypes. *European Review of Social Psychology, 18*(1), 1–53. doi.org/10.1080/10463280701489053

Oswald, F. L., Mitchell, G., Blanton, H., Jaccard, J., & Tetlock, P. E. (2013). Predicting ethnic and racial discrimination: A meta-analysis of IAT criterion studies. *Journal of Personality and Social Psychology, 105*(2), 171–192. doi.org/10.1037/a0032734

Pager, D. (2007). The use of field experiments for studies of employment discrimination: Contributions, critiques, and directions for future research. *Annals of the American Academy of Political and Social Science, 609*, 104–133.

Pager, D., & Pedulla, D. S. (2015). Race, self-selection, and the job search process. *American Journal of Sociology, 120*, 1005–1054.

Pager, D., & Shepherd, H. (2008). The sociology of discrimination: Racial discrimination in employment, housing, credit, and consumer markets. *Annual Review of Sociology, 34*, 181–209.

Pager, D., Western, B., & Bonikowski, B. (2009). Discrimination in a low-wage labor market: A field experiment. *American Sociological Review, 74*, 777–799.

Payne, B. K., Vuletich, H. A., & Lundberg, K. B. (2017). The bias of crowds: How implicit bias bridges personal and systemic prejudice. *Psychological Inquiry, 28*(4), 233–248. doi.org/10.1080/1047840X.2017.1335568

Petty, R. & Briñol, P. (2020). A process approach to influencing attitudes and changing behavior: Revisiting classic findings in persuasion and popular interventions. In J. Forgas, W. D. Crano, & K. Fiedler (Eds), *Applications of social psychology* (pp. 82–103). New York: Routledge.

Quillian, L., Pager, D., Hexel, O., & Midtbøen, A. H. (2017). Meta-analysis of field experiments shows no change in racial discrimination in hiring over time. *Proceedings of the National Academy of Sciences, 114*(41), 10870–10875.

Rachlinski, J. J., Johnson, S. L., Wistrich, A. J., & Guthrie, C. (2009). Does unconscious racial bias affect trial judges? *Notre Dame Law Review, 84*(3), 1195–1246.

Reber, A. S. (1989). Implicit learning and tacit knowledge. *Journal of Experimental Psychology: General, 118*(3), 219–235. doi.org/10.1037/0096-3445.118.3.219

Rubinstein, R. S., & Jussim, L. (2019). *Stimulus pairing and statement target information have equal effects on stereotype-relevant evaluations of individuals*. Manuscript submitted for publication.

Rubinstein, R. S., Jussim, L., & Stevens, S. T. (2018). Reliance on individuating information and stereotypes in implicit and explicit person perception. *Journal of Experimental Social Psychology, 76,* 54–70. doi.org/10.1016/j.jesp.2017.11.009

Ryan, C. L., & Bauman, K. (2016). *Educational attainment in the United States: 2015.* U.S. Census Bureau, Current Population Reports, P20–578.

Sabin, J. A., & Greenwald, A. G. (2012). The influence of implicit bias on treatment recommendations for 4 common pediatric conditions: Pain, urinary tract infection, attention deficit hyperactivity disorder, and asthma. *American Journal of Public Health, 102*(5), 988–995. doi.org/10.2105/AJPH.2011.300621

Schimmack, U. (2019). The Implicit Association Test: A method in search of a construct. *Perspectives on Psychological Science.* doi.org/10.1177/1745691619863798

Schmader, T., Bergsieker, H. B., & Hall, W. M. (2020). Cracking the culture code: A tri-level model for cultivating inclusion in organizations. In J. Forgas, W. D. Crano, & K. Fiedler (Eds), *Applications of social psychology* (pp. 334–355). New York: Routledge.

Schwarz J. (1998, September 29). Roots of unconscious prejudice affect 90 to 95 percent of people, psychologists demonstrate at press conference. *University of Washington News.* Retrieved from www.washington.edu/news/1998/09/29/roots-of-unconscious-prejudice-affect-90-to-95-percent-of-people-psychologists-demonstrate-at-press-conference/

Stanley, D. A., Sokol-Hessner, P., Banaji, M. H., & Phelps, E. A. (2011). Implicit race attitudes predict trustworthiness judgments and economic trust decisions. *Proceedings of the National Academy of Sciences, 108*(19), 7710–7715. doi.org/10.1073/pnas.1014345108

Talaska, C. A., Fiske, S. T., & Chaiken, S. (2008). Legitimating racial discrimination: Emotions, not beliefs, best predict discrimination in a meta-analysis. *Social Justice Research, 21*(3), 263–296.

Walton, G. M., & Brady, S. T. (2020). "Bad" things reconsidered. In J. Forgas, W. D. Crano, & K. Fiedler (Eds), *Applications of social psychology* (pp. 58–81). New York: Routledge.

Zigerell, L. J. (2018). Black and White discrimination in the United States: Evidence from an archive of survey experiment studies. *Research & Politics.* doi.org/10.1177/2053168017753862

17

CRACKING THE CULTURE CODE

A Tri-Level Model for Cultivating Inclusion in Organizations

Toni Schmader, Hilary B. Bergsieker and William M. Hall

People are increasingly finding themselves living, learning, and working in a diverse world. Although increased exposure to, tolerance of, if not preference for diversity poses political challenges (Forgas & Lantos, this volume), it also presents important opportunities for cultural innovation. As a key example, organizations are increasingly motivated to diversify their workforce and capitalize on the potential benefits that diverse teams can have for creative problem solving and innovation (Galinsky et al., 2015; Phillips, Mannix, Neale, Gruenfeld, 2004). One challenge of working in diverse environments is that—even in the absence of explicit intergroup biases or prejudice—deep-rooted and perhaps evolutionarily determined inclinations toward homophily (Cosmides, Tooby, & Kurzban, 2003; McPherson, Smith-Lovin, & Cook, 2001; see also van Vugt et al., this volume) can lead people to seek out working relationships with similar others and avoid those who are different. These biases are exacerbated when the culture of the organization is defined by and adheres closely to the preferences, interests, and working styles of the majority. For those who have a devalued minority identity in these settings, the result can be a feeling of alienation that can lead them to self-select out of domains where they experience a lack of fit (Schmader & Sedikides, 2018; Woodson, 2015).

In the present chapter, we seek to understand what it means to have an inclusive organizational culture by considering a tri-level model of culture as consisting of: (1) *institutional* policies, (2) the beliefs and attitudes of *individuals*, and how these institutional features and individual beliefs play out in (3) the *interpersonal interactions* between people. We apply these ideas to specifically understand feelings of alienation and exclusion that women experience in male-dominated fields in science, technology, engineering, and math (STEM). Not only do these fields offer highly lucrative and intellectually rewarding careers, they are also key economic drivers of society. Thus, when there are systemic factors that undermine gender inclusion, women's career autonomy is threatened, the gender wage gap grows larger, and societies fail to maximize their intellectual resources. In engineering, for example, a field that is 80 percent male in North America, women show disproportionately higher rates of attrition (Corbett & Hill, 2015). Low numeric representation per se can deter women from STEM fields (Murphy, Steele, & Gross, 2007). However, some traditionally male-dominated occupations (e.g., law, medicine, life science) have been markedly quicker to desegregate than others (e.g., engineering, computer science; Carli, Alawa, Lee, Zhao, & Kim, 2016), suggesting that the culture of the latter fields may impede women's entry and advancement. Indeed, women who choose to leave engineering and technology careers after clearly having demonstrated both an interest in and talent for the field often attribute their departure to problems of ill-fitting organizational culture (Fouad & Singh, 2011; Margolis & Fisher, 2003). As social psychologists, how can we better understand what it means to have an inclusive culture, and what methods can we use to achieve cultural change (see also Fiedler, this volume)?

Culture and Mutual Constitution

Humans have an evolutionarily adaptive capacity to form, maintain, and affirm cultures (Henrich, 2015). These cultures then shape individuals' sense of identity (Markus & Hamedani, 2007). The prevailing understanding is that cultures are embedded systems that both define and are defined by the identities of the individuals in that society and are formed and reformed through social interactions and relationships (Markus & Kitayama, 2010). Through this process of mutual constitution, shared cultural norms are partly created by the beliefs, attitudes, and preferences of the majority or dominant groups. The stronger the majority, the more likely that the group's beliefs and practices become polarized as similar individuals interact with one another and reinforce each other's shared tendencies (Isenberg, 1986). Once created, these norms for what to believe, what to like, and how to behave become codified in both explicit and implicit ways. These norms then have the power to shape the way in which people perceive and interact with one another. Those interactions, as well as broader cultural beliefs and shared attitudes, then also have the power to change individuals' own attitudes, beliefs, self-views, and behavior.

Although cultural psychologists have typically used these ideas to frame our understanding of people from different societies, subcultures, or regions of the world, these same basic processes are likely to prove useful for understanding the culture of organizations. More practically, we might better isolate the levers for changing organizational culture by importing social-psychological theory of what defines a culture (see also Fiedler, this volume). Here we focus on three distinct but interconnected levels of organizational culture: the institutional, interpersonal, and individual levels. First, we describe how each level potentially contributes to the experienced culture of an organization. We then use this framework to discuss how different kinds of interventions could change workplace culture. Although organizations (and cultures more generally) ideally promote equity for all regardless of gender, age, ethnicity, and other demographic markers of identity, the reality is that many of these groups still face subtle and not so subtle barriers to their belonging and authenticity (Schmader & Sedikides, 2018). The processes we describe may apply broadly to many contexts and dimensions of identity, however the primary illustration we use involves changing organizational culture in highly male-dominated careers (such as engineering, finance, and technology) to become more gender inclusive.

The Institutional Level: Organizational Policies and Practices

The culture of an organization is signaled by its policies, procedures, and expressions of organizational identity (Schein, 2004). Just as individuals leave clues to their own personality in the digital and physical spaces they inhabit (Gosling, Ko, Mannarelli, & Morris, 2002), organizations also broadcast aspects of their culture in their websites, promotional materials, and physical layout of their workspaces. Many organizations aim to present an image of inclusion by using images of diverse people (Pippert, Essenburg, & Matchett, 2013; Swan, 2010), or even by explicitly and prominently displaying a diversity mission statement, already a common corporate practice by the mid-1990s (Kelly & Dobbin, 1998).

These efforts on the part of organizations to advertise an inclusive ideology are then used by perceivers to make assumptions about the culture of an organization (Brady, Kaiser, Major, & Kirby, 2015; Kaiser et al., 2013; Purdie-Vaughns, Steele, Davies, Ditlmann, & Crosby, 2008). In fact, diversity statements can create the impression of an egalitarian workplace culture so effectively that perceivers come to doubt that biases can still exist in those environments and penalize targets who report instances of discrimination when they do occur (Kaiser et al., 2013). Such institutional cues to inclusion not only shape the perceptions of outside observers, but also signal fit (or lack thereof) for those who would typically be underrepresented. Members of devalued groups habitually attend to cues related to *social identity contingencies*, namely, the judgments, stereotypes, opportunities, constraints, and treatments tied to one's social identity in a given setting (Purdie-Vaughns et al., 2008). Research increasingly finds in educational settings, for example, that physical reminders of a "typical student," institutional practices that preference only one way of learning, or syllabus statements referencing an entity orientation to success, can all be cues that trigger a reduced sense of belonging or authenticity for students from underrepresented groups (Cheryan, Plaut, Davies, & Steele, 2009; Stephens, Hamedani, & Townsend, 2019; Fuesting et al., 2019; Schmader & Sedikides, 2018).

In organizational settings, companies ideally institute diversity policies and practices, not only to signal an inclusive culture, but in a sincere effort to attract and retain diverse talent. Analysis of these practices at hundreds of organizations over time suggests that some of these strategies (when not merely "window dressing," see Kaiser et al., 2013) are indeed effective for boosting diversity in leadership positions (Kalev, Dobbin, & Kelly, 2006). Most notably, evidence-based best practices include engaging in active recruitment of diverse candidates; making hiring and promotion committees accountable for their record of diverse selections; and appointing equity, diversity, and inclusion officers to manage these efforts. These types of institutional initiatives, on average, boost the representation of women and minorities into management positions (Kalev et al., 2006). In addition, these and other inclusion-oriented policies may signal that the culture of the organization (or at least its leadership) values inclusion. For example, even when women or minorities are underrepresented in an organization, simply knowing that the organization has a stated interest in promoting diversity can make that company seem like a more desirable place to work for members of underrepresented groups (Purdie-Vaughns et al., 2008; Hall, Schmader, Aday, Inness, & Croft, 2018).

The Individual Level: Implicit and Explicit Beliefs, Biases, and Self-Views

Cultures are broad networks of norms, beliefs, and attitudes that guide the behavior of individuals. Thus, the emergence of organizational culture involves the dynamic interplay of top-down influences, such as the formal mission or policies set by leadership, and bottom-up attitudes, beliefs, and actions of individual employees. Although it is tempting to parse the variance between institutional and individual biases (Jussim, Careem, Honeycutt, & Stevens, this volume), because policies and practices are established and maintained by individuals within a culture, the two are likely to be inextricably linked. Through a cycle of mutual constitution, the actions of individuals help to create, perpetuate, and change the culture as a function of their own preferences, biases, self-views, and life experiences. From this logic, organizations that have a broader representation of women or minorities are likely to also have (at least on average) more favorable attitudes toward diversity policies and cultural practices that favor their own group. Indeed, members of marginalized groups attend closely to numeric representation as a cue to an environment's inclusiveness (Murphy et al., 2007; Purdie-Vaughns et al., 2008). Although different disadvantaged groups will not necessarily band together automatically to support all forms of diversity and inclusion, they are more likely to support broad-based policies of inclusion when reminded of their shared disadvantage with other marginalized groups (Cortland et al., 2017). Moreover, given the power of leaders to set influential norms (Cheng, Tracy, Foulsham, Kingstone, &

Henrich, 2013), the benefits of diverse representation for an inclusive workplace culture will most strongly be realized when the diversity of representation occurs in positions of leadership throughout the organization rather than within lower-status roles within the organizational hierarchy (Bartol & Zhang, 2007).

Increased diversity of representation can contribute to a more inclusive workplace culture but is neither necessary nor sufficient for creating a culture of inclusion. Understanding why involves acknowledging that cultures dwell in the minds of individuals at both implicit and explicit levels (Markus & Kitayama, 2010; see also Forgas & Lantos; and Wohl & Stefaniak, this volume). At an implicit level, people learn automatically activated associations to social categories based on some combination of group members' actual representation in different roles and one's own salient experiences with them (Asgari, Dasgupta, & Cote, 2010; Asgari, Dasgupta, & Stout, 2012). For example, although implicit measures such as the Implicit Association Test are not without critique (Jussim et al., this volume), the implicit association of "science" (vs. "arts") with "male" (vs. "female") is sensibly correlated with cross-national variability in gender gaps in both math performance (Nosek et al., 2009) and science representation (Miller, Eagly, & Linn, 2015).

Furthermore, in line with other dual-process views of attitudes and beliefs (Petty & Briñol, this volume), these implicit associations can diverge strongly from people's explicitly reported beliefs and attitudes toward the same groups (Nosek, 2005). Even women with successful careers in engineering exhibit a significant tendency to associate their concept of "engineering" (vs. "family") more with "male" than with "female" (Block, Hall, Schmader, Inness, & Croft, 2018). But these implicit associations do not only reflect the realities of women's underrepresentation in engineering (and overrepresentation in managing family life), they can also be internalized to shape women's own views of themselves. For example, the automatic tendency to associate science and engineering more with male than female correlate with women's lower ratings of self-confidence, self-efficacy, and organizational commitment in science, math, and engineering (Block et al., 2018; Stout, Dasgupta, Hunsinger, McManus, 2011; Nosek, Banaji, & Greenwald, 2002).

That implicit stereotypes and attitudes can be internalized by members of underrepresented groups to shape their own beliefs about gender and themselves means that simply boosting representation will not guarantee an increasingly inclusive organizational culture. For example, in studies that have documented gender biases in evaluative or hiring contexts, these biases have been exhibited both by women and men (Madera, Hebl, Dial, Martin, & Valian, 2018; Moss-Racusin, Dovidio, Brescoll, Graham, & Handelsman, 2012), and as a function of enacting the assumed biases held by other sexist leaders (Vial, Dovidio, & Brescoll, 2019). Notably, however, individuals act within a broader cultural context. Simply associating Science and Men at an implicit level, does not automatically lead to expressions of bias or discriminatory actions toward women in science (Crandall & Eshleman, 2003; Devine, 1989; Fazio, 1990). Rather, the surrounding cultural context can either license these implicit biases to shape behavior and decision-making, or cue perceivers to suppress or counteract them (Forbes, Cox, Schmader, & Ryan, 2012; Murphy, Kroeper, & Ozier, 2018; Murphy & Walton, 2013).

Recent research demonstrates this dual process accounts for how implicit and explicit beliefs interact to predict women's outcomes in STEM (Régner, Thinus-Blanc, Netter, Schmader, & Huguet, 2019). In a unique field study, members of 39 different evaluation committees took part in a study of gender bias in their real-life selections for women and men into elite scientific research positions. Approximately half the committee members completed measures of their implicit science=male stereotypes and their explicit beliefs about the reasons for gender disparities in science. Over the course of the year-long study, committees' tendency to promote women into elite research positions did not simply correlate with the implicit science=male associations of their members. Rather, their implicit associations (averaged across committee members) only translated into adverse impact for women in the competition if, at an explicit level, committee members (on average) did not believe that external barriers such as discrimination partly explain women's underrepresentation in science. In other words, the committees who rejected the notion that bias is a problem were the ones who showed a relationship between their implicit biases and behavior. Among those committees who believed that women face barriers to their advancement, the strength of their implicit associations was unrelated to their decision-making. Notably, these effects emerged independently of the representation of women on selection committees.

These findings imply that, just as individuals can successfully regulate their own implicit stereotypes and attitudes when motivated to do so (Cunningham et al., 2004), groups may also dynamically regulate the biases of their members. In fact, the social presence of others who share these same associations but deny their importance might even meta-cognitively validate relying on these implicit stereotypes when making decisions (Petty & Briñol, this volume). In contrast, in the presence of shared explicit norms for inclusion, implicit associations might cease to have much impact on behavior or, in some cases, even lead to efforts to boost the representation of minority candidates. This is likely why studies of hiring biases among egalitarian-minded academic scientists sometimes find a bias in hiring female over male candidates when applicants are similarly highly qualified (Williams & Ceci, 2015). It is important to note, however, that meta-analyses suggest that when candidates' qualifications are more ambiguous, biases in hiring are more likely to favor members of the advantaged group (Koch, D'Mello, & Sackett, 2015).

The Interpersonal Level: Daily Interactions Between People

Most attention given to organizational culture—both in academic literature and public discourse—focuses on what institutions themselves can do either to change their culture by enacting new policies, communicating inclusive values from leadership, or educating individual employees through diversity training. An organizational focus certainly makes sense in light of evidence that organizational culture is signaled, in part, from the overt and covert messaging, policies, and practices that are created and maintained at the level of the institution. Likewise, an individual focus is appealing to private industry because of the increased liability posed by the discriminatory conduct of bad actors. However, adopting a social-psychological understanding of culture entails recognizing that culture is also communicated through the *interactions* of individuals with each other within a cultural-defined setting (Mead, 1934; see also Kovera, this volume, for a similar argument as it relates to biases in the legal system). People's emotional well-being and general satisfaction with life are heavily impacted by their daily interactions with co-workers (Lim, Cortina, & Magley, 2008). When people leave an organization or even a career path due to concerns with the culture, these day-to-day interactions are likely to be where cultural mismatches are most strongly felt.

Some of the interpersonal experiences that signal a lack of inclusion are overt instances of hostility, harassment, or feeling that others are undermining one's work (Berdahl, Cooper, Glick, Livingston, & Williams, 2018). For example, relative to men, women are more likely to experience acts of aggression (Baron & Neuman, 1996), bullying (Rayner & Hoel, 1997), incivility (Andersson & Pearson, 1999), emotional abuse (Keashly, Harvey, & Hunter, 1997), sexism (Cortina, 2008), and sexual harassment (Berdahl & Raver, 2011). Even in the absence of explicitly negative interactions, however, a less-than-inclusive workplace culture can manifest in subtler ways. For example, after interacting with male peers who hold implicitly sexist associations with women, female engineering students perform more poorly on a test of their engineering skills (Logel et al., 2009). Women experiencing these subtle but negative effects of bias on their performance were oblivious to how their male partners' dominant and flirtatious behavior undermined their performance.

In addition to the effects of subtle sexism, women in male-dominated workplaces sometimes feel isolated from informal networks where they could otherwise build relationships and learn about new opportunities (Bartol & Zhang, 2007; Forret & Dougherty, 2004). Organizational literature "strongly suggests that women do not have equal access to social capital because they are often excluded from the social networks most important for power acquisition and career success" (Wang, 2009, p. 33). Women seek connections both with socially similar co-workers (women) and high-status co-workers (typically men), but a dilemma arises in men's reciprocation of these choices: "If network contacts are chosen according to similarity and/or status considerations, [women] are less desirable network choices for men on both counts" (Ibarra, 1992, p. 440). Moreover, in male-dominated workplaces, even some women report avoiding other women (Derks, Van Laar, & Ellemers, 2016) and denigrating female-focused networking events. For example, a large-scale series of focus groups analyzing women's underrepresentation in engineering observed:

> For years [these female engineers] had avoided women's networking events because they were "packed with lawyers and HR types," not people in the "business of the business." If one of these female engineers walked into a room filled with women, she promptly walked back out. As one explained, "By definition nothing important is going on in this room: In this company men hold the power." These women seemed to have learned to avoid and look down on other women.
>
> *The Athena Factor;* Hewlett et al., 2008; p. 11

Due either to perceivers' prejudices and stereotypes or to targets' own stigma consciousness, interactions between members of diverse groups can be plagued by feelings of *social identity threat*, namely, concerns about negative evaluation based on one's group membership (Steele, Spencer, & Aronson, 2002; Vorauer, 2006). For women working in male-dominated STEM environments, feelings of social identity threat can arise when women sense a lack of complete acceptance and respect from male colleagues (Hall, Schmader, & Croft, 2015; Hall, Schmader, Aday, & Croft, 2019). These findings come from a series of daily-diary studies examining how day-to-day interactions in STEM workplaces cue women's experience of identity threat. Notably, across three distinct samples, the effect of these daily interactions on women's experience of social identity threat was unique to women's conversations with male colleagues about work-related topics and not rooted in how men and women relate to or perceive each other in general (Hall et al., 2019). Men did not report similar levels of identity threat if they feel a lack of respect during conversations with women or other men. And these effects, which reflect within-person variability due to specific conversations, cannot be explained by individual differences in women's stigma consciousness. Rather, something subtle seems to be happening in some of the women's conversations with men in STEM settings that makes their gender salient.

These concerns about identity threat seem to carry important consequences: On those days when women report less acceptance from male colleagues, they also report a greater experience of psychological burnout, an effect statistically mediated through feelings of social identity threat (Hall et al., 2019). These effects parallel but extend earlier findings that used a more objective measure of workplace conversations with a smaller sample of scientists (Holleran, Whitehead, Schmader, & Mehl, 2011). In that study, an electronically activated recorder (EAR) was used to sample workplace conversations between male and female academic researchers as they went about their normal work week. Among men, those who spent more time talking about research with male colleagues reported feeling more engaged in their work—an intuitive finding. Among women, however, those who spent more time talking about research with male colleagues reported feeling less engaged in their work.

Of course, one could argue that the interpersonal factors affecting women's daily workplace experiences have little to do with the culture of an organization and more to do with idiosyncratic bad encounters with a few biased co-workers. Although such explicitly negative interactions do occur, our evidence suggests that they do not drive these effects (Hall et al., 2019). Rather the rules of engagement for workplace interactions are, at least in part, shaped by the cultural norms signaled by the organization (Hall et al., 2018). Organizations adopting inclusive workplace policies may create a stronger norm for respectful and inclusive interactions among diverse individuals. Indeed, our own research indicates that women working in engineering report feeling less daily social identity threat to the extent that their organization has more gender-inclusive policies in place. Critically, this relationship is mediated by women's reports of experiencing more accepting and respectful daily interactions with their male colleagues in organizations with more gender-inclusive policies (Hall et al., 2018). In sum, cultural norms may be signaled at the institutional level and represented in the minds of individuals, but they are often experienced by diverse people as the manner in which people interact with one another.

Cultivating an Inclusive Culture

Organizational culture not only forms but also evolves through the dynamic interplay of institutional, individual, and interpersonal factors. The simple understanding that culture exists at these three levels can help provide a playbook for how best to change the culture of an organization. It also implies that different types of change might be better targeted at different levels, and that change at one level can variously catalyze change or encounter inertia at another level. Although our focus in this chapter has been on norms for inclusion, these same three interrelated levels can also be applied to understand the power of social norms in other contexts. For example, aggressive behavior among children can be reduced by interventions directed at classroom policies, interpersonal interactions, or individual impulse control (Krahé, this volume), and problems of adolescence are best tackled by multilevel interventions (Crano & Ruybal, this volume).

At the institutional level. As already mentioned, organizational science suggests that certain institutional policies are effective for increasing the representation of diverse leaders in an organization. Although these policies might have tangible benefits for some individuals, they might only result in meaningful cultural change if most people in the organization are aware of and support these policies. Our own research suggests that women and men who perceive that others' attitudes toward gender-inclusive institutional policies have improved over time come to feel a greater sense of value fit with the organization, which in turn predicts an increase in women's organizational commitment (Hall et al., 2019). This research suggests that merely enacting policy changes toward inclusion will prove insufficient unless organizations educate their employees about the value of those policies.

Institutional changes can also be informed by more recent social-psychological evidence about identity safety. Organizations can aim to de-bias their workplaces by looking for ways they can signal inclusive organizational values. This process can include websites, office imagery, pronouns, land acknowledgements, accessibility, bathroom facilities, and properly-sized equipment (Chaney & Sanchez, 2018; Murphy & Taylor, 2012). To effect change, these updates must seem sincere, not like hollow or disingenuous gestures (Kaiser et al., 2013). Moreover, we typically look to leaders and those in higher-status positions to define norms and values (Cheng et al., 2013). Thus, leaders and the institutions they represent have the power to create signals of inclusive culture that manifest in the norms of how people interact. When these policy changes and messages are enacted to signal a true organizational value toward inclusion, such cues may instil a stronger sense of fit for those who are traditionally likely to be devalued in that space (Schmader & Sedikides, 2018).

At the individual level. Another common strategy for changing the culture of an organization involves targeting the biases and beliefs in the minds of individuals. Equity, diversity, and inclusion training is not only common practice, but also a burgeoning business, with such programs now offered at over half of mid-sized and large US companies (Dobbin & Kalev, 2016), often emphasizing implicit or "unconscious" bias (Onyeador, 2017). As with many efforts to import ideas generated from academic research into practice (Fiedler, this volume), up until quite recently, there has been little to no evidence demonstrating that these training programs indeed work (Jussim et al., this volume; Paluck, 2006). Indeed, initiatives narrowly targeting individual "wrongdoing" in isolation may backfire: A recent review finds that sexual harassment training programs can in some cases decrease the number of women in management (Dobbin & Kalev, 2019). An additional challenge arises when combatting implicit bias, because implicit associations prove quite resistant to long-term change among adults who have had a lifetime to internalize cultural associations (Lai et al., 2014, 2016). If the goal is to actually change individuals' stereotypes and attitudes, successful interventions may need to target younger age groups who are still forming categories and associations between them (Baron & Banaji, 2006; Gonzalez, Dunlop, & Baron, 2017).

However, if the ultimate aim is to change intrinsically motivated behavior rather than implicit associations, then successful interventions might equip individuals with strategies to recognize and control their automatically activated responses (Carnes et al., 2015; Devine et al., 2017; Forscher, Mitamura, Dix, Cox, & Devine, 2017; Moss-Racusin et al., 2018). For example, in an extensive program of research, Devine and colleagues have been carrying out "Breaking the Bias Habit" workshops that educate individuals about the nature of automatic and controlled processes in bias, and teach people specific strategies for bias identification and control. A gender-bias version of this intervention carried out with academic scientists not only increased awareness and self-efficacy to control one's biases, but also boosted the proportion of women hired by 18 percentage points (a marginally significant increase) in the two years after the workshop took place (Carnes et al., 2015; Devine et al., 2017). In contrast to this face-to-face training program, the typical format for organizational diversity training is often online—to scale easily across many sites and employee schedules, but individual online training has much more limited success (Chang et al., 2019).

Individually-focused interventions that seek to foster more inclusive cultures rightfully target the deeply ingrained stereotypes and attitudes that can subtly bias behavior and decision-making. However, another valuable approach can be found in mindset interventions aimed at shifting the perspective of those who are disadvantaged or negatively stereotyped (Walton & Brady, this volume). When applied to boost the academic achievement of lower socioeconomic or ethnic minority students, these interventions work by helping students reframe academic difficulties or feelings of isolation as a normal part of transition (Walton & Cohen, 2011), or by encouraging a more growth-oriented mindset (Yeager et al., 2016). For example, in a recent large-scale intervention with nearly 1,000 incoming undergraduate students, a mindset intervention aimed at encouraging a growth orientation to challenges and setbacks led to a 30–40 percent reduction in the achievement gap between students from socially/economically advantaged versus disadvantaged backgrounds (Yeager et al., 2016). These efforts to reappraise negative experiences are also thought to be a beneficial strategy to boost women's sense of inclusion and self-efficacy in STEM (Walton, Logel, Peach, Spencer, & Zanna, 2015). For example, when anxiety is reframed as being potentially beneficial to performance, women and minorities perform better, even in a context where they otherwise might experience stereotype threat (Johns, Inzlicht, & Schmader, 2008; Schmader, Forbes, Zhang, & Mendes, 2009).

We contend that efforts to change or reframe the beliefs and behaviors of individuals in an organization are more likely to succeed when accounting for other levels in this model of organizational culture. For example, mindset interventions effectively counteract the reduced feelings of self-efficacy and inclusion experienced by members of marginalized groups, but will be of only limited value if broader institutional or interpersonal biases still exist as norms. In addition, institutional policy changes will only be effective if they have an effect on individual decision-making or interpersonal interactions. For example, some of the most effective policies to promote inclusion are organizational accountability programs that incentivize careful decision-making (Kalev et al., 2006). The policy to track and report clear metrics helps to circumvent perceivers' tendencies to sometimes fall back on implicit associations when overwhelmed by complex hiring and promotion decisions (Bohnet, 2016; Bohnet, van Geen, & Bazerman, 2015; Uhlmann & Cohen, 2005). Thus, combining Devine's "Break the Bias Habit" program with an accountability policy would likely achieve better results than either initiative alone.

At the interpersonal level. Finally, as interpersonal contexts often provide the proximal conduit for how people feel included, efforts to change the culture of an organization would do well to target efforts directly at this level as well. In fact, social psychology has a long and largely successful tradition of reducing intergroup biases in applied settings using positive intergroup contact (Sherif & Sherif, 1953; Pettigrew & Tropp, 2006). Guided by Gordon Allport's (1954) recommended recipe for successful contact, interventions in schools, workplaces, and conflict settings have sought to orchestrate successful contact between individuals from diverse backgrounds by placing them on a level playing field, working together toward a common goal. Other key ingredients catalyzing effective contact include support from institutional leadership and the potential for real social connections or even friendships between the interacting individuals. These are not necessary, but rather facilitating conditions: Experimental efforts to create contact can reduce intergroup biases even with only some of these ingredients in place (Pettigrew & Tropp, 2006, 2008). Although contact experiences are more effective at reducing the negative intergroup attitudes held by the majority or higher-status group (Tropp & Pettigrew, 2005), some laboratory evidence suggests that a structured positive contact experience helps minority group members more readily rebuild trust after an intergroup transgression (Bergsieker, 2012).

Although the intergroup contact literature underscores the general effectiveness of contact for changing attitudes, it is notably underutilized in most interventions aimed at creating a more inclusive workplace culture for women in male-dominated workplaces. This omission likely reflects an assumption that lack of contact is not the problem facing interactions between women and men. For example, whereas situations of intergroup conflict often include antipathy toward the other group, men's attitudes toward women tend to be positive to begin with (Krys et al., 2018). Moreover, contact that creates "friendship potential" (as recommended by Pettigrew, 1997), risks merely inviting the opportunity for unwanted sexual advances.

However, the manner in which men and women interact in male-dominated workplaces might bear more similarity to other intergroup contexts than has been recognized previously. First, because women can often feel excluded from or overlooked in organizational networks, and organizations often show substantial gender segregation at different status levels (Ibarra, 1992), the assumption that close contact already occurs in the work context might not be true. Second, although people feel warmth toward women in traditional roles (e.g., housewives), stereotypes and attitudes about successful working women are notably less warm (Fiske, Cuddy, Glick, & Xu, 2002) and may reflect backlash (Rudman & Glick, 2001). Finally, well-publicized efforts to create more opportunities for women in these fields risk giving the impression that certain career opportunities and rewards are distributed in a zero-sum fashion between men and women (Kuchynka, Bosson, Vandello, & Puryear, 2018), setting the stage for perceptions of realistic intergroup conflict over resources (Dover, Major, & Kaiser, 2016).

Thus, although intergroup contact has not typically been employed as a means to change the culture of male-dominated workplaces, interventionists may find some of these strategies useful. In particular, education about gender biases could be effectively combined with interpersonal dialogues that elicit greater perspective-taking and mutual understanding to instil a shared goal of creating more inclusive workplace cultures by working together. However, positive intergroup contact and intergroup harmony can also reduce disadvantaged individuals' support for institutional changes (Dixon, Levine, Reicher, & Durrheim, 2012; Hasan-Aslih, Pliskin, van Zomeren, Halperin, & Saguy, 2019). Thus, contact approaches might be successfully paired with institutional remedies to changing culture as well.

Acting at these three levels to cultivate more inclusive organizational cultures offers broad benefits that extend beyond the intervention "targets." Research suggests that efforts to include individuals from a given underrepresented group can create spillover benefits for other disadvantaged individuals. For example, a recent randomized control trial of diversity training focused exclusively on gender biases improved employees' attitudes and behaviors (e.g., mentoring) toward racial minorities in the workplace (Chang et al., 2019). After a separate intervention project targeting gender bias in academia, not only women but also men in participating departments, reported greater comfort when bringing up family issues, and even receiving more appreciation for their research months after the training (Carnes et al., 2015). Similarly, environments with less homophobia also benefit straight men by reducing suspicion about their identity claims and weakening gender-stereotypic constraints on their behavior (Oakes, Eibach, & Bergsieker, 2019). Just as all-inclusive multiculturalism garners more support from Whites than traditional diversity messaging (Jansen, Otten, & van der Zee, 2015; Stevens, Plaut, & Sanchez-Burks, 2008), highlighting the non-zero-sum nature of gender inclusion can underscore its value for everyone, leading to more support and proactive involvement from a broad array of diverse individuals.

The Need for More Research

This chapter provides a brief overview of what social psychology might uniquely contribute to our understanding of how to change organizational cultures to become more inclusive. We have structured this review around conceptualizing organizational cultures as comprising three interrelated institutional, individual, and interpersonal levels. Using the specific example of women's experiences in male-dominated STEM careers, we reviewed empirical evidence suggesting that cues at each level have the potential to signal either the presence or absence of an inclusive culture. The implication, of course, is that interventions aiming to change the culture of an organization can target any of these levels and may be most successful if they integrate efforts across levels.

The evidence summarized to make these points often comes from studies with clear limitations either on their ability to explain causal processes or to generalize findings to real-world situations. Organizational studies of inclusive workplace policies have the benefit of summarizing actual data from the field, but often omit measures of employees' own attitudes, experiences, and outcomes. Such research helps illustrate how policies and practices can change representation, but leaves important gaps in our knowledge of how they directly change the culture of the organization itself. For example, when an organization adopts new gender-inclusive policies, to what degree do these changes have a causal role in changing the norms by which men and women interact in the workplace?

Social-psychological studies, conversely, often provide controlled experimental tests of contextual or social cues that boost feelings of belonging or reduce intergroup biases, but these mechanisms still need to be tested in organizational settings to examine real-world outcomes (see also Fiedler, this volume). Finally, research efforts are often isolated to just one of these levels, seldom trying to examine the interrelations among these levels within a broader cultural system. For example, does an experimental manipulation designed to educate people about gender bias, combined with intergroup contact to foster respect and mutual understanding, increase employees' support for policy changes that might help to institutionalize an inclusive culture?

Granted, examining all aspects of this model at once, within a field setting, using rigorous experimental methods is an expensive if not an impossible proposition. And yet, understanding how our basic social science of inclusion translates to organizational cultural change requires moves in this direction. Conducting such research requires considerable investment from and/or partnership with the organizations that stand to benefit from this work. These partnerships have the benefit of leveraging financial commitments made by organizations hoping to better understand and implement cultural change. But the relationships between researchers and partnering organizations can also help keep researchers accountable for asking questions that are clearly relevant. This research presents clear risks and pitfalls: It is costly not only from a budgetary perspective but also in requiring considerable time and effort, which can be difficult to commit when students and junior researchers need a brisk, consistent rate of publications to secure and keep jobs (Cialdini, 2009).

A second risk involves compromising one's objectivity on the questions and the science in the face of organizations or other funders hoping for positive results. In response, researchers need to emphasize the uncertainty of the research process alongside the value (societal and financial) of using evidence-based methods to accurately identify what does and what does not work to change organizational culture. Despite these risks, clear intellectual and societal benefits can arise when we as social scientists begin putting our ideas to the test in the very environments where they stand to make a difference. We encourage researchers and practitioners with an interest in the science of cultural change to work collaboratively toward this goal.

Conclusions

We have proposed that inclusive organizational cultures form and evolve through the dynamic interplay of institutional, individual, and interpersonal factors. Through an integration of theories from social, cultural, and organizational psychology, we have unpacked how, through a process of mutual constitution, inclusive organizational cultures can emerge. An implication of our approach is that an individuals' biases cannot be fully understood without also attending to facts of the cultural context (i.e., outside of the mind) and, similarly, an organization's culture cannot be understood without reference to the biases in the minds of individuals. Thus, interventions are likely to fail when they aim to merely free people from prejudicial representations while not acknowledging the dominant social, material, and structural facts of the context. To fully leverage the power of a diverse workforce, organizations must make efforts to collectively constitute an inclusive culture through individual psychological tendencies, patterns of social relationships, and institutional policies and practices. Taken together, our approach offers a framework promoting inclusion and maximizing human potential in organizational contexts, and in society more broadly.

Author Note

This chapter was supported by a grant (895–2017–1025) from the Social Sciences and Humanities Research Council to the first and second authors.

References

Allport, G. W., (1954). *The nature of prejudice*. Cambridge, MA: Cambridge University Press

Andersson, L. M., & Pearson, C. M. (1999). Tit for tat? The spiraling effect of incivility in the workplace. *Academy of Management Review, 24*, 452–471.

Asgari, S., Dasgupta, N., & Cote, N. G. (2010). When does contact with successful ingroup members change self-stereotypes? A longitudinal study comparing the effect of quantity vs quality of contact with successful individuals. *Social Psychology, 41*, 203–211. doi.org/10.1027/1864-9335/a000028

Asgari, S., Dasgupta, N., & Stout, J. G. (2012). When do counterstereotypic ingroup members inspire versus deflate? The effect of successful professional women on young women's leadership self-concept. *Personality and Social Psychology Bulletin, 38*, 370–383. doi.org/10.1177/0146167211431968

Baron, A. S., & Banaji, M. R. (2006). The development of implicit attitudes: Evidence of race evaluations from ages 6 and 10 and adulthood. *Psychological Science, 17*, 53–58. doi.org/10.1111/j.1467-9280.2005.01664.x

Baron, R. A., & Neuman, J. H. (1996). Workplace violence and workplace aggression: Evidence on their relative frequency and potential causes. *Aggressive Behavior, 22*, 161–173.

Bartol, K. M., & Zhang, X. (2007). Networks and leadership development: Building linkages for capacity acquisition and capital accrual. *Human Resource Management Review, 17*, 388–401.

Berdahl, J. L., Cooper, M., Glick, P., Livingston, R. W., & Williams, J. C. (2018). Work as a masculinity contest. *Journal of Social Issues, 74*(3), 422–448.

Berdahl, J. L., & Raver, J. L. (2011). Sexual harassment. In *APA handbook of industrial and organizational psychology, vol 3: Maintaining, expanding, and contracting the organization* (pp. 641–669). Washington, D.C: American Psychological Association.

Bergsieker, H. B. (2012). *Building, betraying, and buffering trust in interracial and same-race friendships.* (Doctoral dissertation, Princeton University). ProQuest Dissertations and Theses (1039542921).

Block, K., Hall, W. M., Schmader, T., Inness, M., & Croft, E. (2018). Should I stay or should I go? Women's implicit stereotypic associations predict their commitment and fit in STEM. *Social Psychology, 49*, 243–251. doi.org/10.1027/1864-9335/a000343 (Supplemental).

Bohnet, I. (2016). *What works.* Boston, MA: Harvard University Press.

Bohnet, I., Van Geen, A., & Bazerman, M. (2015). When performance trumps gender bias: Joint vs. separate evaluation. *Management Science, 62*, 1225–1234.

Brady, L. M., Kaiser, C. R., Major, B., & Kirby, T. A. (2015). It's fair for us: Diversity structures cause women to legitimize discrimination. *Journal of Experimental Social Psychology, 57*, 100–110. doi-org.ezproxy.library.ubc.ca/10.1016/j.jesp.2014.11.010

Carli, L. L., Alawa, L., Lee, Y., Zhao, B., & Kim, E. (2016). Stereotypes about gender and science: Women ≠ scientists. *Psychology of Women Quarterly, 40*, 244–260.

Carnes, M., Devine, P. G., Manwell, L. B., Byars-Winston, A., Fine, E., Ford, C. E., ... Sheridan, J. (2015). The effect of an intervention to break the gender bias habit for faculty at one institution: A cluster randomized, controlled trial. *Academic Medicine, 90*, 221–230. doi.org/10.1097/ACM.0000000000000552

Chaney, K. E., & Sanchez, D. T. (2018). Gender-inclusive bathrooms signal fairness across identity dimensions. *Social Psychological and Personality Science, 9*, 245–253. doi.org/10.1177/1948550617737601

Chang, Edward H., Milkman, K. L., Gromet, D., Rebele, R., Massey, C., Duckworth, A., & Grant, A. (2019). *Can an hour of online diversity training promote inclusive attitudes and behaviors at work?* Manuscript under review.

Cheng, J. T., Tracy, J. L., Foulsham, T., Kingstone, A., & Henrich, J. (2013). Two ways to the top: Evidence that dominance and prestige are distinct yet viable avenues to social rank and influence. *Journal of Personality and Social Psychology, 104*, 103–125.

Cheryan, S., Plaut, V. C., Davies, P. G., & Steele, C. M. (2009). Ambient belonging: How stereotypical cues impact gender participation in computer science. *Journal of Personality and Social Psychology, 97*, 1045–1060.

Cialdini, R. B. (2009). We have to break up. *Perspectives on Psychological Science, 4*, 5–6. doi.org/10.1111/j.1745-6924.2009.01091.x

Corbett, C., & Hill, C. (2015). *Solving the equation: The variables for women's success in engineering and computing*. Washington, D.C: American Association of University Women.

Cortina, L. M. (2008). Unseen injustice: Incivility as modern discrimination in organizations. *Academy of Management Review, 33*, 55–75.

Cortland, C. I., Craig, M. A., Shapiro, J. R., Richeson, J. A., Neel, R., & Goldstein, N. J. (2017). Solidarity through shared disadvantage: Highlighting shared experiences of discrimination improves relations between stigmatized groups. *Journal of Personality and Social Psychology, 113*, 547.

Cosmides, L., Tooby, J., & Kurzban, R. (2003). Perceptions of race. *Trends in Cognitive Sciences, 7*(4), 173–179. doi-org.ezproxy.library.ubc.ca/10.1016/S1364-6613(03)00057-3

Crandall, C. S., & Eshleman, A. (2003). A justification-suppression model of the expression and experience of prejudice. *Psychological Bulletin, 129*, 414–446. doi.org/10.1037/0033-2909.129.3.414

Cunningham, W. A., Johnson, M. K., Raye, C. L., Gatenby, J. C., Gore, J. C., & Banaji, M. R. (2004). Separable neural components in the processing of black and white faces. *Psychological Science, 15*, 806–813.

Derks, B., van Laar, C., & Ellemers, N. (2016). The queen bee phenomenon: Why women leaders distance themselves from junior women. *The Leadership Quarterly, 27*(3), 456–469. doi.org/10.1016/j.leaqua.2015.12.007

Devine, P. G. (1989). Prejudice and stereotypes: Their automatic and controlled components. *Journal of Personality and Social Psychology, 56*, 5–18.

Devine, P. G., Forscher, P. S., Cox, W. T. L., Kaatz, A., Sheridan, J., & Carnes, M. (2017). A gender bias habit-breaking intervention led to increased hiring of female faculty in STEMM departments. *Journal of Experimental Social Psychology, 73*, 211–215. doi.org/10.1016/j.jesp.2017.07.002

Dixon J., Levine M., Reicher S., Durrheim K. (2012). Beyond prejudice: Are negative evaluations the problem and is getting us to like one another more the solution? *Behavioral and Brain Sciences, 35*, 411–425. doi:10.1017/S0140525X11002214

Dobbin, F., & Kalev, A. (2016). Why diversity programs fail and what works better. *Harvard Business Review, 94*(7–8), 52–60.

Dobbin, F., & Kalev, A. (2019). The promise and peril of sexual harassment programs. *Proceedings of the National Academy of Sciences, 116*, 12255–12260.

Dover, T. L., Major, B., & Kaiser, C. R. (2016). Members of high-status groups are threatened by pro-diversity organizational messages. *Journal of Experimental Social Psychology, 62*, 58–67. doi-org.ezproxy.library.ubc.ca/10.1016/j.jesp.2015.10.006

Fazio, R. H. (1990). Multiple processes by which attitudes guide behaviour: The MODE model as an integrative framework. In M. Zanna (Ed.), *Advances in experimental social psychology* (Vol. 23, pp. 75–109).

Fiske, S. T., Cuddy, A. J. C., Glick, P., & Xu, J. (2002). A model of (often mixed) stereotype content: Competence and warmth respectively follow from perceived status and competition. *Journal of Personality and Social Psychology, 82,* 878–902. doi. org/10.1037/0022-3514.82.6.878

Forbes, C. E., Cox, C. L., Schmader, T., & Ryan, L. (2012). Negative stereotype activation alters interaction between neural correlates of arousal, inhibition and cognitive control. *Social Cognitive and Affective Neuroscience, 7,* 771–781. doi.org/10.1093/scan/nsr052

Forret, M. L., & Dougherty, T. W. (2004). Networking behaviors and career outcomes: Differences for men and women? *Journal of Organizational Behavior, 25,* 419–437.

Forscher, P. S., Mitamura, C., Dix, E. L., Cox, W. T. L., & Devine, P. G. (2017). Breaking the prejudice habit: Mechanisms, timecourse, and longevity. *Journal of Experimental Social Psychology, 72,* 133–146. doi.org/10.1016/j.jesp.2017.04.009

Fouad, N. A., & Singh, R. (2011). *Stemming the tide: Why women leave engineering.* University of Wisconsin-Milwaukee, Final Report from NSF Award, 827553.

Fuesting, M. A., Diekman, A. B., Boucher, K. L., Murphy, M. C., Manson, D. L., & Safer, B. L. (2019). Growing STEM: Perceived faculty mindset as an indicator of communal affordances in STEM. *Journal of Personality and Social Psychology.* doi. org/10.1037/pspa0000154.supp (Supplemental).

Galinsky, A. D., Todd, A. R., Homan, A. C., Phillips, K. W., Apfelbaum, E. P., Sasaki, S. J., ... Maddux, W. W. (2015). Maximizing the gains and minimizing the pains of diversity: A policy perspective. *Perspectives on Psychological Science, 10,* 742–748. doi. org/10.1177/1745691615598513

Gonzalez, A. M., Dunlop, W. L., & Baron, A. S. (2017). Malleability of implicit associations across development. *Developmental Science, 20,* 1–13. doi.org/10.1111/desc.12481

Gosling, S. D., Ko, S. J., Mannarelli, T., & Morris, M. E. (2002). A room with a cue: Personality judgments based on offices and bedrooms. *Journal of Personality and Social Psychology, 82,* 379–398.

Hall, W. M., Schmader, T., Aday, A., & Croft, E. (2019). Decoding the dynamics of social identity threat in the workplace: A within-person analysis of women's and men's interactions in STEM. *Social Psychological and Personality Science, 10,* 542–552.

Hall, W., Schmader, T., Aday, A., Inness, M., & Croft, E. (2018). Climate control: The relationship between social identity threat and cues to an identity-safe culture. *Journal of Personality and Social Psychology, 115,* 446–467. doi.org/10.1037/pspi0000137

Hall, W., Schmader, T., & Croft, E. (2015). Engineering exchanges: Women's daily experience of social identity threat in engineering cue burnout. *Social Psychological and Personality Science, 6*(5), 528–534.

Hasan-Aslih, S., Pliskin, R., van Zomeren, M., Halperin, E., & Saguy, T. (2019). A darker side of hope: Harmony-focused hope decreases collective action intentions among the disadvantaged. *Personality and Social Psychology Bulletin, 45,* 209–223. doi. org/10.1177/0146167218783190

Henrich, J. (2015). *The secret of our success: How culture is driving human evolution, domesticating our species, and making us smart.* Princeton, NJ: Princeton University Press.

Hewlett, S. A., Luce, C. B., Servon, L. J., Sherbin, L., Shiller, P., Sosnovich, E., & Sumberg, K. (2008). The Athena factor: Reversing the brain drain in science, engineering, and technology. *Harvard Business Review Research Report, 10094,* 1–100.

Holleran, S. E., Whitehead, J., Schmader, T., & Mehl, M. R. (2011). Talking shop and shooting the breeze: A study of workplace conversation and job disengagement among STEM faculty. *Social Psychological and Personality Science, 2*(1), 65–71. doi-org.ezproxy.library.ubc.ca/10.1177/1948550610379921

Ibarra, H. (1992). Homophily and differential returns: Sex differences in network structure and access in an advertising firm. *Administrative Science Quarterly, 37,* 422–447.

Isenberg, D. J. (1986). Group polarization: A critical review and meta-analysis. *Journal of Personality and Social Psychology, 50,* 1141–1151. doi.org/10.1037/0022-3514.50.6.1141

Jansen, W. S., Otten, S., & van der Zee, K. I. (2015). Being part of diversity: The effects of an all-inclusive multicultural diversity approach on majority members' perceived inclusion and support for organizational diversity efforts. *Group Processes & Intergroup Relations, 18,* 817–832.

Johns, M., Inzlicht, M., & Schmader, T. (2008). Stereotype threat and executive resource depletion: Examining the influence of emotion regulation. *Journal of Experimental Psychology: General, 137*(4), 691–705. doi-org.ezproxy.library.ubc.ca/10.1037/a0013834

Kaiser, C. R., Major, B., Jurcevic, I., Dover, T. L., Brady, L. M., & Shapiro, J. R. (2013). Presumed fair: Ironic effects of organizational diversity structures. *Journal of Personality and Social Psychology, 104,* 504–519. doi.org/10.1037/a0030838

Kalev, A., Dobbin, F., & Kelly, E. (2006). Best practices or best guesses? Assessing the efficacy of corporate affirmative action and diversity policies. *American Sociological Review, 71,* 589–617.

Keashly, L., Harvey, S., & Hunter, S. (1997). Emotional abuse and role state stressors: Relative impact on resident assistants' stress. *Work and Stress, 11,* 35–45.

Kelly, E., & Dobbin, F. (1998). How affirmative action became diversity management: Employer response to antidiscrimination law, 1961 to 1996. *American Behavioral Scientist, 41,* 960–984.

Koch, A. J., D'Mello, S. D., & Sackett, P. R. (2015). A meta-analysis of gender stereotypes and bias in experimental simulations of employment decision making. *Journal of Applied Psychology, 100*(1), 128–161. doi-org.ezproxy.library.ubc.ca/10.1037/a0036734

Krys, K., Capaldi, C. A., van Tilburg, W., Lipp, O. V., Bond, M. H., Vauclair, C.-M., … Ahmed, R. A. (2018). Catching up with wonderful women: The women-are-wonderful effect is smaller in more gender egalitarian societies. *International Journal of Psychology, 53*(Suppl 1), 21–26. doi.org/10.1002/ijop.12420

Kuchynka, S. L., Bosson, J. K., Vandello, J. A., & Puryear, C. (2018). Zero-sum thinking and the masculinity contest: Perceived intergroup competition and workplace gender bias. *Journal of Social Issues, 74,* 529–550. doi.org/10.1111/josi.12281

Lai, C. K., Marini, M., Lehr, S. A., Cerruti, C., Shin, J.-E. L., Joy-Gaba, J. A., … Nosek, B. A. (2014). Reducing implicit racial preferences: A comparative investigation of 17 interventions. *Journal of Experimental Psychology: General, 143,* 1765–1785. doi.org/10.1037/a0036260

Lai, C. K., Skinner, A. L., Cooley, E., Murrar, S., Brauer, M., Devos, T., … & Simon, S. (2016). Reducing implicit racial preferences: II. Intervention effectiveness across time. *Journal of Experimental Psychology: General, 145,* 1001–1016.

Lim, S., Cortina, L. M., & Magley, V. J. (2008). Personal and workgroup incivility: Impact on work and health outcomes. *Journal of Applied Psychology, 93,* 95–107.

Logel, C., Walton, G. M., Spencer, S. J., Iserman, E., von Hippel, W., & Bell, A. (2009). Interacting with sexist men triggers social identity threat among female engineers. *Journal of Personality and Social Psychology, 96,* 1089–1103.

Madera, J. M., Hebl, M. R., Dial, H., Martin, R., & Valian, V. (2018). Raising doubt in letters of recommendation for academia: Gender differences and their impact. *Journal of Business and Psychology* (First Online). doi.org/10.1007/s10869-018-9541-1

Margolis, J., & Fisher, A. (2003). *Unlocking the clubhouse: Women in computing.* Cambridge, MA: MIT Press.
Markus, H. R., & Hamedani, M. G. (2007). Sociocultural psychology: The dynamic interdependence among self-systems and social systems. In S. Kitayama & D. Cohen (Eds.), *Handbook of cultural psychology* (pp. 3–46). New York: Guilford.
Markus, H. R., & Kitayama, S. (2010). Cultures and selves: A cycle of mutual constitution. *Perspectives on Psychological Science, 5,* 420–430.
McPherson, M., Smith-Lovin, L., & Cook, J. M. (2001). Birds of a feather: Homophily in social networks. *Annual Review of Sociology, 27,* 415–444.
Mead, G. H. (1934). *Mind, self and society* (Vol. 111). Chicago, IL: University of Chicago Press.
Miller, D. I., Eagly, A. H., & Linn, M. C. (2015). Women's representation in science predicts national gender-science stereotypes: Evidence from 66 nations. *Journal of Educational Psychology, 107*(3), 631–644. doi-org.ezproxy.library.ubc.ca/10.1037/edu0000005.supp (Supplemental).
Moss-Racusin, C. A., Dovidio, J. F., Brescoll, V. L., Graham, M. J., & Handelsman, J. (2012). Science faculty's subtle gender biases favor male students. *PNAS Proceedings of the National Academy of Sciences of the United States of America, 109,* 16474–16479. doi.org/10.1073/pnas.1211286109
Moss-Racusin, C. A., Pietri, E. S., Hennes, E. P., Dovidio, J. F., Brescoll, V. L., Roussos, G., & Handelsman, J. (2018). Reducing STEM gender bias with VIDS (video interventions for diversity in STEM). *Journal of Experimental Psychology: Applied, 24,* 236–260.
Murphy, M. C., Kroeper, K. M., & Ozier, E. M. (2018). Prejudiced places: How contexts shape inequality and how policy can change them. *Policy Insights from the Behavioral and Brain Sciences, 5,* 66–74.
Murphy, M. C., Steele, C. M., & Gross, J. J. (2007). Signaling threat: How situational cues affect women in math, science, and engineering settings. *Psychological Science, 18,* 879–885.
Murphy, M. C., & Taylor, V. J. (2012). The role of situational cues in signaling and maintaining stereotype threat. In M. Inzlicht & T. Schmader (Eds.), *Stereotype threat: Theory, process, and application* (pp. 17–133). Oxford: Oxford University Press.
Murphy, M. C. & Walton, G. M (2013). From prejudiced people to prejudiced places: A social-contextual approach to prejudice. In C. Stangor & C. Crandall (Eds.), *Frontiers in social psychology series: Stereotyping and prejudice.* New York, NY: Psychology Press.
Nosek, B. A. (2005). Moderators of the relationship between implicit and explicit evaluation. *Journal of Experimental Psychology: General, 134,* 565–584. doi.org/10.1037/0096-3445.134.4.565
Nosek, B. A., Banaji, M. R., & Greenwald, A. G. (2002). Math = male, me = female, therefore math ≠ me. *Journal of Personality and Social Psychology, 83,* 44–59. doi.org/10.1037/0022-3514.83.1.44
Nosek, B. A., Smyth, F. L., Sriram, N., Lindner, N. M., Devos, T., Ayala, A., & Greenwald, A. G. (2009). National differences in gender-science stereotypes predict national sex differences in science and math achievement. *Proceedings of the National Academy of Sciences, 106,* 10593–10597.
Oakes, H., Eibach, R., & Bergsieker, H. B. (2019). *How closets create climates of suspicion: Stigmatizing environments raise doubts about claims to majority identity.* Manuscript in preparation.

Onyeador, I. N. (2017). *Presumed unintentional: The ironic effects of implicit bias framing on Whites' perceptions of discrimination* (Unpublished doctoral dissertation). Los Angeles, CA: University of California.

Paluck, E. L. (2006). Diversity training and intergroup contact: A call to action research. *Journal of Social Issues, 62,* 577–595. doi.org/10.1111/j.1540-4560.2006.00474.x

Pettigrew, T. F. (1997). Generalized intergroup contact effects on prejudice. *Personality and Social Psychology Bulletin, 23,* 173–185.

Pettigrew, T. F., & Tropp, L. R. (2006). A meta-analytic test of intergroup contact theory. *Journal of Personality and Social Psychology, 90,* 751–783. doi.org/10.1037/0022-3514.90.5.751

Pettigrew, T. F., & Tropp, L. R. (2008). How does intergroup contact reduce prejudice? Meta-analytic tests of three mediators. *European Journal of Social Psychology, 38,* 922–934. doi.org/10.1002/ejsp.504

Phillips, K. W., Mannix, E. A., Neale, M. A., & Gruenfeld, D. H. (2004). Diverse groups and information sharing: The effects of congruent ties. *Journal of Experimental Social Psychology, 40*(4), 497–510. doi-org.ezproxy.library.ubc.ca/10.1016/j.jesp.2003.10.003

Pippert, T. D., Essenburg, L. J., & Matchett, E. J. (2013). We've got minorities, yes we do: Visual representations of racial and ethnic diversity in college recruitment materials. *Journal of Marketing for Higher Education, 23,* 258–282.

Purdie-Vaughns, V., Steele, C. M., Davies, P. G., Ditlmann, R., & Crosby, J. R. (2008). Social identity contingencies: How diversity cues signal threat or safety for African Americans in mainstream institutions. *Journal of Personality and Social Psychology, 94,* 615–630.

Rayner, C., & Hoel, H. (1997). A summary review of literature relating to workplace bullying. *Journal of Community & Applied Social Psychology, 7,* 181–191.

Régner, I., Thinus-Blanc, C., Netter, A., Schmader, T., & Huguet, P. (2019). Implicit bias predicts promoting fewer women in science when evaluators deny discrimination. *Nature Human Behavior, 3,* 1171–1179. doi.org/10.1038/s41562-019-0686-32019

Rudman, L. A., & Glick, P. (2001). Prescriptive gender stereotypes and backlash toward agentic women. *Journal of Social Issues, 57,* 743–762.

Schein, E. H. (2004). *Organizational culture and leadership.* San Francisco, CA: Jossey.

Schmader, T., Forbes, C. E., Zhang, S., & Mendes, W. B. (2009). A metacognitive perspective on the cognitive deficits experienced in intellectually threatening environments. *Personality and Social Psychology Bulletin, 35*(5), 584–596. doi-org.ezproxy.library.ubc.ca/10.1177/0146167208330450

Schmader, T., & Sedikides, C. (2018). State authenticity as fit to environment: The implications of social identity for fit, authenticity, and self-segregation. *Personality and Social Psychology Review, 22,* 228–259. doi.org/10.1177/1088868317734080

Sherif, M., & Sherif, C. (1953). *Groups in harmony and tension.* New York, NY: Harper.

Steele, C. M., Spencer, S. J., & Aronson, J. (2002). Contending with group image: The psychology of stereotype and social identity threat. In *Advances in experimental social psychology* (Vol. 34, pp. 379–440). San Diego, CA: Academic Press.

Stephens, N. M., Hamedani, M. G., & Townsend, S. S. M. (2019). Difference matters: Teaching students a contextual theory of difference can help them succeed. *Perspectives on Psychological Science, 14,* 156–174. doi.org/10.1177/1745691618797957

Stevens, F. G., Plaut, V. C., & Sanchez-Burks, J. (2008). Unlocking the benefits of diversity: All-inclusive multiculturalism and positive organizational change. *The Journal of Applied Behavioral Science, 44,* 116–133.

Stout, J. G., Dasgupta, N., Hunsinger, M., & McManus, M. A. (2011). STEMing the tide: Using ingroup experts to inoculate women's self-concept in science, technology, engineering, and mathematics (STEM). *Journal of Personality and Social Psychology, 100*, 255–270. doi.org/10.1037/a0021385

Swan, E. (2010). Commodity diversity: Smiling faces as a strategy of containment. *Organization, 17*, 77–100.

Tropp, L. R., & Pettigrew, T. F. (2005). Relationships between intergroup contact and prejudice among minority and majority status groups. *Psychological Science, 16*(12), 951–957.

Uhlmann, E. L., & Cohen, G. L. (2005). Constructed criteria: Redefining merit to justify discrimination. *Psychological Science, 16*(6), 474–480.

Vial, A. C., Dovidio, J. F., & Brescoll, V. L. (2019). Channeling others' biases to meet role demands. *Journal of Experimental Social Psychology, 82*, 47–63.

Vorauer, J. D. (2006). An information search model of evaluative concerns in intergroup interaction. *Psychological Review, 113*, 862–886.

Walton, G. M., & Cohen, G. L. (2011). A brief social-belonging intervention improves academic and health outcomes of minority students. *Science, 331*(6023), 1447–1451. doi.org/10.1126/science.1198364

Walton, G. M., Logel, C., Peach, J. M., Spencer, S. J., & Zanna, M. P. (2015). Two brief interventions to mitigate a "chilly climate" transform women's experience, relationships, and achievement in engineering. *Journal of Educational Psychology, 107*(2), 468–485. doi-org.ezproxy.library.ubc.ca/10.1037/a0037461.supp

Wang, J. (2009). Networking in the workplace: Implications for women's career development. *New Directions for Adult and Continuing Education, 122*, 33–42.

Williams, W. M., & Ceci, S. J. (2015). National hiring experiments reveal 2:1 faculty preference for women on STEM tenure track. *PNAS Proceedings of the National Academy of Sciences of the United States of America, 112*(17), 5360–5365. doi-org.ezproxy.library.ubc.ca/10.1073/pnas.1418878112

Woodson, A. (2015). *The politics of normal: A critical race inquiry into the lived experience of civic disempowerment.* Michigan State University: Curriculum, Instruction, and Teacher Education.

Yeager, D. S., Walton, G. M., Brady, S. T., Akcinar, E. N., Paunesku, D., Keane, L., ... Dweck, C. S. (2016). Teaching a lay theory before college narrows achievement gaps at scale. *PNAS Proceedings of the National Academy of Sciences of the United States of America, 113*(24), E3341–E3348. doi-org.ezproxy.library.ubc.ca/10.1073/pnas.1524360113

INDEX

academic probation 63–7
addiction 4, 107–19
adolescence 15, 124–41, 207–23
adolescent depression 207–23; drug involvement in 210–11; marijuana use and 212–13; media research and 221–3; parental influences on 215–19; and self-medication 211–12, 213–15; and suicide 208–9
adolescent smoking 112–13
advertising 5, 115, 117, 281
aggregation levels 31–2
aggression xviii, 2, 15, 124–38; anger regulation and 128–9; development of 125–6; environmental risk factors of 129–31; executive deficits and 126–7; intrapersonal risk factors of 126–7; media and 129–31; and peer relations 131–3; prevention of 136–7; social risk factors of 133–6; theory of mind and 126–8
air pollution 32–3
alcohol abuse 26, 109, 111, 114, 146, 148, 149, 209, 211, 218
anchoring effects 25, 35
anger regulation 125, 126, 128–9, 131, 135, 137
anthropology 8, 40, 45
anxiety 8, 45, 48, 49, 63, 67–8, 73, 161, 173, 174, 188, 189, 191, 193, 197, 208, 211, 213, 293, 296
appetitive behaviors 15, 143, 144–5, 149, 150, 152, 153

applied social psychology 1–17; application vs theory in 2–4; history of 4–6; ideological assumptions of 6–7; individual vs group focus of 9–10; mistaken assumptions of 6–12; nominalist fallacy in 10–11; representative design in 12–13
applied vs basic research 5, 23–36
appraisal processes 189, 199, 296
assumptions about human nature 7–8, 10, 40
attachment theory 14, 187–201; applications of 191–3; basic concepts of 187–9; broaden-and-build cycle of 189–91; in counselling and psychotherapy 193–5; in education 195–7; in health and medicine 197–8; in leadership and management 198–9
attitude change through persuasion 5, 82–99, 108–9, 207, 221–2; elaboration model of 83–4; and intentions 84–5; and personal involvement 86–9; and popular interventions 97–8; and prejudiced attitudes 85–6; and sports performance 91–3
attitudes 5, 14, 16, 73, 82–99, 107, 108, 109, 111, 112, 114–16, 155, 194, 198, 200, 216, 218, 221, 232, 234, 236–41, 276–8, 284–6, 293, 297, 299, 313–19, 324, 335–9, 340, 344–7
attitudes to democracy 277–8
autonomy 47, 199, 272, 300, 333

bad events 58–9, 61, 62
"bad" things reconsidered 58–72; and academic feedback 67–8; close relationships and 69–30; education and 63–4; and health 68–9; and mindset interventions 60–2; paradigmatic examples of 63–6; and re-framing 6–62; and test-taking 67–8; trauma and 69
base-rate neglect 26–7
behavioral confirmation 233, 238–40, 242, 243
behavioral priming 12
behavioral synchrony 14, 161–78
biased hypothesis testing 235–7
biological determination of behavior 7–8
blood alcohol levels 26, 109, 111, 114, 146, 148, 149, 209, 211, 218
brain-to-brain synchrony 169–70
Brexit 272, 273, 284, 302
broaden-and-build cycle of attachment security 189–91

cannabis effect 212, 214, 215; *see also* drug abuse; marijuana use
child-parent relations 207–23
clinical interactions xviii, 2, 12, 15, 161–78, 207
close relationships 46, 52, 69–70, 167, 178, 190, 200
cognitive biases 10, 44, 83–4
cognitive dissonance 240, 241
collapse of democracy in Hungary 273–86
collective emotions 267–90, 292–309
collective memory 303
collective narcissism 16, 267–90, 303; and in-group favoritism 271–2; and political beliefs 270–1; and political preferences 281–2, 283–7; and populism 272–3; measurement of 271–2
collective narratives 293–304
collective nostalgia 16, 291–304; and social misrepresentations 293–5; applied social psychology of 295–7; populism and 300–2; sentimental longings and 297–300
collective nostalgia and populism 300–2
communism 275, 299, 300
computer-mediated communication 107–19
conditional samples 26–7
conformity 4, 301, 327
conspiracy theories 3, 50, 51, 272, 281, 286
construct validity 314–16

consumer behavior 14, 31, 32, 44, 113, 116, 150, 151–2, 200
consumption and reward 142–55
corruption 273–4, 278
crime 32, 231, 241, 242, 243, 244, 284, 315, 316, 324
criminal justice system 231–45
cultural determinism 8–9

decision-making 25, 26, 41, 234–5
democracy 265–78
depression 4, 15, 207–10, 211–12, 213–15, 216–23; and drugs 210–11
desire 142–55
development of aggression 125–6
developmental mismatch 44
diabetes 46
digital revolution 42
discrimination 4, 10, 271, 297, 313, 319, 320, 321, 322, 323–7
distributed learning 24
diversity 2, 4, 17, 301, 326, 327, 334, 336, 337, 338, 340, 343, 344, 346
division of labor 42, 48
drug abuse 207–23
drugs and depression 210–11

eating and drinking behavior 142–55; appetitive stimuli and 144–5; consumption and reward stimulation and 144–6; and desire 147–9; experimental findings on 148–50; grounded cognition theory of 143–5; and marketing 149–52; and mindfulness interventions 153–4
eating disorders xviii, 2, 14, 46, 47, 142–55
economic decisions 32, 71
education and attachment 195–7
educational interventions 63–7
effective reframing 71–2
elaboration likelihood model 82–99; and goal-behavior correspondence 93–4; and intentions 84–5; and personal involvement 86–7; popular interventions of 97–9; and prejudiced attitudes 85–6; and sports performance 91–2; validation of 90–7
emotional well-being 250–9
environmental challenges 51–2
epidemiology 15, 45, 47
epistemology 3, 10–11
ethnocentrism 4

evolutionary mismatch 3, 14, 40–54; evidence for 45–6; and health 51–2; in politics 49–50; and public policy 52–3; psychological mechanisms o 41–4; in relationships 46–7; in work 48–9; in social psychology 46–8
evolutionary psychology 8, 9, 10, 14, 40–54, 291
evolutionary rationality 3, 7, 8, 41
executive function 125, 126–8, 136, 137
existential anxiety 162, 163, 294, 296
expectancy effects 231–45
experimenting society 3, 6
external vs internal validity 12–13, 312
eyewitness identification 2, 24
eyewitness testimony 231, 241–4

face recognition 24
Facebook 16, 47, 250–9; and well-being 251–4
fake news 3
falsifiability 11
fascism 267
fear based communication 115–16
fertility 45, 47
food marketing 150–1
forensic psychology 2, 4, 15, 231–145, 324, 327
France 24, 268, 30, 304

game-based messaging 116–17
Germany 25, 124, 302
goal-behavior correspondence 93–4
Great Britain 268, 272–3, 285, 302
great psychotherapy debate 163–4
grounded cognition theory of desire 143–4
groups vs individuals 9–10
guilt 8, 209, 233, 236, 240, 241, 296, 304

health and attachment 196–8
health interventions 68–9
health related communication 14, 107–19
helplessness 65, 71, 209, 210
historical narratives 292, 294, 298
historical representations 16
historical traumas 275–6
history of applied social psychology 1, 2, 4–5
Hitler 268, 275, 284
HIV 27, 30
homesickness 295
hopelessness 209
hormonal changes 168, 208

human nature 7–8, 10, 40
Hungary 16, 268, 274–87, 299

identity loss 296
identity politics 9–10
ideological assumptions of applied social psychology 6–7
immigration 16, 294, 297, 299
implicit associations test 312–28; construct validity of 314–16; and discrimination 323–5; effect size of 317–18; interpreting 'bias' in 318–19; and racial inequality 320–2; predictive validity of 319–20; psychometric issues of 316–17
implicit associations 4, 12, 16
implicit attitudes 312–28
implicit bias 312–28
implicit stereotypes 338–9
implicit vs explicit beliefs 337–8
inclusion in organizations 334–40; and daily interactions 340–1; and individual beliefs 337–8; and organizational culture 335–6; and organizational policies 336–7
inclusive organizational culture 342–5
individuals vs groups 9–10
Industrial Revolution 42
in-group favoritism 10, 16, 269, 270, 271–2, 278, 284, 286, 293, 302–3
intelligence testing 2, 6–7
intention to use doping substances 84–5
intergroup behavior 10, 16, 296, 299, 304
internal vs external validity 12–13, 25
international society of applied psychology 5
internet porn 44, 47, 52
interpersonal behavior 340–2
interpersonal expectancy effects 232–4
interpersonal synchrony 161–78; and brain-to-brain synchrony 169–70; chronic processes in 172–3; empirical research on 173–5; and linguistic synchrony 168–9, 175–6; and movement synchrony 166–7, 173–4; phasic processes in 170–1; and psychotherapeutic alliance 162–4; and physiological synchrony 167–8; tonic processes in 171–2
IQ 7
IT technology 4

jury decision making 15–16, 233, 234–5, 240–1
jury selection 232, 234–5
just world beliefs 277–8

language and interpersonal synchrony 168–9, 175–6
leadership 5, 49–50, 198–200, 299, 301
learning paradigms 4
legal psychology 2, 4, 15, 231–145, 231–45, 324, 327; behavioral confirmation effects in 238–41; eyewitness identification in 241–4; interpersonal expectancy effects in 232–3; jury selection and decision making in 234–5
liberalism 267, 268, 270, 274, 275, 284, 301
linguistic analyses 16, 278–80
linguistic synchrony 168–9, 175–6

machine learning 4
marijuana use 212–13, 215, 217
marital conflict 70–1
Marxism 9, 10, 11, 256
mating 14, 44, 46, 47, 188
meaning in life 296
media research 221–2
medical diagnosis 26–7
mental representations and political behavior 269–70
meta-cognition 90–1
MeToo movement 31–2
micro-aggression 12
mind modules 8, 9
mindfulness based training 153–4
mindset interventions 60–4
mistaken assumptions of applied social psychology 6–13
mood effects on cognition 11, 48, 83, 190, 252, 254, 257
motor performance 1, 143, 147, 170, 175
movement synchrony 166–7, 173–5
multilevel design 15, 125, 126, 132, 133, 137, 342
Muslims 269, 270, 297, 299

narcissism 267–87
national anthems 276–7
national identity 276–7, 280
nationalism 276–7
neural evidence for consumption and reward simulation 146–7
nominalist fallacy 10–11, 12
nostalgia 291–304

obedience 13
office of strategic services 5

online social networks 16, 250–9; and emotion 254–6; reasons for using 257–8; and well-being 251–4, 258
organ donation 24–5
organizational behavior xviii, 334–48
output-bound sampling 28–31
overconfidence bias 33–4
overheard communication technique 222

parental effects 14, 15, 208, 215–23
parental influences on marijuana use and depression 215–16
parental warmth 216
patient-therapist relationship 162–3
peer group effects 131–3, 218
person perception 11–12
personal investment 86–8
personality assessment 3
persuasion against tobacco use 107–19
persuasion through fiction 108–9
persuasion 5, 82–99, 108–9, 206, 221–2; elaboration model of 83–4; and intentions 84–5; and personal involvement 86–9; and popular interventions 97–8; and prejudiced attitudes 85–6; and sports performance 91–3
philosophy of science 3
physical exercise 54
physiological synchrony 167–8
placebo effect 73–4
Poland 200, 268, 271, 273, 275, 284, 285, 300
political behavior 267–87, 292–311; and collective nostalgia 292–311
political populism xviii, 2, 267–87
political psychology 10, 12, 14, 16, 32, 43, 49–50, 76–7, 267–87, 292–311
populism xviii, 2, 16, 267–87, 300–1; applied social psychology of 295–7; and collective narcissism 267–90; and collective nostalgia 291–304; in Hungary 273–6; in-group favoritism and 271–2; and political beliefs 270–1; and political preferences 281–2, 283–7; sentimental longings and 297–300; and social misrepresentations 293–5; in the USA and Britain 272–3
power 94–5
practice vs theory 1, 23–36
predictive validity of IAT 319–20
prejudice 12, 85–6, 312–28
preventing adolescent depression 207–23

primates 41–2, 43
problem drinking 295
propaganda 5, 268, 269, 270, 274, 281–2, 284, 286
psychoactive substances 207
psychoanalysis 11–12
psychotherapeutic alliance 164–5
psychotherapy 161–78; attachment theory in 193–5; and brain-to-brain synchrony 169–70; chronic processes in 172–3; empirical research on 173–5; interpersonal synchrony in 161–78; and linguistic synchrony 168–9, 175–6; and movement synchrony 166–7, 173–4; phasic processes in 170–1; and physiological synchrony 167–8; tonic processes in 171–2
public policy 43, 52–3
purchasing decisions 29
Purkinje effect 3

racial inequality 4, 312–28
rational vs irrational judgments 26
real vs unreal 118–19
reframing bad events 60–4
reframing challenges 58–9
refugees 297
regression effects 24, 33–5
regression trap 33–4
relationships 3, 46–7, 187–201
representative design 12–13
resource depletion 61
risk assessment 26–8
risk factors for aggression 126–8, 133–5
Russia 268, 299, 300, 304

sampling theory 25–7, 32–3
schizophrenia 213
scientific paradigms 6
selective forgetting 298
self and identity 293
self-blame 209
self-categorization 302
self-evaluations 280
self-fulfilling prophecy 219
self-medicating hypothesis 213–14, 215
self-medication and depression 211–12, 213–15
signal detection theory 3
situationist bias 7–8
social decision making 14, 43
social exclusion 17
social facilitation 1
social identification 296

social identity 2, 10, 293, 302, 303, 336, 341
social identity threat 341
social inclusion 334–52
social interaction 231–45
social judgments 25, 26, 29–30
social media xviii, 2, 3, 47, 52, 250–9
social networks xviii, 16
sports performance 91–2
Stalin 268
Stanford prison study 13
stereotype accuracy 9
stereotype threat 12
stereotypes 9, 12, 312–28
suicide 207–23
superstition 42
sustainability 51–3
Sydney Symposium of Social Psychology xix–xx
symbolic ability 291

teenage suicide xviii, 1, 207–27
the in-sync model 170–1
theory and practice 1, 2–3, 23–36
theory of mind 126–7
theory of planned behavior 221
therapeutic relationships 15, 161–81
tobacco addiction 107–19
tobacco regulation 112–13
translational research 6, 13–14, 23–36; and aggregation levels 32–3; and base-rate neglect 26–7; and output-bound sampling 28–30; and the regression trap 33–4; sampling theory approaches in 25–32; and unrealistic optimism 34–5
trauma 63, 69, 195, 275–6
Trump 268, 284, 301, 302
Turkey 268, 274

values 6, 86, 87, 270, 274, 275, 276–8, 287, 293, 294, 296, 299, 301, 322, 337, 340, 343
video games and public health 14, 109–12
violence in the media 129–31
virtual reality 14, 107–19
virtual transportation model 108–9, 113–15
voir dire 235–7, 238–40

willing suspension of disbelief 108
wisdom of crowds 23, 24
wise interventions 14, 58–64
workplace culture 17, 48–9, 334–50
World War II 304